New Frontiers in Regional Science: Asian Perspectives

Volume 71

This series is a constellation of works by scholars in the field of regional science and in related disciplines specifically focusing on dynamism in Asia.

Asia is the most dynamic part of the world. Japan, Korea, Taiwan, and Singapore experienced rapid and miracle economic growth in the 1970s. Malaysia, Indonesia, and Thailand followed in the 1980s. China, India, and Vietnam are now rising countries in Asia and are even leading the world economy. Due to their rapid economic development and growth, Asian countries continue to face a variety of urgent issues including regional and institutional unbalanced growth, environmental problems, poverty amidst prosperity, an ageing society, the collapse of the bubble economy, and deflation, among others.

Asian countries are diversified as they have their own cultural, historical, and geographical as well as political conditions. Due to this fact, scholars specializing in regional science as an inter- and multi-discipline have taken leading roles in providing mitigating policy proposals based on robust interdisciplinary analysis of multifaceted regional issues and subjects in Asia. This series not only will present unique research results from Asia that are unfamiliar in other parts of the world because of language barriers, but also will publish advanced research results from those regions that have focused on regional and urban issues in Asia from different perspectives.

The series aims to expand the frontiers of regional science through diffusion of intrinsically developed and advanced modern regional science methodologies in Asia and other areas of the world. Readers will be inspired to realize that regional and urban issues in the world are so vast that their established methodologies still have space for development and refinement, and to understand the importance of the interdisciplinary and multidisciplinary approach that is inherent in regional science for analyzing and resolving urgent regional and urban issues in Asia.

Topics under consideration in this series include the theory of social cost and benefit analysis and criteria of public investments, socio-economic vulnerability against disasters, food security and policy, agro-food systems in China, industrial clustering in Asia, comprehensive management of water environment and resources in a river basin, the international trade bloc and food security, migration and labor market in Asia, land policy and local property tax, Information and Communication Technology planning, consumer "shop-around" movements, and regeneration of downtowns, among others.

Researchers who are interested in publishing their books in this Series should obtain a proposal form from Yoshiro Higano (Editor in Chief, higano@jsrsai.jp) and return the completed form to him.

Mukunda Mishra • Subrata Saha •
Madhabendra Sinha
Editors

Public Policies and Sustainable Development in Post-Reform India

Regional Responses and the Way Forward

Springer

Editors
Mukunda Mishra
Department of Geography
Dr. Meghnad Saha College, Itahar
Uttar Dinajpur, West Bengal, India

Subrata Saha
Department of Economics
Raiganj University
Uttar Dinajpur, West Bengal, India

Madhabendra Sinha
Department of Economics and Politics
Visva-Bharati University
Santiniketan, West Bengal, India

ISSN 2199-5974 ISSN 2199-5982 (electronic)
New Frontiers in Regional Science: Asian Perspectives
ISBN 978-981-99-3695-3 ISBN 978-981-99-3696-0 (eBook)
https://doi.org/10.1007/978-981-99-3696-0

This Springer imprint is published by the registered company Springer Nature Singapore Pte Ltd.
The registered company address is: 152 Beach Road, #21-01/04 Gateway East, Singapore 189721, Singapore

Foreword

India's decision to choose the path of development through nationwide planning guided by the Planning Commission was the first major landmark in her post-colonial history. When the First Five Year Plan was launched in 1951, the eyes of the whole world were focused on India, so to speak. A very poor, overpopulated country with abysmally low literacy rate was boldly undertaking the experiment of rapid development through comprehensive planning. And the political system remained non-autocratic—a unique fusion of Soviet type technocratic intervention and Western style parliamentary democracy. This was certainly one of the most ambitious projects in the developing world. Winston Churchill had predicted with characteristic arrogance (and ignorance) that independent India would collapse into chaos within a decade. He was proved shatteringly wrong and by the end of the First Plan (1956) growth rate of real GDP per capita was already considerably above the pathetic 0.1 per cent averaged over the last half century of British rule. One Plan followed another producing a mixed array of results with numerous positives and several negatives. Eventually, the negatives threatened to overwhelm the positives and by the early 1990s, through an unfortunate conjunction of adverse external shocks (the Kuwait War mainly) and persistent policy mismanagement, the economy was on the verge of collapse.

External help saved the situation and led to the Rao-Singh Reforms of 1991—the second major landmark in the country's post-independence trajectory. Comprehensive reforms across the board attempted to sweep away the inefficiencies that had accumulated over the previous decades and ushered in a new era of market-led development with the State relegated to an enabling role.

The seventy fifth years of Independence may be considered as a natural vantage point for an overview of achievements and failures. Although the literature on post-reform India is voluminous, there is always scope for fresh perspectives, given the dynamics of a very complex, heterogeneous economy. Some age-old issues continue to be of relevance, while new ones have emerged in the wake of major policy moves such as National Health Policy of 2017, National Education Policy of 2020, and the Sustainable Development Goals to be met by the deadline of 2030. All of these are competently discussed in this volume. Particularly interesting is the role of digital education in schools and Massive Open Online Course in general. Additional aspects that receive good treatment include the performance of the banking sector, social protection for vulnerable groups of workers, and empowerment of women as a promoter of gender equality and public policy as a protector of the environment.

The book with its wide coverage promises to be of great usefulness to serious students, teachers, and researchers interested in the evolution of the modern Indian economy.

Soumyen Sikdar has been a Professor of Economics at the Indian Institute of Management (IIM) Calcutta, Kolkata, India. He obtained his undergraduate and master's degrees from Presidency College and the University of Calcutta, respectively, and his Ph.D. from the University of Minnesota, USA. He has more than 40 years of experience in teaching and research and has been a Visiting Professor at Shenzhen University, China, and the Institute of Social and Economic Research, Osaka University, Japan. Professor Sikdar has authored numerous research publications in internationally respected journals and three books on macroeconomics and globalization released by international publishers. His research interests include industrial organization theory, open economy macroeconomics, and development economics.

Indian Institute of Management
Calcutta, Kolkata, West Bengal, India
15 March, 2023

Soumyen Sikdar Ph.D.

Preface

Emphasizing the rational exploitation of natural systems to use the biological natural resources within limits to ensure those resources are available for use by future generations underpins the concept of sustainable development in the 1980s. However, social scientists have been witnessing that although the "idea" of achieving development with ensured sustainability is noble, the path is critical enough for the economic, social, and environmental agendas to walk abreast. Post-colonial states like India have been finding themselves in a challenging position to generate broadly shared economic well-being and quality of life through creating and utilizing physical, human, financial, and social assets. Undoubtedly, the capacity of these states is linked to the available economic resources; however, on the one hand, the evolving relations between the political executive and the bureaucracy and the state and civil society, on the other, do matter. Thus, the political system evolved in India crucially determines the capacity of the state to implement its programs.

The core objective of sustainable development aspires to the implementation of utopian intellectual constructs, which is historically evident to have rarely been attempted by any states to execute. India is not an exception. While the market forces dominate, whether of goods, services, or capital, the socioeconomic system of the state propagates away from the producing and defending principles of justice and legitimacy. Within two decades since the Rio Declaration on environment and development, the standard socioeconomic analysis entails the concept of sustainable development firmly. However, the principle of securing long-term economic progress by linking it with environmental protection could be successful through actions and its implementation in practice, which is still muted. Given the urgency of the development process should be abreast of sustainability; it needs concrete actions.

In India, the economic reforms, initiated significantly during 1991–93, with the opening up of both the domestic and external economy, have continued since June 1991 and were accompanied by intense intellectual and political debates. Detractors contend that the poor have not been benefited as desired and that the growth has encouraged inequality and joblessness to trigger major social and political problems. Although the per capita GDP growth rate rose an average of 1 percentage point in the post-reform period, commentators perceive that the post-reform growth process has been inequitable. Equity, no matter what form it is, has always been the bullseye to India's intellectuals, politicians, and policymakers. While the mobilization of the huge population to the next orbit of income, employment, education, and health is a significant challenge for India to achieve the SDG within the given timeframe, the strategies have also been transforming remarkably during the post-reform period in terms of motive, goal, and coverage. Though it is unsurprising that economic growth is a proxy for welfare in India, it does not warrant development for all and development for a long time.

The book provides a holistic insight into multiple perspectives of public policies in achieving sustainable development by 2030, particularly in India. This volume is organized into four broad sections containing a total of 22 chapters. A chapter-by-chapter brief description will be convenient for the readers to connect with the book before reading it.

Part I (Chaps. 1–4) presents a detailed analysis of the economic reforms, public policy moderation, and sustainability. Chapter 1 is a prelude to stepping into the discussion of public policy intervention in the post-reform period. It synthesizes the context of the economic reform in India and discusses the impacts of the economic reforms on the balance of payments crisis and how it helped to boost export, import, and productive efficiency. The following chapter (Chap. 2) analyzes the implications of institutional participatory governance on the green economy and socio-political and environmental sustainability. The study provides an outcome of new forms of governance which are perceived by society as the modes of the technological orientation of green economic, social, political, environmental, scientific, and technological action. The next chapter (i.e., Chap. 3) focuses on discussing how democracy, governance, and public policy can work to drive sustainable development agendas of the country for better outcomes. Chapter 4 intends to study how the acceleration in the GDP growth rate has an impact on the trends of poverty and inequality and how the social protection system acts sustainably to reduce poverty and prevent it from falling back into poverty across the life cycle.

Part II (Chaps. 5–10) demonstrates multiple facets of public policies in achieving sustainable development, particularly in India. While Chapter 5 examines long-term assurance, planned purposes, and strategic consistency through vertical and horizontal management and explains the systematic relationship between democracy, governance, and sustainable development, the next chapter (i.e., Chap. 6) puts an attempt to re-examine the global policy interventions to achieve sustainable development through environmental education or environmental studies and education for sustainable development focusing on the curricular and pedagogical aspects in the Indian state of West Bengal. The following chapter (Chap. 7) discusses the necessity for reimagining Women Resource Zone (WRZ) and provides various practices and recommendations that would help achieve SDGs. Chapter 8 explores the relationship between agricultural sustainability and women since women in India and other agro-economy-based developing nations play an important role in the agricultural sector—from sowing seeds to cutting crops, the same women face domestic violence and deprivation, keeping the development for all in an equitable way questionable.

The next chapter in this section (i.e., Chap. 9) intends to focus on the nature and specificity of weavers of West Bengal and also studies the trends of transformation in the textile industry with a critical review of the current policies. Chapter 10 attempts to measure the well-being of the elderly people of India by considering their economic dependency, living arrangements, and physical mobility with a quest for ensuring sustainability for all—across gender, age, and socioeconomic strata.

Part III (Chaps. 11–14) covers a detailed discussion of how the public policies in the post-reform period have been acting to revitalize the education sector. Chapter 11 focuses on the issues and challenges of digital inclusion in school education in the post-pandemic period in India, which brings forth vital social consequences. Chapter 12 focuses on the prospects and challenges involved in implementing the new education policy through a sample survey in the Kolkata Metropolitan of India. The next chapter in this section (i.e., Chap. 13) attempts to discuss how the introduction of Massive Open Online Courses (MOOCs) impacts the education system of India as a supplement to face-to-face education, which has historically been practiced in the country. Chapter 14 tries to analyze the educational attainment of the tea plantation workers along with their children and also puts a major focus on bringing out the reason behind the drop-outs of their children amidst the existence of provisions the clause in the current policies along with multiple initiatives and schemes announced by the state to prevent the drop-outs.

Part IV (Chaps. 15–22) is vast and diverse; it highlights public policy interventions in India toward social and economic transformations. Chapter 15 intends to examine the dynamic relationships between human capital, physical capital, and economic growth, which shows how GDP plays a vital role in determining health, education, and gross capital formation. Chapter 16 examines the short-run and long-run relationship between GDP and imports, exports, and FDI. Chapter 17 speaks about the empowerment level of SHG women and also tries to analyze the evolution of public policies regarding women empowerment. The next chapter (i.e., Chap. 18) examines the importance of women in the participation of labor-force, which is very important to eliminate gender inequality resulting in the achievement of sustainable development. Chapter 19 places a major focus on discussing the evaluation of the performances of the public and private sector commercial banks of India during the post-reform era. The following chapter (i.e., Chap. 20) attempts to discuss the government-sponsored social security programs, including ration card, MGNREGA, PMJDY, and RSBY that have a significantly higher contribution to the poor of vulnerable areas mainly the coal mining areas of Jharkhand state of India where elite capture of public welfare programs is common but social safety net is quite critical. The following chapter (i.e., Chap. 21) aims to investigate how the Electronic Service Quality (ESQUAL) of online banking services works at the bottom of the pyramid of consumers of West Bengal, considering eight districts of the state. Chapter 22 tries to explore the major items and areas which would help human resources to result in empowerment and progress sustainably. It also focuses on studying the potential of human empowerment that affects quality and innovation in public enterprises.

In a nutshell, this volume incorporates critical reviews from the benchmark events from the 1990s policy of opening up of the economy, post-reform fiscal and monetary policies to 2016s policies of demonetization, 2017s National Health Policy (NHP 2017), 2020s National Education Policy 2020 (NEP 2020), policies relating to ecosystem services and green technology manifestation, which combinedly simulate the system to address sustainable development through its public policies and uphold it as the dominant and structuring narrative to resolve the existing conflicts and ensure societies to develop amidst a harmonious world that is reconciled with nature. Unlike many other utopian visions that would develop against, alongside, or without the states' action, the editors of this volume firmly believe that the specificity of sustainable development is to place the state at the heart of its execution.

Itahar, India | Mukunda Mishra
Raiganj, India | Subrata Saha
Shantiniketan, India | Madhabendra Sinha
28 February 2023

Acknowledgments

Collective effort for more than 2 years has made this book possible. We are sincerely thankful to all of our friends and families, colleagues, students, and all others concerned that this venture would not have been completed without whose advice, mental support, and inspiration to write.

We express our most profound sense of indebtedness to Professor Soumyen Sikdar, Indian Institute of Management Calcutta, Kolkata, West Bengal, India. We are thankful to him for his kind advice and valuable time writing the 'Foreword' for this volume.

We are thankful to Professor Yoshiro Higano of the University of Tsukuba, Japan, for allowing this space for our volume in the Springer Series of *New Frontiers in Regional Science: Asian Perspectives,* in which he has been disseminating his role as the Editor-in-Chief with profound support to us whenever needed.

Expository reviews, thoughtful remarks, and valuable shreds of advice on the manuscripts of so many scholarly minds remain unparalleled in selecting manuscripts for the volume and substantially upholding the quality of the content within its folds. The Editors must mention the name of **Prof. Anil Bhuimali**, former Vice Chancellor of Raganj University and Professor of Economics at the University of North Bengal; **Prof. Sanchari Roy Mukherjee**, former Vice Chancellor of Raiganj University and Balurghat University and Professor of Economics in the University of North Bengal; **Prof. (Retd.) M. Thangaraj** of the School of Economics, University of Madras; **Prof. S. Pulla Rao** of Andhra University; **Prof. Partha Pratim Sengupta** of the National Institute of Technology (NIT) Durgapur; **Prof. Anjan Chakraborti**, Professor-Director of UGC HRDC; and **Prof. Govinda Chowdhury**, Department of Economics in the University of North Bengal; **Prof. Hasan Dinçer** of Istanbul Medipol University; **Prof. Jitendra Sahoo** of the University of Gour Banga; **Prof. Sankar Majumder** and **Dr. Achiransu Acharyya** of Visva-Bharati University; **Prof. Abhijit Dutta** of Sikkim University; **Dr. Anjan Ray Chaudhury** of Durgapur Government College; **Prof. Ramesh Chandra Das** of Vidyasagar University; **Dr. Amit Kundu** of Coochbehar Panchanan Barma University; **Dr. Manas Naskar** of Raiganj University; **Dr. Partha Mukhopadhyay** of Steel

Authority of India Limited; **Dr. Ujjal Protim Dutta** of Rangia College; **Dr. Rajib Bhattacharyya** of Goenka College of Commerce and Business Administration; **Dr. Sreemanta Sarkar** of Bidhan Chandra College and many more for their commendable roles and responsibilities at the different stages of the publication process.

The role of the contributing authors is precious in an edited volume. We convey our sincere thanks to all contributors for offering us the opportunity to include their valuable works in this volume. Their prompt response and active cooperation have made this volume successful on time.

Constructive editorial advice and constant support from Yutaka Hirachi, *The Senior Editor in Economics, Operations Research & Statistics, Springer Japan*, remains unparalleled. We acknowledge the support of the entire team of Springer Nature associated with the publishing process, disseminating their respective roles as perfectly as ever.

Disclaimer

The authors of individual chapters are solely responsible for ideas, views, data, figures, and geographical boundaries presented in the respective chapters of this book, and these have not been endorsed, in any form, by the publisher, the editor, and the authors of foreword, preambles, or other chapters.

Contents

Editors and Contributors

About the Editors

Mukunda Mishra is an Assistant Professor, Department of Geography, and designated Vice Principal of Dr. Meghnad Saha College in West Bengal, India. The college is affiliated with the University of Gour Banga. Dr. Mishra completed his postgraduate studies in Geography and Environmental Management at Vidyasagar University (receiving top rank in both the B.Sc. and M.Sc. panels of merit) and held a Ph.D. in Geography from the same University. He was selected for the prestigious National Merit Scholarship by the Ministry of Human Resource Development, Government of India. His research chiefly focuses on analyzing unequal human development, regional planning, and multi-criteria predictive model building. He has more than 12 years of hands-on experience in dealing with development issues at the ground level in various districts of eastern India. Dr. Mishra has in his credit to publish one monograph and four edited research volumes so far from the house of Springer Nature. Dr. Mishra has more than 30 research articles and book chapters published in the journals and books of international repute. Besides serving as the reviewer of several reputed journals published by Springer Nature and Elsevier Inc., he is continuing as the Managing and Publishing Editor of Ensemble, a UGC-CARE (India) enlisted journal of repute, since its inception to date.

Subrata Saha was awarded a Ph.D. in Economics from the University of North Bengal. Dr. Saha specializes in issues of fiscal policies and effects of structural changes on fiscal relationships in Southeast Asian Countries and India. The area of research interest is Public Finance, Health and Education, and Time Series Econometrics. He is a member of the editorial board of UGC-CARE listed journal ENSEMBLE and a life member of the Indian Econometric Society and Indian Economic Association. Dr. Saha is presently working as an Associate Professor of Economics at Raiganj University, West Bengal, India. He has supervised four M. Phil. and one Ph.D. and presently supervising four Ph.D. scholars at Raiganj University. He has contributed several research papers to National and International Journals and edited research volumes. Besides, he has authored two books to his credit. IRDP, India, has awarded him with the prestigious Sarvepalli Radhakrishnan Lifetime Achievement National Award in 2018 in recognition of his contribution to his research activities, and in 2021, World Education Congress has awarded him West Bengal Education Leadership Award 2021 toward promoting educational excellence.

Madhabendra Sinha is an Assistant Professor at the Department of Economics and Politics, Visva-Bharati (A Central University), Santiniketan, India; and prior to that he served as an Assistant Professor at the Department of Business Administration, Raiganj University, India. He has been a Senior Research Fellow and Ph.D. in Economics at the National Institute of Technology Durgapur, India. He obtained M.Sc. and M.Phil. in Economics from the University of Calcutta, India, and qualified UGC-NET in Economics. His research interests include open economy economics, development economics, and applied econometrics. He has credits of a couple of research publications in several reputed journals including Journal of Policy Modeling (Elsevier), Social Indicators Research (Springer), Economic Papers (Wiley), Global Business Review (Sage), Applied Intelligence (Springer), Margin: JAER (Sage), Journal of Asian and African Studies (Sage), IJEED (Inderscience), etc. He contributed a number of book chapters published by Springer, Routledge, Emerald, IGI Global, etc. He has participated in several workshops and presented research papers in various conferences and seminars organized by ADBI, IGC, IITs, IIMs, ISI, DSE, IIFT, BIBM & UNCDF, RIS-EXIM Bank, etc. in India, Japan, France, and other countries. He acted as reviewers of different journals published by Taylor & Francis, Wiley, Emerald, and Sage. He organized a number of workshops and seminars on research methodology and other issues and gave invited lectures in different universities.

Contributors

Nufazil Altaf Department of Humanities, Social Science and Management, NIT Srinagar, Srinagar, Jammu and Kashmir, India

Pradip Banerjee Indian Institute of Management (IIM) Indore, Indore, Madhya Pradesh, India

Ranjan Banerjee Himalaya Drug Company, Kolkata, West Bengal, India

Anindya Basu Department of Geography, Diamond Harbour Women's University, Sarisha, West Bengal, India

Shivani Bhardwaj Sathi all For Partnership (SAFP), E09 Anandlok Housing Society, Mayur Vihar Phase I, New Delhi, India

Mudaser Ahad Bhat Department of Data Science, Christ University, Lavasa-Pune, India

Susmita Bhattacharyya Department of Sociology, University of Calcutta, Kolkata, West Bengal, India

Diganta Biswas Post Graduate Council, Raiganj University, Raiganj, West Bengal, India

Nilendu Chatterjee Department of Economics, Bankim Sardar College, Kolkata, West Bengal, India

Susmita Chatterjee Manindra Chandra College, Kolkata, West Bengal, India

Samhita Chaudhuri Department of Geography, Bijoy Krishna Girls' College (Affiliated to University of Calcutta), Howrah, West Bengal, India

Pinki Das Centre for the Study of Regional Development, School of Social Sciences, Jawaharlal Nehru University, New Delhi, India

Sujoy Kanti Ghoshal Department of Economics, St. Joseph's College, North Point, Darjeeling, West Bengal, India

Md. Nijairul Islam Department of Education, Gazole Mahavidyalaya (Affiliated to University of Gour Banga), Malda, West Bengal, India

Aamir Jamal Department of Economics, University of Kashmir, Srinagar, Jammu and Kashmir, India

Bappaditya Koley Department of Geography, Bankim Sardar College, Kolkata, West Bengal, India

Anusri Kundu Department of Geography, Diamond Harbour Women's University, Sarisha, West Bengal, India

Santanu Mallick Department of Commerce (Hindi Shift), Banwarilal Bhalotia College, Asansol, West Bengal, India

Siddhartha Sankar Manna Department of Political Science, University of Gour Banga, Malda, West Bengal, India

Mukunda Mishra Department of Geography, Dr. Meghnad Saha College, Itahar, Uttar Dinajpur, West Bengal, India

Ajit Mondal Department of Education, West Bengal State University, Barasat, Kolkata, West Bengal, India

Partha Naskar Netaji Subhas Administrative Training Institute, Kolkata, West Bengal, India

Anindita Nath Department of Geography, Bankim Sardar College, Kolkata, West Bengal, India

Rajendra Narayan Paramanik Department of Humanities and Social Sciences, Indian Institute of Technology Patna, Patna, Bihar, India

Debdas Rakshit Department of Commerce, The University of Burdwan, Burdwan, West Bengal, India

Chandan Roy Raiganj Surendranath Mahavidyalaya, Uttar Dinajpur, West Bengal, India

Sudeshna Roy Centre for the Study of Regional Development, School of Social Sciences, Jawaharlal Nehru University, New Delhi, India

Bhaswati Saha Department of Sociology, Kalyani Mahavidyalaya, Kalyani, Nadia, West Bengal, India

Subrata Saha Department of Economics, Raiganj University, Uttar Dinajpur, West Bengal, India

Jitendra Sahoo Department of Political Science, University of Gour Banga, Mokdumpur, Malda, West Bengal, India

Sreemanta Sarkar Department of Economics, Bidhan Chandra College, Asansol, West Bengal, India
Department of Commerce, The University of Burdwan, Burdwan, West Bengal, India

Tanmoy Sarkar Department of Geography, Gazole Mahavidyalaya, Malda, West Bengal, India

Ahana Sen Department of Management, Raiganj University, Raiganj, West Bengal, India

Subhasis Sen Balaji Institute of Technology & Management (BITM), Sri Balaji University Pune (SBUP), Pune, Maharashtra, India

Raju Singha Department of Education, Dr. Meghnad Saha College (Affiliated to University of Gour Banga), Uttar Dinajpur, West Bengal, India

Madhabendra Sinha Department of Economics and Politics, Visva-Bharati University, Santiniketan, West Bengal, India

Sandeep Sundas Department of Economics, Raiganj University, Uttar Dinajpur, West Bengal, India

M. C. Omar C. Vargas-González Instituto Tecnológico de México, Campus Cd. Guzmán, Cd. Guzmán, Jalisco, Mexico

José G. Vargas-Hernández Instituto Tecnológico Mario Molina Pasquel y Henríquez, Unidad Académica, Zapopan, Zapopan, Jalisco, Mexico

Arun Kumar Yadav Monitoring and Evaluation (M&E) Office, Patna, Bihar, India

Vidya Yadav Department of Geography, College of Commerce, Arts and Science, Patliputra University, Patna, Bihar, India

Kumari Youkta Department of Humanities and Social Sciences, Indian Institute of Technology Patna, Patna, Bihar, India

Abbreviations

AABY	Aam Admi Bima Yojana
AAY	Antyodaya Anna Yojana
ACABC	Agri-Clinics and Agri-Business Centre
AECC	Ability Enhancement Compulsory Courses
AfDB	African Development Bank
AHP	Analytical Hierarchical Process
APMAS	Andhra Pradesh Mahila Abhivruddhi Society
ASEAN	Association of South East Asian Nations
BCCL	Bharat Coking Coal Limited
BOP	Balance of Payment
BPL	Below Poverty Line
CADFWF	Central Agricultural Development Fund for Women Farmers
CAST	Conflict Assessment System Tool
CBCS	Choice-Based Credit System
CBD	Convention on Biological Diversity
CEC	Consortium for Educational Communication
CEDAW	Convention for the Elimination of All Forms of Discrimination against Women
CEDICAM	Integral Campesino Development Center of the Mixteca
CEE	Central and Eastern European countries
CHCDS	Comprehensive Handloom Cluster Development Scheme
CI	Concentration Index
CRC	Convention on the Rights of the Child
CRPD	Convention on the Rights of Persons with Disabilities
DBT	Direct Benefits Transfer
DESD	Decade of Education for Sustainable Development
DIET	District Institute of Education and Training
DPSP	Directive Principles of State Policy
EAG	Empowered Action Group (States)
ECCE	Early Childhood Care and Education
EE	Environmental Education

EGSS	Environmental Goods and Services Sector
EPA	Environmental Protection Authority (of Ethiopia)
ESD	Education for Sustainable Development
ESQUAL	Electronic Service Quality
EU	European Union
EVS	Environmental Studies
EWS	Economically Weaker Sections
FAO	Food and Agriculture Organization
FDI	Foreign Direct Investment
FDP	Faculty Development Programme
FERA	Foreign Exchange Regulation Act
FFP	Fund For Peace
FSI	Fragile State Index
GCED	Global Citizenship Education
GDP	Gross Domestic Product
GNP	Gross National Product
GEE	Green Economic Efficiency
GGEI	Global Green Economy Index
GOI	Government of India
GRC	Gender Resource Center
GRG	Gender Resource Gap
GST	Goods and Services Tax
GTI	Green Technology Innovation
HEI	Higher Education Institution
HR	Human Resources
HWCWS	Handloom Weavers' Comprehensive Welfare Scheme
IAY	Indira Awas Yojana
ICDS	Integrated Child Development Services
ICT	Information and Communications Technology
IEEP	International Environmental Education Programme
IFAD	International Fund for Agricultural Development
IFPRI	International Food Policy Research Institute
IGNDPS	Indira Gandhi National Disability Pension Scheme
IGNOU	Indira Gandhi National Open University
IGNWPS	Indira Gandhi National Widow Pension Scheme
ILO	International Labour Organization
IMF	International Monetary Fund
INFLIBNET	Information and Library Network Centre
IPSrC	Integrated Programme for Senior Citizens
IRDP	Integrated Rural Development Programme
ITUC	International Trade Union Confederation
IUCN	International Union for Conservation of Nature
LCA	Life Cycle Assessment
LCSA	Life Cycle Sustainability Assessment

MAW	Middle-Aged Women
MBT	Mobile-Based Training
MDG	Millennium Development Goal
MGNREGS	Mahatma Gandhi National Rural Employment Guarantee Scheme
MHRD	Ministry of Human Resource Development
MoLE	Ministry of Labour and Employment (India)
MOOC	Massive Online Open Courses
NIM	Net Interest Margin
MPCE	Monthly Per Capita Expenditure
MPI	Multidimensional Poverty Index
MYRADA	Mysore Resettlement And Development Agency
NABARD	National Bank for Agriculture and Rural Development
NACDAOR	National Confederation of Dalit and Adivasi Organisation
NCERT	National Council of Educational Research and Training
NCEUS	National Commission for Enterprises in Unorganized Sector
NCF	National Curriculum Framework
NCF	National Curriculum Framework
NCTE	National Council for Teacher Education
NEP	National Education Policy
NFBS	National Family Benefit Scheme
NFCFDC	National Scheduled Castes Finance and Development Corporation
NHDP	National Handloom Development Programme
NIOS	National Institute of Open Schooling
NIPUN	National Initiative for Proficiency in Reading with Understanding and Numeracy
NITI	National Institution for Transforming India
NITTTR	National Institute of Technical Teachers Training and Research
NMAET	National Mission on Agricultural Extension and Technology
NMSA	National Mission for Sustainable Agriculture
NOAPS	National Old Age Pension Scheme
NPE	National Policy on Education
NPTEL	National Programme on Technology Enhanced Learning
NRDWP	National Rural Drinking Water Programme
NRHM	National Rural Health Mission
NULM	National Urban Livelihood Mission
OBC	Other Backward Caste
OECD	Organisation for Economic Co-operation and Development
OPHI	Oxford Poverty and Human Development Initiative
PACS	Primary Agricultural Cooperative Societies
PFLS	Periodic Labour Force Survey
PLA	Plantations Labour Act
PMEGP	Prime Minister's Employment Generation Programme
PMGKY	Pradhan Mantri Garib Kalyan Yojana

PM-KMY	Pradhan Mantri Kisan Maandhan Yojana
PMMMNMTT	Pandit Madan Mohan Malaviya National Mission on Teachers and Teaching
PPS	Probability Proportional to Size (Sampling Technique)
PSB	Public Sector Bank
PVB	Private Sector Bank
RAY	Rajiv Awas Yojana
RBI	Reserve Bank of India
REES	Revitalization of EE in Schools
RMSA	Rashtriya Madhyamik Shiksha Abhiyan
ROA	Return on Assets
ROE	Return on Equity
RSBY	Rashtriya Swasthya Bima Yojana
RTE	Right to Education (Act)
RVY	Rashtriya Vayoshri Yojana
SAARC	South Asian Association for Regional Cooperation
SAG	Scheme for Adolescent Girls
SC	Scheduled Caste
SD	Sustainable Development
SDG	Sustainable Development Goal
SDZ	Sustainable Development Zone
SEEA	System of Environmental-Economic Accounting
SHG	Self-Help Group
SIDBI	Small Industries Development Bank of India
SJSRY	Swarna Jayanti Shahari Rozgar Yojana
SMAM	Sub-Mission on Agricultural Mechanization
SSA	Sarva Shiksha Abhiyan
SSS	Social Security Schemes
ST	Scheduled Tribe
TAM	Technology Acceptance Model
TBI	Tea Board of India
TEEB	The Economics of Ecosystems and Biodiversity
TEQIP	Technical Education Quality Improvement Programme
TFP	Total Factor Productivity
TPDS	Targeted Public Distribution System
TSC	Total Sanitation Campaign
UG	Under Graduate (Degree)
UGC	University Grants Commission
UHC	Universal Health Care
UNDESA	United Nations Department of Economic and Social Affairs
UNDP	United Nations Development Programme
UNEP	United Nations Environment Programme
UNESCAP	United Nations Economic and Social Commission for Asia and the Pacific

UNESCO	United Nations Educational, Scientific and Cultural Organization
UNICEF	United Nations International Children's Emergency Fund
UNRISD	United Nations Research Institute for Social Development
USDA	United States Department of Agriculture
USTAD	Upgrading the Skills and Training in Traditional Arts/Crafts for Development
VAWG	Violence Against Women and Girls
WBSCL	West Bengal Swarojgar Corporation Ltd
WCED	World Commission on Environment and Development
WEAI	Women's Empowerment in Agriculture Index
WHO	World Health Organization
WRZ	Women Resource Zone
WSC	Women Struggle Committee
YSS	Yarn Supply Scheme

List of Figures

List of Tables

Part I
Economic Reforms, Public Policy Moderations and Sustainability

Chapter 1
Contextualizing the 1990s' Economic Reforms in India: A Politico-Economic Narrative

Tanmoy Sarkar and Mukunda Mishra

1.1 Introduction

In the economic history of independent India, July 1991 is considered as a benchmark. It is marked by a drastic shift in economic policy following bold economic and policy reform decisions by the Rao-led Government of India (GOI). The ripples of the conventional wisdom of economic reform of 1991 have been arguably prevailing in the country till date, and the policy decisions followed by every succeeding cabinet of the GOI, irrespective of political ideology, have curved its way since decades back.

The democratically elected first-ever Government in Independent India had many more challenges. In 1950, India was a newly independent nation with only 14% literacy, one-seventh of the world population with a meager per capita income, and three-fourths population engaged in the primary agricultural sector with primitive tools and techniques (Adhia 2015). The colonial past of the country has had a significant impact on its territorial disputes and also contributed to poverty, illiteracy, and structural distortions. The Nehru-led government had the challenge to counter and shape the crystallization of the colonial economic structure that led to poverty, underdevelopment, and a dependence on and subordination to Britain (Chandra et al. 2000). The colonial history and pro-Britain policies stagnated the Indian agricultural sector in large part of the country. The early years after independence (1947–1964) were devoted to reconstructing the nation, to shape its polity, economy, and society. Nehru focused on modern industrial transformation, agricultural revolution, and

T. Sarkar
Department of Geography, Gazole Mahavidyalaya, Malda, West Bengal, India

M. Mishra (✉)
Department of Geography, Dr. Meghnad Saha College, Itahar, Uttar Dinajpur, West Bengal, India

M. Mishra et al. (eds.), *Public Policies and Sustainable Development in Post-Reform India*, New Frontiers in Regional Science: Asian Perspectives 71,
https://doi.org/10.1007/978-981-99-3696-0_1

implementation of five-year centralized planning for India to be self-reliant. In the colonization-driven underdeveloped scenario, firstly, India approached import substitution industrialization to develop, protect, strengthen, and encourage the local economy and to reduce the dependency on developed nations. The economic policy of India was set to counter foreign capital domination. The introduction of land reforms by abolishing the Zamindari system for the potential use of land and social justice appeared as one of the most remarkable reforms (Basu 2008; Dey Biswas 2014). Introducing cooperatives, especially service cooperatives, was another important step by the government to focus on growth, welfare, and equity.

Moreover, the Nehru Government's expenses for the pro-poor and welfare approach led to the debt crisis. The operationalization of the so-called Nehruvian socialism with the mixed economy model of centrally planned development initially evolved into a serious domestic economic crisis and finally consequent in the balance of payment (BOP) crisis in 1957 (Chandra et al. 2000). On the eve of independence, this crisis was further intensifying due to divestment by foreign business houses from their holdings in the nation and halting of domestic investment in India.

DeLong (2003) criticized Nehru's Fabian socialism turn, centralized form of planning, and bureaucratic red tape (License Raj) for India's stagnated development and rampant corruption along with massive inefficiency. On the other part, the uniqueness of Indian development consensus with rapid industrial transformation within a democratic electoral government system led to an uncharted path that must be considered (Chandra et al. 2000). The mixed economic model in the early years after independence aimed to encourage the private and public sectors in a fashion where the coexistence was complementary to each other, and the development of private sectors allowed freedom as much as possible within the periphery of the National Plan. After the abolition of the British Raj, Indian industrial policy and economic development started to be governed by the "License Raj." The industrial policy resolution of 1956 and the Second Five-Year Plan came up with a new resolution and restrictions for foreign capital and private sector dominance.

Though the Nehru-Mahalanobis strategy put thrust on heavy and capital goods industries in the Second Five-Year Plan that led to more importance on the public sector, import substitution policy was taken to reduce foreign capital dependence, boosting Indian domestic capital investment and getting self-reliance. It was the decision in response to that time. Labor-intensive and capital-promoting community projects in the agricultural sector, along with community development programs (CDP) and development of cooperatives, were taken to respond to the then massive unemployment situation. Nehru-Mahalanobis emphasized growth with equity and assumed that higher growth could encourage higher levels of equity. The complicated industrial "License Raj" and control system were set up with the objectives of leading development along centrally planned lines, reducing foreign dependency and monopoly, protecting domestic entrepreneurship and small industry, and channelizing the resource following the government-directed priorities to reduce regional imbalance (Chandra et al. 2000). The situation led to the balance of payment (BOP) crisis in 1956–1957. The government decided to impose stringent import and foreign exchange controls to overcome the acute shortage of foreign exchange.

Table 1.1 Indices of industrial production in India: 1951–1979[a]

Industrial group	1951	1961	1971	1978–1979
General	55	109	153	186
Textiles	80	103	106	110
Basic metals	47	119	209	144
Machinery	22	121	373	208
Electrical machinery	26	110	405	162

Source: Government of India (1980); Johnson (1983); Adopted from Chandra et al. 2000, p. 481

[a]1960 = 100 (for 1951–1971) and 1970 = 100 (for 1978–1979)

However, the overall Indian economy performed impressively well compared to the colonial period. India's gross national product (GNP) showed an average growth rate of about 4% per annum between 1951 and 1964–1965 (Chandra et al. 2000). The domestic savings and investment rate showed remarkable growth from 1951 to 1965. Apart from the industrial sector, the agricultural front had been going through a reform process that started after independence. Large infrastructural investments in irrigation, power, and community development initiatives at the village level were implemented, and the development strategy centered around the land reform strategy in the 1960s. The indicative form of planning in the agricultural sector allowed farmers to make output and investment decisions with a serious thrust to achieve self-sufficiency in food grains. However, the impressive agricultural growth was not enough to match the escalating population demand for food, and India had to rely heavily on imports. The situation was altered after adopting modern industrial output and modern technology, using high-yielding variety (HYV) seeds, adopting mechanized farm tools, developing irrigation facilities, etc., in the form of the green revolution since the mid- and late 1960s. The industrial front showed comparatively faster growth due to the import substitution of consumers, capital, and intermediate goods (Table 1.1).

The share of investment in GDP and population growth rate is considered an important parameter to determine the growth scenario of a country, and India was significantly lacking in both of these parameters (DeLong 2003). There are several illustrations considering the limited economic growth and overall inefficiency in India during the Nehruvian dynasty. The impact of post-World War II also could not be ignored. Nehru's attraction to Fabian socialism and central planning contributed to the stagnant situation though there are some counterarguments also. The alternate argument is that the welfare policy consideration of Nehru for the deprived and poorest section of the country was the demand of time and space where extreme poverty, utmost unemployment, and serious social and economic inequality prevailed (Dandekar 1988). Therefore, India's policy decision was framed with the objectives of achieving decent growth, boosting social justice, and attaining self-reliance (Kaushal 1979). The "License Raj" undoubtedly affected the private sector economy, and the inefficiency in resource mobilization limited the promotion of policy efficiency in India.

1.2 Departure from the Nehruvian Legacy (1965–1991)

After the demise of Jawaharlal Nehru in 1964, Lal Bahadur Shastri took over as Prime Minister of India. The failure of the Third Five-Year Plan (1961–1966) was explicit. India had already experienced the India-China war in 1962. This period started with two massive monsoon failures in 1965 and 1966, and the agriculture-dependent Indian economy massively underperformed. Apart from these successive two climate hazards, the Sino-Indian War of 1962 and the Indo-Pak War of 1965 caused havoc on the Indian economy. The inflation was sharply elevated to around 12% from 2% in 1963, and the fiscal deficit was markedly increased. In his brief 19-month period of prime ministership, Shastri had to face violent anti-Hindi agitation in South India (1965), the country's worst-ever food crisis, and the crushing economy after the military escalation of the Sino-Indian border disputes, and most importantly, he had to face a continuous fragmented consensus within his party since his charge. His strong leadership in the most crisis-ridden period in India is worth appreciation. He tried to shift the focus to agricultural growth rather than heavy industries. Amidst those crises, his focus on food security and the role of agricultural scientist M.S. Swaminathan made India free from the dependency on the USA for food aid that, in turn, was supposed to influence the country's foreign policy autonomy. The introduction of "green revolution," under the leadership of Lal Bahadur Shastri and Indira Gandhi, revolutionized the food and agricultural sector of India with complete self-reliance. After the success of the green revolution, the country experienced the success of the white revolution in the dairy sector through the cooperative movement.

The importance of the development of the private sector, increase in foreign investment, and market-oriented approach to production were being considered by the government, but a lack of bold reform decisions could not make such change in the scenario. After the death of Shastri, Indira Gandhi took over the charge as Prime Minister of India in 1966. Indira Gandhi-led Indian Government had the challenge of responding to devaluation, economic turbulence, and inflationary recession. The BOP crisis triggered the need for import liberalization to get external assistance. The problems of exploding population and escalating unemployment were not resolved; however, the successive two wars against China and Pakistan greatly burdened the Indian economy. The Indian rupee was devalued by 36.5% in 1966 to reduce the gap between domestic and external prices, promote development, and get economic discipline. This devaluation encouraged the competitive market approach to address the country's trade economy and balance of payments.

Along with devaluation, several existing special export promotion schemes providing import entitlements against exports and the scheme for tax credit certificates were abolished. GOI had the plan to slow down the monetary expansion, simplification, and rationalization of import tariffs and policy designed to shape the improvement in the BOP position (Srinivas 2017). The Fourth Five-Year Plan was rescheduled in 1969 as the GOI declared a "plan holiday," and three consecutive annual plans were taken in response to the severe drought for 2 years and two wars with China and Pakistan on the borderland. The primary objective was to accelerate exports and to find a way for efficient utilization of industrial assets. The devaluation decision in 1966 was accompanied by several import liberalization decisions. However, the outcome was not satisfactory as expected.

Post-1967 India experienced several national political events, which in turn influenced the economy at large. While Indira Gandhi got a landslide setback in March 1971 election with the "Garibi Hatao Desh Bachao" (i.e., "remove poverty, save the country") campaign and took over the charge as Prime Minister of India, the radical socialist policies came into force to complement the populist democratic prepoll slogan. However, in the long run, these made some distortions in the way of reform. Government control was increased with the nationalization of banks, insurance (1972), and coal industry (1973). The objective of bank nationalization was to regulate bank lending towards the agricultural sector and to align the banks' move to the government's welfare policy direction. Bank credit in the rural economy was markedly picked in the post-nationalization period. However, the politically influenced economic pathways started causing economic pressure on the banking system.

The introduction of the Foreign Exchange Regulation Act (FERA) in 1973 put severe restrictions on foreign capital investment and made it difficult for the functioning of foreign companies in India. In addition, the policies of acquiring loss-making industries built more pressure on the economy. Although these decisions worked as the remedy for unemployment and stressful economic conditions, they paved the way for the BOP crisis in the coming days.

The 1971 Census of India estimated the population at 548.2 million, and the workforce was measured at 184 million, with which agriculture contributed 68.3% of the workforce (Kumar 2021). The green revolution was already in force, and it was mainly concentrated in a few pockets. The sharply elevated share of agricultural laborers (24% in 1961 to 37.8% in 1971) clearly indicated that small farmers were losing land. However, agricultural growth has been recorded as the highest in India after independence under the leadership of Mrs. Gandhi (Kundu 2016), and the green revolution had a pivotal role to play.

Inequality in every sector continued to grow. Underdevelopment, unemployment, and poverty were everywhere, but few pockets had the greater possibility of responding rapidly compared to others. With limited opportunity and limited funds, the government had to consider the places that looked promising for development. The vision of the trickle-down effect actually continued to accelerate the rural-urban divide as infrastructural investments were concentrated mainly in the urban areas. The per capita income in India declined by 0.9% in 1971–1972 though the state's income grew slightly by 1.4% (Kumar 2021).

The Fourth Five-Year Plan (1969–1974) was introduced in response to a devaluation, drought condition, and inflationary recession and had the vision of self-reliance with an ambitious goal of 5.6% growth. But the War with West Pakistan, the independence of Bangladesh, a massive flood of refugees from East Pakistan (Independent Bangladesh) and the subsequent economic pressure on India, the Asian oil crisis of 1973, and successive monsoon failure were the major obstacles against the achievement of this five-year plan. The political rhetoric of welfare politics continued to govern the economic policies during the tenure of Indira Gandhi. The industrial sector did not experience a major setback during Mrs. Gandhi's tenure. However, several industrial policies had been taken to boost investment, including new industrial licensing regulations to reduce control over small investment (CIA 1973), but the control over large firm investment remained tight. The CIA report mentioned that the Monopolies and Restrictive Trade Practices Act (1970) became law, which reads:

> "... any investment by firms with greater than 200 million of assets, or by firms with assets with assets of more than Rs. 10 million that control more than one-third of the market for a particular project, must be approved by the government"—CIA (1973)

Apart from this licensing raj and direct controls, several policies were reformed to include several financial measures to provide more government control over private investment. Mrs. Gandhi's political vision of employment maximization with restrictive policy by the protection of labor-intensive, inefficient, traditional techniques in village industries was thought to be responsible for the slowdown in the industrial growth—from 6% in 1968–1979 to 4% growth of industrial output in 1972 (CIA 1973). The process of long-term bureaucratic screening and rigid government process to consider applications for new direct investment was continued rather more intensified in the tenure of Mrs. Gandhi. The objective of progressive and steady Indianization of foreign firms continued to slow down industrial growth to a large extent.

We must remember that the economic policy was not always economically decided; rather, it had been on the political situation, the demand for democracy, and the ineluctability of the electoral voting process. Prior to the 1980s, interventionist policies, import controls (Bhagwati and Desai 1970), and discouraging entrepreneurship were the features of the government's economic policies.

After the assassination of Prime Minister Indira Gandhi, her son Rajiv Gandhi took charge as PM and continued from 1984 to 1989. Rajiv Gandhi-led government had taken primary initiatives to encourage the import of capital goods by relaxing the bureaucratic red tape of industrial regulations. Moreover, the tax system was also regularized, and the attitudinal shift in government vision to encourage all entrepreneurial initiatives boosted a belief in national and international industry stakeholders. India experienced an economic boom in the 1980s with the policy shift towards trade liberalization and relaxation of "License Raj" in investment, though the growth rate was highly variable throughout the decade. Joshi and Little (1994) emphasized the role of fiscal expansion financed by internal and external borrowing to boost economic growth. The unsustainable economic growth in the 1980s was "fuelled by a build-up of external debt that culminated in the crisis of 1991" (Ahluwalia (2002). The liberalization policy initiatives of the 1980s provided the necessary groundwork for the forthcoming 1991 reform in India. A major pace in policy decisions to consider industrial relaxation was considered during 1985–1988. GDP growth achieved a remarkable peak at 7.6% during 1988–1989 to 1990–1991 (Panagariya 2004). The export had marked a remarkable growth at 14.4% during

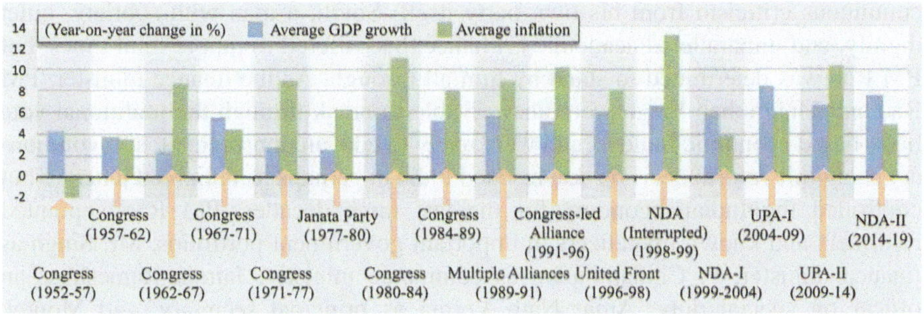

Fig. 1.1 A brief history of the Indian economy and the ruling government in center, 1947–2019. (Source: Prepared from the World Bank data, https://data.worldbank.org/)

1985–1990 from 1.2% during 1980–1985 (Fig. 1.1). Reducing the share of government in canalized imports, expansion in the number of the capital goods items in the OGL list, several export intensives, reduction of interest rate on export goods, duty-free imports of capital goods for selected thrust areas, relaxation in the industrial controls, and realization of exchange rate contributed towards the way of reform.

1.3 The Economic Reform in 1991: Expectations and Realities

The economic reforms in 1991 were not abrupt; the preparation had started in the 1980s. The growth rate took off a pace in the 1980s as the immediate effect of a few liberalizing attitudes of the Rajiv Gandhi-led government. The change in official attitude regarding the policy of encouragement despite discouraging the "investment" and the entrepreneurial economy was the key to sustaining the economic growth in India, irrespective of the major policy shift in 1991 (DeLong 2001; Rodrik and Subramanian 2004). Dr. Manmohan Singh's 1991 historic budget speech acknowledged the contribution of the policy and development initiatives taken by former Prime Ministers since 1947, and the policy shift in 1991 was not sudden. The Nehruvian policy of mixed economy (Kumar 2017) has had a great contribution to paving the way forward to adopt a reform in 1991 as it must not be considered a piecemeal decision.

After Rajiv Gandhi-led Congress government, India had two coalition governments led by Vishwanath Pratap Singh (December 2, 1989, to November 10, 1990) and Chandra Shekhar (November 10, 1990, to June 21, 1991). After these coalition-led unstable phases, P.V. Narasimha Rao was sworn in as India's premier on June 21, 1991. The massive fiscal and BOP crisis that was continuously building up since independence climaxed in 1991. And Manmohan Singh took charge of the finance minister on June 22, but his primary statements on economy and inflation were not supposed to be from a canny politician. PM Rao had to face a sharp attack and continuous criticism from his own party itself. Singh, a man with sobriety, quiet dignity, and unparalleled academic brilliance, had offered to quit several times, but PM Rao was determined to stand by him all through. As the finance minister, PM Rao and Manmohan Singh were unswervable to break through the traditional vote bank-based economic mindset and were ready to take an unprecedented, revolutionary economic reform decision that rescued India in perhaps its unlighted juncture but controlled the Indian economy for the last three decades. PM Rao appointed reformers and known liberalizers in important government portfolios: Mr. Singh as finance minister, P. Chidambaram as commerce minister, Jairam Ramesh as an officer on special duty, Amar Nath Verma as principal secretary, and Montek Singh Ahluwalia appointed as a commerce secretary. India was going through a profound macroeconomic crisis and an acute shortage of foreign exchange reserves that was a potential threat to the sustainability of growth. Due to several external and internal factors like the Gulf War and oil price hike in the international market, the political instability in India was extremely high; capital inflow sharply declined as the lack of international confidence in Indian economy. The entire country was in search of a leader who could make bold decisions and will respond to the macroeconomic imbalances. In June 1991, the nation had the exchange only to pay for just 2 weeks of imports (Ramesh 2015, also cited in Kumar 2017). And finally, on July 24, 1991, Manmohan Singh[1] presented the "historic" budget speech:

> "... There is no time to lose. Neither the Government nor the economy can live beyond its means year after year ... Any further postponement of macro-economic adjustment, long overdue, would mean that the balance of payments situation, now exceedingly difficult, would become unmanageable, and inflation, already high, would exceed limits of tolerance. For improving the management of the economy, the starting point, and indeed the centre-piece of our strategy, should be a credible fiscal adjustment and macro-economic stabilisation during the current financial year to be followed by continued fiscal consolidation thereafter ... Macro-economic stabilisation and fiscal adjustment alone cannot suffice. They must be supported by essential reforms in economic policy and economic management as an integral part of the adjustment process, reforms which would help to eliminate waste and inefficiency and impart a new element of dynamism to growth processes in our economy."

In his budget speech, Dr. Manmohan Singh outlined the thrust of the reform process. The great economist speculated that a reform is essential:

- To increase the efficiency and international competitiveness of industrial production
- To utilize for this purpose foreign investment and foreign technology to a much greater degree than the country has done in the past
- To increase the productivity of investment
- To ensure that India's financial sector is rapidly modernized

[1]See the Union Budget, Ministry of Finance, Government of India. Available at https://www.indiabudget.gov.in/bspeech.php.

- To improve the performance of the public sector so that the key sectors of Indian economy are enabled to attain an adequate technological and competitive edge in a fast-changing global economy

There is ample literature during the late 1990s and the first decade of the new millennium that have analyzed the "reforms" critically on the ground of what we "expected" and what actually "happened." While those "sky-kissing expectations" have been verified with the "ground-rooted realities," most of them concluded with the lists of "unfulfillment" from the reform. 1990s' economic reform is, like many other such earlier reforms in India and abroad, certainly not a "panacea" to work equally to resolve all possible issues.

While a popular expectation is often set that trade liberalization encourages economic activity and hence raises production and employment, it sounds somewhat unrealistic to expect immediate benefits through such a channel. The ground reality is that the trade liberalization that implies increased foreign competition leads to the closure of less competitive firms, and therefore job losses and income reduction in the initial phase are a hard reality (Siggel and Agrawal 2009). Trade liberalization in the initial post-reform years has shrunk India's manufacturing base in terms of value addition and employment (Nambiar et al. 1999). However, the scenario changes in the long run. Indian economy started experiencing increased productivity, competitiveness, and accelerated growth since the mid-1990s. Moreover, amidst the break of the "dream" of revamp of production, import liberalization came forward to challenge the historically prevailed syndrome of "high protection-high cost-poor quality" in the production system.

There are objections about the non-materializing of rapid and sustained growth of output and employment; getting the industrial base narrowed; finding the employment growth in the 1990s negative in 5 out of 9 years; and stagnancy of labor productivity after 1995/1996, despite getting increased in the early 1990s and many more (Chaudhuri 2002). Alongside, there was a decline in debt/equity ratios in the majority of industries, especially in new firms consequent to financial reform. The matter of TFP decline was mainly attributed to trade and licensing reforms. However, the reform facilitated the industrial sector in expanding its capacity (Balasubramanyam and Mahambre 2001). While Ahluwalia (2002) considers the 1990s' reform as gradualist, it raises the query of whether it is attributed so by design or the consequence of political constraints. Still, the cumulative impact of 1990s' reform was substantial, and it was successful in creating the basis for accelerated growth.

1.4 Bringing Efficiency for Politico-Economic Leadership in South Asia

The collapse of the multipolar and bipolar geopolitical world has made inevitable changes in both the economic and the security model globally. While the earlier security models were mostly based on the balanced confrontation between the powers or superpowers and their allies, the current security is envisaged as the interdependence and cooperation between states. Moreover, globalization, liberalization, and established institutional structures work as essential stimuli. Similarly, economics in the pre-Cold War world was discussed mostly on a national scale and, to a large extent, a self-sufficient model, which has now significantly included the possibilities of significant external cooperation and foreign affairs agendas. It embraces both the hard (i.e., military) and soft (i.e., nonmilitary) dimensions, and, in some complex cases, the "soft" are now taking the lead over the "hard"—both at the national and international levels (Zukrowska 1996). As Kukuka (1994) mentioned, the size of the country, stability of the economy, stability of the political system, relations with neighbors, ability to adjust to changing internal and external conditions, institutionalization of external relations, and opening up of the economy are the critical factors for "soft" dimensions, and all these are the deciding factors for a state to emerge as a politico-economic leader of a region. A politically and economically stable India could make it executed successfully in South Asia:

> "The enabling and constraining capabilities of India with regard to promoting regional cooperation in South Asia had been discussed even before the conceptual journey of the South Asian Association for Regional Cooperation (SAARC) began in 1983. India occupies a unique position in the South Asian region. By the virtue of its size, location and economic potential, India assumes a natural leadership role in the region."—Bhasin (2008)

The data of the annual change of GDP and inflation over the last 60 years (1961–2021) of the eight SAARC states (i.e., Afghanistan, Pakistan, India, Sri Lanka, Bangladesh, Bhutan, Nepal, and Maldives), retrieved from the World Bank data portal (https://data.worldbank.org/), makes the scope of a comparative discussion amongst the SAARC states' economic portfolio in the last six decades. Plotting of the annual change in GDP and inflation in India with the backdrop of the maximum (keeping "positive" at the ceiling and "negative" at the floor) change of annual GDP (Fig. 1.2a) and inflation change (Fig. 1.2b) makes meaningful interpretation.

From 1992 onward, India's annual GDP change has always been positive until the severe effect of the Covid-19 pandemic on the economy to find a negative change (−7.484%) in 2020. Indian economy witnessed a consistently stable trend since the reform, except abrupt declines from +5.471% (in 1996) to +2.071% in 1997; from +6.851% (in 1999) to +1.965% in 2000; from +6.093% (in 2007) to +1.630% in 2008; and from +7.013% (in 2010) to +3.818% in 2011 to fall into a consecutive declining trend between 2017 and 2020 (i.e., from +6.980% in 2016 to +5.56% in 2017, +5.302% in 2018, +2.6797% in 2019, and −7.48% in 2020) (Fig. 1.2a). While situating the Indian GDP trend within the GDP scenario of the ambient SAARC nations, the post-reform Indian GDP trend looks more robust and consistent than its neighbors.

The trend of post-reform inflation in India is somewhat straightforward up to 2003. There was a gradual and consistent decline of inflation (GDP deflator as annual %) from 1991 (13.751%) to 1999 (3.068%), and it stayed almost stable up to 2003 (3.867%). It was followed by a rising curve to reach the highest in that spell

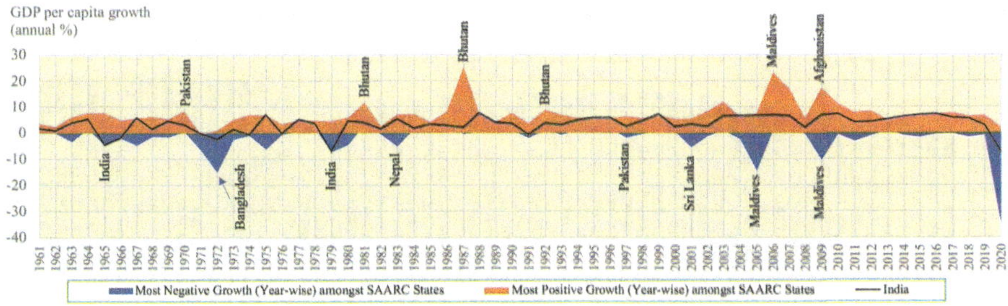

(a)

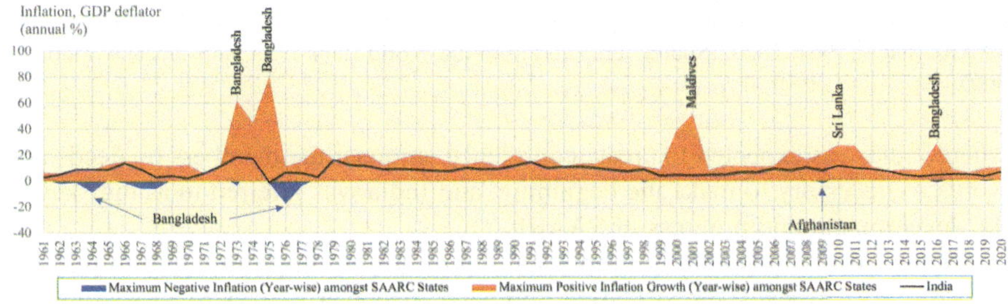

(b)

Fig. 1.2 The most positive and negative annual change in (**a**) GDP and (**b**) its deflator across the last 60 years (1961–2020) in the states of South Asia and India, 1961–2020. (Source: Prepared from the World Bank Data, https://data.worldbank.org/)

in 2010 (10.527%) and then gradually declined to 2.390% in 2019. This trend is robust without any abrupt rise like the Maldives in 2001 (50.892%), Afghanistan in 2007 (22.527%), Pakistan in 2009 (20.666%), Sri Lanka in 2010 (26.934%), Nepal in 2011 (26.397%), and Bangladesh in 2016 (27.850%) (Fig. 1.2b).

The 1990s' economic reform in India took place amidst a rapidly changing global political and economic scenario during the post-Cold War era. While a number of states erupted into internal conflict, another significant number of postcolonial states allowed partial or total liberalization of their commercial regime at the bilateral or less-than-multilateral level (Fawcett 1995; Ravenhill 2008). Alongside, the diminishing trend of "superpower relations" was opening up prospects for regionally preeminent powers to adopt more overt managerial roles in their respective regions (Ayoob 1991). At the recession of the superpowers, the successful practice of the open-market economy and multilateral economic cooperation system was prevailing in many parts of the globe—the Organization for Economic Cooperation and Development (OECD) in the West with Anglo-Saxon members, the noticeable success of the transforming economies of China, the little dragons of East Asia along with their neighbors in the Association of South East Asian Nations (ASEAN), and open economic and trade policies in Latin America, notably in Mexico, were the major propounders. However, better late than never, the South Asian nations took up until 1985 to form the South Asian Association of Regional Cooperation (SAARC),

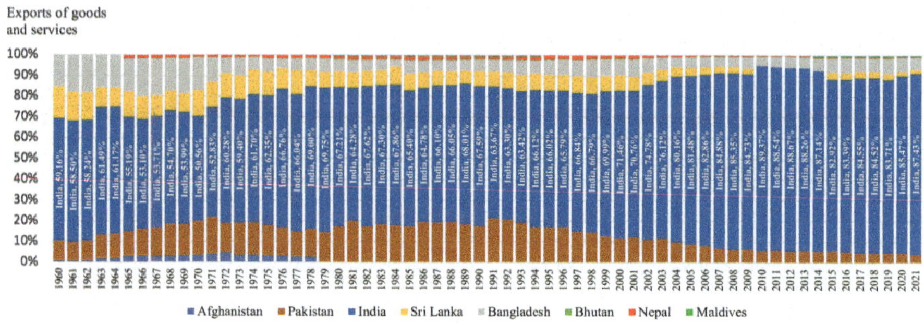

Fig. 1.3 Share of exports of goods and services in the last 60 years (1961–2020) amongst the SAARC states, 1961–2020. (Source: Prepared from the World Bank Data, https://data.worldbank.org/)

where India was expected to create confidence amongst the members by deeds and words so necessary to make the beginning, and India was referred to as the "key to the development and progress of SAARC."[2]

Amidst several cohesive and tensional forces, 1990s' economic reform of India played a critical role. The structural approach to power considers an advantaged position to India in South Asia historically. India, sharing its international borders with all South Asian countries, enjoys a vital physical link in the region, sharing 72% of the land surface, with 77% of the population of the South Asia (Bhasin 2008).

Amongst the SAARC states, India's export figure had been conspicuous historically (Fig. 1.3). However, the introduction and/or expansion of several export incentives, especially after 1985, helped imports directly when imports were tied to exports and indirectly when relaxing the foreign exchange constraint:

> "Exporters were given REP licenses in amounts that were approximately twice their import needs and thus provided a source of input imports for goods sold in the domestic market. The key distinguishing feature of the REP licenses was that they allowed the holder to import items on the restricted (and therefore those outside of the OGL or canalized) list and had domestic import-competing counterparts. Even though there were limits to the import competition provided through these licenses, as exports expanded the volume of these imports expanded as well. This factor became particularly important during 1985–90 when exports expanded rapidly."—(Panagariya 2004)

Joshi and Little (1994) ascribed those export incentives as the "quasi-Southeast Asian-style" reforms which included the following:

- 50% of business profits attributable to exports were made income tax deductible in the 1985 budget and were extended to 100% in 1988.
- Interest rate on export credit was reduced to 9%, which was 12% earlier

[2]Address by His Majesty Junius Richard Jayewardene, President of Sri Lanka, at the Fourth SAARC Summit, Concluding Session, 29–31 Dec. 1988, Islamabad, Pakistan, *From SARC to SAARC: Milestones in the Evolution of Regional Cooperation in South Asia* (1980–88) Vol. I, SAARC Secretariat, Kathmandu

- In April 1988, access for exporters to imported capital goods was increased by widening the list of those available on OGL and by making some capital goods available selectively to exporters without going through "indigenous clearance." Assurance was given that the incentives announced in the export-import policy would not be reduced for a period of 3 years.

Now, we should focus on the political stability or fragility in South Asia. The Fragile State Index (FSI) is developed by the Fund for Peace (FFP), an independent, nonpartisan, 501(c)(3) nonprofit research and educational organization that works to prevent violent conflict and promote sustainable security. The FSI has its original methodological concept rooted in FFP's Conflict Assessment System Tool (CAST), developed in the 1990s to help policymakers and field practitioners better understand and measure conflict drivers and dynamics in complex geopolitical environments.[3] The FSI is based on a total of 12 indicators—three cohesion indicators (i.e., C1: Security Apparatus; C2: Factionalized Elites; and C3: Group Grievance); three economic indicators (i.e., E1: Economic Decline; E2: Uneven Economic Development; and E3: Human Flight and Brain Drain); three political indicators (i.e., P1: State Legitimacy; P2: Public Services; and P3: Human Rights and Rule of Law); and three social and cross-cutting indicators (i.e., S1: Demographic Pressures; S2: Refugees and IDPs; and X1: External Intervention). Based on CAST's comprehensive social science approach, data from three main streams (i.e., preexisting quantitative datasets, content analysis, and qualitative expert analysis) is triangulated and critically reviewed to obtain final scores for the FSI. While the index inherently ranks different countries to visualize how some are more fragile or more stable than others, the FSI score (where a higher FSI score denotes higher fragility) of the SAARC states has been picked up for the years of 2006, 2011, 2016, and 2021 (Table 1.2).

While the efforts of liberalization, preferential trade agreements, politico-economic union formations, etc. were empowering the multilateral economic integration, the issues of political fragility of the states were excerpting disintegrative force that had serious repercussions not only for those particular states and their people but also for their neighbors. Postcolonial states in South Asia and the states in sub-Saharan Africa had been witnessing alarming political fragility historically (Fig. 1.4). These have emerged from ethnic tensions, civil wars, or several forms of revolution; whatever the cause might be, they resulted in complex humanitarian emergencies.

South Asia has remained the epicenter of border disputes, military movements, armed standoffs and skirmishes, and even war during the postcolonial era. Since the early 1960s, there has existed an alliance between China and Pakistan. After formally resolving all of its boundary disputes with China through the Sino-Pakistani Agreement of 1963, Pakistan started receiving Chinese military assistance in 1966. It was followed by the formation of a strategic alliance in 1972 and the launch of economic cooperation in 1979 that has been making China the

[3] See the FSI Methodology Handbook available on the URL: https://fragilestatesindex.org/wp-content/uploads/2017/05/FSI-Methodology.pdf.

Table 1.2 Fragile State Index score and rank of the SAARC states in the years 2006, 2011, 2016, and 2021

	FSI 2006		FSI 2011		FSI 2016		FSI 2021	
Country	Rank	Score	Rank	Score	Rank	Score	Rank	Score
Afghanistan	10th	99.8	7th	107.5	9th	107.9	9th	102.1
Bhutan	39th	87.9	50th	85	78th	77.6	96th	68.3
India	93rd	70.4	76th	79.3	70th	79.6	66th	77
Maldives	n.a.	n.a.	91st	75.6	91st	74	99th	67.6
Sri Lanka	25th	92.4	29th	93.1	43rd	87.7	55th	80.5
Pakistan	9th	103.1	12th	102.3	14th	101.7	29th	90.5
Bangladesh	19th	96.3	25th	94.4	36th	90.7	39th	85
Nepal	20th	95.4	27th	93.7	33rd	91.2	51st	82.2

Source: Official website of the Fragile State Index, https://fragilestatesindex.org

largest supplier of armaments and the third largest trading partner overall to Pakistan. Gradually, Beijing took a central part of Islamabad's foreign policy. On the military front, the People's Liberation Army and the Pakistan Armed Forces started sharing a notably close relationship. While Beijing started supporting Pakistan's position on the Kashmir conflict, Islamabad started seconding the Chinese stance on the Xinjiang controversy, the sovereignty of Tibet, and the Taiwan issue. The conflicting and competing interests between India and the China-Pakistan alliance resulted in a complex situation in South Asia. Amidst the power tussle between the USA, the "defending champion," and China, a strong contender for sharing the domination, the emergence of an economically and politically strong India as the regional politico-economic leader of South Asia could be the solution for peace and stability in the entire region, the cornerstone of which was laid in the 1990s' economic reform.

1.5 Conclusion

1990s' India, which was then emerging as the regional politico-economic leader, has transformed itself into the fifth largest economy of the world within the latter three decades by virtue of effective democratic governance, rational public policies, and internal political stability. An overly regulated economy, inadequate state capacity, complex state-society relations, and limited rationalization across state and society writ large, most of which persisting since India's emergence as an independent nation, pose challenges to its accelerated growth. However, the post-reform period has demonstrated the country's ability to achieve multidimensional success in terms of improving its economic performance and comprehensive regional integration, coupled with sustaining its democracy successfully. From the abysmal 3.5% annual growth until the 1980s, the reforms accelerated the improving 5.5% growth rate to

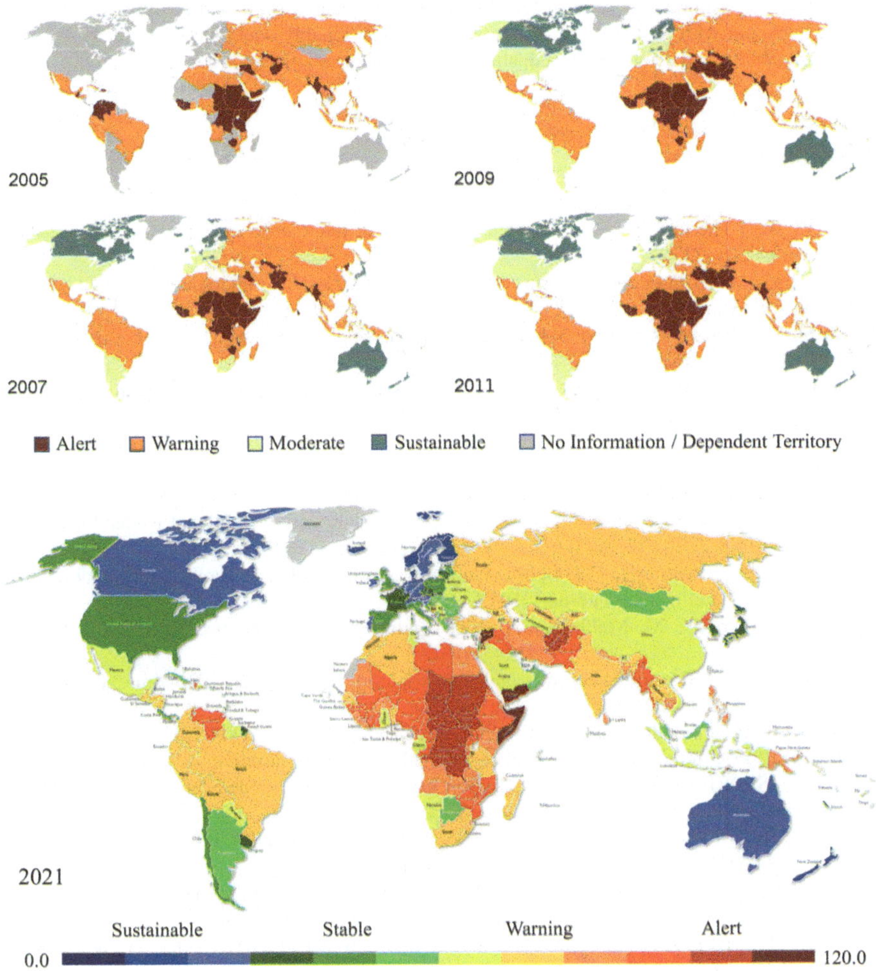

Fig. 1.4 The status of political fragility across the world, and, especially to the South Asia, as envisaged by the Fragile State Index (FSI), developed by the Fund for Peace (FFP), an American nonprofit, nongovernmental research and educational institution, founded in 1957

the 7% demonstrated since the new millennium. The country is determined to expand specific forms of collaboration, evidenced by its efforts to build strategic partnerships with more than 30 different countries globally. Presently, India has been advocating in a focused way to enact policies and build institutions towards ensuring self-reliance (*atmanirbhar*) in all facets of the economy. Its goals are multi-dimensional and broad, as mentioned by the Prime Minister of India that,

> when India speaks of becoming self-reliant, it doesn't advocate a self-centred system. India's self-reliance is concerned with ensuring the whole world's happiness, cooperation and peace. A quarter of a century ahead of the economic reform, India's role in successfully

blending the democratic governance, the self-reliant economy, and the robust effort of peace-making with an advantageous geostrategic positionality sounds promising in advocating stability and achieving sustainability in South and Southeast Asia.

References

Adhia N (2015) The history of economic development in India since independence. Educ About ASIA 20(3):18–22

Ahluwalia M (2002) Economic reforms in India since 1991: Has Gradualism Worked? J Econ Perspect 16(3):67–88

Ayoob M (1991) India as a regional hegemon: external opportunities and internal constraints. Int J. XLVI.(31):Summer; 420

Balasubramanyam VN, Mahambre V (2001) India's economic reforms and the manufacturing sector, Lancaster University working paper 2001/010

Basu K (ed) (2008) The Oxford companion to economics in India. Oxford University Press, New Delhi

Bhagwati J, Desai P (1970) India: planning for industrialization. Oxford University Press, London

Bhasin M (2008) India's role in South Asia: perceived hegemony or reluctant leadership? Indian Foreign Affairs J 3(4):72–88. http://www.jstor.org/stable/45340757

Central Intelligence Agency (1973) Indira Gandhi's economic policies: intelligence memorandum, directorate of intelligence, February 1973

Chandra B, Mukherjee M, Mukherjee A (2000) India after Independence 1947–2000. Penguin Books

Chaudhuri S (2002) Economic reforms and industrial structure in India. Economic and Political Weekly, pp 155–162, January

Dandekar V (1988) Indian economy since independence. Econ Polit Wkly 23(1–2):41–50

DeLong JB (2001) India since independence: an analytic growth narrative

Dey Biswas S (2014) Land rights formalization in India; examining de Soto through the lens of Rawls theory of justice. FLOOR Working paper 18. p. 16

Fawcett L (1995) Regionalism in historical perspective. In: Fawcett, Hurrell A (eds) Regionalism in world politics. Oxford University Press, Oxford, pp 9–36

Government of India (1980) India: a reference annual. GOI, New Delhi, p 312

Johnson BLC (1983) Development in South Asia. Harmondsworth, p 136

Joshi V, Little IMD (1994) India: macroeconomics and political economy: 1961–91. World Bank, Washington, DC

Kaushal G (1979) Economic history of India 1757 to 1966. Kalyani Publishers, New Delhi

Kukuka J(1994) Bezpieczeæstwo mi¢ędzynarodowe w Europie,rodkowej po zimnej wojnie, Uniwersytet Warszawski, Instytut Stosunków Międzynarodowych, Warszawa 1994

Kumar SB (2017) P.V. Narasimha Rao: the precursor of the era of economic reforms in India. Indian J Public Adm 63(4):616–630. https://doi.org/10.1177/0019556117726824. SAGE publications. http://journals.sagepub.com/home/ipa

Kumar, A. (2021). The 1970s Indian economy: a period of growing strains and the nation's fight against poverty; https://thewire.in/history/indian-economy-1971-poverty-bank-nationalisation-indira-gandhi

Kundu T (2016) How India fared under Indira Gandhi. https://www.livemint.com/Politics/UZVGcQyJMZ3t5ZJLNZRcMO/How-did-India-fare-under-Indira-Gandhi.html

Nambiar RG, Mungekar BL, Tadas GA (1999) Is import liberalisation hurting domestic industry and employment? Econ Polit Wkly, February, pp 417–424

Panagariya A (2004) India in the 1980s and 1990s: a triumph of reforms. IMF Working Paper

Ramesh J (2015) To the brink and back: India's 1991 story. Rupa Publications India, New Delhi, p 4

Ravenhill J (2008) Regionalism. In: Ravenhill (ed) Global political economy, 2nd edn. Oxford University Press, Oxford, pp 172–209

Rodrik D, Subramanian A (2004) From 'Hindu growth' to productivity surge: the mystery of the Indian growth transition, working paper No. 10376, NER, March, http://www.nber.org/papers/w10376

Siggel E, Agrawal P (2009) The impact of economic reforms on Indian manufacturers: evidence from a small sample survey. Working paper series no. E/300/2009, Institute of Economic Growth

Srinivas V (2017) The economic history of India: India and the International Monetary Fund 1944-2017. Special lecture at the National Archives of India dated 21/7/2017

Zukrowska K (1996) International organizations in new conditions. Polish Quart Int Affairs 5(3–4): 81–98

Dr. Tanmoy Sarkar is an Assistant Professor in the Department of Geography of Gazole Mahavidyalaya (College) in Malda, West Bengal, India. The college is affiliated with the University of Gour Banga. Dr. Sarkar completed his postgraduate studies in geography and environment management, specializing in remote sensing and GIS at Vidyasagar University. He was awarded Ph. D. from Raiganj University. His research chiefly focuses on the application of geospatial tools and techniques and multi-criteria predictive models in addressing physical and human processes on the spatial framework. He has been teaching geographical science at the undergraduate level for more than 10 years. He has working experience as an investigator in different research projects sponsored by DST and ICSSR. Dr. Sarkar has published three research papers in reputed journals, published by Springer Nature.

Dr. Mukunda Mishra is an assistant professor in the Department of Geography and designated Vice Principal of Dr. Meghnad Saha College in West Bengal, India. The college is affiliated with the University of Gour Banga. Dr. Mishra completed his postgraduate studies in geography and environmental management at Vidyasagar University and holds a Ph.D. in geography from the same university. He was selected for the National Merit Scholarship by the Ministry of Human Resource Development, Government of India. His research chiefly focuses on analyzing unequal human development and creating multi-criteria predictive models. He has more than 10 years of hands-on experience in dealing with development issues at the ground level in various districts of eastern India. Dr. Mishra has in his credit one monograph and three edited research volumes so far from the house of Springer Nature, and he has more than 25 research articles and book chapters published in the journals and books of international repute. Besides serving as the reviewer of several reputed journals published by Springer Nature and Elsevier Inc., he is continuing as the Managing and Publishing Editor of Ensemble, a UGC-CARE (India) enlisted journal of repute, since its inception to date.

Chapter 2
Green Economy, Sociopolitical and Environmental Implications of Institutional Participatory Governance

José G. Vargas-Hernández and M. C. Omar C. Vargas-González

2.1 Introduction

The green economy is a multi-level concept of governance. Governance refers to the act of governing and the series of acts undertaken by people to shape, affect, and guide the acts of others to jointly rule and control the public consequences of human activities and natural events (Gordon 1991; Dean 1999). Governance is a term used in political sciences since the twentieth century defined as the formal centralized political institutions intended to govern publicly managed problems and concerns issues that respect the interests and identities of the communities. However, the notion of the polity as the substance of politics is being disconnected from the traditional sites, territorial connotations, and formal political institutions (Hajer 2003).

Political ecology analyzes the environmental governance in the green economy at their multi-level structures of power and politics, such as the green economy (Adger et al. 2001). Governance factors with respect to institutional frameworks may facilitate a transition to a green economy (Droste et al. 2016). Participatory governance is determined by the theoretical perspective adopted and by the stance towards the actors taken. Institutional participatory governance induces positive changes in the distribution of public resources and services that impact the green economy, sociopolitical and ecological-environment reshaping of the society, and creation of new values.

J. G. Vargas-Hernández (✉)
Instituto Tecnológico Mario Molina Pasquel y Henríquez, Unidad Académica, Zapopan, Zapopan, Jalisco, Mexico
e-mail: jose.vargas@zapopan.tecmm.edu.mx

M. C. O. C. Vargas-González
Instituto Tecnológico de México, Campus Cd. Guzmán, Cd. Guzmán, Jalisco, Mexico

M. Mishra et al. (eds.), *Public Policies and Sustainable Development in Post-Reform India*, New Frontiers in Regional Science: Asian Perspectives 71,
https://doi.org/10.1007/978-981-99-3696-0_2

Environmental research contributes to sustainable economic development. Revolutionary changes in a brief period of time have an impact on the green economic, social, political, and environmental development at the local level. Green economics, circular economy, and bio-economy must be assessed within cross-cutting metrics of environmental, social, and economic sustainability, such as the Changing Wealth of Nations by the World Bank (Lange et al. 2018). The project analysis of the green economy explores the conceptual and methodological framework for the implementation and monitoring of the dimensions (Loiseau et al. 2015), the critical factors for practices of the green economy (Pitkänen et al. 2016), and the governance factors and institutional frameworks to facilitate transitions to a green economy (Droste et al. 2016).

The complexity and diversity of the environment of the earth are the features of economic systems in local policy and decision-making processes. The eco, intellectual, political, and moral categories of institutional participatory governance are addressed by green economics to provide holistic solutions to economic, social, and environmental problems. On the other hand, neoclassical economics is considered an instrument that imposes a set of values for economic, social, and environmental control as the foundations for the commodification of nature, leading to poverty because it does not aim to maximize equity, freedom, and utility.

Governance is a term related to economics further developed in fields such as institutionalist economics, administrative sciences, and political sciences (Williamson 1996; Benz and Dose 2010; Mayntz and Scharpf 1995; Marks et al. 1996). An interdisciplinary social science observes institutional participation and transformation in situ and in practice. The scientific observations may become political. Regulative political formation and decision-making processes are characterized by negotiation among a multitude of stakeholders, economic agents, and political actors at all levels embedded in this process and outsourced at functional and differentiated institutional governance (Jachtenfuchs and Kohler-Koch 2010, p. 69). Attempts have been made to order and govern the processes of negotiation among the actors and participants to get involved and develop a shared sense of understanding and dialogue of the problems and issues at stake.

The green economy is an extension of the conventional mainstream neoclassical economic approach to encompass distributional social equity and environmentally sustainable quality objectives (Bateman 1997, p. 37). Given their inherent tendency towards weak frameworks, most of the green economy approaches are in their infancy and challenging the policy-making measurements of positive effects of economic policies through the interactions between the environment and the economy. Moreover, these approaches do not embrace the discourses of going beyond GDP, accepting the need for a complement.

The practical balance between social and environmental equity in green economics is beyond distributional equity, ensuring a social transformation achieved through the process and at the end rather than an economic analysis of distribution activities (Kennet and Heinemann 2006). Monitoring the transformations of the green economy extends to collecting data on traditional and conventional economic and environmental sectors.

Recommendations to improve the measurement for green economy transformations should consider including more availability of data and cheaper, faster, broader, and wider frameworks for measuring the interactions among the economy, society, and environment (Georgeson et al. 2017). Society, economy, and environment recognize the role of the green economy to be foundational and operate within the global biosphere, as the initiative The Economics of Ecosystems and Biodiversity (TEEB) (Folke et al. 2016; Ten Brink et al. 2012).

The meaning and aim of green economics are creating conditions required to create the economic conditions to develop social and environmental justice to benefit the earth-wide nature, human and nonhuman species, and socio-ecosystems. Green economic background, inherent to natural and social sciences, grounds in social and environmental justice. Green economics offers some emerging questions on the rationale of the background to the implementation of social and environmental justice while addressing reversing habitat destruction. Green economics has an inclusive scope to implement the means for change of social and environmental justice as the attainments of ends that reconcile contradictory choices between justice and the environment.

Thinkers in green economics argue that there is a link between poverty and inequality, and therefore, improvement of equality ends up poverty and enhances environmental justice by overcoming environmental degradation. Mainstream economics has some considerations pertaining to green economics, environment, and energy (Reardon 2007). The essential criteria for the adoption of sustainable environmental regulation and green economy efficiency are green energy production and consumption, labor policies and socio-economic development policies, resource efficiency, and green industry development (Naseer et al. 2021). Post-Keynesian economics does not always include the environment in its analysis because any nonorthodox deviation from mainstream orthodoxy is opposed instead of examining the social and environmental elements (Mearman 2007).

Participation of economists, political scientists, sociologists, politicians, elected officials, bureaucrats, urban planners, other relevant actors, and stakeholders culminates a wide range of expertise and practices across diverse sectors. Therefore, practices concerning an ideal type of governance and participation may confirm discrimination regarding the meaning of different institutional and political notions concerning urban field practices. However, participatory institutions do not always follow the law and regulations to accomplish their functions, more when they are dominated by the agenda of local politicians, failing to address the complexity of socio-economic problems of the community such as violence and poverty, showing the existing distance between the law and the current exercising of state authority. Global large corporations are agents of hegemony and power (Gramsci 1932–1934), becoming undemocratic and lacking transparency as being the causes of socio-economic and environmental problems. Corporations that are not socially responsible for society become immoral (Bakan 2004, p. 35).

The basic assumptions regarding politics and science in participatory governance of organizations lead to governablity that is phrased on how to govern (Gordon 1991: 7). It is considered as a bricolage of ideological and empirical dynamics underlying the economic, social, political, and technological contexts. Participatory governance knowledge and practices as the ways of acting and thinking at once, focusing on the agency of joint learning and action, occur in a place around political-life concerns and power in spheres of action in the economy, society, politics, and science, constituted in simultaneous processes of mutual shaping (Flyvbjerg 2001).

International funding agencies drive institutional participatory governance pushing for rules to advance good governance. Radical participation's assumption of representation is that it kills citizenship and makes them inactive individuals cutting the ability of community fellowship, self-governance, shared public goods, mutual deliberation, autonomy, and social justice.

The socio-economic and ecological environment of participatory governance influences and sets the parameters for the potential impact on the internal workings of participatory governance institutions. The meaning of participatory governance summarizes the theoretical influences of participation forms and the debates on contention areas, description, location, and scope guided by the arguments of politics, political sociology, development studies, and economic institutionalism. Governance theory is the core attribute of participatory governance that engages in governing problems by encompassing practical applications and solutions in diverse practices stemming from diverse participation uses within discourses.

The notion of public participation is approached by the practical development theory that implements the social theory of interpersonal relations orientation developed by social sciences (Schutz 1958). The practical implication of this theory is building public participation based on trust. The theory of interpersonal relations orientation developed by Schutz (1958) and further detailed by Bormann (1990) assumes that individuals as members of society participate in social, economic, and political activities, creating a dialogue with other persons. The concept of a green economy is related to different economic theories aiming at environmental, economic, and social benefits.

This analysis is presented in sections. The first part analyzes the green economic implications to continue with the social, followed by the social and environmental implications.

2.2 Green Economic Implications

The green economy results in the improvement of well-being and social equity, reducing environmental risks and ecological scarcities (UNEP 2011a). The environmental economy deals with the efficient use of natural resources. The concept of a green economy is attractive to business organizations and governments with the aim of implementing economic growth, mitigating environmental damage, providing employment, and introducing green industries (Borel-Saladin and Turok 2013). The green economy focuses on areas identified as elements of the enhancement of stocks and flows of natural capital and efficient renewable energy and natural resources, environmental technologies, green manufacturing, waste management, transport, buildings, tourism, and cities (UNEP 2011a).

The concept of the "green economy" was created by Pearce et al. (1989) for the UK's Department for the Environment. The notion of a green economy appeared in 1989 in Pearce's Blueprint for a Green Economy, the British environmental economist (Pearce et al. 1989). The United Nations Environment Programme (UNEP) is an international organization that plays a leading role in developing and promoting a green economy defined as the results in the improvement of human well-being and social equity, reducing ecological scarcities and environmental risks, and being the engine for economic growth, through the generation of jobs and poverty eradication (UNEP 2011b, page 1). The emerging concept of the green economy implies a strong intersection between the economy, social, and environmental dimensions leading to provision of guidance by broadening the consistent notions of inclusive green economy and inclusive green growth with the recognition of the environmental limits within the green economy. The implementation of these concepts integrates economic, social, and environmental dimensions and poverty eradication into green economy policies (UNDESA and UNDP 2012).

The UNEP Green Economy synthesis for policy-making downplays substitutability in the trade-off between economic growth and environmental sustainability (UNEP 2011a). The multisectoral nature and complexity of the green economy require a co-integration of policy-making bridging spatial planning with practical implementation related to a multiplicity of factors such as environment, energy, innovation, agriculture, housing, and transport, depending on the context (Droste et al. 2016).

Green economy policy and strategy agenda supported by technological economies implemented through schemes aimed to protect and modernize economic sectors offer solutions to developed as well as less developed economies, which results in the transformation of management, governance, and control of natural resources. Comprehensive green economy policies and strategies are displayed in approaches reflecting the different approaches towards green economic transformations in terms of the promotion of sustainable environmental technology sectors, low-carbon developments, and circularity enhancement. Green economy policies and strategies focus on the origin of environmental degradation in the current economic system and propose decisions and aim towards the transition to achieve economic growth, social equity, and environmental sustainability (Droste et al. 2016). The green economy is an economic system that is consistent with keeping the economy with socio-environmental conditions and within socio-ecological limits. It is an environmental-economic perspective that seeks to achieve a sustainable society.

The conceptual framework of the green economy is a radical transition for efficient, environmentally friendly, resource- and energy-saving technologies leading to reduction of gas emissions, mitigation of the effects of climate change, and tackling of resource depletion and environmental degradation (Jänicke 2012). Resource-efficient growth falls short of the global environmental and social challenges. Resource efficiency and green purchasing are the best strategies for a green economy efficiency and development of environmental regulation. Regulations are a new dimension partially based upon knowledge to assess the societal significance. Knowledge is socially and politically robust and accepted.

Participatory governance practices have positive effects on the creation of new values, equal distribution of natural resources, and sharing of economic and socio-ecological responsibilities (Wampler and McNulty 2011). Participatory governance practices are emerging in specific circumstances, practices, activities, etc., affecting the discourses and ordering of the governed and ordered issues at stake and also affecting the existing formal institutions. Focus on practices limited to key incidents in the location of participatory governance in the form of diachronic and synchronic forms.

The public environmental field is a unit of analysis in participatory governance practices shaping relationships of contestation regarding the expressions of joint rule and judgment (Fox and Miller 1997). Resource sharing connected at all levels may ensure the implementation of new models of institutional participatory governance based on the subsidiary principles to prepare the foundations to implement other different participatory approaches that include cultural diversity, human rights, sustainability, and participatory democracy to enhance economic and socio-ecological development.

The green economy principles, documented at the Rio+20 outcome, however, did not clarify the policy measures to be implemented, a gap that is being filled by the green economy literature leading to the implementation of emerging green economy policy toolkits and instruments to design, implement, monitor, evaluate, and experience climate change and environmentally sustainable policies. Many of the green economy initiatives are related to Rio+20, towards the green economy and better governance, contributing to building sustainable development policies and strategies (EU Communication 2011). Development changes in science and innovation towards the ecological economy and environmental economics under a Green Economy Model are intended to control climate change and global warming.

Based on the analysis of the concepts of green economy and green growth given by international organizations, Borel-Saladin and Turok (2013) conclude that the green economy provides the required tools to transform economic activities into healthy and inclusive economic environments. Economic growth as a concept in green economics is reserved to be used for natural resources that are abundant and grow without any destruction, as in environmental economics.

The economic growth, supported by innovation and development supported by changes in the ecological economy, and environmental economics, leads to a green economy aimed at controlling climate change and global warming. Green economics is a complex and vast field of a general nature and is related to topics such as green political economy, social and environmental justice, intergenerational equity, and stakeholder theory, including organics and durability of goods.

The nature of civil society organizations is linked to organizational economics as they need resources and capabilities to function as active agents in participatory governance institutions. The nature of participatory governance institutions is to support the environment. The adoption of participatory governance institutions focuses more on programs to fit between the local needs and rules. The rules, norms, processes, and procedures are varied in participatory governance institutions that have effects on the outcomes. The institutional rules must be adapted and adopted to solve problems and have an impact on the participatory governance program.

The adoption of participatory institutions is in response to the economic, financial, and political crisis or a transition to a democratic regime. Organizations may attend participatory meetings to keep informed about development projects and to promote the public good. This sphere is referred more to emotions and sentiments than rational arguments and instrumental economics of rational choice, based on knowledge use and created for decision-making in open spaces that include a diversity of participants. Institutions are relevant to create conditions for planning economic development. The diversity of institutional participatory governance programs demonstrates the needs of local communities. New forms of institutional participatory governance may be in developing regions (Allegretti and Herzberg 2007). Participatory governance institutions are facing some challenges to achieving the desired outcomes, despite increasing the scope of the problems. Reforms of horizontal and public participatory arrangements among political actors, economic agents, and other stakeholders involved in the decision-making process within vertical and top-down representative democracy may sustain more flexible institutions, structures, and processes. Variations in the institutions of the state, civil society, and economic development make sense to adopt or adapt institutional participatory governance, an analysis of economic and social actors within a comprehensive definition of civil society (Lovan et al. 2004).

Economic actors get involved in governing processes in coherence with inclusive practices at local and regional participatory governance spaces framed by fiscal dependence and support from private partners to achieve competitiveness goals (Newman and Thornley 2005). Public participation in participatory budgeting should be favorable to all the political actors, economic agents, and stakeholders, which keep evolving in the right direction to become a process of participatory democracy (Rabouin 2009, p. 97). Participatory budgeting program includes the component of social justice that develops economic, financial, political, and social connections among the residents of a community. Emerging institutional and participatory governance experiences may function better at certain economic thresholds in the developing world and other economic environments that are hosting and influencing participatory governance in experiments such as participatory planning and budgeting. Institutional governance constraints are often deemed intractable in the supply side of economics, failing to reach the socially excluded and poor groups, despite laws and regulations.

The environmental regulations for green economy efficiency could be analyzed based on the analytical hierarchical process (AHP). The AHP is an evaluation process technique used by Naseer et al. (2021) to reduce uncertainty in decision-making through environmental regulation and green economy efficiency. The analytical hierarchy process is used to identify, analyze, and rank the green economy efficiency criteria and alternatives for the growth and enforcement of environmental regulations and green economy efficiency.

Green economy visions and discourses vary between continents and nations (United Nations Environment Programme (UNEP) 2011a; AfDB 2012; UNESCAP and Asian Development Bank and United Nations Environment Programme 2012). Economic and social actors of the nation-state participate in dynamic economic and social networks stretching across national boundaries. A functional approach of cross-border institutional participatory governance determines the effects (Ulrich 2016). The new forms of participatory governance institutions are created and developed from sociopolitical engagement, relationships, and interactions forged in networks.

The green economy and environmental dimension have strong links in practice to governance approaches at national and local policy levels in which the green economy is considered the pathway to the three dimensions of sustainability, the environment, economic, and social. Network governance and network management are notions that capture the interactions between the state and civil society and the ability of the state to govern in the complexity and uncertain transnational economic and social networks (Mayntz 1993; March and Olsen 1995; Kickert et al. 1997; Rhodes 1995; Pierre and Peters 2000).

Regional integration based on neo-functionalism intergovernmental approaches and multi-level governance regarding inclusiveness and participatory governance emphasizes the cooperation rationale among the administrative elites, cross-border economic agents, and political actors involved in functional bargaining and technocratic regulation (Ulrich 2016). Participatory institutions may have different impacts on political parties, rivals or not.

From a transborder perspective, economic transnationality focuses on the governance of global companies in economic zones. The active role of a cross-border and transnational governance structure is framed as economically and people-oriented institutions towards achieving more cohesion, competitiveness, and innovation. Changes in governance practices privilege the relationships with other economic interests. Using the different participatory governance approaches is crucial for more inclusive policies that make a difference in the lives of ordinary people on key issues related to economic policies and the sustained deepening of democracy. Landscape-level shifts of the multi-level perspective are of growing relevance to justify green economic policies, such as in the case of environmental policy for climate change.

There is no specific strategy to promote greener economies that must be targeted to the political, economic, social, and environmental situation. Instead, the green economy implements strategies to improve sustainable environmental development growth outcomes (ICMA 2019). A varied array of diagnostic tools and instruments for process guidelines of green economic policies and strategies are available to be implemented by developed and developing countries to deliver outcomes across economic, social, and environmental dimensions at the levels of national and local governments. Local governments may improve the business environment and the quality of life (ICMA 2019). Local, regional, and national government authorities need to be supported by legal and political instruments for governance.

In some less developed countries, the configuration of transition towards a green economy reflects the institutional development of the historical struggles over the governance of natural resources. The economic and industrial policy overlaps with the environmental problems. Shifts in landscape imperatives at a multi-level perspective related to climate change provide legitimacy for green economy policies that create a supportive environment. Informal and formal participation are manifestations of struggles over political legitimacy related to government-led participation exercises.

2.3 Social Implications

Green economy addresses socio-environmental needs to leverage ecosphere and lithosphere material and immaterial benefits, although the societal outcomes beyond the land use are limited, and there is no unmistakable evidence of decoupling economic growth from the impacts of environmental sustainability (Vadén et al. 2020; Ward et al. 2016). Green economy incorporated the idea of decoupling of the rates of change in economic output and the environmental assets used up in that process (Pearce 1991). Resource decoupling breaks the link between the environmental "bad and economic good" (OECD 2002).

Participatory governance practices are connected to the political democratic structures to solve social problems, improve the institutions, and use public resources from a sustainable co-governance practice. Citizens find value in participatory practices in individual participation and local government practices reflecting their social and political preferences. Citizens have the knowledge and abilities both to rule and to be ruled (Aristotle 1976) and to administer themselves by governing free men. Citizens are engaged in the participatory model of governance, although the public does not have enough possibilities to contribute. Citizens engage in participatory governance even though the public at large cannot always participate and contribute. Any change in the process of institutional participatory governance leads to changes in the outcomes, as in the situation emerging from an individual more confident in their interest in politics, which may bring an important procedural impact. Any model of sustainable participatory governance must bring decision-making closer to citizens on issues related to the project implementation. Exploring an innovative model of participatory local decision-making and governance seems to have many challenges.

The typology of civil society organizations that are working within the participatory governance context may be based on the density of social capital contribution to participatory institutions and their embeddedness in civil society. Of course, a certain type of institutional participatory governance initiative is more likely to result in positive effects in specific contexts. Most of the institutional participatory governance programs are organic and induced by local governments. Government at all levels can experience both bottom-up and top-down efforts to promote and enhance participatory governance. However, many cases of institutional participatory governance are a mix of the elements of these categories, top-down and bottom-up. Civil society organizations may have a contestation and demanding rights history and links to political parties with a strong link to citizens that shape participatory institutions, despite that it is more likely to be dominated by political parties or government officials. The scope of participatory governance and its implications with cultural heritage are needed including trust, ethics, respect, political, professional and social will, a legal framework, transparency and access to information, education and training for the actors involved, and funds for promoting participation (Voices of Culture 2015: 12). Different and broad array of social and political actors contribute to increasing citizen participation emerging in different contexts. Local government leaders and political and social actors adopt this institutional participatory governance supported by strong incentives to establish robust participation.

Local government officials and political and social activists rely upon social networks using formal and informal governance arrangements. An induced institutional participatory institution depends on the political will of government officials and politicians committed to implementing and supporting the institutions. Government officials, politicians, and social leaders can be motivated by strong incentives to promote institutional participatory governance. Envisioning multiple futures as a political act has political implications.

Institutional participatory governance arrangements incentivize reconsideration among boundaries between the different spheres and fields such as the case of the public consequences of food production, distribution, commercialization, and consumption that may become a political conflict leading to the redesign of food safety regulations. The participation patterns have different forms, including informal participation relying on traditional means such as public relations, mass media, political lobbying, and other forms, not necessarily conventional forms of participation beyond the legal border.

Welfare economics, environmental economics, Buddhist economics, and post-autistic economics (Kennet and Heinemann 2006, pp. 84–89) are sister disciplines contributing to green economics. Social resource and service localization is one consequence of welfare state dissolution, and in post-transitional countries, it is a shift of the managerial logic of governance based on market principles to govern public resources and services. Best practices can be transformed into guiding principles aimed at a need for creativity for government officials, politicians, and civil society activists. The green economy results in improved human well-being and social equity while significantly reducing environmental risks and ecological scarcities (UNEP 2011a). Social well-being improvements may result from participatory governance more than other factors such as economic growth. Green economy advocates the leverage of ecological processes that occurs in natural and seminatural systems to enhance the social well-being of human beings by promoting low-carbon energies without jeopardizing the environmental sustainability of the ecosystems (D'Amato and Korhonen 2021). The GDP growth driven by some greenness is not a real indication of a green economy because it does not prove to deliver changes in natural resource management, reduction of gas emissions, resource depletion and environmental degradation, changes in consumption patterns, and mitigation of climate change.

The emerging movements of nongovernmental organizations, social organizations, and movements, and local government officials, participate in initiatives of participatory local governance. Development and equality in opportunities between noninstitutional and institutional public, private, and social sectors require the involvement of stakeholders in participatory governance (Švob-Đokić 2004a, 2004b; Katunarić 2003, 2004, 2007; Vidović 2012, 2014, 2017; Mišković 2015; Vidović and Žuvela 2016; Žuvela 2016; Barada et al. 2016). In the institutional context, partnerships between the public, private, and social sectors at regional and local levels are mixed structural arrangements dealing with management and governance under the inter-sectorial participatory principles. Biosecurity, spatial resilience, management and governance, systemic environmental and production risks, etc. are only a few fields that benefit from the green economy and bio-economy.

Green production capacity is beyond green technology innovation (GTI) to encompass the socio-economic and environmental activities in the economy. Green economy, circular economy, and bio-economy should create and develop a solid framework at all levels of organizational contexts. The bio-economy aims at the growing economic sectors not necessarily environmentally benign, based on biological material inputs, nature-based instead of fuel-based products such as agroecological crops, forest products, etc., which may be contested by biodiversity loss and land-use management.

The development of participatory governance practices in the context of an institutional framework may reflect the lack of legal basis only determined for some of the institutions. Empowered participatory governance (EPG) is part of a solution to the democratic erosion, political passivity, and social privatization (Fung and Olin Wright 2003) supported by efficient and participative institutions aimed to transform governance based on bureaucratic organization and administration and political representation. This situation lies more in the contentious nature of political concerns of social movements than in the institutional design and styles of politics.

2.4 Environmental Implications

The philosophy of green economics is the management of nature and the management of the environment. Green economics builds on evolved, more recent thinking to analyze economic, social, political, and environmental concerns of reality by means of holistic, multidisciplinary, complex, and very-long-term methods. Green economics criticizes neoclassical economics and proposes a reform bringing core drivers, principles, and assumptions of ecology, social and environmental justice, and equity.

Social and environmental justice, addressed by Lawson (2007), ends the fragmentation in alternative economics, leading to the development of robust green economics with the argument that a sustained and systematic ontological analysis is required, meaning to study the nature of the real domain. Furthermore, the nature and role of institutional participatory governance are growing in co-governance processes (Abers 2000; Goldfrank 2011; McNulty 2011; Wampler 2007). Lawson defends the principles and thesis of patriarchy and accumulation underlying green economics as a science.

Green economics interconnect all human activities and the whole planet, becoming an overarching science of human interactions through an economic system focused on the environment and combining socio-economic-technological knowledge in dynamic analysis of the physical environment. The current economic system of overstimulated consumption and unrestricted economic growth is unsustainable: it impoverishes people, exacerbates inequality, and destroys the environment. Awareness of consumer environmental protection increases with the upgrading of consumption structure concentrated on green products to promote green economic growth.

Eco-design products for zero waste production consider the environmental impacts of life cycle products, take-back, and reuse. Life cycle assessment (LCA) is the tool for assessing the environmental impacts of products and services from the cradle to the grave (Finnveden et al. 2009). Life cycle sustainability assessment (LCSA) is the integration of economic, environmental, and social aspects with the concept of life cycle assessment (Guinée et al. 2011; Heijungs et al. 2010). The environmental extended input-output model explains the interdependencies and environmental impacts between the different economic sectors (Kitzes 2013).

On the other hand, green economics promotes "fairness, equity, participation, and democracy with social and environmental justice at its core" (Kennet and Heinemann 2006, p. 70). Institutional participatory governance is considered a means to enhance complex political and social democratization processes. Regarding the nature of participation, the issues to consider are the participants, modalities of adoption, supportive environment, and promoting participation. Green economics takes a longer term perspective to discount and restitute natural resources to be used by future generations through the knowledge of environmental and natural sciences, economics, archeology, and anthropology to develop a holistic and multidisciplinary analysis of economic decision-making.

Green economics reformulates the concept of demand to make more effective consumption in accordance with the real supply of natural resources and more efficient distribution concerns of the impacts on the value and supply chains by the embedded social, environmental, and human costs; economies of scale; equity; transparency; complexity; locality; ethical values; and diversity (Kennet 2004, 2005; Scott Cato and Kennet 1999). Green economic efficiency (GEE) benefits the economy, society, and environment. Green products and services benefit the consumer's lifestyle, natural environment, communities, and society by developing and strengthening a political framework. The environmental goods and services sector (EGSS) measures green economy transformations with limited potential, and therefore it does not consider the potential of green economy for creating economic innovation and restructuring economic activities, as well as the complexity of economic contributions to identify producers using standard statistical classifications (Eurostat 2009, 71). The environmental goods and services sector (EGSS) treated as the target leads to output distortion (Hood 2012).

The precautionary principle states that the activities raising harmful threats to human health or the environment are critical to green economics, and precautionary measures must be taken even in the absence of scientific proof (Kennet and Heinemann 2006, p. 70). The measures of environmental goods and services sector (EGSS), green R&D, environmental innovation, and green patents are part of the OECD framework (OECD 2014). The environmental goods and services sector (EGSS), as a section of the System of Environmental-Economic Accounting (SEEA), is related to green economy opportunities but does not accurately reflect the scale of green economy opportunities and transitions.

Environmental expenditure measurement should measure the advancement of opportunities in the green economy. The environmental goods and services sector (EGSS) methodology challenges to measure national green economic performance. The measurement performance of a narrow environmental goods and services sector (EGSS) focus should be improved, leading to the structural transformation of the green economy. The proponent of the activity should bear the burden of the proof in a process that must be open, informed, and democratic, including all the affected parties and involving the full range of alternatives, including no action.

Substitute indicators of the transformational green economy are a flexible, irrelevant framework and have a lower utility that allows not to measure the interactions between the economy and environment and inequality, which are transformational issues. For example, the Netherlands Environmental Assessment Agency developed an indicator to assess changes in the quality and quantity of the ecosystems (Davies et al. 2015; Ten Brink et al. 2012). Macro-meso levels of green economics include metric indicators for social, environmental, and economic dimensions, such as the Global Green Economy Index (GGEI) (Citizen Dual 2021), which assesses perception and performance in cities and nations, and the green growth indicator framework (OECD 2021), to assess national progress.

To improve measurements of green economy transformations, it is recommended to measure beyond the GDP broadening to measure the interactions of economy, society, and environment and use alternative measurement approaches, new methodologies, and sources of available data.

2.5 Conclusion

The green economy is a multi-level concept of governance. Improvement of economic, social, environmental, and ecological goals can be addressed through green economy and growth conceptual approaches to design co-integrated policies and implement strategies to find solutions. The economic, sociocultural, environmental, and institutional participatory governance issues have impacts on green economy efficiency. Transitioning from traditional economic development models to green economy to attain green economy efficiency supported by the patterns and structure of economic development, environmental regulations, implementation, and execution are relevant factors. The analysis of participatory institutions of governance is complex but rich with a potentially profound change because of the implications of the new interactions between citizens and government officials. The ongoing debates on green economics frameworks and practices are relevant for the societal, economic, and environmental reorganization aimed at achieving gas emission reductions, social and environmental justice, socio-environmental sustainability, and stable economic growth. Emerging institutional participatory governance programs as organic experiences from the bottom-up, implementers, political parties, and committed leaders should consider the issue of environmental sustainability.

Furthermore, political parties are a driving force to attract local citizens into top-down participatory governance processes. Political parties must engage citizens in institutional participatory governance experiences and address financial hardships, apathy, etc. Political parties from the left promoted participatory institutions that have expanded ties to citizens to improve governance.

The green economy and growth concept have not shared understanding on ongoing debates sustaining contrasting definitions reflecting the different perceptions of the economy-socio-ecological environment relationships. The green economy is a term that must reflect different social, economic, environmental, and cultural contexts. The analytical hierarchical process decision-making framework is a model used to implement green economy efficiency and evaluate green economy efficiency criteria for sustainable economic, social, and environmental growth.

The new forms of governance are perceived by society as the modes of ordering the teleological orientation of economic, social, political, and scientific activities. New participatory institutions embedded in the rule structure and the political-economic interests are reflecting the interests of designers to facilitate the participation of citizens and civil society organizations. New models of institutional participatory governance in emerging institutions with social mandate happen to exist working with and for people.

The key elements of any platform and network structure for institutional participative activities must be inclusiveness, solidarity, socio-interculturality, etc., aimed to bring together all levels of governmental institutions; social, civic society, and community organizations; business; citizens; political actors; economic agents; and other stakeholders. Furthermore, the effectiveness of the participation of actors and stakeholders in the processes is the element to achieve economic, social, and political sustainability, which must be developed to build and maintain the dialogue and trust based on access, standing, and influence among all the participants (Senecah 2004:22).

Moral concerns incorporated into green economics include the foundations of economic, social, and environmental inclusiveness and justice, fairness, equity, and access. Institutional participatory governance can be tackled for socially inclusive public service delivery, supported by the theory of change framework that integrates supply and demand governance. Between governance and participation, there is an ideal and formal inclusion of noninstitutional actors into public action processes by the initiative of political leadership. Political leadership rules the participatory governance of the several types of inclusion procedures at local levels but not at regional scales. The theory-led approaches have operational implications for integrating demand and supply in institutional participatory governance committed to transforming social institutions.

Economic measurements of green economic transformations and measurable improvement of the relationships among society, environment, and economy are areas that require improvement. The current measurements of the green economy have limitations to full engagement between them. Other limitations are the scale measurement of responses to environmental and climate changes and supply-side measurement of the aggregate impact of economic activities on the environment to track the transformations of the green economy.

References

Abers R (2000) Inventing local democracy: grassroots politics in Brazil. Lynne Rienner Publishers, Boulder

Adger WN, Benjaminsen TA, Brown K, Svarstad H (2001) Advancing a political ecology of global environmental discourse. Dev Chang 32:681–715

African Development Bank (AfDB) (2012) Facilitating green growth in Africa: perspectives from the African Development Bank. www.afdb.org/fileadmin/uploads/afdb/Documents/GenericDocuments/Facilitating_Green_Growth_in_Africa__Perspectives_from_the_African_Development_Bank_June_2012.pdf. Accessed 24 July 2015

Allegretti G, Herzberg C (2007) Participatory budgets in Europe: between efficiency and growing local democracy. Transnational Institute, Amsterdam, The Netherlands. http://www.tni.org/briefing/participatory-budgets-europe

Aristotle (1976 [1958]) Politics, book I. Trans. B. Jowett. New York: Washington Square

Bakan J (2004) The corporation – the pathological pursuit of profit and power. Constable

Barada V, Primorac J, Buršić E (2016) Osvajanje prostora rada. Uvjeti rada organizacija civilnog društva na području suvremene kulture i umjetnosti. Zaklada "Kultura nova, Zagreb

Bateman I (1997) Environmental and economics appraisal. In: Riordon O (ed) Environmental management for environmental science. Addison Wesley

Benz A, Dose (2010) Governance - Regieren in komplexen Regelsystemen. Eine Einführung. VS Verlag für Sozialwissenschaften, Wiesbaden

Borel-Saladin JM, Turok IN (2013) The green economy: incremental change or transformation? Environ Policy Governance 23:209–220

Bormann E (1990) Small group Communication: theory and practice. Harper & Row, New York

Citizen Dual (2021) https://dualcitizeninc.com/global-green-economy-index/

D'Amato D, Korhonen J (2021) Integrating the green economy, circular economy and bioeconomy in a strategic sustainability framework. Ecol Econ 188:107143. https://doi.org/10.1016/j.ecolecon.2021.107143. (https://www.sciencedirect.com/science/article/pii/S0921800921002019)

Davies KK, Fisher KT, Dickson ME, Thrush SF, Le Heron R (2015) Improving ecosystem service frameworks to address wicked problems. Ecol Soc 20:37. https://doi.org/10.5751/ES-07581-200237

Dean M (1999) Governmentality—power and rule in modern society. Sage, London

Droste N, Hansjürgens B, Kuikman P, Antikainen R, Leskinen P et al (2016) Supporting innovations for the transition towards a green economy: an analysis of governance factors and government intervention in five European cases. J Clean Prod 135:426–434. https://doi.org/10.1016/j.jclepro.2016.06.123

EU Communication (2011). Rio +20: towards the green economy and better governance COM (2011) 363 final, https://eurlex.europa.eu/LexUriServ/LexUriServ.do?uri=COM:2011:0363:FIN:EN:PDF
Eurostat (2009) The environmental goods and services sector: a data collection handbook. Eurostat, Luxembourg
Finnveden G, Hauschild MZ, Ekvall T, Guinée J, Heijungs R et al (2009) Recent developments in life cycle assessment. J Environ Manag 91:1–21
Flyvbjerg B (2001) Making social science matter: why social inquiry fails and how it can succeed again. Cambridge University Press, Cambridge
Folke C, Biggs R, Norstrom AV, Reyers B, Rockstrom J (2016) Social-ecological resilience and biosphere-based sustainability science. Ecol Soc 21:41. https://doi.org/10.5751/ES-08748-210341
Fox CJ, Miller HT (1997) The depreciating public policy discourse. Am Behav Sci 41(1):64–89. https://doi.org/10.1177/0002764297041001006
Fung A, Olin Wright E (2003) Thinking about empowered participatory governance. In: Fung A, Olin Wright E (eds) Deepening democracy. Institutional innovations in empowered participatory governance. The real utopias project IV. Verso, London and New York, pp 3–45
Georgeson L, Maslin M, Poessinouw M (2017) The global green economy: a review of concepts, definitions, measurement methodologies and their interactions. Geogr Environ 4(1):e00036
Goldfrank B (2011) Deepening local democracy in Latin America: participation, decentralization, and the left. Pennsylvania State University Press, University Park, PA
Gordon C (1991) Governmental rationality: an introduction. In Burchell, G. C. Gordon, P. Miller (eds.) The foucault effect. Studies in governmentality. London: Harvester Wheatsheaf
Gramsci A (1932–1934) Some theoretical and practical aspects of economism, http://www.marxists.org/archive/gramsci/editions/reader/q13-18.htm. Accessed Jan 17 2006
Guinée JB, Heijungs R, Huppes G, Zamagni A, Masoni P (2011) Life cycle assessment: past, present, and future. Environ Sci Technol 45:90–96
Hajer MA (2003) Policy without a polity: policy analysis and the institutional void. Policy Sci 36(2):175–195
Heijungs R, Huppes G, Guinée JB (2010) Life cycle assessment and sustainability analysis of products, materials, and technologies. Toward a scientific framework for sustainability life cycle analysis. Polym Degrad Stab 95(3):422–428
Hood C (2012) Public management by numbers as a performance-enhanced drug: two hypotheses. Publ Admin Rev 71:S85–S92
ICMA (2019) Growing a green economy | icma.org [WWW document]
Jachtenfuchs M, Kohler-Koch B (2010) Governance in der Europäischen Union. In: Benz, A. und Dose, A. (Hg.): Governance - Regieren in komplexen Regelsystemen eine Einführung. Wiesbaden VS, Verl. Für Sozialwissenschaften, p. 69–93
Jänicke M (2012) Green growth: from a growing eco-industry to economic sustainability. Energy Policy 48:13–21
Katunarić V (2003) Decentralization in Southeast Europe: objectives, instruments, practices. A methodological paper for (comparative) research on cultural policy commissioned by policies for culture. Available online at: http://www. policiesforculture.org/dld/PfC_VKatunaric_SEEDecentralisation.pdf (2/2/2018)
Katunarić V (2004) Toward the new public culture. In: Švob-Đokić N (ed) Cultural transitions in southeastern Europe. Culturelink joint publication series no 6. Institute for International Relations, Zagreb, pp 19–43
Katunarić V (2007) Lica kulture. Antibarbarus, Zagreb
Kennet M (2004) How do current purchasing methods in large international companies affect stakeholders? Research to investigate the effect of purchasing trends and practices on people and the planet, corporate social responsibility and environmental Management Conference, University of Nottingham Jubilee Campus, 28–29 June, conference proceedings

Kennet M (2005) How do the current purchasing and supply chain methods in large international companies affect stakeholders? Contrasting stakeholder theory and green economics using a holistic approach, conference proceedings, Devonshire Hall, University of Leeds Business and Sustainable Environment, 4–6 September

Kennet M, Heinemann V (2006) Green economics: setting the scene. Aims, context, and philosophical underpinning of the distinctive new solutions offered by green economics. Int J Green Econ 1(1/2):68–102

Kickert WJM, Klijn E, Koppejan JFM (1997) Managing complex networks. Strategies for the public sector. Sage, London

Kitzes J (2013) An introduction to environmentally extended input-output analysis. Resources 2: 489–503

Lange G, Wodon Q, Carey K (2018) The changing wealth of nations 2018: building a sustainable future. World Bank, Washington, DC. https://openknowledge.wor ldbank.org/handle/10986/2 9001

Lawson T (2007) An orientation for green economics? Int J Green Econ 1:250

Loiseau E, Saikku L, Antikainen R, Leskinen P, Pitkänen K et al (2015) Conceptual framework and methodological tools used by green economy. J Cleaner Production 139:361–371

Lovan R, Murray M, Shaffer R (2004) Participatory governance. Planning, conflict mediation and public decision-making in civil society, Ashgate, Aldershot

March JG, Olsen JP (1995) Democratic governance. The Free Press, New York

Marks G et al (1996) European integration from the 1980's: state centric v. multi-level governance. J Common Mark Stud 4(3):341–378

Mayntz R (1993) Policy-Netzwerke und die Logik von Verhandlungssystemen. In: Héritier A (ed) Policy-Analyse. Kritik und Neuorientierung, PVS Sonderheft 24. Westdeutscher Verlag, Opladen, pp 39–56

Mayntz R, Scharpf FW (1995) Steuerung und Selbstorganisation in staatsnahen Sektoren. Campus, Frankfurt am Main

McNulty S (2011) Voice and vote: decentralization and participation in post Fujimori Peru. Stanford University Press, Stanford

Mearman A (2007) Post Keynesian economics and the environment: waking up and smelling the coffee burning? Int J Green Econ 1(3/4):374–380

Mišković D (2015) Kontekst kao sadržaj. In: Vidović, D. (ed) Radna bilježnica za društveno-kulturne centre: povodom Radnog skupa "Prema institucionalnom pluralizmu: Razvoj društveno-kulturnih centara," Zagreb, 12. – 14. studenoga 2015. Zagreb: Zaklada "Kultura nova." pp. 5–18

Naseer S, Song H, Aslam MS et al (2021) Assessment of green economic efficiency in China using analytical hierarchical process (analytical hierarchical process). Soft Comput 2021:2489. https://doi.org/10.1007/s00500-021-06507-5

Newman P, Thornley A (2005) Planning world cities. Palgrave Macmillan, Basingstoke

OECD (2021). Green growth indicators. https://www.oecd.org/greengrowth/green-growth-indicators/

Organisation for Economic Co-operation & Development (OECD) (2014) OECD green growth studies: green growth indicators. OECD Publishing, Paris

Organisation for Economic Co-Operation and Development (OECD) (2002) Indicators to measure decoupling of environmental pressure from economic growth. OECD 2002:4. http://www.oecd.org/officialdocuments/displaydocumentpdf?cote=sg/sd(2002)1/final&doclanguage=en. Accessed 3 Sep 2012

Pearce D (1991) Green economics. Environ Values 1:3–12

Pearce DW, Markandya A, Barbier EB (1989) Blueprint for a green economy. Earthscan, London

Pierre J, Peters (eds) (2000) Debating governance: authority, steering and democracy. Oxford University Press, Oxford

Pitkänen K, Antikainen R, Droste N, Loiseau E, Saikku L, Aissani L, Hansjürgens B, Kuikman PJ, Leskinen P, Thomsen M (2016) What can be learned from practical cases of green economy?

Studies from five European countries. J Clean Prod 139:666–676. https://doi.org/10.1016/j.jclepro.2016.08.071
Rabouin L (2009) Démocratiser la ville: Le budget participatif: De Porto Alegre à Montréal. Lux Éditeur, Montreal
Reardon J (2007) Comments on green economics: setting the scene. Aims, context, and philosophical underpinnings of the distinctive innovative solutions offered by green economics. Int J Green Econ 1(3/4):532–538
Rhodes R (1995) The new governance: governing without government. Political Studies 44:652–667
Schutz W (1958) FIRO: a three dimensional theory of interpersonal behaviour. Reinhart, New York, NY
Scott Cato M, Kennet M (1999) Green economics: beyond supply and demand to meeting People's needs. Aberystwyth, Green Audit
Senecah SL (2004) The trinity of voice: the role of practical theory in planning and evaluating the effectiveness of environmental participatory processes. In: Depoe SP, John WD, Elsenbeer MFA (eds) Communication and public participation in environmental decision making. State University of New York Press, New York, NY
Švob-Đokić N (2004a) Introduction. In: Švob-Đokić N (ed) Cultural transitions in Southeastern Europe. Culturelink Joint Publication Series No 6. Zagreb. Institut za međunarodne odnose, pp 1–7
Švob-Đokić N (2004b) Cultural contexts in transition processes. In: Švob-Đokić N (ed) Cultural transitions in southeastern Europe. Culturelink joint publication series no 6. Institute for International Relations, Zagreb, pp 7–19
Ten Brink P, Mazza L, Badura T, Kettunen M, Withana S, (2012) Nature and its role in the transition to a green economy. The economics of ecosystems and biodiversity (TEEB), Geneva, Switzerland
Ulrich P (2016) Institutionalizing (cross-border) citizenship on subnational level - the European grouping of territorial cooperation (EGTC) as new administrative space for participatory and functional governance in Europe. Federal Governance 13(1):11–39. https://nbn-resolving.org/urn:nbn:de:0168-ssoar-48532-2
UNDESA, UNDP (2012) Synthesis of national reports on Rio+20, UN Department of Economic and Social Affairs and the UN Development Programme. http://sustainabledevelopment.un.org/
United Nations Economic and Social Commission for Asia and the Pacific (UNESCAP), Asian Development Bank and United Nations Environment Programme (2012) Green growth, resources, and resilience: environmental sustainability in Asia and the Pacific. United Nations and Asian Development Bank, Bangkok
United Nations Environment Programme (UNEP) (2011a) Towards a green economy: pathways to sustainable development and poverty eradication. United Nations Environment Programme, Nairobi
United Nations Environment Programme (UNEP) (2011b) Towards a green economy: pathways to sustainable development and poverty eradication. A synthesis for policy makers http://www.unep.org/greeneconomy/GreenEconomyReport/tabid/29846/Default.aspx
Vadén T, Lähde V, Majava A, Järvensivu P, Toivanen T, Hakala E, Eronen JT (2020) Decoupling for ecological sustainability: a categorisation and review of research literature. Environ Sci Policy 112:236–244. https://doi.org/10.1016/j.envsci.2020.06.016
Vidović D (2012) Razvoj novonastajućih kultura u gradu Zagrebu od 1990. do 2010. Zagreb: Filozofski fakultet Sveučilišta u Zagrebu. Doctoral Thesis
Vidović D (2014) New models of cultural centres—case of Croatia. The 8th international conference on cultural policy research – Iccpr2014. Hildesheim: UNESCO Chair "Cultural Policy for the Arts in Development"
Vidović D (2017) Novonastajuće kulturne prakse u Hrvatskoj. In: Jakovina T (ed) Dvadeset pet godina hrvatske neovisnosti – kako dalje? Centar Miko Tripalo, Zagreb, pp 483–496

Vidović D, Žuvela A (2016) Participatory governance as a driver for inclusive cities. In: Imperiale F, Vecco M (eds) 7th Annual Research Session. ENCATC. October 5–7, 2016. Valencia, Spain. Cultural Management Education in Risk Societies – Towards a Paradigm and Policy Shift? Book Proceedings. ENCATC, Brussels, pp 356–365. http://research.gold.ac.uk/19075/1/ENCATC_Va¬lencia2016_Proceedings.pdf. Accessed 3 Sep 2018)

Voices of Culture (2015) Brainstorming report. Participatory governance in cultural heritage. Structured dialogue between the European Commission and the cultural sector. http://www.goethe.de/mmo/priv/14903520-STANDARD.pdf. Accessed 2 Feb 2018

Wampler B (2007) Participatory budgeting in Brazil: contestation, cooperation, and accountability. Pennsylvania State University Press, University Park

Wampler B, McNulty SL (2011) Does participatory governance matter? Exploring the nature and impact of Participatory reforms. Woodrow Wilson International Centre for Scholars, Washington

Ward JD, Sutton PC, Werner AD, Costanza R, Mohr SH, Simmons CT (2016) Is decoupling GDP growth from environmental impact possible? PLoS One 11:e0164733. https://doi.org/10.1371/journal.pone.0164733

Williamson OE (1996) Economics and organization: a primer. Calif Manag Rev 38(2):131–146. https://doi.org/10.2307/41165836

Žuvela A (2016) Krojeno po mjeri? Prakse i tendencije kulturnog obrazovanja u Hrvatskoj. Zaklada "Kultura nova, Zagreb

Dr. José G. Vargas-Hernández is a professor at the University Center of Economic and Administrative Sciences of the University of Guadalajara, Mexico. Besides, he serves as the member of the National System of Researchers (Level I) in his country, and he is the visiting scholar at Laurentian University, Sudbury, Ontario, Canada; University of California-Berkeley; and Carleton University, Ottawa, Canada. He has also served as a professor of the Doctorate in Administrative and Organizational Sciences, La Salle University, Autonomous University of Durango, and as an Academic Advisor of the Doctorate in Administration of the Autonomous University of Aguascalientes. His research area is organizational economics, and he is associated with the research project entitled "Conacyt and BMBF (Germany) Business bio-economics in urban areas" at CUCEA-UDG and Kaiserslautern University, Germany, and RE-CITY EUROPEAN UNION research project on "Reviving shrinking cities - innovative paths and perspectives towards livability for shrinking cities in Europe." There are more than 1000 research articles, authored by him, which is published in international journals, edited research volumes, and conference proceedings of repute, and he has authored 23 books so far. He has also served as the editor of several journals of academic significance.

M. C. Omar C. Vargas-González is a Professor and Head of the Department of Systems and Computing at the Technological National of Mexico Campus Ciudad Guzmán, professor of Telematics Engineering at the University Center of the South of the University of Guadalajara, with a master's degree in computer systems. He has received training in Entrepreneurship and Multidisciplinary Innovation at Arizona State University (2018) as well as a diploma in Ecosystems of Innovation and Entrepreneurship from the Harvard University School of Business. He currently conducts research in diverse areas such as entrepreneurship, economics, statistics, mathematics, and information and computer sciences; has collaborated in the publication of more than 15 articles in magazines; and directs innovation and technological development projects.

Chapter 3
Democracy, Governance, and Public Policy: The Trio for Ensuring India Towards Sustainable Development Agendas

Jitendra Sahoo

3.1 Introduction

The infrastructure of a state is not just a matter of building up roads, schools, power grids, etc.; equally, it is a question of strengthening democratic governance, bringing new policies, and maintaining the rule of law. Alongside, without the accountability of not only the government to its people but also the people among themselves, there is no hope for a viable democratic state (Ki-moon 2009). The concept of development administration emerged after the Second World War and thrived the modern nations for their reconstruction with a target to provide equal status to the common people by bringing their socio-economic developments. Therefore, all the independent countries started their planning of development through varieties of projects and policies. The development of a country is only possible with an effective governance system, and it also brings success to every government. Generally, the country's development depends upon sound human resource management; proper use of physical, capital, and natural resources; as well as scientific discoveries and inventions of new technology.

In India, controversies have wrapped around many major developmental and infrastructural projects—Sardar Sarovar Dam on River Narmada, the Chilika Lake in Odisha, the Konkan Railways, the East Coast Road, and the establishment of many heavy industrial sites. These created several hazards through environmental degradation and uprooting humans from their native places. This dichotomy reflects the essence of the debate around sustainable development. The mechanism of resolving all these conflicts between the environment and development and the actual way-outs will indicate whether the term sustainable development is implementable

J. Sahoo (✉)
Department of Political Science, University of Gour Banga, Mokdumpur, Malda, West Bengal, India

M. Mishra et al. (eds.), *Public Policies and Sustainable Development in Post-Reform India*, New Frontiers in Regional Science: Asian Perspectives 71,
https://doi.org/10.1007/978-981-99-3696-0_3

in a country like India or not. But now, the term "sustainable development" is a buzzword not only in India but also all over the world. The world is going through serious problems. People continue to fight wars among themselves, terrorist activities are increasing day by day, and popular opinions are suppressed by many governments. The cry for popular democracy is everywhere, but it is crushed by despots who insist on maintaining order rather than improving living conditions. Yes, people need to be governed to avoid anarchy and chaos. However, what makes a good government versus an oppressive one? The answer is that democracy, good governance, and public policy need to work hand in hand. These three are considered as the best suitable way to ensure sustainable development agendas in the world and, obviously, for India.

When our thought concerns future generations, all the developed and developing countries consider the ethos of sustainable development. The Brundtland Commission's Report in 1987 advocated that the development process has been initiated by the developing countries with the beginning of liberalization, privatization, globalization with mechanization, and industrialization (Pattanaik 2016). But all these are also responsible for the degradation of the environment and therefore put a question on the growth model and what steps the nation-states are taking for the future world. Because of the acceleration in economic growth, the nation-states are really distorting the natural resources and inflicting harm on the environment by clearing forests, converting agricultural lands to urban sites, extracting groundwater excessively, polluting the air by using vast numbers of vehicles, and emitting pollutant gases from industries, dust from construction works, heat from household electric devices, and smoke due to the burning of paddy husk. However, in its ethical form, the term "sustainable development" simply signifies not cheating our children and neighbors, including creatures and animals. Therefore, sustainable development aims at development in such a manner that all the policies, programs, projects, and activities lead to a positive change in the socio-economic and ecological spheres without causing any harm to our natural resources in current times or during the future.

The objectives of the present essay are to explore the meaning of democracy, governance, and public policy; secondly, to find out the nature of democracy in India, which is most suitable for bringing sustainable development to our country; thirdly, to explain the process of governance with SMART[1] qualities that are really fit for sustainable development in India; and finally, to examine the public policies and institutions solely responsible for bringing sustainable development agendas in India.

[1] SMART governance has a great importance in modern administration; it signifies the following: (i) simplification of government rules and regulations through the use of ICT providing citizen-friendly administration; (ii) morality is the cardinal principle in administration with ethical value advancement of anti-corruption measures; (iii) accountability of authorities for public services; (iv) responsiveness means speedy delivery of services; and (v) transparency in providing information to the citizens as and when it is needed.

3.2 Research Questions and Methods

Research questions in social science are the cardinal principles for finding the solutions that social scientists want to explore. The present essay is concerned with addressing a few questions that have been mentioned below:

- Are democracy, governance, and public policy sufficient to bring sustainability to the developing world, particularly in India?
- What is the role played by these "trio" during emergencies?
- Whether the government of India is working to bring sustainable development in accordance with the guidelines given by international organizations?
- Whether these three are working together with a favorable ambiance, especially in India?

Since time immemorial, academic society has been curious enough regarding every social event, and they use different methods to understand it. This study is entirely based on qualitative methods and purely based on secondary sources.

3.3 Democracy

Democracy comes from two Greek words: "*demos*," which means "people," and "*krates*," which means "rule," which are conjugated to signify the "power of the people." Therefore, democracy is a political system where the ultimate power lies in the hands of the people (Kotler 2016). The people have the power to say "yes" or "no" for or against any policies, laws, rules, and regulations made by the elected government. This is only possible because they elect their representatives through periodic elections, and the government is formed only to think for their betterment.

Good government has a better chance if candidates have the right to run for election and if citizens have the right to choose their leaders in a systematic manner according to the law of the land. However, democracy is not a simple system. It requires more than that just running free elections, as the following:

- It requires citizens who are knowledgeable
- It requires a free assembly of citizens to discuss issues and, when needed, organize a peaceful protest.
- It requires a free press and two or more political parties that can freely advertise and debate their proposals and their promises before the common people

The United States represents such a democracy. It was founded by a set of brilliant individuals who chose to fight for independence from Great Britain and form a new Republic, as Abraham Lincoln said, "it's the government of the people, by the people, and for the people" (Rout 1988).

On 11 June 1776, the US Congress appointed a "Committee of Five," membered by John Adams, Benjamin Franklin, Thomas Jefferson, Robert R. Livingstone, and

Roger Sherman from Massachusetts, Pennsylvania, Virginia, New York, and Connecticut, respectively. In the "Declaration of Independence," the committee stated that truths to be self-evident, that all men are equal, that they are endowed by their Creator with certain unalienable rights, and that among these are life, liberty, and the pursuit of happiness (Kotler 2016). And these principles are still continuing in the law of the land and also still in the minds of the people of the United States and also have been appreciated worldwide.

But as per my observation, I would like to emphasize when Rout (1988) highlighted the statement on democracy, referring to Mazzini, as the government of the best and wisest, for the progress of all and through all, and these sayings are nowadays the buzzword like Sabka Sath and Sabka Vikas with Sabka Viswas, i.e., *our strength is our vitality, our strength is our solidarity, our vitality is the spirit of nation first—always first* (HT 2019). Again, Rout liked the statement of democracy given by Seeley as a government in which everybody has a share. This gives a moral boost to every person to participate in the decision-making process.

When the question comes to our mind, what "democracy" actually means to citizens and why it matters were also solved as one could distinguish between the "minimal" and "maximal" perceptions of democracy. The former signifies the "means," i.e., democracy depends upon fair elections, respect for human rights, and universal adult suffrage. Therefore, civil liberties like freedom of speech, right to vote, political participation, free and transparent elections, and accountability are the primary features of the minimalist definitions of democracy. These features minimize the chances of abuse by governments through a process of checks and balances. On the other hand, the latter not only highlights the means but also focuses on the "ends" like justice, fairness, transparency, responsiveness, and wiping out all types of unethical attitudes like corruption in administration, providing qualitative service to the people, guarantying public safety and social security, etc. (Vinod and Meena 2013).

When we look into the principles of Indian democracy, the Preamble of the Constitution highlights several democratic principles:

- The nature of Indian democracy is based upon sovereign, socialist, secular, democratic, and republic. It assures its citizens' social, economic, and political justice. It offers liberty of thought, expression, belief, faith, and worship. It provides equality of status and opportunity to all people. It strives to promote fraternity among all citizens assuring the dignity of the individual and the integrity of the nation.
- The people of India enjoy the ultimate source of sovereignty. Our Constitution also provides the Fundamental Rights to the People and Independence of the Judiciary and Election Commission of India. The "people" are considered as an "end" and "state" as the "means" in the democratic system.
- It has also adopted the principle of the welfare state, and it establishes a federal political structure with wide unitary features.
- Apart from these, India has adopted parliamentary democracy. Here, democracy is based on sovereignty. People can exercise their power in democracy. They elect

their representatives through periodic elections, and the government remains responsible to the common mass for its every omission and commission. The real authority rests in the cabinet, but the cabinet is responsible to the legislature, which refers to a control mechanism we call legislative control over the executive and vice versa. And also, judiciary has a vital role in controlling the legislature as well as the executive.
- The Constitution also introduces the system of universal adult franchise to all citizens without any discrimination.
- Decentralizing powers and establishing Panchayat Raj[2] at the village level are also democratic features under the purview of the Indian Constitution.

Since the Constitution of India was in place after its independence, the state has been witnessing many hindrances in the way of upholding the ethos of democracy—poverty, unemployment, population explosion, unhealthy role of political parties, slow and uneven economic development, communalism, alienation from the center, cancer of corruption, decline of various democratic institutions, elite-mass gap, ethnic problems, growing political violence, cross-border terrorism, politics of reservation, anti-reservation movements, and many more. Most recently, it is the COVID-19 pandemic that appeared as the real threat not only to Indian democracy but also to the entire world.

Discipline, hard work, thrift, saving, and lack of ostentation in living are as essential for democracy. Unfortunately, it is a painful truth that lack of discipline characterizes many parts of India's national life. It manifests in many ways, of course, more significantly in students' behaviors in educational institutions, industrial strikes, destruction of public property by antisocial elements, alarming rise in the incidence of crime and violence, and, above all, our attitude towards our duty.

Therefore, we should maintain and control all our individual activities in a democratic way. As per my observation, the only solution is governance; that is, good governance in the form of SMART governance is the need of the time for the development of any country of the world.

Democracy aims to establish the government "of the people, by the people, and for the people." Irrespective of the direct or indirect form of democracy, the will of the people becomes the rule of the land, and always the representatives who are elected by the people are ethically concerned with thinking about the betterment of the people. Again, the people's representatives are always thinking about the development of the people through long-term policies to save the entire human civilization, and it is possible only there is the spread of democratic principles in the world.

---

[2]The Panchayati Raj system in India is considered as the pillar of democratic principles where self-rule, i.e., the rural people, elect their representatives by themselves for their development. Part IV of the Indian Constitution, i.e., Art. 40, says: "The state shall take initiatives to organise village panchayats and empower them with such powers and authority as may be necessary to enable them to function as units of self-government." Through constitutional 73rd Amendment Act, 1992, the three-tier Panchayati Raj system has been started in India.

Democracy is most suitable for bringing sustainable development in a country because it is enough for the country to run elections, every citizen can get the right to vote, citizens are free to speak and exchange their views, they can raise their voices in a peaceful manner, they can freely practice any religious beliefs according to their own choice, and the country has the provision of freedom of the press so that the media persons can report their news and opinions freely. Democracy provides a better chance for decent shelter with food, cloth, and shelter; facilitates health care; benefits the sound educational system both for men and women; and provides good opportunities for entertainment and safe travel within the boundary of the country by bringing various policies and developmental projects taking into account the future perspectives of its citizens (Kotler 2016).

3.4 Governance

The term "governance" originated from the Greek word "*Kybernan*," which implies "to steer and to pilot or be at the helm of things." In the late 1970s, Harlan Cleveland used the term "governance" for the first time, and to him, people think more about "governance" and less about the "government" (Mahi 2020).

Kautilya, an ancient Indian polymath, elaborates on the traits of the king of a well-governed state as the happiness of his subjects lies in his happiness; in their welfare, his welfare; whatever pleases himself, he does not consider as good, but whatever pleases his subjects, he considers as good (Sharma and Susmita 1998).

In Greek political theory, Mahajan gives his credit to Plato for developing the concept of the *Philosopher King* as the ideal ruler and Aristotle as the first person to deal with the concept of "governance" when he classified the political systems into three broad categories. He explained the administrative system according to the role of the rulers: rule by one man is considered a monarchy, and its perverse form is known as tyranny; if there is the rule of few persons, it is an aristocracy, and its perverse form is an oligarchy; finally, where there is the rule by many people, it is a polity, but its perverted form will be a democracy (Mahajan 2013).

To understand the meaning and role of governance, Pal has quoted the sayings of Rhodes (Mahi 2020) that in public administration, there are six essential uses of governance:

- As the minimal state
- As corporate governance
- As the new public management
- As self-organizing networks
- As a socio-cybernetic system
- As good governance

Here, the minimal state refers to the size of the government being reduced due to privatization. Corporate governance leads to individual's responsibilities towards their activities as assigned. New public management leads to the introduction of markets, customers, and competition and signifies more governance and less government. Self-organizing networks identify the involvement of different interdependent actors in the delivery of welfare services. The introduction of a socio-cybernetic system signifies multiple actors interacting with each other for each and every activity of government. Finally, good governance brings reforms in the administrative process, civil services, intermingling of public-private partnerships, deduction in overstaffing, greater use of nongovernmental organizations, etc.

Another vital contribution to the field of governance was made by Stroker (1998), who explained the theory of governance with five crucial propositions: Firstly, it is a set of institutions working beyond government; secondly, it delimits the boundaries of taking responsibility by individual departments; thirdly, it identifies the collective involvement of institutional activities; fourthly, it advocates the autonomy of organizations; and finally, it recognizes the ability to get things done not only through government but also by any means.

Governance has a variety of use in today's world; it emphasizes hierarchies, markets, and networks; it is used in the form of public governance, global governance, good governance, meta governance, E-governance, and M-governance. It has basic characteristics like participation, predictability, accountability, transparency, responsiveness, consensus orientation, equity and effectiveness, and efficiency. It has a wider perspective and dimensions in the political, legal, administrative, economic, and social sectors. As far as its political dimension is concerned, it deals with the exercise of power, conduct of political representatives, political parties, functioning, and many other activities. In its legal or judicial sphere, it has its basic principles like the rule of law, citizen-friendly police, easy access to justice, and judicial services. In administrative matters, it emphasizes managing human resources very smoothly by providing basic services, easy management of human resources, good financial management, transparency in administrative activities through the use of IT, etc. In the economic sphere, it denotes the financial governance, business environment, primary support sector, etc. In social and environmental matters, it always looks into the welfare of the poor and vulnerable sections and gives importance to the role of civil society and media in the management of the environment (DARPG 2009). Therefore, we can say that this governance is an important instrument for ensuring sustainable development in India.

3.5 Public Policy

The third pillar of the sustainable agenda in India nay the world is public policy. The term public policy is a combination of two words—"public" and "policy." In general, public policy means a course of action by the government in response to the common people for their betterment. Shukla identified the statement of Dye that public policy is whatever governments choose to do or not to do (Haridwar 2021). Therefore, public policies are governmental decisions or actions having specific goals and objectives to fulfill towards the advancement of the country's economy, educating common people, proper utilization of resources, scope for scientific inventions-discoveries, bringing transparency in administration, introduction of good governance through E-governance, and all-round development not only for the country itself but also to make an eco-friendly world. In India, many institutions are there to play significant roles in policy-making—Legislature, Executive, Cabinet, and Cabinet Secretariat, Prime Minister and Prime Minister's Office (PMO), National Institution for Transforming India (NITI Aayog), other state governments, etc.

3.6 Theoretical Analysis

Several models, e.g., the systems model, institutional model, elite-mass model, group model, rational policy-making model, and many more, explain the functions of public policy in its ideal form (Sapru and Sapru 2021).

Political system, as developed by Easton, is an integral part of every society, which he called the authoritative allocation of values (Varma 2017). In his system approach, he has pointed out that inputs are observed as sociopolitical-economic and physical products of the environment and are accepted into the system in the form of demands and supports. Here, the demands are made by individuals and groups to change some aspects of the environment, which affects public policy. In a political system, supports consist of customs, rules and regulations, policies, laws, etc., which leads to the basis of the existence of a political community. The environment is shown towards the boundaries of the political system, and at the core of the political system, there are institutions and personnel for policy-making. In the political system, outputs constitute the values in the form of public policies, and finally, there will be a provision of feedback, which indicates the modification of public policies for a better environment.

Institutionalist models opine that the institutions in the form of government institutions directly impact public policies (Johari and Gupta 2021). Therefore, they consider public policies as the outcome of government institutions. Constitutional government and democracy are a remarkable outcome as explained by intuitionalist models of public policy where he argued that public policies are formulated, implemented, and enforced by the government institutions because of three reasons:

- Public policies get legal sanctions through government institutions
- Public policies are applicable universally
- It has its coercion

The elitist model of public policy signifies a few groups and individuals having the power or influence to change or bring new public policies (Johari and Gupta 2021). Advocates opined that power as those who occupy the command posts and elite is the by-product of the institutional landscape. Another eminent scholar said that public policy under the influence of elites is really dominated by the best educated, wealthiest, and most powerful elites (Sapru and Sapru 2021).

The group theory of public policy advocates that group pressures result in bargaining, negotiating, competition, understanding, and compromising among powerful groups, where the major groups make their own interactions among themselves and pressure the government to fulfill their demands. According to its advocates, an interest group is a shared attitude group that makes certain claims upon groups in society; such a group becomes political if and when it makes a claim through or upon any of the institutions of government (mentioned in Sapru and Sapru 2021). Therefore, public policy is influenced by various groups having wealth, organizational strength, leadership, and easy access to decision makers.

The rational policy-making models emphasize that policy-making is a choice among policy alternatives, which means choosing one best option among several policies, which are more suitable for the concerned group of individuals or society. Another exponent has said that a policy is rational when it is most efficient, i.e., if the ratio between the values it achieves and the values it sacrifices is positive and higher than any other policy alternative (Haridwar 2021).

Finally, the mixed approach advocated that there is a mixture of both the application of techniques and political processes (Johari and Gupta 2021). They have set out the nine steps in public policy, which they say as "mixed":

- Deciding to decided
- Deciding how to decide
- Issue definition
- Forecasting
- Setting objectives and priorities
- Option analysis
- Policy implementation, monitoring, and control
- Evaluation and review
- Policy implementation, succession, or termination

The analysis of the above public policy models reveals the importance of public policy in public administration and bringing sustainable development. The success and growth of any country depend upon the success of policy formulation, execution monitoring, and policy analysis. In independent India, this trend emerged with the launching of five-year plans after the framework of the Indian Constitution. Various goals and targets have been finalized, and the Government of India (GOI) has been rendering its best efforts to achieve those. Many hurdles have been faced—wars with Pakistan and China, declaration of national emergencies and other state emergencies, a lot of hue and cry still going on frequently concerning environmental pollution, employment generation, healthcare facilities, rural developments, communalism, regionalism, sectarianism, tribalism, population explosion, etc. Apart from all these, India is successfully marching ahead because of its effective public policies. Indian democracy is now full of aspirations, and people are now proactive; they consider themselves as they know more and demand more from the government. Therefore, the current demands from the people with regard to the development and emerging national, international, and environmental challenges have raised issues to which our public policies are responding in an effective manner (Bidyut and Chand 2020).

The Government of India has formulated a number of policies having particular reference to the environment, employment, education, and public health. As far as policies with regard to checking the major ecological issues like air-water-noise pollution, deforestation, loss of biodiversity, and solid waste, the Government of India has taken effective policies: Water (Prevention and Control of Pollution) Act, 1974, 1975, 1977, 1978; Air (Prevention and Control of Pollution) Act 1981, 1982; Environment (Protection) Rules 1986; Hazardous Wastes (Management and Handling) Rules 1989; Manufacture, Storage and Import of Hazardous Chemicals Rules 1989; Forest (Conservation) Act, 1980 and 1981; Forest Rights Act 2006; National Forest Policy 1988; Wildlife Protection Rules, 1995; Public Liability Insurance Act 1991; National Environment Tribunal Act 1995; National Environment Policy 2006; National Water Policy 2002; Biological Diversity Act 2002; and Wetland Conservation and Management Rules, 2017.

As far as the policies made with regard to education are concerned, the Indian Government has drawn landmark steps to strengthen the intellectual capacities of the people. As education comes under the concurrent list, both the center and the states have shared responsibilities for education, but overall responsibility is vested in the hands of the central government. Major steps in this regard are the University Education Commission 1948, the Education Commission 1948–1949, the Secondary Education Commission 1952–1953, the formation of the NCERT in 1961, establishment of IITs by the Nehru Government through the scientific policy resolution, Kothari Commission 1964–1966, National Education Policy 1986, National Programme of Action 1992, Yashpal Committee 1992–1993, RTE Act 2009, New Education Policy 2020, etc. (Bidyut and Chand 2020).

While public health is concerned, the Government of India has also taken many policies and formed many committees in this regard like Bhore Committee (1946), Muralidhar Committee 1962, Chadha Committee 1963, Mukherjee Committee 1965, Jungalwalla Committee 1967, Kartar Singh Committee 1973, Srivastava Committee 1975, and Rural Health Scheme 1977. Since independence, massive campaigns have started against malaria, TB, smallpox, leprosy, filariasis, cholera, dengue, etc. Recently, India has successfully checked the COVID-19 situation in our country and is also capable of supplying vaccines to other countries of the world. National Health Policy 1983, National Health Policy 2002, National Rural Health Mission 2005, and National Health Policy 2015 are significant steps taken by the Government of India in this regard (Bidyut and Chand 2020).

Employment is another thrust area that brings stability to the socio-economic condition of the people, especially to the poor, marginalized, and underprivileged sections. Therefore, the Government of India has taken several programs and policies in this regard like the Rural Man Power 1960–1961, Pilot Intensive Rural Employment Project 1972, Small Farmers Development Agency 1971–1972, Marginal Farmers and Agricultural Labourers' Scheme 1978, Food for Work Programme 1977, National Rural Employment Programme 1980, Rural Landless

Employment Guarantee Programme 1983, Jawahar Rozgar Yojana 1993–1994, Jawahar Gram Samridhi Yojana 1999–2000, Sampoorna Grameen Rozgar Yojana (SGRY) 2001–2002, National Food for Work Programme 2004, and Mahatma Gandhi National Rural Employment Guarantee Act (MGNREGA) 2006 (Bidyut and Chand 2020).

3.7 Sustainable Development Goals and Inclusive Policy in India

The Sustainable Development Goals (SDGs) came into force in the month of January 2016, and these have been guiding and monitoring the UNDP policies and will give fund for it until 2030. India, being a signatory to it, is committed before the global community to reduce all forms of inequalities and atrocities from the world; therefore, the GOI is always working on eradicating poverty, unemployment, population explosion, and any kinds of discrimination among the people of the entire world and always tries to promote peace and tranquility and establishment of effective and accountable institutions and provide justice to all on the earth (Shashi 2019).

As far as the provisions of the Indian Constitution are concerned, it is the duty of the government to protect the interests of the marginalized people, especially the Scheduled Castes and the Scheduled Tribes and other weaker sections. Therefore, the present government has taken initiatives with regard to the weaker sections and marginalized people in the sphere of education, health, hygiene, gender equality, livelihood, entrepreneurship, electrification, safe drinking water, standard of living, sanitation, rural development, etc. Some most-needed pro-women programs launched by the GOI are the following:

- *Beti Bachao Beti Padhao,* launched on 22 January 2015, to bring gender equality through protecting girl children and ensuring that they are being educated adequately
- *Swadhar Greh Scheme,* launched in 2001, to rehabilitate women in difficult circumstance by providing the shelter, food, clothing, counseling, training, and clinical and legal aid
- *Scheme for Adolescent Girls* (SAG) through the Integrated Child Development Services (ICDS), devised in 2010, to provide special attention to adolescent girls
- *Pradhan Mantri Matru Vandana Yojana* as an initiative for providing the maternity benefits since January 2017

To protect the health and hygienic conditions of women and provide for the inclusive benefits of women in every sphere, the government has taken schemes like *Ujjwala Yojana*, Mahila (i.e., Women) Police Station, Mahila E-Haat, and Mudra (i.e., Currency) Loan. Under the Swachh Bharat (i.e., Clean India) Scheme, the government provides toilets for each household to protect the dignity and safety of women. For the benefit of the Scheduled Castes (SC) and Scheduled Tribes (ST) and to protect their interests, especially for the students, there are provisions like Babu Jagjivan Ram Chhatrawas Yojana (BJRCY), Pre-matric Scholarship, and free coaching for preparation of competitive examinations. The National Backward Classes Finance and Development Corporation (NBCFDC) has various schemes, such as micro-credit finance for the people of Scheduled Castes.

The Ministry of Tribal Affairs focuses on the social and economic development of Scheduled Tribes in the country and their empowerment. For the expansion of education, there is a provision for setting up Eklavya Model Residential Schools for the tribal students, equipped with hostels, staff quarters, playgrounds, and laboratory facilities. There is a provision like Dr. Ambedkar Central Sector Scheme of Interest Subsidy on Educational loans for students from the Other Backward Classes (OBC) and Economically Backward Classes (EBC) desiring their overseas study to acquire M.Phil. and Ph.D. degrees. There are also many government schemes for the minorities for their social, economic, and educational developments, including pre-matric and post-matric scholarship, *Padho Pardesh Scheme*, *Nai Udaan*, *Jiyo Parsi Scheme*, *Seekho aur Kamao*, *Nai Manzil Scheme*, Upgrading the Skills and Training in Traditional Arts/Crafts for Development (USTTAD) Scheme, and *Hamari Dharohar Scheme*. For Economically Weaker Sections (EWS), the GOI has launched Ayushman Bharat Programme, National Nutrition Mission, 10% reservation in the employment sector, Pradhan Mantri Shram Yogi Maandhan Scheme, PM-KISAN scheme, etc. For the greater interests of the Divyangjan (i.e., physically handicapped), several programs have also been launched by the GOI, including the Unique Disability Identification Project, the National Award for Empowerment of Persons with Disabilities, the Accessible India Campaign, etc.

3.8 Policy Intervention for Sustainable Development

During the independence, India's economy was in a position of underdeveloped one. However, planned economic development initiatives have helped achieve the stage of developing economies, and now we are moving towards developed ones. In the words of Kaushik Basu, former chief economist of the World Bank: "Ultimately an economy has to be evaluated not according to the country's economic growth, but it is being evaluated in terms of what happens to the poor, unprivileged people" (Basu 2004). All the discussions so far finally excerpt that successful linkage between democracy, governance, and public policy is the key to ensuring the interests of the poor, and, evidently, the betterment of the majority of the country could bring sustainable development for India. Our direct experience and observation since the last 70 years of independence give us a crystal idea. Within this time, some most significant steps taken by the Government of India appeared as the benchmark in transforming India towards a better place of living (Gautam 2018):

- Controller of Capital issues, 1947
- Minimum Wages Act, 1948
- Factories Act, 1948
- Development Finance Institutions, 1948
- Banking Regulation Act, 1949
- Planning Commission, 1950
- Finance Commission, 1951
- Industries (Development and Regulations) Act, 1951
- State Bank of India Act, 1955
- Oil and Natural Gas Division, 1955
- Essential Commodities Act, 1955
- Industrial Policy Resolution, 1956
- Institutes of Technology Act, 1961
- Food Corporations of India, 1965
- Agricultural Price Commission, 1965
- Special Economic Zones, 1965
- Public Provident Fund, 1968
- Nationalization of Banks, 1969
- Nationalization of General Insurance, 1972
- Abolition of Right to Property, 1978
- Consumer Protection Act, 1986
- Prevention of Corruption Act, 1988
- Disinvestment Policy, 1991
- National Telecom Policy, 1994
- Electricity Regulatory Commission Act, 1998
- Insurance Regulatory and Development Authority (IRDA) Act, 1999
- Information Technology Act, 2000
- The Prevention of Money Laundering Act, 2002
- National Rural Employment Guarantee Act (MGNREGA), 2005
- Pradhan Mantri Jan Dhan Yojana, 2014
- Aadhar Act, 2016
- Banknote Demonetisation, 2016
- The Central Goods and Services Tax (GST) Act, 2017

In the year 2015, the world leaders adopted 17 Sustainable Development Goals in their 2030 Agenda and presented a road map for future development with a focus on the eradication of poverty, environmental sustainability, peace, prosperity, etc. The NITI Aayog of India has come up with a single measurable index to track the progress of all the states and union territories in India, accepting 13 SDGs out of 17 (Civil Service Chronicle September 2019).

3.9 Concluding Observation

Global environmental concerns have resulted in the remarkable growth of international environmental law in the post-Stockholm Conference period. As a signatory member of the convention, there has been a close interlink between international laws, national laws, and municipal/panchayat (local government) laws of the country. Bhopal Gas Tragedy in December 1984 is often considered as a point after which India came forward for the rapid development of environmental laws in India. The Supreme Court of India, with the power of judicial activism, made it possible in many cases. The intellectual and progressive personalities have tied the entire human race into various knots to bring environmental balance to this planet.

On the one hand, a section of people are ensuring ever-higher standards of living, keeping the most basic needs of the majority of the population under severe economic and environmental strain. However, there is a lack of holistic thinking among people on how to manage their socio-economic affairs in the present world. Still, there is high hope that principles like democracy, governance, and public policy ensure sustainable development agendas in India. As India celebrates the year 2022 as "Azadi Ka Amrit Mahotsav" and within these 75 years of independence, it has transformed itself from an underdeveloped to a developing country with outstanding achievement in reaching the fifth largest economy in the world. If India needs to accelerate into a developed and high-human-development country, it needs to speed up reforms in all fields. It may be in the form of *Ayushman Bharat* or the NIPUN (National Initiative for Proficiency in Reading with Understanding and Numeracy) *Bharat* or gender budgeting or skills mission or any other scientific innovations with maximum governance and minimum government by empowering all the stakeholders—public or private, and philanthropic or common citizens, with a target to clear timelines and rigorous monitoring of progress and course rectification in order to achieve holistic socio-economic and human development goals set forth under the SDG 2030.

References

Basu K (ed) (2004) India's emerging economy: performance and prospects in the 1990s and beyond. Oxford University Press, New Delhi

Bidyut C, Chand KP (2020) Public administration in a globalizing world theories and practices. SAGE Texts, New Delhi

Civil Service Chronicle (2019) India's Progress towards the SDGs, Vol. XXXI No.3, p. 67

DARPG (2009), State of governance-a framework for assessment, New Delhi

Gautam C (2018) 70 policies that shaped India (1947–2017). Observer Research Foundation

Haridwar S (2021) Public policy and administration in India. Mahaveer Publications, Dibrugarh, Assam

HT (2019), After Sabka Saath, Sabka Vikash, Sabka Viswas: Modi's message of inclusion, https://www.hindustantimes.com/editorials/after-sabka-saath-sabka-vikas-win-sabka-vishwas-modi-s-message-of-inclusion/story-6i8Lo7ve0ibklPOR7E4jqI.html Accessed 14 April 2022

Johari, Gupta (2021) Public policy and administration in India. Vishal Publishing Co., Jalandhar
Ki-moon B(2009) Remarks to the security council on Tmor-Leste. http://www.un.org/. Accessed 10 April 2022
Kotler P (2016) Democracy in decline rebuilding its future. SAGE, London
Mahajan VD (2013) Political theory. S. Chand & Company Ltd., New Delhi
Mahi P (2020) Rural local governance and development. SAGE Texts, New Delhi
Pattanaik BK (2016) Introduction to development studies. SAGE Texts, New Delhi
Rout BC (1988) Political theory and ideology. Panchashila, Bhubaneswar, India
Sapru RK, Sapru Y (2021) Public policy: formulation, implementation and evaluation. Sterling Publishers (P) Ltd, New Delhi
Sharma LN, Susmita S (1998) Kautilyan indicators of good governance, IIPA Journal. https://journals.sagepub.com/doi/abs/10.1177/0019556119980302?journalCode=ipaa. Accessed 29 March 2022
Shashi R (2019) Development with inclusive policy, Yojana (Sept. 2019), pp. 58–62
Stroker G (1998) Governance as thory: five propositions. Int Soc Sci J 50(155):17–28
Varma SP (2017) Modern political theory. VIKAS Publishing House Pvt. Ltd., New Delhi
Vinod MJ, Meena D (2013) Contemporary political theory. PHI Learning Private Ltd., New Delhi

Dr. Jitendra Sahoo is currently working as Professor and Head, Department of Political Science, University of Gour Banga, Malda, West Bengal, India. He has more than 20 years of teaching experience at the UG and PG levels. He has obtained two master's, one in political science and another in public administration, and was awarded M.Phil. and Ph.D. degrees from Utkal University, India. He is actively engaged in research work; has participated and presented papers in various national and international conferences, seminars, and webinars; has contributed 15 articles in different national and international journals; and has written 26 chapters in edited books. Dr. Sahoo has co-authored two books, and he has edited seven books which were published by the publishers of national and international repute. His areas of research interest are governance at local and national level, public administration, society and polity in India, etc. He is a life member of Indian Political Science Association and West Bengal Political Science Association. Currently, he is also a member of Board of Editors of UGC-Care List Journal ENSEMBLE and a member of Board of Editors in a peer-reviewed multidisciplinary research journal ANWESHAN.

Chapter 4
Social Protection Under the Aegis of Public Policy in India: A Step Toward Sustainability in Post-reform Period

Sujoy Kanti Ghoshal

4.1 Introduction

The role of social protection systems is instrumental in not only reducing poverty but also preventing people from falling (back) into the vortex of poverty across the life cycle (Bastagli et al. 2016; Scott et al. 2014). In India, poverty has significantly reduced (Planning Commission of India 2013) over time, but a large proportion of the population remains chronically poor. However, inequality started to rise (World Bank 2011; Himanshu 2007) during the 1990s. With the acceleration in GDP growth rate[1] in India in recent decades and the trend in poverty and inequality, growth has increased the focus on sustained growth. The social protection system is a significant step toward sustainability. During the initial phase of liberalization, social protection measures were neglected, but this began to change in the mid-1990s.

International Labour Organization (ILO 1952) addressed social security as protective measures against social and economic distress throughout the life cycle. ILO's approach to social security was criticized for being limited to the experience of developed countries (Sarkar 2004). Understanding the concept of social protection is vital. However, the concept of social security varies from country to country (Goswami 2011). In this context, Jean Dreze and Amartya Sen argue that, in developing countries, social security should be seen more as pro-poor measures implemented through public means (Sen and Dreze 1989).

In developing countries like India, social security is best understood as pro-poor measures that can be promotional, preventive, and protective (Sarkar 2004). Unfortunately, India fails to provide for 24.4% of its total population the social welfare

[1] See https://data.worldbank.org.

S. K. Ghoshal (✉)
Department of Economics, St. Joseph's College, North Point, Darjeeling, West Bengal, India

M. Mishra et al. (eds.), *Public Policies and Sustainable Development in Post-Reform India*, New Frontiers in Regional Science: Asian Perspectives 71,
https://doi.org/10.1007/978-981-99-3696-0_4

supports; whereas, 46.9% of the global population, who are the most vulnerable citizens, fails to receive social welfare aid (ILO 2021). Nevertheless, data shows that gaps in social protection coverage are often associated with a fiscal deficit of 1.72% of GDP (Ministry of Finance, Govt. of India 2012).

Social security is not only a human right but also an economic and social necessity.[2] The social security legislation in India derives its strength and spirit from the Directive Principles of the State Policy as contained in the Constitution of India. India has a plethora of social protection schemes, both at the central and state levels, which cater to different segments of the population. The ambit of these schemes is quite ample, covering basic education and health, employment promotion, workers' social security, and food and nutrition security or almost the entire realm of social policy, including workers' rights at work. However, the coverage has not expanded due to the formalization of the workforce. Recently, the Government of India has initiated major Labour Law Reforms in the country.

4.2 Progress in Building the Social Protection Systems: Global Outlook

Social protection provides contingencies of modern life sickness, unemployment, old age, dependency, industrial accidents, and invalidism against which the individual cannot be expected to protect himself and his family by his own ability or foresight (Bhatnagar 1984). Globally, the development of social protection systems over the last few decades has been progressing significantly. The United Nations adopted the Sustainable Development Goals (SDGs), also known as the Global Goals in 2015, to implement nationally appropriate social protection systems for all, including floors, for reducing and preventing poverty by 2030 (UN 2017; UNRISD 2016). However, a global consensus on the important role of coherent and effective social protection systems is vital. In this context, an emerging global consensus reflected in the strategic frameworks of major international and multilateral organizations (e.g. FAO 2017; UNICEF 2012; World Bank 2012; ILO 2012b; WHO 2010; OECD 2009) aims at building inclusive and sustainable social protection systems that are closely coordinated with other social and economic policies.

Building strong and sustainable social protection systems is vital. Here, various international bodies have been moving forward to reach SDGs. Development partners—bilateral donors and multilateral agencies, including the United Nations, and multilateral financial institutions—engage in social protection in different ways, applying different emphases that reflect their individual mandate (Devereux and Roelen 2016). The World Bank focuses on social protection as a means of reducing poverty and enhancing pro-poor economic growth; the UNICEF sees it as a tool for

[2]The joint UN web platform on Social Protection and Human Rights provides useful resource on this topic; see http://www.socialprotection.humanrights.org.

achieving child well-being and children's right to social security and extending coverage to all (ibid.).

Social protection is a core pillar of the ILO mandate on social justice and decent work. The ILO's Social Security (Minimum Standards) Convention, 1952 (102); the Social Protection Floors Recommendation, 2012 (No. 202); and other international social security standards are at the heart of the UN's work of supporting countries to turn the human right to social protection into reality.

The IMF did not interfere directly with social protection until recently. In the wake of the global financial crisis, it has supported spending on social safety nets in select countries (IMF 2019). The UNDP views social protection as a key tool to transform its strategic vision to help countries achieve the simultaneous eradication of poverty and significant reduction of inequalities and exclusion into reality, as stated in its Strategic Plan 2014–2017 (UNDP 2014). Department for International Development's (DFID) work on social protection helps deliver its strategic objectives to "Tackle extreme poverty and help the world's most vulnerable" and "Strengthen resilience and response to crises" (DFID 2019).

Social protection helps in the realization of human rights, which are enshrined in the Universal Declaration of Human Rights, international conventions, and national constitutions. However, sustainable and equitable growth cannot be achieved in the absence of strong social protection policies, which guarantee at least a basic level of social security to all in need through a nationally defined social protection floor and the progressive extension of the scope and level of social security coverage (ILO's Social Protection Floors Recommendation 2012a, No. 202).

Despite substantial progress in the extension of social protection, the fundamental human right to social security remains unfulfilled for the large majority of the world's population. India is one of the largest welfare states in the world. The Government of India has accepted the international commitment that arises from the ratification of the Covenant of Social, Economic, and Cultural Rights of the United Nations. This Covenant, inter alia, recognizes the right of everyone to social security, including social insurance. India is also a signatory to several other significant conventions, such as the Convention for the Elimination of All Forms of Discrimination Against Women (CEDAW),[3] the Convention on the Rights of the Child (CRC),[4] and the Convention on the Rights of Persons with Disabilities (CRPD).[5] India has also ratified some Conventions of the ILO regarding social security, including the Workmen's Compensation (Occupational Diseases)[6] (No. 18 and revised Convention No. 42 of 1934); Equality of Treatment (Accident

[3]CEDAW guides the work of UN women for gender equality and empowering all women.

[4]CRC or UNCRC sets out the civil, political, social, health and cultural rights of children.

[5]CRPD or UNCRPD intended to protect the rights and dignity of persons with disability.

[6]Workmen's Compensation (Occupational Diseases) (Revised Convention No. 42 of 1934), a General Conference of the ILO for the partial revision of the workmen's compensation for occupational diseases.

Compensation)[7] (No. 19 of 1925); and Equality of Treatment (Social Security)[8] (No. 118 of 1962). However, ILO Convention 102[9] has not been ratified by India.

4.3 Social Security in India: Moving Toward Inclusive Progress

The ILO's notion of social security includes nine core contingencies—sickness, maternity, employment injury, unemployment, invalidity, old age, death, need for long-term medical care, and supporting families with children—that lead to stoppage or substantial reduction of earnings. The Indian Constitution adopted in 1951 contains all the ingredients obliging the state to move toward the realization of socio-economic rights. Although India is not a signatory to ILO Convention 102, it has well-established social security systems providing varying degrees of coverage in several of the nine branches of the Convention.

In this context, in providing the facilities of these schemes, the Government of India has been facing a fiscal challenge. Appropriate design and effective implementation, which involve improved accountability of all those implementers and proactive measures to reach the most vulnerable segments of the population, are also major barriers.

The trends in poverty, inequality, and growth rate have significant implications for social protection policies and programmes. Several areas that do not have a significant place in India's social protection system are increasingly demanding greater interventions in light of India's changing economic conditions. After liberalization, in the initial phase, social protection measures were neglected, but this began to change in the mid-1990s when there was an expansion in the budget for rural employment generation and social assistance programmes.

The growing importance of social protection is reflected in the Government of India Common Minimum Programme[10] and 11th Five-Year Plan[11], which commit to the institutionalization of programmes as legal rights continue upscaling of interventions, and proposals to expand new types of social protection interventions to the large unorganized sector.

---

[7]Equality of Treatment (Accident Compensation, No. 19 of 1925), a General Conference of the ILO for the equality of treatment for national and foreign workers as regards workmen's compensation for accidents.

[8]Equality of Treatment (Social Security, No. 118 of 1962), a General Conference of the ILO for the equality of treatment of nationals and non-nationals in social security.

[9]ILO Convention 102 is the flagship of all ILO social security conventions that establishes worldwide-agreed minimum standards for all nine branches of social security.

[10]Government of India Common Minimum Programme (2004) is a document outlining the minimum objectives to tackle the needs of India's poor through NREGA, Midday meals.

[11]11th Five-Year Plan (2007–2012) emphasize on increased resources and priority for social protection commitment to a more inclusive growth model.

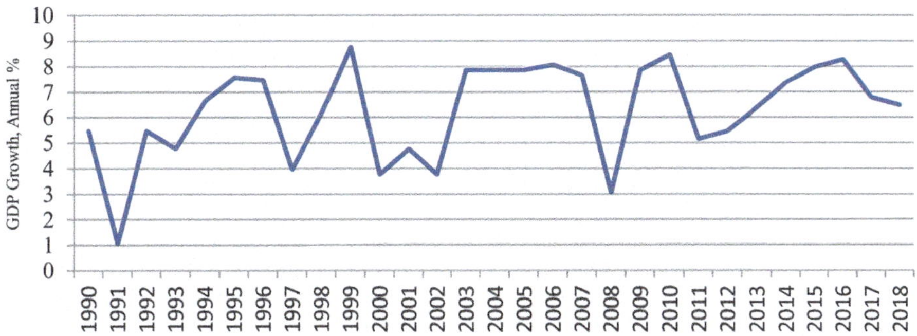

Fig. 4.1 Trend in GDP growth rate in India. (Source: Prepared by the author based on the World Bank Data)

In India, most social security provisions remain limited to formal employment. However, various studies have shown the need for social security for informal sector workers. In this context, Labour Law Reforms in the country in recent years have been a major step by the Government of India toward an inclusive social protection system.

4.4 Social Protection Systems in India: A Reflection from Data

India will undoubtedly continue its strong commitment to a social protection system that seeks to serve vulnerable and disadvantaged people. The trends in poverty, inequality, and growth rate have significant implications for social protection policies and programmes. In this context, there is a need to formulate strategies and deepen the ongoing policy reorientation of the Indian social protection system to meet the changing and increasingly diverse needs of its population.

However, for meaningful social protection policies and programmes, there is a need for the collection, compilation, and analysis of data on social protection measures. But the collection of reasonably accurate data on social protection measures is a challenging task.

Here, the statistical study mainly follows the secondary data, which is largely sourced from the World Bank, the Planning Commission of India, the NSS, and the ILO. In India, the GDP growth rate has been accelerated, especially since the 1990s (Fig. 4.1).[12] With the increasing GDP growth rate, poverty has fallen from 37.2% to 21.9% (Table 4.1). However, inequality started to rise during the 1990s, particularly in urban areas (Table 4.2). Data shows that the share of people protected by at least one social protection in India is significantly low compared to the world population

[12] https://data.worldbank.org/indicator/NY.GDP.MKTP.KD.ZG?locations=IN&start=1962

Table 4.1 Below poverty line trends in India

Year	Percentage of persons		
	Rural	Urban	National
2004–2005	41.8	25.5	37.2
2009–2010	33.8	20.9	29.8
2011–2012	25.7	13.7	21.9

Source: Planning Commission of India (2013)

Table 4.2 Inequality trends in India

Year	Rural	Urban	National
1983	0.32	0.34	0.32
1987–1988	0.30	0.35	–
1993–1994	0.29	0.34	0.30
2004–2005	0.30	0.38	0.33

N.B. Gini coefficients calculated using NSS data
Source: World Bank (2011), Himanshu (2007)

Table 4.3 People protected by social protection systems including floors (in percentage)

Indicator	World	India
Total Beneficiaries of at least one Social Protection (excluding health)	46.9	24.4
Children	26.4	24.1
Maternity	44.9	41.5
Unemployment	18.6	0.0
Work Injury	35.4	3.7
Disability	33.5	5.6
Old-age Pension	77.5	42.5
Contributors to Pension	32.5	15.5
Vulnerability	28.9	16.4
Universal Health Coverage	65.6	55.0

Sources: ILO (2021) World Social Protection Database, based on SSI; ISSA/SSA, social security programmes throughout the world; ILOSTAT, ECLAC, IMF, WHO, WB, UNDP, UNICEF, completed with national data sources. See URL https://wspr.social-protection.org

(Table 4.3). Low coverage of social protection is mainly due to a deficit in public expenditure. However, some improvement is seen in the share of public expenditure by the centre—from 1.30% of GDP in 2001–2002 to 1.73% of GDP in 2011–2012 (Table 4.4). Unfortunately, the share of expenditure on public health is unexpectedly low (Table 4.5).

4.5 Moving Forward: Selective Social Protection Schemes in India

India's surge in growth and rapid expansion in public spending in the past decade has created new possibilities for its social protection system. In addition, India's growth has raised expectations from the population of the social protection system.

Table 4.4 Public expenditure by centre on social security schemes (% of GDP)

Indicator	2001–2002	2006–2007	2011–2012
Total Rural Employment	0.22	0.35	0.38
Total Social Assistance programme (National Social Assistance Programme and Social Security Scheme)	0.05	0.09	0.11
Total Housing (Rural and Urban)	0.10	0.07	0.13
Total Food Security (ICDS, MDM, PDS)	0.92	0.76	1.08
Total Employment Promotion (Training, SJSRY, PMEGP)	0.01	0.02	0.02
Total—All Programmes	1.30	1.29	1.72

Source: Expenditure Budget Vol-II of various ministries and departments, Union Budget, Ministry of Finance, Govt. of India (2012)

Table 4.5 Public health and social protection expenditure (in percentage)

<table>
<tr><th colspan="2">Indicator</th><th>World</th><th>India</th></tr>
<tr><td colspan="2">Total Expenditure on Social Protection (excluding health)</td><td>12.9</td><td>1.4</td></tr>
<tr><td rowspan="3">Total Expenditure on Social Protection Systems (including floors), by Broad age group</td><td>Children</td><td>1.1</td><td>0.1</td></tr>
<tr><td>Working-age population</td><td>3.6</td><td>0.3</td></tr>
<tr><td>Old age</td><td>7.0</td><td>0.3</td></tr>
<tr><td colspan="2">Health Expenditure (Domestic General Health Expenditure, WHO)</td><td>5.8</td><td>1.0</td></tr>
</table>

Sources: ILO (2021) World Social Protection Database

In India, central and state levels recognize the need for a more effective and relevant social protection system, and there has been considerable innovation in social protection policy and delivery systems in recent years. However, financial constraints and poor delivery systems are still a concern.

The Government of India has initiated a number of social protection programmes for which a major part of the finances is also drawn from the federal budget. These programs span the entire life cycle of poor individuals and cover various dimensions, such as health, education, food security, shelter, employment, and livelihoods. Here, the major social protection programmes launched by the central government and currently being implemented in India are summarized in Table 4.6.

4.6 Conclusion

In developing countries like India, people are inadequately covered under the existing social protection system. The acceleration in the growth rate in India in recent decades has gone hand in hand with a decline in poverty. However, increasing inequality and chronic poverty persist significantly. In India, social protection has been seen more broadly as pro-poor measures implemented through public means. The ILO addressed social security as a protective measure against abrupt reduction

Table 4.6 Major social protection schemes of the central government

Name of scheme	Objective	Target group	Coverage	Nature of scheme
Education, nutrition, and health support for preschool and school-aged children				
Sarva Shiksha Abhiyan (SSA)	To support universal enrolment and retention of children in elementary schooling and to support the provision of quality education	6–14-year-old children in elementary schools	All government-financed elementary schools	Non-statutory, but supports the implementation of the Right to Education Act
Integrated Child Development Scheme (ICDS)	Improvement in the nutritional and health status of children 0–6 years through a package of services providing nutritional and health support to children and pregnant and lactating mothers	All children in the eligible age group and pregnant and lactating mothers in areas served by ICDS centres	Services provided to 7.48 crore children under 6 years and 1.8 crore pregnant and lactating mothers	Non-statutory but major components are part of the proposed National Food Security Act
National Programme of Mid Day Meal in Schools	National programme of mid day meal in schools	School-going children in all recognized schools and educational centres providing primary, upper-primary, or non-formal education	12 crore children in about 12 lakh schools	Non-statutory but major components are part of the proposed NFSA
Social health protection				
National Rural Health Mission (NRHM) (now National Health Mission)	Provision of accessible, affordable, and accountable health services, in coordination with states, through a decentralized and convergent approach	Rural and now urban population		Non-statutory

Rashtriya Swasthya Bima Yojana (RSBY)	To protect poor families from major health shocks that involve hospitalization through insurance for which beneficiaries only pay a nominal registration fee	Below Poverty Line Poor families and other families of informal workers to whom coverage has been extended	3.42 crore smart cards issued by March 2013 covering almost half of BPL families	Semi-statutory
Total Sanitation Campaign (TSC)	To accelerate sanitation coverage in rural areas and to develop community-managed environmental sanitation systems	All rural families with an incentive to Below Poverty Line families		Non-statutory
National Rural Drinking Water Programme (NRDWP)	To provide solutions for safe drinking water to all rural households			Non-statutory
Food security				
Targeted Public Distribution System (TPDS)	Stabilization of food prices and provision of subsidized foodgrains to poor households	Three-tier provision of subsidized cereals and other essential commodities (APL, BPL, and Antyodaya or destitute households)	36.2% households in 2009–2010 (NSS estimates)	Non-statutory at present but will become part of the proposed NFSA
Employment and livelihood security for the rural and urban poor				
Mahatma Gandhi National Rural Employment Guarantee Scheme (MGNREGS)	Provision of up to 100 days of employment in public works to rural households demanding manual employment and creation of public assets	All rural households demanding unskilled manual employment in public works	24% rural households provided employment (2009–2010 survey)	Statutory, with nearly 90% contribution by the central government, remaining by states

(continued)

Table 4.6 (continued)

Name of scheme	Objective	Target group	Coverage	Nature of scheme
National Rural Livelihood Mission (Ajeevika) (from June 2011) [reformed Swarna Jayanti Gram Swarozgar Yojana or SGSY)	To reduce poverty by enabling the poor households to access gainful self-employment and skilled wage employment through strong grassroots institutions (self-managed self-help groups (SHGs) and federated institutions)	Below Poverty Line rural poor in self-help groups	Since inception in 1999, 42.69 lakh SHGs formed. During 2010–2011, 21.09 lakh persons received assistance (69.5% women)	Non-statutory
Swarna Jayanti Shahari Rozgar Yojana (SJSRY)/ National Urban Livelihood Mission (NULM)	Creation of employment through specified public work activity and through assistance to women self-help groups and individual female and male micro-entrepreneurs	Urban poor (BPL) individuals and (women) members of SHGs	17.2 lakh urban poor and women SHG members assisted in setting up enterprises; 23.61 lakh poor given skill training; 797.35 lakh man days of employment generated up to December 2011	Non-statutory
Prime Minister's Employment Guarantee Programme (PMEGP)	Generation of employment through assistance in the form of margin money subsidy in setting up of micro-enterprises	Urban and rural micro-entrepreneurs	3.8 crore jobs during 2008–2012	Non-statutory
State-assisted pensions for the poor (National Social Assistance Programme—NSAP)				
National Old Age Pension Scheme (NOAPS)	Provision of pensions	Poor persons (Below Poverty Line) above 60 years (provision of food assistance under Annapurna Scheme to persons eligible under NOAPS but not getting it)	1.65 crores (2012–2013)	Semi-statutory

Indira Gandhi National Widows' Pension Scheme (IGNWPS)	Provision of pensions	Poor widows (Below Poverty Line) between 40 and 64 years	84 lakhs (2012–2013)	Semi-statutory
Indira Gandhi National Disability Pension Scheme (IGNDPS)	Provision of pensions	Poor disabled persons (Below Poverty Line) between 40 and 64 years	12 lakhs	Semi-statutory
Housing for the poor				
Indira Awas Yojana (IAY)	Construction of dwelling units and upgradation of existing unserviceable kutcha houses by providing grant-in-aid	Rural people Below Poverty Line belonging to SCs/STs, freed bonded labourers, and non-SC/ST categories	27.15 and 22.30 lakh houses in 2010–2011 and 2011–2012, respectively	Non-statutory
BSUP/IHSDP Rajiv Awas Yojana (RAY)	Urban housing/basic services/ slum upgradation		10 lakh dwelling units built or under construction (2005–2012)	Non-statutory
Life and disability cover for the poor				
Aam Admi Bima Yojana (AABY)	Life, accident, and disability cover to the main breadwinner	Agricultural labour families; age of insured 18–59 years	82 lakhs insured by September 2009	Semi-statutory
National Family Benefit Scheme (NFBS) (component of the NSAP)	One-time benefit on the death of breadwinner	BPL families	4.5 lakhs	Semi-statutory

Source: Compiled by the author from annual reports of the ministries, budget of the GoI, draft 12th plan, and official websites of the schemes

or stoppage in income resulting from sickness, maternity, employment injury, unemployment, disability, old-age death, and provision for medical care. Though India is not a signatory of ILO Convention 102, the Government of India has introduced several policy initiatives to extend social security benefits to the people. Some progress has been made, but not enough, especially for the disadvantaged section.

Research has shown that a comprehensive social security net in developing economies can enhance labour market efficiency and stimulate sociopolitical and economic growth (Justino 2003). The Indian workforce comprises a huge informal/unorganized sector. According to the International Trade Union Confederation, India is amongst the ten worst countries in the world in terms of worker rights in 2020 (ITUC 2020). However, recent Labour Law Reforms in the country are a significant step to moving forward for sustainability.

Various welfare schemes can lead to socially inclusive and sustainable progress. The report of the National Commission for Enterprises in Unorganized Sector (NCEUS) commissioned by the Government of India suggested a way forward and asserted that providing social security should not be seen as a burden on the economy and, instead, is an important bedrock for a developing country to build form (NCEUS 2007). The recent COVID-19 pandemic is posing an unprecedented challenge to the social protection systems of countries across the globe. The pandemic has exposed the vulnerability of those not adequately protected from its socio-economic consequences. Without proper action, global poverty and inequality will deepen significantly—no exception in India. Unfortunately, in India, informal workers are particularly at risk, covered by neither social assistance nor social insurance. However, in responding to the crisis, Indian polity has used social protection policies to protect public health, jobs, and incomes. The Government of India has extended coverage of existing benefits, improved or introduced new ones, adapted administrative and delivery mechanisms, and mobilized additional financial resources. The Government of India has declared the Pradhan Mantri Garib Kalyan Yojana (PMGKY), a relief package to support poor and vulnerable people and ensure that their basic needs are met. The package comprises both the implementation of new social protection interventions and adaptation of pre-existing benefits through the programmes such as Mahatma Gandhi National Rural Employment Guarantee Scheme (MGNREGS), Antyodaya Anna Yojana, Indira Gandhi National Old Age Pension Scheme, and Building and Construction Workers' Fund managed by state governments. The announcement of a measure expanding health insurance for healthcare workers is also a significant step.

References

Bastagli F, Hagen-Zanker J, Harman L, Barca V, Sturge G, Schmidt T, Pellerano L (2016) Cash transfers: what does the evidence say. A rigorous review of programme impact and the role of design and implementation features. ODI, London, 1(7)

Bhatnagar D (1984) Labour welfare and social security legislation in India. Deep and Deep Publications, New Delhi, pp 46–47
Devereux S, Roelen K (2016) Hot topics in social protection
DFID (2019) Department for International Development single departmental plan
FAO (2017) Social protection framework: promoting rural development for all
Goswami VG (2011) Labour and Industrial Law. Edn. Central Law Agency, Allahabad, p.3
Government of India Planning Commission (2013) Press note on poverty estimates, 2011–12
Himanshu (2007) Recent trends in poverty and inequality: some preliminary results. Econ Polit Wkly 42(06):497–508
ILO (1952) Social security (minimum standards) convention (No. 102). International Labour Organization
ILO (2012a) Social security for all: building social protection floors and comprehensive social security systems. The Strategy of the International Labour Organization
ILO (2012b) Social security for all: The strategy of the International Labour Organization
ILO (2021) World Social Protection Database. https://wspr.social-protection.org
IMF (2019) Guidaence note on IMF engagement on social safeguards in low-income countries. International Monetary Fund, Washington, DC
ITUC (2020) ITUC global rights index. International Trade Union Confederation
Ministry of Finance (2012) Report of the committee on roadmap for fiscal consolidation. New Delhi
NCEUS (2007) Report on conditions of work and promotion of livelihoods in the unorganized sector. National Commission for Enterprises in the Unorganized Sector
OECD (2009) Promoting pro-poor growth: social protection
Sarkar S (2004) Extending social security coverage to the informal sector in India. Social Change 34(4):122–130
Scott L, Hanifnia K, Shepherd A, Muyanga M, Valli E, Network CPA (2014) How resilient are escapes out of poverty. CPAN Challenge Paper, 2
Sen A, Dreze J (1989) Hunger and public action. Clarendon Press
UN (2017) Progress towards the sustainable development goals: report of the Secretary-General, E/2017/66
UNDP (2014) Changing with the world: UNDP strategic plan 2014–17. United Nations Development Programme, New York
UNICEF (2012) Integrated social protection systems: enhancing equity for children
UNRISD (2016) Policy innovations for transformative change: UNRISD flagship report 2016, Geneva
WHO (2010) The World Health Report: Health systems financing: the path to universal coverage
World Bank (2011) Perspectives on poverty in India: stylized facts from survey data
World Bank (2012) Resilience, equity and opportunity: the World Bank's social protection and labour strategy

Sujoy Kanti Ghoshal (Ph.D. in Economics) is the faculty, St. Joseph's College, University of North Bengal, West Bengal. His area of specialization is development economics. He has more than 15 research papers published in reputed national and international economics and other social science journals and edited books. He has also presented papers in national and international seminars. He is a life member of the Indian Economic Association and Bengal Economic Association.

Part II
Facets of Public Policies in Achieving Sustainable Development

Chapter 5
Is Democracy a Precursor to Sustainable Development? Reflections on the Accomplishment of SDGs in India

Siddhartha Sankar Manna and Mukunda Mishra

5.1 Introduction

"Democracy" has been interrelated with high levels of human capital, lower inflation, political stability, and developed economic liberty and choices. It is essential to state that democracy has been strongly linked with economic bases of growth, like education levels and life span, through the development of educative organizations and health care. The worldwide debate on democracy has been more and more marked by growing mistrust of democratic organizations, systems of practices, and elected governments. However, with Sustainable Development Goal (SDG) 16, a global effort is underway to "promote peaceful and inclusive societies for sustainable development, provide access to justice for all, and build effective, accountable and inclusive institutions at all levels." This chapter emphasizes an opportunity on the guidelines of the 2019 UN Economic and Social Council ministerial segment to accelerate arrangements around developing Goal 16 and promote a thematic dialogue of democracy. As there has not been a unique or universal pattern of democracy, and each state must seek to attain the ideal type of democracy that performs for its conditions, there are essential features of commonalities to qualify the democracies and representative forms of government.

Governance is a fundamental mode of a system that affects development. It endorses the "accountability, transparency, efficiency, and the rule of law" in different stages. It lets effective management of human capital, natural resources, and economic resources for reasonable and sustainable development and ensures

S. S. Manna
Department of Political Science, University of Gour Banga, Malda, West Bengal, India

M. Mishra (✉)
Department of Geography, Dr. Meghnad Saha College, Itahar, Uttar Dinajpur, West Bengal, India

M. Mishra et al. (eds.), *Public Policies and Sustainable Development in Post-Reform India*, New Frontiers in Regional Science: Asian Perspectives 71,
https://doi.org/10.1007/978-981-99-3696-0_5

involvement in policymaking procedures of civil society. Democratic governance denotes the system of control and rule of the regime in certain times of conflicts, demands, and collective demands that foster the developing process and progressive management in a representative form of government. It brings specific management processes and arrangements. A system of governance accomplished the collective sense and a multidimensional plan arranged by the government for sustainable development. Sustainable development (SD) claims that the existing use and practice of resources should reduce the degree of harm and loss to the future usage of resources in society.

In the context of democratic governance, SD has been considered the promise of a political retort and response to various issues or problems, and governance is the coordination and synchronization of that response. So, governance is the system in which SD can be nurtured and shaped. From an economist standpoint, as SD has been the key to the stable development of the money economy, it must confirm that development should occur without destroying the ecological balance. Furthermore, the existing development should not compromise on the requirements of the future generations. Due to civil society's involvement and more extensive participation, transparency and accountability have been essential features of the issues and dialogue on governance.

The World Bank (1994) denotes "governance" as all practices of controlling and exercising authority in the distribution of wealth. The governance issues have consequently been meticulously linked with the procedures and apparatuses through which people can get into wealth and resources. These comprise matters of property rights, social relationships, and gender, as well as social capital through which people access resources (World Bank 1994). Although policies have succeeded in building the scope of management at lower stages, changing power and controlling relationships have become more complex and challenging. Democracy represents a peaceful transfer of power through electoral procedures. It depends on receptive and accountable governance, ensures the rule of law, and safeguards human rights and participation of people in the political and decision-making processes. These democratic methods reinforce a peaceful and balanced society. The governance functions would be effective with the existing democratic principles and democratization procedures. It seeks to consolidate governance by introducing inclusive and responsible organizations and vigorous civil society. They stimulate the human rights, impartiality, and rule of law and advocate public involvement in sociopolitical procedures. Whilst all these are set together, democracy and governance are found to be interlinked and interconnected; one is meaningless without the other.

5.2 Public Policy: Scope of Intervention

Public policy has been considered a plan of action assumed and pursued by the administration and government. Public policy can usually be depicted as an arrangement of rules, controlling actions, procedures of functions, and a given subject proclaimed by an administrative unit or its legislatures. Public policy can be generally defined as a system of laws, regulatory measures, courses of action, and funding priorities concerning a given topic promulgated by a governmental entity or its representatives. Policies that have good consequences, benefitting a large number of people, may not be the "right" ones if they violate the fundamental rights of individuals guaranteed in the Constitution of India. A strategy of action is adopted by administrative representatives to attain certain extensive purposes affecting a considerable section of the citizen in the state. Public policy inputs shape a government's policy decisions and strategies to address problems. Public policy goals can be broad and high-minded or narrow and self-serving. The government uses public apparatuses involving the combination of incentives and penalties to prompt citizens to act in ways that achieve policy goals. Public policy effects are the outcomes arising from government regulation.

Public policy is goal oriented, and it considers the response of the political system to the challenges and issues emerging from the society and environment. It is generally articulated by administrative management and government authorities. Various measures are used to categorize several forms of public policies based on functions and works like education, physical condition, transport, line of work and business, public security, and ecological protection. Theodore J. Lowi, the American political scientist, in one of their articles entitled "*American Business, Public Policy, Case Studies and Political Theory*," pointed out four categories of policy (Lowi 1964), i.e., (i) *distributive*, (ii) *redistributive*, (iii) *regulatory*, and (iv) *constituent*. *Distributive policies* refer to allocating resources for a definite section of society and state. It incorporates all government's public support and welfare programs, e.g., adult education plans, food relief, social protection, and employment opportunities. It encompasses the distribution of goods and services to members of society.

Redistributive policies have been an important factor of stratagems for diminishing disparity and inequity that help promote sustainable development in its three different fields in society, i.e., economic, social, and environmental. Kohler (2015) illustrated that in a redistributive policy framework, costs are borne by a relatively small number of groups or individuals; still, benefits are expected to be enjoyed by different groups in society. The redistributive policies include assistance for education and health care; temporary assistance for needy families, e.g., income support; food programs like the supplementary nutritional aid program; and many other avenues through which the public are benefitted.

In contrast, a *regulatory policy* regulates companies and organizations to protect the public. It denotes the decree of aimed rules and regulations, usually accompanied by several authoritative apparatuses for rigorous care and imposing obedience in the field of public policy. The primary purpose of the regulatory plan is to ensure the regulatory functions for common interests. There have been two types of regulation, i.e., (i) economic and (ii) social. It bounds the activities.

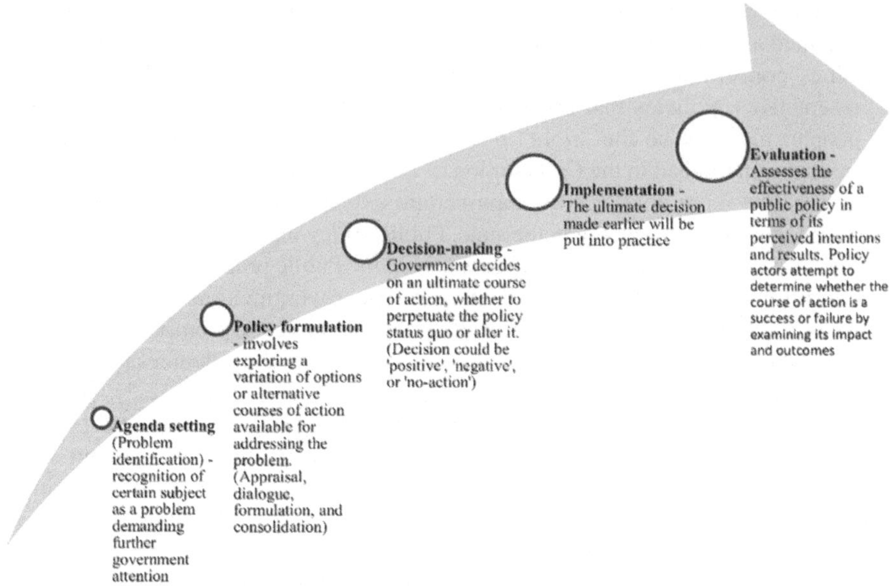

Fig. 5.1 Schematic presentation of the five stages of the Public Policymaking model. (**Source:** Compiled by the authors following Anderson (1974))

Constituent policies form the decision-making and policymaking power units or are interrelated with laws and regulations. Constituent policies as well deal with the fiscal rule in certain conditions. These policies may include forming government organizations and setting up rules or actions for a government organization. It relates to the formulation of regulations for distributing power and authority between the present and future government strategies.

The policy cycle has been an instrument used to consider the development and progress of a policy. It can also be regarded as a "stagist approach," "stages heuristic," or "stages approach" (Laswell 1971). It is thus a rule of thumb rather than the actual reality of how policy is created, but it has been influential in how political scientists look at policy in general. Harold Lasswell, the renowned American political scientist and communications theorist, amplified this type of model theory. He had categorically assumed the widespread pattern of the policy series and divided the procedure into seven different stages. He revealed the crucial questions of how and why public policies should be formulated and made (Laswell 1971). The policy seeks to coordinate this process with underlying policy application with the stages extending across (Howlett 2011) (i) intelligence, (ii) promotion, (iii) prescription, (iv) invocation, (v) application, (vi) termination, and (vii) appraisal.

On the other hand, Anderson (1974) postulated another form of public policy in his "Public Policymaking" (Fig. 5.1). He has pointed out the following stages:

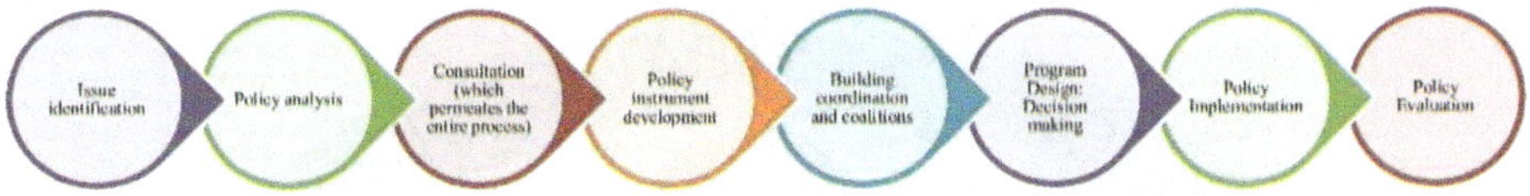

Fig. 5.2 Schematic presentation of the eight-step policy model. (**Source:** Compiled by the authors following Bridgman and Davis 2004)

- Agenda setting
- Policy formulation
- Decision-making
- Implementation
- Evaluation

In the scope of public policy, Peter Bridgman, the senior officer in the Queensland Public Service and Professor at the Australian National University, with his co-author Glyn Davis, postulated an eight-step policy in their book entitled "*The Australian Policy Handbook*" (Bridgman and Davis 2004) (Fig. 5.2):

- Issue identification
- Policy analysis
- Consultation (which permeates the entire process)
- Policy instrument development
- Building coordination and coalitions
- Program design: decision-making
- Policy implementation
- Policy evaluation

The conceptual pattern of public policy introduced by Bridgman and Davis (2004) has been an experimental and interactive aspect. It is deliberately regulating and not meant to be analytic. In this regard, the policy cycles have been generally categorized as assuming a classical approach (Fig. 5.3). There is a tendency to describe procedures from the authorities' viewpoint for policymaking and decision makers. Hence, some postpositivist intellectuals challenge the cyclical models as impassive, impractical, and idealistic, favoring systemic and more complicated models (Young and Mendizabal 2009). They think about a broader scope of units or actors involved in the policy system that comprises the arrangements of civil society, mass media, academicians, organizations for policy research, corporations, campaigners, etc.

The United Nations Development Program (1997) defines governance as the exercise and implementation of economic, political, and administrative authority to deal with the activities of the state at different stages. It includes the state apparatuses, methods of functions, and organizations through which people and a group of people enunciate their welfare and interests, carry out their legal rights, fulfill their responsibilities, facilitate their changes, and recognize the essential features of good governance: involvement, rule of law, consensus orientation, equality, efficiency,

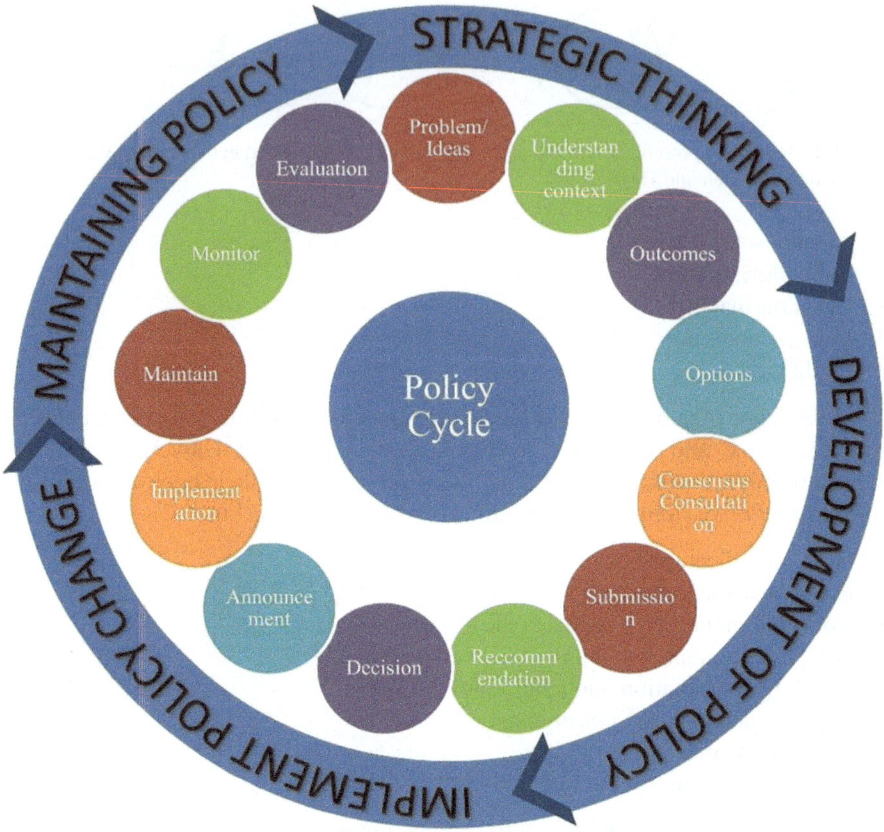

Fig. 5.3 The classical approach of the policy cycle. (**Source:** Compiled by the authors)

responsiveness and effectiveness, responsibility, and planning concept. The notion of governance can be understood regarding regional sustainable development policymaking and decision-making (Berger 2003) or relating to the rule of law (Sachiko and Durwood 2005).

The United Nations Development Programme (UNDP) has also provided for the development of good governance by concentrating on the following six different areas (Fig. 5.4):

- Parliamentary development
- Assistance with electoral systems and processes
- Improvement of access to justice and human rights
- Promotion of access to information
- Support for decentralization and local governance
- Reform of public administration and civil service

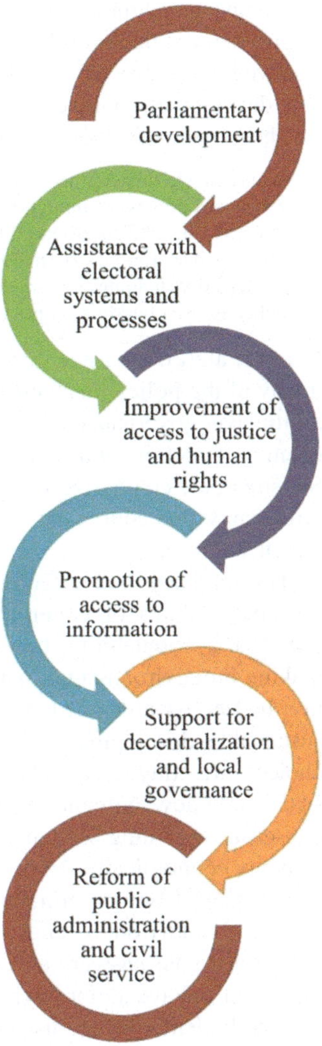

Fig. 5.4 Key areas to be focused on ensuring good governance. (**Source:** Compiled by the authors following the UNDP)

5.3 Good Governance for Ensuring SD

The idea of sustainable development has been an effective plan in international policy. It encompasses long-term influence and development programs from global to local. Although global and nationwide assurances have been stated several times, the conventional paradigms of governance, controlled by the regulatory authority of recognized state organizations, have not been well prepared to execute the changes that sustainable development indicates and showed their limits, assuming the more and more intricate nature and worldwide scope of today's sustainability issues and challenges. For addressing the increasingly multifaceted challenges and matters of sustainable development, a planned and strategic methodological approach is needed to provide a suitable outline and context for a cohesive vision of all mechanisms involved in the process and development. The responses are made through sustainable development policies.

The Commission for Sustainable Development opines that (Kardos 2012):

> "a sustainable development strategy is defined as a coordinated, participatory and iterative (repeating) process of thoughts and actions to achieve economic, environmental and social objectives in a balanced and integrated manner at the national and local levels, a tool for informed decision-making that provides a framework for systematic thought across sectors and territory, helping to institutionalize processes for consultation, negotiation, mediation and consensus building on priority societal issues where interests differs."

Kemp et al. (2005) argue that the government has been revealed by the government in any of the policy mechanisms, and it is a significant encounter to ensure that the multiplayer governance rules exemplify dimensions for sustainability-oriented organization, direction, and redirection and offer a realistic logic of idea and obligation. SD strategies emphasize the systematic and organizational features of a repetitive governance procedure where the system of arrangement should function a gradually significant role.

Transparency and effective public involvement in policymaking have been essential features of governance for sustainable development. It is important to state that accountability, transparency, and democratic empowerment in decision-making on environmental matters were included in "Principle-10" of Rio Declaration in 1992 (Kardos 2012). In this regard, Kardos (2012) rightly pointed out that sustainable development is of critical importance for all citizens, as it engages choices affecting essential aspects of our lifestyles. In this context, achieving sustainable development depends on what kind of role society plays in reaching a consensus regarding sustainable development vision, goals, and objectives, in spite of many economically, environmentally, and socially driven interests. A three-unit commitment from government, trade, and civil society is essential to successfully engage all individuals, and worldwide responsibility should be shifted to groups with immediate answers and unique focus. Emerging alliances above seem to be important to have a more dynamic force, as statecraft's institutional mechanism has frequently demonstrated its constraints. There are clear decision-making procedures at the level of public authorities, as well as civil society participation in decision-making processes, in a good governance system.

In this case, decentralization requires increased effectiveness. It has been desired, in addition to a better amalgamation of purposes and activities, both (Kardos 2012) (i) *vertically* (i.e., across international, national, and sub-national levels of government) and (ii) *horizontally* (i.e., between the entities of a particular tier of government). For vertical integration, Mihaela Kardos mentions the following:

- The arrangement of the most important ecological effects of rules and actions
- The formation of a structure of negotiation and discussion
- Sectoral policies for modification

- Policies of activities
- Financial policies and monitoring schemes

For horizontal integration, he suggests the practice of durable sustainability policies for sectoral realms; specific governing organizations entrusted with total management, control, and oversight of the coordination of the integration procedure; communication programs; and nationwide action schemes with levels of feedback and reconsideration and resolution of the clash. In this context, Lafferty (2002) presents some recommendations for vertical and horizontal principles within the range of ecology.

The Sustainable Development Goals (SDGs), or Global Goals, have been a set of 17 interrelated global goals planned to be a proposal to attain an improved and more sustainable future for people. The United Nations General Assembly (UN-GA) introduced the SDGs in 2015 (United Nations 2015). These goals, recognized as Agenda 2030, have been planned to be attained by 2030. The 17 SDGs are (i) No Poverty; (ii) Zero Hunger; (iii) Good Health and Well-being; (iv) Quality Education; (v) Gender Equality; (vi) Clean Water and Sanitation; (vii) Affordable and Clean Energy; (viii) Decent Work and Economic Growth; (ix) Industry, Innovation, and Infrastructure; (x) Reduced Inequality; (xi) Sustainable Cities and Communities; (xii) Responsible Consumption and Production; (xiii) Climate Action; (xiv) Life Below Water; (xv) Life on Land; (xvi) Peace, Justice, and Strong Institutions; and (xvii) Partnerships for the Goals.

Like many other issues, e.g., poverty, educational attainment, nutrition, and public health services, which are historically unequal at the sub-national level, SDG achievement also appears to be substantially unequal across the state (Fig. 5.5). This unequal pattern reinforced the belief of the planners that the SDG cannot be achieved by India until and unless they are achieved at the sub-national levels. The rising concern of intervening up to the sub-national level is, though theoretically sounds easy, a challenging task indeed in a federal state like India.

> "In a federal country like India, states, with defined powers over a wide range of subjects, have, over the years become the primary drivers of development. In fact, the SDGs with their focus on equality, inclusion, and the principle of 'leave No One Behind', make the states essential actors with crucial roles. However, the wide diversities among the Indian states in localizing the SDG Agenda in their respective development planning- implementation-advocacy-evaluation strategies, has created the need to document the varied localization processes in different states and the lessons learnt, which will help to accelerate the country's drive to achieve the 2030 Agenda."—NITI Aayog [1]

India seeks to reveal the responsibility of the SDGs for the convergence with the nationwide development program as exposed in the proclamation of Sabka Saath Sabka Vikaas (Collective Efforts for Inclusive Development). India followed the

[1] See the "Acknowledgement" by Sanyukta Samaddar, Adviser, Sustainable Development Goals Division, NITI Aayog, Government of India, in the report entitled "Localising SDGs: Early Lessons from 2019" by NITI Aayog, Government of India, in partnership with the United Nations; URL: https://www.niti.gov.in/sites/default/files/2020-07/LSDGs_July_8_Web.pdf.

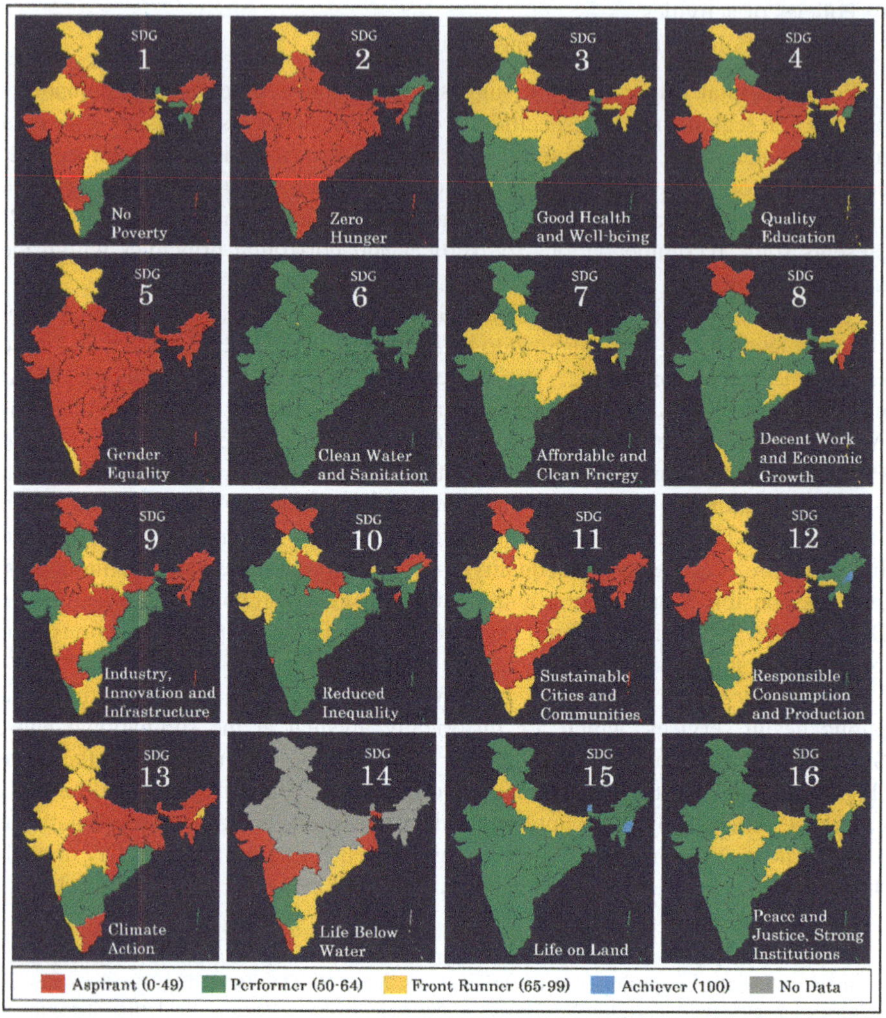

Fig. 5.5 SDG 1–16 across Indian states, 2019–2020. (**Source:** Compiled by the authors from the report entitled SDG India: Index and Dashboard 2019–2020, published by the NITI Aayog, Govt. of India, in partnership with the United Nations)

dynamic policies of the SDG localization paradigm on adoption, execution, and supervision at the state and district levels. India engages several sub-national and regional administrations, civil society organizations, local groups, people in vulnerable conditions, and the private sector. The government of India has taken several initiatives and made several arrangements to tackle ecological degradation and environmental disasters.

The following plans and programs further represent India's development across the SDGs:

- **Aatmanir Bharat (Self-reliant India):** India has effectively lifted over 271 million people out of multidimensional poverty through economic development and empowerment. The Government of India (GoI) takes various measures to diminish inequalities among marginalized and vulnerable people, like access to nutrition, child health, education, sanitation, drinking water, electricity, and housing. These measures have led to decreased disparities in society. Besides, different skill enhancement and vocational training for the rural population, particularly for women, result in not only an economic well-off for a larger population but also making resilient and self-reliant societies throughout the country.
- **Swachh Bharat (Clean and Healthy India):** The Indian Government launched the Swachh Bharat Mission on 2nd October, 2014, with the goal of achieving 100% sanitation and hygiene in villages across the country. This sanitation program and campaign lower the rates of child and maternal mortality. It is important to note that 100 million toilets were constructed in rural areas of India under this program. In addition, this mission seeks to attain "open-defection free" in all villages of India. The government emphasizes the health care protection scheme, i.e., Ayushman Bharat (the world's largest health protection scheme), that provides health care facilities and services. It serves approximately 500 million people in India, covering 100 million families. [2]
- **Samagra Bharat-Saksham Bharat (Inclusive and Entrepreneurial India):** This initiative promotes social inclusion through nutrition, health care, social protection, and expansion of enterprise and service activities:
  - Enhance employability (need-based training)
  - Open routes of progression
  - Develop industry-benchmarked standards
  - Independent assessments
  - Quality assurance
  - Provide credible certification
  - Assist in employment/self-employment
- **Satat Bharat–Sanatan Bharat (Sustainable India):** India has taken several environmental policies to reduce environmental pollution and ecological calamities. It develops effective energy schemes, robust arrangements to tackle ecological disasters, and an organized ecosphere. In the project of Sanatan Bharat, India planned to electrify 100% of its villages. The electrification of its villages decreases CO_2 emissions by 38 million per year. It has provided pure cooking gas to 80 million marginalized families and set an objective to establish 450GW of renewable power and reinstate 26 million hectares of the disgraced landscape by 2030. In this regard, India concentrated on the development of disaster management infrastructure and solar systems.
- **Sampanna Bharat-Samriddh Bharat (Prosperous and Vibrant India):** India has been one of the fastest rising and developing marketplaces with many young

[2] See the website https://swachhbharat.mygov.in/.

people. It seeks to create innovative strategies for the development of trade systems. It aims to increase the gross domestic product (GDP) of India. By introducing this policy, the GDP development was 2.72 trillion from 2018 to 2019. India targets and attempts to attain nearly a USD 5 trillion economy by 2025. It is a growing innovation and trade system. India seeks to develop inclusive and sustainable development by motivating manufacturing, structuring the organization, inciting investments, improving entrepreneurship, and promoting technological modernization.

5.4 The Democracy and SD Knot

The *representative democracy theory* and the *participatory democracy theory* are two distinct approaches to studying democracy. Is it more important to have a representative democracy or a participatory democracy for long-term growth? Participation happens in all different forms of democracies, but the differences lie in the form and depth of that participation. Although including stakeholder input in development has been emphasized in academic literature, it has been less common in actual practice. Most attempts to incorporate stakeholder input into the development process have been poorly planned and led by those at the top and have focused solely on the social and technical components of a project. In Burkina Faso, this held true during President Thomas Sankara's first year in office. However, despite his success in mobilizing and including people in the implementation of initiatives to conserve water—a vital and limited resource in this Sahelian country—they were alienated from the decision-making framework and had no involvement in the planning of the programs themselves. In this context, the observation of Landell-Mills seems to be relevant—"the leaders led, and the people are supposed to follow" (Munslow and Ekoko 2007).

SD and democracy share some common ground and are interconnected in practice. They are committed to inclusive decision-making and the empowerment of all members of society to shape the way we live and the outcomes we seek. Present political and democratic processes will need to acclimate toward achieving SD. However, there are tensions and contradictions between the two concepts that must be settled first. The challenges of attempting to tackle complex issues and the demand for a very wide variety of political affairs or involvement are two pressures on our existing modern democracies that suggest our democratic government and practices like to develop. It is possible and even likely that democratic principles and sustainable development goals will overlap. They can rely on one another and help each other out. The two share a common understanding of the importance of citizen participation in shaping the society's course of action and determining its desired objectives. A rapid democratic response and wide levels of creativity are both possible in a democratic system. Using democratic contests and safety measures, SD can be made fair, legitimate, and credible to society.

In a world where wealth is unequally distributed, and natural resources are threatened by global warming, democracy faces a bleak future. SD is, in other words, essential for healthy democracies. However, existing democratic governments are not necessarily tied to SD. Participatory democracies and SD get it on with each other frequently. On the one hand, the concept of participation can be understood as a practical increase in focus in development practice; on the other hand, it can be understood as a fundamental reorganization of political authority. From there, we can talk about the myths surrounding the concept of "empowerment." Decentralization, which is a precursor to increasing participation and empowerment, is evidently a challenging argument to put into action. Few of the potential mechanisms for empowering the public have succeeded in giving ordinary people meaningful decision-making authority. A return of power to the individual may turn out to be an artificial construct.

Ikuo Kabashima summarized his model as follows (Munslow and Ekoko 2007):

- The greater the supportive participation by less privileged groups, the more continuity and stability in government.
- The greater the continuity and stability in government, the greater the economic development if other economic factors are held constant.
- The greater the economic development, the greater the opportunity for redistributing income from the more privileged to the less privileged.
- The greater the redistribution, the more supportive participation and stability in government.

Fundamentally, there is a division among those who consider the problem of political power to be important and others who claim that social engagement is an effective instrument in achieving SD at an objective level (the very first three views). Friedman (1992) makes a compelling case for the necessity of transforming "social" to "political" participation. Those who feel that their political voice is not being heard or whose economic and social goals are not being met are calling for greater levels of individual agency. La Palombara and Weiner (1966) have revealed that countries with varying degrees of plurality and levels of national unity have all seen demands for involvement. Lanni (2017) made the observation that governments are hesitant to fully accept involvement and participation due to the various challenges that this demand creates. Research conducted by the World Bank (1990) showed that if people were involved in the process of determining what projects should be undertaken rather than just carrying them out, it might lead to an unrealistic rise in aspirations.

Robert (1983) argued for a radical shift toward people-centered development, in which people are the focus rather than the end result of progress. Development, according to Korten (1984), refers to a process through which individuals in a society expand their personal and organizational capabilities to mobilize and manage resources in order to achieve sustainable and rightly allocated gains in their quality of life compatible with their own ambitions. Sandbrook says openly (Munslow and Ekoko 2007): "human-centred development, though admirable in principle, lacks a plausible political approach to achieve its recommended socio-economic transformation."

Some advocates of SD theory have attempted to link environmental degradation with the suppression of human rights (in this case, the right to own property) in order to justify their policies. The concept of "environmental rights" has been developed by Leach and Mearns (see Clover 2005) into a comprehensive theoretical framework. Human rights violations (both public and private) are blamed for the current state of affairs. The lack of a strong civil society makes it easier for people's rights to be denied or violated. Increasing social engagement, strength of civil society, and acceptance of people's rights are all expected to result from easing political restrictions; these factors, in turn, will promote development and better ecological sustainability. Effective utilization of resources, including certain indigenous knowledge, will be fostered rather than discouraged. Since half of the people do not have jobs, the new democratic government will have to work hard to protect and promote citizens' rights to look for and keep jobs, especially in the informal economy.

The solution lies in reorganizing government at the national level. According to Friedman (1992), this is the core concept behind the term "empowerment." There are probably three different approaches that could be taken in this kind of situation. The first is decentralized, with more authority resting at the neighborhood level in matters such as project management and the formulation of neighborhood-specific plans for economic growth. The second factor is the development of civil society, which has helped to make the government more answerable and cut down on corruption. The last thing that needs to be done is to secure people's civil and political rights. Chambers and Leach place special emphasis on the value of people's ownership of their own land. The Butare Colloquium on Human Rights and Economic Development has highlighted the connection between respect for human rights and economic growth in Francophone, Africa (Hannum 1979). The right to life, the right to work in safe conditions, the right to education, and the right to govern natural resources to ensure that basic human needs are met are all included in this list, as determined by the participants. Guaranteeing these rights should be carried out in a manner that prevents state intervention or manipulation.

5.5 Challenges in Attaining Sustainable Development

The emergence of socio-economic differences, demographic complexes, and technological and environmental tendencies have affected the development challenges. These tendencies complement each other's behaviors, which creates some challenges and problems. These tendencies are considered the fundamental changes that transmute society and significantly impact individuals. SD has not been correctly achieved due to several types of sociopolitical problems and hurdles:

- Rise of illiteracy rate
- Weak infrastructure
- Deficiency of monetary resources to carry out sustainable development scheme
- Lack of human resources
- Inadequacy of drinking water
- Lack of housing facilities
- Disparities in per capita income
- Corruption
- Lack of health facilities
- Population growth
- Gender disparity
- Lack of sufficient food
- Natural disasters and incidents can create a threat to sustainability
- Ethno-religious struggles
- Nonexistence of efforts at a municipal level
- Misuse of natural resources
- Absence of hi-technologies
- Environment change

There are several policies to overcome these challenges, and problems for SD emerged in this social phenomenon. The following factors could overcome the obstacles and hurdles:

- Strict reduction in the utilization of nonrenewable resources
- Halting the depletion of resources
- Investment in substitute sources of energy and power
- Safeguarding human rights
- The practice of the finest accessible knowledge
- Making plans properly to help the children grow into responsible and accountable citizens

5.6 Conclusion

In this chapter, we pointed out several types of challenges and prospects by introducing redistributive policies to benefit sustainable development. A system of governance that accomplishes both the collective sense and a multidimensional plan is arranged by the government for sustainable development. Sustainable development claims that the existing use and practice of means should reduce the degree of destruction and loss to the future usage of resources in society. The study finds some suggestive sanctions for adopting planned methods of the SDS in democratic governance. Despite several limitations, the study develops the system of relationships between democracy, government, and sustainable development policies.

It depends on receptive and accountable governance, ensures the rule of law, and safeguards human rights and participation of people in the political and decision-making processes. These democratic methods reinforce a peaceful and balanced society. Operative governance would be effective with the existence of democratic principles and democratization processes. It seeks to consolidate authority by introducing inclusive and responsible organizations and vigorous civil society. Redistributive and other strategies restructure the essential framework for diminishing inequity and overthrowing the illegitimate practice of natural resources. The reforms required for the different economic and political economy patterns recognize the inherent economy of society and the environment that seeks to maximize human welfare and human security.

Our exploration of the relationship between democracy and sustainable development has focused on a number of issues. The academic debate leads one to conclude that there is no strict correlation between democracy and sustainable development, but there are a number of pathologies awaiting the unwary. This implies that a flexible policy approach needs to be adopted. Perhaps the strongest argument that can be made for encouraging increased popular participation in some form is the ill-effects on state-society relations attendant upon the record of so many states under authoritarian personalized rule. Whilst the jury on the academic debates may still be out, the key global decision makers seem to have reached some conclusions. The World Bank is now placing emphasis on its conditionality lending on good governance rather than democratization. Western governments are lessening their pressure upon "stubborn" countries to democratize, and witness the current situation in Africa in Nigeria, Algeria, and Cameroon, and above all of China in Asia, where the annual rate of economic growth appears stuck in double figures whilst Russia languishes way behind.

Some items in the total package of democratic ideas are capable of being prioritized and made acceptable in helping to build SD, in particular transparency in the management of resources, protecting human rights and social participation. The United Nations Development Programme has devised its package of human development indicators by which all countries are evaluated. Perhaps, the widespread acceptance of this concept of "human development" indicators is the best hope that there is an encouragement for some of the democratic ideals within the sustainable development package.

References

Anderson P (1974) Lineages of the absolutist state. Verso, London

Berger G (2003) Reflections on governance: power relations and policy making in regional sustainable development. J Environ Policy Planning 5(3):219–234

Bridgman P, Davis G (2004) The Australian policy handbook. Allen & Unwin, ISBN: 9781741142204

Clover, Jenny. (2005). Human-centred environmental security: the link between environmental care and the creation of a more secure society, https://www.researchgate.net/publication/237324126_Human-centred_environmental_security_The_link_between_environmental_care_and_the_creation_of_a_more_secure_society. Accessed 14 March 2023

Friedman M (1992) Capitalism and freedom. University of Chicago Press

Hannum H (1979) The Butare Colloquium on human rights and economic development in Francophone Africa: a summary and analysis. Universal Human Rights 1(2):63–87

Howlett M (2011) Designing public policies: principles and instruments. Routledge

Kardos M (2012) The reflection of good governance in sustainable development strategies, 8th international strategic management conference. Proc Soc Behav Sci 58:1166–1173. www.sciencedirect.com. Accessed 27 April 2022

Kemp R, Parto S, Gibson R (2005) Governance for sustainable development: moving from theory to practice. Int J Sustain Dev 8. https://doi.org/10.1504/IJSD.2005.007372

Kohler P (2015) Redistributive policies for sustainable development: looking at the role of assets and equity, DESA working paper no. 139 ST/ESA/2015/DWP/139, https://www.un.org/esa/desa/papers/2015/wp139_2015.pdf. Accessed 18 April 2022

Korten DC (1984) Community organization and rural development: a learning process approach, Public Administration Review, https://courses.washington.edu/pbaf531/Korten_LearningProcessApproach.pdf. Accessed 14 Mar 2023

La Palombara J, Weiner M (eds) (1966) Political parties and political development. Princeton Univ. Press, Princeton, NJ

Lafferty WM (2002) Adapting government practice to the goals of sustainable development BT - Improving Governance for Sustainable Development, OECD Seminar, 22–23 Nov 2001. In: Improving Governance for Sustainable Development, OECD Seminar, 22–23 Nov 2001. OECD, Paris

Lanni A (2017) Sartori, the theoretician of democracy who brought logic to politics, published on 11th April, 2017, https://www.resetdoc.org/story/sartori-the-theoretician-of-democracy-who-brought-logic-to-politics/. Accessed 14 Mar 2023

Laswell H (1971) A pre-view of policy sciences. Elsevier, New York

Lowi TJ (1964) American business, public policy, case-studies, and political theory. World Politics 16(4):677.–693+695+697+699+701+703+705+707+709+711+713+715 (28 pages), Cambridge University Press, https://www.jstor.org/stable/2009452. Accessed 18 April 2022. https://doi.org/10.2307/2009452

Munslow B, Ekoko F (2007). Is democracy necessary for sustainable development? Democratization, file:///C:/Users/ugb/Downloads/3-Is%20democracy%20necessary%20for%20SD%20(1).pdf. Accessed 18 April 2022

Robert C (1983) Rural development: putting the last first. Routledge Taylor & Francis Group, London and New York

Sachiko M, Durwood Z (2005) Rule of law, good governance and sustainable development. seventh international conference on environmental compliance and enforcement

UNDP (1997) Promoting democracy through reform. http://www.undp.org/governance/index.htm

United Nations (2015) Resolution adopted by the General Assembly on 25 September 2015, transforming our world: the 2030 Agenda for Sustainable Development. Accessed 18April 2022

World Bank (1990) World development report 1990, https://openknowledge.worldbank.org/server/api/core/bitstreams/8a00844a-9661-539f-9662-cee8b4ffd046/content, Oxford University Press. Accessed 14 Mar 2023

World Bank (1994) Governance: the world bank's experience. Washington, DC: The World Bank. https://documents1.worldbank.org/curated/en/711471468765285964/pdf/multi0page.pdf. Accessed 18 April 2022

Young J, Mendizabal E (2009) Helping researchers become policy entrepreneurs. Overseas Development Institute, London

Dr. Siddhartha Sankar Manna is an Assistant Professor in the Department of Political Science at the University of Gour Banga. He was awarded with the Ph.D. from the Vidyasagar University. The focal theme of his research is the analysis of international relations, political theory, democratic politics, and human development. He has published more than 20 papers in reputed national and international journals.

Dr. Mukunda Mishra is an assistant professor in the Department of Geography and designated vice principal of Dr. Meghnad Saha College, affiliated to the University of Gour Banga in West Bengal, India. Dr. Mishra completed his postgraduate studies in geography and environmental management at Vidyasagar University and holds a Ph.D. in geography from the same university. He was selected for the National Merit Scholarship by the Ministry of Human Resource Development, Government of India. His research chiefly focuses on analyzing unequal human development and creating multi-criteria predictive models. He has more than 10 years of hands-on experience in dealing with development issues at the ground level in various districts of eastern India. Dr. Mishra has in his credit one monograph and four edited research volumes so far from the house of Springer Nature, and he has more than 25 research articles and book chapters published in the journals and books of international repute. Besides serving as the reviewer of several reputed journals published by Springer Nature and Elsevier Inc., he is continuing as the Managing and Publishing Editor of Ensemble, a UGC-CARE (India) enlisted journal of repute, since its inception to date.

Chapter 6
Environmental Education in Public Education Sector in India, Especially West Bengal: Policy and Practice Towards Sustainability

Ajit Mondal and Md. Nijairul Islam

6.1 Introduction

The realization of the human race for the importance of the environment and its connection with development and quality of human life in the global community accentuate the concept of sustainable development (SD). SD formally emerged out of numerous environmental movements on the global level under the aegis of the United Nations (UN). However, it gained wide-reaching popularity with the publication of the report on "Our Common Future," by the World Commission on Environment and Development, popularly known as the Brundtland Commission, in 1987. Environmental education (EE) or environmental studies (EVS) have become a vehicle for awakening awareness about man's essential relationship with his environment. Environmental education implies education through the environment, about the environment, and for the environment. EE looks at the environment holistically—natural, social, and man-made (Deshmukh 2014). Environmental education aims at revealing the growing concerns about the environment and its associated problems and examining the development and growth-related issues from an environmental approach (Tilbury 1995). EE primarily aims at building a global community that is well informed pertaining to the biophysical environment and its related problems, making the public aware of how to channelize our efforts towards their solution (Stapp et al. 1969). Several initiatives have recently been in operation in India, formally within the curriculum frameworks for school education,

A. Mondal
Department of Education, West Bengal State University, Barasat, Kolkata, West Bengal, India

M. N. Islam (✉)
Department of Education, Gazole Mahavidyalaya (Affiliated to University of Gour Banga), Malda, West Bengal, India

M. Mishra et al. (eds.), *Public Policies and Sustainable Development in Post-Reform India*, New Frontiers in Regional Science: Asian Perspectives 71,
https://doi.org/10.1007/978-981-99-3696-0_6

to bring home the significance of EE. Though the call for the promotion of much-needed knowledge, skills, and values about the protection and conservation of the environment is well contextualized in the school education system, EE is not wholly unknown to the Indian system of education:

> "Traditional Indian philosophies, which date back to several thousand years, have always upheld environmental protection as important, restraining the consumption of natural resources, living in harmony with the natural environment, caring for all living organisms and future generations and advocating developmental modes that are in harmony with the environment." (Ravindranath 2007: p. 193)

Gradually, there has been a trend of international academia showing more and more interest in the role of education in sustainable development (Blum 2015; UNESCO 2014). Education in general, and EE in particular, has been identified as playing an essential role in instilling and arousing environmental consciousness and knowledge, skills, attitudes, and values in learners and moving towards a sustainable world. EE intends to achieve the cardinal objective of sustainable development, i.e., to reduce the world's acute poverty level by ensuring healthy livelihoods that decrease resource reduction, environmental deprivation, cultural disorder, and social unrest (Barbier 1987).

Since the last four decades, the Government of India, through its various ministries, along with the directorates of education at the state level and various NGOs, has taken up many programs and policy initiatives to introduce EE to school and college-going learners across the country. The National Policy on Education (NPE), 1986, for the first time, emphatically advocated for the need to make learners aware of environmental issues by integrating it into the educational process at all levels of education. Accordingly, the National Curriculum Framework for Elementary & Secondary Education, 1988, aimed to equip the school curriculum with lessons on know-hows about protecting the environment, care for nature, environmental pollution, and energy conservation (NCERT 1988: p. 6). Accordingly, this framework advocated for the introduction of environmental studies (EVS) as a subject at the primary level. Meanwhile, the drive for universalizing environmental education in India started with the interference of the Supreme Court of India as a consequence of an application filed by Shri M. C. Mehta in 1991 as a public interest litigation. The Court directed the government to introduce the study of the environment as a compulsory subject in schools and colleges (Sharma and Kanaujia 2020: p. 206).

The Supreme Court observed in its judgment in the writ petition number 860 in 1991:

> "We accept on principle that through the medium of education, awareness of the environment and its problems related to pollution should be taught as a compulsory subject." (The Supreme Court of India 1991)

The Court issued directions to all state governments and education boards across India to compulsorily introduce the study of the environment in a graded way for all classes up to the secondary level from the academic year 1992–1993 and put the onus on the National Council of Educational Research and Training (NCERT) to formulate a model syllabus of EE for various grades, and directed the University

Grants Commission (UGC) to rationalize the practicability of making this compulsion in undergraduate (UG) level and recommended a course on EVS (ibid).

Immediately, to give effect to this judgment, the Environment Education in School Systems and Greening of Textbooks was initiated by the Ministry of Environment and Forest (MOEF) with the support of the World Bank.

A national project, titled Environmental Education in the School System (EESS), was visualized just after the development of a discussion paper, "Revitalization of EE in Schools (REES)" in 1998, and its subsequent discussion took place among all the states in a meeting (Sharma and Kanaujia 2020). Later, the National Curriculum Framework for School Education 2000 also put stress on knowing the environment as a whole, how to eradicate environmental hazards, and how to preserve the environment (NCERT 2000: p. 40). Accordingly, it prescribed to introduce the environmental studies, encompassing the natural and social elements of the environment from classes III to V. It also offered full autonomy to schools to utilize locally developed curriculum and learning resources for classroom transactions of the same (ibid: p. 65).

In compliance with the Supreme Court's order in December 2003, the NCERT also prepared a model syllabus for EE. The Supreme Court asked NCERT to oversee the implementation of its order as a nodal agency (The Supreme Court of India 2003). On 13 July 2004, the Supreme Court further mandated the adoption of the syllabus developed by the NCERT for Class I to XII across India (The Supreme Court of India 2004). In fact, it is one of the few verdicts by the Court on EE/EVS that has been applied to the entire formal education system in India.

In 2005, the National Council for Teacher Education (NCTE) again recommended that EE should be introduced as a compulsory course at all levels and stages of teacher education, including vocational and physical education programs (NCTE 2005: p. 15). Concurrently, "the National Curriculum Framework (NCF) adopted an infusion approach to introduce compulsory EE in schools into the curricula of all disciplines while ensuring that adequate time is earmarked for pertinent activities" (Sharma and Kanaujia 2020).

The Position Paper: National Focus Group on Habitat and Learning (NCERT 2006) speculated:

> "The main focus of EE should be to expose students to the real-life world, natural and social, in which they live; to enable them to analyse, evaluate, and draw inferences about problems and concerns related to the environment; to add, where possible, to our understanding of environmental issues; and to promote positive environmental actions in order to facilitate the move towards sustainable development. To achieve these goals, the curriculum may be based on: Learning about the environment; Learning through the environment; Learning for the environment." (NCERT 2006: pp. 4–5)

The discourse on education for sustainable development (ESD) has strengthened in the international stratum. Notably, target 4.7 of the sustainable development goals (SDGs) emphasizes:

> "By 2030, ensure all learners acquire knowledge and skills needed to promote sustainable development, including among others through education for sustainable development and sustainable lifestyles ... and culture's contribution to sustainable development." (United Nations 2015)

The UN has recognized ESD as a central component of the Agenda 2030. In general, ESD is a "key enabler" of all the SDGs, but in particular, it is an effective vehicle for achieving Sustainable Development Goal 4 (UNESCO 2020: p. 3). In consonance with the spirit, the National Education Policy (NEP) 2020 of India utters that SDG 4 (Target: Ensure inclusive and equitable quality education and promote lifelong learning opportunities for all) can be achieved by 2030 through reconfiguring and rebooting the education system substantially to foster learning (Government of India 2020: p 3).

However, turning this mandate into practice requires a paradigm shift from the mode of life, which we have been leading through the lessons learnt in the classrooms. Undoubtedly, an array of advocacies and suggestions has been forwarded, but the question still persists on its practice. Against this backdrop, this chapter intends to re-examine the policy and practice of EE for sustainable development in post-reform India, with special reference to the state of West Bengal. It encompasses the global perspective on the EE and ESD for sustainable development and national policies on ESD before and after the reform period. It also analyzes the current status of curricular and pedagogical aspects of EDS through EE/EVS in public educational institutions from primary to UG level in West Bengal.

6.2 EE and ESD: The Global Perspective

The concept of sustainable development was popularized at the United Nations Conference on the Human Environment, held in Stockholm in 1972 (Barbier 1987), although it succeeded in drawing global attention with the publication of the Brundtland Report in 1987. Education has been recognized as a powerful tool for realizing SD since the concern of the UNESCO on environmental issues, with the formation of the IUCN (International Union for the Conservation of Nature, now the World Conservation Union) in 1948, for the preservation of the natural environment (Leicht et al. 2018).

The first discussion on EE at a global platform took place at the Biosphere Conference, convened by the UNESCO in 1968 in Paris. The conference recommended holding a meeting for formulating curricula for all grades, providing technical training, and escalating awareness of global environmental issues. Such a meeting, entitled "Environmental Education in the School Curriculum," conducted by the IUCN along with the UNESCO in Nevada in 1970, proposed the definition of EE in the following way:

> "Environmental education is the process of recognizing values and classifying concepts in order to develop skills and attitudes necessary to understand and appreciate the inter-relatedness among man, his culture and his biophysical surroundings. Environmental Education also entails practice in decision-making and self-formulating of a code of behaviour about the issues concerning environmental quality." (IUCN 1970: p. 11)

In 1969, William B. Stapp and his students at the University of Michigan formally developed and published the aim of EE as producing a community that is well informed of the biophysical environment and its related harms, conscious and motivated to work towards their eradication (Stapp et al. 1969 as cited in Shimray 2016).

In 1972, the United Nations Conference on the Human Environment in Stockholm, Sweden, for the first time, attended the significance of the environment and its linkage with the development and quality of human life (Mondal 2020). During the conference, the countries' representatives debated mainly from these preparatory reports and finally adopted 26 principles and 109 recommendations in order to affirm the linkage between ecological, economic, and social concerns and to envisage some possible ways of acting (Boudes 2011). The Stockholm Declaration called for a common outlook and common principles to motivate and lead people of the world towards the preservation and enrichment of the human environment. In tune with this spirit, Principle 19 suggested EE as an approach to education in the following way:

> "Education in environmental matters, for the younger generation as well as adults, giving due consideration to the underprivileged, is essential in order to broaden the basis for an enlightened opinion and responsible conduct by individuals, enterprises and communities in protecting and improving the environment in its full human dimension. It is also essential that mass media of communications avoid contributing to the deterioration of the environment, but, on the contrary, disseminate information of an educational nature on the need to protect and improve the environment in order to enable man to develop in every respect." (United Nations 1973: p. 5)

Recommendation 96 of this conference also made a call for the introduction of EE as a means to address environmental concerns across the globe. This recommendation stressed:

> "... to establish an international program in environmental education, interdisciplinary in approach, in school and out of school, encompassing all levels of education and directed towards the general public, in particular the ordinary citizen living in rural and urban areas, youth and adult alike, with a view to educating him as to the simple steps he might take, within his means, to manage and control his environment." (ibid: p. 24)

In response to the recommendation mentioned above, the UNESCO and the United Nations Environment Programme (UNEP) initiated the International Environmental Education Programme (IEEP), which was mainly crafted to arouse reflection on environmental concerns worldwide, initiate actions, and draw international cooperation in this area (UNESCO 1984). During the first phase (1975–1977), activities of the IEEP towards the awareness of EE at the global level through a series of international and regional workshops led to the International Workshop on Environmental Education at Belgrade in 1975 and the Belgrade Charter of 1975. The goal, as cited in this charter, was:

> "... to develop a world population that is aware of, and concerned about, the environment and its associated problems, and which has the knowledge, skills, attitudes, motivations and commitment to work individually and collectively toward solutions of current problems and the prevention of new ones." (UNESCO-UNEP 1976)

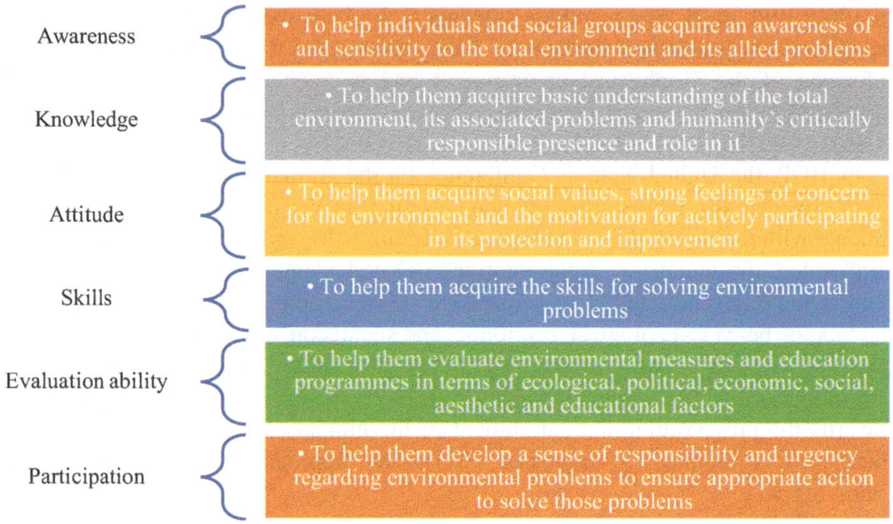

Fig. 6.1 Objectives of EE as per Belgrade Charter (**Source:** UNESCO-UNEP 1976)

The Belgrade Charter reiterated certain objectives of EE, which is presented in Fig. 6.1.

The first Intergovernmental Conference on Environmental Education convened by the UNESCO, in association with the UNEP in 1977, held in Tbilisi, ratified the Belgrade framework and prepared the Tbilisi Declaration, which stressed EE as interdisciplinary and holistic in nature and application. It should be adopted as an approach to education as a whole, encompassing a shared relationship between the human and natural worlds. Tbilisi Declaration, thus, became the global text for implementers and practitioners in the domain of EE all over the world. Nations across the globe started introducing and promoting EE through the development of curricula, courses, and training programs. Besides, the IEEP, during its second phase (1978–1980) and third phase (1981–1983), initiated a series of training workshops, seminars, programs, and projects and published a newsletter entitled "Connect" and books, such as "Trends in Environmental Education" (1977) and "Environmental Education in the Light of the Tbilisi Conference" (1980).

In spite of taking numerous initiatives at various levels, it was felt that EE failed to address social and economic issues such as poverty, excessive consumption, and underdevelopment. It could not even effectively address prevailing environmental issues. These compelled the world to think of a more holistic and all-encompassing approach to EE, which would help tackle serious environmental concerns and which would be, at the same time, socially viable. Such realization ultimately resulted in the introduction of the concept of "sustainable development" (Shimray 2016).

In 1987, the World Commission on Environment and Development (WCED), for the first time, drew global attention to the concept of SD, reiterated in its report "Our Common Future" (Brundtland Report). The report emphasized how social and

Table 6.1 Four goals of Chapter 36 of Agenda 21

• "Promote and improve access to quality basic education so that citizens acquire the knowledge, skills and values they need to improve the quality of their lives in their communities.
• Reorient education programmes from pre-school to university so that the education provided leads to acquiring more principles, knowledge, skills, perspectives and values related to environmental, societal and economic sustainability.
• Develop public understanding and awareness of sustainability to ensure active, knowledgeable and responsible actions of citizens locally, nationally and internationally.
• Provide training to businesses, industry and all sectors of the workforce in sustainability practices so that they may adopt sustainable modes of production and consumption."

Source: UNESCO 2018: p. 32

economic factors helped in solving environmental problems. Chap. 2 of WCED, entitled "Towards Sustainable Development," began with a comprehensive definition of SD:

> "Sustainable development is development that meets the needs of the present without compromising the ability of future generations to meet their own needs. It contains within it two key concepts:
> - the concept of 'needs', in particular the essential needs of the world's poor, to which overriding priority should be given; and,
> - the idea of limitations imposed by the state of technology and social organization on the environment's ability to meet present and future needs." (United Nations 1987)

This definition has been significantly accorded with several other international initiatives, such as the IUCN, the Tbilisi Declaration, the International Education Programme, the UN Conference on Environment and Development of 1992, the Earth Summit, Agenda 21 (Chapter 36), Millennium Development Goals, Dakar Framework for Action: Education for All, and Decade of Education for Sustainable Development (2005–2014), in which education and learning occupy the central means of approaches to SD (Alexandar 2012).

With the publication of the report "Our Common Future," the Brundtland Commission advocated for organizing a global conference to reassess the developmental status of the signatory countries pertaining to sustainable development and to formulate the principles of a global plan of action towards sustainable development in the future. Accordingly, in 1992, in Rio de Janeiro, Brazil, the United Nations Conference on Environment and Development, popularly known as the "Earth Summit," was held. This conference crafted a 40-chapter global plan of action under the caption of "Agenda 21" to make the globe ready to face the challenges of the twenty-first century. Each of the 40 chapters included education as a cross-cutting theme in the implementation strategies (UNESCO 2012 & 2018). Chapter 36 (Promoting education, public awareness, and training) formed the basis of education for sustainable development (ESD). Chapter 36 spells out four goals of education, training, and public awareness for SD, as shown in Table 6.1.

Agenda 21 also envisaged:

> "Education is critical for promoting sustainable development and improving the capacity of the people to address environment and development issue ... Both formal and non-formal educations are indispensable to changing people's attitudes so that they have the capacity to

> assess and address their sustainable development concerns ... Education is critical for achieving environmental and ethical awareness, values and attitudes, skills and behaviour consistent with sustainable development and for effective public participation in decision-making." (United Nations 1992: p. 264)

The International Commission on Education, under the chairmanship of Edgar Faure, in its report "Learning to Be: The World of Education Today and Tomorrow" in 1972, suggested remoulding education for generating "a learning society capable of building its democracy, building equality, and building its sustainable future" (UNESCO 2018). While the concept of SD was realized since the publication of the report of the Brundtland Commission in 1987, education as an indispensable medium for achieving SD started gaining significance since the emergence of Agenda 21. It has also been prominently reiterated in the "Dakar Framework for Action, Education for All: Meeting our Collective Commitments" adopted in the World Education Forum (26–28 April 2000, Dakar):

> "Education is (...) the key to sustainable development and peace and stability within and among countries, and thus an indispensable means for effective participation in the societies and economies of the twenty-first century." (ibid 2000b: p. 8)

In 2000, the UN community not only re-emphasized the principles of SD, embedded in Agenda 21, but also dedicated to the realization of eight Millennium Development Goals (MDGs) encompassing concerns related to the environment, poverty, education, gender equality, etc. Notably, MDG 7 ("Ensure environmental sustainability") clearly implies SD (Elliot 2006). Ten years later, to catalyze education as an indispensable component for realized SD, the World Summit on Sustainable Development (WSSD), held in 2002 in Johannesburg, projected the period 2005–2014 as the "Decade of Education for Sustainable Development" (DESD). Later, the UN Sustainable Development Summit from September 25 to 27, 2015, held at the UN headquarters in New York, set 17 SDGs and 169 targets to be realized over the next 15 years. The new set of ambitious goals and targets mainly seeks to achieve the unreached MDGs. Irina Bokova, Director-General of the UNESCO, ascribed education as an essential tool for achieving global sustainable development goals and opined that education should be placed at the center of our efforts in adapting to changes and transforming the world we live (UNESCO 2015). Qian Tang, Assistant Director-General for Education UNESCO, also observed that:

> "Education is explicitly formulated as a stand-alone goal—Sustainable Development Goal 4. Numerous education-related targets and indicators are also contained within other Sustainable Development Goals (SDGs). Education is both a goal in itself and a means for attaining all the other SDGs. It is not only an integral part of sustainable development, but also a key enabler for it. That is why education represents an essential strategy in the pursuit of the SDGs." (ibid 2017: p. 1)

Thus, education is conceived as a key driver for the achievement of all 17 SDGs as education contributes to the vision of sustainable global development (UNESCO 2015). However, let us have a look at the nexus between EE and ESD in terms of creating a more sustainable world. Since the articulation of Chapter 36 of Agenda 21, there has been a shift in environmental education, and it adopted the term

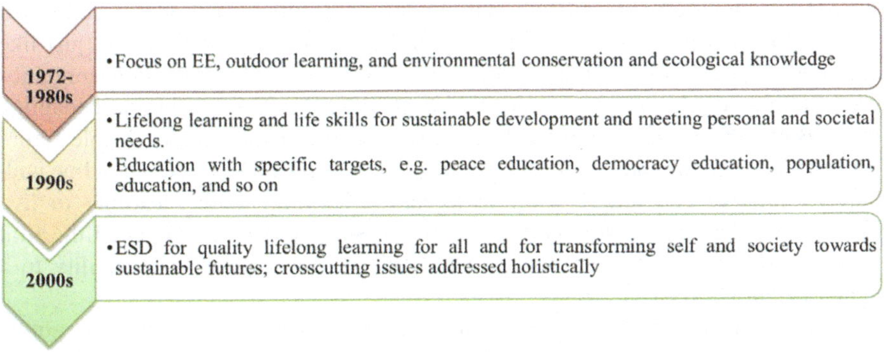

Fig. 6.2 Gradual shift in the concept towards ESD from EE (**Source**: UNESCO 2018)

Table 6.2 Differences and similarities between EE and ESD

Differences	Similarities
"ESD teaches all the spheres of sustainability – environment, society, and economy, with an underlying dimension of culture. EE focuses more on the environment." "ESD has four thrusts: (1) access to and retention in quality basic education; (2) reorienting existing education programmes; (3) increasing public awareness and understanding; and (4) providing training. EE primarily works in thrusts two and three."	"There are, of course, similarities between how ESD and EE are currently practised. For example, both EE and ESD have an environmental component." "Both EE and ESD call for participatory learning and the use of pedagogies that promote higher order thinking skills, support decision-making, and stimulate the formulation of questions. Both EE and ESD have a values component."

Source: UNESCO 2012: p. 44

"education for sustainable development" (ESD) in the course of SD in many countries (Mondal 2020). Figure 6.2 summarizes the gradual shift of the concept towards ESD from EE.

Sustainability has three dimensions, encompassing environmental, societal, and economic sustainability. Concurrently, ESD also covers these three aspects (Mckeown and Hopkins 2003, 2005). Agenda 21 attached importance to economic and human development and, at the same time, protecting the environment. The goal has been shifted to searching for an appropriate approach to environmental protection and, at the same time, easing human suffering. Thus, Agenda 21 gives a sounder understanding of the linkage between human development and environmental protection in terms of sustainability (Mckeown and Hopkins 2003).

Broadly speaking, ESD implies education for transforming society with an eye on making society more sustainable. However, ESD is not just an adjectival education. It is an overarching paradigm that directs and shapes the core disciplines, second-tier disciplines, and adjectival education in order to enable them to contribute to a more sustainable future (UNESCO 2012).

A substantial analysis of the fundamental documents on EE points out some similarities and many differences between EE and ESD (Table 6.2).

ESD has emerged out of EE. Environmental educators, who at first supported ESD, had shown interest in ESD in the post-Rio period. In addition, EE, just like other educational fields—human rights education, peace education, and economics of education—contributes to the development of ESD with content and pedagogy (ibid). Both EE and ESD will work upon a common vision—a sustainable future (Shimray 2016). Ultimately, all educational activities must be carried out in line with the five aims of education—learning to know, learning to do, learning to live together, and learning to transform oneself and society. UNESCO added the fifth pillar, "learning to transform oneself and society," to achieve sustainability to a greater extent (UNESCO 2012).

Whatever form EE has taken, what is to be emphasized is to raise public understanding about the environment and human development and its associated concerns and to promote environmental values and a sense of responsibility towards making the globe more sustainable (United Nations 1992). However, education will be a powerful medium for creating a sustainable future only when the prevalent educational enterprise is reoriented towards addressing SD through appropriate curriculum implementation and provision of sharing knowledge among all sectors of society (UNESCO 2012). EE and ESD are different, yet they correspond to each other in terms of achieving SD (Mckeown and Hopkins 2007). Both EE and ESD have encompassed a common and entangled vision, and it does not matter which term we use within our practices (Monroe 2012). However, a balance between the economic and social disciplines with the environmental one should be prioritized for creating a more sustainable future. This balance comes out of a shared dialogue among environmental educators, economic educators, social studies, and science educators (Mckeown and Hopkins 2005).

6.2.1 Concept of SD in the Educational Policies in India in the Post-reform Period

Traditionally, India has been a sustainable society. From the historical and cultural perspectives, it can be claimed that social values and attitudes among the Indians have been in tune with the environment. Its reflections can be found in our literature and religious texts. All these writings replicate the recognition that a quality human life heavily depends on the quality of the environment (Sarabhai 2004). After Independence, the Government of India incorporated many of these practices and thoughts in its own Constitution by putting accountability upon its citizens for the protection and improvement of the environment (CEE 2007; Sarabhai 2004). The Constitution of India sufficiently includes mandates related to the protection and preservation of the environment (Vardhan 2014). It endorses the concept of sustainability by enjoining the state and the citizens through the following Articles under the Constitution of India (Table 6.3).

Table 6.3 Constitutional mandates on protection and preservation of the environment

Article	Mandates
Article 17	The State shall regard the raising of the level of nutrition and the standard of living of its people and the improvement of public health as among its primary duties and, in particular, endeavor to bring about prohibition of the consumption except for medicinal purposes of intoxicating drinks and of drugs which are injurious to health.
Article 48	The State shall endeavor to organize agriculture and animal husbandry on modern and scientific lines and shall, in particular, take steps for preserving and improving the breeds and prohibiting the slaughter of cows and calves and other milch and draught cattle.
Article 48-A	The State shall endeavor to protect and improve the environment and to safeguard the forests and wildlife of the country.
Article 51-A (g)	It is the duty of every citizen of India to protect and improve the natural environment, including forests, lakes, rivers, and wildlife, and to have compassion for living creatures.

Source: The Constitution of India

The Constitution has adequately put the environment and its protection in line with the legacy of our deep-rooted values and traditions, and its provisions have been evolving and growing with time. In addition, the Government of India has incorporated the principles of sustainability in the national education policies and various developmental plans and programs. EE in all curriculum implementation programs in the domain of Indian formal education can be traced back to the Report of Education Commission of 1964–1966, which recommended that teaching science in primary school should be directed towards promoting a sound understanding of the fundamental concepts, principles, and issues related to the physical and biological environment (Government of India 1966: p. 366). Afterward, "Curriculum for the Ten-Year School: An Approach Paper" and "Curriculum for the Ten-Year School: A Framework" (the first national curriculum framework for school education in India) brought out by the NCERT in 1975 put due emphasis on the need for EE, cutting across the entire gamut of school education through appropriate subject disciplines.

Environmental issues in India have appeared as a priority area in terms of policy statements, plans, and strategies, particularly after 1980, with the establishment of an independent Ministry of Environment and Forests in 1985 (Sonowal 2009). The previous efforts and policy initiatives, both at the central and state levels, gained impetus when NPE 1986 recommended to reorient the educational system towards the establishment of EE more formally in the school curriculum and integrated the core value of environmental protection into the teaching of many school subjects (Sarabhai and Chhokar 2009). NPE 1986 was the first national policy that stated that "protection of the environment," like other values, such as "equality of the sexes" and "removal of social barriers," should be promoted through the common core elements cutting across subject areas based on the guidelines of a national curriculum framework (Mondal and Mete 2014). In addition, the policy emphasized:

> "There is a paramount need to create a consciousness of the environment. It must be permeate all ages and all sections of society, beginning with the child. Environmental consciousness should inform teaching in schools and colleges. This aspect will be integrated in the entire educational process" (Government of India 1986: para 8.15).

Later, NCERT developed "National Curriculum for Elementary and Secondary Education: A Framework" in 1988, based on the policy reforms embedded in NPE 1986. This framework emphatically stated that school curricula should promote awareness. This framework emphatically stated that school curriculum should promote an awareness of the means and ways of protecting the environment, preventing environmental pollution and preserving energy, and realizing the interdependence between the environment and the animal kingdom, including the human being, for survival, growth, and development (NCERT 1988). It also made, for the first time, an effort to introduce EE into the school curriculum, infusing environmental issues within the whole gamut of school subjects. In 1993, the Department of Education in Science and Mathematics of NCERT undertook a project to analyze the school curricula developed by the NCERT, as a part of the implementation of NPE 1986 for identifying the EE concepts and activities vis-à-vis the universal objectives of EE, as agreed at the Tbilisi Conference (NCERT 1993). In the same year, "Learning Without Burden: Report of the National Advisory Committee (1993)" recommended the introduction of the infusion approach of environmental education in order to avoid the addition of load by adopting a separate subject approach (Shimray 2016). In its "Curriculum Framework for Quality Teacher Education" in 1998, the NCTE clearly spelled out the urgency to make teachers and teacher educators aware of some emerging issues, such as protection of the environment, checking environmental pollution, instilling environmental values, and increasing legal literacy (NCTE 1998). Accordingly, teacher education programs at the secondary stage and the senior secondary stage included EE as one of the optional courses.

In response to the writ petition (civil) no. 860 of 1991 between M.C. Mehta vs. Union of India and others, the Hon'ble Supreme Court stated in its direction no. 4:

> "We accept in principle that through the medium of education, awareness of the environment and its problems related to pollution should be taught as a compulsory subject . . . we would require every State Government and every Education Board connected with education up to the matriculation or stage even intermediate colleges to immediately take steps to enforce compulsory education on environment in a graded way." (The Supreme Court of India 1991)

This directive underlines the implication of environmental concerns for which our pursuit of sustainable development across the globe has started. This is also a significant indicator for a country like India, where a sizeable proportion of people depend on environmental resources to maintain their livelihoods (NCERT 2006: p. 28).

Meanwhile, being discontented with the non-conformity of the former order of 1991 pertaining to introducing EE compulsorily by the states at all levels of formal education, the Supreme Court on 18 December, 2003, again ordered:

> "We also direct the NCERT which is a respondent herein to prepare a module (model) syllabus to be taught at different grades and submit the same to this Court by the next date of hearing so that we can consider the feasibility to introduce such syllabus uniformly throughout the country at different grades" (The Supreme Court of India 2003).

On 13 July 2004, the Hon'ble Court again directed:

> "The syllabus prepared by the NCERT for class I to XII shall be adopted by every state in their respective schools. ... the NCERT be appointed as a nodal agency to supervise the implementation of the Court's order" (The Supreme Court of India 2004).

Acting on this directive, the NCERT published the National Curriculum Framework (NCF) in 2005, and EE emerged in the form of "Habitat and Learning" under the Position Paper: National Focus Group on Habitat and Learning in this framework (NCERT 2006). The NCF discussed the concerns related to the environment and placed the environment at the center of children's learning. This framework stated:

> "Environmental degradation proceeds at an unprecedented pace, we are beginning to realise the importance of taking good care of our habitat. Humankind must, therefore, make an attempt to comprehend its roots, to re-establish links with its habitat, and to understand and take good care of it. In substance and spirit, then the theme ' Habitat and Learning' is equivalent to environmental education. These significant concerns are best realised by infusing the components of environmental education as part of different disciplines while ensuring that adequate time is earmarked for pertinent activities. This approach can be meaningfully employed in the treatment of content in Physics, Mathematics, chemistry, Biology, geography, History, political science, health and physical education, art, music etc. Activities constructed for life situations become a meaningful means for the engagement of learners." (ibid 2005: p. 64)

The "Habitat and Learning" Focus Group recommended:

> "The main focus of EE should be to expose students to the real-life world, natural and social, in which they live; to enable them to analyse, evaluate, and draw inferences about problems and concerns related to the environment; to add, where possible, to our understanding of environmental issues; and to promote positive environmental actions in order to facilitate the move towards sustainable development. To achieve these goals, the curriculum may be based on: Learning about the environment; Learning through the environment; Learning for the environment." (ibid 2006, pp. 4–5)

The Focus Group identified six major areas for action as a road map—curricular revision; material development; use of conventional media and taking advantage of information and communication technology (ICT); teacher preparation; evaluation system; and school habitat (ibid). Ultimately, Like NCFSE 2000, NCF 2005 also suggested introducing EVS as a subject for classes I–V and infusing environmental issues into various subject areas (Ravindranath 2016: p. 97).

Although the Hon'ble Supreme Court emphasized the need to teach EE as a compulsory subject at all levels and stages of school education, the latest NCF adopted the approach to infusing the components of environmental education as part of different disciplines. Consequently, NCERT, representing schools in India, filed a supplementary affidavit on 26 November 2007 in favor of substantiating the order of the Supreme Court with this approach. In compliance with the Court's direction, NCERT explained why EVS should be a compulsory component of the curriculum. The affidavit submitted by the NCERT was accepted by the Supreme Court on 3 December 2010, and the matter of the writ petition was deemed to have been resolved (Menon 2012). However, EE existed within the gamut of the school curriculum in many forms prior to the intervention by the Supreme Court, but the Court's directives created a force to the implementation of EE in the landscape of formal education of India (Sonowal 2009; Almeida and Cutter-Mackenzie 2011).

Concurrently, the National Curriculum Framework for Teacher Education (NCFTE) 2009, prepared by the NCTE under the caption "Towards Preparing Professional and Humane Teacher," also encompassed the concerns and issues pertaining to environment. It observed:

> "In order to develop future citizens who promote equitable and sustainable development for all sections of society and respect for all, it is necessary that they be educated through perspectives of gender equity, the perspectives that develop values for peace, respect the rights of all, and respect and value work. In the present ecological crisis, promoted by extremely commercialized and competitive lifestyles, teachers and children need to be educated to change their consumption patterns and the way they look at natural resources." (NCTE 2009: p. 13)

It also suggested that a pedagogy course on EVS should include the following:

> "Philosophical and epistemological basis of EVS as a composite area of study that draws upon the sciences, social sciences and environmental education; acquainting student teachers with children's ideas of their physical and social world so that these can later be interpreted for classroom instruction; helping student teachers develop the ability to plan comprehensive units that do not compartmentalize knowledge but view it holistically" (ibid: p. 37).

Many concerns and issues pertaining to EVS have been taken into consideration in this framework, but it does not make reference to the infusion approach of environmental education in the curriculum or the pedagogy component which NCF 2005 recommended (Shimray 2016).

It was NPE 1986 that, for the first time, focused on the necessity of promoting an environmental orientation to education at all levels. After 12 years of introducing the National Curriculum for Elementary and Secondary Education: A Framework 1988, in response to the phenomena of globalization and liberalization, the National Curriculum Framework for School Education, 2000, reoriented education towards global citizenship and human rights, environmental issues, and promotion of environmental values within the subjects like history, geography, and languages (NCERT 2000).

It can be reasonably claimed that the endeavors to institutionalize EE at all stages of school education in India have been concretized with the directives of the Supreme Court in 1991. The Court also gave a directive to the UGC to introduce an elementary course on the environment in all disciplines of a college education. Accordingly, the UGC developed a "Six Months Module Syllabus for Environmental Studies for Undergraduate Courses" in 2003 to implement compulsorily in all the universities and their affiliated colleges across India. The UGC also prepared "Textbook for Environmental Studies for Under Graduate Courses of all Branches of Higher Education" in 2004. The book intends to create pro-environmental attitudes and modify the behavioral patterns and lifestyles of the youth (Ravindranath 2016). Many universities have already introduced the UGC module at the college level as a common course for UG students, irrespective of the discipline, since 2005. Technical universities and colleges have also introduced EVS as a compulsory subject in all programs of study (ibid: p. 97). In 2017, the UGC again formulated an eight-unit module syllabus for "Ability Enhancement Compulsory Courses (AECC-Environmental Studies)" under a choice-based credit system (CBCS) for implementing EVS in UG course of all branches of higher education in universities and colleges.

6.2.2 *SD as Reflected in NEP 2020*

As the first national education policy of the twenty-first century, NEP 2020 laid down an array of policy reforms in school and higher education systems in the country. Five founding pillars of this policy (i.e., access, equity, affordability, accountability, and quality) have been embedded in harmony with the principles of Agenda 2030 for sustainable development in order to develop a resilient and robust education system in India (Kumar et al. 2020). An equitable quality education is a key to the realization of SD of any nation. Accordingly, this policy proposes some policy statements to overhaul the whole gamut of Indian education, including its curricular structure, regulation, and governance, in order to create a robust and vibrant system that is in alignment with the lofty goals of the twenty-first-century education, including SDG 4. The policy states:

> "This Policy envisions ensuring equitable access to quality education to all students, with a special emphasis on SEDGs . . . the approach to equity and inclusion must be common across school and higher education" (Government of India 2020: p. 41).

In response to today's rapidly changing world, the policy maintains that all students should acquire certain skills and capacities to become "good, successful, innovative, adaptable, and productive human beings." These skills include:

> "Scientific temper and evidence-based thinking; creativity and innovativeness; sense of aesthetics and art . . . knowledge and practice of human and Constitutional values; gender sensitivity; Fundamental Duties; citizenship skills and values; knowledge of India; environmental awareness including water and resource conservation, sanitation and hygiene; and current affairs and knowledge of critical issues facing local communities, States, the country, and the world" (ibid: p. 15).

To make this effective, the policy intends to introduce contemporary subjects such as artificial intelligence, design thinking, holistic health, organic living, environmental education, and global citizenship education (GCED) at relevant stages to develop these skills in students (ibid). The policy proposes an appropriate integration of "environmental awareness and sensitivity towards its conservation and sustainable development" within the school curricula to make EE an integral part. It also recommends including "areas of community engagement and service, environmental

Table 6.4 Vision on ESD in NEP 2020

• "ESD will require the entire education system to reconfigure and reboot to support and foster learning so that all of the critical targets and goals of the 2030 agenda for sustainable development can be achieved" (p 3).
• The policy will "develop knowledge, skills, values, and dispositions that support responsible commitment to human rights, sustainable development and living, and global well-being, thereby reflecting a truly global citizen" (p 5).
• All B.Ed. programs will "appropriately integrate environmental awareness and sensitivity towards its conservation and sustainable development, so that environment education becomes an integral part of school curricula" (p 23).
• In the higher education level, EE "will include areas such as climate change, pollution, waste management, sanitation, conservation of biological diversity, management of biological resources and biodiversity, forest and wildlife conservation, and sustainable development and living" (p 37).

Source: NEP 2020

education, and value-based education" within the curricula of all higher education institutions (HEIs). The policy reiterates certain ambitious visions and future plans regarding initiating and nourishing ESD in various stages of formal education (Table 6.4).

NEP 2020 puts priority on the desirable knowledge, skills, values, and attitudes that can empower individuals to make an adequate contribution to the realization of SD. It accords with the truth that to create a more sustainable world, individuals must become sustainability changemakers. Hence, to materialize the policy visions related to sustainability principles, curriculum frameworks at all levels, along with teacher education programs, should soon be in place. This theoretical framework regarding injecting awareness in learners of the burning environmental issues and making them fit citizens of a sustainable world must also accompany the right road map and program of action by the department of education, both at the central as well at state/UT level.

6.3 Present Status of Curricular and Pedagogical Aspects of SD Through EE/EVS in the Public Education Sector in West Bengal: Primary to UG Level

In response to the mandate of the Supreme Court and the guidelines framed by NCF 2005, EE/EVS is now being taught from primary to UG level in all government-sponsored/aided educational institutions of all the states/UTs of India. In the state of West Bengal, the scenario of teaching-learning of this subject has been discussed in the following sections:

6.3.1 Primary Level (Class/ Standards I–V)

Though no separate book has been prescribed in classes I and II for EE, an attempt has been made in "*Aamar Boi: Pratham, Dwitiya ebong Tritiya Parba*" (i.e., "My Book: 1st, 2nd, and 3rd Stage") to familiarize the children with the world around them (Government of West Bengal 2021a). They will learn about trees, fruits, flowers, animals, birds, rivers, and sky in a collaborative, child-centric, activity-based, and integrated method, keeping in line with the objectives stated in NCF 2005 and Right to Education (RTE) Act 2009. Colorful pictures and rhymes have been used to make these books attractive and catch the messages contained therein by the children.

For classes III, IV, and V, separate textbooks on EE, titled "*Aamader Paribesh*" (i.e., "Our Environment") are supplied to the schools by Paschimbanga Prathamik Shiksha Parshad, School Education Department, Government of West Bengal. All these books have been structured as per the recommendation of the expert committee (Government of West Bengal 2021b). Efforts have been made to promote in the learners a sense of scientific outlook, love for animals, preservation of the pollution-free environment, anti-hunting attitude, etc. Let us have a look at the topics related to EE in these books (Table 6.5).

In these books, colorful illustrations have been incorporated to make them attractive and effective for joyful learning. These textbooks lay emphasis on raising awareness and sensitizing children about environmental issues. They contain relevant ideas commensurate with the age and cognitive-emotive developmental level of children in order to provide them with the necessary knowledge and understanding about their surrounding environment. The main objective is to make pupils curious and inquisitive towards diversity and daily occurrences of the environment, to make their journey smooth from the known world to the unknown one through sense perception. It is expected that they will explore the world around them through simple observation and gradually develop scientific and logical thinking. It is expected that teachers, along with guardians and other members of the community,

Table 6.5 Topics on EE in the textbooks at the primary level

Class III	Class IV	Class V
• Concept on weather • Knowing the things around our habitat • Knowing the sky, with the sun, the moon, and stars • Cloud, rainfall • Air, soil, and water bodies • Importance of plantation	• Living beings and nonliving things surrounding the human habitat • Knowing birds and animals • Interdependence of various plants and animals for sustenance • Atmosphere • Knowing the night sky • Importance of water • Primary knowledge about environment pollution	• Soil • Water • Biodiversity • Environmental resources—forest, mineral, and fuel resources • Knowledge on natural calamities

Source: "*Aamader Paribesh*" for classes III–V, Government of West Bengal

will help the children explore nature joyfully and will awaken their curiosity and scientific temper theoretically as well as with hands-on, collaborative experiences. Regarding the transaction of the content, emphasis has been laid on the need to organize learning in locally specific contexts, which will provide more concrete and meaningful experiences to children. The scope for conducting hands-on activities—in and outside the classroom—is also there. Pictures, charts, models, etc. will be used in the classroom for concretizing learners' perceptions. Audiovisual media may also be used for effective learning. Activity tasks for learners have been incorporated at the end of each chapter.

6.3.2 Upper-Primary Level (Class/Standards VI–VIII)

For the teenager learners of classes VI–VIII, textbooks on EE, titled "*Paribesh o Bijnan*" (i.e., "Environment and Science"), are supplied to the learners by Paschimbanga Madhyashiksha Parshad (Government of West Bengal 2021c). These books have also been structured keeping in mind the recommendations of NCF 2005 and RTE Act 2009. The syllabi on EE at this stage (Table 6.6) are a natural continuation of the concepts already acquired by the learners at the primary level.

It is presumed that children at this stage will learn through observation, and the textbooks will further help them know nature joyfully. Teachers, along with guardians, will help them explore nature, awakening their wonder and curiosity, and scientific temper. Concept, amalgamated with hands-on experience, will concretize their learning. Measures will be taken to grow their imagination and interest in peer learning. Teaching programs will be organized in such a way that may help them construct knowledge on different aspects of the environment. In these textbooks, open-ended questions have been incorporated to make the learners explorative. Detailed instruction on conducting easy, low-cost scientific experiments inside and

Table 6.6 Topics on EE in the textbooks at the upper-primary level

Class VI	Class VII	Class VIII
• Interdependence of living beings and nonliving things in nature • Natural occurrences around us • Biodiversity and its classification • Nonliving things in nature • Evolution of life • Habit and habitat of some animals and reptiles • Concept on waste and its management	• Concept on eco-friendly sources of energy • Role of nonliving things in environment • Environmental crises and conservation of environment • Weather cycle • Relation between environment and public health	• Natural occurrences and their logical explanation • Environmental crises and conservation of environment • Flora and fauna around us • Endangered animals and birds, and their protection

Source: "Paribesh o Bijnan" for classes VI–VIII, Government of West Bengal

outside the classroom has also been given. Overall, it is an integrated approach of teaching-learning, correlated with other domains of scientific knowledge, such as biology, physics, chemistry, and geography. In such a pedagogical approach, there is enough scope for the formation of abstract concepts in the learners through analogy and metaphor. Teachers should have a clear idea of concept learning and knowledge construction in learners, and accordingly, he/she will facilitate them in exploring the environment.

6.3.3 Secondary Level (Class/Standards IX and X)

At this stage, no separate book on EE has been prescribed. Lessons on the environment have been embedded across subjects like life science, physical science, geography, and history. "*Jiban Bijnan o Paribesh*" (i.e., "Life Science and Environment"), "*Bhouta Bijnan o Paribesh*" (i.e., "Physical Science and Environment"), "*Itihaas o Paribesh*" (i.e., "History and Environment"), and "*Bhugol o Paribesh*" (i.e., "Geography and Environment")—all these books, both for classes IX and X, are intended to familiarize learners with various aspects of nature and environment, integrated with the different topics of the core subjects concerned (Government of West Bengal 2015). Environmental concepts also extend to language subject areas in order to reinforce the learning and internalization of these concepts (Table 6.7). Mainly classroom lecture is the mode of transaction of these contents.

Moreover, a 60-page book titled "*Paribesher Tare Sakale Aamra*" (i.e., "We are all for Environment") seeks to create consciousness among the learners at this stage through catchy cartoons and rhymes (Government of West Bengal 2017). Learners can easily grasp the messages regarding the need for plantation; diverse ecosystem;

Table 6.7 Topics on environment awareness embedded in various subjects in secondary level

Class IX	Class X
• Diversity of living beings on earth • Environment and its resources • Natural resources, their uses and overuses • Water and sound pollution and its prevention • Causes and management of natural hazards and disasters	• Concern about our environment • Different types of environment pollution • Environment and health issues • Importance of biodiversity and its conservation • Endangered species and their conservation • Concern about ozone layer depletion • Greenhouse effect and global warming • Management of domestic and industrial waste • Sewage disposal and pollution of rivers

Source: Secondary curricula and syllabi for classes IX and X. West Bengal Board of Secondary Education, Government of West Bengal

interdependence of flora and fauna for sustainable development; necessity of preserving water bodies and forests; danger of using plastic materials; need for preservation of water; danger of air, land, and sound pollution; and global warming, which have been beautifully conveyed through illustrious cartoons of the book.

6.3.4 Higher Secondary Level (Class/Standards XI and XII)

This is this stage of diversification; learners may pursue arts, science, or commerce stream. They may also opt for either the academic stream or the vocational stream. During 2007–2013, a higher secondary-level student had to study EVS as a compulsory subject. This subject then carried 100 marks. The entire syllabus used to be taught throughout classes XI and XII. In the school routine, one period used to be allotted per week, and project work could be conducted during vacations and holidays, if necessary. The terminal examination used to be held at the end of class XII. Each student had to compulsorily take the examination in the subject. The distribution of marks was 40 for the theoretical examination and 60 for project work and viva voce. A minimum of 30 marks out of 100 had to be obtained in this examination. Examinees failing to secure the minimum marks in EVS would be declared disqualified in the higher secondary examination (Government of West Bengal 2006). But at present, no provision is there to study EVS compulsorily at this level. Since the academic session 2013–2014, at the time of the introduction of the new syllabus, EVS is now being offered as an optional subject and not compulsory at this level. However, some concepts of EVS are found in optional subjects, such as biology, chemistry, and geography (Government of West Bengal 2013).

6.3.5 Undergraduate (UG Level)

Complying with the mandate issued by the Supreme Court of India in 1991, UGC decided that a 6-month compulsory core module course in EVS for UG courses of all branches of higher education would be prepared and compulsorily implemented in all the universities and colleges of India (UGC 2003). As per the UGC guidelines, the core model syllabus of EVS includes the following eight units to be covered in 50 lectures throughout a semester at the UG level (Fig. 6.3).

The first seven units of the syllabus will cover 45 classroom-based lectures to enhance the knowledge, skills, and attitude of the learners towards the environment. The last unit is based on field activities, which will be covered in five lecture hours and will provide students with first-hand knowledge of various local environmental issues. Field work seeks to move out of the textbook mode of teaching into the realm of practical learning in the field, where the teacher will act as a catalyst to interpret what the students observe or discover in their own environment. The universities/

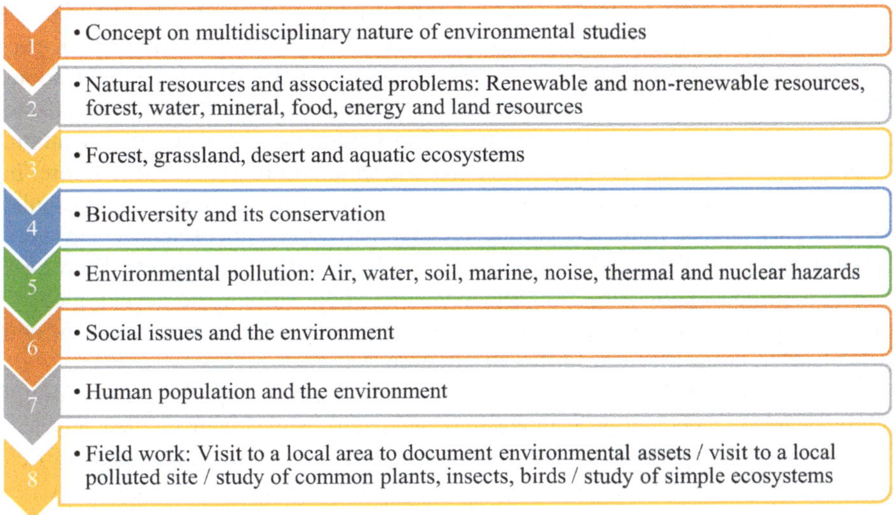

Fig. 6.3 Core model syllabus of EVS at UG level. (Source: UGC 2003: pp. 1–6)

colleges can also draw upon the expertise of outside resource persons for transacting the course (ibid: p 7).

However, in most of the universities in West Bengal, EVS has been included in the UG syllabus as AECC (ability enhancement compulsory course), but there is no uniformity of weightage given to the subject. Some universities assign four credits to this course with 100 marks (four periods of 1 h/week), whereas some universities assign it two credits, with 50 marks (two periods of 1 h/week).

6.4 Suggestions for Bolstering ESD Through EE/EVS

There is no denying the fact that education is the most powerful tool for securing a more sustainable future. It plays a crucial role to enhance the ability of the citizens of tomorrow to find new vistas to a more sustainable world. While they can draw upon experiences of the past to solve the problems of today and tomorrow, still the onus goes to them to engage themselves in a continuous dialogue in the educational process to analyze critically how to get over the present crises facing humanity. Awareness about and protection of the environment are the most essential part of ESD, and it cannot be considered in isolation from the present developmental process. ESD has four thrust areas:

- Improving access and retention in quality basic education
- Reorienting existing educational programs to address sustainability
- Increasing public understanding and awareness of sustainability
- Providing training to all sectors of the workforce

The first two areas primarily involve formal education, while the last two are concerned with nonformal and informal education. In the post-reform period, particularly in the mid-90s of the last century, environmental scientists and educationists thought of ESD as an "adjectival education." However, this perspective failed to encompass the larger understanding of ESD as harnessing all aspects of education, including awareness and training, at the mass level to ensure a sustainable future. In recent times, ESD has been incorporated into many fields of educational curricula, such as EE, human rights education, history, geography, life science, and even language subjects. EE enriches ESD in terms of content and pedagogy. Therefore, in order to impart knowledge and understanding about sustainable development to the future guardians of the earth, they must know their physical environment and strive hard to protect it from further destruction.

In the educational curriculum from KG to UG level, pupils acquire cultural norms, values, and behavior from teachers and peers, as well as from their physical surroundings. Theoretically, the curricula at various levels are saturated with rich concepts on the environment, but practically there remains a wide gap between learning objectives and outcomes. Debates and dialogues galore have already been there regarding the ways to ensure ESD. Let us add the following suggestions as to how we can inject into the learners the practice of ESD through EE:

6.4.1 Reorient Curricula

Policy makers need to identify the knowledge, skills, and values that are central to sustainable development in each of the three components of sustainability—environment, societal, and economic—and incorporate them into the curricula at various stages of education. Biodiversity, climate change, environmental hazards, and their effect on agriculture, economy, etc. should find a due place in the curricula to fulfill the national or local sustainability goals. Spiral curricula may serve this purpose.

6.4.2 Include EE as a Compulsory Subject in the Curricula

The real spirit behind the introduction of EE as a compulsory subject in the curricula from KG to UG level has to be understood by the policy makers and syllabi framers. Along with a separate course on locale-specific EE, the "embedding" of various concepts of EE in other core subjects will do further justice to the course. No specialized teachers would be required to teach the subject; each and every subject teacher would act as an EE teacher. The curricular materials already available could be used for providing necessary content input, as well as desirable experiences to the learners. Attitudinal changes of the learners would be of paramount importance, and this may happen through teachers' resourcefulness and skill in organizing activities for learners and providing them with requisite local-specific materials through community support.

6.4.3 Bring Back EE at the HS Level

A higher secondary level of learning is a crucial juncture when teenagers are turning into adult citizens of this planet. Learners of this stage are full of high energy and idealism. Their consciousness towards the environment may yield positive results. Therefore, EVS should be brought back into the HS curriculum as a compulsory subject.

6.4.4 Encourage Co-scholastic Activities

Co-scholastic activities can convey strong messages on sustainability, addressing the environmental, social, and economic concerns of the community. Special events, such as organizing tree plantation festivals, environmental fairs, music and art festival, community service, dance, and drama, may have positive effects on learners.

6.4.5 Adopt a "Whole-School" Approach

This increasingly popular approach usually contains knowledge, skills, perspectives, and values related to sustainability in the formal curricula. The school runs on sustainability ethos, and the school policies reflect the ethos of environmental, social, and economic sustainability. Interactions between the school and the community are fostered. The school often begins with one sustainability activity, which then leads to the other. Over time, the school becomes habituated to maintaining a number of sustainable practices (UNESCO 2012).

6.4.6 Apply ESD Pedagogies

Pedagogies for ESD include critical thinking, social criticism, and analyses of local issues. Such pedagogies involve debate, discussion, and application of values. Role-playing, drama, music, quiz, storytelling, simulating alternative futures, and such other creative ways of teaching-learning may bring positive change in the behavioral pattern of pupils. Experiential learning techniques will also be effective in teaching topics on SD. The content of EE should begin with the experiential background and immediate environment of the learner and extend itself to national and finally to a global perspective in a graded manner. The investigation, experimentation, and analysis through the discussion should be the way of imparting EE. This may be quite easy if locale-specific examples are included precisely. For younger students, pedagogy can include telling stories from Aesop's Fables, the Jataka Tales, and Panchatantra (Chandiramani 1991) that represent different ways of thinking about the self and others, nature, and the universe.

6.4.7 Include Locale-Specific Materials in EE

While incorporating contents in EE in the school curriculum, take care that the learners get acquainted with their local environmental elements first and then move to national and global environmental issues. There must be logical inclusion of locale-specific materials in EE, given its relevance in the contemporary value system. The program should be arranged so as to enable learners to observe and study their local environment, which might have been affected by various human activities, such as deforestation, use of chemicals in farming, industrial sewage disposal, mining, or quarrying. Care should be taken so that pupils take home lessons learned in the classroom and the field study. Teachers should present to them the issue of environmental crisis as a moral problem in order to nourish eco-friendly attitudes in them.

6.4.8 Teach History and Geography Subjects as "Carriers" of ESD

Efforts to harness the learners' ability to create values should be central to ESD. History and geography, as social science subjects, help pupils appreciate how the environment has been shaped by human activities down the ages and vice versa. These two subjects can act as the "carriers" of various concepts of ESD. Pupils can also apply historical and geographical knowledge and skills to interpret physical as well as social changes in nature.

6.4.9 Adopt Suitable Assessment Tools and Techniques

The foci of the expected learning outcomes of ESD should be developing a deeper understanding of the environmental issues and the ramifications of the same at national and international levels, besides developing the capacity to contribute meaningfully towards strengthening the process of sustainable development. The assessment of learning related to sustainability should not be done with simplistic tools and techniques, such as multiple-choice tests and the like. Essay writing competitions, project works, speeches, excursions, field studies, comparison and drawing of inferences, multimedia presentations, etc. may prove handy in assessing the learning outcomes of a complex topic like sustainability. Rubrics are also useful tools to rate pupils' performance on a wider variety of sustainability topics.

6.4.10 Ensure Participation of the Local Communities

Very active and meaningful support from the community around the educational institutions will be central to the implementation of EE. The school system in isolation may fail to mobilize adequate resources needed for creating any perceptible impact of EE. Moreover, for including the indigenous cultural traditions and ethos in the overall EE curriculum, the contribution of the local community will be of great help.

6.4.11 Encourage "Learning to Live Together"

The aim of learning to live together, set by the UNESCO, must mold learners who can live contributively and, in turn, educate future generations to engage in sustainable development. Through formal and informal education, efforts should be made to discuss the symbiotic relationship between human beings and the natural environment (Sharma 2020: p 50). While it is urgent to equip the learner with accurate facts and information about climate change, ESD should also include the values, interests, and perceptions that students bring into the classroom to create a learning environment that represents different perspectives.

6.4.12 Introduce an Effective Monitoring Mechanism

It is necessary to evolve an effective monitoring mechanism to achieve the desired results in spreading awareness and knowledge, honing skills, habits, and attitudes, and nourishing values among learners, following the proposed curriculum of EE at various stages of education. A suitable monitoring system provides an opportunity for improvement in the planning, implementation, and evaluation procedures of ESD. Its coverage would include the development of teaching-learning materials (TLMs) needed in the pedagogical process, teacher preparation programs, classroom processes, co-scholastic activities, and assessment of pupils' learning outcomes. A system of participatory monitoring to look after qualitative improvement from the national to the grassroots level may prove fruitful in this regard.

6.4.13 Use Mass Media

Mass media mold the minds of millions. With the help of mass and social media, environmental concerns and deterioration, need for the conservation of the environment, etc. should be popularized among the learners.

6.5 Closing Remarks

Environmental concerns and practices in India have been there since the dawn of civilization. However, EE/EVS for ensuring a sustainable future mainly sprang out of the landmark directives by the apex court of the country. There is no denying the fact that the government, in its policy papers, enumerates that ESD for citizens depends on the proper orientation of individuals so that they may utilize natural resources to create a sustainable future. This process calls for required changes in attitude, behavior, knowledge, values, and actions at the mass level to realize a symbiotic relationship between the natural environment and the human race. Unfortunately, the yawning gap between theory and practice, between the lofty ideals enumerated in the policy documents of the government and the outcomes in terms of human actions, still persists.

ESD is earmarked to be an essential part of each and every student's learning process. With this end in view, environmental issues and its conservation were identified as core areas in the curriculum at the school level in NPE 1986 and the subsequent Programme of Action (POA) in 1992. Although many state boards of secondary education in India and the Central Board of Secondary Education (CBSE) emphasized the need to educate future citizens about environmental issues to SD, there has been very little perceptible change in our approach to teaching-learning of EE/EVS. NCF 2000 and 2005 also put great importance on this subject as any other core subject at the school level, but we have still been grossly indifferent in this regard. The subject has never been treated with prime concern; it has always been seen as an auxiliary subject to other scholastic areas like sciences and social sciences. As in West Bengal, in many other states and UTs in India, EE/EVS is taught from class III to VIII compulsorily, and in classes IX and X, in a rather diffused manner; but in the higher secondary level, learners have little opportunity to learn about it as a core subject.

The pedagogical aspect of any subject plays a vital role in the improvement of knowledge and understanding level of that subject among the students, and it also helps to draw their interest in that subject. To make learners environment-conscious, practical classes and field studies are essential. However, in practice, most of the schools neither care for conducting practical classes nor use improved teaching methods, such as the TLMs, to make the subject interesting to the learners. They simply follow the classroom lecture method, and nature study gets neglected. Exhaustive activities in order to sensitize the learners towards environmental crisis are sadly lacking in the present pedagogical practices. Naturally, the learners have inadequate exposure to their habitat. Besides, in the school education system, evaluation of the learning outcomes in any subject is essential. But most of the schools do not consider evaluation in EE/EVS to be as important as evaluation in the core subjects. Failing to clear the test in this subject is generally not considered to be a bar in getting a promotion to the next higher class. Moreover, in almost all schools, there is no specialist teacher for teaching EE/EVS. The prescribed contents and activities of this subject are simply taught by other teachers having no or little domain knowledge.

Given the present environmental crises and the resultant calamities looming large all over the world, it is expected that the authorities concerned will pay due attention to nurturing SD culture in the learners. We all must keep in mind that we have only one green planet to live in, and its existence depends on our dedication to love it, protect and preserve it, and live together with it.

In the efforts towards achieving SDGs, NEP 2020 proposes to reconfigure the entire education system in alignment with the critical targets and goals of Agenda 2030. This policy lays emphasis on ensuring equitable quality education for all to accelerate India's progress towards achieving SDGs. But to promote the concept of sustainable development among learners, it fails to place a sound implementation road map with capacity-building initiatives. All the curricula frameworks should be revised; syllabi, modalities, and resource books should be formulated in line with the SDGs. We need to reconfigure the content materials with local contexts at all stages of the education system. The prevalent evaluation systems on EE/EVS across India require further assessment in light of the twenty-first-century education. Teachers are the key enabler to sensitize children with the need for a sustainable future. Therefore, teachers' capacity building should be enhanced through continuous professional development to facilitate them in updating content knowledge and pedagogical skills in EE/EVS. They should also be empowered with environmentally friendly classrooms that allow students to ponder over environmental concerns. Not only West Bengal but all states/UTs across India should transform the policy reforms in the education sector into practice. Only then can we utilize education as the crucial gateway to sustainable development.

References

Alexandar A (2012) Environmental education for sustainable development in selected schools of Puducherry and Cuddalore regions, India. Unpublished Thesis, Department of Ecology and Environmental Sciences, Pondicherry Central University

Almeida S, Cutter-Mackenzie A (2011) The historical, present and future of environmental education in India. Aust J Environ Educ 27(2):322–329

Barbier E (1987) The concept of sustainable economic development. Environ Conserv 14(2): 101–110

Blum N (2015) Topic guide: education, climate and environment. Doi: https://doi.org/10.12774/eod_tg.march.blumn

Boudes P (2011) United Nations conference on the human environment. In: Newman J (ed) Green ethics and philosophy–the green series: toward a sustainable environment. Sage Publications Inc, New York, pp 410–413
CEE (2007) Environmental education in the Indian school system: status report 2007. Centre for Environment Education, Ministry of Environment and Forests, Government of India, Ahmedabad
Chandiramani GL (1991) Panchatantra. Rupa Publications, New Delhi
Deshmukh N (2014) Environmental education: holistic approach for environment protection and sustainable development in the Indian context. Indian J Public Adm LX(1):137–145
Elliot JA (2006) An introduction to sustainable development. Routledge, London & New York
Government of India (1966) Report of the education commission 1964–66: education and national development. Ministry of Education, Government of India, Delhi
Government of India (1986) National policy on education 1986. Ministry of Human Resource Development, Government of India, New Delhi
Government of India (2020) National education policy 2020. Ministry of Education, Government of India, New Delhi
Government of West Bengal (2006) Circular number 185-SE(HS)/8C-04/06 dated 11.10.2006, West Bengal Council of Higher Secondary Education. Government of West Bengal, Kolkata
Government of West Bengal (2013) Circular number L/Secy/48/2013 dated 27.05.2013, West Bengal Council of Higher Secondary Education. Government of West Bengal, Kolkata
Government of West Bengal (2015) Secondary curricula and syllabi for classes IX & X. West Bengal Board of Secondary Education, Government of West Bengal, Kolkata
Government of West Bengal (2017) Paribesher tare sakale aamra. Department of Forest, Government of West Bengal, kolkata
Government of West Bengal (2021a) Aamar boi: Pratham, dwitiya ebong tritiya parba. West Bengal Primary Education Council, Directorate of School Education, Government of West Bengal, Kolkata
Government of West Bengal (2021b) Aamader paribesh. West Bengal Primary Education Council, Directorate of School Education, Government of West Bengal, Kolkata
Government of West Bengal (2021c) Paribesh o bijnan. West Bengal Board of Secondary Education, Government of West Bengal, Kolkata
IUCN (1970) International working meeting on environmental education in the school curriculum. International Union for Conservation of Nature and Natural Resources (IUCN), Nevada
Kumar K, Prakash A, Singh K (2020) How national education policy 2020 can be a lodestar to transform future generation in India. J Public Aff 21(3):125. https://doi.org/10.1002/pa.250
Leicht A, Combes B, Byun WJ et al (2018) From agenda 21 to target 4.7: the development of education for sustainable development. In: Leicht A, Heiss J, Byun WJ (eds) Issues and trends in education for sustainable development. UNESCO, Paris
Mckeown R, Hopkins C (2003) EE & ESD: defusing the worry. Environ Educ Res 9(1):117–128. https://doi.org/10.1080/13504620303469
Mckeown R, Hopkins C (2005) EE and ESD: two paradigms, one crucial goal. Appl Environ Educ Commun 4:221–224. https://doi.org/10.1080/15330150591004616
Mckeown R, Hopkins C (2007) Moving beyond the EE and ESD: disciplinary debate in formal education. J Educ Sustain Dev 1(1):17–26. https://doi.org/10.1177/097340820700100107
Menon S (2012) School EE in India. Centre for Environmental Education (CEE), Ahmedabad
Mondal A (2020) Environmental education (EE) and education for sustainable development (ESD) towards sustainable development (SD)—a comparative study. Indian J Adult Educ 81(1–2): 31–44
Mondal A, Mete J (2014) Education for sustainable development in India: the policy perspective. University News 52(23):20–28
Monroe MC (2012) The co-evolution of ESD and EE. J Educ Sustain Dev 6(1):43–47. https://doi.org/10.1177/0973408211006001l0

NCERT (1988) National curriculum for elementary and secondary education: a framework. National Council of Educational Research and Training (NCERT), New Delhi
NCERT (1993) Environmental education in the school curriculum developed by the NCERT. National Council of Educational Research and Training (NCERT), New Delhi
NCERT (2000) National curriculum framework for school education: a discussion draft document. National Council of Educational Research & Training (NCERT), New Delhi
NCERT (2006) Position paper: national focus group on habitat and learning. National Council of Educational Research & Training (NCERT), New Delhi
NCTE (1998) Curriculum framework for quality teacher education. National Council for Teacher Education (NCTE), New Delhi
NCTE (2005) Curriculum framework for quality teacher education—a draft. National Council for Teacher Education (NCTE), New Delhi
NCTE (2009) National curriculum framework for teacher education (NCFTE) 2009: towards preparing professional and humane teacher. National Council for Teacher Education (NCTE), New Delhi
Ravindranath MJ (2007) Environmental education in teacher education in India: experiences and challenges in the united Nation's decade of education for sustainable development. J Educ Teach Int Res Pedagogy 33(2):191–206. https://doi.org/10.1080/02607470701259481
Ravindranath S (2016) Environmental education in India – the shifting paradigm. In: Shailaja Gorana RN, Kanaujia RK (eds) Reorienting educational efforts for sustainable development: experiences from South Asia. Springer, Netherlands, pp 89–110
Sarabhai KV (2004) Thoughts on environmental education at the school level. Centre for Environment Education, Ahmedabad
Sarabhai KV, Chhokar KB (2009) Environmental education in India: evolution of education as a tool for sustainable development. In: Taylor N, Littledyke M, Eames C et al (eds) Environmental education in context: an international perspective on the development of environmental education. Sense Publishers, Rotterdam, Netherlands, pp 51–61
Sharma N (2020) Value-creating global citizenship education for sustainable development: strategies and approaches. Palgrave Macmillan
Sharma PK, Kanaujia PR (2020) Journey of green schools in India. In: Gough A, Chi-Kin Lee J, Po Keung Tsanget E (eds) Green schools globally, international explorations in outdoor and environmental education. Springer Nature, Cham, Switzerland, pp 203–226
Shimray C (2016) Teaching environmental education. Sage Publications, New Delhi
Sonowal CJ (2009) Environmental education in schools: the Indian scenario. J Hum Ecol 28(1): 15–36. https://doi.org/10.1080/09709274.2009.11906215
Stapp WB et al (1969) The concept of environmental education. J Environ Educ 1(1):30–34
The Supreme Court of India (1991) M.C. Mehta vs Union of India and Ors, on November 22, 1991, writ petition (civil) no. 860 of 1991 (environmental education case). https://elaw.org/content/india-mc-mehta-v-union-india-wp-8601991-19911122-environmental-education-case
The Supreme Court of India (2003). M. C. Mehta vs Union of India & Ors on December 18, 2003 (Case No.: Writ Petition (Civil) 860 of 1991). https://indiankanoon.org/doc/1419757/. Accessed 20 Aug 2022
The Supreme Court of India (2004) M. C. Mehta vs Union of India & Ors on July 13, 2004 (case no.: writ petition (civil) 860 of 1991). http://education-for-change.blogspot.com/2012/06/ncert-approach-dr-jaishree-sharma-nodal.html. Accessed 20 August 2022
Tilbury D (1995) Environmental education for sustainability: defining the new focus of environmental education in the 1990s. Environ Educ Res 1(2):195–212
UGC (2003) Six-months module syllabus for environmental studies for under graduate courses. University Grants Commission (UGC), New Delhi
UNESCO (1984) Activities of the UNESCO-UNEP international environmental education programme: 1975–1983. UNESCO, Paris
UNESCO (2012) Education for sustainable development: source book. UNESCO, Paris

UNESCO (2014) Sustainable development begins with education: how education can contribute to the proposed post-2015 goals. UNESCO, Paris

UNESCO (2015) Rethinking education: towards a global common good? UNESCO, Paris

UNESCO (2018) Guidebook on education for sustainable development for educators: effective teaching and learning in teacher education institutions in Africa. UNESCO, Paris

UNESCO (2020) Education for sustainable development: a roadmap. UNESCO, Paris

UNESCO-UNEP (1976) The Belgrade charter: a global framework for environmental education. UNESCO-UNEP Environ Educ Newsl 1(1):1–9

United Nations (1973) Report of the united conference on the human environment. United Nations, New York

United Nations (1987) Report of the world commission on environment and development (WCED): our common future. United Nations, New York

United Nations (1992) Agenda 21: Programme of action for sustainable development. United Nations, New York

United Nations (2015) Transforming our world: the 2030 agenda for sustainable development. United Nations, New York

Vardhan PP (2014) Environment protection under constitutional framework of India. Press Information Bureau, Government of India, New Delhi

Dr. Ajit Mondal is an Assistant Professor at the Department of Education, West Bengal State University, Barasat, Kolkata. Formerly, he was attached with the Department of Education, Surendranath College for Women (University of Calcutta). He has published more than 32 papers in peer-reviewed journals and authored five books. He has also edited 12 books on different aspects of education. He has also remarkably contributed articles to the SAGE Open Journal & Journal of Social Inclusion Studies (SAGE Publications), Education 3-13 (Taylor & Francis), Kurukshetra, Yojana (Government of India), the Primary Teacher Journal (NCERT), University News (AIU), and the Mainstream Weekly and Bangladesh Education Journal (BAFED in collaboration with Bangladesh, UNESCO). Policy-making, historical development of education in India, child rights, and right to education fall under the areas of his interest.

Dr. Md. Nijairul Islam was awarded Ph.D. in Education in 2015 from the University of Kalyani, West Bengal, India. The area of his interest includes contemporary issues in the history of education in India, and application of learning styles and multiple intelligences in teaching-learning. Dr. Islam has authored and edited several books on education and published more than 35 articles/research papers in edited books and academic journals of national/international repute, such as Education 3-13 (Taylor & Francis Group/Scopus indexed journal) and University News—a weekly journal of higher education in India.

Chapter 7
Achieving Sustainable Development Goals with Gender Equality: A Hands-On Experience in India

Shivani Bhardwaj and Sudeshna Roy

7.1 Introduction

The realities of the COVID-19 pandemic, politics of orthodox tenets and principles, intolerance, and the society with caste taboo and poverty in the backdrop of the corporate control of resources have further exasperated the gender resource gap (GRG) in India (Bhardwaj and Ghosh 2012). Resources include land, water, and housing with services like education, health, and transport, with access to gainful skills, infrastructure, and natural resources. However, the resources are captured by a few, leaving the excluded increasing, and the number of people at risk, especially in fragile, conflict, and violence-stricken areas, dispossessed more than before (World Bank 2020). The process of mainstreaming gender and the excluded has thus faced an unparalleled setback (UN 2020), and leaving no one behind (UNSDG 2020) seems a challenging convergence.

The movement that strengthened woman's rights to land was steeped into women's unpaid work in agriculture and at home. The farmers' movement in India today has squashed the sharecropper and the marginal and small farmers (BBC 2020). The rich landowner farmers sat in Delhi for months protesting against the corporatization of agriculture. However, the unorganized farmworker and the wage laborers still toil on the soil and spend their energy at building sites without the security of tenure at source or destination areas.

S. Bhardwaj
Sathi All For Partnerships (SAFP), E09 Anandlok Housing Society, Mayur Vihar Phase I, New Delhi, India

S. Roy (✉)
Centre for the Study of Regional Development, School of Social Sciences, Jawaharlal Nehru University, New Delhi, India

M. Mishra et al. (eds.), *Public Policies and Sustainable Development in Post-Reform India*, New Frontiers in Regional Science: Asian Perspectives 71,
https://doi.org/10.1007/978-981-99-3696-0_7

The Labour Codes 2020 of the Ministry of Labour and Employment (MoLE 2020) have been formulated, asking the worker to earn what they can while the woman participation rate declines in India. Violence Against Women and Girls (VAWG) has increased from their known, and they have no place to go to escape assault and indignity. These current anomalies must be considered while recalling that erstwhile calls for local peoples' control of land, water, and forest have not been forgotten. From the local reality, let us now turn our attention to international concerns.

The United Nations General Assembly adopted in 2015 a set of 17 Sustainable Development Goals (SDGs) with specific targets which are to be achieved by 2030 (UN 2015). Sathi All For Partnerships (SAFP) is a Trust that has worked for the past two decades to advocate for spatial solutions based on women's right to resources and building capacities to safeguard the interests of those at risk. At the core of its work lies experience-based thought leadership working on the targeted achievement of SDGs, particularly in goal 5 by advocating inclusion and convergence towards a gender-equal world by planning local areas to contain inclusive projects that address the GRG. SAFP co-created partnerships on access to resources for vulnerable women such as single women. For example, it has convinced an NGO to lease its infrastructure and livelihood assets to a woman Mutual Benefit Trust such that women can experiment with how they will manage it sustainably. It also supports well-being by running support groups. A support group for the COVID-19-stricken people called Kritagyata or gratitude reached out to more than 2000 people, and its support group on mental health connected families in distress with help through local community connect. Since safeguarding policies can provide protection, SAFP took on work to develop policies and training manuals for agencies as well as NGOs looking after organizing workers with the primary aim to facilitate comprehension to strengthen capacities through planned enabling approaches through collaborative efforts. SAFP's primary data through seminal research has been in areas pertaining to child rights, women empowerment, disability, psychosocial and mental health, violence, land rights, safety, and well-being, among others. SAFP advocacy has impacted the planning documents of the country. The governments of Delhi and Kerala adopted the Women Resource Zone (WRZ) ideas to launch projects that continue to serve women and development workers on the ground and have taken aspects of Sustainable Development Zones (SDZs) into their social change agenda (Terragreen 2011). However, the government entity took only one aspect of the concept into their ongoing work. A reiteration needs to be attempted to build on the gains in articulation as well as develop an understanding of how women can gain access to build infrastructure, finance, and natural resources and rebuild their skills in the post-COVID-19 era. Impacting ideas to get recognition of women's land rights and starting programs based on policy change are not enough, and resource utilization by women has to gain prominence for the way inclusiveness will impact sustainability. This piece has to be articulated yet again to strengthen the discourse on gender gaps and resource rights. As women are not a homogenous group, GRG will need to be understood in the context of communities that work and govern themselves within their realm of defined social norms.

The underlying problem is that women who are skilled to nurture life "sustainably" have no skills in managing property and assets as they do have access and ownership of property and control of resources. Women are considered property and saddled with roles through the institution of marriage and family. The gender role of caring for members of the family makes women within the family not free to work on reducing the GRG. Thus, it falls upon the "single" people or those outside the family institution and community leadership to take on the role of addressing the gender resource gap. The above realization made SAFP develop an association with the dispossessed, who were identified as the "orphaned" who have experienced state-sponsored care in orphanages, and the migrant unorganized sector workers as communities on margins in India.

It was important to comprehend the gender differentials in ownership of productive resources and to understand barriers in accessing assets by women from some focus groups, as women are a nonhomogeneous cohort. In addition, age and socioeconomic intersections create a wedge of differences in how women are placed in government policies and in developmental budgets. SAFP realized that change in these policies would require work at the level of practice where a set of excluded women claim their right to resources and ask for their role in implementing the SDGs in their own neighborhoods. Towards this end, SAFP organized consultations and research to articulate the right to resources for women from Tribal, Muslim, and Dalit communities [1] and analyzed the literature on gender resource gaps as shared in the discussion ahead.

7.2 Discussion

Much has been written and analyzed across literature reviews (UNFPA 2005; Sen et al. 2007) about gender inequality being an outcome of the nexus of socioeconomic disparity in resource distribution (Arora 2012) and which is perpetuated by the vicious cycle of gender bias and violence (Jayachandran 2015). Resource empowerment and financial literacy regarding the rights of women are mandated under governmental policy formulations as the inheritance of landed or immovable parental or spousal property and assets. Women are largely deprived of these resources in the Indian patriarchal resource control customs (ICRW 2006; Halder and Jaishankar 2008). They cannot step out of the house and are kept in line through violence inside the home as well as in workplaces and public spaces. Structural violence to which women are subjected in everyday life through types of infrastructure constructed in which women's access, use right, and needs are undermined eventually leads to

[1] Dalit community includes those who are treated as untouchable in India who face discrimination by birth. The word means "oppressed or broken." The Indian courts and government refer to them as Scheduled Castes. Dalit communities have been organized as politically active groups to participate in vote politics. Thus, this identity of being a Dalit is also a self-reference to develop in relation to researched gaps.

gender-biased social practices. There exists systematic deprivation and exclusion of women (IMPRI 2021). Participating in governance is a skillset she learns by swimming against the tide of resource constraints. The women from the margins face more violence as they are needed to provide low-cost labor by maintaining caste hierarchy (Equality Now and NCWL 2021).

There clearly lie challenges in achieving SDGs, as when women are found tapping their potential as change agents and assert their right to be active beneficiaries, they face backlash from administration backed by communal and sectarian forces. To safeguard women from the backlash, men and the transgender community must support the transformative leadership of women from excluded sections. Support is required in the form of mobilization of youth and middle-aged women (MAW) to work together in self-help groups (SHGs). Together, communities need to harness their sets of skills on resource sustainability within a backdrop of a safeguarded enabling environment. Services near home are needed for communities to perform their gendered roles to care for people within the family and community, often known as social reproductive roles; to earn for the family that includes the productive roles; and to sustain resources, which are known as community roles. A change in the existing roles of gender can be brought about by co-creating the infrastructure to care for the family and strengthening the livelihood efficiently such that there is time and energy for each person to perform the community roles.

7.2.1 Land Rights

After a decade of advocacy, woman's land rights were included in the draft land policy of India as official recognition that in the GRG, land remains the most important means of production, and the ownership of land is passed as a tradition to the male in the family (Agarwal 1994). The notion of group land rights in the policy for women is a way to get resources for women outside family and community resource control. The issue of GRG and its linkages with patriarchal control of the robust resource base is a complex contestation rendering most inclusion efforts to lessen impact (Katrak 2006). Yet historically, rights are realized when a system of demand is consistent with legal and moral arguments. SAFP set up the Consult for Women and Land Rights to reach the voice of women across different cultures to advocate to lobby for change in law, policy, and programs in 2003. Within no time, many networks emerged that created the human resource for organizations to support ground-level work, research, and policy reform work on women and land (UNIFEM and SAFP 2008).

A land title in woman's name requires credit, access to services, and an asset base to sustain ownership and control while trying to make land productive and regenerating (Valera et al. 2018; Salcedo-La Vina 2020). Women migrating due to marriage or with their work have to negotiate their right to land differently than men, and thus they remain vulnerable as their ownership of housing and services is even less secure than their land right (Roberts 2021). The discourse of women and land thus incorporates housing and livelihood resources. However, when single women were defined as never married, married and divorced, deserted, widowed, and in partnership with other women/men, the planning unit remained household with the addition of the category of women-headed households. The conceptual clarity on what land rights constituted thus has had a long process, which further got qualified based on gender roles in the management of land, assets, and related resources. Households divide the social reproductive role, productive role, and community roles between men and women, which is often not negotiated based on capabilities and opportunities. Thereby, different members of the household get to experience multiplicity in performing gender roles. The work on gender resource planning was evolving under the policy concerns for gender equality (Beall 1996). Token allocations for land planning for a vending zone for women were attempted by town planners in 2011, and this was a welcome sign. The rural and urban development ministries in India did pick up the idea to increase women's ownership by promoting joint ownership in government allocation of land and housing, but it is yet to adopt a holistic method to compute GRG as a basis of planning projects and area development plans.

7.2.2 Gender Resource Gaps (GRGs)

GRG is multifarious, begins at the family or household level, and escalates into the neighborhood, district, state, and national levels manifested in income, assets, productive relations, access to services, opportunities and spaces, decisions on resource governance, health and education, transport, enterprise development, labor participation, skill training, mobility, information asymmetry, and membership networks. While skills are crucial to managing resources, women remain bound by stereotypical roles (Hentschel et al. 2019).

Following the Harvard Analytical Framework of GRG (Evertzen 2009), SAFP has studied the perceptions about space needs, services, and participation at socio-economic and governance levels that were explored across high, middle, and lower income categories. The forms of GRG were most in spousal income, livelihood opportunities, and space. Therefore, a spatial plan was proposed in District Okhla, Uttar Pradesh, in collaboration with architects from Equal Saree, to make Gender Resource Centers (GRCs) with livelihood interventions connected through safe roads with many public infrastructure for care and production spaces (SAFP et al. 2013).

The designs for the public and private workspaces were co-created with men, which enhanced women's participation in neighborhood activities. This provided an alternative visual image of an inclusive design and use of infrastructure. Participation in a project from its inception builds a web of relationships that can influence utility, usage, and design. Knowledge and attitude based on gender equality first need to be imbibed in both men and women and then be translated into gender-equity practices (Haider 2012). A simple solution to closing the gender gap in space is to provide spaces that women can access more or have exclusive access to. Changes can be brought at the level of public visibility. This visibility will help in transforming patriarchal attitudes. Balancing growth and development against that of protecting the environment and preserving open space need to be merged into the solutions we seek that may eventually close the gender gaps. Training for men to increase their livelihoods and rejuvenation options near home will also help in the swapping of gender roles.

When SAFP presented the design of a women's center that local women designed for the clerics in Okhla who owned land on which the center could be built, they asked us to come after a week. The women's center was designed as a mosque, as women were not allowed inside the mosque to pray. The center design had water points to get uncontaminated, and pure water as the space was designed not just for work but also for the care of adults and children, as well as a space for renting out to earn revenue. After a week, when we sat for a feasibility discussion, we were made to sit in the newly demarcated area within the mosque to initiate the address of gender gaps. The mere articulation of women initiated goodwill from a supportive cleric. Such are the winds of change that inspire ideations towards equality.

7.2.3 GRG for Women in Different Communities and Work Sectors

SAFP partnered with Women Struggle Committee (WSC) and National Confederation of Dalit and Adivasi Organisations (NACDAOR) to compute Dalit women's resource gap (SAFP et al. 2013). The research supported by the Ministry of Women and Child Development, Government of India, was spread over rural and urban areas of five states of Uttar Pradesh, Rajasthan, Bihar, Tamil Nadu, and Punjab, comprising 1000 Dalit and non-Dalit women.

The SAFP Dalit women and resource study revealed that non-Dalit women had more access to resources, such as 19.6% more land, 66.6% more shops/workshops, and 60.6% more livestock besides having more access to healthcare and transport. The research found that Dalit women lag behind in education and skills, credit, and access to natural resources, particularly land, housing, and service, in comparison to non-Dalit women. Even where schemes for scheduled population exist, such as the Special Component Plans, only 25% of Dalit women knew about it. Women's schemes, which did not seem to reach Dalit women, with the exception of those with political patronage, had an awareness of around 58% among Dalit women, whereas only 33% of non-Dalit women were not aware. The Dalit women's resource gap in access to schemes was 25%, with 46% non-Dalit women reporting that they have not benefited from the government or NGO schemes, whereas more than 71% of Dalit women say the same. This is also a considerable gap when additionally, 33% more of the Dalit women feel deprived of services like health, transport, and social get-together, and 20% of Dalit women feel that they have not been benefited by education relative to only 11% of non-Dalit women responding on the same.

Discrimination across different institutional sites, from the household and community to the state and markets, and the pervasive violation of their human rights, implies that even when Dalit women gain access to resources, they are unable to translate it into improved welfare and well-being over a period of time. The proportion of Dalit women is higher in agricultural labor and rearing livestock such as pigs and goats and lower in unpaid domestic chores when compared to non-Dalit women.

The most striking gap was in the missing social networks seemed to be a clear gap for Dalit women to get better employees who continue to work in their caste-based occupations. About 33% of Dalit women claim that being a Dalit is an obstacle to reform as compared to only 11% of non-Dalit women saying so. The need to organize special awareness programs on government schemes for Dalit women and promote their collectives and organizations to empower them and facilitate narrowing the resource gap was felt by both Dalit and non-Dalit women study participants.

The allocation and monitoring of the SC Sub-Plan with mechanisms need to be improved to ensure that 50% of the SCP should be earmarked for Dalit women. Since Dalit people comprise 17% of the population of India, the Gender Budget Guidelines of the Government of India need to make proportionate provisions for SC/ST/Minority women. In this case, 17% allocation for the Scheduled Caste women should be mandatory under the Gender Budgeting by the union and state governments. Furthermore, district development plans should be audited for gender and Dalit equity gaps. Towards this end, the monthly action taken report of the District Collector should be utilized to monitor the reduction of resource gaps for Dalit women by tracking the implementation of all schemes and women components of the budgets.

Other recommendations include setting up an empowered government body to deal with Dalit women's development and protection of livelihood opportunities with special protection mechanisms for the Dalit women who have filed police complaints under the Prevention of Atrocities Act, 1989. [2] The right to livelihoods of Dalit women needs to be protected for specific occupations where Dalit women work as informal sector workers (e.g., manual scavengers, sanitation). Social audit of the government scheme called Mahatma Gandhi National Rural Employment Guarantee Act (MGNREGA), [3] developmental projects, as well as other schemes that can

[2]The Scheduled Castes and the Scheduled Tribes (Prevention of Atrocities) Act, 1989, has been enacted by the Indian Parliament to prevent atrocities, offences, and hate crimes against the scheduled castes and scheduled tribal communities in the country and it is legally punishable under the Indian Penal Code.

[3]Mahatma Gandhi National Rural Employment Guarantee Act 2005 or MGNREGA is an Indian labor law and social security measure that aims to guarantee the "right to work" and alleviate poverty. It aims to enhance livelihood security in rural areas by providing at least 100 days of wage employment in a financial year to at least one member of every household whose adult members

enhance land or infrastructure base related to adequate housing and right to the livelihood needs to be led by Dalit women's organizations.

7.2.3.1 Women from Other Excluded Groups

Women in other excluded groups like indigenous communities, Muslim communities, orphan youth who left care, and unorganized sector workers are in close contact with SAFP. These women have been in communication with each other and have educated themselves on the GRC and its implication for them individually. However, working with each other in groups has been a challenge in the communal, caste-ridden, capitalist, and patriarchal hegemony. Resource scarcity, escalation in the frequency of natural and anthropogenic calamities, economic uncertainty, political turmoil, and social conflicts striking at the heart of religious, ethnic, class, and racial differences have increased the feelings on in-group and out-group and threaten to play a divisive role in social solidarity and harmony.

In a study partnered with the Action Aid Association, SAFP documented a case study of Muslim women and men in 2020. [4] Based on the interactions, the resource gaps and inequalities in access to work opportunities, economic resources, and services like healthcare facilities among Muslim women were found to face discrimination owing to their status of being a religious minority in India.

7.2.4 Middle-Aged Women (MAW)

In another study funded by the Ministry of Women and Child Development (MoWCD) and partnered with Jamia Millia Islamia University, SAFP conducted a situational analysis of the psychosocial well-being among the MAW in the Delhi National Capital Region (NCR) (MoWCD 2018). MAW (45–60 years) are usually a forgotten population group in Indian demographic and health policy and largely remain a blind spot in gender discourse and empowerment programs for safeguarding their interests. The marginalization of MAW stems from deep-rooted patriarchal norms and years of subjugation. Hartmann Heidi (1979) defines patriarchy as hierarchical social relations across gender, which legitimizes men to dominate women, based on the control over "material power" and women's "labor power," by restricting women's "sexuality" and "access to economic resources."

These questions are pertinent as gender-based discrimination and violence against women have a direct impact on a woman's health and well-being. Hence, GRG

volunteer to do unskilled manual work such as making roads, canals, irrigation works, and other assets. Women are guaranteed one-third of the jobs made available under the MGNREGA.

[4] It is an internal/within organizational document report of Action Aid Association and European Union.

cannot be ignored while studying the relevance of well-being in a MAW's life. Subjective experiences constituted from culturally informed knowledge, expectations, and practices are equally essential markers for well-being. Once women cross the reproductive age, the state is silent in both policies and a program for them.

MAW are at the cusp of diminishing youth and approaching old age; hence, it requires attention. Women, especially those over the age of 50 years, face deep injustice, yet tend to stay silent in public, but hardly there is any protest by this age group to draw attention from all concerned to their marginalization and neglect by self, state, and society. Almost all government policies and public sector initiatives target young women who are in the reproductive age group. Even socially, these women suffer at the hands of economic dependence, health-related problems, self-esteem and self-worth issues, technological handicap, mental illnesses, shifting roles, dislocation, domestic violence, sexual abuse, worthlessness, empty-nest syndrome, and repressed sexuality, among many others. Addressing the well-being of women of this age group would lead to reducing old age-related psychological and social issues.

MAW manifest psychosocial disorders almost five times as frequently as men (WHO 2021). Researchers (Malhotra and Shah 2015) believe that the reason behind this difference is more social and psychological rather than physiological. The stress for MAW appears especially severe in our culture, where youth and beauty are greater emphasis on women being purposeful and needful. Thus, the need is to examine the phenomenon of well-being from within cultural context rather than stereotypical generalizations of linking hormones to women of this age.

The SAFP study decrypted whether this invisibility and neglect impact the well-being of MAW, what it is that well-being truly means to these women, how it is that they ensure their well-being, what the psychosocial barriers to well-being are, and how they overcome these barriers. Common psychosocial stressors have severe and long-standing physiological and psychological consequences. Hence, SAFP's study focus was on the manifestations and experiences of women in their day-to-day life domain, which is beyond the conventional issue of health and violence.

The study found GRGs noticed within the neighborhood where in the residential welfare areas (RWA), office space was only a man space as governing bodies rarely had women members and office bearers. Field interactions revealed that evident gaps were witnessed in the pension policies both for widows and for the elderly. Women were finding it difficult to enroll in government beneficiary schemes, and in case the women were already enrolled, there was an irregularity of payment. Safety and security, especially of the elderly, are compromised. Though many legal provisions are there to help women steer out of violence, abuse, and harassment, their awareness was found to be negligible. This is a major gap, as not being aware of their rights and entitlements created a sense of helplessness and vulnerability among them. The most marginalized were the middle-aged widows. The role of the state in terms of ensuring timely old age and widow's pensions is desired. Not being able to benefit from and access these schemes led to frustration, adversely affecting their well-being.

The value of MAW needs to be understood at the core economy of family, community, and nation as a whole. They need to be treated with an asset-based approach, viewing them less as passive recipients of services and more as active contributors and leaders of society. Good governance can ensure the provision of necessary healthcare facilities targeting MAW along with provisions of skill development, which would make these women economically self-dependent and tap their potential. All flagship programs should be gender and age mainstreamed and inclusive, and a percentage of the women's component plan must be earmarked for the use of MAW in the state. Midlife centers on the pattern of geriatric centers must be started in public hospitals as lifestyle diseases such as cancer have a higher likelihood of occurrence during these ages. Government must increase the old age and widow pension allowance owing to the rising cost of living considerably at par with the minimum basic wage. For MAW, awareness and accessibility to information regarding continued education are missing. There should be specially designed courses for women who want to continue adult education.

With digital India initiatives taking center stage, MAW must make themselves technology savvy. RWA and local bodies, both public and private, in a partnership, must take active participation in opening and operationalizing computer teaching centers. Resources for these women can be generated from within the community where MAW who are computer literate could be hired on remuneration to teach those who do not. This helps to generate income for the women resource persons and thus serves a dual purpose.

Local government can build on work to promote well-being by including strategic programming and rethinking service design to build capacity, confidence, and well-being resources. This can be achieved through increasing employment opportunities. The government set up Mahila Shakti Kendra between 2017–2018 and 2019–2020, which caters to empowering rural Indian women with digital literacy, skill development, employment opportunities, health, and nutrition (MoWCD 2016). But there is again a lack of a comprehensive umbrella scheme for middle-aged urban Indian women, which requires utmost policy attention.

7.2.5 Gender-Equal Space for Spatial Planning

SAFP, in collaboration with Equal Saree and Partners, who work with state governments, made sustainable planning models in Kollam, Kerala; Shivpuri, Madhya Pradesh; Dumra, Bihar; and Okhla, Delhi (SAFP et al. 2013). These local area plans addressed GRGs. These plans were presented to State Planning Commissions, District Planners, and elected representatives so that they could allocate GRCs and women-centric projects within the local plan. The roads connecting these project locales could be made safe spaces by allocating women in groups resource packages. These projects with resource packages will involve skill development with infrastructure access and budgets for housing units and women's hostels, production centers, parking, vending, shopping areas, migrant/placement centers with space for exhibition and gardens, and planning including a detailed gender resource plan within the urban or rural plan of any local area development project.

Each local area will have different levels of exclusion that need to be lessened to foster inclusion, as is clear from the SAFP Dalit women and resource gap research. If these gaps are worked through the gender lens, two levels of individual vulnerability and collective exclusion at the socioeconomic level would be mitigated. Specific gaps could be addressed through area development projects that can impact the status of women within their own households. The GRGs at the familial or the household level will be addressed through local climate change adaptation and care service projects that benefit both the community and the household in each neighborhood. These plans should make a visible contribution to women through local governance structures. Greater gender equality can enhance productivity, improve development outcomes for the next generation, and make institutions more representative. Women collectives need to be made within their own neighborhoods where they can choose the partners of the collectives they represent. Each group should be entitled to develop its business plan with immediate steps to legalize its collective entity as an SHG.

The short-term steps below can be developed to make the SHG economically viable:

- Getting a constituency and stakeholders active to take on the process to understand GRGs of different communities and neighborhoods they live and work in.
- Planning inclusion with owners, users, and participant people by livelihood, care, and development visioning exercise to map a way forward benefitting all but keeping the women in charge of 50% of development activity.
- Making the Detail Project Report for projects with Urban Local Bodies and Gram Panchayats to own the process.
- Secure financial, building, and natural resources for neighborhood wellness projects that connect with each other as a district inclusion and gender equality plan.

The long-term steps would include the following:

- Formulate the area and neighborhood plans.
- Setting up information and training services to improve access to resources for the community under women's ownership.
- Data generation for community livelihood based on the regeneration of local resources.
- Women's cooperatives (for placement and productive and care services).
- Establishing neighborhood care services through GRCs that are linked across the district for social infrastructure development that increases productivity and safety.

7.3 Conclusion

Resources have been maintained differentially within communities through a state-supported patriarchal structure, which needs to demonstrate now that it wears a constitutional hat of equality. The existence of a GRG is a violation of the constitutional obligation of the state. The existence of GRGs varies across spatial location, hierarchies, gender, and socioeconomic intersections indicating that the stakeholders are unaware of the nature and quantum of GRGs and are deprioritized in policy towards it. Thus, it is the local communities who must rise up and recognize their potential and contribute towards the creation of WRZs in a participatory manner at their micro spatial levels, neighborhoods, and localities, thereby bringing together resource pooling and democratic accessibility and agency over it, aimed at gender equality, helmed at transparency and accountability. WRZs are located within the regional plans and have equal access across gender to both natural resources and built-up infrastructure (Bhardwaj and Ghosh 2012).

However, policy and planning-level solutions proposed at the macro level, i.e., at National Planning Commission, National Institution for Transforming India (NITI Aayog) level, or local or district, city, or village level, require training to document GRG at the smallest unit area to monitor the reduction of the gap. Towards this social, economic, and political will, to impact local area plans with inclusive planning is essential. How will local area plans be made for more gender equality is a big question that can be answered only through an individual quest for equality, sustainability, and safety.

In the 75 years of India's Independence, we should remember the passion that each Indian had to be self-sustained and self-reliant. The COVID-19 pandemic has made each person learn that independence is within a web of co-dependence. The value of collaboration and collective engagement has increased profoundly. The palpable need to increase the safety net for children, the disabled, the infirm, and the non-mobilized has been mobilizing. It is recommended to document shreds of evidence on discrimination, strengthening children and women safeguarding and monitoring. Girl children must be provided opportunities to be the leaders against mobilizing forces of patriarchy, capitalism, and commonality. Herein, middle-aged and single women must take to leadership roles and form SHGs in steering their community resources, teaching and training about vulnerabilities, identifying risks and barriers to protection, and mobilizing agency among children, youth, and themselves at family and neighborhood levels, thereby empowering the local and grassroots-level groups to assist, back, and advocate each other during times of peace, conflict, and emergencies. Thus, WRZs and GRCs within the framework of sustainable development-inclusive local area plans will prevent GRGs, protect communities from vulnerabilities and violence, and promote equitable safeguarding to sustain global and local resources.

If policy change does not come forth and political parties fail to work towards WRZ, then this work will go on at the local level. This is exemplified by Santhal women whom SAFP met in March 2022. These Indigenous women, like other tribals, have little or no access to land through inheritance. Through their Mutual Benefit Trust, they not only earn a livelihood through agriculture and vending but also manage and maintain a community center on land and grant from the village land. This center is utilized for their meetings and is also available to the community to congregate for their activities. The Panchayat organizes funds for maintaining this infrastructure, while the women manage the daily upkeep of the premise. A woman member residing in the neighborhood has the key to the center. The women in this Panchayat have successfully organized themselves into agriculture producers' groups with assistance from Badlao Foundation. They also get the motivation to pursue newer livelihood options by investing in each other through their saving and credit schemes. These Santhal women have been able to collectively pursue justice for their members and their daughters when the marriage breaks down. This is a direct result of the training they got in through the access, control, and management of their group and this center. The women have developed skills to nurture financial resources while empowering themselves and their children. They now look forward to not only managing themselves but also taking charge of resources, especially human resources of their village, by maintaining safe migration registers to know where each person within their community network is and how safe and secure they are.

These Santhal women have taken on the challenge of addressing the gender resource gap (GRG) that is entrenched in the culture and mindset of both their community and the governance system through short-term and long-term strategies. The women and girls, with the support of men in government, and corporate and civil society actors need facilitation to converge existing initiatives at micro and macro levels to ensure that they yield power to track migration and compute the resource flow from their land so that they participate with equal stakes in sustaining resources, including the human resource of the area, that is alienated at present.

References

Agarwal B (1994) A field of one's own: gender and land rights in South Asia. Cambridge University Press, New York

Arora RU (2012) Gender inequality, economic development and globalisation: a state level analysis of India. J Dev Areas 46(1):147–164

BBC (2020) What has brought Indian farmers to the streets? December 3rd 2020. British Broadcasting Corporation. https://www.bbc.com/news/world-asia-india-55157574

Beall J (1996) Urban governance: why gender matters. UNDP gender in development programme. https://www.gdrc.org/u-gov/doc-whygendermatters.html

Bhardwaj S, Ghosh R (2012) Women's resource zones (WRZ): a sustainable approach to governance. Innovative approaches to land governance and management: evidence on implementation and impact. Paper presented at annual World Bank conference on land and poverty; April 23–26, 2012

Equality Now and NCWL (2021) Eliminating caste-based sexual violence in India. Recommendations for the prevention of sexual violence againt Dalit women and girls. August. National Council of Women Leaders. https://live-equality-now.pantheonsite.io/wp-content/

uploads/2021/11/ELIMINATING-CASTE-BASED-SEXUALVIOLENCE-IN-INDIA-Recommendations-August-2021.pdf
Evertzen A (2009) Gender tools. Netherlands Development Organization. http://gadegender.nl/Bibliographies/Gender%20tools.htm
Haider H (2012) Helpdesk research report: changing attitudes and behaviours in relation to gender equality. GSDRC, pp 1–20
Halder D, Jaishankar K (2008) Property rights of Hindu women: a feminist review of succession laws of ancient, medieval, and modern India. J Law Religion 24(2):663–687. http://www.jstor.org/stable/25654333
Hartmann Heidi I (1979) The unhappy marriage of Marxism and feminism: towards a more progressive union. Capital Class 12(2):1–33. SAGE. https://doi.org/10.1177/030981687900800102
Hentschel T, Heilman ME, Peus CV (2019) The multiple dimensions of gender stereotypes: a current look at men's and women's characterizations of others and themselves. Front Psychol 10. https://doi.org/10.3389/fpsyg.2019.00011
ICRW (2006) Property ownership and inheritance rights of women for social protection—the South Asia experience. Synthesis report of three studies. International Centre for Research on Women, New Delhi
IMPRI (2021) How does violence become a part of a city's infrastructure? Youth Ki Awaaz
Jayachandran S (2015) The roots of gender inequality in developing countries. Annu Rev Econ 7: 63–88. https://doi.org/10.1146/annurev-economics-080614-115404
Katrak KH (2006) Politics of the female body: post-colonial writers of the third world. Rutgers, University press, New Brunswick, New Jersey and London
Malhotra S, Shah R (2015) Women and mental health in India: an overview. Indian J Psychiatry 57(2):S205–S211. https://doi.org/10.4103/0019-5545.161479
MoLE (2020). The industrial relation code. The gazette of India. Part II. Ministry of Labour and Employment, Government of India. New Delhi. https://labour.gov.in/labour-codes
MoWCD (2016). Mahila Shakti Kendra Scheme. No. 26/13/2016. Ministry of Women and Child Development, Government of India. New Delhi
Roberts B (2021) Securing Women's land rights: challenges and solutions. Landsea. https://www.landesa.org/securing-womens-land-rights-challenges-and-solutions/
Salcedo-La Vina C (2020) Beyond title: how to secure land tenure for women. World Resources Institute. https://www.wri.org/insights/beyond-title-how-secure-land-tenure-women
Sathi All For partnerships (SAFP), Equal Saree and TAAL (2013) The next steps towards rural women resource zone in Shivpuri, Madhya Pradesh. Delhi
Sen G, Ostlin P, George A (2007) Unequal, unfair, ineffective and inefficient gender inequity in health: why it exists and how we can change it. Final report to the WHO Commission on Social Determinants of Health. September 2007. IIMB & Karolinska Institute
Terragreen (2011) The hand that rocks the cradle. How women in rural India are redefining the gender roles. October, pp. 28–33
UN (2015) Transforming our world: the 2030 agenda for sustainable development. A/RES/70/1. United Nations. Geneva
UN (2020) Policy brief: the impact of Covid-19 on women. April 9th. United Nations. Geneva
UNFPA (2005) Frequently asked questions on gender equality. United Nations Population Fund. https://www.unfpa.org/resources/frequently-asked-questions-about-gender-equality
UNIFEM, SAFP (2008) Overview of civil societies engagement with women's control and ownership of productive assets and resource. Discussion paper. New Delhi
UNSDG (2020) Leave no one behind. United Nations Sustainable Development Group. United Nations, Geneva
Valera HGA., et al. (2018) Women's land title ownership and empowerment: evidence from India. ADB Economics Working Paper Series No 559, September: 1–25

WHO (2021) Gender and women's mental health. World Health Organization, Geneva. https://www.who.int/teams/mental-health-and-substance-use/gender-and-women-s-mental-health
World Bank (2020) Supporting the most vulnerable: scaling up support to address fragility, conflict, and violence. November 16th. Results Brief. https://www.worldbank.org/en/results/2020/11/16/supporting-the-most-vulnerable-scaling-up-support-to-address-fragility-conflict-and-violence

Dr. Shivani Bhardwaj is among the founders of SAFP, Pravah, Nirmana, and National Alliance for Labor Rights, and a global forum called the Consult for Women and Land Rights (CWLR). She worked as Gender Advisor Royal Embassy of Norway in India, Habitat International Coalition, IDS, Plan International, DFID, Save the Children (UK), GIZ, and Indo-German Social Service Society and is on the board of three development organizations. She works for a mental wellness support group at the local levels mentoring youth. She has authored numerous publications on training, safeguarding, land rights, and gender resource gap.

Dr. Sudeshna Roy is awarded with a Ph.D. from Jawaharlal Nehru University and is an independent social science research and development professional and SAFP Associate. She has worked in various government and nongovernment organizations. She is a prolific writer having interests and authorship on gender, health, livelihood, urbanization and urban sociology, and marginalized people.

Chapter 8
Agricultural Sustainability and Women: Indian Scenario

Diganta Biswas and Bhaswati Saha

8.1 Introduction

Women have been playing a vital role in the entire firming process in India—from sowing the seeds to the cutting of crops. The number of farms operated by women has more than doubled since 1978. In 2009, the World Bank, FAO, and IFAD found that over 80% of rural smallholder farmers worldwide were women; this was caused by men migrating to find work in other sectors (Robinson-Pant 2016). As per the study conducted by the FAO in 2011, the share of women in the agricultural labour force ranges from about 20% in the Americas to almost 50% in Africa. The global average is dominated by Asia. Within Asia, the sub-regional averages range from about 35% in South Asia to almost 50% in East and Southeast Asia. The Asian average is dominated by China, where the female share of the agricultural labour force has increased slightly during the past three decades. The female share in India has remained steady at just over 30%, exceeding 50% in Bangladesh. However, interestingly, in Malaysia, there is a declining female labour share in agriculture. Women comprise almost 50% of the agricultural labour force in sub-Saharan Africa. The averages in Africa range from just over 40% in Southern Africa to just over 50% in Eastern Africa (Doss and SOFA Team 2011). In India, the Economic Survey of 2017–2018 shows that 78% of Indian's employed women work in the agricultural field, and 50% of rural women are agricultural labourers.[1] Unfortunately, it is quite

[1] Growing Migration by Men is Causing "Feminisation" of Agriculture Sector, Says Economic Survey. See https://pib.gov.in/Pressreleaseshare.aspx?PRID=1518099.

D. Biswas (✉)
Post Graduate Council, Raiganj University, Raiganj, West Bengal, India

B. Saha
Department of Sociology, Kalyani Mahavidyalaya, Kalyani, Nadia , West Bengal, India

M. Mishra et al. (eds.), *Public Policies and Sustainable Development in Post-Reform India*, New Frontiers in Regional Science: Asian Perspectives 71,
https://doi.org/10.1007/978-981-99-3696-0_8

understandable that they suffer from several issues—domestic violence, deprivation of the right to property, uneven distribution of household work, etc. Apart from these stumbling blocks at home, they are also subjected to many discriminations in the fields. It ranges from unequal remuneration for work, sexual harassment, lack of institutional support and safety nets, non-availability of credit, and lack of training opportunities up to the reluctance to maternity issues, evidently the recent incidents of removal of the uterus of some of the women farmers in Maharashtra in recent times[2] and many more which are unreported.

8.2 Objectives

Attainment of agricultural sustainability is linked to the upliftment of *economic, social,* and *environmental* policy frameworks linked to farming activities. Agricultural sustainability is at the heart of the UN's 2030 Agenda and the first fundamental step to securing zero hunger. Sustainability in agriculture is considered from three dimensions of sustainability: economic, social, and environmental.[3] At this backdrop, this chapter aims:

- Firstly, to study the concept of sustainable agricultural system
- Secondly, to explore the relationship between agricultural sustainability and women
- Thirdly, to find out how this problem may be resolved under the Indian legal framework

8.3 Conceptualizing Sustainable Agricultural System

Sustainable agricultural systems are those production models that are able to produce foods that are adequate in quality and quantity, ensure a fair economic remuneration for the farmers, and help safeguard the agricultural soil and natural resources. In other words, sustainability means "seeking a long-term maintenance of the agricultural production and soil fertility while reducing environmental risks related to those very same agronomic practices".[4] Sustainability in agriculture is the first fundamental step to securing zero hunger. This idea is considered from three dimensions of

---

[2]Kundan Pandey, "They stole my womb": Doctors mislead thousands of women to get their uterus removed. See https://www.downtoearth.org.in/news/health/-they-stole-my-womb-doctors-mislead-thousands-of-women-to-get-their-uterus-removed-69579, accessed on 4th December, 2021, at 3 PM.

[3]The 2030, Sustainable Development Goal Agenda, 2030 indicator 2.4.1.

[4]Barilla, C. F. N. (2011). New Models for Sustainable Agriculture. *Barilla Center for Food & Nutrition: Parma, Italy,* Pg. 46

sustainability: *economic*, *social*, and *environmental*.[5] Sustainable agriculture is based on a large number of agricultural practices that are already known. The knowledge available, comprised of scientific knowledge and proven practices, crystallized into some excellent and practical guiding principles that are the foundation of genuinely sustainable farming. It has been discovered that the application of traditional farming practices, and a proper crop rotation in particular, ensures environmentally sustainable production. The next step is the "actual measurement in the field" of the most favourable cropping systems, which will be compared to traditional ones. The next step is to directly involve farmers and industry experts so that the concepts of sustainability and productivity come to be part of corporate strategies as two absolutely reconcilable aspects of agricultural production.[6] The promotion of sustainable agriculture and gender equality is within the 17 Sustainable Development Goals (SDGs), but advancements and setbacks about the complexities generated by the intersection of these issues seem to have been overlooked by the United Nations Agenda for "peace and prosperity for people and the planet" (Sachs 2012). In short, these guidelines include:

- Farming of a wider range of plant species
- Systematic use of crop rotations
- Minimized mechanical working of the land
- Maintenance of a protective cover on the surface of the organic soil
- Optimized use of organic and inorganic fertilizers
- Integrated management of pests and diseases through appropriate practices
- Efficient management of water resources

In the next section, it is pertinent to discuss some of the well-organized models of sustainable agriculture involving women that are globally appreciated.

8.3.1 Models of Sustainable Agriculture

There are different models of agriculture[7] considered as sustainable agriculture in the world. A few of them are as follows[8]:

---

[5] *The 2030, Sustainable Development Goal Agenda, 2030 indicator 2.4.1.*

[6] Supra Note 4, Pg. 53.

[7] A complete classification of "agricultural models" should start from the definition of typical situations regarding the use of key inputs, such as genetic resources: traditional local varieties, modern varieties obtained by conventional breeding, hybrids, and GMOs; water resources: rain-fed cultivation and crop irrigation; energy resources: labour intensive and highly mechanized; soil resources (quantity): extensive farming and intensive agriculture; soil resources (quality): zero/minimum tillage and conventional ploughing; nutritional resources: organic fertilizers, natural fertilizers, and inorganic and synthetic fertilizers; and the fight against pathogens and weeds: biological control, integrated pest management, and fight against synthetic chemical products.

[8] Supra Note 4, Pg. 34.

8.3.1.1 The United States

In the late 1990s, the USDA of the United States established the national organic standards.[9] This model features the use of mechanization and monoculture and a ban on the use of fertilizers and pesticides, which means greater protection of land, water, and consumers.

The case of Earthbound Farms in Carmel (California, USA): Drew and Mayra Goodman founded Earthbound Farms with two and a half acres of raspberries and vegetables in Carmel, California. In 1986, they started the retail sale of ready-made salads and now have become the major producers of organic products and the most successful in the world, billing up to 450 million dollars in 2006. In 2011, at Earthbound Farms, 36,000 acres were cultivated. They avoid the use of "333,000 pounds (about 150,000 kg) of toxic and persistent pesticides and more than 11,200,000 pounds (about 5000 tons) of chemical fertilizers". Moreover, they claim to "save about 1.8 million gallons (about 7000 L) of oil by avoiding the use of pesticides and fertilizers made from petroleum, and to fight global warming by avoiding the release of carbon dioxide, a major greenhouse gas, into the atmosphere, equivalent to that produced by about 7800 cars".[10]

8.3.1.2 Mexico

In Mexico, since the beginning of its colonization about 500 years ago, due to large-scale deforestation, the area has become one of the most eroded in the world. According to scientists, up to five meters of the active layer of the soil may have been lost, and 80% of the soil has eroded, amounting to 500,000 acres of land.[11] At this, the CEDICAM, founded in 1980 by Jesus Leon and a group of farmers in Mixteca, began its reunification work in order to reconstruct the local ecosystem through the adoption of sustainable agriculture. They planted one million native trees in the Mixteca region to combat erosion and conserve the local biodiversity. Leon also turned to the use of the ancient indigenous practice of constructing canals to harvest rainwater and prevent runoff. Hundreds of miles of canals were built by a small number of peasants, who thus also increased their shared capital, in addition to water availability. Leon also promoted the use of greenhouses to produce vegetables for families and educated farmers about sustainable/basic agricultural practices. Now, traditional agricultural practices and local diet are valued more highly than foreign products over there.[12]

---

[9] Supra Note 4, Pg. 40.

[10] Supra Note 4, Pg 41.

[11] Supra Note 4, Pg. 32–33.

[12] Supra Note 4, Pg. 32–33.

8.3.1.3 Kazakhstan

In Kazakhstan, particularly in northern Kazakhstan, no-tillage (or ***zero-tillage***) is a technique used in a highly conservative concept of agriculture. It had a very rapid diffusion from 2007 to 2008. The zero-tillage farmers use special machines that can grind up crop residues and leave them on the soil surface, even if it means leaving heaps of stubbles on the ground. These two methods have proven very effective in maintaining soil moisture high and reducing erosion due to wind and water. The savings that came out of the non-cultivation of soil is often reinvested in the purchase of herbicides. However, zero-tillage farming is more susceptible to weeds because the weeds are not removed mechanically as in other agricultural models.[13]

8.3.1.4 North Korea

In the Democratic People's Republic of Korea (DPRK), the period suitable for cultivation is limited due to the harsh climate, with temperatures ranging from − 19 °C in winter to 25 °C in summer. The soils ended up typically poor in organic matter and phosphorus. At this point, the government encouraged the adoption of cropping systems that were an alternative to traditional monoculture. From September 2002 until November 2005, the FAO carried out a project on conservation agriculture and food security aimed at obtaining food security involving training farmers involving experts on conservation agriculture practices to increase yields in a sustainable manner. Conventional tillage, for example, had been replaced by no-till technologies and cropping systems that, among other things, included green manure and cover crops.[14]

8.3.1.5 New Zealand

In 1993, a study was conducted in New Zealand to assess the differences between biodynamic and conventional farming in terms of soil fertility and profitability. Interestingly, 85% of the biodynamic farms presented better soil structure in terms of ventilation, drainage, and preparation of the seedbed. Almost all areas of biodynamic cultivation obtained a higher amount of organic matter in the soil compared to conventional agriculture farms. Consequently, the carbon-nitrogen ratio and the available nitrogen were greater in areas of biodynamic farming.[15] Generally, since the biodynamic products were sold at a 25% higher price, and if the price were to

[13] Supra Note 4, Pg. 35.

[14] Supra Note 4, Pg. 36–37.

[15] Organic agriculture combines tradition, innovation, and science for the benefit of the environment and promotes fair relationships, as well as a good quality of life, for all involved (IAASTD, 2009).

increase further, it would have a significant impact on the financial sustainability of the biodynamic and organic[16] farm.[17]

8.3.1.6 Ethiopia

The "Tigray Project" created in 1996 in northern Ethiopia, where the diversity of crops is traditionally very high, is one of the projects that demonstrates how the adoption of organic agriculture can substantially increase yields and, at the same time, result in increased access to food by the population groups. It was an experiment conducted by farmers and experts who wanted to find out if a community-based ecological approach for the restoration of soil and the improvement of production through ecological principles improves the living conditions of poor small farmers. An FAO publication of the "Tigray Project" in 2010 listed its main activities: *training courses and follow-up for the preparation and use of compost*, including the monitoring of the impact on production; starting up the activity of soil and water conservation; reduction of grazing and feeding of animals with fresh herbs and woody plants; creation of community ponds, small dams, and river diversions, in order to collect and store water for use in the dry season; promotion of water harvesting, beekeeping, and use of bio-pesticides based on local knowledge; support for families with female heads of the household and composed of elderly people (the poorest of the poor), through the provision of seeds, spices, and training courses for the cultivation of fruit trees and plants used as fodder to be sold locally; training courses for unemployed women who have completed compulsory education, enabling them to acquire the necessary skills to enter the work world; and sharing of experiences through cross visits and promoting the use of new and simple technologies and tools that are easy to find and use (such as foot pumps) (Bockel et al. 2012).

For the "Tigray Project", the Institute for Sustainable Development, in collaboration with the Ministry of Agriculture and Rural Development and the Environmental Protection Authority (EPA) of Ethiopia, adopted the principle of Extension Services.[18]

---

[16]Biodynamic farming has the non-use of chemicals and synthetic fertilizers in common with organic farming, but instead uses manure as fertilizer, and then calls for the rotation of crops, pest control carried out in a natural way, and diversification of crops and livestock. However, biodynamic farming differs from organic farming and other agricultural models in the preparation of compost and plant protection products.

[17]Supra Note 4, Pg. 39.

[18]Technique based on direct and constant technical assistance to farmers, keeping the world of research in touch with that of the field technicians.

8.3.1.7 Ecuador

In Ecuador,[19] nature and sustainability are treated as integral components of development. The project, namely, Sustainable Agriculture with Gender Inclusion and Participation, running in the municipal area of Quito, is a noteworthy initiative undertaken to improve food security, urban agroecology, climate change adaptation, and nutrition. This project, by promoting sustainable practice in agriculture and use of vacant land for the growth of food, is protecting the city's natural surroundings and forests, pursuing joint environmental governance, sustainable land management, and integrated human development. The programme has been working together with women and female-headed households through training courses, technical assistance, and support resources. Nearly 352,600 people are benefitted from the programme, comprising 56,000 urban farmers, 85.71% of whom are women, and 170,000 consumers. The project promotes and validates alternative and sustainable land management approaches through the implementation of climate change adaptation actions. It also ensures food and nutrition security and universal health access, which are essential for poverty eradication and climate-resilient sustainable development. The project fosters sustainable and safe agricultural production and agribusiness, with a focus on micro-enterprise management and access to different markets. Additionally, it improves participants' earnings by generating jobs, as well as helping them to save money by consuming their own products. Since the start of the project, 16,700 participants have been trained, 2500 urban gardens have opened, and 110 urban agriculture start-ups have been promoted with 105 different food products.

8.3.1.8 Italy

In Italy, the study conducted by the Barilla on Italian durum wheat showed that the correct application of knowledge and agricultural practices not only helps in improving crop yields and quality of products, thus allowing to increase the income generated by crops, but also helps reduce the environmental impacts (up to 40% less greenhouse gas emissions) due to increased efficiency of fertilization. In light of the results of this study, Barilla developed "Ten Commandments" for the cultivation of durum wheat: a list of guiding principles for farmers who are facing the complex challenges of sustainable agriculture. It is also shown how to correct agronomic practices and contribute to the reduction of environmental impacts, thus enabling optimum production both qualitatively and quantitatively.[20]

---

[19] Sustainable Agriculture with Gender Inclusion and Participation | Ecuador. See the website under the URL https://unfccc.int/climate-action/momentum-for-change/women-for-results/sustainable-agriculture-with-gender-inclusion-and-participation-ecuador, accessed on 12th December, 2021, at 1 PM.

[20] Supra Note 4, Pg. 55.

Alternate crops: Plant durum wheat in a favourable crop rotation. Monoculture and rotations exclusively of cereal crops are, in fact, the cause of high environmental impacts and low profitability.

Work the soil with respect for it: Choose the tillage in a flexible manner, using tools and depth of working that are adapted to the specific conditions, climate, and cropping system in which durum wheat is inserted, according to the following guidelines.

Use the best variety: Choose the variety to be sown in relation to the cultivation area and expectations in terms of productivity and technological quality.

Use only certified and tanned seeds: Only certified seed ensures varietal identity (production capacity, technological quality, and resistance to adversity) and seed quality (purity, germination).

Sow at the right time: Each variety has an ideal time of planting, which can vary according to the cultivation area and weather conditions.

Use the right amount of seeds: Choose the density of sowing in relation to the variety, area, time of sowing, and soil conditions, since planting too thickly prevents the crop from making the best use of resources, promotes the development of diseases, and causes enticements.

Restrain weeds in a timely manner: The treatment must be timely and appropriate to the type of weeds present and the environmental conditions and cropping practices.

Dosage of nitrogen according to the needs of the plant: The use of nitrogen fertilizer should be adequate, both in terms of quantities supplied and periods in which they are used.

Protect the plant from disease: Carry out the treatments of defence in relation to the conditions of risk, and adopt a comprehensive strategy that involves all aspects of cultivation.

Extend sustainability to the farming system: Place the cultivation of the durum wheat in the cropping system (rotation) without limiting it to the context of individual crops, but rather apply sustainability measures to the overall management of the farm.

8.4 Agricultural Sustainability and Women

Women have been playing a crucial role in the entire agricultural process. With women predominant at all levels—production, pre-harvest, post-harvest processing, packaging, and marketing—of the agricultural value chain, to increase productivity in agriculture, it is imperative to adopt gender-specific interventions. Many women in Indian villages today are responsible for the integrated management of farming activities parallel to and use of diverse natural resources to meet daily household needs. Therefore, it needs a discussion over the contribution of women to farming activities.

8.4.1 *Special Roles of Women Farmers*

Men and women have different roles within livelihood systems that comprise farms and gardens, common property "resources such as pastures and forested lands, as well as protected areas. Men and women often have different knowledge about and preferences for plants and animals. For example, women's criteria for choosing certain food crop seeds may include cooking time, meal quality, taste, resistance to bird damage, and ease of collection, processing, preservation, and storage. Men are more likely to consider yield, suitability of flora and fauna, range of soil types, and ease of storage. Both are essential for human welfare. Now, in the following section, we should look over some of the notable roles of women involved in farming.

8.4.1.1 Conservation of Agro-Biodiversity (Conservation of Flora and Fauna)

Women play a lead role in biodiversity conservation and sustainable use. Women conservers should be enabled to continue their conservation ethos by providing support for essential infrastructure. They are the most important user and preserver of agro-biodiversity because, as farmers, rural women are responsible for growing and collecting food and for deciding how to use diverse natural resources to fulfil daily household needs (crops and wild plants, tree products, wild and domesticated animals). Unfortunately, today, the locally varied food production systems are under threat, including local knowledge and culture and skills of men and women farmers. Today, more than 90% of crop varieties have disappeared from farmers' fields; half of the breeds of many domestic animals have been lost.[21] With this decline, agro-biodiversity is disappearing; the scale of the loss is extensive. With the disappearance of harvested species, varieties, and breeds, a wide range of unharvested species also disappear.

The role of women in conserving agro-biodiversity has been recognized internationally on several occasions. The Convention on Biological Diversity (CBD)[22] has recognized "the vital role that women play in the conservation and sustainable use of biological diversity" and affirms "the need for the full participation of women at all

[21] Some 75% of plant genetic diversity has been lost over the extended period as farmers worldwide have left their multiple local varieties and "landraces" for genetically uniform, high-yielding varieties; 30% of livestock breeds are at the risk of extinction: 6 breeds are lost each month. Today, 75% of the world's food is generated from just 12 crops and 5 animal species. Of the 4% of 250,000 to 300,000 known plant species that are edible, only 15–200 are used by humans and only 3 (rice, maize, and wheat) contribute to nearly 60% of calories and proteins obtained by humans from plants. Animals provide some 30% of human requirements for food, and 12% of the population live almost entirely on products from ruminants. (Available at http://www.fao.org/3/y5609e/y5609e02.htm, accessed on 20th October, 2020, at 2.32 PM)

[22] The 1992 Rio Earth Summit, popularly known as the Convention on Biological Diversity, is dedicated to promoting sustainable development.

levels of policymaking and implementation for biological diversity conservation". It describes "ecosystem" as "a dynamic complex of plant, animal, and micro-organism communities and their non-living environment acting as a functional unit".

Decision V/6 suggests an ecosystem approach as defined by 12 principles and 5 operational guidelines. The CBD considers that a general application of the ecosystem approach will help achieve a balance of three objectives: conservation, sustainable use, and fair and equitable sharing of the benefits arising out of the utilization of genetic resources. While this definition is meant to give the widest possible scope for discussions related to biological diversity, specific reference to agro-biodiversity can be found in Decision V/5 (Settle 2020).

8.4.1.2 Nature of Involvement of Women in Farming Activities

In general, the following are the major farm and off-farm roles performed by women both in hill and plain villages. Now let us overview the different farm activities in which women are involved (Table 8.1).

8.4.1.3 Hurdles of Farm: Women and Agricultural Sustainability

Women constitute close to 65% of all agricultural workers. An even greater share, 74% of the rural workforce, is female. Despite their hard labour in the field, women are not officially counted as farmers and are labelled as either "agricultural labourers" or "cultivators" (Mohan 2020a).

Generally, three aspects of gender relationships are in existence in the farm sector, i.e. (i) *organization of production;* (ii) *organization of labour;* and (iii) *subordination of women in agriculture in India with the involvement of state or state agencies* (Raj and Aruna 2008). Keeping these things in mind, it may be clearly stated that unless adequate safety arrangements are made for women farmers in India, particularly when the feminization of agriculture has become a prominent picture in India, it is challenging to achieve agricultural sustainability. Gender inequality undermines progress toward sustainable agricultural development across multiple dimensions. Today, farming women face difficulty in access to land ownership, extension services, and finance. Agricultural credit, for instance, is critical for farmers to manage the seasonality of agricultural income and expenditures and to invest in technologies and long-term farm improvements. According to a report published by the International Food Policy Research Institute in 2011, women have less access to agricultural extension services and face barriers to accessing high-capital inputs such as seeds, fertilizers, and equipment (Raney 2011). On top of these limitations, women also lack access to less tangible benefits such as skilled labour, connections to other farmers, and linkages to potential buyers and suppliers. Since, in most cases, women tend to own smaller farms than men, they are far less likely to receive government agricultural subsidies, which target large producers of cash crops. All these factors reinforce and institutionalize gender inequality in farming (Belarmino

Table 8.1 Agriculture and nature of involvement of women

Sl. No.	Pre-sowing and sowing role/s	Inter-cultivation role/s	Harvest and post-harvest role/s	Allied agriculture role/s	Marketing of agricultural commodities
1	Cleaning and preparing of the field/s during pre-monsoon period	Irrigation	Reaping of crops	Cleaning of cattle shed/s	Collecting crops and vegetables
2	Levelling of the land	Separation of new ginger plants from mother ginger (only for ginger cultivation)	Collecting of crops	Feeding and grazing the cattle	Weighing and bagging of crops and vegetables
3	Preparation of compost and cow dung manure	Weeding	Thrashing (in hill area threshing is done by male persons)	Breeding	Marketing of flower, vegetables, fruits, etc. (in few cases)
4	Carrying of composed manure and seeds to the field	Earthling for maize	Winnowing, drying, and cleaning of grains	Storing cow dung for fuel and manure	
5	Preparing of the seedbed (for paddy cultivation)	Preparation and application of organic fertilizer/manuring	Stacking the straw (for paddy)	Taking care of sick cattle	
6	Sowing of seeds	Taking care of plants	Sieving	Getting and storing cattle feed and dairy equipment	
7	Observation of the seedbed	Watching standing crops	Storing and treating of grain and seeds	Cooking food for farm labourers	
8	Maintaining the agricultural implements	Getting knowledge about plant diseases, pruning, staking, water management		Supervising farm work/s	
9	Selection and treatment of seeds including hulling			Discussion with other farmers/specialists about agriculture/allied agriculture operations	

(continued)

Table 8.1 (continued)

Sl. No.	Pre-sowing and sowing role/s	Inter-cultivation role/s	Harvest and post-harvest role/s	Allied agriculture role/s	Marketing of agricultural commodities
10	Transplantation			Evaluation of printed materials/ listening to radio for farm/allied farm information	

Source: Prepared by the authors

and Schaedel 2019). Hence, a gender-responsive and human rights approach is crucial to strengthening the technical capacities of urban and peri-urban farmers and forming human capital. The ideas of sustainable agricultural development should involve the following (La Vina et al. 2007):

- Empowerment of poor farmers
- Integration of the ideas of poverty alleviation and environmental goals
- Promotion of sustainable agricultural practices to protect ecosystems
- Promotion of better governance of the agricultural sector

However, unfortunately, when we look at this section of supplier of food, it is pretty understandable that they are suffering due to several reasons, e.g. domestic violence, deprivation of the right to property, and uneven distribution of household work as their male counterparts are mostly found reluctant to shoulder the responsibility. Apart from these stumbling blocks at home, in the fields also, they are subjected to a great number of discriminations starting across unequal remuneration for work, sexual harassment, lack of institutional support and safety nets, non-availability of Kisan Credit Card, lack of training facilities, reluctance to maternity issues, and so on.

Now, let us look over the different types of difficulties faced by farm women in India:

Non-sharing of Domestic or Household Activities by the Male Counterpart

A group of persons who normally lived together and took food from a common kitchen constituted a household.[23] Rural women of all ages spend much of their day engaged in domestic chores, including collecting water and firewood, processing and preparing food, traveling and transporting, and caregiving. A typical day sees poor

[23] Reducing rural women's domestic workload through labour-saving technologies and practices. See the website under the URL https://www.ifad.org/documents/38714170/40196082/Teaser_workload_web.pdf/c8b175be-f4cf-4f97-a3bf-d6720cc08aaf, accessed on 20th June, 2020, at 7.42 PM.

rural women working up to 16 h, or even longer in some cases, performing many tasks while the male partners are mostly reluctant to shoulder the household responsibilities. Thus, fewer adult women at home means fewer hands to help with domestic work. Unfortunately, the bulk of their work at home and their role in subsistence farming are often unremunerated.[24] Vulnerable households—such as female- or child-headed, or those with members who are elderly, disabled, or suffering from a long-term illness—are particularly afflicted with domestic drudgery owing to relatively weakened labour capacity, lower income, and a limited asset base. The household activities include fetching water for her family, cooking and cleaning for all the members of the family, taking care of all the family members, and working as a hired farmhand during planting and harvest seasons. All these tasks are unpaid and restrict a woman's time and mobility. A heavy domestic workload often leads to "*time poverty*",[25] which is a primary reason why women in rural economies are marginalized and young women migrate to urban areas in search of a better life (Bardasi and Wodon 2010). It restricts their opportunities in education, training, farming, off-farm employment, and development processes and limits the income that they can bring in and have control over at home. These factors undermine women's participation in decision-making at home and in the community and perpetuate the inequitable balance of workloads between men and women. A reduced domestic workload through sharing of domestic responsibilities by male members of the family and through labour-saving technologies and practices means women need less assistance from their children, giving the children more time for school and play, and women can perform more productive activities to generate income and improve household food and nutrition security. These activities include:

- Paying attention to the health, nutrition, and well-being of women and their families
- Family farming (crop production and processing, small livestock production)
- Fish processing/trading and aquaculture, vegetable gardening
- Selling and buying goods in the local market
- Off-farm employment

Women also have more time to participate in training, self-help groups, and community-based organizations, which in turn will empower them with a greater

[24] Id.

[25] Time poverty means "working long hours and having no choice to do otherwise". It results from the combination of two conditions:

"First, the individual does not have enough time for rest and leisure once all working hours are accounted for.

Second, the individual cannot reduce his/her working time without either increasing the level of poverty of his/her household or leading his/her household to fall into monetary poverty due to the loss in income or consumption associated with the reduction in working time (if the household is not originally poor)".

(Source: Bardasi, E., & Wodon, Q. (2010). Working long hours and having no choice: Time poverty in Guinea. *Feminist Economics*, *16*(3), 45–78.)

voice and influence over their lives. According to the OECD data, women spend 577% more time in a day on household work than men in India.[26] In India, women are involved in unpaid work to look after their household work and children, which shares 3.1% of the national GDP.[27]

Lack of Access to the Property (Land)

Historical barriers that prevent women from owning profitable assets, such as companies, farms, and even houses, are pervasive around the world. For example, until 1850, American married women had no legal right to own land, and in Brazil, women had their right to land made official only in 1988. In 2010, the Nicaraguan Government finally adopted legal measures to improve rural women's access to credit in order to facilitate their path toward land ownership.[28] An extensive literature review confirms the link between increasing women's land rights and poverty reduction. Land rights can also be seen as a key factor in rural households seeking economic migration. A recent report from FAO analysed the synergies of land rights in Niger and how it affected the majority rural population vis-à-vis food security and sustainable agriculture development (Ignaciuk and Tun 2019). Even in the twenty-first century, women acquire land primarily through marriage and inheritance rather than by individual purchase. In most cases, husbands have more direct control over joint assets, including land. Even female inheritance of farmland is still limited because male relatives are favoured due to their perceived capacity to successfully manage farm work (La Vina et al. 2007). In India, only 10–20% of landholders are women. Due to that reason, it is rare for female farmers to enter into a farming agreement that restricts them to higher earnings.

Difficulties in Accessing Credit Facilities

Since credit is an important matter closely linked to proportionate collateral and also a matter of policy decision of the government, to protect the interests of the farming women, the government must come forward. Another approach is to develop innovative strategies to improve access to credit and agricultural services for marginalized farm populations. This requires strategic investment in public goods and programmes that benefit marginalized populations. These include rural infrastructure, education and health services, credit, subsidized inputs, information, and extension programmes.

[26] Gender inequality—how domestic responsibilities are keeping India's women away from workforce, increasing inequality, available at amp.scroll.in, accessed on October 25, 2020.

[27] Inequality has female face in India, women's unpaid work worth 3.1% of GDP: OXFAM, available at www.thehindu.com, accessed on October 25, 2020.

[28] Supra Note 25.

Lack of Access to Training on Advanced Technologies

The women farming community has little access to training in advanced technologies. Though more programmes are utilizing mobile technologies to deliver services, women's access to such technologies continues to lag behind that of men. They are still involved in arduous activities when such kinds of activities could have been easily avoided.

Lack of Access to Market Information

Since women are mostly involved in house activities after returning from the field, in most cases, they suffer from a lack of information about the market.

Legal Bottlenecks Concerning Repayment of Loans Inherited After Husband's Death

According to the NCRB, India reported suicides of 10,677 persons in the farming sector during 2020, accounting for 7% of total suicides (153,052) in the country. In 2016, it recorded suicides of 11,379 persons in the sector. It declined to 10,655 in 2017, 10,349 in 2018, and 10,281 in 2019 (Mohan 2020b). The main cause of suicide among female farmers arises typically that a large number of women farmers from farm households inherit massive debts after their husband's death.

Inequal Remuneration with Male Workers

Inequal remuneration is again a prominent feature in the agricultural sector all over the world.

8.5 Indian Approach

In India, the feminization of agriculture has been a recognized phenomenon. It calls for policies aiming at gender-specific intervention to raise the productivity of small farm holdings, integrate women as active agents in rural transformation, and engage men and women in extension services with gender expertise. Eying at the same, the Economic Survey, 2017–2018, pointed out that many measures have been taken to ensure mainstreaming of women in the agriculture sector (Sunder 2020). It recommends:

- Earmarking at least 30% of the budget allocation for women beneficiaries in all ongoing schemes/programmes and development activities

- Initiating women-centric activities to ensure that the benefits of various beneficiary-oriented programmes/schemes reach them and focusing on women self-help group (SHG) to connect them to micro-credit through capacity-building activities and to provide information and ensure their representation in different decision-making bodies (Sunder 2020)

Interestingly, the Central Budget of 2018–2019 addressed this issue.[29] Further, in India, the idea of sustainable agriculture is embedded into the Constitution of India and other statutory and policy initiatives.

8.6 Organization/Reorganization of Agriculture

The Constitution of India, under Article 48 of the Directive Principles of State Policy (DPSP), reads:

> "The State shall endeavour to organise agriculture and animal husbandry on modern and scientific lines ... and take steps for preserving and improving the breeds, and prohibiting the slaughter, of cows and calves and other milch and draught cattle."

Additionally, the Government of India, at different times, initiated several schemes to empower the farming community in general but not women farmers in particular. So, we need to look at the deficiencies in the system for farm women and the measures of the Government of India and its provinces to empower them.

8.6.1 Social Security

The Constitution of India, 1950, delineates the different social security measures under Part IV, i.e. in the Directive Principles of State Policy. Echoing with the Preamble, Article 38 reads: "State to secure a social order for the promotion of welfare of the people by securing and protecting as effectively as it may......".[30] The provision under the same Article also states, "the State shall, in particular, strive to minimize the inequalities in income and endeavor to eliminate inequalities in status, facilities, and opportunities ...".[31] The Constitution under Article 42 directs for just and humane conditions of work and maternity leaves. Article 43 speaks about the living wage, etc. for the workers, and Article 47. The duty of the State is to raise the level of nutrition and the standard of living and to improve public health. The State

---

[29] Growing Migration by Men is Causing "Feminisation" of Agriculture Sector, Says Economic Survey. See the website under the URL https://pib.gov.in/Pressreleaseshare.aspx?PRID=1518099, accessed on 12th December, 2021.

[30] Art. 38(1), The Constitution of India, 1949.

[31] Art. 38(2), The Constitution of India, 1949.

shall regard the raising of the level of nutrition and the standard of living of its people and the improvement of public health as among its primary duties. Further, on the statutory front, the following instruments are noteworthy. Interestingly, in addition to the Constitutional Directives under Part IV of the Constitution, "*Directive Principles of State Policy*", the Social Security Act 2008 provides social security for the unorganized sector. Mostly women labourers get helpless in their old age, including other labourers who do not get actual health benefits, minimum wages, etc. Additionally, the Women Farmers' Entitlements Bill, 2011,[32] was introduced in the Rajya Sabha by agricultural scientist M.S. Swaminathan. The salient features of the Bill need careful discussion (Swaminathan 2011).

The Bill was the first to define a woman farmer.[33] A woman can be considered a "woman farmer" irrespective of marital status and land ownership. Section 6 of the Bill says that every woman farmer should have equal ownership of and inheritance **rights over land** acquired by her husband, his share of the family property, or his share of land transferred through a government land reform or resettlement scheme.

Alongside, Section 8 says that women farmers, who have a Woman Farmer Certificate, would be entitled to a Kisan Credit Card,[34] which was so far only available to male farmers. They would also have the **right to credit and other kinds of financial support** for agricultural activities.

The Bill says about the setting up of a **Central Agricultural Development Fund for Women Farmers (CADFWF), which would** be used to develop women-friendly farming technologies, train women farmers, organize capacity-building programmes, create market facilities and rural godowns, and set up crèches and day care centres, among other things. The government must also frame a social security scheme for women farmers that cover old-age pension.[35] Besides, it ensures each State to setting up a Women Farmers' Entitlement Board and a District Vigilance Committee to monitor and implement the objectives of the Bill. State governments should provide mechanisms for the grievance redressal of women farmers at the block and district levels.

---

[32]Prof. M.S. Swaminathan, Rajya Sabha member (2007–2013), proposed the "Women Farmers Entitlement Bill" in the year 2011, but unfortunately the Bill was lapsed in 2013.

[33]A woman living in a rural area, who is primarily involved in agricultural activity but does non-agricultural activity occasionally, is a woman farmer (Sect. 2(f), The Women Farmers' Entitlements Bill 2011).

[34]The Kisan Credit Card (KCC) scheme is a credit scheme introduced in August 1998 by Indian public sector banks to issue Kisan Credit Card to the farmers of India. This model scheme was prepared by the National Bank for Agriculture and Rural Development (NABARD) on the recommendations of the R.V. Gupta Committee.

[35]Section 9, the Women Farmers' Entitlements Bill, 2011.

8.6.2 Financial Assistance Programme

The PM Kisan is a Central Sector Scheme with 100% funding from the Government of India. It became operational on 1st December 2018. Under the Scheme, income support of INR 6000 per year in three equal instalments will be provided to small and marginal farmer families (husband, wife, and minor children) having combined landholding/ownership of up to 2 hectares. The state government and UT administration will identify the farmer families who are eligible for support as per scheme guidelines. The fund will be directly transferred to the bank accounts of the beneficiaries.[36] Recently, the government has declared to provide the KCC under the Scheme.[37] The Scheme includes some exclusions. However, in West Bengal, under the Krishak Bandhu Scheme, the government has announced to provide financial aid of Rs. 5000 per acre to each of these families every year in two instalments, which includes both farmers and agricultural labourers.[38]

8.6.3 Crop Insurance

The issue of crop insurance is crucial in the context of natural calamities, crop failure, etc. In India, both at the central and the state levels, the system of crop insurance has been introduced. The Pradhan Mantri Fasal Bima Yojana was launched on 18th February 2016 and is an important development in this regard. The scheme aims to provide insurance coverage and financial support to the farmers in the event of failure of any of the notified crops as a result of natural calamities, pests, and diseases. It also aims to stabilize the income of farmers to ensure their continuance in farming. The scheme involves premium payments by the farmers in

[36] Available at https://pmkisan.gov.in/, accessed on 12th October, 2020, at 09.52 PM.

[37] Circular-1-20/2018 Credit-1 (Part) dated 6th February, 2020.The developed nations offer huge subsidies to agriculture which, at times, exceed 200 per cent of the production value, despite the 5 per cent *de minimis* (*de minimis* support indicates the maximum level of trade-distorting subsidies that can be given by a country to its agricultural sector (aggregate measurement of support or AMS—measures to support prices and subsidies directly linked to production)) prescribed, while for developing countries, it is 10 per cent. A joint paper by India and China has revealed that rich nations, including the USA, the EU, and Canada, have been consistently giving trade-distorting subsidies to their farmers, *more than 90 per cent of global aggregate measurement of support (trade-distorting subsidies) entitlements amounting to nearly $160 billion ... which is beyond their de minimis* (Amiti Sen, Rich nations have cornered 90% of farm subsidy entitlements: India-China study, see the website under the URL https://www.thehindubusinessline.com/economy/rich-nations-have-cornered-90-of-farm-subsidy-entitlements-indiachina-study/article9785329.ece, accessed on 26th October, 2020, at 10.15 PM).

[38] IANS| Kolkata, Mamata announces life insurance and financial aid for Bengal farmers. See the website under the URL https://www.business-standard.com/article/news-ians/mamata-announces-life-insurance-financial-aid-for-bengal-farmers-118123100823_1.html, accessed on 26th December, 2020.

favour of PMFBY, which varies from 1.5 to 5% of the sum assured or actuarial rate (whichever is less) by the farmers. The risks which are covered under the insurance include the following[39]:

Standing Crop: Yield loss due to non-preventable risks, such as natural fire, lightning, storm, hailstorm, typhoon, hurricanes, tornado, floods, landslides, and inundations; drought and dry spells; pests/diseases, etc.

Prevented Sowing/Planting Risk: In this case, insured farmers of a notified area are prevented from insured crop sowing or planting because of deficit/adverse rainfall, and thereby, up to 25% of the sum insured is payable to the farmers as indemnity claims.

Post-harvest Losses: Insurance cover for a maximum period of 14 days is available for the crops which are cut and spread to dry in the field post-harvesting against cyclone/cyclonic rains and unseasonal rains in the country.

Localized Calamities: Coverage from losses that occur due to some identified localized risks—hailstorms, landslides, and inundations which eventually affected isolated farms in the notified area.

However, the coverage does not include wars and nuclear risks, malicious damage, riots, theft, act of enmity, and grazing and/or destruction by domestic or wild animals.

In this connection, the Government of West Bengal introduced the Bangla Shasya Bima on 15th February 2019.[40] Under this scheme, the government would provide crop insurance coverage to farmers, especially for the Kharif-season crops. This scheme is supervised by the Department of Agriculture of West Bengal. Through this scheme, the WB Government aims to reduce the suicide rate of farmers, which occurs when farmers lose in their agriculture. This scheme is expected to prevent farmers from falling into the debt trap.

8.6.4 Problem of Distress Selling

If we closely observe the section of people involved in agricultural activities, most of them have poor formal educational legacy though they have the solid skill to carry on farming activities. Moreover, it is also noticeable that they are suffering from proper bargaining capacity. Additionally, there remains an information asymmetry between the farmers selling their produces and the buyers. Consequently, most of the time, they surrender to the middlemen and end up being deprived of getting the due value of their skill and labour behind farming activities. Hence, the participation of local government in the marketing of agricultural commodities is crucial. The

[39]Pradhan Mantri Fasal Bima Yojana. See the website under the URL https://pmfby.gov.in/pdf/New%20Schemes-english_.pdf, accessed on 14th December, 2020.

[40]Bangla Shasya Bima. See the website under the URL banglashasyabima.net › downloadk2, accessed on 14th December, 2020.

Government of India, on a number of occasions, has attempted to address the situation. Recently, a scheme was launched by the Government of India on May 10, under which farmers will get Rs. 8000 per acre every year as crop investment support.[41] Some of such attempts are as below:

The Farmers (Empowerment and Protection) Agreement on Price Assurance and Farm Services Act, 2020: Section 5 states that the price to be paid for the purchase of farming produce may be determined and mentioned in the farming agreement itself, and in case such price is subject to variation, then, such agreement shall explicitly provide for (a) a guaranteed price to be paid for such products; (b) a clear price reference for any additional amount over and above the guaranteed price, including bonus or premium, to ensure best value to the farmer, and such price reference may be linked to the prevailing prices in specified APMC yard or electronic trading and transaction platform or any other suitable benchmark prices. Further, Section 9 states that a farming agreement may be linked with insurance or credit instrument under any scheme of the Central Government or the State Government or any financial service provider to ensure risk mitigation and flow of credit to farmer or sponsor or both.

The Farmers' Produce Trade and Commerce (Promotion and Facilitation) Act, 2020: It attempts to ensure the following:

- To provide for the creation of an ecosystem where the farmers and traders enjoy the freedom of choice relating to sale and purchase of farmers' produce, which facilitates remunerative prices through competitive alternative trading channels
- To promote efficient, transparent, and barrier-free interstate and intrastate trade and commerce of farmers' produce outside the physical premises of markets or deemed markets notified under various state agricultural produce market legislation (Sect. 8.4)
- To provide a facilitative framework for electronic trading (Sects. 8.5 and 8.7)

8.6.5 Insurance Coverage

The farming community, which is vulnerable economically, should be brought under insurance coverage.

Life insurance: Compensation for the death of the farmer to the family members has been a matter of planning in the mind of the government. The farmers should be provided with life insurance as a measure of social security. In March 2018, the Government of Telangana announced a mega health-cum-life insurance scheme for farmers. Under this scheme, the ryots would be provided a cover of INR 5 lakh per annum for healthcare and hospitalization as well as in case of death. The families of

[41] This state just approved Rs. 5 lakh insurance cover to farmers; see the website under the URL https://www.zeebiz.com/india/news-this-state-just-approved-rs-5-lakh-insurance-cover-to-farmers-48770, accessed on 15th December, 2020.

these farmers will be paid the amount if the farmer dies of any accident or natural cause.[42] Gradually, the other Indian states introduced life insurance schemes under different nomenclature, e.g. Krishak Bandhu and Rythu Bandhu. In West Bengal, the government announced life insurance under a state-sponsored "Krishak Bandhu" scheme in 2019. The scheme extends life insurance coverage of INR 2 lakh for each of the state's farmers aged 18–60 years. In case of their death, be it natural or unnatural, the families are covered.[43]

Facilities of health insurance: Article 39(e) provides for the health and strength of workers, men, and women. Additionally, the MS Swaminathan Committee recommended inter alia to provide affordable health insurance and revitalize primary healthcare centres. The Ayushman Bharat project initiated by the Government of India is an attempt to address the issue, offering insurance coverage of Rs. 5 lakhs for the insured's family.

8.6.6 Maternity Issues

Article 39(e) speculates that *citizens are not forced by the economic necessity to enter avocations unsuited to their age or strength.* The Janani Suraksha Yojana (JSY) is a safe motherhood intervention under the National Health Mission. It is being implemented with the objective of reducing maternal and neonatal mortality by promoting institutional delivery among poor pregnant women. The scheme, launched on 12 April 2005 by the Hon'ble Prime Minister, is under implementation in all states and union territories (UTs), with a special focus on Low Performing States (LPSs). It offers financial assistance up to INR 2000 in rural while INR 1400 in urban areas.[44] In this connection, the incidents of removal of the uterus of some of the women farmers in Maharashtra in recent times that have been reported in Indian electronic and print media portray the two issues—income insecurity as well as prioritizing of livelihood over the reproductive right of women in agriculture.

---

[42] KCR Announces Mega Insurance Schemes for Farmers; see the website under the URL https://www.icicilombard.com/insurance-information/home-insurance-info/article/kcr-announces-mega-insurance-schemes-for-farmers, accessed on 14th December, 2020.

[43] Mamata announces life insurance, financial aid for Bengal farmers; see the website under the URL https://www.business-standard.com/article/news-ians/mamata-announces-life-insurance-financial-aid-for-bengal-farmers-118123100823_1.html, accessed on 15th December, 2020.

[44] Janani Suraksha Yojana (JSY), URL https://www.nhp.gov.in/janani-suraksha-yojana-jsy-_pg, accessed on 12th December, 2020.

8.6.7 Social Securities and Old-Aged Farmers

The ***Pradhan Mantri Kisan Maandhan Yojana (PM-KMY)*** is a government scheme meant for old-age protection and social security of small and marginal farmers (SMF).[45] All small and marginal farmers having cultivable landholding up to 2 hectares falling in the age group of 18–40 years, whose names appear in the land records of states/UTs as on 1st August 2019, are eligible to get benefits under the scheme. The applicants between the age group of 18 and 40 years will have to make monthly contributions ranging between INR 55 and INR 200 per month till they attain the age of 60. Under this scheme, the farmers would receive a minimum assured pension of INR 3000 per month after attaining the age of 60 years, and on the incidence of death, the spouse of the farmer shall be entitled to receive 50% of the pension as a family pension. Family pension is applicable only to a spouse.

8.6.8 Land Rights

In many parts of India, there are restrictive land leasing laws that do not provide the facilities and security to the farmers and do not ensure the tenure of tenancy between the landowner and the person who is engaged with the land for the cultivation of crops. It causes difficulties for landless and poor marginal farmers to access the land (Deo 2020). The Scheme for Doubling Farmers' Income[46] recommended that the agricultural land leasing act to ensure private sector investments in agriculture. This scheme provides leasing of land that will ensure the landowner and farmers' security regarding the ownership of landowners and security of tenure for tenants. This also provides the terms and conditions regarding the lease, and farmers can access insurance bank credit (Sharma 2020). However, in this context, the Model Land Leasing Act, 2016, introduced by the NITI Aayog, Govt. of India, also does not specify the lease periods and the rights of the landowner lessor and lessee agricultural farmers. Further, the Government of West Bengal's scheme, namely, "Nijo Griha, Nijo Bhumi",[47] entitles ownership of five decimals of land per family of houseless agricultural labourers, artisans, and fishermen, which is provided by the Government of West Bengal.

---

[45] Pradhan Mantri Kisan Maandhan Yojana; see the website under the URL https://pmkmy.gov.in/scheme/pmkmy, accessed on 14th December, 2020.

[46] The government is on track to achieving the target of doubling farmers' income by 2024 and recent farm reforms, including setting up of a Rs. 1 lakh crore agri-infra fund, which are steps in that direction. NITI Policy Paper No. 1/2017.

[47] **Scheme Nijo Griha, Nijo Bhumi;** see the website under the URL https://wb.gov.in/government-schemes-details-nijogriha.aspx, accessed on 10th December, 2020.

8.6.9 *Inequal Remuneration*

Article 39(d) of the Indian Constitution provides that there is equal pay for equal work for both men and women. In India, during 1990–2000, the average wage rate paid to men was INR 54.46 up to Rs. 70.37 in 2006–2007. However, in 2013, the average wage rate went to Rs. 193. However, the average wage rates have increased from 40.64 in 1990–2000 to Rs. 144.6 in 2013–2014 (Das 2020). The Union Labour Ministry decided to fix the minimum wage rates for unskilled agricultural labour, including women agricultural workers, at Rs. 350 per day in C-class towns which were to be effected from November 1, 2016.[48]

The West Bengal Government has fixed the minimum wage rates in the agricultural sector, which was effected from January 2020 to June 2020. The minimum wage rates are set as INR 247 (without food) and INR 230 (with food) for unskilled agricultural labour, including women, and for skilled agricultural labour, it is INR 299 (without food) and INR 282 (with food).

8.7 Other Schemes

Apart from the above gender-neutral approaches, the Government of India, over the period of time, has introduced a number of schemes, specifically for women farmers, which are as below:

National Mission on Agricultural Extension and Technology (NMAET): The objective of the National Mission on Agricultural Extension and Technology (NMAET) is to restructure and further strengthen agricultural extension, thereby enabling the delivery of appropriate technology and improving agronomic practices to farmers. Under this, the Sub-Mission on Agricultural Mechaniszation focuses on farm mechanization. The Mission will specifically cater to the requirements of small and marginal farmers through various institutional arrangements like custom hiring, mechanization of preselected villages, subsidy for the procurement of machines and pieces of equipment, and more.

Agri-Clinics and Agri-Business Centres (ACABC): Under the Scheme, 44% back-ended composite subsidy is announced toward the cost of the project to women as compared to 36% to men.

Special Programme for Women Farmers: One day specially allocated to cover areas of core competence of women farmers in programmes of All India Radio and Doordarshan.

[48] https://economictimes.indiatimes.com/news/economy/policy/government-to-fix-minimum-wage-rate-farm-worker-to-get-rs-350-a-day/articleshow/55120666.cms?utm_source=contentofinterest&utm_medium=text&utm_campaign=cppst, accessed on 15th December, 2020.

Procurement of Agricultural Machinery and Equipment: Different types of subsidies have been introduced for women to buy agricultural machinery, e.g. tractors and power tillers.

Integrated Scheme for Agricultural Marketing: This Scheme allows 33.33% subsidy (on capital cost) for women as compared to 25% for men.

National Mission for Sustainable Agriculture (NMSA): Under this scheme, at least 50% of the allocation is to be utilized for small, marginal farmers, of which at least 30% are women beneficiaries/farmers.

Sub-Mission on Agricultural Mechanization (SMAM): Under this scheme, training programmes on gender-friendly equipment for women farmers are to be conducted by farm machinery training and testing institutes.

National Organic Farming Project, Vision 2025 : In January 2016, the Ministry of Commerce and Industry urged the government to show "total commitment" and promote organic farming. Organic farming has the potential to generate a revenue of INR 45,000 crore per annum and more (Aggarwal 2018). There is an urgent need to increase the coverage area under organic farming. Unfortunately, today, the organic sector gets barely $500 crores. Moreover, the National Organic Farming Projects (the Paramparagat Krishi Vikas Yojana) and the Mission Organic Value Chain Development for North Eastern Region cover very little ground. The area under organic farming is 23.02 lakh hectares, a mere 1.27% of the total cultivation land in India (181.95 million hectares) (Upadhyay 2020). The need of the hour is to switch priorities and subsidies from chemical to organic farming as shown by the State of Sikkim (the World's First Organic State and the Gold Medallist Winner of the UN Future Policy Awards).[49]

An "inclusive and transformative agricultural policy" is the call of the day. The Economic Survey 2017–2018 speculates that the growing rural-to-urban migration by men creates the possibilities of "feminization" in the agriculture sector, with an increasing number of women in multiple roles as cultivators, entrepreneurs, and labourers. Therefore, the following measures have been taken to ensure mainstreaming of women in the agriculture sector[50]:

- Earmarking at least 30% of the budget allocation for women beneficiaries in all ongoing schemes/programmes and development activities.
- Initiating women-centric activities to ensure that the benefits of various beneficiary-oriented programmes/schemes reach them.
- Focusing on women self-help group (SHG) to connect them to micro-credit through capacity-building activities and to provide information and ensure their representation in different decision-making bodies.

[49] Sonam Taneja, Sikkim is 100% organic! Take a second look; see the website under the URL https://www.downtoearth.org.in/news/agriculture/organic-trial-57517.

[50] Growing Migration by Men is Causing "Feminisation" of Agriculture Sector, Says Economic Survey; see the website under the URL https://pib.gov.in/Pressreleaseshare.aspx?PRID=1518099, accessed on 21st March, 2020, at 8.54 PM.

- Recognizing the critical role of women in agriculture, the Ministry of Agriculture and Farmers Welfare has declared the 15th of October of every year as Women Farmer's Day.

Interestingly, in case of Nandini Sundar vs. the State of Chhattisgarh,[51] the Supreme Court of India has aptly observed:

> "the State is the provision of Security to all its citizens, without violating human dignity. This would necessarily imply the undertaking of tasks that would prevent the emergence of great dissatisfaction, and disaffection, on account of the manner and mode of extraction, and distribution, of natural resources and organization of social action, its benefits and costs."

The Court also stated, "Policies that run counter to that essential truth are necessarily destructive of national unity and integrity". The term farmer has been defined as an individual engaged in the production of farming produce by self or by hired labour or otherwise, and includes the Farmer Producer Organisation.[52] Recently, the Supreme Court of India, in August 2020, through Justice Arun Mishra, clarified that the daughter also has the right to parental property in an undivided Hindu family. The Court stated that if one person has one daughter and one son, and if the person had died before the amendment to the Hindu Succession Act, 2005, the daughters have an equal share over the property. Even if the daughters who have already been deprived of an equal share of their deceased father's property, they also have the equal right to claim.[53]

8.8 Conclusion and Suggestions

The government must adjust its policy on the various facets of livelihood activities so that the benefits of such investments reach the groups that need them. It requires to have tailored services and targeted delivery, including gender-sensitive and pro-poor targeting. This will, in turn, support better, more sustainable agriculture and, in the end, a better landscape for all. At this, the following may be recommended:

- The unequal division of labour and inequitable workloads are central issues to be considered in developing policies and programs. Sensitizing people toward sharing of rural women's domestic workload by the male members of the families.
- Promotion of research for the development of labour-saving technologies and practices in agricultural activities.
- Attempt to corporatize the sector and extend binding the sector through legislation in line with the Plantation Labour Act, 1951, and the division of roles on the basis of gender following the model as described under the Factories Act, 1948.

---

[51] (2011) 7 SCC 547 (Paragraph 25).

[52] Section 2(e) of the Farmers (Empowerment and Protection) Agreement on Price Assurance and Farm Services Act, 2020.

[53] Vineeta Sharma v. Rakesh Sharma (2020) 9 SCC 1.

- Compulsory introduction of maternity benefits for which a cess may be introduced in the pattern of construction cess from the purchaser/consumers of crops through the vendors of such crops. The local governments must be activated in this regard.
- Compulsory visits at sites of agricultural production by the officials of the department of labour if the land is under corporate farming or contract farming. Anganwadi workers may be engaged in the collection of data regarding the health of the farmers.

The Bhamashah Model[54] in the state of Rajasthan may be followed to extend the benefits to farm women. Supply of potable drinking water at the doorstep of the farmers and a proper irrigation system should be developed, extending the coverage of more land under irrigation.

Introduction of a system is needed involving the local government in the process of renting agricultural land to safeguard the interests of the owners, bargadars (tenants), and local agricultural labourers attached to such land, if any, while dealing with the corporate entities.

There should be stable procurement of a variety of crops by the government and declared MSP with a component of remunerative price (at least 50% of the price of crops) for each crop the farmers produce. Here, we require to be alert as to the benefit that must not end up benefiting traders instead of farmers to distort markets like Madhya Pradesh's Bhavantar Bhugtan Yojana.[55]

Unfortunately, in many states of India, a farm labourer does not get wages[56] as per the Minimum Wages Act, 1948. Just like any labourer, a farm labourer is entitled to a living wage as directed by the Constitution of India, and the local government must ensure the same. At this, the relevance of the Act becomes questionable.

---

[54]This scheme had trifold objective of financial inclusion, women empowerment, and effective delivery of benefits. Bank accounts and Bhamashah cards had to be made in the name of female head of the house. The card could be used for transferring all cash benefits directly to the bank accounts, which required biometric authentication as the platform of authentication.

[55]The Bhavantar Bhugtan Yojana (BBY) was launched in October 2017 in MP, which intends farmers who register under the scheme are compensated only if their selling price (SP) is lower than the government-set minimum support price (MSP). The actual amount of compensation or deficiency payment made to a farmer is determined by a modal price. (*Modal price is a marker of average market price within the state and markets outside the state where the commodity is traded.*)

[56]According to Section 2(h) of the Minimum Wages Act, 1948, the term wages means all remuneration capable of being expressed in terms of money, which would if the terms of the contract of employment expressed or implied were fulfilled be payable to a person employed in respect of his employment or of work done in such employment and includes house rent allowance but does not include (i) the value of any house accommodation supply of light water medical attendance or any other amenity or any service excluded by general or special order of the appropriate government; (ii) any contribution paid by the employer to any person fund or provident fund or under any scheme of social insurance; (iii) any travelling allowance or the value of any travelling concession; (iv) any sum paid to the person employed to defray special expenses entailed on him by the nature of his employment; or (v) any gratuity payable on discharge.

Strengthening land tenure rights among poor rural women farmers is a must. If a woman cannot enjoy control over land, she cannot be in charge of her own livelihood or destiny.

Since women enjoy significantly less access to the market, the marketing of crops through self-help groups (SHGs) can be a good vehicle in this regard. The SHGs must involve themselves to ensure the smooth participation of women in agricultural activities, access to market information, and agricultural knowledge; they must sensitize the male family members to participate in domestic household work and allow women participation in the decision-making process for farm management activities.

References

Aggarwal M (2018) Andhra Pradesh's push for zero budget natural farming inspires others, Conserving Agro-biodiversity, Environment and Health, 27 September, 2018, see the website under the URL: https://india.mongabay.com/2018/09/andhra-pradeshs-push-for-zero-budget-natural-farming-inspires-others/. Accessed 16 Nov 2020

Bardasi E, Wodon Q (2010) Working long hours and having no choice: time poverty in Guinea. Fem Econ 16(3):45

Belarmino K, Schaedel M (2019) Seeds of inequality: women in sustainable agriculture, See the website under the URL https://www.openglobalrights.org/seeds-of-inequality-women-in-sustainable-agriculture/. Accessed 11 Sep 2020, at 2.37 PM

Bockel L, Tinlot M, Branca G (2012) The carbon footprint of the agricultural growth project (AGP) in Ethiopia. FAO Obtenido desde. http://www.fao.org/fileadmin/templates/ex_act/pdf/case_studies/draft_aout2012-clear.pdf

Das A (2020) Trends in wage rates in rural India. https://fas.org.in/trends-in-wage-rates-in-rural-india/. Accessed 11 Nov 2020

Deo S (2020) Millions of Indian farmers benefit from formalized land leasing law, see the website under the URL: https://news.trust.org/item/20191024103311-pc9w6/. Accessed 14 Sep 2020

Doss C, SOFA Team (2011) The role of women in agriculture. Food and Agriculture Organization of the United Nations

Ignaciuk A, Tun C (2019) Achieving agricultural sustainability depends on gender equality. Washington, DC, International Food Policy Research Institute

La Vina, A., Fransen, L., Faeth, P., & Kurauchi, Y. (2007). Agricultural subsidies, poverty, and the environment

Mohan T (2020a) A field of her own, See the website under the URL: https://indianexpress.com/article/opinion/columns/indian-women-farmers-agriculture-sector-patriarchy-land-ownership-4781311/. Accessed 12 Oct 2020 at 2.39 PM

Mohan V (2020b) Suicides of agricultural labourers rise by 18%: NCRB report, See the website under the URL: http://timesofindia.indiatimes.com/articleshow/87344897.cms?utm_source=contentofinterest&utm_medium=text&utm_campaign=cppst. Accessed 21 Oct 2020

Raj MK, Aruna D (2008) Women farmers of India. NBT India

Raney T (2011) The state of food and agriculture. Women in agriculture: closing the gap for development, 2

Robinson-Pant A (2016) Learning knowledge and skills for agriculture to improve rural livelihoods. UNESCO Publishing

Sachs JD (2012) From millennium development goals to sustainable development goals. Lancet 379(9832):2206–2211

Settle W (2020) Ecosystem management in agriculture: principles and application of the ecosystem approach, See the website under the URL: http://www.fao.org/3/Y4586E/y4586e12.htm. Accessed 20 Oct 2020, at 2.32 PM.

Sharma YS (2020) Government rolls out a model act to legalize land leasing, see the website under the URL: https://economictimes.indiatimes.com/news/economy/policy/government-rolls-out-a-model-act-to-legalize-land-leasing/articleshow/51808345.cms?from=mdr. Accessed 11 Dec 2020

Sunder S (2020) India economic survey 2018: farmers gain as agriculture mechanisation speeds up, but more R&D needed, see the website under the URL: https://www.financialexpress.com/budget/india-economic-survey-2018-for-farmers-agriculture-gdp-msp/1034266/. Accessed 22 Dec 2020

Swaminathan MS (2011) The women farmers' entitlements bill. See the website under the see the website under the URL: https://dillichalo.in/the-women-farmers-entitlements-bill-2011/. Accessed 24 Dec 2020

Upadhyay V (2020) Back to basics, Uttarakhand to criminalize usage of chemical fertilizers, see the website under the URL: https://www.newindianexpress.com/nation/2019/nov/15/back-to-basics-uttarakhand-to-criminalize-usage-of-chemical-fertilisers-2061831.html. Accessed 25 Oct 2020

Dr. Diganta Biswas is currently working as the Secretary, Postgraduate Council, Raiganj University, Raiganj, WB, and is enriched with the experience of teaching totalling more than 12 years at institutions like Department of Law, University of North Bengal, and School of Law, Christ University, Bangalore, Karnataka, in different capacities who has completed his Ph.D. from the University of North Bengal. The title of his thesis is "Impact of corporatisation of agriculture on farmers' right to land and seed protection in West Bengal during 2000–2010". He has more than 30 publications in his credit with a book entitled "Eminent Domain and Private Property".

Dr. Bhaswati Saha is currently working as an Assistant Professor, Department of Sociology, Kalyani Mahavidyalaya, Kalyani, WB, and has teaching experience of more than 10 years in different capacities. She completed her Ph.D. with a topic entitled "Nature of Participation of Women in agriculture in plains of the district of Darjeeling" from the University of North Bengal. She has a good number of publications in her credit.

Chapter 9
Sustainability of Weavers Communities of West Bengal: Investigating the Role of Public Policy Interventions

Samhita Chaudhuri and Susmita Bhattacharyya

9.1 Introduction

The concept of sustainability, in general, is related to the communities. Communities sustain on renewable and nonrenewable resources. Health, well-being, security, safety, societal life, economy, cultural life, and livelihoods ideally need a fresh and pure environment. Handloom constitutes one of the crucial craft-based sectors in India, characterized by traditional technology, a long historical legacy, enriched artistry, and hereditarily transmitted skills. However, despite its importance in the employment sector, it declined in terms of the number of weavers from 65.5 lakh workers and 34.87 looms in 1995–1996 to 43.3 lakh workers and 23.77 lakh handlooms in 2009–2010 (third Handloom Census, 2009–10). Outdated skills of the weavers, lack of training, village-based morphology, and inability to adapt to the changing global market are major reasons, along with low-priced products of power looms and uncertain export market, the most cited reasons for this decline (Menon 1999; Mukund and Syama Sundari 2001; Solanki 2008, Subrahmanya 2011, Bhattacharya and Sen 2018). In the post-liberalized period, there was an estimated engagement of 64.37 lakh people in 25.75 lakh power looms in 2016–2017 (Bhattacharya and Sen 2018).

More than four million weavers make their livelihood in connection to handloom industries in India; among them, around half are living below the poverty line, facing disposition between the prospect and real suffering in the context of the contemporary sociocultural scenario. Development Commissioner of Handicrafts,

S. Chaudhuri
Department of Geography, Bijoy Krishna Girls' College (Affiliated to University of Calcutta), Howrah, West Bengal, India

S. Bhattacharyya (✉)
Department of Sociology, University of Calcutta, Kolkata, West Bengal, India

M. Mishra et al. (eds.), *Public Policies and Sustainable Development in Post-Reform India*, New Frontiers in Regional Science: Asian Perspectives 71,
https://doi.org/10.1007/978-981-99-3696-0_9

Government of India (4th All India Handloom Census, 2019–2020 (n.d.)), mentioned that crafts or handicrafts are "both objects of utility and objects of decoration" and are defined as "items made by hand, often with the use of simple tools, and that are generally artistic and/or traditional in nature" (4th All India Handloom Census, 2019–2020 (n.d.)). Regardless of the production of high-value-added products, skilled labor artisans of Bengal's handloom industry work within the periphery of the "informal sector" under an insecure work environment in addition to an ill-paid segment due to subsidiary position in the value chain (Scrase 2003). Handloom products are artistically recognized as the cultural essence of the glorious heritage of Bengal with an enthusiastic manifestation of creative designs with respect to the niche market, which attracts affluently biased for buying these precious items. Henceforth, there should be an incessant journey of remaking human agency in the conceptual framing of "technoscape" and "financescape" as Appadurai (2002, pp. 46–64) expressed both of the concepts in the context of West Bengal's silk weaving industry. According to the Handloom Census of India, 2009–2010 (3rd Handloom Census, 2009–2010 (n.d.)), about 38.47 lakh adult people are recorded as handloom weavers and workers who worked in 23.77 lakh handlooms in the country. Out of the 38.47 lakh adult weavers and allied workers, about 78% are women. Alongside, the classification finds that around 10% belong to the Scheduled Caste (SC), 18% are Scheduled Tribe (ST), and 45% are from Other Backward Caste (OBC). However, the Indian handloom industry is providing a livelihood for womenfolk, sometimes direct engagement in the production system as well as employing them as marginal workers during peak season (Shazli and Abdul 2014; Rao et al. 2018; Reddy 2019). About 82% of handloom working households are enumerated as weavers involving at least one member engaged in the weaving activity. Approximately 53% of handloom workers are included in commercial production, with 16% of households as a combination of domestic and commercial purposes (Shukla 2011).

Handloom sector records as the second major provider of employment to the people, next to agriculture, in India (Report of Ministry of External Affairs, Government of India. Sep 22. 2020). It is vibed within the country and abroad due to gorgeous designs, motifs, and color combinations. These traditional craft industries passed through many *ups and downs* with the sentiments of regionality, cultural viewpoints of the creators, and political patronage. However, after independence, planners and policymakers realized the importance of the traditional industry sector and adopted the path of modern industrialization to improve national economic conditions on a blended economic platform of state-centered planning. Here, regional specificity in cultural artistry got highlighted; thus, state-centered development revolved around handloom and handicraft specializations. The government considered taking importance by setting up Khadi and Village Industries Commission, Handicrafts Board, Handloom Board, Coir Board, Central Silk Board, etc. by the 1950s and 1960s with the primary objective of developing and empowering rural people (Baishya 2019; Raihan 2010; Mishra et al. 2021).

The budgetary allocation of funds for the upgradation of handloom agencies under various schemes has been a new addition in this regard. Some important schemes are National Handloom Development Programme (NHDP), the Comprehensive Handloom Cluster Development Scheme (CHCDS), Handloom Weavers' Comprehensive Welfare Scheme (HWCWS), and Yarn Supply Scheme (YSS).

Human life and the environment are closely linked, and due to increasing industrial growth and technological advancement, people have exploited natural resources more than before, which has caused environmental damage and resource depletion and accentuated adverse global climatic changes. Hence, a way should be identified to reduce environmental degradation in the contemporary period to secure the well-being of every community during the present and for future generations as well. The World Commission on Environment and Development set three aspects in this regard—economic, social, and environmental—and identified four key areas—sustainable production and consumption, climate change and energy usage, scarcity of natural resources, and sustainable communities (Report of the World Commission on Environment and Development 1987). Maintaining existing urban resources through community culture and traditions is the vital aim of the latter one. In every production process, the maximum attention is always on lowering the production cost and increasing efficiency (Asmah et al. 2015; Kovács 2018; Mondal 2022). However, manufacturers, designers, and retailers often neglect the environmental impact of such discourses of production.

This study analysis will allow researchers to go beyond the gap between weavers and the rest of society and the interactive ensemble of related social groups, technologies, institutions, and knowledge practices that constitute the weaving culture of West Bengal. As most related studies focus on the geographical nature of places and economic and industrial aspects of handloom industry, this study ventures to identify the socio-economic aspects of heritage weaves of Bengal in regards of the contemporary condition of weaving community and proving some policy implications for upgrading the present scenario. This study investigates the dichotomy of application of indigenous knowledge and modern technology in the production process from the respondent's response, which makes it a unique one. This study also opens a wide range of arena for further research in the field of handloom industry of West Bengal in general and Santipur cotton textile industry in particular.

9.2 Objectives and Methodology

The broad objectives of the present study are to explore the nature and specificity of weavers in the state of West Bengal in India and to highlight their transformation trends in the present context. This handloom industry in West Bengal provides widest avenue for employment opportunities in rural areas. The reservoir of handloom silk is concentrated in some states of India like North-Eastern states together accounting for more than 60% handloom households followed by West Bengal with more than 4 lakh constituting about 15% (3rd Handloom Census, 2009–2010 (n.d.)). In the share of female adult (18 years and above) handloom workers among all states of India, West Bengal's share is the second highest after Assam (3rd Handloom Census, 2009–2010 (n.d.)). Bengal handloom is famous for its rich heritage, unique craftsmanship, exclusive artwork made by hand, and diversity of products on a variety of fabrics, which enjoy the artistry through the hand of skilled weavers of Bengal. This study revolves around the handloom weavers of this state as the products are now popular worldwide for its intricate weaving and colorful appearance. The popular products range from Murshidabad silk, Baluchari weaving, Kantha embroidery, and Santipur and Dhaniakhali cotton sarees. Santipur is assigned for its glorious tradition in handloom products, especially cotton sarees, which is famous not only in Bengal but also all over India.

The study is based on primary data collected from Santipur, Nadia district of West Bengal. The sample size is 50. The study also depends on secondary sources like books, journals, blogs, and newspaper articles.

Handloom products of Bengal as art forms can be expressed as an exquisite platform of words and tales for the articulation of the cultural heritage of India. The glorious heritage of artworks is associated with the livelihood pattern and prospect of weavers living in West Bengal, with special reference to the Santipur cotton textile sector in the Nadia district. For the matter of persistence, weavers of this district have adopted sustainability, flexibility, conversion, and product diversification concerning their sociocultural creativity, indigenous knowledge system for permanence, and skill management through the hereditary system (Parthasarathy 1999). Multidimensionality in form, content, and technicalities is the way to achieve sustenance in the world of fashion and design to a global extent.

The work of the weavers of Santipur as a form of folk art with enriched cultural presence and hereditary value can be linked with the process of glocalization for the powerful existence of regional and national platforms. This sector is dominated by an intersection of several steps of productive activities with the prominent presence of stakeholders. The chain of activities involves a series of subdivisions within the sphere of production involving the initial raw materials to the finished products. The mutual interdependence of several hierarchies in the production system ultimately creates a value chain. Institutional market and strategic undertaking of handicraft production should coincide with the demand drive for exploration of the livelihood of weavers of Bengal. The sector is focused on human labor power with respect to the energy-intensive hereditary skill of production. Traditional glory of Indian cultural products is merged with assimilating power of "Appropriation, Collaboration, Provenance, and Identity" (Lunde 2018), considering the international platform. In general, the outline of motifs and designs is drawn in a dark color like black, blue, or red thread. Motifs are dominated by scenes from rural daily life like flowers, animals, birds, trees, and sceneries; another trend is prominent in the sphere of artwork of the products, which has a focus on historical figures. This natural fiber-made ordinary textile product is appropriate for daily uses, whereas costly intricate designs with a gorgeous presentation in mixed base materials are related to ritualistic expression and ceremonial existence.

9.3 Review of Literature

While comprehending any "handmade object and its maker," significant areas of concern may be the location of the creation, the values of the creator, the value chain economy, and the processes of transition. The art of embroidery was perceived as a social activity due to group involvement in a single piece of art. In analyzing stitch and artwork, the socio-economic patterning of geo-cultural sole in production takes a significant role within the transformed frame of cultural sustainability. Bengal's handloom works are recognized as crafts that form the cultural identity of the whole eastern part of India, preserving the age-old folk tradition in the context of individual artistic performance. To Kundu and Chakrabarti (2008), community collaboration and surveillance, mutual faith, and trust take a significant place in the processes of organizing different layers of hierarchical and nonhierarchical contracts, especially within the informal sector. The existence of numerous strata of hierarchies involves intermediaries engaged within the domain of Bengal's handloom with special reference to *Kantha* work.

In the cultural map of Bengal, the cotton textile product is documented as one of the precious handloom products with gorgeous as well as artistic propensity venturing the national boundary. With a specific bearing on cultural identity in developing countries, artisanal industries can add a new dimension to the sphere of economic development as well as a sustainable employment opportunity (Nash 1993; Liebl and Roy 2004). To Fowler (2004), as an effect of mechanization, the livelihood of the weavers is considerably endangered by commercialization and product diversification. The artistry of the artisans is consistently coupled with recent skills and techniques, and hence the use of technical know-how can neither be related to the categorization of "traditional industry," nor can the workers be acknowledged as "indigenous people." The concept of "*lokavidya*" is the knowledge of the common people proposed by Sahasrabudhey and Sahasrabudhey (2001), where integration of skills is linked with untrained as well as uneducated, but with the access of indigenous knowledge, they can attempt for transcending the limited local periphery of regional artwork. For example, in "Baluchari of Mallabhum," Das and Mukhopadhyay (1995) engraved a detailed analysis of the sociocultural context and economic dimension of Baluchari weaving. The eternal dialectics between the handloom and power loom has been considered the central focus of their discussion. The issue of modernization in the textile industry of Bengal was highlighted by Chandra (2004) in the 90th chapter of his book "Mallabhum Bishnupur" in describing the legend of Baluchari and Swanachari of Bishnupur. Banerjee and Chakrabarti (2020) emphasized the beginning of industrial production with the help of power loom as a double-edged sword to the handloom producers. The weaving techniques of Bengal utilizing the wooden pit looms have persisted unchanged with minimum modification in the changed context of rapid technological progression.

9.4 Nature and Specificity of Weavers of West Bengal

Heterogeneity characterizes the West Bengal handloom sector with an emphasis on ongoing transformation through the initiation of the power loom. In the contemporary economic order, there is a tendency for several artisans to exit, connecting workers and small traders from the sector with the consequential descending stress on earnings. Another possibility is seen among them where there is anticipation for adopting competitive strategies for persistence in the market, including exaggeration in searching for uniqueness of the handloom products through originality in design, upgrading in the excellence of product, and technology development. Changes in lifestyles and market scenarios illustrate that handloom weaving is no more a feasible profession. The production has been reducing, although there is demand in the domestic market for handloom products. Contemporary handloom products are currently utilizing dyed polyester filament yarn and blended yarns. The use of such yarns instead of natural fiber and the use of machined power to weave an astounding assortment of clothes and handloom products have played bewilderment with regional identities. Members of the weaving community are enthusiastic to carry on their long-established weaving art with an aspiration of a robust support system to intensify production and distribution strategy with the intention of better livelihood by practicing their heritage craft. The youngsters of their family are familiar with the heritage craft since childhood. The younger generation is more educated and has been unenthusiastic about accepting weaving as a profession mostly. It is an urgent necessity to attract them through a variety of awareness programs.

People related to the handloom industry in India may be in different categories based on their work performance during the production process—weavers, investors, intermediaries, and customers. Weavers are the makers who create new objects by applying their inherited skills in rural or semirural living conditions. They apply their traditional knowledge, which they have achieved from earlier generations, about the weaving process. In India, with a rich cultural tradition, rural weavers with a storehouse of traditional knowledge have the capability to expertise in this field. The weaving process takes its shape with the supply of raw materials to the weavers. For this purpose, weavers depend on cooperatives, local suppliers, and sometimes certain government agencies (like Khadi and Village Industries Commission). From this point, weavers may be categorized as independent or dependent.

Independent weavers have the advantage of controlling the whole production process by their own. In contrast, the dependent weavers are in an unprivileged condition, as master weavers or intermediaries take all the opportunity and control the terms and conditions of payment for the finished product after completing the rigorous process done by the weavers. Dependency, thus, is due to the payment structure to the weavers in accordance with the *ups* and *downs* of the market price. Independent weavers are also direct sellers, while dependent weavers depend on other bodies to sell the produce (Fig. 9.1 and Table 9.1). When any intermediaries

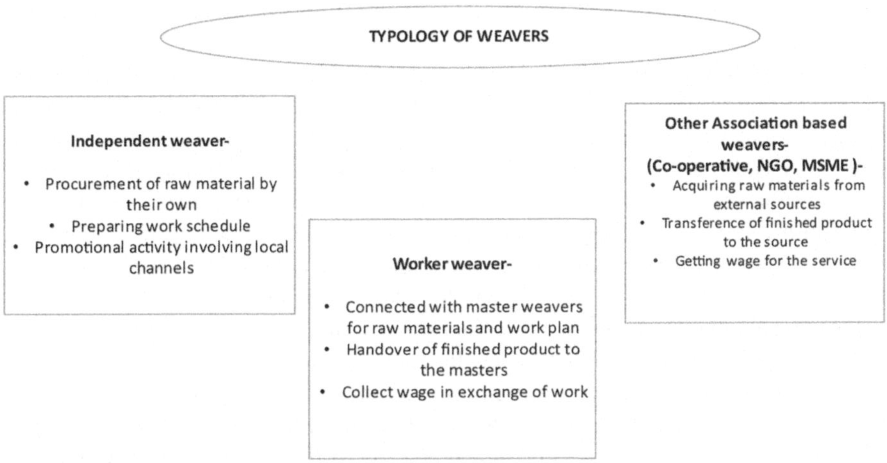

Fig. 9.1 Types of weavers. (Source: Prepared by the authors)

Table 9.1 Classification of weavers

Type	Details	Characteristics for production		Characteristics during selling
1	Independent weaver	Acquiring the raw materials by own		Directly sell their products to buyers and earn money directly
2	Dependent weaver	Depend on external source for supply of yarn	On master weaver	Master weavers, who sell the product and give money to weaver
			On middlemen	Middlemen sell the products and, after keeping their share, give a small portion of selling amount to the weaver
			On government agencies	The cooperative society, from where weavers take the selling amount at government prices

(**Source**: Prepared by the authors)

are involved in the process, they are more concerned about their share and exploit the psychology of weaver.

Another way of categorizing weavers is based on their skill and knowledge of weaving intricate designs—master weavers and helpers. Master weavers sometimes own the looms and prepare attractive designs as per the requirements of customers and the demand of the market. To some extent, training is provided to master weavers to upgrade their skills and knowledge from different governmental or private organizations under various schemes and strategies. Master weavers are necessary to become well equipped to keep pace with the demand of the contemporary globalized world by improving their design pattern, fabric selection, and creation of the end product. The unskilled village people are called helpers who assist the master weaver during the production process at the loom. They have to abide by the rules of the master weaver during the preparation of design cards, different types of works, and information about the market demand and customer taste.

The third categorization approach is based on genders—men and women—while the fourth one is based on participation—main and marginal weavers. In general, women workers who are engaged in the weaving process generally work for silk yarn processing, dyeing, and other additional work and mainly join hands during peak season and as supporting hands. This cottage industry offers women the opportunity to work in their homely atmosphere after completing their domestic chores, and another important feature is that they usually lack direct access to wages as weaving is done inside their household. The Third National Handloom Census (2011) reveals that women constituted about 78% of the weaving community.

With this backdrop of inheritance, the Indian handloom sector conventionally exhibits the cultural legacy concerning innovation in pioneering designs and motifs. The Mughal period in India was recognized as the initial phase of the handloom sector in India with a focus on the amalgamation of distinct cultural inheritance in terms of geographical specificity for the existence of finished products. Indian handloom sector emerged in several regions with the support of emperors, including nawabs, maharajas, and rajas (Dasgupta 2000). A considerable part of rural people depends on the handloom industry to ensure livelihood as the most significant and the chief cottage industrial sector (Annual Report, 2002–2003, Ministry of Textiles (n.d.); Kumar and Kundu 2017; Mustaquim et al. 2018). The Indian Government has recognized the handloom sector as a rural enterprise with the inclusion of a variety of schemes for improving the finished product (FICCI Report on Indian Handloom Industry 2019).

9.5 Trends of Transformation

The noted transformation of the world on a considerable scale was marked in Bengal on the platform of traditionality in the contemporary era. Though some handloom crafts or industries were unable to continue in their own traditional way (Roy 2007) of their economic persistence, mechanization has brought to the forefront the coexistence of indigenous knowledge in a modern version. The factory system and expansion of trade and commerce on a global scale should be viewed as responsible factors for the probable destruction of the traditional craft industries in several regions of India. In contemporary India, the rapid rate of urban growth and subsequent sociocultural and economic processes brought principal changes in the handloom sector. Design-intensive crafts and skilled handloom weavers, especially in cotton textile weaving, had to confront the threat of mechanized power loom products in the periphery of technological adjustment. Sometimes, the generational transfer of indigenous knowledge and regional specificity became a severe issue in community sustainability. Ramaswamy (2002) pointed out that unavoidable factors of consumerism resulted in negative impacts like starvation deaths, suicides, and a sense of alienation among the surviving weavers.

Table 9.2 Focus on indigenous knowledge (based on the response of respondents)

Application of indigenous knowledge	Complete dependence	Partial dependence	Complete avoidance
Number (%)	20 (40%)	25 (50%)	5 (10%)

Source: Prepared by the authors

Table 9.3 Relationship with technology (based on the response of respondents)

Role of technology	Supportive	Non-supportive	Mixed role
Number (%)	40 (80%)	6 (12%)	4 (8%)

Source: Prepared by the authors

Table 9.4 Medium of production (based on the response of respondents)

Production process	Hand made	Machine made	Mixed
Number (%)	5 (10%)	40 (80%)	5 (10%)

Source: Prepared by the authors

Table 9.5 Reason of shifting towards new mode (On Respondent's Responses)

Reasons	**Cost**	**Time**	**Demand**
Number (%)	42 (84%)	6(12%)	2(4%)

Source: Prepared by the authors

A primary survey done on the Santipur weavers' community reveals the fact about the transformation of their industry. Table 9.2 focuses on several issues related to their production intricacy. It is revealed from the survey that the majority of the weavers are in favor of partial dependence on indigenous knowledge in textile products (Table 9.3), and the majority of them opine that technology plays a supportive role for them (Table 9.4). Alongside this, the preference for machine-made products is clearly noticed in this context (Table 9.5). Interestingly, cost-effectiveness distinctly appears as the principal reason for shifting the weavers towards newer modes.

9.6 Creativity and Artistic Representation of Weavers Engaged in the Cotton Textile Sector of West Bengal

In the Santipur saree weaving process, the majority of work is done by males due to the prevalence of intricate weaving techniques, intense demand for production, and strenuous workload (Ganguly and Ganguly 2015). It can be represented as a distinctive as well as an exquisite illustration of intricate motifs of the aesthetic exhibition. Typically, common motifs include gods and goddesses; animals like ducks, fishes, and peacocks; and floral and geometric patterns; in reality, the focus of design and motifs can be associated with anything and everything in the context of the creators' imagination. Textile-related artifacts can be associated with differential techniques, and patterns of weaving surfaced by the practical application of indigenous knowledge and age-old hereditary traditions. For the sake of conversion, traditional artwork is attempting to resurge following new adoption of production techniques, marketing strategy, and ongoing trends of customer preference. Gangotra (1998) opined that motifs and designs are weaved or embodied through embroidery irrespective of gender-based collection of fashion items.

The aim of the artwork has a focus on the narration of a tale involving the emotion and expression of the artisan. Mostly, the weavers are women, inclusive of all classes as the work including leisure time. In wealthy families, exquisite cotton saree with traditional artistry is considered a heritage gift for the next generation, whereas cotton sarees are also linked with daily necessities for the middle and lower middle class. Some of the regional customs become genuinely significant for making this artwork, and the workers related are recognized as "home-based workers."

In the new phase of commercialization, the traditional belief system has undergone a thorough change—artisans have to work the whole night to meet the demand pressure of the market. In this age of post-liberalization, the heritage art of handloom work should venture for new tastes of rejuvenation with flexible adaptations in capturing the market segment for creating a balance between aesthetic presence and rigid market struggle. Hence, the Indian heritage product—"cotton sarees of Bengal"—can be recognized as a global sustainable product not only for the weavers' community but for the artisans also.

9.7 Government-Aided Welfare Schemes for Weavers

The effect of economic liberalization, intense competition with power-loom, emergence of cheaper materials, rising credit prices, shifts in customer tastes, and alternative employment have created a challenge for weavers in the handloom sectors of the whole country. The Ministry of Textiles of the Government of India is implementing several schemes to revive and develop handloom sectors in different parts of the country (Annual Report 2017–2018, Min. of Textiles, GOI (n.d.)). Some of these are Handloom Weavers' Comprehensive Welfare Scheme (HWCWS), National Handloom Development Programme (NHDP), Block Level Cluster Projects, Comprehensive Handloom Cluster Development Scheme (CHCDS), Yarn Supply Scheme (YSS), Handloom Weavers Comprehensive Welfare Scheme, and many more. For example, HWCWS provides accidental and disability insurance coverage to handloom weavers/workers. Other schemes also provide various measures to improve the situation of weavers' communities. Besides, the Ministry of Textiles has signed Memorandums of Understanding with Open University and Open Schooling to secure educational facilities for the weavers and their families by offering continuing education programs through accessible and flexible learning opportunities. Secondary and senior secondary level education with specialized subjects on design, marketing, business development, and other supports is offered through distance learning mode not only to weavers but also to their children for career progression. Women learners belonging to handloom weavers' families of Scheduled Caste (SC), Scheduled Tribe (ST), and Below Poverty Line (BPL) categories are supported by providing reimbursement of some amount of the fee towards admission in various courses (Compendium Of Handloom Schemes (2021), Dutton et al. (2004), Report on Handloom Weavers, Ministry of Textiles (2019), India Handloom Brand on the National Handloom Development Corporation Ltd. Website (n.d.))

Another important initiative was the Handloom Marketing Assistance, which provides a marketing platform and financial assistance to the handloom agencies/ weavers to sell their products directly to the consumers. In 2015, India Handloom Brand was launched by the hon'ble Prime Minister of India for the branding of high-quality handloom products, with the goal of increasing the production of niche handloom products with high-quality, eco-friendly raw materials, authentic traditional designs, and environment-friendly production process (Kaushik and Jain 2015).[1]

Thus, numerous policies and schemes are trying to help the handloom sector to sustain a standard handloom fabric output level and improve the income level for the weavers, and to manage the negative situation (Shyamsundarachary and Sreenivas 2017). In the state of West Bengal, the pivotal role of marketing handloom products is vested to the West Bengal State Handloom Weavers' Cooperative Society Ltd. (*Tantuja*) and Paschim Banga Resham Shilpi Samabay Mahasangha Ltd. (*Resham Shilpi*). They obtain handloom products from individual weavers as well as primary weavers' cooperative societies and sell their products from their retail outlets as well. The West Bengal Handloom Circuit Development Scheme (state sector) and the Integrated Skills Development Scheme (central sponsored) provided skill development training to 96,115 weavers and allied workers at the cost of Rs. 44.11 crores. During 2016–2017, 22,280 (cumulative 65,821) weavers and allied workers have been reported training under West Bengal Handloom Circuit (Annual Administrative Report, 2016–2017 of Directorate of Textiles).

9.8 Conclusion

To maintain the sustainable nature of the textile industry, the Indian Government emphasized the textile sector as the principal aspect. In the contemporary world, the eco-friendly nature of textile materials and the sustenance of weavers depending on this industry require the creation of environment-friendly products. They should have the aptitude to contribute to the society holistically without obstructing

[1]National Handloom Development Corporation Ltd. Website, https://www.nhdc.org.in/internal.aspx?menuid=2&CatID=64 retrieved on 14/10/2022; Report posted by the Ministry of Textiles, 2019.

biodiversity. Therefore, the focal concern of each production unit is directed towards the appropriate management of natural resources. In the textile sector, from the processing of raw fiber to finished products, the same feature is being observed with a special focus on incorporating traditional knowledge and regional cultural essence from its commencement of the sector. The Indian textile sector, in general, and handloom products, in particular, Indian heritage products, provide a livelihood to the most rural and semirural marginalized people as the country's most capable and significant resource-creating sector.

Sociocultural regeneration and all-inclusive alteration are now associated with the magnificent creation of the traditional Indian handloom industry. Artisans should have to be habituated with a prime concern on product diversification and transformation, amalgamating several items. The list of products of artisans engaged in handloom works encompasses various new entries in accordance with the demands in the market. Hence, they should be aware of the present and ongoing trends of the market scenario with a prospect of the expanding market, focusing on an elaborated supply chain. For a broader commercial setup, customers' preferences and choices are taken into significant consideration to turn it into a positive endeavor. Established shops, showrooms (private and government), fairs, exhibitions, and expos are popular platforms for the representation of Bengal's cotton textile products to passionate buyers. Major areas of this sector are the incorporation of indigenous knowledge of weaving communities and their economic viability during the entire course of production. The impact or reintroduction of the cooperative system to maintain the sustainability components of the weavers' community can be viewed as areas of future research. In reality, with the increasing incorporation of the sustainability concept in society, some changes are seen in the textile sector, where traditional modes of production with indigenous techniques of several communities are being used to produce sustainable textiles.

References

3rd Handloom Census of India 2009–10 (n.d.) Development Commissioner (Handlooms) Ministry of Textiles Government of India

4th All India Handloom Census 2019–2020 (n.d.). https://ruralindiaonline.org/en/library/resource/fourth-all-india-handloom-census-2019-2020/

Annual Report, 2002–03, Ministry of Textiles, government of India (n.d.) http://texmin.nic.in/pdf/ar03_c05.pdf

Annual Report 2017–18, Ministry of Textiles, Government of India (n.d.) http://texmin.nic.in/sites/default/files/AnnualReport2017-18%28English%29.pdf

Appadurai A (2002) Disjuncture and difference. In: Inda JX, Rosaldo R (eds) The anthropology of globalization: a reader. Blackwell Publishers, pp 46–64

Asmah AE, Okpattah V, Dominic H (2015) Improving the efficiency of the traditional loom. Eur J Basic Appl Sci 2(4)

Baishya D (2019) Empowering women weavers by up-gradation of handloom industry of Assam through microfinance. Int J Innov Technol Explor Eng 8(12):1511

Banerjee A, Chakrabarti G (2020) Exploring the effects of globalization on silk weaving tradition of Bishnupur region in West Bengal, India. oriental Anthropol 20:1–22

Bhattacharya R, Sen S (2018) Pride and prejudice: the condition of handloom weavers in West Bengal. Background $aper – 16, Azim Premji University

Chandra M (2004) Mallabhum Bishnupur. Sudhangshu Sekhar Dey, Dey's Publishing, Kolkata

Compendium Of Handloom Schemes-Office of the Development Commissioner for handlooms Ministry of Textiles, Govt. of India Udyog Bhawan, New Delhi, 2021

Das P, Mukhopadhyay A (1995) Baluchari of Mallabhum, National Institute of science, technology and development studies, "village artisans science" Project, Council of Scientific and Industrial Research (CSIR), Kenduadihi, Bankura, West Bengal

Dasgupta B (2000) Trade in pre-colonial Bengal. Soc Sci 28(5/6):47

Dutton et al (2004) Transforming enterprise. The economic and social implications of information technology. MIT Press, Cambridge

FICCI (2019) Report on Indian handloom industry. https://www.ficciflo.com/wp-content/uploads/2019/03/Indian-Handloom-Industry-Final.pdf

Fowler B (2004) Preventing counterfeit craft designs. In: Finger JM, Schuler PE (eds) Poor people's knowledge: promoting intellectual property in developing countries. World Bank and Oxford University Press, pp 113–131

Gangotra (1998) SanskritiEvem Kala (Hindi). Haryana Sahitya Acadami, Panchkula, pp 147–152

Ganguly M, Ganguly A (2015) A study on anthropometric measurement, socio-economic conditions & occupational health problems of baluchari shari weavers of Bishnupur International. J Current Res 7(07):17,722–17,729

Handloom Weavers, Ministry of Textiles (2019), Posted On: 13 Dec 2019. https://pib.gov.in/PressReleasePage.aspx?PRID=1596372. Accessed 14 Oct 2022

India Handloom Brand on the National Handloom Development Corporation Ltd. Website (n.d.). https://www.nhdc.org.in/internal.aspx?menuid=2&CatID=64. Accessed 14 Oct 2022

Kaushik N, Jain M (2015) Impact of government schemes on handloom weavers at Maheshwar, M.P. Int J Manag Stud II(1)

Kovács G (2018) Methods for efficiency improvement of production and logistic processes. Research Papers Faculty of Materials Science and Technology Slovak University of Technology 26:55–61. https://doi.org/10.2478/rput-2018-0006

Kumar D, Kundu D (2017) Origin and development of cottage industries in India: a study in pre-Independence era. Res Social Sci Technol 7:2249–2496

Kundu A, Chakrabarti S (2008) Some microeconomic aspects of informal sector enterprises: field-based evidence from West Bengal. Arthavijñāna J Gokhale Inst Politics Econ Poona (India):209–238. https://doi.org/10.21648/arthavij/2008/v50/i3/115432

Liebl M, Roy T (2004) Handmade in India: traditional craft skills in a changing world. In: Finger, Schuler (eds) Poor people's knowledge: promoting intellectual property in developing countries. World Bank and Oxford University Press, pp 53–73

Lunde MB (2018) Sustainability in marketing: a systematic review unifying 20 years of theoretical and substantive contributions (1997-2016). AMS Rev 8:85–110. https://doi.org/10.1007/s13162-018-0124-0

Menon ST (1999) Psychological empowerment: definition, measurement, and validation. Can J Behav Sci / Revue canadienne des sciences du comportement 31(3):161–164. https://doi.org/10.1037/h0087084

Mishra A, Das P, Sangma WSN (2021) Handlooms micro-enterprises for empowerment of women in Meghalaya. Int J Curr Microbiol App Sci 10(01):2493

Mondal A (2022) Design approach to enhance manufacturing efficiency of the handloom sector in Northeast Zone

Mukund K, Syama Sundari B (2001) Traditional industry in the new market economy: the cotton handlooms of Andhra Pradesh. Sage Publications, New Delhi

Mustaquim M, Islam W, Asif (2018) Way to immersing handloom cottage industry in Ambarpur Village of Murshidabad District: a geographical study. Int J Manag Stud:145. https://doi.org/10.18843/ijms/v5i3(4)/16

Nash JC (ed) (1993) Crafts in the world market: the impact of global exchange on middle American artisans. SUNY Press

Parthasarathy R (1999) Tradition and change: artisan producers in Gujarat. J Entrep 8(1):45–65. https://doi.org/10.1177/097135579900800103
Raihan M (2010) Handloom: an option to fight rural poverty in Bangladesh. Asia-Pacific J Rural Dev 20:113–130. https://doi.org/10.1177/1018529120100108
Ramaswamy V (2002) Alien weave – crafts vs consumerism. India Int Centre Quart 29(2)
Rao et al (2018) Involvement of women in handloom segment: an empirical study with reference to Krishna District, Andhra Pradesh. Am Econ Social Rev 3(1). https://doi.org/10.46281/aesr.v3i1.137
Reddy DN (2019) XXIX gender and economic policy discussion forum, May 2019. Institute of Social Studies Trust, New Delhi
Report of the World Commission on Environment and Development - Our Common Future (1987). https://sustainabledevelopment.un.org/milestones/wced
Report on "Make-In-India program weaving India's way towards Atmanirbharta" by the Economic Diplomacy Division, Ministry of External Affairs, Government of India (2020). https://indbiz.gov.in/make-in-india-program-weaving-indias-way-towards-atmanirbharta/
Roy T (2007) Out of tradition: master artisans and economic change in colonial India. J Asian Stud 66(4):963
Sahasrabudhey S, Sahasrabudhey C (2001) The Lokavidya standpoint [Hindi]. LokavidyaPratishtha Abhiyan, Varanasi
Scrase TJ (2003) Precarious production: globalisation and artisan labour in the third world. Third World Q 24(3):449–461
Shazli T, Abdul (2014) Female work participation in handloom industry-a case study of Mubarakpur town, Azamgarh District, U.P
Shukla R (2011) Census weaves rich handloom data. https://economictimes.indiatimes.com/view-point/census-weaves-rich-handloom-data/articleshow/7440632.cms?utm_source=contentofinterest&utm_medium=text&utm_campaign=cppst
Shyamsundarachary R, Sreenivas A (2017) Schemes and programmes of handloom industry in India – a study. World Wide J Multidiscip Res Dev 3(12):4–8
Solanki SS (2008) Sustainability of rural artisans. Econ Polit Wkly 10:24–27
Subrahmanya MHB (2011) Technological innovations and firm performance of manufacturing SMEs: determinants and outcomes. ASCI J Manag 41:109–122

Dr. Samhita Chaudhuri is presently working as Assistant Professor in Geography at the Bijoy Krishna Girls' College, Howrah, West Bengal, India. She visited Thailand under the ICSSR-NRCT Scholar Exchange Programme. Her research interests are cultural geography, population geography, urban and regional planning, and women's studies. She has First Class in Geography at the PG level and has done her doctoral studies from the University of North Bengal, India. Her present research is based on cultural aspects of India. Her recent publications are edited volumes on (i) Resource Management: Human and Natural, (ii) Gender Roles and Caste Effects in Indian Social Setup, (iii) District Profile of Darjeeling, and (iv) Cultural Geography. Her recent book is Festivals: A New Avenue for India-Thailand Cultural Linkage. She has presented papers on various national and international conferences.

Dr. Susmita Bhattacharyya is Assistant Professor in the Department of Sociology, University of Calcutta. She has her master's degree in sociology from the University of Calcutta and Ph.D. from Jadavpur University. Area of her research is linked with cultural studies. Her interest areas are sociology of literature, media, Indian sociological thought, research methodology, and industrial sociology. She is engaged in several kinds of writing endeavors in pure academics as well as in sociocultural activities.

Chapter 10
Perceived Health Status Among Elderly in India: Leveraging Public Policies to Achieve SDG-3

Kumari Youkta and Rajendra Narayan Paramanik

10.1 Introduction

In order to achieve balanced and sustainable development and to realize human rights, all sustainable development goals (SDGs) were set by countries worldwide. SDGs call for leaving no one behind. Their motive was to make development more inclusive so that it could address the needs of each and every segment of society, especially those who are most vulnerable—including older persons.

Many countries are facing the problem of the ageing population. India is not an exception to it. Continuously declining fertility rates along with falling mortality rates have led to an abnormal rise in the size of the elderly population (Rajan et al. 2003). United Nations Population Fund projected that India's elderly population will likely increase by 19% of the total population by the year 2050. The rapidly changing demographic structure may lead to economic, social, and health-related challenges, which would require timely intervention from the government's side. United Nation Organization has taken the initiative in the form of SDGs that aims to attain health and well-being for all. However, the elderly population requires special attention due to their greater vulnerabilities, poor health, unemployment, and financial insecurity.

In the past few decades, the Indian economy and society have been witnessing substantial changes (Ghosh and Husain 2010). Due to growing inequality, urbanization, and modernization, extended family culture is on the verge of extinction, and consequently, older people are getting more dependent on their families (Ranjan and Kumar 2003; Visaria 2001). In the Indian context, researchers are more focused on

K. Youkta (✉) · R. N. Paramanik
Department of Humanities and Social Sciences, Indian Institute of Technology Patna, Patna, Bihar, India
e-mail: youkta_1921hs08@iitp.ac.in

M. Mishra et al. (eds.), *Public Policies and Sustainable Development in Post-Reform India*, New Frontiers in Regional Science: Asian Perspectives 71,
https://doi.org/10.1007/978-981-99-3696-0_10

studying economic independence, living arrangements, and the prevalence of morbidity among the elderly. Hence, very little information we have from the literature about their perceived health status (Ghosh and Husain 2010). Rajan (2006) has presented an overview of the scenario of ageing in India. Rajan and Kumar (2003) have examined the association between economic independence and the quality of life of elderly people in India. Alam and Mukherjee (2005) and Albert et al. (2005) further extended the literature by establishing the relationship between poverty, the severity of illnesses, and the lack of autonomy among older people. Similar studies have been conducted in other South-East Asian countries also in which the prevalence of morbidity among older people were found to be determined by socio-economic correlates like caste, income, education, etc., and the availability of health facilities (Kumar 1996; Kumar 1999; Kumar 2003; Rajan 2006 and Alam 2006).

Although the above-mentioned works have their own limitations, they were helpful in creating a base on the discussed issue. This chapter tries to examine the determinants of self-reported health of the elderly in India. Older people's state of economic independence, living arrangements, and physical mobility are included as focal independent variables in the study.

The rest of the chapter is organized as follows—Sect. 10.2 deals with materials and methods used in the study; Sect. 10.3 describes the significant findings; and Sect. 10.4 presents the concluding remarks.

10.2 Materials and Method

10.2.1 Data

The present study has drawn data from the 75th round of the National Sample Survey on Social Consumption in India which was conducted between July 2017 and June 2018 and has covered almost every district in India. A total of 113,823 households were interviewed. A close-ended structured questionnaire and a stratified multi-stage sampling design were adopted for the survey.

Since the study addresses the determinants of the perceived health status of older people in India, so first of all, we merged the household file with 113,823 observations and the individual file with 555,352 observations to get a sample of 555,352 individuals. Then, from this entire information of individuals, we filtered out the information of older people (age equal to or greater than 60 years) only for our study. Thus in this way, we reached our final sample of 42,762 elderly.

10.2.2 Key Measures

Self-reported health or perceived health status has been employed as an outcome variable in the study. Respondents were asked, "What is your perception about current health status?" They answered on an ordinal scale, given three options to choose from—Option 1: Excellent/ Very good; Option 2: Good/ Fair; and Option 3: Poor. Our key independent variables are economic independence, living arrangements, and physical mobility. We have also incorporated some socio-economic factors of older people, such as age, gender, size of household, literacy, and per-capita health expenditure, in our study to make it more informative and elaborative.

10.2.3 Empirical Strategy

In order to study the impact of living arrangements, economic independence, physical mobility, and several other socio-economic factors like literacy, gender, size of household, per-capita health expenditure, etc., on self-reported health of older people in India, an ordered logistic regression model has been used. Since the outcome variable, perceived health status is ordered in nature, denoting very good/ excellent, fair/good, and poor categorizations, the ordered logistic regression model appeared to be most appropriate.

10.3 Results and Discussion

Table 10.1 reports the characteristics of the studied population. A total of 555,115 individuals were interviewed, out of which the information of 42,762 elderly individuals was relevant as per the objective of the study. The average age of the entire elderly population was found to be 67 years. The number of males and females was the approximately equal proportion in the sample, and 54% of them were illiterate. 90% of the population had their own house and an average of 5 members in the family. The per capita health expenditure of the elderly in India is approx. Rs. 2467. A significant portion of the studied population is financially dependent (46.98%), and most were physically mobile (92.4%).

Table 10.2 presents the results of the ordered logistic regression model, which has been used to examine the association between socio-economic and demographic characteristics of the elderly on their self-reported health status. Results reveal a strong and positive association between the ages of older people on their poor perception of self-health. This is quite obvious that with age, the incidence of chronic illnesses also increases substantially (Gupta and Sankar 2003; Rajan 2006; Mini 2009; Alam 2009). This is why as they grow older, the tendency to report poor health status by them also increases. Several studies done so far also emphasize the significant age effect on poor perceived health status (Kelleher et al. 2003).

Ample shreds of the literature suggest that educational attainment helps the elderly in shaping positive perceptions about their own health status (Chou and Chi 2002; Gupta and Sankar 2003; Mini 2009; Alam 2009). Educated, elderly

Table 10.1 Descriptive statistics of the studied sample

Variables	No. of observations	Mean/ percentages	Standard deviation
Age	42,760	67.51846	6.809641
Household size	42,760	5.074465	2.631948
Gender	42,760		
Male Female		49.08 50.92	
Education	42,760		
Illiterate Literate		54.11 45.89	
Per capita health expenditure	42,760	2467.925	1972.857
Economic Independence	42,753		
Independent Partially dependent Fully dependent		30.08 22.94 46.98	
Place of stay	42,753		
Own house Other's house		90.61 9.39	
Living arrangement	42,760		
With spouse and other members		50.27	
With spouse only Without spouse Alone		14.10 31.48 4.16	
Physical mobility	42,753		
Immobile Confined to home Move using wheelchair Mobile		1.37 5.53 0.63 92.47	

Source: Author's calculation

people generally get involved in social gatherings and healthy leisure time activities, which helps in reducing the chances of depression in them, and thus they are more likely to rate their health status positively (Varshney 2007). The results in our study align with the literature mentioned above. We have also found literate elderly people reporting better health status.

It is a well-established fact that across the lifespan, gender acts as an organizing principle of social life (Rossi 1985). In India, the miserable condition of women is driven by their poor control over assets and illiteracy (Husain and Ghosh 2017). Their work does not get proper recognition at the workplace as well as at their homes. They themselves seldom recognize their contributions to household activities (Agarwal 1996). Due to social influences and prolonged deprivation, females are conditioned to disadvantages and poor health status. Thus in our study also, we have found women reporting better health status as compared to their male counterparts.

Table 10.2 Ordered logistic regression results

Variables	Coefficient	SE	*P* value	95% CI
Age	0.0557815	0.0017043	0.000	[0.0524412, 0.0591219]
Household size	−0.0462724	0.0048049	0.000	[−0.0556898, −0.036855]
Gender				
Male [ref.]				
Female	−0.1746732	0.0267103	0.000	[−0.2270246, −0.1223219]
Education Illiterate [ref.]				
Literate	−0.2012543	0.0249275	0.000	[−0.2501112, −0.1523974]
Log per capita health expenditure				
	−0.181846	0.0204159	0.000	[−0.2218605, −0.1418316]
Economic Independence Independent [ref.]				
Partially dependent Fully dependent	0.5176932 0.970339	0.0326022 0.0316489	0.000 0.000	[0.4537941, 0.5815923] [0.9083082, 1.03237]
Place of stay Own house[ref.]				
Other's house	0.0636529	0.038702	0.100	[−0.0122017, 0.1395075]
Living arrangement With spouse and other members [ref.]				
With spouse only Without spouse Alone	0.2170256 0.0788618 0.4429903	0.0423987 0.0531791 0.0949631	0.000 0.138 0.000	[0.1339257, 0.3001255] [−0.0253673, 0.1830908] [0.2568661, 0.6291145]
Physical mobility Immobile[ref.]				
Confined to home Move using wheelchair Mobile	−0.9629956 −1.220548 −2.681242	0.1034233 0.1517186 0.0965597	0.000 0.000 0.000	[−1.165701, −0.7602897] [−1.517911, −0.9231852] [−2.870496, −2.491989]

Note: *CI* Confidence Interval, *[ref.]* Reference category, *SE* Standard error
Source: Author's calculation

Existing studies highlight the importance of the economic condition of the elderly in determining their health status (Alam 2008; Ghosh and Husain 2010; Guilmoto and Rajan 2002; Mini 2009; Rajan and Kumar 2003). Economic dependency is like a restriction on the demand and healthcare needs of older people. If they are not economically independent, they have to rely entirely on their caretakers for their health-related decision-making (Singh et al. 2013). The findings of this study comply with the existing literature. Elderly populations who are either partially or fully dependent have a greater likelihood of rating their health as poor one as compared to those older males or females who are financially independent.

Older people who live in an extended or intergenerational family setup generally have large social connections with friends, neighbours, relatives, etc. This social support has a positive impact on the self-rated health of the elderly (Heidrich and Ryff 1993; Sugisawa et al. 1994; Varshney 2007). The findings of our study also substantiate it. As compared to those older people who live along with spouse and family members both, those who live alone or in old age homes are more likely to report poor health status. Also, the larger the household size, the lesser the possibility of rating poor health status.

Physical activity has a vital role in keeping both body and mind in balance. Nowadays, it is a crucial part of a healthy lifestyle. In our study, we have found that older people who are not completely immobile or are not confined to bed only have a greater likelihood of rating their health as better one.

10.4 Contemporary Policies for the Elderly

Several attempts have been made internationally and within India to insure healthy ageing and quality life for elderly population. The Madrid Plan of Action and the United Nations Principles for Senior Citizens adopted by the UN General Assembly in 2002, the Proclamation on Ageing and the global targets on ageing for the Year 2001 adopted by the General Assembly in 1992, the Shanghai Plan of Action 2002 and the Macau Outcome document 2007 adopted by United Nations Economic and Social Commission for Asia and the Pacific (UNESCAP) form the basis for the global policy guidelines to encourage governments to design and implement their own policies from time to time. Later on, the United Nations (UN) General Assembly declared 2021–2030 as the UN Decade of Healthy Ageing and asked World Health Organization (WHO) to lead the implementation. The UN Decade of Healthy Ageing is a global collaboration bringing together governments, civil society, international agencies, professionals, academia, the media, and the private sector for 10 years of concerted, catalytic, and collaborative action to foster longer and healthier lives. The UN Decade of Healthy Ageing (2021–2030) seeks to reduce health inequities and improve the lives of older people, their families and communities through collective action in four areas: changing how we think, feel, and act towards age and ageism; developing communities in ways that foster the abilities of older people; delivering person-centred integrated care and primary health services responsive to older people; and providing older people who need it with access to quality long-term care.

Since independence the Indian government has been committed to supporting the old people in our society with certain interventionist welfare methods. The year 1999 was declared by the UN as the International Year of Older Persons followed on 13th Jan 1999, by the Government of India approving the National Policy for Older Persons for accelerating welfare measures and empowering the elderly in ways beneficial to them. Maintenance and Welfare of Parents and Senior Citizens Act, 2007 provides legal sanctions to the rights of the elderly. In addition, constitutional provisions for old age security, old age pension, establishing old age homes, expanding geriatric services, liberalizing housing policy for elders have also been undertaken. Several programmes and schemes were launched by various ministries to support elderly in India such as Integrated Programme for Senior Citizens (IPSrC) to provide grants-in-aid for proper functioning and maintenance of Senior Citizens Homes popularly known as Old Age Homes to the Implementing Agencies, Rashtriya Vayoshri Yojana (RVY) launched on first April 2017 to provide senior citizens, belonging to Below Poverty Line category and suffering from age-related disabilities/infirmities, with such physical aids and assisted living devices which can restore near normalcy in their bodily functions, Senior Citizens' Welfare Fund—introduced in the budget announcement 2015–16 under which a welfare fund was created to be utilized for such schemes, for promoting financial security of senior citizens, health care and nutrition of senior citizens, welfare of elderly widows, schemes relating to Old Age Homes, Short Stay Homes and Day Care of senior citizens, etc., for the promotion of the welfare of senior citizens, Senior Citizen Health Insurance Scheme (SCHIS)—implemented in the year 2016 to provide health insurance cover of Rs. 30,000/– which is available to senior citizens, in additional to the coverage of Rs. 30,000/– under Rashtriya Swasthya Bima Yojana, etc.

Undoubtedly, we are not lacking in policies and programmes targeting old-age people but in proper implementation of these interventions. This inefficiency gets created basically due to corruption, lack of awareness among beneficiaries, complex procedure of availing these services, etc. Thus along with the launching new policies and plans, a simultaneous effort is required to be made to monitor its implementation, spread awareness among beneficiaries, and assess its outcome in timely fashion.

10.5 Conclusion

This study attempts to investigate the factors that determine the poor self-rated health of older people (both male and female) in India. Older peoples' socio-economic and demographic characteristics have been used as focal independent variables in the study. The findings of the study are pretty appealing and suggest that older people, if economically independent and living with a spouse and other family members, have a higher likelihood of rating their health as a fair one. Financial dependency snatches the autonomy of decision-making from them. So they must depend on their caretakers to make decisions for them. The presence of spouse and other family members around them does not let them feel lonely, which helps in reducing the chances of depression in them. This may be the reason behind the negative association between the family size of the elderly and their poor rating of health also. Older people who are physically active in their daily life and are not confined to bed, home or are physically immobile are more likely to rate their health as fair. As educated people are more active in their social lives and enjoy quality leisure, we found educated people self-assessed them healthier in our study. On the other hand, women were found to report poorer health status than their male counterparts and with age tendency of rating poor health status increases for older males and females. Thus, it can be said that ageing poses a number of challenges not only for governments and society but also for the older persons themselves. Thus, to meet these challenges, they urgently require targeted policy measures and anticipatory measures to prepare the country as a whole for meeting these challenges.

The present study reports some limitations also. The outcome variable, which is representative of older people's health status, is self-reported and is based on individuals' personal experiences (Sen 2002). Thus, it is a subjective measure that varies from person to person and is sometimes debatable to be used as a measure of health status among scholars. But in global public health literature, self-reported health measure has faced validity (Subramanian et al. 2009), and voluminous literature supports its applications. Several other factors like social networks, community characteristics, and many other factors can have an impact on older people's self-rated health, but due to data-related constraints, we are not able to incorporate them in our study.

References

Agarwal B (1996) A field of one's own: gender and land rights in South Asia. Cambridge University Press

Alam M (2006) Ageing in India: socio-economic and health dimensions. Academic Foundation, New Delhi

Alam M (2008) Ageing, socio-economic disparities and health outcomes: some evidence from rural India (working paper E/290/2008). Institute of Economic Growth, Delhi, India

Alam M (2009) Ageing, socio-economic disparities and health outcomes: some evidence from rural India. Indian J Human Dev 3(1):47–76

Alam M, Mukherjee M (2005) Ageing, activities of daily living disabilities and the need for public health initiatives: some evidence from a household survey in Delhi. Asia-Pac Popul J 20(2): 47–76

Albert SM, Alam M, Nizamuddin M (2005) Comparative study of functional limitation and disability in old age: Delhi and New York City. J Cross Cult Gerontol 20:231–241

Chou KL, Chi I (2002) Successful aging among the young old, old-old and oldest-old Chinese. Int J Aging Hum Dev 54:1–14

Ghosh S, Husain Z (2010) Economic independence, family support and perceived health status of elderly: recent evidence from India. Asia-Pac Popul J 25(1):47–77

Guilmoto CZ, Rajan SI (2002) District level estimates of fertility from India's 2001 census. Econ Polit Wkly 37:665–672

Gupta I, Sankar D (2003) Health of the elderly in India: a multivariate analysis. J Health Population Dev Countries. www.longwoods.com/home.php?cat=394

Heidrich SM, Ryff CD (1993) Physical and mental health in later life: the self-system as mediator. Psychol Ageing 8(3):327–338
Husain Z, Ghosh D (2017) Analysis of perceived health status among elderly in India: gender and positional objectivity. In Cross-cultural and cross-disciplinary perspectives in social gerontology. Springer, Singapore, pp. 177–202
Kelleher C C, Friel S, Nic G. S et al (2003) Socio-demographic predictors of self-rated health in the Republic of Ireland: findings from the National Survey on lifestyle, attitudes and nutrition, SLAN. Soc Sci Med 57: 477–486
Kumar V (ed) (1996) Aging—Indian perspective and global scenario. All India Institute of Medical Sciences, New Delhi
Kumar PV (1999) Elderly women in rural India: need for policy intervention. Help Age India 5(3)
Kumar SV (2003) Economic security for the elderly in India: an overview. J Aging Social Pol 15(2–3):45–65
Mini GK (2009) Socioeconomic and demographic diversity in the health status of elderly people in a transitional society, Kerala, India. J Biosoc Sci 41(4):457–467
Rajan SI (2006) Population ageing and health in India. Centre for Enquiry into Health and Allied Themes, Mumbai, India
Rajan SI, Kumar S (2003) Living arrangements among Indian elderly: new evidence from National Family Health Survey. Econ Polit Wkly 38(1):75–80
Rajan SI, Sarma PS, Mishra US (2003) Demography of Indian aging, 2001-2051. J Aging Soc Policy 15(2):11–30
Rossi AS (ed) (1985) Gender and the life course. Aldine de Gruyter, New York
Sen A (2002) Health: perception versus observation. Br Med J 324:860–861
Singh L, Arokiasamy P, Singh PK et al (2013) Determinants of gender differences in self-rated health among older population: evidence from India. SAGE Open 3(2):2158244013487914
Subramanian SV, Subramanyam MA et al (2009) Are self-reports of health and morbidities in developing countries misleading? Evidence from India. Soc Sci Med 68:260–265
Sugisawa H, Liang J, Liu X (1994) Social networks, social support and mortality among older people in Japan. J Gerontol 49(1):S3–S13
Varshney S (2007) Predictors of successful ageing: associations between social network patterns, life satisfaction, depression, subjective health, and leisure time activity for older adults in India. Unpublished doctoral dissertation, University of North Texas, August
Visaria P (2001) Demographics of ageing in India. Econ Polit Wkly 36(22):1967–1975

Kumari Youkta is a Doctoral student in the Department of Humanities and Social Science at Indian Institute of Technology, Patna, India. Her research interest lies in economics of health, public health, and development studies.

Dr. Rajendra Narayan Paramanik is an Assistant Professor of Economics and Finance in the Department of Humanities and Social Science at Indian Institute of Technology Patna, Bihar, India. Dr. Rajendra specializes in the area of macro-dynamic modelling, Time series analysis, International Economics and Finance and has published several research articles in leading journals.

Part III
Steps Toward Revitalizing the Education Sector

Chapter 11
Digital Inclusion in School Education in India: Key Issues and Challenges

Subhasis Sen

11.1 Introduction

The Covid-19 pandemic has made us realize the significance of technology in our day-to-day life with special emphasis on teaching and learning the school curriculum at home (Seufert et al. 2021). Information and communication technologies (ICTs) have become the support for lifelong learning opportunities (Melinte 2012). Wu and Huang (2011) explain that students' learning achievement in the environment of information technology (IT) education using cloud computing has been better than that in the traditional educational environment. A model for integrating ICT in the professional development of teachers in Bangladesh shows two perspectives—on the one hand, the challenges in the use of ICT among teachers, and, on the other hand, the benefits to the teachers, trainers, and policymakers who are directly or indirectly accountable for teachers' professional development (Khan 2014). Qualitative research by Reyes Jr. and Kheng (2015) has attempted to explore how school stakeholders cope with educational transformations by using research instruments to understand the sense-making experiences of stakeholders through focus group discussions, interviews, and observations. In Turkey, however, it has been found that smartphone use by preschoolers or babies is mainly meant for playing games rather than learning activities (Genc 2014). In Romania, ION (2012) observed that there is a demand for a more attractive instructional process for the new generation of students who are already familiarized with using personal computers, navigating the internet, and browsing mobile phones. In a mobile-based training (MBT) environment, learners can access information using software applications specific to mobile

S. Sen (✉)
Balaji Institute of Technology & Management (BITM), Sri Balaji University Pune (SBUP), Pune, Maharashtra, India
e-mail: subhasis.sen@bitmpune.edu.in

M. Mishra et al. (eds.), *Public Policies and Sustainable Development in Post-Reform India*, New Frontiers in Regional Science: Asian Perspectives 71,
https://doi.org/10.1007/978-981-99-3696-0_11

devices. E-learning educational settings across the globe range from hi-tech classrooms with vast resources to schools in developing countries with no IT access (Resta 2011). Digital competence refers to confidence and expertise in IT skills for work, leisure, and communication (European Commission 2007). The Government of India's Digital Inclusion Policy builds on three key pillars, mainly catering to services for the untapped needs of people, public services to underprivileged masses, and developing an infrastructure to deliver services like education (IT for Change 2008). In spite of the growing digital trend in the industry, a survey by Euromonitor International (2019) showed that the growth in possession of personal computers by households for the year 2014–2019 in India was 48.4%, Romania accounted for 18.8%, Bolivia reached 43.1%, and Turkey accounted for 8.6%. On the other hand, the growth in the percentage of population covered by Mobile-Cellular Networks during the year 2014–2019 in India was 4.1%, Romania accounted for 0.1%, Bolivia showed −0.8%, and Turkey reached 2%. The data reflects that there is a problem with digital inclusion in emerging economies. Analytics like Schoology (learning management system) has been able to track the time students spend on digital resources, submitting assignments, etc. Even in the corporate world, employees are widening the scope of learning by opting for massive online open courses (MOOCs), and employers are offering such courses to train their staff with requisite skills (Euromonitor International 2017). Education providers in schools like Educomp, Tata ClassEdge, Pearson, and TeachNext have been coming up with interaction software to aid teachers in classroom teaching (Frost and Sullivan 2016). In a study by Muirhead (2000) on Canadian schools, 13 teachers from online schools were interviewed. It revealed that developing the scope and reliability of the technology and improving access to digital academic content are essential to nurture students experiencing online education effectively. The findings from a regression analysis carried out by Wang et al. (2019) explained no connection between school-level factors and use of digital learning resources. In the previous studies, it is also observed that there have not been many studies pertaining to digital support while encouraging student engagement by meeting their psychological needs (Chiu 2021). Therefore, this chapter aims to bridge the gap between traditional and digital school education, especially in emerging markets, and determine the expectations of the stakeholders involving schoolteachers, students, and parents related to digital inclusion for policy decision-making.

11.2 Past Research on Digital Usage in School Education

Recommendations of a study by Kong et al. (2014) highlighted the goals for the twenty-first-century e-learning skills, linkages between society and school, exposure to digital technologies for school education, and training of teachers to adapt technologies in the classroom. In a qualitative study, audiovisual classroom as evidence and focus group discussions were used followed by a Web-based questionnaire administered for teachers to understand the attitude towards ICT for routine activities and the confidence in utilizing them and to assess whether any change in teaching perception happens concerning knowledge and skills imparted to academicians (Popova and Fabre 2017). A content analysis by Olofsson et al. (2018) concluded that schools need to effectively use ICT with respect to their daily activities like writing, documenting, storing, and peer support. The findings of a study by Crompton (2017) using the thematic synthesis method showed that educators need to realize the potential of technology while using it in teaching and learning. Three types of resources identified for sound technology integration are training, access to mobile devices, and technical assistance. A study indicated that smartphone usage in schools could positively influence students' learning (Philip and Garcia 2015). In the midst of the Covid-19 pandemic and a need for distance (online) education, teachers must equip themselves with technology-related constructive learning activities primarily to improve the problem-solving skills of students (Sailer et al. 2021).

When students and teachers are put into adversities for carrying out academics during the pandemic, transformative digital competence evolved as a necessity to tackle demanding situations (Aagaard and Lund 2020). A study by Damşa et al. (2021) attempted to find out how teachers acted on the fast mobilization of both digital knowledge and skills. In the article by Teri (2022), Business Research Company reported the progress of the global digital publishing market as USD 36.29 billion in the year 2021 and it is expected to grow by USD 68.81 billion in 2026. Digital publishing in the education sector is projected to grow by USD 10.55 billion in the forthcoming years, with maximum contribution expected from the school level. The cognitive technologies that would rein in the future are artificial intelligence, machine learning, expert systems, and robotic process automation, leading to cost reduction for content creation and speeding up of the publication process. Simultaneously, the e-learning and m-learning (mobile learning) segment showing a growth of USD 18.23 billion in 2019 is estimated to value at USD 58.5 billion by 2025, as reported by Market Data Forecast.

11.3 Research Questions

The research questions addressed derived from past research studies are the following:

- RQ1: What is the awareness level and learning experience among the primary and secondary school students while using digital devices and applications?
- RQ2: What are the issues and challenges pertaining to digitization in school education among teachers from emerging economies?

11.4 Methodology

The research study here primarily deals with a content analysis considering qualitative data and is exploratory in nature. Content analysis is effective in the context of justifying established patterns that support existing theories and discovering or identifying patterns for formulating new theories. It has been the tool for analyzing communications and advertising studies for many years (Kolbe and Burnett 1991). The content analysis focuses on published text, pictures, or video clips as the source of data (Hair Jr. et al. 2016). Primary data has been collected using a non-probabilistic sampling technique and by conducting semi-structured in-depth interviews with 26 school students and 10 schoolteachers in India, whereas the secondary data has been referred from journal articles and cases relevant to school education. The validity of the qualitative data has been tested using an adequate referencing method (Gay et al. 2008). A checklist matrix of content analysis adapted from Miles and Huberman (1994) in this study has highlighted the conditions supporting digital inclusion for students and teachers in school education.

11.5 Results and Analysis

- Table 11.1 depicts that there is a need for digital inclusion in every subject for student understanding, especially when school education is offered online, owing to the Covid-19 pandemic situation.
- Figure 11.1 shows a high level of interest among students in digital learning since the words which are prominently derived are learning, interesting, wonderful, and amazing while interviewing them.
- Figure 11.2 depicts that difficulties faced by students are minimal. However, there are a few health issues identified in digital usage, like eyes being stressed due to light emission from electronic devices.
- Figure 11.3 reflects that students take a lot of interest while working with software applications like PowerPoint, Word, and Excel and computer languages like Java, Python, and C++.

Table 11.1 Multiple response analysis of students' learning through usage of software applications and games in school education

Subject	Percentage (%)
Science	24
Mathematics	21
English	21
Geography	10
Foreign languages (French, German, etc.)	8
History	5
General awareness	3
Other courses	8

Source: Primary Data collected by the author

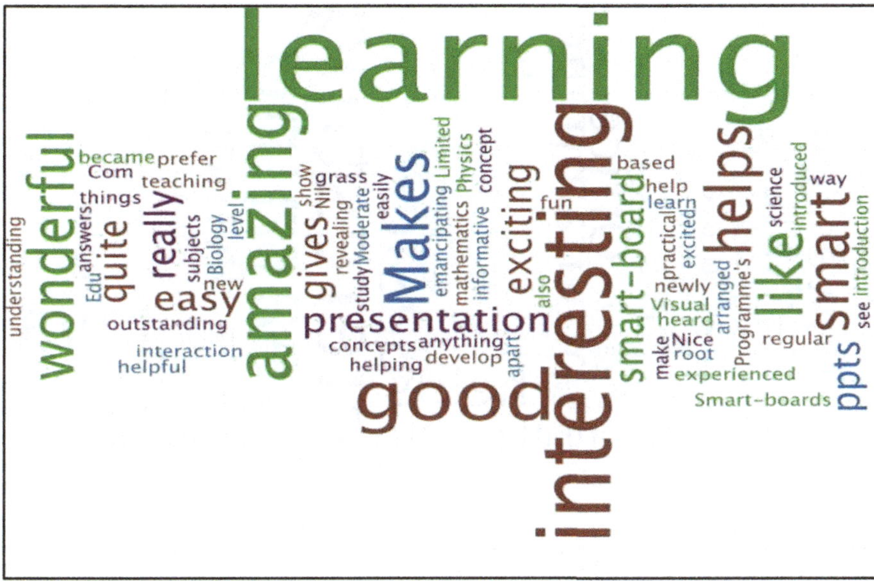

Fig. 11.1 Word Cloud of digital experience among students in school education. (Source: Prepared by the author from the Primary Data)

Fig. 11.2 Word Cloud of difficulties faced by students while using digital devices for academic activities. (Source: Prepared by the author from the Primary Data)

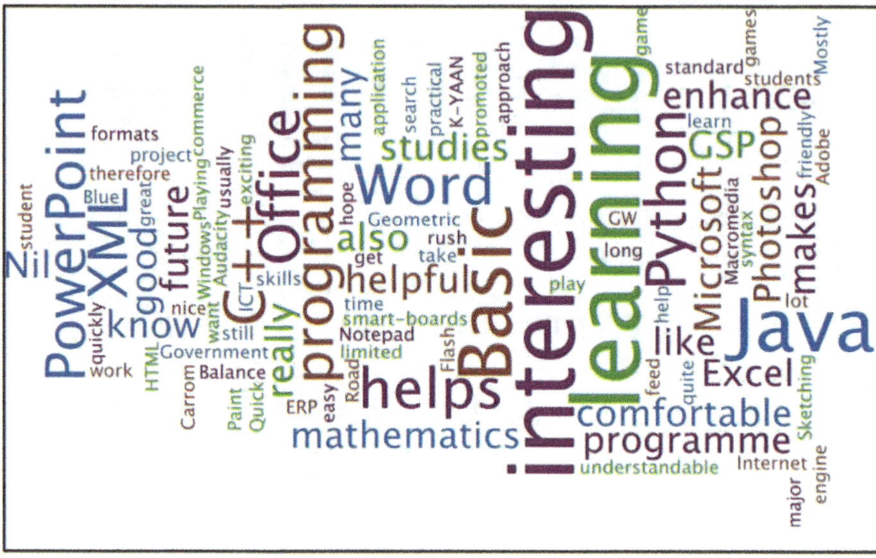

Fig. 11.3 Word Cloud of software application usage and learning experience among students. (Source: Prepared by the author from the Primary Data)

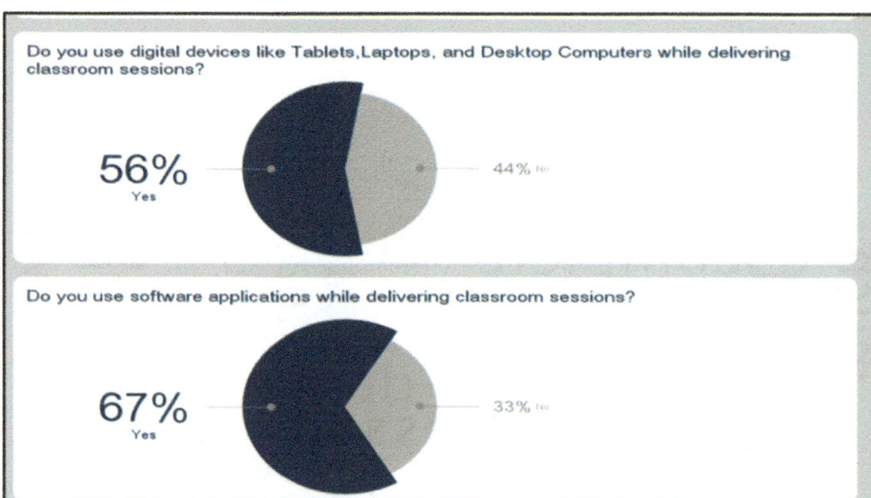

Fig. 11.4 Digital usage among teachers. (Source: Prepared by the author from the Primary Data)

- Figure 11.4 shows that mostly teachers are using digital devices and software applications while delivering sessions, but there are schools where ICT infrastructure are inadequate for proper usage.

Fig. 11.5 Word Cloud of digital experience among teachers in school education. (Source: Prepared by the author from the Primary Data)

- Figure 11.5 shows that there is a mixed reaction among teachers using digital devices and applications. App-based learning and smart board usage are appreciated. On the other hand, the lack of availability of relevant software and infrastructural problems are causing an interruption in digital inclusion.
- Figure 11.6 depicts the difficulties faced by teachers like internet speed, lack of network support, and bigger screens, whereas a few of them have stated that not many issues or problems have been faced occasionally. Digital inequality at home during Covid-19 (González-Betancor et al. 2021) for delivering school education is a big challenge in remote corners of India.

11.6 Findings and Discussions

Major findings of different research studies reveal that the biggest challenges to adopting the use of new technologies in less developed countries are hardware compatibility, complexity, language barriers, lack of electricity, computers, internet access, and engagement of trainees, which include the inability to understand the advantages of IT applications (Richardson 2011). A stepwise regression analysis has proved that ICT infrastructure influences schools differently in urban and rural areas (Lu et al. 2015). A study has shown that parental ICT attitude influences primary

Fig. 11.6 Word Cloud of difficulties faced by teachers while using digital devices for academic activities. (Source: Prepared by the author from the Primary Data)

school children's digital adoption (Aesaert et al. 2015). Education is presently facing a critical challenge in terms of building digital culture and citizenship (Vélez and Zuazua 2017). Children in third and fourth grades use the internet for recreation or playing games, whereas students in fourth and sixth grades focus their internet usage on online communication and socialization. The same behavioral pattern exists while they use mobile phone devices. The primary data analysis using the Word Cloud reflects that students are eager to learn using digital devices and applications, followed by interesting, amazing, and wonderful topics as expressed by them. Students face the least difficulty in using digital devices while dealing with assignments, homework, and examinations. There have been challenging situations among teachers while using ICT devices for delivering sessions in schools, like infrastructure, speed of internet, and networking. In spite of such difficulties, still, teachers appreciate their digital experiences in educating children. The checklist matrix of content analysis adapted from Miles and Huberman (1994) has summarized the perspectives as high satisfaction level, low difficulty, and moderate usage of digital devices and software applications for students, whereas moderate satisfaction level, serious difficulty, low usage of digital devices, and moderate use of software applications in case of teachers delivering classroom sessions. The checklist matrix representing content analysis is given in Table 11.2.

Table 11.2 Conditions for supporting digital inclusion in school education

Condition	For students	For teachers
Satisfaction	High	Moderate
Difficulty	Low	High
Digital device usage	Moderate	Low
Software applications/games/app usage	Moderate	Moderate

Source: Adapted from Miles and Huberman (1994)

11.7 Conclusion

The outcome of this content analysis would largely benefit the policy decision makers, vendors of digital solutions, teachers, and students of educational institutions around the world. A model discussed in the study refers to professional development, competencies, growing educational beliefs, and the school's vision and policy directed towards ICT that can positively impact technology usage (Vanderlinde et al. 2014). A conceptual framework developed in Accra Technical University, Ghana, has increased ICT use among teachers and students to a great extent (Asabere et al. 2017). The study here has identified the issues concerning and conditions supporting digital experience for students and teachers in school education. However, the integration of ICT can be studied further with respect to digital inequality at home, which primarily covers the socio-economic status (SES) of both students and teachers. There is a need for robust digital technology to conduct online classroom sessions and examination processes across India. Further to this study, the UNESCO (2013) stated, "ICT must go beyond issues of equipment availability and connectivity; it is necessary to move towards the issue of uses and their impacts on learning." Finally, the chapter can be concluded with the statement, following Flórez-Aristizábal et al. (2019), that the motivation of a child grows through the use of technology in a playful manner.

References

Aagaard T, Lund A (2020) Digital agency in higher education. Transforming teaching and learning. Routledge, London & New York

Aesaert K, Nijlen DV, Vanderlinde R, Tondeur J, Devlieger I, Braak JV (2015) The contribution of pupil, classroom and school level characteristics to primary school pupils' ICT competencies: a performance-based approach. Comput Educ 87:55–69

Asabere N, Togo G, Acakpovi A, Torgby W, Ampadu K (2017) AIDS: an ICT for integrating teaching, learning and research in technical university education in Ghana. Int J Educ Dev Using Inf Commun Technol 13(3):162–183

Chiu TKF (2021) Digital support for student engagement in blended learning based on self-determination theory. Comput Hum Behav 124:106909. https://doi.org/10.1016/j.chb.2021.106909

Crompton H (2017) Moving toward a mobile learning landscape: presenting a mlearning integration framework. Interact Technol Smart Educ 14(2):97–109

Euromonitor International (2017) Passport: digital consumer in India
Damşa C, Langford M, Uehara D, Scherer R (2021) Teachers' agency and online education in times of crisis. Comput Hum Behav 121, ISSN 0747-5632,:106793. https://doi.org/10.1016/j.chb.2021.106793
Euromonitor International (2019) Passport—economies and consumers annual data. National Statistics/International Telecommunications Union (ITU)
European Commission (2007) The key competences for lifelong learning—a European framework (annex of a recommendation of the European Parliament and of the council of 18 December 2006 on key competences for lifelong learning). European Communities, Brussels
Flórez-Aristizábal L, Cano S, Collazos CA, Benavides F, Moreira F, Fardoun HM (2019) Digital transformation to support literacy teaching to deaf children: from storytelling to digital interactive storytelling, telematics and informatics. 38:87–99. https://doi.org/10.1016/j.tele.2018.09.002
Frost & Sullivan (2016) Digital Education in India, Frost Perspectives, Information & Communication Tech
Gay LR, Mills GE, Airasian P (2008) Educational research: competencies for analysis and applications. Pearson Education USA, Upper Saddle River, NJ
Genc Z (2014) Parents' perceptions about the mobile technology use of preschool aged children. PRO 146:55–60
González-Betancor SM, López-Puig AJ, Cardenal ME (2021) Digital inequality at home. The school as compensatory agent. Comput Educ 168:104195. https://doi.org/10.1016/j.compedu.2021.104195
Hair JF Jr, Celsi M, Money A, Samouel P, Page M (2016) Essentials of business research methods. Routledge USA, New York
Ion AM (2012) Influence of ICT development on education. Informatica Economicá 16(1):154–163
IT for Change (2008) Digital inclusion policies: some lessons from India. Association for Progressive Communications. https://www.apc.org/sites/default/files/APCProPoorKit_CaseStudy_SomeLessonsFrom_India_EN.pdf. Accessed 23 Nov 2022
Khan SH (2014) A model for integrating ICT into teacher training programs in Bangladesh based on TPCK. Int J Educ Dev Using Inf Commun Technol 10(3):21–31
Kolbe RH, Burnett MS (1991) Content analysis research: an examination of applications with directions for improving research reliability and objectivity. J Consum Res 18:243–250
Kong SC, Chan TW, Griffin P, Hoppe U, Huang R, Kinshuk, Looi CK, Milrad M, Norris C, Nussbaum M, Sharples M, So WMW, Soloway E, Yu S (2014) Game based learning for 21st century transferable skills: challenges and opportunities. J Educ Technol Soc 17(1):70–78
Lu C, Tsai C, Wu D (2015) The role of ICT infrastructure in its application to classrooms: a large scale survey for middle and primary schools in China. Educ Technol Soc 18(2):249–261
Melinte IE (2012) The impact of information and communication technologies on education and training. Outlook on Communication 2(2):104–106
Miles MNB, Huberman AM (1994) Qualitative data analysis: an expanded sourcebook. SAGE, Thousand Oaks, CA
Muirhead WD (2000) Online education in schools. Int J Educ Manag 14(7):315–324
Olofsson AD, Lindberg OJ, Fransson G (2018) Students' voices about information and communication technology in upper secondary schools. Int J Inf Learn Technol 35(2):82–92
Philip TM, Garcia A (2015) Schooling mobile phones: assumptions about proximal benefits, the challenges of shifting meanings, and the politics of teaching. Educ Policy 29(4):676–707
Popova I, Fabre G (2017) Digital inclusion of secondary schools' subject teachers in Bolivia. Int J Educ Dev Using Inf Commun Technol 13(3):41–56
Resta P (2011) TWG 4: global awareness. Briefing paper presented at the EDUsummIT 2011 meeting, Paris
Reyes VC Jr, Kheng CS (2015) School stakeholders' experience with navigating ICT policy reforms in Singapore. Int J Inf Commun Technol Educ 11(4):83–96

Richardson JW (2011) Challenges of adopting the use of technology in less developed countries: the case of Cambodia. Comp Educ Rev 55(1):8–29

Sailer M, Murböck J, Fischer F (2021) Digital learning in schools: what does it take beyond digital technology? Teach Teach Educ 103:103346. https://doi.org/10.1016/j.tate.2021.103346

Seufert S, Guggemos J, Sailer M (2021) Technology-related knowledge, skills, and attitudes of pre- and in-service teachers: the current situation and emerging trends. Comput Hum Behav 115: 106552. https://doi.org/10.1016/j.chb.2020.106552

Teri T (2022) Tracking the relentless digital momentum in India. Publishers Weekly 269(29)

UNESCO (2013) Enfoques Estratégicos Sobre Tics en Educación en América Latina y el Caribe, Enfoque Estratégico Sobre Tics. En Educación En América Latina Y El Caribe

Vanderlinde R, Aesaert K, Braak JV (2014) Institutional ICT use in primary education: a multilevel analysis. Comput Educ 72:1–10

Vélez AP, Zuazua II (2017) Digital literacy and cyberconvivencia in primary education. PRO 237: 110–117

Wang J, Tigelaar DEH, Admiraal W (2019) Connecting rural schools to quality: rural teachers' use of digital educational resources. Comput Hum Behav 101:68–76

Wu CF, Huang LP (2011) Developing the environment of information technology education using cloud computing infrastructure. Am J Appl Sci 8(9):864–871

Dr. Subhasis Sen is a professor (MBA, M.Phil., PhD in marketing) and a researcher with around 25 years of working experience both in the academics and corporate sectors. The areas of his expertise include marketing research, sports management, rural marketing, services marketing, sales and distribution management, business analytics, and digital marketing. Dr. Sen has published research papers in Scopus and ABDC indexed international journals and participated as Track Chairperson and Paper Presenter in reputed international conferences hosted by IIM Bangalore; Indian Institute of Science, Bangalore; Indian School of Business, Hyderabad; Rosen College of Hospitality, Orlando (USA); and XLRI, Jamshedpur. Presently, he is also guiding MBA and PhD students in research work at Sri Balaji University, Pune, Maharashtra.

Chapter 12
Scope of Standardization of the Teacher Education Program Within the Purview of India's National Education Policy 2020

Anusri Kundu and Anindya Basu

12.1 Introduction

Education is not only limited to young pupils, but those who train their minds also need modernized training. To enable teachers to discharge their responsibilities more effectively, the role of teacher education is significant (Aggarwal 1988). Verma (2009) acknowledged that teacher training did not achieve a stage of development equal to the education of other professionals like doctors, engineers, or lawyers. However, gradually, teacher education programs have started to become more structured. The primary purpose of teacher education is to create an informed and sophisticated approach to inculcate theoretical knowledge and technical applicability with equal emphasis (Yadav and Sumbul 2006). An educational institution performs a significant function of providing learning experiences to lead its students from the darkness of ignorance to the light of knowledge. Teachers are key personnel in the institutions that play a vital role in bringing about this transformation. Teacher education program covers teachers at all levels of education, namely pre-primary, primary, elementary, secondary, higher secondary, and tertiary. The requirements of students from a structured education system vary at each level. Construction of the relevant knowledge base for each stage of education seeks a high degree of academic and intellectual understanding of matters related to teacher education at each stage. Evidently, no nation develops without the quality of its education system, which is highly dependent on the quality of its teachers. Often much is discussed about the performance and accountability of teachers; if the molding of young teaching aspirants can be done through systematic knowledge imparting and moral training about being responsible, then the entire teacher education system will become more meaningful for society. In this context, the National Educational Policy 2020 tries to

A. Kundu · A. Basu (✉)
Department of Geography, Diamond Harbour Women's University, Sarisha, West Bengal, India

M. Mishra et al. (eds.), *Public Policies and Sustainable Development in Post-Reform India*, New Frontiers in Regional Science: Asian Perspectives 71,
https://doi.org/10.1007/978-981-99-3696-0_12

restore the credibility of teacher education programs for providing skilled and receptive teachers to the future generation.

12.2 Institutionalization of Teacher Education in India

Teacher education is an essential component of the Indian education system. It is closely associated with society—its beliefs and cultural traits. Apart from constitutional objectives and directive ethics of the state policy, the socio-economic situation and changing aspirations of the youth are some factors that call for a suitable response from the existing education system and provide the perspective within which teacher education programs need to be observed (NCTE 1997).

It was the Charter Act (1698) that initiated the conversation about education for the first time. The first formal Teachers Training Institution was set in India by Danish Missionaries at Serampore, Bengal (Adaval 1984). In 1849, Alexander Duff started out a standard teacher training department at Calcutta. A regular training department first began in 1851 at Poona College, followed by similar ones at Surat and Agra (Aggarwal 1988).

In 1904, the resolution of the then government on Indian educational policy was passed, and it pinpointed the need for having an artwork-based teaching approach to reduce the students' tendency to depend upon rote learning. Following this guideline, in 1906, a Secondary Training College was set up in Bombay (Nair 2006).

The Central Advisory Board of Education was revived in 1935 to look into education-related issues and emphasize eradicating mass illiteracy (Mukerji 1968). Again, in 1944, the Board chalked out an educational reform plan popularly called the "Sargent Scheme," which underlined the need for more trained teachers (Kundu 1988). It was suggested that one teacher was essential for every 30 pupils in pre-basic and junior primary school, every 25 students in senior basic schools, and every 20 pupils in high schools (Reddy 1998).

After independence, the Central Institute of Education, a pioneer teacher education institution in the country, began functioning in Delhi. By 1948, the Government Training College at Allahabad was developed into the Government Central Pedagogical Institute (Shankar 1984). The Ministry of Education, Government of India, selected University Education Commission under the chairmanship of Dr. S. Radha Krishnan in 1948, and its report was submitted in 1949 (NCTE 1997).

In 1960, the Second All India Conference was held at Mysore, which viewed teacher training from a broader standpoint and culminated in the concept of "Education for Training" (Mehta 1998). Since then, there has been a wave of workshops, seminars, symposia, and conferences generating debates and discussions regarding suitable changes to be implemented in the sector of teacher education (Mangla 2001).

The Report of the Secondary Education Commission in 1953 recommended three types of teacher training institutions in the country—primary or basic, secondary, and graduate teachers' training institutions (NCERT 2005). Nevertheless, the

Commission recommended that the training institutions should be only of two types—one for those who have taken the Secondary School Leaving Certificate, for whom training should be of 2 years under a separate Board, and the other for graduates for whom the period of training should be of one academic session which would be affiliated to universities (NCTE 1998).

Education Commission (1964) was constituted under the chairmanship of Prof. D.S. Kothari, the then Chairman of the University Grants Commission, which indicated that a sound program for teachers' education is essential for the holistic development of education (Rao 2001). Accordingly, the Commission gave its approval for teacher training with the following visions:

- Removing the isolated training institutions and merging them with the general stream under the universities
- Improving the value of education programs and training establishments
- Expanding training services
- Making suitable provisions for the continuing expert schooling of all teachers
- Creating proper interventions both at the center and the states for the preservation of the standards of teacher education

It additionally advised for an intensive emphasis on development programs of training institutions of all standards, correspondence education, in-service education, and formation of training institutions of formidable size (Deb 2004).

The Government of India set up a Committee of Members of Parliament on Education (1967) under the chairmanship of Shri Ganga Sinha to ponder the record and formulate the draft of a statement on the National Policy on Education (NPE) (MHRD 1992). In the year 1983, the National Commission on Teachers was established, followed by a Programme of Action (1986 and a revised one in 1992) by the Ministry of Human Resource Development, keeping the spirit of the National Policy on Education (Dubey 1997).

The NPE, 1986, calls for a substantial improvement in the conditions of work and the quality of teachers' education. The policy also emphasizes the teachers' accountability to the pupils, their parents, and the community and to their own profession. The Programme of Action (POA) 1986 spelled out the main aspects of the strategy for the implementation of these postulations. The prescriptions of the POA 1986 continued to be of relevance and need to be acted upon with vigor and determination (Khanna 2005).

The National Knowledge Commission (2008) identified the education of teachers as a major area of concern since both pre-service and in-service training of school teachers were tremendously insufficient and poorly accomplished in maximum states. It further stated that pre-service training had to be stepped up and in-service training needed to be more flexible to deal with the shortage (Gupta 1980).

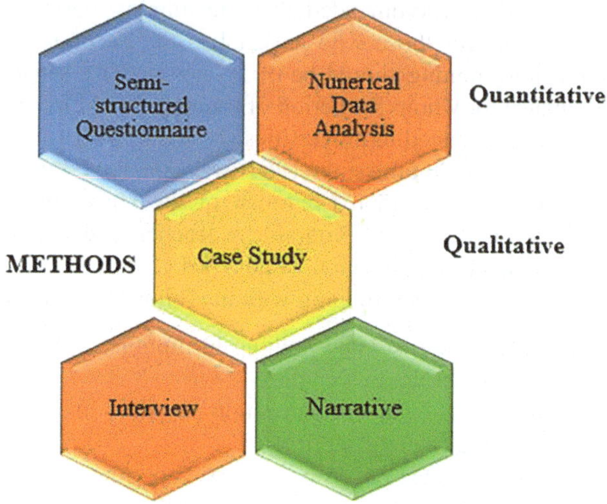

Fig. 12.1 Methodological framework involved in the study. (Source: Drawn by the authors)

12.3 Objectives

Teaching profession is taken in very high regards by several developed countries and for that a detailed, modernized teacher education program is often implemented ensuring the quality. The basic premise of the study is to appraise the teacher education program involved in educating and training the teacher-trainees for high schools, in today's rapidly changing times. The objectives are to assess the relevancy of the teacher education program in India from contemporary perspective, keeping its regional needs in mind; to gauge whether the framework of teacher education program is at par with international standards; and to assess the pros and cons associated with the impending implementation of the policy principles of NEP 2020.

12.4 Methodology

The research is based on an extensive literature survey covering the aspects of previous policy frameworks of India regarding teacher education programs and current educational policy principles. To analyze how far the present teachers' education policy in India mirrors the international benchmark in comparison to the similar programs which are in place in other developed countries like Australia, China, Japan, Turkey, the UK, and the USA has been taken into account. A primary survey involving the stakeholders like management authorities and present students of teacher education institutions, i.e., trainee teachers, was taken into account to weigh the strengths and weaknesses associated with the proposed 4-year integrated B.Ed. course under the purview of the newly mooted NEP 2020. The study adopts a mixed method including quantitative and qualitative methods (Fig. 12.1). The primary data was collected by survey using semi-structured questionnaires. As a part of the qualitative methods, researchers have considered incorporating case studies, interviews, and narratives.

To carry out the perception study, the collection of primary data involved all 19 teacher education institutions of Kolkata city, including government (6), government-aided (6), and private institutions (7). For a better understanding of discernment, management authorities (19) were categorized into government, government-aided, and private.[1] A total of 210 students were surveyed during the study through snowball sampling, comprising 136 female and 74 male students through online questionnaire circulation. Students were categorized based on gender, as the profession of teaching in India traditionally (e.g., women are significantly overrepresented in the profession of elementary educators) and technically (e.g., vacancy statements in the recruitment of teachers) excerpted a gendered narrative.

One-way ANOVA is applied to bring out the perception of managerial authorities of the colleges about the course in point through three broad facets—structural aspect, curriculum aspect, and student aspect. It involves nine, eight, and five parameters, respectively, for those aspects (Fig. 12.2). All the statistical analysis has been done through Excel v2013 and IBM SPSS v23.0.

12.5 Study Area

Since the teacher training institutes (B.Ed. colleges) of India function under the same regulation and face similar ground realities, an in-depth perception analysis in any area will act as a prototype. In order to get a deep understanding of the selected phenomenon, the study selects the city of Kolkata, West Bengal, India—a leading urban center of India which hosts several teacher training institutes (Fig. 12.3).

12.6 Rationale Behind the National Education Policy 2020

The National Education Policy (NEP), 2020, which the Union Cabinet approved on 29 July, 2020, was formulated as part of the Seventeenth Plan adopted by the Government of India for sustainable development in 2015. The NEP 2020 proposed by the Union Government, is a policy that is able to describe the Indian education system in different aspects, and its main objective is to improve the quality of Indian education. One of the most significant aspects of this policy is the proposed

[1]Government colleges are entirely funded and administered by the state government, whereas government-aided colleges get partial financial aid from the state government and need to follow certain governmental regulations like stipulated fee structure and specified recruitment policy, while private colleges are completely run by individual managerial authorities who often take exorbitant fees from the student to provide quality education as well as for profit maximization.

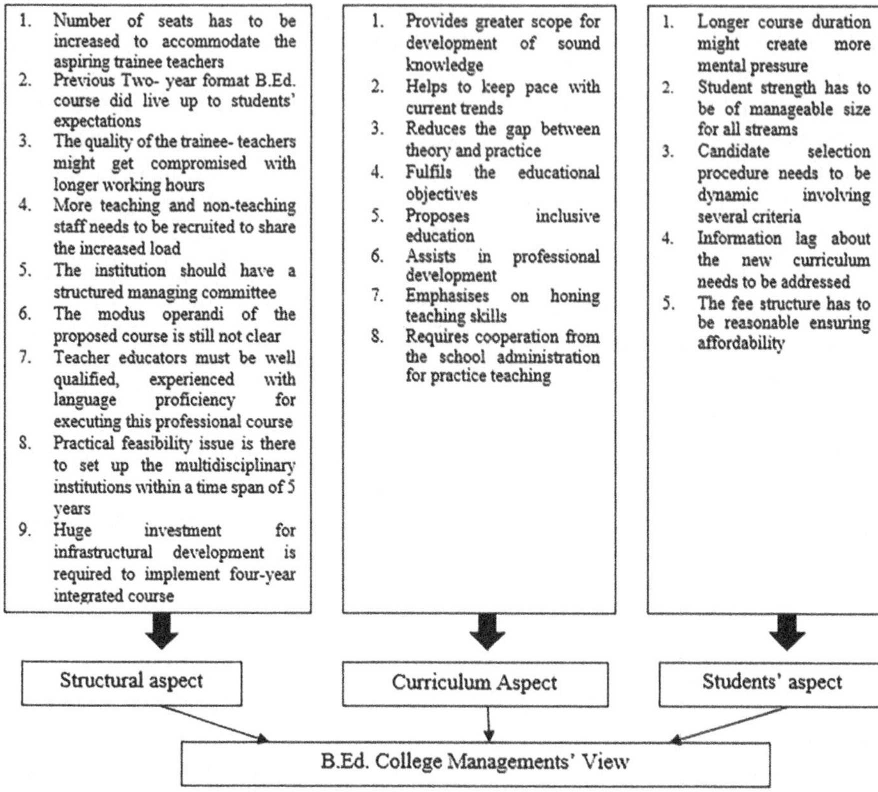

Fig. 12.2 Parameters involved in perception studies of the managerial bodies of teacher training institutions. (**Source**: Prepared by the authors)

allocation of 6% of GDP of the country to education. The policy is committed to bringing about a radical change in the education system from a structural and functional point of view and covers the entire range from pre-primary to higher education. Many developed countries worldwide have formulated their own education policies and infrastructure capable of sustaining the trend of sustainable development in the field of education.

Similarly, such a policy with groundbreaking changes was needed to make India at par in terms of educational capability. The education policy states that it is not only the responsibility of the central or state government to meet the growing demand for education but also that private educational institutions should be more generous and proactive in providing educational services to all sections of society. This education policy has also made various proposals in the field of the higher education system. Because if primary education is the foundation, higher education will be the future of the country. One of the dimensions of this higher education is the teacher education system, which has established a close link between primary and higher education. Because on the teacher's shoulder, the responsibility of

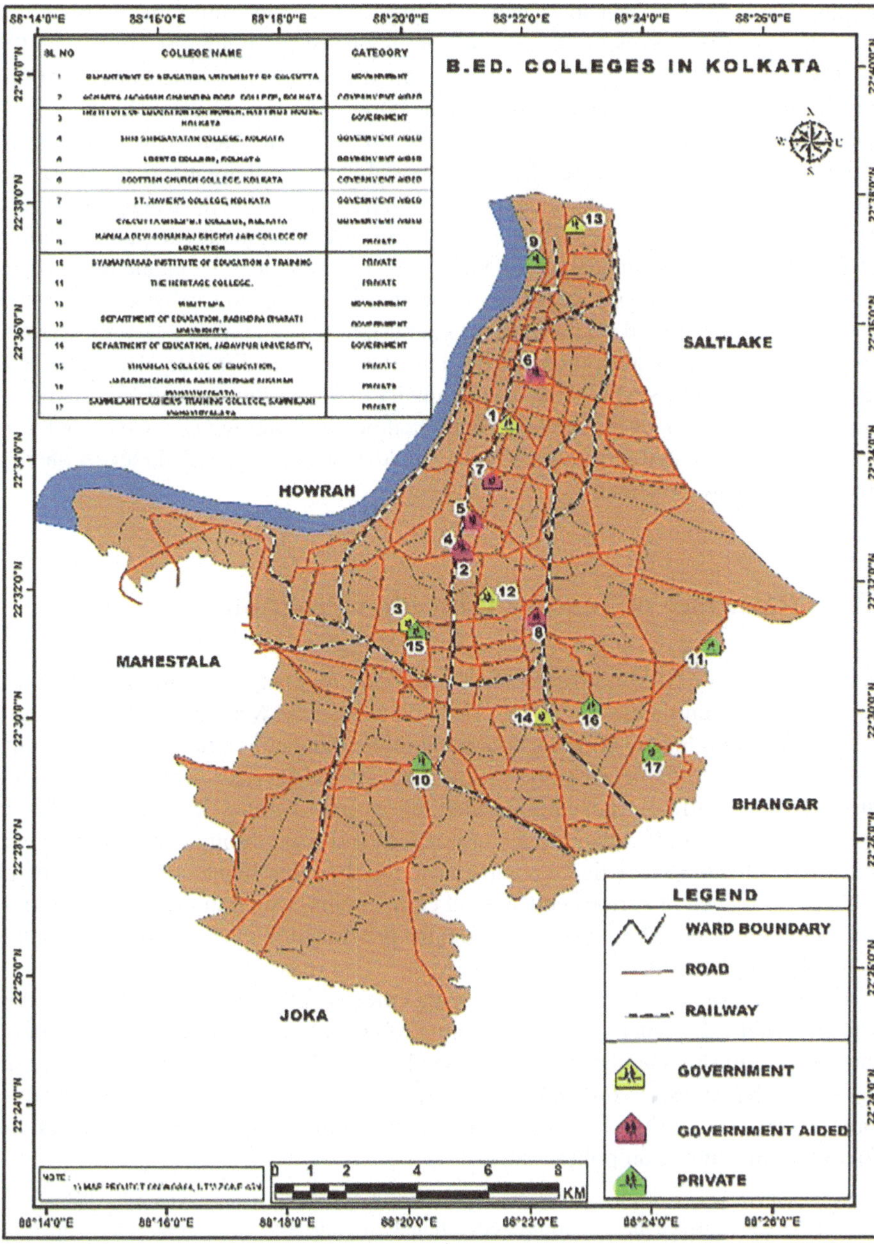

Fig. 12.3 Distribution of teacher training institutes in the city of Kolkata, West Bengal, India. (**Source**: NCTE 2020)

creating an educated, sensible, and sensitive future generation lies. Therefore, restructuring of the teacher education system is one of the main objectives of NEP 2020. Chapter 15 of NEP 2020 gives a detailed description of teacher education, emphasizing the two issues—teacher education program and teaching profession (Government of India, 2020). One of the pillars of the entire education system is the teacher; through the teacher, it is possible to implement all plans of the education system. However, in a developing country like India, the teacher is blamed for failing to reach the expected level of student success, especially in public schools (Atherton and Kingdom 2010). In this case, the student's spontaneity is often hampered even in primary stages, as instead of grasping the subject matter, too much emphasis is placed on mechanical memorizing. The current education system has to be student-centered, with the teacher playing an active role. Therefore, the new education policy seeks to change the quality of the teacher education system in a way that not only makes the teacher's qualifications internationally standard but also makes the education system at the primary, middle, secondary, and higher secondary levels much more practical.

12.7 Relevance of Teacher Education Program

According to Ball (1999), despite socio-economic diversity, education policies are based on two main themes—market price and efficiency. Market penetration in the field of education means bringing education in the competitive field, and as a result, competition is created between the various educational services in the private sector through which different educational institutions try to impart education of better quality or take resort to advanced technology. In this way, through an invisible race, education is made to face fierce competition. On the other hand, competency refers to the performance of various educational components, which in fact determines the quality of education. These two issues fuel the privatization of education, making the sector highly competitive.

This education policy also wants to change the concept of education. Education is not just a biblical science; the core meaning of education lies in the acquirement of knowledge and skills by the students—this idea the NEP seeks to spread at all levels of society. Therefore, in this policy, the autonomy of teachers has been reduced to some extent so that the students get maximum rights in all spheres of education. Therefore, the education policy states:

> "The main objective of education will be to achieve the goal of universal education and this goal must be achieved through primary education. If this objective is achieved by 2050, then other aspects of this education policy will become relevant to the interests of the students. And in order to achieve this goal, the basic need for education must first be achieved."

Teachers are one of the key players in making the primary education system effective at all levels of society. The main goal of the teacher is not only to teach the student to read and write but also to ensure that the student can become a socially, culturally, and morally worthy citizen of society. Therefore, the overall development of the student and, at the same time, the development of education will be possible only when it is possible to improve the quality of the teacher. Therefore, for the teacher to become a worthy guide, all kinds of help and support must be provided institutionally.

12.8 Highlights of Teacher Education Programs Across the Globe

Around the world, those countries which are aiming to create a high-quality teaching standard realize that there must be a strong association between planning, execution, and standard of teacher education (Darling-Hammond and Lieberman 2012). In Australia, there is a strong demand for the teacher education program, and all the universities have high admission requirements; applicants must have high grade points and volunteer work experience in any school (Burns and McIntyre 2017). The whole system is run by the government authorities to give equal chances to all the candidates, including the minority population, and the primary objective behind that is to have teaching faculties from diverse backgrounds (Gitomer 2007).

The United States established National Board for Professional Teaching Standards in 1987 to develop the quality of the teaching force through the issuance of teaching licenses based on teacher preparation (Zeichner 1993). A professional body supervises this entire assessment and certification process. Every university initiates clinical learning for beginner teachers in special teacher training schools for trainee teachers who need to prove themselves as skilled teachers through various assessments (Walsh 2001). In the teacher training programs, few innovative models for advanced student teaching strategies are introduced, and besides that, various practical knowledge like classroom management skills and communication with parents are also imparted (Darling-Hammond et al. 2005).

In Japan, a formal teacher education program began in 1949. There are national, public, and private colleges that are responsible for training secondary school teachers (Hirotoshi 2015). In these colleges, several kinds of courses are running, like child education, human development education, and professional schools of teacher education, and they provide pre-service and in-service teacher education programs also. Besides, various developmental short courses are provided to the trainee teachers to enhance teacher's skills and proficiency (Fukumoto 2009).

In China, a teaching aspirant needs to apply to the Bureau of Education if he or she wants to become a teacher. Before applying, they must have either a teacher education certificate or equivalent qualifications. In addition, trainee teachers should have completed a teacher training program, including mandatory specialization courses, intensive training courses, and a 6-month practice teaching course. The specialized courses aim to develop teachers' expert knowledge and skills in a particular subject. Both the teacher education commissions should sanction subject area courses and training courses in universities and the Ministry of Education (MOE 2011). There are mainly two types of teacher education programs in China: the first one is a 5-year undergraduate education program, the second is a graduate degree, and a 1-year full-time (or 2-year, part-time) master's degree in the education program. Often, these institutions offer short-term classes for teachers who need in-service training after the application to the Bureau of Education (Leung et al. 2015). In China, all kinds of education-related courses, graduate credit programs, and training teachers from kindergarten to high school level have become the responsibility of all colleges and universities (Tsung et al. 2015).

In Turkey, teacher education programs are handled by the Council of Higher Education and implemented by the universities' faculties of education. This program was renewed in 2006–2007. A flexible curriculum has been made that includes various courses like field and field education courses, teaching profession knowledge, and general culture courses (Erdem 2015). Furthermore, in the practical training course, the implementation of school experience and teaching practice courses are executed in cooperation with the Ministry of National Education (Table 12.1).

12.9 Key Recommendations of the National Education Policy (2020) on Teacher Education

The necessary steps recommended by the National Education Policy (2020) are the following:

12.9.1 Bringing Teacher Education Courses Under the University

According to the policy, teacher training can only be completed if the teacher training degree is administered through a multidisciplinary college or university and the B.Ed. program is designed by a 4-year integrated education system to complete pedagogical theory and practical training through a certain number of stages.

12.9.2 Coexistence of Dual Degrees

The National Education Policy states that, at the university level, a 4-year integrated B.Ed. program will offer undergraduate studies in a variety of subjects, where students will study with their chosen subject. In other words, the work of teacher

Table 12.1 Comparing key features of contemporary teacher education program in various countries

Parameter	Australia	China	Japan	Turkey	UK	USA
Duration	4 years	5 years	4 years	4 years	3–4 years	4–5 years
Minimum qualification	Higher secondary education	Higher secondary education	Higher secondary education	Higher secondary education	Undergraduate degree	Higher secondary education
Admission procedure	Average marks of higher secondary examination	Entrance test	Entrance test	Percentage of higher secondary examination	Interview and marks of higher secondary examination	GPA (grade point average) and interview
Pattern/ structure	Graduation with B.Ed.	Graduation with B.Ed.	Graduation with B.Ed.	Graduation with B.Ed.	Graduation with B.Ed.	Graduation with B. Ed.
Practice teaching	Up to 1 year	6 months	4–20 weeks	21–25 days	Up to 1 year	Up to 10 months

(**Source:** Compiled by the authors based on Burns and McIntyre 2017; Walsh 2001; Hirotoshi 2015; Leung et al. 2015; Erdem 2015)

training will continue along with gaining skills in certain subjects. As the dropout rate in education declines, so does the number of committed teachers.

12.9.3 Ways to Increase Teacher Efficiency

Given the demands of the present society and technological development, a radical change is needed in the entire education system, which will help enhance teachers' efficiency. However, the policy does not mention any step where the contribution or importance of the teacher as a measure of the quality of education is undeniable. There was no mention of any workshop or development program to enhance the professionalism of teachers. For example, in 2015–2016, only 1% of primary school teachers participated in any type of training (DISE 2017).

Arrangements have been made to make teachers more responsible for the overall development of the students. Based on the type of work, special changes will be made in terms of tenure, various benefits of pension, etc. For example, based on the evaluation of the work of teachers, just as they may be given different benefits, different convenient services can be discontinued at any level of employment. According to the education policy, teachers who have done outstanding work must be recognized and promoted, and their salaries are increased. In order for every teacher to be able to apply their best skills in the field of education, they need to be constantly encouraged, and their work needs to be properly evaluated and recognized. A committee should be constituted by the central and state governments to properly evaluate the teachers. This committee will give priority to the evaluation of a particular teacher in a particular school, his attendance rate, participation in various activities, review from his colleagues, etc.

12.9.4 Development of Women's Education

However, the detailed observations and performance appraisals for teachers in many cases reflect the view that teaching is not a creative endeavor but that the quality of teaching depends on a thorough calculation of various rewards or punishments. In encouraging such thinking, another significant point to keep in mind is that female teachers are overrepresented in primary education in India. So, if, for some reason, these women continue to feel neglected in terms of various assessments or are actually neglected, it can have a far-reaching effect on the development of women's education.

12.9.5 Instruction to Close Down Substandard Individual Teacher Training Centers

The National Education Policy 2020 has decided to close all the nonfunctioning independent teacher training institutes across the country by 2023, aiming to produce teachers scientifically and effectively through teacher education programs across the country. In that case, such institutions will have to transform themselves into multidisciplinary higher education centers by 2030, with the introduction of a 4-year integrated B.Ed. program. This whole matter will be done under the supervision of the National Higher Education Regulatory Authority and the State Education Commission, which will in fact determine the quality of teacher education.

According to the policy:

> "to ensure integrity, transparency, and efficiency of resources, a 'light but strong' regulatory framework needs to be put in place to maintain the effectiveness and uniqueness of the teacher education course and at the same time enable students to enter the course through due process. Which will give birth to skilled and enterprising teachers as a guide for future generations." (Sharma 2020)

This is one of the most important decisions in the national education policy because if all the B.Ed. colleges are included in the multidisciplinary higher education center or university, then B.Ed. section will continue its existence only as a department.

12.9.6 Changes in the Admission Process for Teacher Education Courses

According to the new policy, in order to be admitted to this course, each student has to take an entrance test for a specific subject and qualification, which will be recognized by the National Testing Agency.

12.9.7 Increasing Responsibilities for the Varsities' Education Departments

The new education policy recommends that the university education department take on more responsibilities, as the education department needs to coordinate with the rest of the subject, creating schoolteachers as well as teachers who will be trained. Various other courses related to education should be introduced, and they should also be monitored.

In this regard, it is pertinent to mention that this education policy calls for the integration of pre-primary classes with first and second grades. But no specific road map has been given on how to prepare teachers for this. In that case, there is some ambiguity as to what kind of methods and technology can be used for the regular recruitment of teachers or whether training can be imparted to teachers through distance education.

12.9.8 Requirement of Teachers for Teacher Education Program

According to the National Education Policy 2020, teachers of all subjects should be recruited in the education department, and priority should be given to Ph.D. degree holders, so that the education department can become diverse from all sides. This kind of diversity will help in enhancing the identity of the teachers.

12.10 Perception Towards National Educational Policy 2020: Across the Board

The theoretical discussions are not enough to realize the gravity of the matter, as the policy change is going to impact the stakeholders directly; their perception of the changing scenario is of utmost importance.

12.10.1 Perception Study Regarding 4-Year Integrated B.Ed. Course Involving the Trainee Teachers

In Kolkata, the B.Ed. students from different study semesters have given their opinions regarding the restructuring of the teacher education program as mentioned in NEP 2020. The number of female respondents is more as female trainee teachers are much higher in number than their male counterparts throughout the district. This scenario is the same across the country, making school teaching a gendered vocation as very few male students likely opt for B.Ed. course at such a young age, primarily due to societal constructs of patriarchy, comparatively lower remuneration, and longer course duration. But interestingly, the perception study (Fig. 12.4) shows that both female and male students are positive about this integrated course, as they think that restructured B.Ed. course will act as an educational strategy, being more specific and goal oriented, and may create more job opportunities. So, male trainee teachers feel that more young people will likely opt as there is a chance to get employment quickly with this integrated 4-year course with a lesser total course duration if viewed alongside the present B.Ed. course of 2 years after 3 years of traditional graduation course.

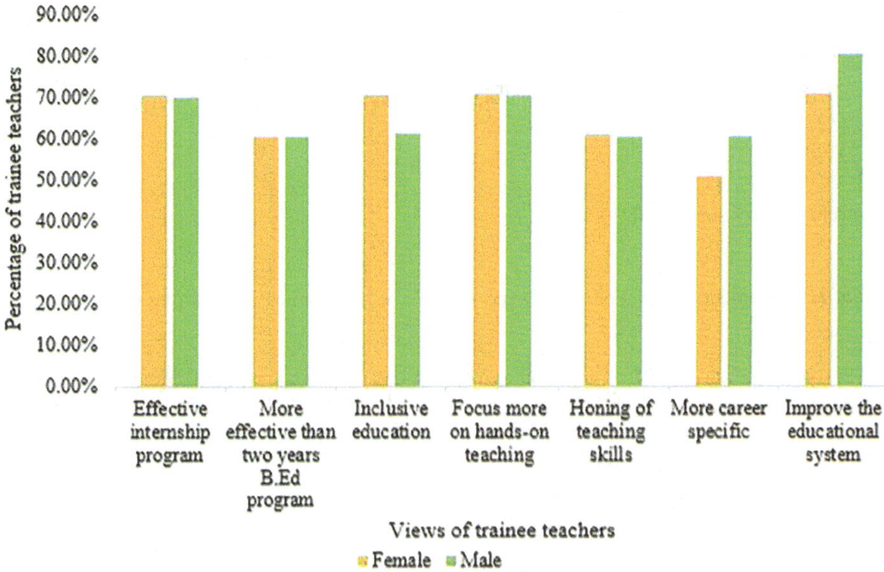

Fig. 12.4 Gender-wise perception of trainee teachers towards 4-year integrated B.Ed. course, Kolkata, West Bengal. (**Source**: Prepared by the authors)

Though the foundational principles of NEP 2020 are access, equity, quality, affordability, and accountability, the majority of the students (almost 80% of the respondents), to some extent, are concerned about affordability. They fear a steep rise in tuition fees hampering access and equity towards quality education for all. Moreover, since a complete overhaul of the entire system is needed within a short period, they fear that the private players will impose a higher fee structure to improve the much-needed infrastructure.

12.10.2 Perception Study Regarding 4-Year Integrated B.Ed. Course Involving the Managerial Authorities

The total organizational structure of teacher education institutions varies based on management category. In order to get the views of managerial authorities of the colleges towards this particular course, researchers have designed their interpretations based on three categories: structural aspect, curriculum aspect, and student aspect. A genuine concern arises to know the difference between government, government-aided, and private B.Ed. colleges in terms of managerial views concerning the implementation of 4-year integrated B.Ed. program. For this purpose, a one-way ANOVA has been applied.

Nine items have been selected to determine whether the college managements are aware and willing to set up the newly formed course and where they actually stand

Table 12.2 Descriptive statistics of structural aspect from the managerial viewpoint

Summary				
Groups	Count	Sum	Average	Variance
Government college	6	183	30.5	5.9
Government-aided college	6	182	30.33333	5.866667
Private college	7	251	35.85714	6.142857

(**Source:** Primary survey, 2021–2022)

Table 12.3 Comparison of scores on the perspective of management from different institutions

ANOVA						
Source of variation	SS	df	MS	F	P-value	F crit
Between groups	130.9411	2	65.47055	10.94705	0.00101	3.633723
Within groups	95.69048	16	5.980655			
Total	226.6316	18				

(**Source:** Primary survey, 2021–2022)

Table 12.4 Descriptive statistics of curriculum aspect from a managerial viewpoint

Summary				
Groups	Count	Sum	Average	Variance
Government college	6	157	26.16667	4.166667
Government-aided college	6	177	29.5	7.9
Private college	7	193	27.57143	18.95238

(**Source:** Primary survey, 2021–2022)

Table 12.5 Comparison of scores on the perspective of management from different institutions

ANOVA						
Source of variation	SS	df	MS	F	P-value	F crit
Between groups	33.63659	2	16.8183	1.546087	0.243286	3.633723
Within groups	174.0476	16	10.87798			
Total	207.6842	18				

(**Source:** Primary survey, 2021–2022)

(Fig. 12.2). The descriptive summary of these items has been presented in Table 12.2. The results demonstrated (in Table 12.3) that the F value is "10.94," which is higher than the critical value of F, i.e., "3.63" at the 0.05 level of confidence. This result confirms that a significant difference exists among government, government-aided, and private B.Ed. colleges in terms of execution of integrated B.Ed. course.

For the curriculum aspect, eight items (Fig. 12.2) have been selected based on which management's view was evaluated concerning the new curriculum transaction. The summary showed that the F value is "1.54," which is higher than the critical value of F, i.e., "3.63" at 0.05 level of confidence (Tables 12.4 and 12.5). Therefore,

Table 12.6 Descriptive statistics of students' aspect from the managerial viewpoint

Summary				
Groups	Count	Sum	Average	Variance
Government college	6	98	16.33333	5.866667
Government-aided college	6	81	13.5	9.1
Private college	7	123	17.57143	1.285714

(**Source:** Primary survey, 2021–2022)

Table 12.7 Comparison of scores on the perspective of management from different institutions

ANOVA						
Source of variation	SS	df	MS	F	P-value	F crit
Between groups	55.24185	2	27.62093	5.353696	0.016592	3.633723
Within groups	82.54762	16	5.159226			
Total	137.7895	18				

(**Source:** Primary survey, 2021–2022)

it concludes that no significant difference exists among government, government-aided, and private B.Ed. colleges, in terms of opinions regarding the curriculum of integrated B.Ed. course.

One of the prime foci of management is students' well-being and educational benefits. Regarding the students' aspect, different college managements think differently. Five items (Fig. 12.2) have been taken into consideration to measure this aspect, which actually delivers insight into management's thoughts about students (Table 12.6). As shown in Table 12.7, the results demonstrated that the F value is "5.35." It is higher than the critical value of F, which is "3.63" at 0.05 level of confidence. So, a significant difference exists among government, government-aided, and private B.Ed. colleges in terms of students' benefits in new integrated B.Ed. course.

From the above results, it can be said that government B.Ed. colleges are in a better position to implement newly reformed B.Ed. course as it is easier for them to adapt the fresh curriculum through a new system as they will receive direct aid from the government to start and continue the whole procedure. Also, they have adequate infrastructure to some extent, while private institutions need to generate funds for initiating the course, which is the most challenging part from their side.

12.10.3 Ground Realities

One of our samples, a second-semester student from a private B.Ed. college, who comes from a mediocre family, shared her views exclusively. After completing an M.A. from a government-aided college, she was trying to get enrolled in a government or aided B.Ed. college. However, due to fewer seats in government colleges, she could not find the chance despite those fairly good marks in her postgraduate scorecards. As a result, she was forced to opt for a private B.Ed. college, but the main constraint faced was the high course fees. That college agreed to give admission on an installment basis payment of fees. She excerpts her views, "one entrance test should be introduced for getting admission in B.Ed. and number of seats should also be increased. It will encourage more students with a good academic score towards this course and the teaching profession. It will also give every student the equality of opportunity." *[Interviewed on 6th July 2021 by the first author]*

Our other interviewee, a member of the management of a reputed government degree college in the city, opines, "Within the year 2030, I couldn't guess how far it is possible to make our college a multidisciplinary institution. At a time, we have to run 4-year integrated B.Ed. course, B.Ed. course of the previous mode, general degree course, both honours and program. For this transformation, we need huge capital, infrastructure, buildings, and teaching and non-teaching staff, and till now, we have not received any detailed framework from the government on how to process this huge work and how to execute it." *[Interviewed on 9th July 2021 by the first author]*

A fourth-semester student from a government B.Ed. college opines, "It will be very helpful for students like us who want to pursue the teaching profession as a career from the beginning. We do not need to search for several colleges and their admission forms after completing a higher degree, like post-graduation. It will be easier for the students who are focussed on being teachers; once they get the chance, they will be qualified as successful trainee teachers within less time also, as now we spend three years for graduation and another two years for B.Ed. The new course will save an important year which will be definitely supportive for students." *[Interviewed on 12th July 2021 by the first author]*

A teacher-in-charge (i.e., a teacher who temporarily acts as the principal) of a government-aided college showed an assorted approach towards the NEP 2020, especially the teacher education program. She appears to be a little bit confused regarding their duties for implementing the new policy. She stated, "I am not in a condition to give comments regarding this new issue as I do not know where we shall go, how to merge the stand-alone colleges, and how to manage all the courses in this limited time and space. *[Interviewed on 13th July 2021 by the first author]*

12.11 Conclusion

This study makes an attempt to analyze and explore the dynamic alterations of the teacher education program, which is proposed in the agenda of the NEP 2020. All the recommendations of this current policy concerning teacher education have been assessed through a modest comparison with the systems, successfully implemented in other countries. Also, it is validated by the views of different stakeholders involved with the system of teacher education. All the progressive countries instituted B.Ed. in such a manner that high standard in the teaching profession is ensured and the trainee teachers are able to meet the expectations of the future generation.

This new policy has been framed to meet that kind of international criteria for the trainee teacher education program so that a world-class standard can be achieved through the development of a much-needed quality teaching force.

Traditionally, the Indian education system has been plagued by race, religion, caste, class, gender, and various social inequalities. But in spite of all this, in order to maintain national unity and harmony, the foundation stone of equality and justice must be laid in the education system. Therefore, the NEP 2020 seeks to redesign the education system in such a way that this newly created education system can serve as a key determinant in the development of society and the formation of a democratic federal structure. The importance of teacher training in our society is immense because the teacher is a pillar of the society on whose efficiency and foresight the future of the whole country depends. The contribution of teachers in maintaining such national unity and sensitivity is undeniable. Teacher education program always has a direct influence on human improvement. It can also be led to high commitment and spirit in the school environment. However, with the expansion of teacher education institutes, the assurance of quality has been challenged, which is the basic requirement in the knowledge society. The expected standard can only be achieved by establishing an innovative, flexible organization that can adjust quickly to changes in its environment and is capable of learning. As a whole, quality assurance of teacher education may be ensured by involving every stakeholder because the contributions of everyone are essential and interrelated; still, the plan is subject to continuous review and revision.

It is said that the teacher represents an intellectual community in society, so much so that the quality of the education system depends on the quality of the teachers. Thus, the role of the teachers should be critical to any reforms designed to improve quality education. However, the way in which the teacher education program is being transformed may be a safe passage for privatization to come dominating in the field of education amidst the new-liberalism ascendancy. Although this newer education policy promises to restore the lost credibility of teachers to a greater extent, it also keeps further challenges to the transforming society through its complexity of architecture, certain vagueness in the execution end, and more space for dubious privatization in teachers' training system.

References

Adaval SB (1984) Analytical study of teachers' education in India. Amitabh Prakashan, Allahabad

Aggarwal JC (1988) Teachers' role, status, service conditions and education in India. Doaba House, New Delhi

Atherton P, Kingdom G (2010) The relative effectiveness and costs of contract and regular teachers in India. CSAE Working Paper Series 2010-15, Centre for the Study of African economies, University of Oxford

Ball S (1999) Global trends in education reform and the struggle for the soul of the teacher! Paper presented at the British Educational Research Association annual conference, University of Sussex. Brighton, September 2–5, 1999

Burns D, McIntyre A (2017) Empowered educators in Australia: how high-performing systems shape teaching quality. Jossey-Bass, San Francisco, CA
Darling-Hammond L, Lieberman A (2012) Teacher education around the world: changing policies and practices. Routledge, New York
Darling-Hammond L, Holtzman DJ, Gatlin SJ, Heilig JV (2005) Does teacher preparation matter? Evidence about teacher certification, teach for America, and teacher effectiveness. Educ Policy Anal Arch 13(42):3–51
Deb K (2004) The changing scenario of teacher education. In: Singh MS (ed) Quality impact in teacher education. Adhyayan Publishers and Distributors, Delhi, pp 60–64
District Information System for Education (2017) Elementary education: trends in India 2015–16. National Institute of Educational Planning and Administration, New Delhi
Dubey A (1997) Commercialization of education in India: policy, Law and Justice. A.P.H. Publishing Corporation, New Delhi
Erdem M (2015) Comparative education systems. In: Balcı A (ed) Turkish education system, 5th edn. Pegem publishing
Fukumoto K (2009) The development of teachers' competency standards in Japanese universities of education, developing the capacity of arts education practitioners, Core competencies of arts education practitioners
Gitomer D (2007) Teacher quality in a changing policy landscape: improvements in the teacher Pool. Educational Testing Service, Princeton, NJ
Government of India (2020) New education policy. Ministry of Human Resource Development, New Delhi
Gupta SP (1980) A study of the in-service teaching needs of the secondary teacher educators. NCERT, New Delhi
Hirotoshi Y (2015) Estimation of future demands for school teachers and the prospects of teacher education. Shuppan, Kyodo
Khanna P (2005) Changing scenario of higher education: challenges to quality assurance and sustenance. Univ News 43(7):48–62
Kundu CL (1988) Indian year book on teacher education. Sterling Publishers Pvt. Ltd., New Delhi
Leung FKS, Wong ASC, Leung CCY (2015) Overview of education system in Hong Kong. http://timssandpirls.bc.edu/timss2015/encyclopedia/countries/hong-kong-sar. Accessed 14 Nov 2021
Mangla S (2001) Teacher education: trends and strategies. Radha Publications, New Delhi
Mehta AC (1998) Education for all India: enrolment projections. National Institute of Educational Planning and Administration (NIEPA) and Vikas Publishing House Pvt. Ltd., New Delhi
Ministry of Human Resource Development (MHRD) (1992) Revised national policy on education. Government of India, New Delhi
MOE (2011) Teacher's law of the People's Republic of China. http://old.moe.gov.cn/publicfiles/business/htmlfiles/moe/moe_2803/200907/49852.html. Accessed 27 Jan 2022
Mukerji SN (1968) Education of teachers in India, vol II. S. Chand and Company, Delhi
Nair AS (2006) The changing face of teacher education. The CTE National Journal, Bhopal
National Council for Teacher Education (NCTE) (1997) Report on manpower planning for teacher education: central expert group on manpower planning for teacher education. NCTE, New Delhi
National Council for Teacher Education (NCTE) (1998) Teacher education in Delhi, Current Status, Issues and Future Projections, New Delhi
National Council of Educational Research and Training (2005) National curriculum framework. NCERT, New Delhi
National Council of Teacher Education (NCTE) (2020). Annual Report 2020–2021, New Delhi: NCTE
Rao VK (2001) Teacher education. A.P.H. Publishing Corporation, New Delhi
Reddy RS (1998) Principles and practices of teacher education. Rajat Publication, Delhi
Shankar U (1984) Education of Indian teachers. Sterling Publishers, New Delhi

Sharma R (2020) Review of national education policy 2020 with specific reference to teacher education. Working Papers 2020-35-04, Voice of Research. https://ideas.repec.org/p/vor/issues/2020-35-04.html

Tsung HJ, Che DL, Kuan MC, Chen YL (2015) Overview of education system, teachers, teacher education and professional development. http://timssandpirls.bc.edu/timss2015/encyclopedia/countries/chinese-taipei. Accessed 21 Jan 2022

Verma SK (2009) Teacher education: quantity vs. quality. Paper presented at national seminar on self financing teacher education: need and problem, Babe Ke College of Education, Mudki, 2009

Walsh K (2001) Teacher certification reconsidered: stumbling for quality. The Abell Foundation, Baltimore

Yadav SK, Sumbul R (2006) Teacher education in India: issues and concerns. Univ News 44(40): 146–161

Zeichner KM (1993) Traditions of practice in U.S. pre-service teacher education programs. Teach Teach Educ 9(1):1–13

Anusri Kundu is pursuing Ph.D. in Geography, Diamond Harbour Women's University. She is working as Assistant Professor in the Department of B.Ed., Syamaprasad Institute of Education and Training (affiliated to WBUTTEPA). The author did her Graduation in Geography (Hons.) and Postgraduation from the University of Calcutta with good academic record. Later, she obtained B. Ed. and M.Ed. from the University of Calcutta. She had started her career of teaching as a guest lecturer in geography at Surendranath College. She has qualified the National Eligibility Test exam. She has also participated in national and international seminars and presented research papers in various occasions and also contributed papers in various journals and books.

Dr. Anindya Basu has been working as Assistant Professor in the Department of Geography, Diamond Harbour Women's University, since 2017. Previously, from 2011, she served as an Assistant Professor in Women's Christian College, Kolkata. She has been a rank holder in bachelor's and master's degree program in geography from the University of Calcutta and UGC-Junior Research Fellow recipient. She has also received PG Diploma in RS-GIS from Jadavpur University. She has keen interest in sociopolitical geography, urban-environmental issues, and tourism geography. Basu has presented a number of papers in national and international conferences and seminars, apart from publishing several research papers and book chapters.

Chapter 13
The Implementation of Massive Open Online Courses (MOOCs) in India: An Initiative Toward Quality Education for Sustainable Development

Raju Singha

13.1 Introduction

A look at the history of Indian education reveals three distinct eras. The education system of the Brahmanic and Buddhist eras is referred to as the ancient Indian education system, which was primarily Pathshala and Tol centric. [1] Medieval education essentially refers to the Islamic era's educational system, which was primarily focused on Maktab and Madrasa. [2] The modern era of education in India

[1] In the early Indian educational system, the Pathshala and the Tol were the two learning institutions. Essentially, Pathshalas served as the primary level institutions. The teaching of basic literacy and handwriting to children took place in these institutions. Generally speaking, these institutions were constructed in the neighborhood on the verandah of the grocery store, underneath a tree, or in any other deserted and empty space. In ancient India, there were tols or secondary schools. Any child could enroll in Tol after completing his education at Pathshala. As well as teaching the fundamental lessons, the local Guru or Acharya would also recite verses from the Veda, Gita, and Upanishad while imparting a variety of useful life lessons. In educational institutions run by Pathshala and Toll, Sanskrit was the language of instruction.

[2] During the Islamic era, Muslim educational institutions were called Madrasas and Maktabs. Maktabs were primary schools of Islamic learning. It was connected with some mosque. During the reign of Emperor Akbar, Maktabs became more popular like Pathshalas of ancient Vedic era. The curriculum of the Maktab was writing, reading, memorizing verses of the Holy Quran, etc. It can be said that the Maktab was one of the means of spreading mass education among the Muslim masses of that era. Madrasas were institutions of higher learning during Islamic rule in the Middle Ages as in the Vedic period. Madrasas were usually associated with mosques. Madrasas were equivalent to colleges. A madrasa was established in almost every major city. Most of the madrasas were patronized by noble Muslim families and the then emperors.

R. Singha (✉)
Department of Education, Dr. Meghnad Saha College (Affiliated to University of Gour Banga), Uttar Dinajpur, West Bengal, India

M. Mishra et al. (eds.), *Public Policies and Sustainable Development in Post-Reform India*, New Frontiers in Regional Science: Asian Perspectives 71,
https://doi.org/10.1007/978-981-99-3696-0_13

primarily refers to the colonial education system of British-ruled India and its follow-up in the post-colonial period with certain amendments and extensions. During this time, the concept of modern schools, colleges, and universities emerged in India. After nearly two centuries of the ruling, the country was declared independent. India's educational institutions are gradually modernized, and the demand for education among the people of the country has also been increasing gradually. As a result, it becomes unfeasible to provide "education for all" in the scarce formal education system.

India has made education for all citizens a national priority. Article 45 of the Constitution, which went into effect on January 26, 1950, declared unequivocally that all boys and girls in the nation, ages 6–14, would receive free and compulsory primary education within 10 years of its adoption. Three strategic directions can be used to explain the idea of universal education in India. All countrywide students aged 6–14 are guaranteed access to all educational facilities, which is known as universal provision. Universal enrollment refers to keeping pupils enrolled in school at least until they have completed 8 years of primary education. Universal enrollment refers to making sure that all boys and girls aged 6–14 are enrolled in primary school. Keeping in mind the idea of Education for All in India, the Central and State Governments have taken various steps from time to time.

In order to strengthen primary education, the first All India Education Commission (1964–1966) in independent India placed a strong focus on school complex and work experience, among other things. In the National Education Policy of 1986, which came later, there were initiatives like the scheme Operation Blackboard, the establishment of District Institutes of Education and Training (DIET) in every district for the training of primary teachers, and a focus on Early Childhood Care and Education (ECCE). The Government of India launched the District Primary Education Program (DPEP) in 1994, with the main goals of the program being the establishment of more new primary schools, the implementation of Operation Blackboard, the recruitment of more qualified teachers at primary institutions. To provide every children in primary schools with cooked foods at mid-day in schools, the National Program of Nutrition Support to Primary Education (Presently known as PM-POshan SHAkti Nirman, PM-POSHAN) was introduced in 1995. Additionally, the Sarva Shiksha Abhiyan (SSA) initiative was started in 2000 with the intention of educating all of India in order to achieve the Millennium Development Goals (MDG) set forth by the UNO in 2000. Its goals were to ensure that everyone should get a minimum of 4 years of primary education by 2003, 5 years of primary education by 2007, and 8 years of primary education by 2010. The Right to Education Act (RTE Act-2009) is a crucial endeavor to implement universal primary education. This Act declares that all children between the ages of 6 and 14 have a fundamental right to education under Article 21-A of the Constitution.

In India, efforts are being made to make secondary education universal in addition to elementary education. The Mudaliar Commission issued significant suggestions in 1952–1953 to alter the objectives, course offerings, and organizational framework of secondary education. The Rashtriya Madhyamik Shiksha Abhiyan (RMSA) was also introduced in 2009 with the goal of making secondary education universal by the year 2017 and retaining all students in secondary school by the year 2020. Its objectives include providing girls and boys aged 15–16 with a quality secondary education, eradicating gender disparity in the secondary education sector, and making secondary education universal by 2020.

In this light, a new educational concept emerged in India, where all students are recognized for their educational opportunities. As society never remains static, science and technology advancements have made the educational system dynamic. In light of science and technology, the modern educational system has also undergone revolutionary changes. One of them is the utilization of ICT in the education system. The online education system is the most recent version of the Indian educational landscape in the twenty-first century. Online education essentially means that a student has the opportunity to fulfill all of his or her educational needs based on internet connectivity. One such online education is Massive Open Online Courses (MOOCs).

Massive Open Online Courses (MOOCs) were introduced through the SWAYAM platform in 2017, and they quickly gained popularity within the Indian educational system. MOOCs maintain an asynchronous learning environment and an online course format. MOOCs were widely used both before and after the pandemic outbreak. Without a question, the corona pandemic has had a significant negative influence on the formal education system at schools, colleges, and universities. However, because MOOCs are online courses that have been widely adopted since their inception, the pandemic plays no direct or unfavorable influence in this situation. However, throughout this pandemic, students in India have gained some understanding of hybrid learning and the necessity of ICT or e-readiness abilities. In the discussion, the author has only tried to explore the Indian initiatives toward MOOCs and whether MOOCs can provide quality education? Hence this part is not included in the discussion.

Sustainable development is a concept that comes up repeatedly in our discussions in this age of globalization. Realizing the importance of sustainable development, the United Nations (2015) mentioned a total of 17 sustainable development goals (SDGs) at a general meeting attended by 197 countries throughout the globe. Quality education is the fourth of the 17 Sustainable Development Goals, ensuring inclusive and equal opportunities in education and promoting lifelong learning for all people, regardless of caste, creed, religion, or gender. In India, "quality education" refers to an education that allows a person to grow as a skilled, positive thinker, a contributing member of society, and a participant in the national cause.

In this chapter, the author intended to find out the significance of MOOCs in quality education in India. The discussion has been divided into two segments. In the first part, I tend to explain what Massive Open Online Courses (MOOCs) are and what initiatives have the Indian Government taken to promote and develop MOOCs. In the second part, I have attempted to explore whether MOOCs are successful in providing quality education in India.

The definition of MOOCs is hidden within its acronym. MOOCs can be defined as free course of study that is made available to a large number of people via the internet. In 2008, David of the University of Prince Edward in Canada and Bryan

Alexander of the National Institute for Technology in Liberal Education first coined the term MOOC (Nisha and Senthil 2015), and it became well-known and popular in 2012. There are two concepts regarding MOOCs—one is cMOOCs and xMOOCs. "cMOOCs" are based on the theory of connectivism [3] and emphasis community learning through social media like blogs and wikis to construct their own knowledge. "xMOOCs," on the other hand, are based on the concept of traditional classroom teaching, in which students are given assignments, quizzes, and pre-recorded video to help them maintain their skills and meet their educational needs. Several top universities around the world, including the prestigious Stanford University, MIT, and Harvard University, were among the first to offer xMOOCs to students.

Before the successful online course run in India, various initiatives were taken for the application of ICT in education, such as the National Digital Repository by IGNOU, and Vidya Vahini, a scheme for integrating ICT in the rural school curriculum. The main objective of such an initiative was to use ICT in education to reach out to more boys and girls. Also on the list is EDUSAT, an educational satellite of the Government of India that broadcasts various educational programs for students. Information and Library Network Centre (INFLIBNET) is a center that creates digital integration among university libraries throughout the country under the aegis of the University Grants Commission (UGC). Its basic aim is to make a modern revolution in the library system of the country to optimum utilization of the information. Various other ICT initiatives have also been taken, but despite taking so many initiatives, the real purpose was being thwarted due to lack of awareness. In view of the popularity of online courses in different countries of the world and the demand of students, the Government of India has taken some effective steps in this regard.

13.2 National Programme on Technology Enhanced Learning (NPTEL)

NPTEL is a project funded by the Ministry of Human Resource Development (MHRD) of India, established in 2003. This project was formed by a joint venture of seven Indian Institute of Technology (IITs) (Bombay, Delhi, Kanpur, Kharagpur, Madras, Guwahati, and Roorkee) and Indian Institute of Science (IISC), Bangalore (http://nptel.ac.in) to offer engineering and science online courses in India

[3] A brand new concept in learning theories is the theory of connectivism. The concept of this learning theory was introduced by George Siemens and Stephen Downes in the year 2009 (Siemens and Downs 2009). In today's age of science and technology, education is not confined to four walls. According to this theory, a network is created between students with the help of digital technology and students get the opportunity to learn in a collaborative way. Connectivism can be said to be "A learning theory for the digital age" (Siemens 2005). Sthephen Downes described it as "...the thesis that knowledge is distributed across a network of connections, and therefore that learning consists of the ability to construct and traverse those networks." (Downes 2007, para. 1)

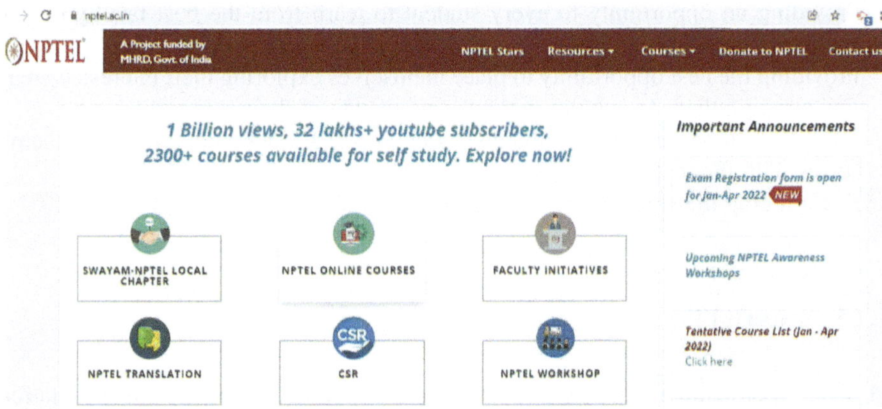

Fig. 13.1 A screenshot of the initial version of NPTEL homepage providing information and access to interested learners for the online courses of their choice. (**Source**: https://nptel.ac.in/, accessed on 03 Jan 2022)

(Fig. 13.1). In the first phase, between 2003 and 2008, NPTEL focused on five core disciplines: Civil Engineering, Computer Science & Engineering, Electrical Engineering, Electronics & Communication Engineering, and Mechanical Engineering. Between 2009 and 2014, the second phase focused on developing the engineering and core science courses that were launched in the first phase, as well as 600 web and video content also created on all major science courses for undergraduate and postgraduate students. Since March 2014, NPTEL began to offer MOOCs on the core science disciplines and engineering courses with the objective of mass enrollment from every corner of the country. Very recently, on 24 July 2018, NPTEL signed a Memorandum of Understanding (MOU) with the All India Council for Technical Education (AICTE) to offer online certification courses for Faculty Development Programme (FDP). Presently NPTEL is conducting many MOOCs courses on various topics of Science and Engineering through 4223 Local Chapters (LC) throughout the country. [4]

The major objectives are as follows:

[4] National Program on Technology Enhanced Learning (NPTEL), which provides self-study engineering, humanities, and science stream courses, is one of the national-level coordinators of SWAYAM platform to conduct MOOCs in India. With the permission of the college administration, NPTEL is establishing Local Chapters (LC) in numerous colleges across India in order to promote online learning and encourage students to enroll in online courses. Local Chapters can be thought of as the wings of NPTEL. The college's established Local Chapters are overseen by a faculty member known as the Single Point of Contact (SPOC). The SPOC of each Local Chapter (LC) is constantly kept up to date by NPTEL's activities. NPTEL time to time host events in colleges affiliated with Local Chapters (LC) to increase awareness among the higher education faculties and students about NPTEL and its features, online courses, and different workshops.

- Providing an opportunity to every student to learn from the best faculty of the country (http://nptel.ac.in).
- Providing the best opportunity to place themselves exploring their interested area.
- Encouraging them to acquire in-depth knowledge of their subjects.
- Providing an opportunity for Indian students to SELF-assess and compare themselves with the rest of the world.
- Encouraging the student's self-directed learning.

13.3 mooKIT

Massive Open Online Courses (MOOCs) have undoubtedly opened a new vista for aspiring, committed, and interested learners to upgrade their knowledge and skills and gain familiarity with the new knowledge world. However, in a rural country like India, where the majority of the population lives in rural areas, the internet system is a significant issue. IIT Kanpur developed a lightweight Massive Open Online Courses (MOOCs) management system that uses open-source technology to offer "Connectivist MOOCs" (cMOOCs) in 2012 with keeping this connectivity issue in mind (Connectivist MOOCs). This management system was initially seeded by the Technical Education Quality Improvement Programme (TEQIP), Kanpur IIT. [5] In recent times, the mooKIT (Fig. 13.2) has been substantially funded by Pandit Madan Mohan Malaviya National Mission on Teachers and Teaching (PMMMNMTT), a scheme under the Ministry of Human Resource Development (MHRD), Govt. of India (Nic 2022). It gives the learner a visual indication of a bad connection, and they can use other content delivery options provided by mooKIT, such as streaming only audio and playing it in sync with the slides (Chauhan and Goel 2017). The purpose of building this management system is to promote online teaching learning in low bandwidth and low computing situations. Presently the mooKIT is providing more than 60 online courses with more than 2 lakh enrolled learners from more than 90 countries across the globe. Commonwealth of Learning has prepared a systematic architecture of mooKIT (Perris 2015) (Fig. 13.3).

Continuing Education Centre (CDC), IIT, Kharagpur, and Commonwealth of Learning (COL) jointly delivered MOOCs in 2014 and used a systematized architecture developed by Commonwealth of Learning (COL). The mooKIT consists of two parts, such as

- Content Management System (CMS)
- Learning Management System (LMS)

The Drupal content management framework oversees the Content Management System (CMS). The Drupal content management system is a completely free and open-source programme. Whereas the Drupal interface makes it simple for users to

[5] See: https://www.mookit.in/about, Retrieved 18 October 2022.

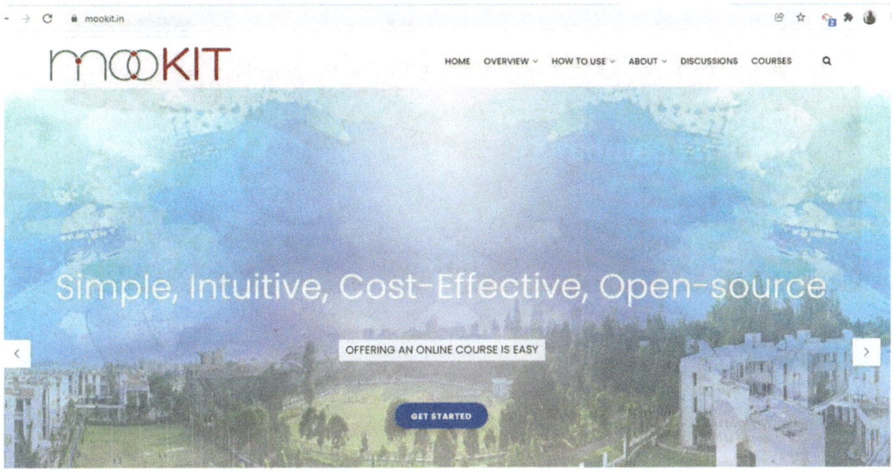

Fig. 13.2 Home page of mooKIT, Kanpur IIT. (Source: https://www.mookit.in/, accessed on 03 Jan 2022)

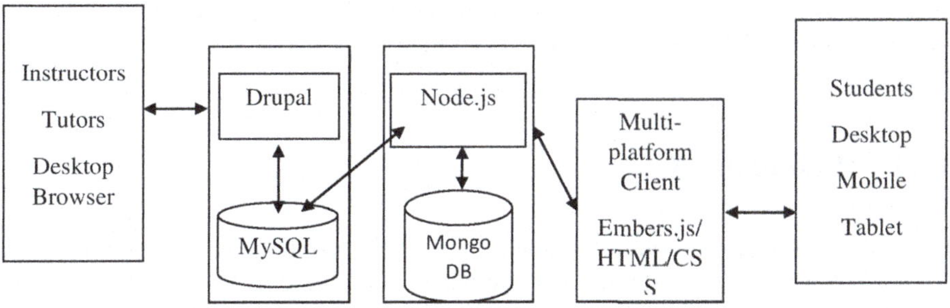

Fig. 13.3 mooKIT Architecture. (Source: https://openbooks.col.org/mooconmoocce/, accessed on 04 Jan 2022)

manage and publish material (Drupal 2014). Where a lot of students join, this management system increases RAM to help with scalability. By shifting the user system's intricate calculations, the issue of user traffic in the server or database can be reduced in this.

The second component of the mooKIT architecture is the Learning Management System (LMS). Learners as well as instructors can access and download content here. In this system, the learner can interact with the instructor through charts, forums, and email. All the units of the main course are listed by week, and the learner can easily download the pdf, see the video and the green icon indicates whether the video has been viewed or unviewed. Learners query option and existing quarries or response can also be seen in each lecture unit. Besides, the number of particular queries in each unit can also be seen. Additionally, five channels are

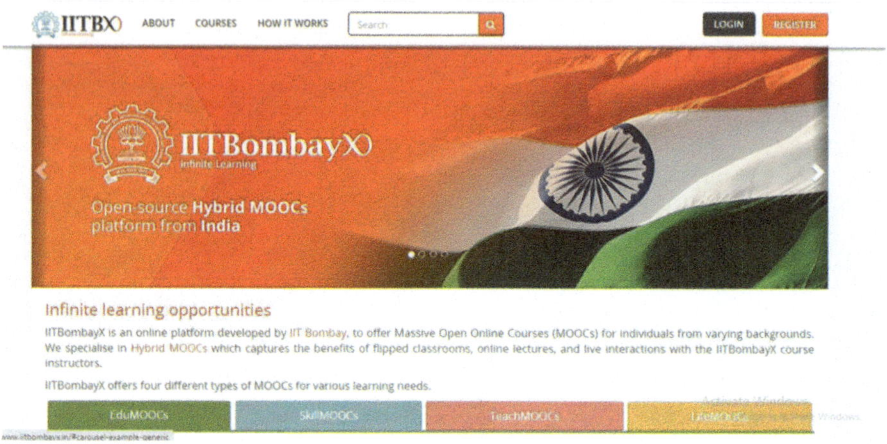

Fig. 13.4 Home page of IITBombayX. (Source: https://www.iitbombayx.in/, accessed on 04 Jan 2022)

employed to keep instructors and students in touch—Video Lectures; Video Assignments; Forums; Chat Sessions; and Contact mail.

13.4 IITBombayX

Under the National Mission on Education through Information and Communication Technology (NME-ICT), IIT Bombay launched a MOOCs platform in 2014 to offer various Massive Open Online Courses (MOOCs) across the country (Fig. 13.4). It offers four types of MOOCs to meet the needs and interests of learners:

- EduMOOCs: EduMOOCs provide opportunities for learners who want to learn more or improve their knowledge.
- LifeMOOCs: LifeMOOCs play a significant role in the lifelong learning of people in various professions.
- SkillMOOCs: SkillMOOCs provide training aimed at improving learners' skills in a specific field, which aids their professional development.
- TeachMOOCs: Teachers can use TeachMOOCs to improve their pedagogical knowledge and teaching skills in the field of the teaching-learning process.

Until the first week of January 2023, IITBombayX has successfully completed more than 700 MOOCs in the field of education, lifelong learning, skill, and teaching. Table 13.1 shows the four types of archived MOOCs that are listed in the domains.

Table 13.1 The archived MOOCs into different domains by IITBX

Types/domain	Animation	Communication	Computer science	Design education	Education and teacher training	Engineering	Finance	Skill development
Education	00	09	45	51	51	76	76	76
Life	00	00	00	00	01	01	01	01
Skill	07	25	30	30	30	32	36	47
Teach	00	01	02	02	19	27	27	27
Total MOOCs	**07**	**35**	**77**	**83**	**101**	**136**	**140**	**151**

(**Source**: Compiled by the author, up to 2021)

13.5 Study Webs of Active Learning for Young Aspiring Minds (SWAYAM)

SWAYAM is an independent digital MOOCs platform run by the Ministry of Human Resource Development (MHRD), Government of India, and it is the largest online MOOCs platform in the country to date (Fig. 13.5). SWAYAM MOOCs provide Indian universities with the opportunity to offer up to 40% of the entire course, and students can earn up to 40% credit transfer to their parent institutions' final grade sheets. The University Grants Commission (UGC) published a concept note in 2016 on developing MOOCs using the SWAYAM portal. As a result, SWAYAM MOOCs use a four-quadrant approach to deliver and develop their courses. With the help of a flow chart (Fig. 13.6), the four-quadrant approach may be explained well.

Since MOOCs are online courses with no opportunity for teacher–student face-to-face interaction, it is obvious that traditional pedagogy cannot suit the needs of learners in these types of courses. In this context, the UGC published a concept note in 2016 on creating and delivering MOOCs, while the Indian government's Ministry of Human Resource Development (MHRD) published guidelines on the four-quadrant approach to pedagogical design of MOOCs in 2017. According to the guidelines, MOOCs delivered by SWAYAM must follow four-quadrant pedagogical methodologies. Quadrant-I refers to an online tutorial that must include video demonstrations, audio and video recordings, and animations with accurate transcriptions. Case studies, e-books, self-instructional materials (SEM), research articles, and journals are all considered to be part of quadrant-II. The discussion forum, the center of any MOOC, is referred to in Quadrant-III. Where the coordinators and learners can communicate digitally on a regular basis. It is a forum where students may ask questions and raise concerns about the courses in front of their peers and

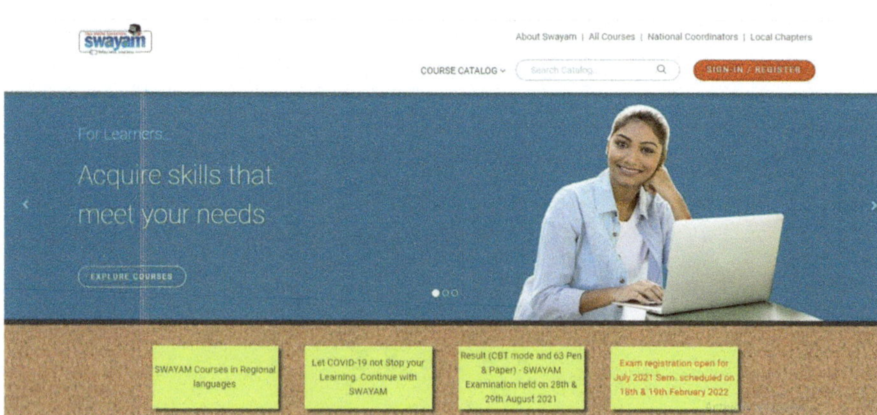

Fig. 13.5 Home page of SWAYAM MOOCs. (Source: https://swayam.gov.in/, accessed on 04 Jan 2022)

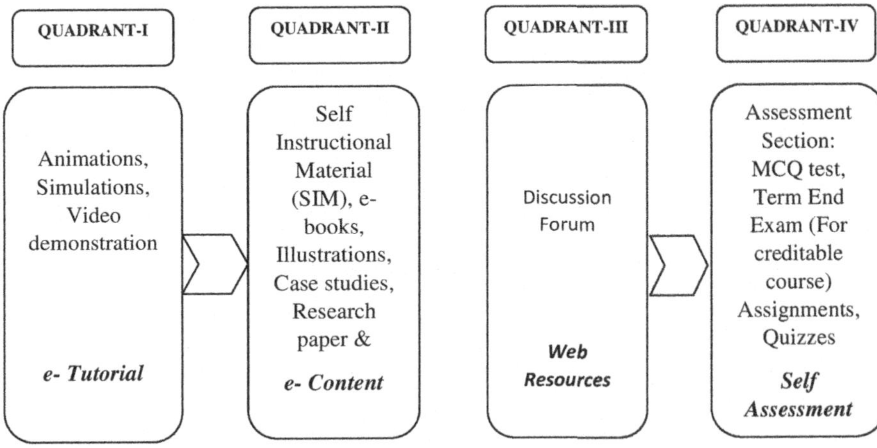

Fig. 13.6 The four quadrant approach in MOOCs. (Source: Instructions for MOOC development and delivery. https://ugc.ac.in/pdfnews/8449573_Intruction-Manual.pdf)

coordinators. The portion for assessment is Quadrant-IV. It includes multiple-choice questions, quizzes, FAQs, fill-in-the-blank questions, and more.

SWAYAM MOOCs have nine national-level coordinators who offer a variety of MOOCs in a variety of programs. The nine coordinators (Table 13.2) at the national level are as follows:

- All India Council for Technical Education (AICTE)
- Consortium for Educational Communication (CEC)
- Indira Gandhi National Open University (IGNOU)
- Indian Institute of Management Bangalore (IIMB)
- National Council of Educational Research and Training (NCERT)
- National Institute of Open Schooling (NIOS)
- National Institute of Technical Teachers Training and Research (NITTTR)
- National Programme on Technology Enhanced Learning (NPTEL)
- University Grants Commission (UGC)

13.6 How Far Are MOOCs Successful in Disseminating Quality Education in India? A Case Study

In this part, I have attempted a case study to determine whether Massive Open Online Courses (MOOCs) in India provide quality education. This case study is based on the perception of eight learners who have enrolled in a MOOCs certificate program offered by IGNOU for the 2021 session. In order to conduct a thorough

Table 13.2 Summary of all the national-level coordinators of SWAYAM MOOCs with courses and enrollments

National coordinators	Programme	Partnering institutes	Completed courses	Students enrolled	Successful certification	Ongoing courses	Students enrolled
AICTE	Self-Paced and International Courses	07	131	280,628	10,233	74	613,750
UGC	Non-Technical Postgraduate	133	263	284,766	9289	NIL	NIL
CEC	Undergraduate	19	587	1,235,001	9691	150	99,218
NCERT	School Education	08	112	234,526	NIL	28	1731
IGNOU	Certificate and Diploma	03	111	226,547	1440	140	56,541
IIMB	Management Studies	03	105	329,250	3383	23	17,813
NITTTR	Teacher Training Programme	03	70	183,997	961	22	5573
NIOS	School Education	01	174	3,132,625	NIL	42	12,048
NPTEL	Engineering	26	3496	16,008,172	1,059,004	594	784,942
Total			5049	21,915,512	1,094,001	1073	1,591,616

(**Source**: Compiled by the author, up to 2021)

investigation, the author used purposive sampling. Each learner was interviewed separately over the telephone. The researcher has reviewed some research articles pertaining to the aforementioned areas in order to establish the standards of quality education in MOOCs and to create an interview schedule. Greece's teachers are prepared to enroll in MOOCs for their career and professional growth, according to a survey study by Bakogianni et al. (2020) that looked into the subject. The majority of the professionals are prepared to enroll in MOOCs in the future for their academic excellence and skill training, according to a study by Tsabedze and Tella (2020) on the use of MOOCs among Eswatini's library professionals. The study found that the professionals are willing to enroll in MOOCs for their academic excellence and skill training. In a related study, Tahiru and Kamaludeen (2018) discovered that 67% of the 190 postgraduate students at Kuala Lumpur Public University expressed their opinion that MOOCs are beneficial to upgrade their skills and make specialize in the particular program. Respondents were asked open-ended questions on the following parameters:

- Leadership Quality
- Skill Training
- Professional Growth and Development
- Academic Excellence
- Industry Exposure

The author introduces himself to each learner and informs them of the purpose of the present study. The educational qualifications and certificate programs of learners are listed below. L1, L2, and so on are used to protect the privacy of the learners (Table 13.3).

13.6.1 Research Approach

This is a case study with only eight students, and it is a qualitative study in which the author has done thematic analysis from his own point of view. The author tries to find out what learners think about the quality of education in MOOCs. It is already mentioned that the samples have been chosen by purposive sampling technique. The fundamental drawback of qualitative research is that the conclusions cannot be extrapolated to a larger population with the same degree of certainty (Ochieng 2009); rather, it aims to create detailed and illustrative information in order to comprehend the different facets of the subject being studied (Queirós et al. 2017). Being a qualitative study, the researcher has placed a greater emphasis on the study's in-depth data. In qualitative research, which employs purposive sampling (non-probability sampling), it is not always possible to evaluate unbiased data. According to the study's objectives, the researcher selected those samples which were most important for the present study. SWAYAM MOOCs are online course, and the Ministry of Human Resource Development (MHRD), the Government of India, and Chennai IIT keep all student information. It is not feasible to obtain

Table 13.3 The educational qualification and enrolled program of the samples

Learners interviewed	Educational qualification	Program enrolled	Date and time of interview
L_1	Undergraduate	Teaching and Learning	22.01.2022
L_2	Undergraduate	Teaching and Learning	22.01.2022
L_3	Postgraduate	Teaching and Learning	24.01.2022
L_4	Undergraduate	Science of Teaching	24.01.2022
L_5	Undergraduate	Science of Teaching	24.01.2022
L_6	Undergraduate	Science of Teaching	28.01.2022
L_7	Postgraduate	Science of Teaching	28.01.2022
L_8	Postgraduate	Science of Teaching	28.01.2022

(**Source**: Compiled by the author, up to 2021)

information on the students who have registered and enrolled for MOOCs. Therefore, only eight currently enrolled MOOC participants from two separate programs (Teaching and Learning and Science of Teaching) have been selected by the researcher from his friends circle and colleagues. The study has been delimited by the following ways: (1) for the current analysis, the researcher only took into account two MOOCs, (2) only eight students were interviewed by the researcher, and only those students who had registered for the 2021 academic session were taken into account. The study's findings may provide National Coordinators (NC), Course Coordinators (CC), and organizations responsible for formulating policy with information on the quality of MOOCs but cannot be generalize to a larger population with the same degree of assurance (Ochieng 2009).

13.6.2 Learners' Perception About Leadership Quality

The leader is the person who can persuade his followers to complete a specific task. Seven out of eight learners supported the statement that "by this type of online courses, leadership quality cannot be developed." Whereas only one expressed his/her observation in support of the statement that "this program can teach me something new that I can teach my little ones." Learners, in this case, have excerpted a negative stance, and the MOOCs course is likely to be perceived as unable to deliver enough content or skill which could augment the participants' leadership quality.

13.6.3 Learners' Perception About Skill Development

One of the main goals of MOOCs is to develop learners' skills in their chosen fields. However, nearly all participants come to believe that such courses are incapable of developing any of these abilities. One learner stated, "A skill is acquired through practical work, but there is no such opportunity in this case," "I participate in quizzes, assignments, and discussion forums, but I don't see any application," another learner expressed. Most of the learners believe that in face-to-face education, where there is the direct involvement of the teacher and scope of proper supervision, could have been a better opportunity for acquiring the development of skills which is regretfully absent in online education, making it limited in getting the degree obtained keeping the true purpose of the course unfulfilled.

13.6.4 Learners' Perception About Professional Growth and Development

Despite the fact that none of the aforementioned samples is engaged in any profession, the majority of learners express their enthusiasm for professional growth and development through MOOCs. They believe that making themselves enrolled in these types of courses will help them succeed in their later careers. One learner commented, "I'm not sure if this degree will be useful in the future, but I've learned some new things that may be useful for me."

13.6.5 Learners' Perception About Academic Excellence

Academic excellence is one of the criteria for quality education. The excellence of students' knowledge domains is one of the goals of MOOCs. Almost every learner agrees that MOOCs online courses help improve their academic performance. One learner commented, "I found it very effective to gain my knowledge and academic excellence." While seven out of eight interviewees ascribed these types of courses to helping them achieve academic excellence, learners commented that they enrolled in this course for the purpose of gaining new knowledge and academic excellence and that they are very fortunate to be receiving the same.

13.6.6 Learners' Perception About Industry Exposure

Various MOOC platforms in India offer a variety of industry-related courses. Significantly, those courses have a large number of students enrolled. However, most students believe that in a face-to-face system, they could have gained industrial exposure through such practical experience, whereas this is seldom the case in online courses. MOOCs do not provide industry exposure, according to all of the students. However, the remaining three of the eight interviewees believe that if industry-related MOOCs can sign MOU with any industry and learners have the opportunity to work practically, then MOOCs can be used to gain industry exposure.

13.7 Discussion

Analyzing the data from the above-mentioned case study, it is evident that students are skeptical about the quality of the education provided via MOOCs. One of the goals of MOOCs is to help children develop skills, but most of the participants in this study believe that such courses will not help them develop any skills. The majority of students believe that taking this type of course will help them achieve academic excellence and knowledge. The majority of students state that they enrolled in this course in order to gain new knowledge. Overall, MOOCs were created with the goal of allowing a large number of people to learn at the same time. It is said that there is always darkness beneath the lamp. Similarly, while the number of students enrolled in MOOCs is large, the completion rate is low. As a result, one of the causes of this massive dropout could be a lack of high-quality education. As a result, MOOC developers and course coordinators should be prepared to develop MOOCs while keeping in mind the various aspects of quality education. As a result, the high dropout rate may decline, and the learners will be able to use quality education to create a sustainable knowledge world.

13.8 Conclusion

The introduction of online courses has undoubtedly caused a revolution in the Indian educational system. Along with traditional education, online teaching learning has been able to create a virtual learning environment. The Indian government has launched various schemes to introduce various types of online courses. MOOCs are one such project in the twenty-first century. Despite the fact that such courses are introduced with a larger goal in mind, they fail to provide students with quality education. Future research should look into how such courses can provide students with a high-quality education. Furthermore, dropout rates in such courses are as high as 95%. In this case, the reasons for dropout should be investigated, and a specific policy is implemented. The pedagogy of MOOCs courses differs significantly from traditional education, so it is necessary to examine how the digital pedagogy of MOOCs can be presented to students more easily.

The regulatory bodies of the Indian educational system may find the above discussion and findings useful in formulating policies regarding online education.

This discussion may also serve as a means of reflection for policymakers, platforms that offer MOOCs, MOOCs developers, MOOCs coordinators, and research students interested in understanding the quality features of MOOCs.

References

Bakogianni E, Tsitouridou M, Kyridis A et al (2020) MOOCs in teachers' professional development: examining teacher readiness. Acad Ther 18:9–40

Chauhan J, Goel A (2017) An overview of MOOC in India. Int J Comput Trends Technol 49(2): 111–120. https://doi.org/10.14445/22312803/ijctt-v49p117

Downes S (2007) What connectivism is. http://halfanhour.blogspot.com/2007/02/what-connectivism-is.html. Accessed 21 Nov 2022

Drupal (2014) About Drupal website. https://www.drupal.org/about. Accessed 15 Nov 2022

Nic LP (2022) Department of higher education, Government of India, Ministry of Education. https://www.education.gov.in/en/pmmmnmtt. Accessed 18 Oct 2022

Nisha F, Senthil V (2015) MOOCs: changing trend towards open distance learning with special reference to India. J Libr Inf Technol 35(2):82–89

Ochieng PA (2009) An analysis of the strengths and limitation of qualitative and quantitative research paradigms. Probl Educ 21st Century 13:13–18

Perris K (2015) Massive Open Online Course (MOOC) on MOOCs. Course Evaluation

Queirós A, Faria D, Almeida F et al (2017) Strengths and limitations of qualitative and quantitative research methods. Eur J Educ Stud 3(9):369–387. https://doi.org/10.5281/zenodo.887089

Siemens G (2005) "Connectivism: a learning theory for the digital age" (PDF). Int J Instruct Technol Distance Learn 2:1–9

Siemens G, Downs S (2009). http://www.elearnspace.org/blog/. Accessed 21 Nov 2022

Tahiru M, Kamaludeen R (2018) Exploring MOOC acceptance and readiness among postgraduate students at a higher learning institution. IIUM J Educ Stud 6(1):69–81

Tsabedze V, Tella A (2020) Awareness and use of massive open online courses among library and information science professionals in Eswatini. J Electron Resour Librariansh 32(4):253–266

Mr. Raju Singha is an assistant professor in Department of Education at Dr. Meghnad Saha College, Itahar, U/D, West Bengal since January 2017. His research interest includes ICT in education, and he is currently enrolled in PhD on the title of Massive Open Online Courses (MOOCs) at Indira Gandhi National Open University (IGNOU), New Delhi, India.

Chapter 14
Education Attainment Policy and Practices: A Study on Tea Plantation Workers and Their Children of Kurseong Tea Estate in Darjeeling District of West Bengal, India

Sandeep Sundas and Subrata Saha

14.1 Introduction

The major tea manufacturing states in India are Assam, West Bengal, Tamil Nadu, and Kerala, contributing 97.48% of tea produced in India (Tea Board of India 2019–2020). West Bengal ranks second in tea production in India. The major tea-producing regions of West Bengal are Darjeeling, Terai, and Dooars. Darjeeling is renowned for its tourism and its tea production. Tea plantation is however believed to have originated in China; the tea planting in the district of Darjeeling began in 1841 by Dr. Campbell, a civil surgeon of the Indian Medical Service. During 1850s, the commercial plantation and development of tea began. Studies reveal that the initial tea plantation on a commercial basis was started in Darjeeling by the British at Tukvar, Aloobari, and Steinthal tea estates during 1852 (Khawas 2006a, b). Tea plantation is a labour-intensive industry, so labourers were engaged in tea production, plucking, processing, and manufacturing of tea. Initially, the tea plantation in Darjeeling was restricted to only four tea gardens during 1860–1864, and it significantly rose to 39 tea estates in 1866, 56 tea estates in 1870, and 113 tea estates in 1874 (Khawas 2006a, b). Darjeeling tea is available as black tea, green tea, and oolong tea. Darjeeling tea became the first Indian product to receive a Geographical Indication of Goods (vide the Registration & Protection Act of 1999) in 2004–2005 through the Indian Patent Office. According to the Tea Board of India, 'Darjeeling Tea' can only be referred to tea that has been cultivated, grown, produced, manufactured, and processed in tea gardens in the hilly areas of Sadar subdivision, only hilly areas of Kalimpong subdivision consisting of Samabeong Tea Estate, Ambiok Tea Estate, Mission Hill Tea Estate, and Kumai Tea Estate, and Kurseong

S. Sundas (✉) · S. Saha
Department of Economics, Raiganj University, Uttar Dinajpur, West Bengal, India

M. Mishra et al. (eds.), *Public Policies and Sustainable Development in Post-Reform India*, New Frontiers in Regional Science: Asian Perspectives 71,
https://doi.org/10.1007/978-981-99-3696-0_14

subdivision excluding the areas in jurisdiction list 20, 21, 23, 24, 29, 31, and 33 comprising Siliguri subdivision of New Chumta Tea Estate, Simulbari and Marionbari Tea Estate of Kurseong Police Station in Kurseong Subdivision of the District of Darjeeling in the State of West Bengal (Khawas 2006a, b). The distinguishing feature of Darjeeling tea is its distinctive flavour and medicinal properties.

Tea is among the most demanded beverages, but the conditions of the labourers that grow tea are among the most deprived, exploited, and vulnerable ones. The socio-economic problems of tea garden workers are worth considering. The tea plantation industry is responsible for providing a major source of livelihood for the people of Darjeeling and has to take care of the workers effectively. Tea plantation workers are mostly illiterate, and the majority of the children of tea plantation workers have either completed formal education or are dropouts from mid-secondary schooling and higher secondary education. The effectiveness of various acts and regulations concerning the welfare of the workers is worth considering now. Moreover, poor medical facilities, social security, and poor educational opportunities add to the miserable living conditions of the tea plantation workers. The tea garden workers are mostly oblivious of their rights and are unaware of sanitation, health, and hygiene. Education works as a pillar for the upliftment of any socially backward class or area, but education is given the least importance by the management and the tea plantation workers.

Being a labour-intensive industry, it provides a major source of livelihood to the people of Darjeeling hills. There are workers who have been working in the tea plantation industry for more than four decades. The industry provides employment opportunities from generation to generation. In the tea plantation, sector employment of women workforce is more than that of men. But it is very unfortunate to observe the living condition and educational attainment of the workers and their children, which is abysmally low. The tea plantation labour lacks awareness, and is isolated and vulnerable to chronic diseases. Among the plantation labour, the women workers are even worse affected due to various issues like unavailability of the toilet at working place or unclean toilet for men and women, drinking water problem, sanitation, and hygiene.

According to the Human Development Index, which is a measure of three indices—life expectancy, literacy, and standard of living, education is an important index of measurement. Better education induces the consciousness of better sanitation and hygiene; It increases the quality of life—thereby, it caters to upthrust the life expectancy and also creates better employment opportunities to increase the standard of living. The education of women becomes very crucial; if a mother is educated, the mother will take care of their children properly and may educate the child with respect to sanitation and hygiene, consumption habits, including minimum necessary nutritional requirements by following a particular diet plan, augmenting the health condition of a child and can also give extra attention to their children's education. Best hygiene is also seen as an improvement in health conditions or prevention of chronic diseases.

Education is a crucial factor of development, and ensuring the right to educate children is considered pivotal to safeguarding human rights. Education of the children of the tea plantation labour is safeguarded under Plantation Labour Act 1951, but not all tea estates within the country consider providing education to all to be that important. Though provisions for primary schools within the tea estates as per the Plantations Labour Act, 1951 are ensured by management in most of the tea estates; but post-primary and secondary schools are lacking within the tea estates, and plantation workers face difficulty in sending their children far for education post-primary. Though the plantation worker considers education as the most important but lack of support from the management and financial constraints act as major obstacles. In the quest for better employment opportunities, the children of the tea plantation labour move out to cities. As per a report published in the Hindustan Times on September 3, 2015, the children of the workers have been missing, and it is doubted that they have fallen prey to traffickers in Assam due to their economically weaker background.

Thapa (2012) observed that 44%, 43%, and 13% of children belonging to self-employed, permanent, and casual tea plantation workers households, respectively, are studying.

Khawas (2006a, b) conducted a significant study with regard to education and concluded from the selected sample of tea garden households over 55% had completed elementary levels of education, followed by less than 15% completing their secondary level of education and less than 2% had attended higher secondary. However, the percentage of the population who had attended college or further education was abysmally low. According to Plantation Labour Act 1951, the employer, under the direction of the state government, may provide suitable educational opportunities in the estates if in any plantation, the number of children of the plantation workers aged 6–12 years exceeds 25 in number. According to a survey conducted by Regional Labour Offices, North Bengal Zone, out of 273 surveyed tea estates, 231 tea estates had provisions for schools. 143 tea estates had access to the vehicle for school-going children. There were no labour welfare offices in 175 tea estates, followed by 125 tea estates that had no canteen facility. [1] As per the report, the percentage of children in the age group 6–14 years attending government school was 56.1%, while 0.3% of children between ages 6 and 14 years were not attending school at all (Annual Status of Education Report, West Bengal 2022).

The auspicious article of the Constitution of India for the ‘rights’ of children to free and compulsory education and the Education Act, 2009 guarantee the promotion of free and mandatory elementary education to all children aged between 6 and 14 years is considered as the fundamental right of children. The ratio of government to private schools in India is in the ratio 7:5. As per the resources of the United Nations International Children Emergency Fund (UNICEF) in India, it ensures equal rights to education of all children and considers the essence of quality teachers’

[1] Synopsis on survey of Tea Garden Conducted by Regional Labour Offices under jurisdiction of Joint Labour Commissioner, North Bengal Zone.

recruitment for shaping the children's future. Moreover, the children who were deprived of quality education due to social and economic obstacles, especially girl children belonging to Schedule Caste and Schedule Tribe, differently-abled children, and children with ethnic importance and religious minority groups, were the priority. The girls are, however, more prone to dropping out from schooling due to various factors such as lack of sanitation at school, household chores to be carried out by girls, and travel inconveniences. UNICEF works with government and non-governmental organizations to promote full gender equality and ensures compulsory education for primary and secondary levels. UNICEF in India promotes 8 years of schooling through and rigorous works of Sarva Siksha Abhiyan both at the national and state level, whose priority is to ensure 'education for all' launched in 2001 and Meena Manch in schools in various states in India for girls to boost their level of confidence. [2]

Singh (2013) highlighted the importance of the universalization of primary education and mentioned the importance of Article 26 of 1948, which declared education as a 'human right'. The study urges the importance of education on children's social control and social transformation. The study brought about the relative importance of education rests on pillars like 'learning to know, learning to do, learning to be, and learning to live'. Article 21 A of the Indian constitution, in its 86th amendment, is replaced with article 45. It describes 'rights to education' as the 'Fundamental Right'. The study asserts that the government at both central and state level are making innumerable efforts to expand education in the country. The study, however, poses some serious threats to achieving the goal of 'education for all', such as—gender parity at the elementary level is not met, oblivious attitudes, poverty, population pressure, lack of quality teachers, segregation, lack of funds and language and ethnicity. The possible recommendation to achieve Education for All goals was discussed in the paper giving more importance to *Sarvha Siksha Abhiyan* for promoting and universalization at elementary levels of education, the National Literacy Mission responsible for alleviating illiteracy, more resources flow, effective teaching-learning, marginalized groups of children and children from Schedule Castes and Schedule Tribes.

Islam and Iftekhar (2015) highlighted various 'UNESCO Goals of 2000' focusing on education for all in India. 'Education for All' rests with six different goals, as discussed in the study, which primarily focuses on the expansion of early childhood care education, more specifically to the deprived and the isolated or marginalized groups; all children, especially girls of different ethnic minorities, get access to free and compulsory primary education by 2015; equitable access to learning; enhancement of adult literacy rate, especially for women by 2015, removing all forms of gender discrimination in primary and secondary school by 2005; and, achieve gender parity by 2015 and promoting quality education. The paper shows, with the aid of statistics, that the growth of enrolment of children at primary levels of education was improving.

[2] See: https://www.unicef.org/india/what-we-do/education-for-all.

UNDP encourages all countries to adopt strategies and actions to be taken to achieve the 17 Sustainable Development Goals (SDGs) by 2030. SDG-3 and SDG-4 focus on good health and well-being and quality education, respectively. Quality education is important as far as health and life expectancies are concerned. The correlation between education and health cannot be overlooked. With education, consciousness is gathered regarding all the ill effects of the practice of bad sanitation and hygiene, leading to the deterioration of health and ultimately compromising life expectancy. In the Plantation Labour Act (PLA) 1951 (which applies to Tea, Coffee, Rubber, and Cardamom industries), the education of the children of the workers is prioritized. The Act ensures the education of the children of the plantation workers aged 6 and 12 years; in addition, if the number of plantation workers exceeds 25 in number in any estates, the state government may make rules for the employer to provide education facilities. Apart from PLA 1951, the Tea Board of India (TBI) also takes forward-looking steps to promote the education of the children of the plantation workers. The various schemes of TBI include a number of stipends to meritorious students to support the children of the plantation worker financially. The stipend allotted per student per annum usually does not exceed Rs 40 thousand, and moreover, the amount is equally divided into tuition fees and hostel fees. Secondly, the wards of the tea plantation workers are also encouraged to take vocational training for which financial support is provided by the TBI. The TBI also provides capital grants for the construction of schools and colleges. Thirdly, the scheme for capital grants for educational institutions organizations towards the extension of the school buildings for which 70% of the capital grants or Rs 8 lakhs, whichever is lower, is sanctioned for government-approved secondary schools. Fourthly, a capital grant of 70% or a maximum of Rs 12 lakhs is provided by the TBI for the scheme of capital grants for the construction of the school or college buildings and hostel buildings attached to schools or colleges. The essential criteria to get the funds under this scheme are enrolment of not less than 25% of the children of tea plantation workers. The children of the tea plantation workers must also be provided with concession or scholarship facilities in such institutions. The institution that receives a grant under the scheme must provide vocational training and must have employment potential.

The Tea Producers' Association, a registered voluntary labour organization, started and maintained the scheme for book grants to libraries. The main objective of this scheme is to make books available to needy and deserving students along with school uniforms for the children of the tea plantation workers, especially in the closed/abandoned/locked-out tea gardens. There is also a special scheme named the Nehru Award for the children of tea plantation workers. Under this scheme, a lump sum of Rs 2000 and Rs 2500, respectively, is awarded to the children of the tea plantation workers who secure 75% marks in 10th and 12th standards and whose family income does not exceed 120,000 per annum. Another scheme is there that provides financial assistance for vocational training courses for the children of tea plantation workers and their dependents. Under this scheme, the children and the dependents of tea plantation workers would be provided with a vocational training course for a period of 6–12 months. The grant is disbursed to the institution providing vocational training to a maximum of Rs 1.5 lakhs for a course.

The Global Multidimensional Poverty Index (MPI) was developed in 2010 by the Oxford Poverty and Human Development Initiative (OPHI) and the United Nations Development Programme (UNDP). The MPI has three broad indicators, among which education is one important indicator. The indices of MPI are 10 in number, and education is accessed through years of schooling and child school enrolment. A household is considered deprived if no member in a household has completed 6 years of schooling that is elementary education level or if any school-aged children are not attending school up to class 8. With the objective of ensuring inclusive quality education for all as a basic right, the National Education Policy 2020 was introduced, which restructured the current education system categorizing the various learning stages of children into four categories. The vision of the National Education Policy 2020 is to make the learners provide quality education in order to completely transform the country. The new system of education aims to transform learners into critical thinkers, develop knowledge, and have a sense of sustainable development by working according to the curriculum. The foundation stage is the first stage under the New Education Policy 2020, focusing on building the foundation of the children. The children aged between 3 and 6 years must attain pre-school or playgroup school, and between 6 and 8 years of age, they may go to classes 1 and 2, and this stage of education will be considered as the foundational stage. The next stage will be the preparatory stage which ranges from the age of 8–11 years. The children may attend classes 3–5 in this stage. The third stage will be the middle stage for children aged 11 and 14 years, where they can attend school in classes 6 and 8, and finally, the secondary stage of education for children aged 14 and 18 years attending school in classes 9–12.

14.2 Review of Literature

A study by Bosumatari and Goyari (2013) highlighted that the educational facility provided by the tea plantation management for workers and their children was very poor. This, in turn, reduces their standard of living as most of the workers are unaware of their rights. The study revealed a strong direct relationship between women's educational attainment and the education of their children.

Borah (2013) studied the basic rights of women and tea garden workers according to the provision of the Plantation Labour Act 1951. The study revealed that most of the tea gardens lack better medical facilities. The women are also deprived of maternal benefits. The women workers of the tea garden are unaware of their rights as most of the garden workers possess very low educational attainment resulting in most of the garden workers believing in superstitions.

Thapa (2012) studied the Human Development status of the plantation workers covering the dimensions of education, health, and basic amenities to gauze their standard of living. The study categorizes the workers into permanent, temporary, and small growers. The study was confined to the tea gardens of Darjeeling. The researcher tried to find a correlation between asset ownership and living standard. Her findings suggested that permanent workers are better off in terms of employment status and standard of living. However, small growers were holding better assets possessions. Small growers hold more production assets like cattle and poultry than the consumption assets such as television, mobile, and others. The health status of the plantation workers was good, and the satisfactory educational status of the children of tea plantation workers was also observed.

Khawas (2006a, b) highlighted the problems of Darjeeling tea gardens. The study observed the problems relating to low wage, low standard of living, education for the workers' children, health issues, frequent violence, and strike across tea gardens in the Darjeeling tea industry. Employment was estimated as altogether 52,000 on a permanent basis and 15,000 during the plucking season lasting from March to November. The total employment of women was recorded as 60%. Female labourers were mainly employed for plucking tea. The researcher found that the education level was quite satisfactory. Fifty-five percent of the tea garden workers had the formal education.

Khawas (2006a, b) concluded that, from the selected sample of tea garden households, over 55% had completed elementary levels of education, followed by less than 15% completing their secondary level of education and less than 2% attending higher secondary. However, the percentage of the population who attended college or further education was very low.

Sharma (2005) in his study highlighted the workers among various sub-communities of a particular caste and their socio-economic status. His study revealed that there was a serious breach of the Plantation Labour Act 1951 by the management. Ninety-eight percent of the respondents and their family members were suffering from certain diseases and were consulting doctors. Tea estates are also deprived of health centres and medical facilities. There was no proper access to safe drinking water and a complete absence of health planning. Firewood was the main source of fuel among the tea plantation workers

Paul and Rohatgi (2014) studied the education, income, and health & hygiene of tea garden workers. The study revealed that most of the labour force comprised of women. The study found that the workers had a tough time to get drinking water as they had to walk a considerable distance to fetch water. The residences seem okay with 66% of the workers having pucca houses. The provision of safe sanitation was missing. The unavailability of latrines resulted in open defecation. There were various health issues among tea plantation workers due to ignorance and lack of awareness. There were reports of even death of the workers due to waterborne diseases. Lower income and lower education were also seen as major problems among tea garden workers.

Dutta (2017) examines the essence of the plantation industry as a major source of livelihood employing more than 50% of the women plantation workers. The study aims at examining the role of women tea plantation workers in decision-making in addition to examining the status of tea plantation workers. The major findings of the study revealed that most of the workers attain very low levels of education and suffer various health hazards mainly due to a lack of awareness. There is a serious breach of the Plantation Labour Act 1951.

Sharma (2013) focused on and suggested that the tea tribes were the most exploited and among the most backward tribes in India. The study revealed that they were denied basic amenities of life such as education, healthcare facilities, proper sanitation, and drinking water. Furthermore, the study also highlighted that due to poor educational opportunities, the workers are oblivious and are indulging in large consumption of alcohol.

Bora (2015) studies the condition of women tea plantation workers. The study reflected that the condition of women tea estate workers was not good. Women workers were suffering from various chronic diseases.

Rai (2019), in an empirical study on the socio-economic condition of the plantation workers of Darjeeling tea estates, shows a keen interest in analysing the living condition of the tea plantation workers and highlights that the majority of the labour force belonged to the scheduled tribe (ST) community. The workers' educational attainment was very poor, and most had only an elementary level of education. The history of tea plantations, the associated labour shortage problem, and the in-migration of labours from various areas to work at the tea estates in Darjeeling were discussed in the study. The study observed that workers were compelled to look for an alternative source of income generation mainly due to poor wages from the tea plantation. The author found a serious breach of the Plantation Labour Act 1951 and the incapacity of the trade union to improve the welfare of the tea plantation workers.

Paul (2017), in a study of the literacy pattern of tea plantation workers in Dooars, analysed the study pattern among tea plantation workers. The study brought a comparative difference between the educational attainment of men and women workers and found that women's educational attainment was very poor. Moreover, the study also revealed that illiteracy is a common phenomenon in tea plantation. The school was not properly maintained, which contradicts the MDGs and violation of the Plantation Labour Act 1951. Finally, the study recommended various strategies to augment opportunities in education.

Begum and Islam (2022) studied the educational attainment of tea plantation workers in Assam. Despite various measures being undertaken by the government, the education attainment among the children of tea plantation workers does not show a promising picture. The study was carried out with secondary data from various articles, journals, newspapers, etc.

14.3 Statement of the Problem

While tea is among the most demanded beverage, the conditions of the labourers growing tea are among the most deprived, exploited, and vulnerable ones. The socio and economic problems of tea garden workers are worth considering. The tea plantation industry provides a major source of livelihood for the people of

Darjeeling, who have to take care of the workers effectively. Plantation workers are mostly illiterate, and most of the children of tea plantation workers have either completed formal education or are dropouts from mid-secondary schooling and higher secondary education. The effectiveness of various acts and regulations concerning the welfare of the workers is worth considering now. Poor medical facilities, social security, and poor educational opportunities add fuel to the fire. The tea plantation workers are mostly oblivious to their rights and unaware of sanitation, health, and hygiene. Education works as a pillar for the upliftment of any socially backward class or area, but education is given the least importance by the management and the tea plantation workers. The tea plantation workers and their children have very poor access to education. Education, although considered an important prerequisite for development, is not getting the proper treatment from management and authority. The importance of education is not heeded by plantation workers either. The plantation workers can fight exploitation and deprivation only through enlightenment which comes through education. The workers' interest in providing better education to their children is subject to their financial constraints, which must be addressed by the management, and suitable measures must be adopted to augment the education of the children of tea plantation workers.

14.4 Objectives of the Study

The tea plantation workers and their wards lack educational opportunities, and it was observed that their educational attainment presents a very poor picture. Among the tea plantation workers, the attainment of education at the higher level is very poor; despite parents' efforts to educate their children with their full resources available, the educational attainment among children of workers is not at all satisfactory.

The objective of this chapter is to analyse the literacy pattern among the tea plantation workers and their children and assesses the percentage of children on tea plantations at the higher education level and the percentage of children dropouts at subsequent levels of their academic journey. The study will also aim to find the possible reasons for children's high dropout rate in the tea estates.

14.5 Study Area

A sample of 90 households was selected randomly from three tea estates of Kurseong, a subdivision of Darjeeling district—Castleton tea estate, Makaibari tea estate (Fig. 14.1), and Goomtee tea estate (Fig. 14.2). The study is a case study of Kurseong tea plantation workers.

Fig. 14.1 A snapshot of the tea workers busy with tea leaf collection at the Makaibari Tea Estate. (**Source:** Captured by Sandeep Sundas)

14.6 Methodology

The study is primarily conducted on the basis of primary data collected personally by visiting the tea estates under study. Three tea estates were selected at random from Kurseong tea estates, a subdivision of the Darjeeling district, and from each tea estate, a random selection of 30 households was made, and the study was carried out. The study also uses secondary data. The study is therefore categorized as (a) preparation of a questionnaire; (b) locating three tea gardens at random; (c) conducting a field survey; and (d) analysis of the data.

The study is based on both primary and secondary data. First of all, researchers attempted to choose tea gardens at random from three distant regions of the Kurseong subdivision. Secondly, a questionnaire was prepared to analyse the education of the workers and children of the workers from tea plantation workers' households, and finally, the researcher personally visited the tea garden to collect the numeric data from each tea garden. Once the data is collected, the data is reviewed and analysed by the researcher.

Fig. 14.2 A snapshot of the Goomtee Tea Estate. (**Source:** Captured by Sandeep Sundas)

14.7 Data Analysis and Discussion

Thapa (2012) observed that the educational attainment of the household at a higher level of education is very poor. The majority of the households have upper primary education contributing to approximately 40%, followed by primary education, which is 33%. The education attainment of the children of tea plantation workers in the study area revealed that around 60% of the children go to government schools while 29% go to private schools. Eleven percent of children are not going to either the government or private schools are around 11%.

Table 14.1 shows the age category of the workers in respective tea estates. The respondents across the entire three tea estates majority 22.2% belong to the age group 46–50 years, followed by the respondents with the age group 36–40 years, calculated as 20%. Approximately 19% and 16% of the respondents belong to the age group 41–45 and 31–35 years, respectively.

The age of the respondents in Castleton tea estate majority falls under the age range between 36 and 40 years and is calculated as 30%, followed by age ranging between 46 and 50 years as 26.6% and 31–35 years calculated as 23.3% as represented in Table 14.1. Makaibari tea estate has respondents with a majority age ranging between 36 and 40 years and 41 and 45 years is, 23.3% each. Goomtee tea estates, however, has the majority of the respondents' age ranging between

Table 14.1 Age structure of the respondents (in years)

Castleton Tea Estate	Age/gender	26–30	31–35	36–40	41–45	46–50	51–55	56–60	Total
	Male	NA	2	5	2	4	1	NA	14
	Female	2	5	4	1	4	NA	NA	16
	Total	2	7	9	3	8	1	0	30
Makaibari Tea Estate	Age/gender	26–30	31–35	36–40	41–45	46–50	51–55	56–60	Total
	Male	NA	2	4	1	1	2	2	12
	Female	2	2	3	6	3	1	1	18
	Total	2	4	7	7	4	3	3	30
Goomtee Tea Estate	Age/gender	26–30	31–35	36–40	41–45	46–50	51–55	56–60	Total
	Male	NA	2	1	2	2	2	3	12
	Female	1	1	1	5	6	2	2	18
	Total	1	3	2	7	8	4	5	30

Source: Field Survey by the authors, 2022

46 and 50 years and is measured as 26.6%, followed by 41–45 years measured as 23.33% (Table 14.1).

13.3% of the respondent from the Castleton tea estate belongs to the general category, followed by 3.3% belonging to the scheduled caste (SC), 73.3% to the scheduled tribe (ST) community, and 10% belonging to the Other Backward Category (OBD) in Castleton tea estate. In the Makaibari tea estate, the general category respondents are 16.6%; 26.66% belong to the SC community, 16.6% to the ST, and 40% to OBC. In the Goomtee tea estate, general category respondents are found to be 43.33%, 3.33% SC, and 53.33% of OBCs.

In Castleton tea estate, the majority of the respondents' age falls under the interval of 36–40, which is 30%, followed by the 46–50 years age group, which is 26.66%, and another 23.3% of the respondents belong to the age group of 31–35 years. Makaibari tea estate's maximum respondent belongs to the age group of 36–40 years and 41–45 years which is 23.33% each. In the Goomtee tea estate, however, the majority of the respondents' age ranges between 46 and 50 years and is measured as 26.6%, followed by the age group of 41–45 years measured as 23.33%.

The workers' educational status data is collected and illustrated in Table 14.2. At Castleton tea estate, 33.33% are illiterate, and 33.33% have attained schooling between class V and VIII, followed by 23.33% who have attained education between class IX and X. The attainment of higher education goes on decreasing. Only 3.3% of the tea plantation worker at Castleton tea estate have studied between class XI and XII. In the Makaibari tea estate, the maximum respondent is illiterate (40%); followed by 33.3% of respondents studied between class V and VIII. The attainment of education between class IX–X and XI–XII is, respectively, 10% and 3.33% of the total. In the Goomtee Tea estate, 50% of the respondent have schooling between classes V and VIII, followed by 30% having education between classes I and IV. The number of illiterate respondents is measured as 10%. The above table shows that the

Table 14.2 Education attainment of the workers in the selected tea estates

Castleton Tea Estate	Education/ gender	Illiterate	I–IV	V–VIII	IX–X	XI–XII	XII–Graduation	Total
	Male	3	2	3	5	1	NA	14
	Female	7	NA	7	2	NA	NA	16
	Total	10	2	10	7	1	NA	30
Makaibari Tea Estate	Education/ gender	Illiterate	I–IV	V–VIII	IX–X	XI–XII	XII–Graduation	Total
	Male	4	1	7	NA	NA	NA	12
	Female	8	3	3	3	1	NA	18
	Total	12	4	10	3	1	NA	30
Goomtee Tea Estate	Education/ gender	Illiterate	I–IV	V–VIII	IX–X	XI–XII	XII–Graduation	Total
	Male	1	5	6	NA	NA	NA	12
	Female	2	4	9	3	NA	NA	18
	Total	3	9	15	3	NA	NA	30

Source: Field Survey by the authors, 2022

educational attainment among tea garden workers is extremely poor. Due to lower educational attainment, tea plantation workers are unable to generate other employment opportunities.

Combinedly, approximately 28% of the tea plantation workers were found to be illiterate during the entire study; 17% of the workers have an elementary level of education; 39% possess upper primary schooling between classes V and VIII. Workers who have studied up to classes IX–X was 14%, and a meagre 2.2% have studied up to classes XI–XII. This shows that educational attainment among tea plantation workers is very poor.

The low education attainment among tea plantation workers is a social concern. With low education attainment, the workers lack basic awareness; they accept improper sanitation and basic healthcare facilities, and they also have a low determination to educate their wards.

Moreover, it is revealed in the study that the ratio of women illiterates was maximum compared to the men workers. Table 14.3 will make it more evident. The data from 90 households surveyed across three tea estates in Kurseong shows that the percentage of male and female illiterate respondents was, respectively, 32% and 68%. This clarifies that the education of women workers was poor in comparison to their male counterparts. Since the education of a mother is important for the upliftment of their children, the focus would have been more on educating women. The responsibility of providing education to workers should also be the responsibility of the management, but it has not been covered under the labour welfare mission by the management. 53.33% and 46.7% of the male and female respondents, respectively, have either completed the first 4 years of formal schooling or studied up to the range from class 1 to 4. Male and female respondents studied from classes V to VIII are estimated to be 45.71% and 54.3%, respectively. 38.5% and 61.5% of the male and female respondents, respectively, have education attainment between

Table 14.3 Education attainment of tea plantation workers in percentage across the three tea estates of Kurseong

Education	Percentage	Male	Female
Illiterate	27.8%	32%	68%
I–IV	16.7	53.33%	46.7%
V–VIII	38.9	45.71%	54.3%
IX–X	14.44	38.5%	61.5%
XI–XII	2.2	50%	50%
XII-Graduation	NA	00	00

Source: Field Survey by the authors, 2022

Table 14.4 Education attainment of the wards of the workers completed or currently studying in Castleton tea estate

Education/ gender	Below 4 years	Illiterate	I–IV	V–VIII	IX–X	M. P	H. S	Graduation	Total
Male	4	2	N. A	8	3	1	2	4	24
Female	2	NA	2	4	6	1	NA	14	29
Total	6	2	2	12	9	2	2	18	53

Source: Field Survey by the authors, 2022

IX and X. Table 14.4 shows the educational attainment of the children of the workers, and Fig. 14.3 gives a visual representation of the scenario.

Table 14.4 reflects the education of the workers' children. Castleton tea estate 34% of the children of the plantation worker have completed graduation, followed by 23% approximately are studying between classes V and VIII. The children who have completed 10th and 12th standard are calculated as 3.8% each. However, nearly 14% of the children in Castleton tea estates are not studying at all. Table 14.5 represents the education scenario of the children of the workers in the Makaibari tea estate; only 4% approximately have completed graduation. 10th and 12th standard was completed by, respectively, 6.3% and 37% of the children in the Makaibari tea estate. Table 14.6 highlights the educational attainment in the Goomtee tea estate. Six percent approximately have completed graduation level. Eleven percent and 35% of the children in the Goomtee tea estate, respectively, have completed 10th and 12th level of their academic journey. The attainment of a higher level of education among children of the tea plantation worker is also not at all satisfactory.

From Table 14.7 it is evident that 33.96% of the respondents' wards have completed graduation, followed by 22.64% studying or studying between classes V and VIII. There are illiterates also. 3.77% of the respondents' wards have passed Madhyamik (i.e. class X final examination), and another 3.77% qualified each for the Higher Secondary (i.e. class XII examinations). Table 14.7 also highlights that a mere 4.16% have attained or completed graduation though 29.166% are studying or have studied up to class VIII, followed by 16.66% are studying or have studied up to class X. The percentage of tea plantation workers' wards who have completed their higher secondary (class XII) level is 37.5%.

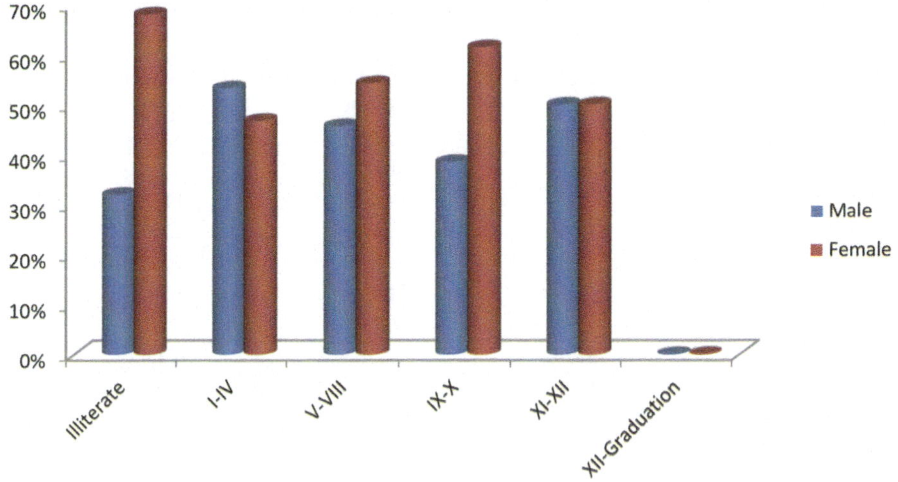

Fig. 14.3 Education attainment among tea plantation workers. (Source: Prepared by the authors from the field survey 2022 datasets)

Table 14.5 Education attainment of the wards of the workers completed or currently studying in Makaibari tea estate

Education/ gender	Below 4 years	Illiterate	I–IV	V–VIII	IX–X	M. P	H. S	Graduation	Total
Male	NA	NA	NA	8	2	2	8	NA	20
Female	1	NA	2	6	6	1	10	2	28
Total	1	NA	2	14	8	3	18	2	48

Source: Field Survey at Makaibari Tea Estate, February 2022

Table 14.6 Education attainment of the wards of the workers completed or currently studying in Goomtee tea Estate

Education/ gender	Below 4 years	Illiterate	I–IV	V–VIII	IX–X	M. P	H. S	Graduation	Total
Male	NA	NA	4	7	3	2	8	2	26
Female	2	NA	3	8	3	5	14	2	37
Total	2	NA	7	15	6	7	22	4	63

Source: Field Survey at Goomtee Tea Estate, February 2022

As per the data observed from the Goomtee tea estate, it is observed that 34.92% have completed the Higher Secondary level, followed by 23.81% attending or have attended classes from classes V-VIII. Again, the enrolment of candidates at higher education levels seems miserable. Only 6.35% of the wards have completed graduate-level of studies. Table 14.8 analyses and compares the tea plantation workers children's education attainment in various tea gardens of Kurseong.

Table 14.7 Education attainment of tea plantation workers children in percentage across 3 tea gardens of Kurseong

Tea estate/education	Castleton Tea Estate	Makaibari Tea Estate	Goomtee Tea Estate
Below 4 years	11.32	2.08	3.17
Illiterate	3.77	0	0
I–IV	3.77	4.166	11.11
V–VIII	22.64	29.166	23.81
IX–X	16.98	16.66	9.5
M.P or equivalent	3.77	6.25	11.11
H.S or equivalent	3.77	37.5	34.92
Graduation	33.96	4.16	6.35
No data found or not studying	13.8	NA	NA

Source: Field Survey by the authors, 2022

Table 14.8 Education attainment of the wards of tea plantation workers according to gender in all the three tea gardens of Kurseong

Gender/class	Boy children	Girl children
Below 4 years	3 (3.37%)	6 (8%)
Illiterate	2 (2.25%)	NA (0%)
I–IV	8 (8.9%)	3 (4%)
V–VIII	23 (25.84%)	18 (24%)
IX–X	11 (12.36%)	12 (16%)
M.P	5 (5.62%)	6 (8%)
H.S	24 (26.97%)	18 (24%)
Graduation	13 (14.61%)	12 (16%)
Total	89	75
Grand total	164	

Source: Field survey 2022

Figure 14.4 indicates that Castleton tea estate has the most number of graduate children of plantation workers and Makaibari tea estate has the least number of graduates children of plantation workers. Moreover, it is very pathetic regarding the enrolment of wards in higher education level though there is a substantial difference between the enrolment of plantation workers children at higher education level among the most and the least number of graduates in the two respective tea gardens.

As per the collected data, it has been observed that the percentage of boy children and girl children of the respondents at Castleton, Makaibari, and Goomtee tea estates are, respectively, 41.50% and 58.49%; 54.16% and 45.83%; and 64.06% and 35.93%.

Let us now analyse the education attainment of boy children and girl children of tea garden workers across three surveyed tea gardens in Kurseong. Table 14.8 is indispensable for the purpose of observing the gender bias, if any, among the tea plantation worker household. The total number of children from 90 respondents' households is 164, of which 89 were boy children and 75 were girl children of

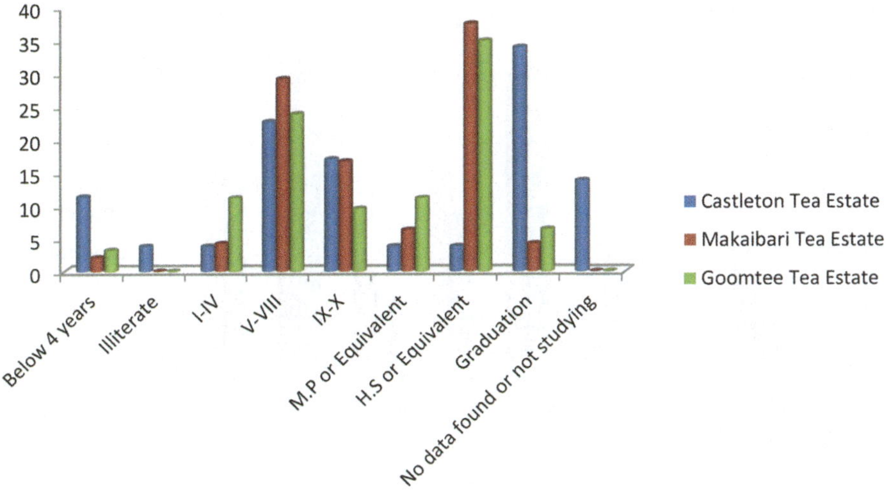

Fig. 14.4 Education attainment of workers wards in three tea estates of Kurseong. (Source: Prepared by the authors from the field survey 2022 datasets)

90 households surveyed. The percentage of boy children is 54.3%, and that of girl children is 45.73%.

Table 14.8 illustrates that the enrolment of girl children at a higher level of education is comparatively higher than that of boy children. Hence the plantation workers do not practice gender bias and would try to educate their children with the best means available to them. As a result, none of the girl children from the respondent family household was illiterate, but some 2.25% of the boy children were found illiterate (Fig. 14.5).

Table 14.9 shows that the children of the workers drop out at the elementary, mid-secondary, secondary, and higher levels of education. Most of the respondents' children were found to discontinue their studies due to various reasons—financial obligations and the urge to work to earn wage, marriage, no awareness, migration, etc.

From Fig. 14.6, it is evident that the dropout rate at the subsequent education level for the girl child is more than the boy child. 20% and 22.53% of the boy children and girl children, respectively, have dropout their studies after either studying up to class XII or after passing the higher secondary level. 11.76% and 12.67% of the respondents' boy children and girl children, respectively, have dropped out after class X or after passing the secondary level of education. 12.94% and 16.90% of the boy and girl children, respectively, have dropped after graduation. Most of the children are either married or engaged in some employment to support the family. 7.05% and 12.67% of boy and girl children have dropped from their studies after attaining up to class XIII.

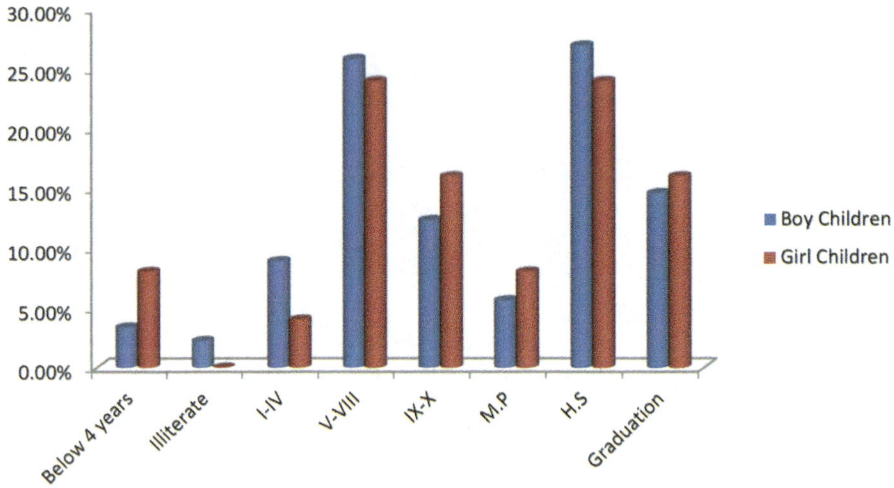

Fig. 14.5 Education attainment of the wards of tea plantation workers according to gender in all the three tea gardens of Kurseong. (Source: Field survey 2022)

Table 14.9 School/college dropouts of wards of tea workers in the three tea estates sorted by genders

Gender/class	Boy children	Girl children	Total
Studying	39 (45.88%)	23 (32.39%)	62
Drop out after class IV	2 (2.35%)	2 (2.81%)	4
Drop out after class VIII	6 (7.05%)	9 (12.67%)	15
Drop out after X or M.P	10 (11.76%)	9 (12.67%)	19
Drop out after XII or H.S	17 (20%)	16 (22.53%)	33
Drop out after graduation	11 (12.94%)	12 (16.90%)	23
Total	85	71	156

Source: Field Survey 2022

14.8 Conclusion

It is observed from the study that the plantation workers, at the most, have upper primary education ranging from classes V to VIII. The enrolment at a higher level of education after this goes on decreasing. The number of children of tea plantation workers studying at present irrespective of the grade of studies was calculated as approximately 46% and 32% for boy children and girl children, respectively. The remaining children dropped out from their studies after various levels of education level primary, upper primary, secondary, higher secondary, and graduation. The children who dropped out after their graduation for boy and girl children, respectively, are 13% and 17%.

There are multiple reasons for such low educational attainment and high dropouts of children of tea plantation workers. Firstly, the attitude of the parents towards

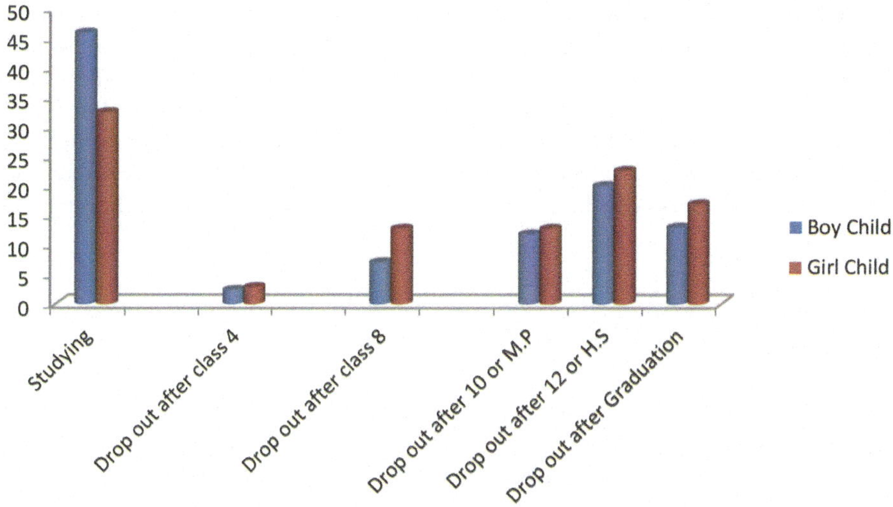

Fig. 14.6 School/college dropouts of the workers' wards. (Source: Field survey 2022)

educating their children; though efforts are made to educate their children with all available means, the influence of parents on children's education is still a primary concern. This is because most of their parents are either illiterate or have completed the basic elementary level of education that appears insufficient to drive their wards toward higher educational attainment confidently.

Secondly, the environment of the tea plantation offers very low welfare to the workers and their family members. With lower wages, lack of basic amenities of life there is a tendency of the children to migrate to cities and abroad in search of better employment opportunities fetching them better earnings, so the children of the workers do not depend on the tea plantation for employment in future.

Thirdly, to support the family financially sometimes the children of the plantation workers are compelled to move out of the estates in search of employment.

Fourthly, the early marriages of girl children make them discontinue their studies.

Fifthly the tendency of children to discontinue their studies after their unsuccessful attempts to clear board examinations as found in the study some children who could not clear their matriculation examination discontinued their studies.

Finally the lack of support from the management and state authorities not to let them decide over choosing educational opportunities.

Education is crucial for the upliftment of individual with full human potential to develop in the society and thereby developing the nation. The indispensable responsibility of the state government and the management of the tea gardens is to identify the crucial factors for the school and college dropouts of the children of the workers.

The management and the state intervention are the need of the hour to augment the education level among tea plantation workers and their children. To achieve the goal of quality education under Sustainable Development Goals, it is required to implement education in the ease of the workers and their children through government intervention. Financial obligation is an important factor for children to discontinue their studies and also to look for better employment opportunities. The wages of the workers need to be upgraded, better housing, better medical facilities, and better social security for the workers and the family members would induce the younger generations to stay and continue working in the tea plantations. Otherwise the glory of tea industry in India will be lost with labour shortages in the times to come shortly.

References

Annual Status of Education Report, West Bengal (2022)

Bora BR (2015) Socio-economic condition of tea garden workers and its impact on women's health with special reference to Teok Tea Estate-Assam. Int J Human Social Stud 3(12)

Borah N (2013) Rights of women workers in the tea garden of Assam. Int Multidiscip J 2(2)

Bosumatari D, Goyari P (2013) Educational status of tea plantation women workers in Assam—an empirical analysis. Asian J Multidiscip Stud 1(3)

Begum S. Islam QF (2022) Education of children of tea garden workers: organizations, provisions and challenges. J Posit Psychol 6(4)

Dutta M (2017) The status of marginalized women tea garden workers in mountain ecosystem of Darjeeling in a globalized village. In: Chand R, Nel E, Pelc S (eds) Societies, social inequalities and marginalization. Springer, Cham, pp 53–70

Islam B, Iftekhar SN (2015) Education for all in India: the present and beyond 2015

Internet (n.d.) darjeelingtea.com, The Himalayan Beacon. darjeelingnews.net

Khawas V (2006a) Socio-economic conditions of tea garden Labourers in Darjeeling Hills. Council for Social Development, New Delhi

Khawas V (2006b) Status of tea garden labourers in eastern himalayas—a case study of Darjeeling Tea Industry. Non ICIMOD Publication

Paul S (2017) Literacy pattern and level of development of the tea garden workers of Dooars region, West Bengal. In: Chaudhuri B (ed) Proceedings of UGC sponsored National Seminar on The Regional Dimensions of Social Development in India: Policy Perspectives, ISBN 978-93-86675-13-2. Ideal International E-Publication

Paul S, Rohatgi S (2014) Socio-economic status and health behavior of tea plantation workers of Dooars region, West Bengal. Geographical Thoughts 12

Rai PC (2019) An empirical study on the socio-economic conditions of the plantation workers in the tea industry of Darjeeling. International Journal of Applied Science and Engineering

Singh JD (2013) Education for all in India: the major issues, challenges and possible enablers. Educationia Confab 2(4):234–240

Sharma K (2005) Sociology of Indian tea industry—a study of inter-ethnic relationship. Mittal Publication

Sharma G (2013) A case study on socio-economic conditions of tea garden labourers-Lohpohia Tea Estate of Jorhat district, Assam. J Human Social Sci 1(3)

Synopsis on survey of Tea Garden conducted by Regional Labour Offices under jurisdiction of Joint Labour Commissioner, North Bengal Zone (n.d.)

Thapa N (2012) Employment status and human development of tea garden workers in West Bengal. Globalization, Development and Plantation Labour in India Routledge

Tea Board of India (2019–2020) Annual Reports

Sandeep Sundas is presently pursuing his doctoral research in the Department of Economics, Raiganj University, West Bengal, India.

Dr. Subrata Saha was awarded with the PhD in Economics from the University of North Bengal. Dr. Saha specializes on issues of fiscal policies and effects of structural changes on fiscal re-lationships in Southeast Asian Countries and India. The area of research interest is Public Finance and Time Series Econometrics. He is a member of the editorial board of UGC CARE listed journal ENSEMBLE and a life member of the Indian Econometric Society and Indian Economic Association. Dr. Saha is presently working as an associate professor of Economics at Raiganj University, West Bengal, India. He has supervised four MPhil and one PhD and presently supervising four PhD scholars at Raiganj University. He has contributed several research papers to National & International Journals and edited research volumes. Besides, he has authored two books in his credit. IRDP, India, has awarded him with prestigious Sarvepalli Radhakrishnan Lifetime Achievement National award in 2018 in recognition of his contribution to his activities towards promoting educational excellence.

Part IV
Public Policy Interventions in Social and Economic Changes

Chapter 15
Contribution of Human and Physical Capital to the Economic Growth in India: Post-reform Scenario

Subrata Saha and Pinki Das

15.1 Introduction

Human capital is one of the most important factors of production, without which the development of a country cannot be possible. It generally is a concept referring to the techniques, skills, and expertise that helps in the productivity of the economy. From a macroeconomic point of view, investment in human capital and physical capital makes capital and labour more productive, facilitates technological innovations, increases returns to capital, and makes growth more sustainable. A person having better education and health can only be considered a human capital because these are the only two factors that provide training and techniques and make a person physically and mentally strong. Investment in labour improves the productivity of human capital, which leads to the economic growth of a country. Gross fixed capital formation is another integral part of gross domestic product, and the economic growth of a country is influenced by gross capital formation. The economic growth of a country is measured as the rise in the amount of capital formation of services and goods of an economy over a while.

Human capital has substantial importance in neo-classical growth theory and endogenous growth theory models. In a neo-classical growth model, Solow (1956) considered that economic growth is a function of capital accumulation in his model and technology as an exogenous factor. A few decades later, the endogenous growth models played an important role in human capital in technological development and economic growth. The endogenous growth model holds the view that investment in human capital and knowledge is a significant contributor to economic growth. According to these new growth models, Romer (1986, 1990), Locus (1988), and

S. Saha (✉) · P. Das
Department of Economics, Raiganj University, Uttar Dinajpur, West Bengal, India

M. Mishra et al. (eds.), *Public Policies and Sustainable Development in Post-Reform India*, New Frontiers in Regional Science: Asian Perspectives 71,
https://doi.org/10.1007/978-981-99-3696-0_15

later other economists examined economic growth through an accumulation of physical and human capital.

Education and health are the only sources that transform a person into human capital. It includes investment in education and health, by which an economy can grow economically, leading to economic growth and development. The development of a country is not possible without physical and human capital. Most developed countries highly depend on physical capital with a deficit of human resources. However, most developing and underdeveloped countries (like India and Bangladesh) have to depend highly on human capital since the larger population size caters to supplying an ample workforce. Improvised technology is also responsible for labour-intensive economies. Higher dependency on physical capital raises unemployment, resulting in a recession in the economy of the country. A human is considered the human capital when he/she possesses proper education and health. It is crucial for the government to emphasize these two factors, i.e. education and health.

An increase in the various factors of human capital does not lead to economic growth always. In a general sense, an increase in expenditure on education and health leads to the development and growth of the economy. However, this is not accepted in every case. Different researchers across the world have studied the same to find whether education expenditure or health expenditure or capital expenditure impacts economic growth; the results were different in different countries. In some countries, it is observed that public education expenditure is the only factor that impacts the GDP (e.g. Abbas 2000; Bawono 2021), while, for some others, health expenditure is the only factor that highly impacts the GDP (Refer those studies). Some studies concluded that gross capital formation has a positive effect on economic growth. Again in some other cases, no education expenditure or health expenditure is seen to impact GDP (e.g. Nyasha and Odhiambo 2019; Sharma 2019; Seshaiah et al. 2018; Basumallik 2017).

India, as of 2021, has been ranked in the sixth position in GDP. Investment in human capital is one of the major factors for the current scenario. Among the sources of human capital mentioned earlier, investment in education and health plays a major role in the growing economy. As per the latest data, the Government of India has been increasing the expenditure on education since 2014. During 2020–2021, about 40% of the Ministry's total allocation, i.e. Rs 39,467 crores, has been allocated to the Department of Higher Education. [1] Since India has a huge population, it is of utmost necessity to increase public expenditure due to the presence of income inequality. The more the investment in education, the higher the population gets educated and contributes to the economic growth of a country. The allocation of such a huge amount to education and health makes us understand that the Indian government has been trying to improve both sectors, which will lead to an increase in human capital

[1] Demand for Grants 2020–2021 Analysis: Human Resource Development, PRS Legislative Research.

and GDP growth. Similarly, an increase in GDP growth also leads to an increase in human capital.

The general finding is that the accumulations of human capital and physical capital have a significant impact on a country's economic growth (e.g. Parika and Singh 2020; Widarni and Bawono 2021). Higher investment in education, health, and physical capital results in economic growth, as evident from previous studies (e.g. Sharma and Sahni 2015; Widarni and Bawono 2021; Karimzadeh and Karimzadeh 2013; Indira and Kumar 2018). Similarly, higher economic growth results in better education and health in a country, as many researchers pointed out earlier (e.g. Sharma and Sahni 2015; Karimzadeh and Karimzadeh 2013). Therefore, the present study intends to investigate (1) the dynamic relationship between Gross Domestic Product (GDP), current health expenditure (HL), secondary school enrollment (ED), and Gross Capital Formation (GC) in India during the period 1997–2019 and (2) to detect the direction of Granger causality among the concerned variables.

The following sections of the present chapter are organized as follows: Section 15.2 discusses micro-level empirical literature. Section 15.3 deals with the data and methodology used in the study, and Section 15.4 depicts the trends in the contribution of human capital and physical capital over the sample period. Section 15.5 demonstrates the empirical results and findings, and Section 15.6 reveals the variance decomposition and impulse response functions. Section 15.7 provides a conclusion and some policy recommendations based on the findings of the present study.

15.2 Literature Review

The research on human capital was commenced by Romer (1988) and Lucas (1998) with the introduction of human capital into their models, and from then, various research studies have continued today. Some studies are concerned with the impacts of gross capital formation on economic growth (e.g. Haldar and Mallik 2010; Shukla 2017; Sharma and Sahni 2015; Sharma 2019). Over the last few decades, numerous studies have been conducted regarding the relationship between gross domestic product, health, and education (Refer those studies), while few studies have been taken on the relationship between gross capital formation and gross domestic product (e.g. Abbas 2000; Parika and Singh 2020; Shukla 2017; Viswanath et al. 2009; Widarni and Bawono 2021; Varkey et al. 2020).

Abbas (2000), in his study, estimates and analyses the effects of human capital on economic growth as a flow and a stock variable for the two countries, viz. India and Pakistan. He also focuses on analysing the effects of effective labour input on economic growth and analysing human capital as an agent in attracting physical capital. The study finds that human capital, measured by the primary schooling enrollment rate, has a positive impact on the economic growth of India. At the same time, it is the higher schooling enrollment rate that has a positive impact on economic growth in Pakistan. It is also found that the stock of human capital is positively correlated to physical capital, implying human capital plays the most crucial role as an agent in attracting physical capital in both countries.

Haldar and Mallik (2010) aim to study the effect of both education and health on human capital investment and also their stock on economic growth. The study finds that investment in education and health plays an important role in the long run per capita GNP growth, and also, the worker's productivity is enhanced by good health and nutrition.

Parika and Singh (2020) examine the association of human capital with economic prosperity and other determinants of economic development in the long and short run which means studying the relationship between human capital and economic growth. The investigators have included several proxy variables, viz. real GDP, human capital index, total trade, and GDP deflator. The study reveals that in the long run, there is a positive and significant impact of human capital and physical capital on economic output. However, in the short run, the level of human and physical capital, trade volume, and fiscal space for the government are determined by the level of economic output.

Shukla (2017) in her study aims to study the role of human capital in economic growth as well as studying the relationship between the same of India from the period 1995 to 2014. The variables used are GDP, health expenditure per capita, gross capital formation, and secondary school enrollment. The study reveals that each of the variables has a positive impact on economic growth, but secondary school enrollment has the greatest role on GDP growth and suggests that increasing funds for education and health is much necessary for sustainable economic growth.

Agrawal and Khan (2020) focus on investigating if there is any relationship between human development and economic growth and also to check whether growth results in human development. The findings reveal that human capital has a positive and significant impact on the economic growth of India.

Maksymenko and Rabbani (2011), in their study entitled 'Economic Reforms, Human Capital and Economic Growth in India and South Korea: A Co-integration Analysis', attempts to study the role of economic reforms and human capital accumulation on post-reform economic growth. The study is based on secondary data, and the data collected for South Korea covers the period of 1966–1967, while it is 1992–2003 in the case of India. The study reveals that human capital accumulation has a significant positive impact on both countries. Also, while the economic reforms positively impact economic growth in South Korea, the same also shows a negative impact in India.

In their study, Idrees and Siddiqi (2013) focus on studying the long-run relationship between public education expenditure and economic growth. The investigators have selected seven developed countries (UK, US, Canada, Germany, France, Italy, and Japan) and seven developing countries (Pakistan, India, China, Turkey, Poland, Russia, and South Africa). The study uses secondary data from various publications (International agencies), and the data used are panel data covering the period of 17 years (1990–2006). The study finds that the impact of public education expenditure on economic growth is more remarkable in developing countries than in developed countries because the marginal productivity of human capital is greater in developing countries.

Nyasha and Odhiambo (2019) focus on studying the literature that assesses the impact of government spending on economic growth. The study finds that the impact of government spending on economic growth varies from country to country. In some countries, the impact is found to be positive, while it is negative for others. Also, for some others, it is also found to have no impact. The study discusses the impact of various countries since 1980.

Indira and Kumar (2018), together, in their study, aim to analyse the trends in public expenditure on higher education and gross enrollment and also analyse the causality between higher education and GDP in India. The study reveals that the higher education sector has been growing, but the increase in expenditure on education is much higher than GDP. It also finds that there is a causal relationship between expenditure on higher education and GDP, implying that an increase in educational expenditure contributes to economic growth.

Khan and Chaudhry (2019) attempt to study the impact of human capital on GDP growth and employment in developing countries. The investigators have used 48 developing countries, among which some are low-income developing countries while the others belong to middle-income developing countries and all developing countries. Based on panel data and fixed effect and random effect models, the study reveals that human capital plays a significant role and contributes as an engine to GDP growth and employment in developing countries.

Sharma and Sahni (2015) in their study (Human Capital and Economic Growth in India: A Co-integration and Causality Analysis) aim to study the causality relationship between human capital investment (education and health investment) and the economic growth of India. The study finds that investment in human capital (education and health) is the main factor that affects the economic growth in the country. Similarly, economic growth also plays an important role in the growth of human capital.

Apergis and Padhi (2013), in their study (Health Expenses and Economic Growth: Convergence Dynamics across the Indian States), try to explore the convergence of real per capita output and health expenses of the Indian states. The investigators have selected 26 states of the country covering the period of 1981–2005 to fulfill the objective. The study finds that the states which form convergent clubs exhibit differences in underlying growth and health expenses factors. An increase in investment in health, either by direct intervention policies or by increasing states' income, is of utmost necessity.

Sharma (2019), in her study, aims to examine the health and education status in both countries from 1970 to 2016, studying the impact of public health expenditure on economic growth and the role of human capital on economic growth. The study reveals that there appears to be a unidirectional causality between public health expenditure and economic growth. Education and health have a positive impact on economic growth in India but a negative impact on China's growth rate.

Sarwar et al. (2020) aim to study the critical aspect of financial development, human capital, and their impact on economic growth. The study covers 83 emerging countries covering the period 2002–2017. The study reveals that financial development and human capital play an important role and positively and significantly impact emerging economies.

Gopalkrishna and Rao (2012) aim to examine the chain relationship between economic growth and human development, the effect of economic growth on human development, and support the role of public expenditure on human development. The study has covered 15 major Indian states and is a secondary data-based study. The study finds that inter-regional disparities in human development have been widening over a long period. However, the states are showing a tendency of convergence to human development. They also found that both public expenditure and human development have a close positive relationship.

Viswanath et al. (2009) estimated the contribution of physical and human capital to economic growth. The study covers 26 Indian states and Union Territories. The study finds that investment in human capital and economic growth has a strong positive relationship.

Widarni and Bawono (2021) investigated the effect of human capital and technology on economic growth in Indonesia. The study considers 35 years (1984–2019) to carry out the objective. The study finds that both human capital and technology positively impact the country's economic growth. Furthermore, it reveals that increasing human capital using education plays the most important role since educational development leads to technological progress and economic growth and development.

Karimzadeh and Karimzadeh (2013) aim to study the effect of foreign trade and human capital on the economic growth of India. For the period 1980–2011. The study finds that there is a significant relationship between trade, human capital, and economic growth. Furthermore, it reveals that any progress in human capital positively affects economic growth. Similarly, an increase in economic growth leads to more employment, income, and profit, i.e. more investment in human capital.

Tamang (2011) attempts to study the relationship between educational expenditure and economic growth in the Indian context. The investigator considers the period 1980–2008 to check the objective. The study reveals that the return per labour due to the increase of physical capital per labour is higher than the return per labour due to an increase in government expenditure on education which means investing in education leads to a lower return than investment in physical capital.

Seshaiah et al. (2018) investigate the impact of general government expenditure on the GDP of India, analyse the trends in general government expenditure and real GDP, and also study the impact of general government expenditure on deficits. The investigators have considered the period of 1980–1981 to 2015–2016. The study finds a negative impact of general expenditure on economic growth post-2008, while there was a positive impact of the former on economic growth post-1991. Non-development expenditure also shares a large proportion of government expenditure.

Gangal and Gupta (2013) analyse the impact of public expenditure on the economic growth of India from 1998 to 2012. The study finds that there is a positive impact of total public expenditure on economic growth. A unidirectional relationship between total public expenditure to GDP and a positive impact of shocks from total public expenditure to GDP and vice versa has been found.

Maitra and Mukhopadhyay (2012) focus on examining the role of public spending on education and health sectors in promoting the GDP of 12 countries in Asia and Pacific over the last three decades—1981–2011. The study finds some of the countries to have co-integrating relations while the same was absent in the rest of the countries.

Zaman et al. (2017) aim to identify the association between life expectancy with health care expenditure and GDP in Bangladesh between 1996 and 2006. The study finds that there exists a direct relationship between GDP and total health expenditure. It is also found that there is no significant relationship between total health expenditure and increasing life expectancy.

Varkey et al. (2020) focus on analysing the relationship between infrastructure and health outcomes and also analysing the impact of health infrastructure on economic growth between 1980 and 2012. It has taken a sample of 15 countries. The study finds that there is a significant positive relationship between Health Infrastructure Index (HII) and Life Expectancy (LE), whereas a significant negative relationship arises between Health Infrastructure Index and Infant Mortality Rate (IMR). Also, at the state level, there is a positive relation between HII and GSDP and HII and LE. On the other hand, a negative relationship has been observed between HII and IMR.

Basumallik (2017) focuses on examining the relationship between health and economic growth in India from the period 1961 to 2015. The study finds that there is no significant relationship between health and economic growth when OLS has been used. But on the other hand, when 2SLS has been employed, a highly significant effect of health on economic growth has been observed.

Most of the empirical studies separately investigated the impact of human capital or physical capital on economic growth in different countries at different times using a different methodology. To the best of our knowledge, no studies have examined the effects of both human capital and physical capital together on economic growth in India. Therefore the present study is an attempt to investigate the contributions of human capital and physical capital to economic growth in India during the period 1997–2019.

15.3 Data and Methods

15.3.1 Data

The present study likes to fulfill the given objective for the period 1997–2019. It uses the data of GDP (annual growth rate), health (current health expenditure as a share of GDP), education (gross percentage of secondary school enrollment), and gross capital formation (gross fixed capital formation as a share of GDP). GDP has been considered as the dependent variable, and the three indicators health, education, and

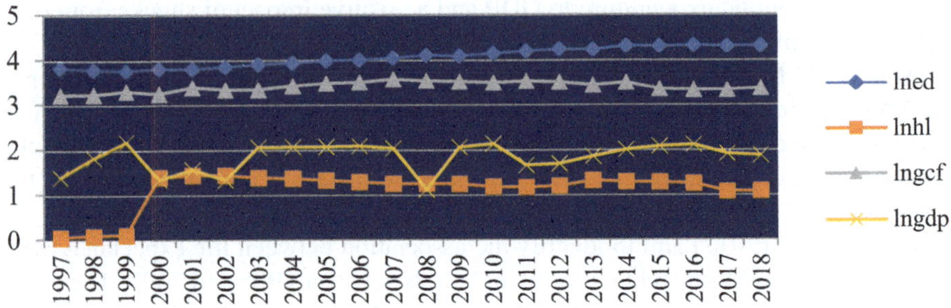

Fig. 15.1 Time plots of GDP, HL, ED, and GC. (**Source:** Plotted by the authors from World Bank data). **Note:** 'lngdp' represents log value of gross domestic product; 'lngcf' signifies log value of gross capital formation; 'lnhl' represents log value of health expenditure; and 'lned' describes log value of education

gross capital formation are the independent variables in the study. The annual data of the given variables have been collected from the original site of the World Bank database and Economic Survey of various rounds (Fig. 15.1). The study shall use the following notations:

- GDP for gross domestic product (annual growth rate)
- HL for current health expenditure as a percentage of GDP
- ED for gross percentage of secondary school enrollment
- GC for gross capital formation

15.3.2 Methods

The study uses E-views 10 software for data analysis. In the first stage, the study has applied the unit root test to investigate the stationarity of four time series datasets. The two techniques, the Augmented Dickey–Fuller Test (ADF) and Phillips–Perron Test (PP), for checking the stationary of the datasets are applied. In the second phase, the study has applied the Autoregressive Distributed Lag Model (ARDL) to find whether any long-run relationships exist among the four variables. Further, lag order selection is based on the Vector Autoregressive model (VAR), and accordingly, Vector Error Correction Estimates (VEC) have been performed. Finally, the VEC granger causality/block exogeneity Wald test has been performed to check whether the independent variables have any impact on the dependent variable or whether the dependent variable impacts the independent variables.

The present study uses the following function:

$$GDP_t = f(HL_t, ED_t, GC_t) \tag{15.1}$$

where GDP_t is a function of health (HL_t), education (ED_t), and Gross Capital Formation (GC_t).

Taking the log value of each variable, the above function may be written as:

$$\log(\mathrm{GDP_t}) = f(\log \mathrm{HL_t},\ \log\ \mathrm{ED_t},\ \log \mathrm{GC_t}) \tag{15.2}$$

Based on the above function, the equation of the econometric model can be developed as follows:

$$\log\ \mathrm{GDP_t} = \alpha + \beta_1 \log \mathrm{HL_t} + \beta_2 \log \mathrm{ED_t} + \beta_2 \log \mathrm{GC_t} + \varepsilon_\mathrm{t} \tag{15.3}$$

The present paper shall estimate the Eq. (15.3) during the study.

The nature of the variables under consideration determines the choice of the estimation process. If all the variables are stationary, then Vector Autoregressive (VAR) model can be used, or if all the variables are non-stationary, then the Vector Error Correction Model (VECM) will be used. However, if one of the variables or more is stationary, i.e. I(0), and other variables are non-stationary, i.e. I(1), then ARDL bound test can be used to examine the long-run relationship between or among the variables.

The ARDL model will help ascertain the long-run relationship among the variables concerned. The ARDL bound test can be applied whether the variables are co-integrated or not.

ARDL equations used in this study are as follows:

$$\begin{aligned}\mathrm{GDP_t} = \alpha_{01} &+ \sum\nolimits_j^m \beta_{1i}\mathrm{GDP}_{t-j} + \sum\nolimits_i^n \beta_{2i}\mathrm{HL}_{t-i} + \sum\nolimits_i^n \beta_{3i}\mathrm{ED}_{t-i} \\ &+ \sum\nolimits_i^n \beta_{4i}\mathrm{GC}_{t-i} + \vartheta_1\end{aligned} \tag{15.4}$$

$$\begin{aligned}\mathrm{HL_t} = \alpha_{02} &+ \sum\nolimits_j^m \beta_{1i}\mathrm{HL}_{t-j} + \sum\nolimits_i^n \beta_{2i}\mathrm{GDP}_{t-i} + \sum\nolimits_i^n \beta_{3i}\mathrm{ED}_{t-i} \\ &+ \sum\nolimits_i^n \beta_{4i}\mathrm{GC}_{t-i} + \vartheta_2\end{aligned} \tag{15.5}$$

$$\begin{aligned}\mathrm{ED_t} = \alpha_{03} &+ \sum\nolimits_j^m \beta_{1i}\mathrm{ED}_{t-j} + \sum\nolimits_i^n \beta_{2i}\mathrm{HL}_{t-i} + \sum\nolimits_i^n \beta_{3i}\mathrm{GDP}_{t-i} \\ &+ \sum\nolimits_i^n \beta_{4i}\mathrm{GC}_{t-i} + \vartheta_3\end{aligned} \tag{15.6}$$

$$\begin{aligned}\mathrm{GC_t} = \alpha_{04} &+ \sum\nolimits_j^m \beta_{1i}\mathrm{GC}_{t-j} + \sum\nolimits_i^n \beta_{2i}\mathrm{HL}_{t-i} + \sum\nolimits_i^n \beta_{3i}\mathrm{ED}_{t-i} \\ &+ \sum\nolimits_i^n \beta_{4i}\mathrm{GDP}_{t-i} + \vartheta_4\end{aligned} \tag{15.7}$$

where, i and j represent the number of lags included in the model. It can be determined empirically based on Akaike Information Criterion and Schwartz

Information Criterion so that the number of lags will be a minimum while, ϑ_1, ϑ_2, ϑ_3, and ϑ_4 are residuals.

The present study uses the VECM to examine the dynamic relationship among four variables and to detect the Granger causal relationship. The following equations of VECM are used in the study.

ρ_1, ρ_2, ρ_3, and ρ_4 are coefficients of error correction terms of Eqs. (15.4), (15.5), (15.6), and (15.7), respectively.

ω_1, ω_2, ω_3, and ω_4 represent the residuals from Eqs. (15.4), (15.5), (15.6), and (15.7), respectively.

Where, i is the number of lags included in the model. It can be determined empirically on the basis of the Akaike Information Criterion and Schwartz Information Criterion so that the number of lags will be minimum while $Z_{it\text{-}1}$, $Z_{2t\text{-}1}$, $Z_{3t\text{-}1}$, and $Z_{4t\text{-}1}$ are error correction terms.

So far as the stability of the model is concerned, CUSUM test and CUSUM-Square test can be used.

15.3.2.1 CUSUM Test

The CUSUM, that is, the cumulative sum of recursive residuals defined as:

$$\text{CUSUM}_\text{t} = \sum\nolimits_{t=k+1}^{r} \widehat{u}_t^{(r)} / \widehat{\delta}_u \tag{15.8}$$

It can also reveal structural changes and is therefore often plotted for $t = K + 1 \ldots T$ in checking a model. The CUSUM was proposed for this purpose by Brown et al. (1975). If the CUSUM wanders off too far from the zero line, this is evidence against the structural stability of the underlying model. A test with a significance level of about 5% is obtained by rejecting stability if CUSUM_t crosses the lines

$$\pm 0.948 \left[\sqrt{T-K} + 2(t-K)/\sqrt{T-K} \right] \tag{15.9}$$

This test is designed to detect a nonzero mean of the recursive residuals due to shifts in the model parameters. The test may not have much power if there is not only one parameter shift but various shifts that may compensate for their impacts on the means of the recursive residuals.

In that case, the **CUSUM Squares** plot is based on the following:

$$\text{CUSUM} - \text{SQt} = \sum\nolimits_{t=k+1}^{r} \left(\widehat{u}_t^{(r)} \right)^2 / \sum\nolimits_{t=k+1}^{T} \left(\widehat{u}_t^{(r)} \right)^2 \tag{15.10}$$

If these quantities cross the lines given by $\pm\, c + (t - K)/(T - K)$, structural instability is diagnosed. The constant c depends on the desired significance level, the sample size T, and the number of regressors in the model.

15.4 Trends in Contributions of Human and Physical Capital

GDP is the value of final goods and services produced in a country during a given period. The present study considers GDP to be the dependent variable. India has been observing quite a fluctuation in the annual GDP growth. The annual GDP growth from 1997 to 2019 has been expressed with the help of a bar diagram in Fig. 15.2. GDP growth in 1997 was 4.05%. It showed an increasing trend to 1999, showing the GDP to be 8.84%. However, it decreased to 3.84% and kept fluctuating till 2002. However, it increased to 7.86% and was capable of maintaining the GDP at 9.23% in both the years 2004 and 2005. The growth rate decreased, but there was not a vast difference till 2007.

However, in 2008, along with the decrease in the GDP of the entire world due to the crash of the Stock Market resulting in recession, India's growth rate decreased to 3.08%. However, it maintained to gain economic growth in the next very year. The growth rate again dropped in the year 2011 and was able to maintain an increasing trend till 2016. After that, it slowly started declining and decreased to 4.04% in 2019.

15.4.1 Health

Health is also one of the most important factors responsible for human capital and economic growth. Along with education, health is also of utmost necessity for the growth of a developing country like India. India has a large population, and as it is not possible to depend on physical capital, it is necessary to maintain the health of the population of the country. Thus, the present study has considered public health expenditure to be one of the independent variables and has been expressed below using a bar diagram.

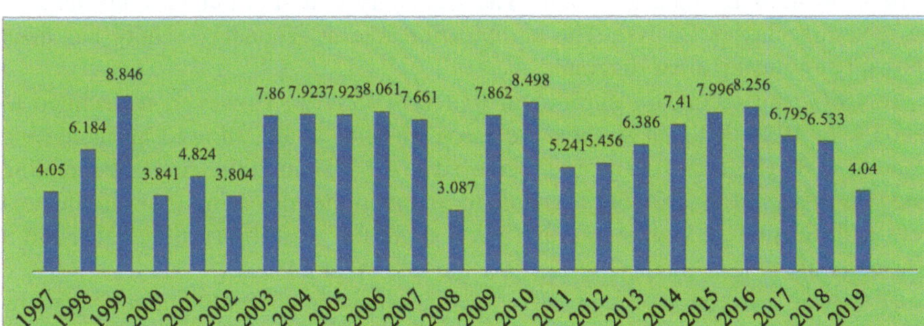

Fig. 15.2 Gross domestic product trends, 1997–2019. (**Source:** Prepared by the authors from World Bank Data)

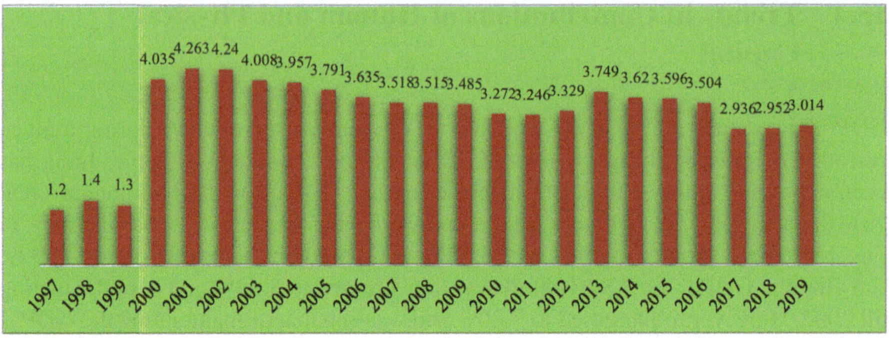

Fig. 15.3 Healthcare expenditure trend, 1997–2019. (Source: Prepared by the authors from World Bank Data)

The amount spent by the government on the public healthcare system has been quite fluctuating over the period 1997–2019 (Fig. 15.3). The share of public expenditure was only 1.2% in 1997. In the first 3 years, slight differences were observed in the expenditure. In 2000, the government increased its public health expenditure to 4.03% and 4.26% in 2000 and 2001, respectively. The government slightly decreased its expenditure to 4.24% in 2002 and kept on decreasing the expenditure till 2011. Statistics shows a decreasing trend in the expenditure level on health, which decreased to 3.24% in 2011. It again increased a bit more than the expenditure carried out in 2011 but kept declining to 3.50% in 2016. However, it dropped to 2.93% in 2017 and showed a slightly increasing trend in 2019 with 3.01%.

15.4.2 Education

Education is one of the most important factors in creating human capital resulting in GDP growth. The study has selected secondary school enrollment as an independent variable to show its impact on GDP. The secondary school in India is considered to be covering classes IX–XII. The participation rate at secondary school has been shown below using a bar diagram.

In 1997, the secondary enrollment rate was 45.83%. However, it declined to 43.03% in 1999. It again slightly increased to 44.87% and showed an increasing trend to 2008 (Fig. 15.4). The rate increased to 60.35% in 2008. A slight declining rate was observed in 2009 but was able to maintain the increasing trend in the next year with 63.11%. It kept increasing, but a slight fall was observed in 2013, and it was certainly able to manage to increase the rate to 74.14%.

However, between 2015 and 2016, fluctuations were observed but at a very low rate. Though the rate has been able to show an increasing trend from 1997 to 2019, i.e. 45.83% to 73.79% respectively, it could not reach to the fullest yet.

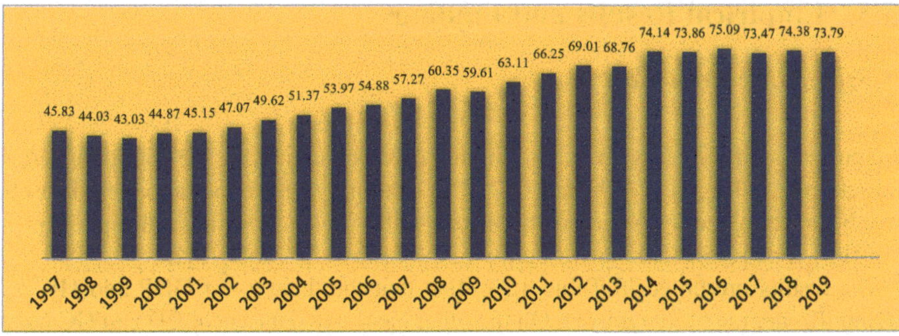

Fig. 15.4 School enrollment, secondary trend, 1997–2019. (**Source:** Prepared by the authors from World Bank Data)

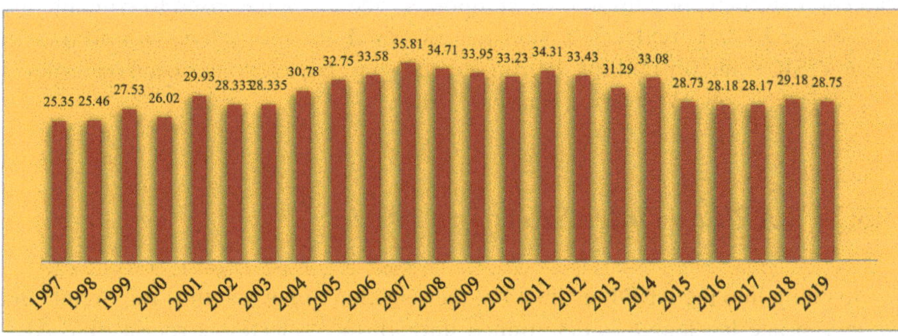

Fig. 15.5 Gross capital formation trend, 1997–2019. (**Source:** Prepared by the authors from World Bank Data)

15.4.3 Gross Capital Formation

Gross capital formation is measured by the total value of the gross fixed capital formation, changes in inventories and acquisitions, and fewer disposals of valuables for a unit or sector. Gross capital has been taken as one of the independent variables along with education and health to determine its impact on GDP.

Gross capital formation also shows a fluctuating trend (Fig. 15.5). In 1997, the gross capital formation was 25.35% which increased to 25.46% and 27.53% in 1998 and 1999, respectively. But in 2000, the rate decreased to 26.02%, and in one go, it increased to 29.93%. It again decreased to 28.33 and showed an increasing trend, and it kept on increasing to 35.81% in 2007. During 2008–2010, rate decreased and maintained at 33.23% in 2010. However, it again showed fluctuations over the next periods and showed almost a constant share with 28.18% and 28.17% in 2016–2017, respectively. It again increased to 29.18% in 2018 and declined to 28.75% in 2019.

15.5 Empirical Results and Findings

15.5.1 Unit Root Test

The present study focuses on examining the relationship among the four time series datasets, viz. GDP, HL, ED, and GC. The stationary and non-stationary datasets have been examined by Augmented Dickey–Fuller Test (ADF) and Phillips–Perron Test (PP). The results are shown below in the following Table 15.1.

The results presented in Table 15.1 state that the datasets of GDP and HL are having I(0) degree of integration. On the other hand, the datasets of ED and GC have I(1) degree of integration. Gross domestic product and health expenditure are stationary at the level, whereas the education enrollment and gross capital formation are non-stationary at the level, as evident from both ADF and PP test results with intercept and intercept with trend assumptions. The lag length used to compute the Augmented Dickey–Fuller test statistics is based on the Schwartz information criterion (SIC), and for Phillips–Perron test statistics, lag length has been determined by applying Newey-West using Bartlett Kernel.

15.5.2 VAR Lag Order Selection Criteria

Before going into the ARDL estimation, the selection of lag length is important, and the appropriate lag length is determined through the 'selection Criteria' like AIC, SIC, LR, HQ, etc. Table 15.2 presents the results of the VAR lag order selection criteria.

It is observed from Table 15.2 that Log L, LR, FPE, HQ, and SC criteria for lag order 1 are significant, but on the other hand, the AIC criterion gives the lowest value as compared to Log L, LR, FPE, HQ, and SC criterion, therefore, lag 2 is being selected for the model because the lower the value of AIC criterion the better the fit of the model. Hence, the result of the lag order selection based on the unrestricted vector autoregressive (VAR) model suggests lag order.

15.5.3 ARDL Bounds Test for Co-integration

For examining the long-run relationship and dynamic interaction among the four concerning variables, the model has been estimated by the Auto Regressive Distributed Lag (ARDL) co-integration procedure developed by Pesaran et al. (2001). The procedure is adopted for the following reasons. First, the bound test is simple as opposed to other multivariate co-integration techniques such as Johansen and Juselius (1990), it allows the co-integrating relationship to be estimated by OLS once the lag order is selected. Second, the bound test procedure does not require the

Table 15.1 Unit root test results

Variable	ADF Intercept		ADF Intercept and trend		PP Intercept		PP Intercept and trend		Degree of integration
	t-stat.	Prob.	t-stat.	Prob.	t-stat.	Prob.	t-stat.	Prob.	
$InGDP_t$	−4.15[a]	0.01	4.21[a]	0.00	−4.08[a]	0.02	−4.15[a]	0.00	I(0) i.e. stationary
$\Delta InGDP_t$	−4.15[a]	0.00	0.32[a]	0.74	4.21[a]	0.00	0.32[a]	0.74	I(0) i.e. stationary
$InHL_t$	−2.64	0.26	3.32[a]	0.00	−4.12[a]	0.01	−2.64[a]	0.01	I(0) i.e. stationary
$\Delta InHL_t$	−2.64[a]	0.01	−0.57[a]	0.56	3.32[a]	0.00	−0.57	0.56	I(0) i.e. stationary
$InED_t$	−0.85	0.94	0.90	0.38	−2.26	0.43	−1.89	0.07	I(1) i.e. non-stationary
$\Delta InED_t$	−0.85	0.40	0.71	0.48	1.92	0.06	1.84	0.08	I(1) i.e. non-stationary
$InGC_t$	−1.45	0.81	1.54	0.13	−1.23	0.87	1.54	0.13	I(1) i.e. non-stationary
$\Delta InGC_t$	−1.45	0.16	−0.83	0.41	−1.45	0.16	−0.83	0.41	I(1) i.e. non-stationary

Source: Computations done by the authors using E-views 10

Notes: ln represents natural logarithm. Δ is the first difference operator. ADF and PP represent Augmented Dicky–Fuller and Phillips–Perron t-statistics. Critical values are obtained from Mackinnon (1996)

[a] Denotes significance at 1%. I(0) is the degree of integration of order zero, i.e. stationary, and I(1) is the degree of integration of order one, i.e. non-stationary series attaining stationary upon first differencing

Table 15.2 VAR lag order selection criteria

Lag	Log L	LR	FPE	AIC	SC	HQ
0	23.22340	NA	1.88e-06	−1.830800	−1.631843	−1.787621
1	90.57126[a]	102.6253[a]	1.47e-08[a]	−6.721072	−5.726289[a]	−6.505179[a]
2	107.4670	19.30940	1.65e-08	−6.806379[a]	−5.015769	−6.417771

Source: Computations done by the authors using E-views 10

Notes: LR: Sequential modified LR statistic (each test at 5% level); FPE: Final prediction error; AIC: Akaike information criterion; SC: Schwarz information criterion; HQ: Hannan-Quinn information criterion

[a] Indicates lag order selected by the criterion

Table 15.3 Results of F-bounds test

Test statistics	Significance	I(0)	I(1)
F-statistics = 5.26	10%	3.47	4.45
$K = 3$	5%	4.01	5.07
	2.5%	4.52	5.62
	1%	5.17	6.36

Source: Computations done by the authors using E-views 10

pre-testing of the variables included in the model for unit root, unlike other techniques, such as Engel and Granger (1987). These techniques require that all the variables be integrated in the same order I(1), i.e. all the variables should be non-stationary. Since the result represents the presence of both stationary i(0) and non-stationary I(0) datasets, the study goes through the Auto Regressive Distributed Lag Model approach (ARDL) to identify the multiple co-integrations among the given variables. Due to the different order of co-integration, it follows the ARDL approach to co-integration. The bound test evidence confirms the long-run relationship. The result of the bound testing approach has been presented in the tables below.

15.5.3.1 ARDL Long-Run Form and Bound Test

Estimated equation:

$$\text{GDP} = f(\text{HL}, \text{ED}, \text{GC}) \tag{15.11}$$

- ARDL (2,1,2,1)
- Optimal lag: 2
- Null hypothesis: No co-integration among the variables

F-Bound test (Table 15.3) shows that the value of F-statistics is 5.26 which is greater than the value of I(0) and I(1) at the 5% level and the result indicates that the concerned four variables are co-integrated. Since the value of t-statistics (Table 15.4) is greater than the value of I(0) and I(1) at the 10% level so we reject the null hypothesis and all the concerned variables have a long-run relationship over the sample period.

Table 15.4 Results of t-bound test

Test statistics	Significance	I(0)	I(1)
t-statistics = −4.11	10%	−3.13	−3.84
	5%	−3.41	−4.16
	2.5%	−3.65	−4.42
	1%	−3.96	−4.73

Source: Computations done by the authors using E-views 10

Table 15.5 Results of F-bounds test

Test statistics	Significance	I(0)	I(1)
F-statistics = 5.26 $K = 3$	10%	3.47	4.45
	5%	4.01	5.07
	2.5%	4.52	5.62
	1%	5.17	6.36

Source: Computations done by the authors using E-views 10

Table 15.6 Results of t-bound test

Test statistics	Significance	I(0)	I(1)
t-statistics = −5.23	10%	−3.13	−3.84
	5%	−3.41	−4.16
	2.5%	−3.65	−4.42
	1%	−3.96	−4.73

Source: Computations done by the authors using E-views 10

15.5.3.2 ARDL Error Correction Regression

Estimated equation:

$$\text{GDP} = \beta(\text{HL}, \text{ED}, \text{GC}) \tag{15.12}$$

- ARDL (2,1,2,1)
- Optimal lag: 2
- Null hypothesis: No co-integration among the variables

The value of F-statistics (Table 15.5) is 5.26, which is greater than the theoretical value of I(0) and I(1) at 5% significant level, and the result indicates that the concerned four variables are co-integrated. Since the value of t-statistics (Table 15.6) is greater than the upper bound value at the 5% level, so the null hypothesis is rejected, implying that all the concerned variables have a long-run relationship during the period of study.

15.5.3.3 Diagnostic Tests

From the Jarque–Bera test, the J. B value is 0.62 (Table 15.7), and since the probability value is 0.73, which is greater than 0.05, the null hypothesis of normality of the residuals is accepted. So the residuals are multivariate normal. Both the LM

Table 15.7 Diagnostic tests summary

Normality J. B value: 0.62, Prob (0.73)
Breusch Godfrey Serial Correlation LM Test: 2.645910, ProbF(2,8) = 0.13
Obs*R-squared: 15.64, Prob. Chi-Square(10) = 0.11
Heteroscedasticity Test (ARCH): 2.918558, Prob.F(10,10) = 0.06
Obs*R-squared: 15.64, Prob. Chi-Square (10) = 0.11

Source: Computations done by the authors using E-views 10

test and Obs*R-squared show a probability value greater than 0.05, which indicates there are no serial correlations among the residuals. Concerning heteroscedasticity, since the probability values of the heteroscedasticity test are 0.06 and 0.11 (Obs*R-squared), which are greater than 0.05, implying that residuals are homoscedasticity.

Summary of the Findings

The results obtained from ARDL bound test suggest that there exists a co-integration among the four variables under consideration. This means that there are stable and long-run equilibrium relationships among the concerned four variables over the period of study. So far as the validity of the ARDL model is concerned, the model which passes through all the diagnostic tests on residuals is valid and stable.

15.5.4 VECM Estimation and Findings

From the above observations, it is clear that there exists a long-run relationship among the variables, but in the short run, disequilibrium may occur among the variables. The present study needs to examine whether such types of short-run disequilibrium converge to long-run equilibrium or not; thus, VECM has been used to generate such short-run dynamics to reach that equilibrium along with causal (Granger) relationship among the variables. The number of lags in the model has been determined based on Akaike Information Criterion (AIC), and the lag order of the model is 2.

To investigate the short-run imbalances and dynamic structure along with short-run Granger Causality among Gross Domestic Product (GDPt), Health expenditure (HEt), Secondary school enrollment (EDt), and Gross capital formation (GCt), VECM is applied. The block exogeneity Wald test has been conducted based on chi-square statistics to further confirm the results obtained from VECM. The results of the VECM have been presented in the following.

15.5.4.1 Co-integration Equation

$$\begin{aligned}\mathrm{GDP}_{t-1} = -71.30 + 25.49\mathrm{HL}_{t-1} + 1.72\mathrm{ED}_{t-1} + 9.05\mathrm{GC}_{t-1} \\ (18.41) \qquad (0.81) \qquad (2.60)\end{aligned} \tag{15.13}$$

Note: The figures in the parentheses are estimated t-statistics.

The results indicate that an increase of 1% point in health care expenditure (HL) will cause an increase of 25.49% points in GDP. Since the t-statistics is insignificant in the education attainment variable, education (ED) has no impact on the gross domestic product. Gross capital formation (GC) is significant at 5%, implying that 1% point increase in gross capital formation will cause an increase of 9.05% points in GDP

The results of the four equations estimated from VECM are presented below.

15.5.4.2 Model 1

When GDP is taken as a dependent variable and HL, ED, and GC are taken as independent variables

$$\begin{aligned}\mathrm{GDP_t} = & -0.17\ (-0.91) + 0.005ECT_{t-1}(0.23) \\ & -0.34\Delta\mathrm{GDP}_{t-1}(-1.29) - 0.23\Delta\mathrm{GDP}_{t-2}(-0.90) \\ & -0.13\Delta\mathrm{HL}_{t-1}(-0.31) + 0.25\Delta\mathrm{HL}_{t-2}(0.58) + 3.78\Delta\mathrm{ED}_{t-1}(0.85) \\ & +2.42\Delta\mathrm{ED}_{t-2}(0.59) - 3.20\Delta\mathrm{GC}_{t-1}(-1.74) + 0.95\Delta\mathrm{GC}_{t-2}(0.59)\end{aligned} \tag{15.14}$$

$R^2 = 0.59, \mathrm{Adj}.R^2 = 0.22, \mathrm{F-statistic} = 1.61, \mathrm{Loglikelihood} = -2.15, \mathrm{AIC} = 1.21$

15.5.4.3 Model 2

When health (HL) is taken as a dependent variable and GDP, ED, and GC are taken as independent variables

$$\begin{aligned}\mathrm{HL}_t = & -0.07\ (-3.30) - 0.04\mathrm{ECT}_{t-2}(-17.38) + 0.12\Delta\mathrm{GDP}_{t-1}(3.87) \\ & +0,04\Delta\mathrm{GDP}_{t-2}(1.26) + 0.20\Delta\mathrm{HL}_{t-1}(3.90) + 0.20\Delta\mathrm{HL}_{t-2}(3.79) \\ & +2.19\Delta\mathrm{ED}_{t-1}(4.06) + 1.67\Delta\mathrm{ED}_{t-2}(3.38) + 0.16\Delta\mathrm{GC}_{t-1}(0.73) \\ & +0.71\Delta\mathrm{GC}_{t-2}(3.63)\end{aligned} \tag{15.15}$$

$R^2 = 0.98, \mathrm{Adj}.R^2 = 0.96, \mathrm{F-statistic} = 66.17, \mathrm{Loglikelihood} = 39.90, \mathrm{AIC} = -2.99$

15.5.4.4 Model 3

When Education (ED) is taken as a dependent variable and HL, GDP, and GC are taken as independent variables

$$\begin{aligned} ED_t = & -0.02\ (1.83) + 0.001ECT_{t-3}(0.55) + 0.04\Delta GDP_{t-1}(2.17) \\ & + 0.03\Delta GDP_{t-2}(1.94) + 0.01\Delta HL_{t-1}(0.54) \\ & + 0.02\Delta HL_{t-2}(0.60) - 0.29\Delta ED_{t-1}(-0.94) + 0.24(0.88) \\ & + 0.10\Delta GC_{t-1}(0.78) + 0.16\Delta GC_{t-2}(1.42) \end{aligned} \quad (15.16)$$

$R^2 = 0.50, \mathrm{Adj}.R^2 = 0.06, \mathrm{F-statistic} = 1.14, \mathrm{Loglikelihood} = 51.50, \mathrm{AIC} = -4.11$

15.5.4.5 Model 4

When Gross Capital Formation (GC) is taken as a dependent variable and HL, ED and GDP are taken as independent variables

$$\begin{aligned} GC_t = & 0.02\ (0.78) + 0.004ECT^4_{t-1}(1.53) + 0.02\Delta GDP_{t-1}(0.65) \\ & + 0.06\Delta GDP_{t-2}(1.76) + 0.13\Delta HL_{t-1}(2.14) \\ & - 0.08\Delta HL_{t-2}(-1.30) - 1.14\Delta ED_{t-1}(-1.78) + 0.21\Delta ED_{t-2}(0.36) \\ & + 0.22\Delta GC_{t-1}(0.83) + 0.08\Delta GC_{t-2}(0.36) \end{aligned} \quad (15.17)$$

$R^2 = 0.58, \mathrm{Adj}.R^2 = 0.22, \mathrm{F-statistic} = 1.58, \mathrm{Loglikelihood} = 36.49, \mathrm{AIC} = -2.64$

Note: The figures in parentheses in Model-1 to Model-4 represent the t-statistics values.

In the GDP model, the coefficient of the error correction term is 0.005 and its t-statistics is 0.23, which is insignificant even at 10% significance level. This indicates that any shock in GDP failed to produce any appreciable change in the long-run relationship that GDP maintained with HL, ED, and GC. The GDP model shows that health expenditure (HLt), school education attainment (EDt), and gross capital formation (GCt) have no impact on Gross Domestic Product (GDPt) as t-statistics values of all the coefficients of lagged independent variables are not statistically significant at 5% level implying no causal (Granger) relationship among the variables. The results indicate that the GDP model is not an appropriate consideration. In the ED model, the coefficient of the error correction term () is not significant even at the 10% level, and this indicates that any shock in ED failed to produce any appreciable change in the long-run relationship that ED maintained with HL, GDP, and GC. The ED model shows that health expenditure (HLt) and gross capital formation (GCt), except Gross Domestic Product (GDP) has no impact on education (EDt) as t-statistics values of all the coefficients of lagged health expenditure and gross capital formation are found to be statistically insignificant at 5% level implying the absence of causal (Granger) relationship among education, health, and gross capital formation, but there exists a weak causal (Granger) relationship between GDP and ED and causality running from GDP to ED. The results indicate that the ED model is not in the short-run equilibrium under consideration.

In the GC model, the coefficient of the error correction term () is 0.004, and its t-statistics is 1.53, which is insignificant even at 10% significance level. This indicates that any shock transmitted through GC failed to produce any significant change in GC around its long-run relationship with GDP, HL, and ED. The GC model shows that first period lagged health expenditure (HLt) is significant at 5% level indicating weak Granger causality running from HL to GC and school education attainment (EDt) and Gross Domestic Product (GDPt) have no impact on Gross Capital Formation (GCt) since all the coefficients of lagged GDP and ED variables are not statistically significant at 5% level implying no causal (Granger) relationship among the variables. The results indicate that there is a problem in the long-run equilibrium relationship in the GC model and the error correction term does not contribute to the changes in GC.

In the health model, the coefficient of error correction term () is negative and highly significant at 5% level based on the standard t-test, which means that the short-run dynamics are in an equilibrium process along with stable long-run relationship among GDP, ED, and HL and contribute to the changes in health. The first period lagged GDP, the first period lagged and the second period lagged education variable (ED), and the second period lagged Gross Capital Formation (GC) are statistically significant at 5% level based on the standard t-statistics values implying there exists Granger causality running from GDP, ED, and GC to HL. Therefore, the results from the health model indicate that GDP, ED, and GC are the granger causes of the changes in health (HL).

15.5.4.6 Summary of the Findings

In view of the results evident from the above four models (Model 1 to Model 4), the health model is considered an appropriate model during the period of study in India. The variables GDP, ED, and GC have significant effects on health (HL) as evident from t-statistics. In the health equation, the high value of R2 signifies that our explanatory variables explain 98% of the variability in the health variable and since the F-statistics is highly significant, implying that the relationship among

HL, GDP, ED, and GC is statically significant. The value of AIC is −2.99, implying better the health model while comparing all four models. In the case of gross domestic product as a dependent variable, it is confirmed that health, education, and gross capital formation have no impacts.

15.5.5 VEC Granger Causality/Block Exogeneity Wald Test

15.5.5.1 Model 1

When GDP is taken as a dependent variable and HL, ED, and GC are taken as independent variables *(Null Hypothesis: HL, ED, and GC have no effects on GDP).*

Since the probabilities of Chi-square statistics for HL, ED, and GC are greater than 0.05 ($P > 0.05$); therefore, the null hypothesis is accepted (Table 15.8). The result indicates the absence of any causal relationship among GDP, ED, HL, and GC, implying that health, education, and gross capital formation are not significant contributors to gross domestic product. The result obtained from model 1, as estimated by VECM is further validated by block exogeneity Wald test.

15.5.5.2 Model 2

When health (HL) is taken as the dependent variable and GDP, ED, and GC are taken as independent variables.

Since the probabilities of Chi-square statistics for GDP, ED, and GC are less than 0.05 ($P < 0.05$); therefore, the null hypothesis is rejected (Table 15.9). The result suggests the causality link running from GDP, ED, and GC to HL, implying that gross domestic product, education, and gross capital formation are significant

Table 15.8 Results of Chi-square test (Model 1)

Excluded	Chi-square	Degrees of freedom	Prob.
D (HL)	0.40	2	0.81
D (ED)	0.89	2	0.64
D (GC)	3.66	2	0.16
All	5.14	6	0.52

Source: Computations done by the authors using E-views 10

Table 15.9 Results of Chi-square test (Model 2)

Excluded	Chi-square	Degrees of freedom	Prob.
D (GDP)	15.09	2	0.00
D (ED)	22.61	2	0.00
D (GC)	13.32	2	0.01
All	49.12	6	0.00

Source: Computations done by the authors using E-views 10

contributors to the health issue. The block exogeneity Wald test confirms the result obtained from model 2 as estimated by VECM.

15.5.5.3 Model 3

When Education (ED) is taken as a dependent variable and HL, GDP, and GC are taken as independent variables.

Since the probabilities of Chi-square statistics for HL and GC are greater than 0.05 ($P > 0.05$); therefore, the null hypothesis is accepted except for gross domestic product ($P < 0.03$) (Table 15.10). The result indicates the absence of any causal relationship among ED, HL, and GC, implying that health and gross capital formation are not significant contributors to education while GDP is a significant contributor to education. The result obtained from model 3 as estimated by VECM is further validated by block exogeneity Wald test.

15.5.5.4 Model 4

When Gross Capital Formation (GC) is taken as a dependent variable, and HL, ED, and GDP are taken as independent variables (Table 15.11).

Since the probabilities of Chi-square statistics for GDP and ED are greater than 0.05 ($P > 0.05$); therefore, the null hypothesis is accepted except health factor ($P < 10\%$). The result demonstrates that there exists no causal relationship between GC, ED, and GDP, implying that education and gross domestic product are not significant contributors to gross capital formation while health Granger causes gross capital formation. The result obtained from model 4, as estimated by VECM is further validated by block exogeneity Wald test.

Table 15.10 Results of Chi-square test (Model 3)

Excluded	Chi-square	Degrees of freedom	Prob.
D (GDP)	6.86	2	0.03
D (HL)	0.75	2	0.68
D (GC)	2.43	2	0.29
All	8.31	6	0.21

Source: Computations done by the authors using E-views 10

Table 15.11 Results of Chi-square test (Model 4)

Excluded	Chi-square	Degrees of freedom	Prob.
D (GDP)	3.17	2	0.20
D (HL)	5.65	2	0.06
D (ED)	3.84	2	0.14
All	10.97	6	0.08

Source: Computations done by the authors using E-views 10

15.5.5.5 Diagnostic Check of VECM Residual

From the AR characteristic roots, it is clear that one root is on the unit circle and all other inverse roots lie within the unit circle. Therefore, the VECM is a stable model. Since the value of J.B test statistics is 8.17 and the probability is greater than 0.05 (5%); therefore, the residuals are normally distributed. To test the serial correlation, the Breusch Godfrey Serial Correlation LM Test is applied since the probabilities are 0.71 and 0.16 for LRE stat with lag order 1 and 2, respectively, which are greater than 5%, so all the residuals are serially uncorrelated. For examining the heteroscedasticity, VEC residual heteroscedasticity test is used. The result confirms that the residuals are homoscedastic with a probability of 0.20, which is greater than the 5% significance level (Fig. 15.6; Table 15.12).

15.5.6 *Stability of the Health Model*

In order to test the stability of the growth model and health model, the CUSUM and CUSUM-square tests are applied (Figs. 15.7 and 15.8). From the CUSUM test and

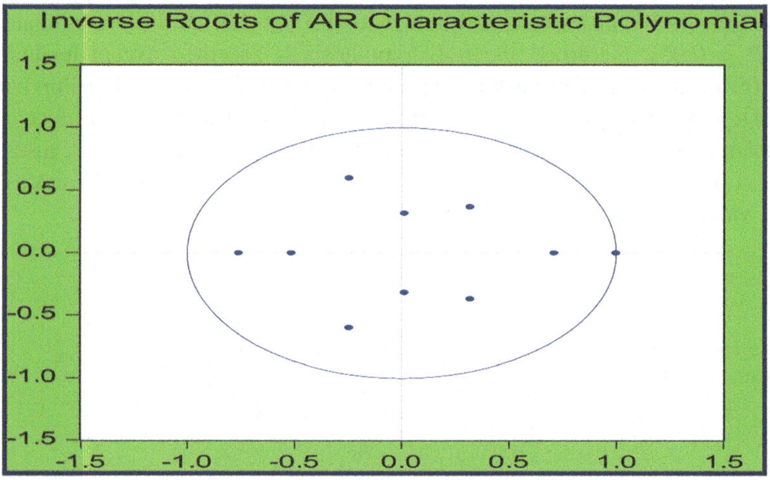

Fig. 15.6 Plots of inverse roots. (Source: Computations done by the authors using E-views 10)

Table 15.12 Summary of diagnostic check of VECM residual

Normality J. B value: 8.17, Prob (0.41)
Breusch Godfrey Serial Correlation LM Test: LRE Stat = 12.43 for lag = 1, Prob (0.71)
For lag = 2 LRE Stat = 21.34 and Prob (0.16)
Heteroscedasticity test (ARCH): 195.65, Prob (0.20)

Source: Computations done by the authors using E-views 10

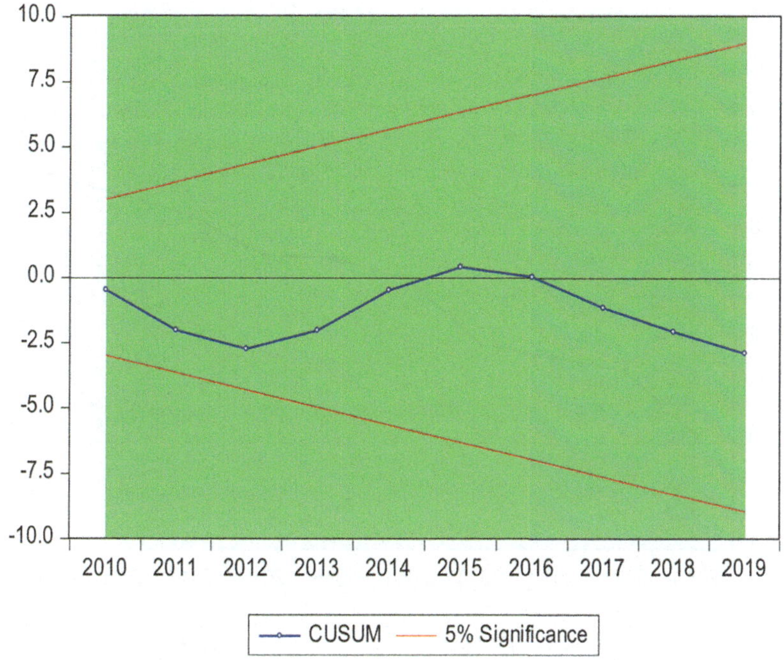

Fig. 15.7 CUSUM test

CUSUM-square test, it is clear that the blue line lies within the 5% critical red lines; therefore, the model is stable over the period of study (Table 15.13). The growth model is also tested stable.

15.6 Variance Decomposition Analysis and Impulse Response Function

Variance Decomposition (VD) and Impulse Response Function (IRF) are used to quantify the relationship between the variables concerned as evident from VECM. In a VECM, variance decomposition analysis reports the proportion variation in each variable as a result of a shock in the variable itself and the shocks in other variables. IRFs show the impact of one standard deviation shock to one variable on other variables and the variable itself.

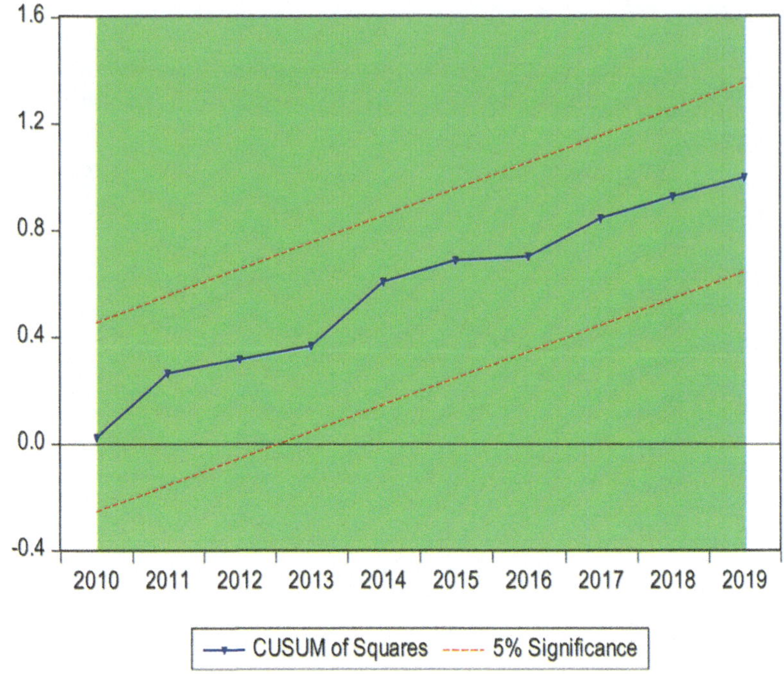

Fig. 15.8 CUSUM—square test

Table 15.13 CUSUM test summary

Period	S.E.	GDP	HL	GC	ED
1	0.381172	100.0000	0.000000	0.000000	0.000000
2	0.476113	84.82762	2.205588	9.292265	3.674524
3	0.552935	76.34195	3.343933	7.270446	13.04367
4	0.634906	79.72287	3.467118	5.530727	11.27929
5	0.733677	79.31611	3.593220	4.157118	12.93355
6	0.809854	78.75360	3.730375	3.422641	14.09339
7	0.889508	78.93328	3.697005	2.870260	14.49946
8	0.962600	79.26697	3.709497	2.453399	14.57014
9	1.033250	79.01359	3.729482	2.141857	15.11507
10	1.098381	79.09929	3.734497	1.909299	15.25692

Source: Computations done by the authors using E-views 10

15.6.1 Variance Decomposition

The results of the variance decomposition of Gross Domestic Product (GDP) from period 1 to period 10 are reported in Table 15.14 and results indicate that 79% of variations in GDP are explained by its shocks since $4 \leq t \leq 10$. Health variable contributes around 4% variations in GDP for the period $5 \leq t \leq 10$ and GC's

Table 15.14 Variance decomposition of GDP

Period	S.E.	GDP	HL	GC	ED
1	0.381172	100.0000	0.000000	0.000000	0.000000
2	0.476113	84.82762	2.205588	9.292265	3.674524
3	0.552935	76.34195	3.343933	7.270446	13.04367
4	0.634906	79.72287	3.467118	5.530727	11.27929
5	0.733677	79.31611	3.593220	4.157118	12.93355
6	0.809854	78.75360	3.730375	3.422641	14.09339
7	0.889508	78.93328	3.697005	2.870260	14.49946
8	0.962600	79.26697	3.709497	2.453399	14.57014
9	1.033250	79.01359	3.729482	2.141857	15.11507
10	1.098381	79.09929	3.734497	1.909299	15.25692

Source: Computations done by the authors using E-views 10

Table 15.15 Variance decomposition of HL

Period	S.E.	GDP	HL	GC	ED
1	0.046531	1.380294	98.61971	0.000000	0.000000
2	0.076608	10.60212	45.30655	0.007542	44.08379
3	0.090559	10.84012	34.49231	5.143572	49.52400
4	0.092699	14.65930	32.92024	5.071688	47.34878
5	0.094147	14.24812	32.08141	5.503788	48.16668
6	0.097079	16.47710	30.18211	8.038026	45.30276
7	0.099884	18.59088	28.52989	10.08513	42.79410
8	0.105223	21.61896	25.71543	13.85807	38.80753
9	0.110458	24.95032	23.34245	16.47858	35.22865
10	0.116582	27.92014	20.95461	19.14009	31.98517

Source: Computations done by the authors using E-views 10

contribution is around 9% at $t = 2$ then begins to decline to 2% in the tenth period. The contribution of ED in explaining the variation in GDP increases from the second period and it reaches around 15% since $2 \leq t \leq 10$. The results suggest that health, gross capital formation, and education are not responsible for explaining the variations in gross domestic product.

In the initial period, i.e. $t = 1$ approximately 99% of the variation in health (HL) is from shocks to the health (HL) itself and then it starts to decline from 45% to roughly 21% since $2 \leq t \leq 10$. The contributions of Gross Domestic Product (GDP) in explaining the variations in health (HL) begin to rise from 1.38 in the initial period ($t = 1$) to roughly 28% in the tenth period (Table 15.15). The contributions of education shock to the variations in health rise till third period at around 50% and start to fall in the remaining periods at around 32%. In health (HL) predicted variance, the contribution of Gross Capital Formation (GC) is almost zero in the initial period and reaches 5% in the third period and then gradually increases from 5% to around 19% for the period $3 \leq t \leq 10$. The results suggest that GDP, ED, and GC have significant effects in explaining the variations in HL.

Table 15.16 Variance decomposition of GC

Period	S.E.	GDP	HL	GC	ED
1	0.055178	2.213769	4.216848	93.56938	0.000000
2	0.090950	8.719973	3.564495	78.73453	8.980999
3	0.117190	15.92023	3.237724	75.22000	5.622040
4	0.136060	17.02138	3.084692	75.31156	4.582368
5	0.156458	18.73507	2.841890	74.76817	3.654875
6	0.174079	20.14632	2.637716	74.03254	3.183431
7	0.190972	21.18919	2.447289	73.69063	2.672884
8	0.206914	22.02371	2.311521	73.31851	2.346261
9	0.222354	22.82716	2.189108	72.92484	2.058889
10	0.236654	23.43078	2.095324	72.62766	1.846242

Source: Computations done by the authors using E-views 10

The forecast error variance of Gross Capital Formation (GC) is more explained by its shocks at around 93% in the initial period and then starts to decline slowly from 93% to roughly 73% for the period $1 \leq t \leq 10$ as evident from the Table 15.16. The contributions of GDP in forecast error variance in Gross Capital Formation (GC) begin to increase from 2% to around 23% until the tenth period while the contributions of education (ED) reach 9% in the second period and then start to fall at around 2% in the remaining period. In making variations in Gross Capital Formation (GC), health (HL) contributes 4% in the initial period and then remains stable at roughly 3% up to the fifth period and then converges to around 2% in the remaining periods. The results indicate the dependence of Gross Capital Formation (GC) on GDP.

15.6.1.1 Summary of the Findings

Because of the results obtained from the variance decomposition of GDP, HL, ED, and GC, it is clear that health (HL), education (ED), and Gross Capital Formation (GC) have no contributions to explaining the variation in Gross Domestic Product (GDP) while Gross Domestic Product (GDP) shocks, education (ED) shocks, and Gross Capital Formation (GC) shocks are found to be significant contributors in explaining the variations of the health (HL) variable. In making the variations to education (ED), Gross Domestic Product (GDP) has more contributions while Gross Capital Formation (GC) has less contribution. In explaining the variations in Gross Capital Formation (GC), Gross Domestic Product (GDP) has some contribution in the long-run while education (ED) and Health (HL) are found to be insignificant contributors.

The same trend or contributions as exhibited from the above findings is depicted in the stacked graph of variance decomposition of GDP, HL, ED, and GC (Fig. 15.9).

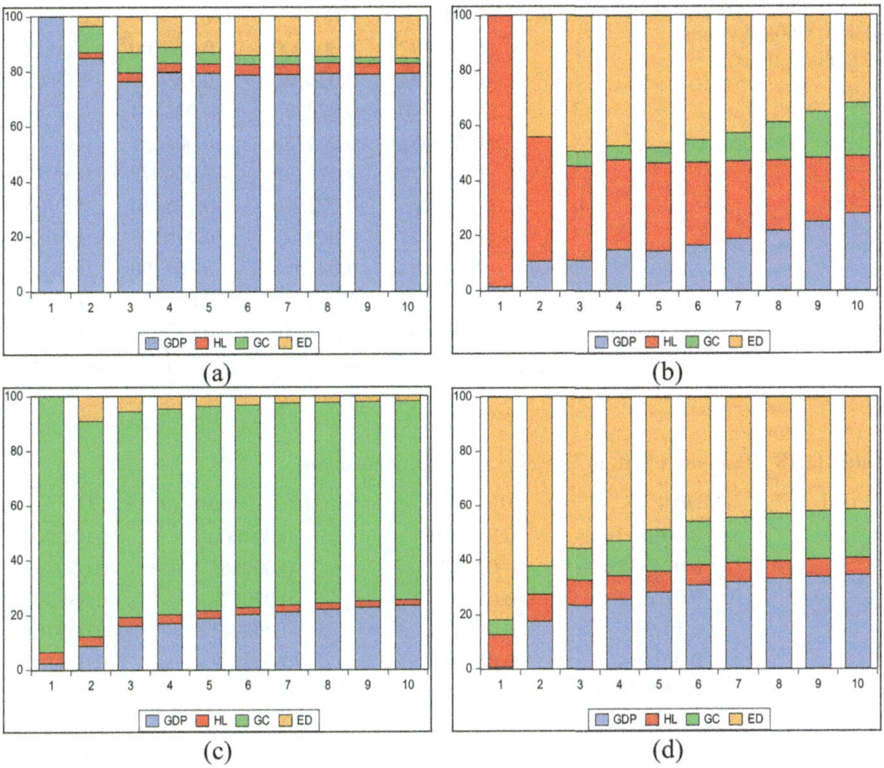

Fig. 15.9 Variance decomposition using Cholesky (*df* adjusted) factors—(**a**) GDP, (**b**) HL, (**c**) ED, and (**d**) GC

15.6.2 Impulse Response Function Analysis

From Table 15.17, it is clear that one Standard Deviation shock to GDP produces a positive change in GDP itself throughout the period. In the initial period, the response of GDP is 0.38 units, and after that, it starts to rise in the fourth and fifth period and then remains stable at around 0.33 units until the tenth period. One Standard Deviation shock to HL, ED, and GC does not produce any changes in GDP in the initial period and the responses of the GDP in the subsequent periods are insignificant as evident from the table. These results indicate that HL, ED, and GC have no effects on GDP fluctuations.

It is observed from Table 15.18 that one Standard Deviation shocks to GDP and ED cause positive changes in HL until the fourth period and after that, the responses of HL start to decline until the tenth period. One Standard Deviation shock to HL causes positive changes in HL itself throughout the period. Then shocks transmitted through GC produce negative changes in HL since $5 \leq t \leq 10$ and before that, it causes some positive changes in HL in the third and fourth periods. The results

Table 15.17 Response of GDP to Cholesky one S.D. innovations

Period	GDP	HL	GC	ED
1	0.381172	0.000000	0.000000	0.000000
2	0.216791	0.070709	−0.145135	0.091266
3	0.202770	0.072277	−0.034124	0.177623
4	0.296583	0.061258	−0.008137	0.074754
5	0.324925	0.073249	−0.009072	0.155407
6	0.299285	0.071586	−0.008416	0.151044
7	0.328671	0.069177	0.016198	0.149299
8	0.331582	0.071558	0.004790	0.152420
9	0.330253	0.073784	0.011552	0.162366
10	0.332763	0.072376	0.012959	0.15652

Source: Computations done by the authors using E-views 10

Table 15.18 Response of HL to Cholesky one S.D. innovations

Period	GDP	HL	GC	ED
1	0.005467	0.046209	0.000000	0.000000
2	0.024338	0.022883	−0.000665	0.050864
3	0.016334	0.013030	0.020528	0.038397
4	0.19254	0.000436	0.003741	0.002705
5	−0.001788	0.003831	−0.007212	0.014161
6	−0.017028	0.000950	−0.016423	−0.000437
7	−0.017376	0.001383	−0.015768	8.20E-05
8	−0.023213	0.000892	−0.022982	−0.005217
9	−0.025506	0.000901	−0.021822	−0.001224
10	−0.027396	−2.95E-05	−0.024307	−0.006998

Source: Computations done by the authors using E-views 10

suggest that a positive shock on GDP, ED, and GC has significant impacts on HL fluctuations.

From Table 15.19, it is clear that one Standard Deviation shock to ED produces positive changes in ED itself throughout the period. In the initial period, the response of ED is 0.02 units and after that, it remains stable at around 0.03 units since $4 \leq t \leq 10$. One Standard Deviation shock to HL, GDP, and GC does produce positive changes in ED throughout the period and the responses of the ED to GDP shocks as evident from the table. These results indicate that HL and GC have no effects on GDP fluctuations, while GDP has caused some changes in ED.

From Table 15.20, it is clear that one Standard Deviation shock to GC produces positive changes in GC itself at roughly 0.06 units throughout the period. In the initial period, the response of ED is 0.05 units and after that, it remains stable at around 0.06 units since $6 \leq t \leq 10$. One Standard Deviation shock to HL and ED does not produce any positive changes in GC throughout the period, and the responses of the GC by GDP shocks are positive since $1 \leq t \leq 10$ as evident from the table. These results indicate that HL and GC have no effects on GDP fluctuations,

Table 15.19 Response of ED to Cholesky one S.D. innovations

Period	GDP	HL	GC	ED
1	−0.001975	0.009235	0.006231	0.024050
2	0.015584	0.007073	0.010175	0.017052
3	0.021077	0.011844	0.014305	0.027900
4	0.022618	0.011960	0.016020	0.029234
5	0.029040	0.012535	0.022231	0.032873
6	0.031814	0.012567	0.021934	0.031430
7	0.033364	0.013204	0.024157	0.035651
8	0.034181	0.013068	0.024477	0.033998
9	0.035836	0.013367	0.025729	0.035739
10	0.035913	0.013430	0.025503	0.035307

Source: Computations done by the authors using E-views 10

Table 15.20 Response of GC to Cholesky one S.D. innovations

Period	GDP	HL	GC	ED
1	0.008210	−0.011331	0.053375	0.000000
2	0.025572	−0.012902	0.060531	−0.027256
3	0.038277	−0.012239	0.061785	−0.005403
4	0.031059	−0.011243	0.060097	−0.008730
5	0.037883	−0.011163	0.066034	−0.006810
6	0.038973	−0.010181	0.064280	−0.008367
7	0.040283	−0.009655	0.066640	−0.003181
8	0.041247	−0.009854	0.067192	−0.005450
9	0.043093	−0.009627	0.068301	−0.003665
10	0.042853	−0.009548	0.067973	−0.004006

Source: Computations done by the authors using E-views 10

while GDP has caused some changes in ED. The results suggest that GDP has some effects on GC while HL and ED have no impact on the changes in GC.

15.6.2.1 Summary of the Findings

All these findings indicate that shocks transmitted through HL, ED, and GC have no effects on GDP while GDP, ED, and GC shocks have brought about significant changes in HL. In the case of ED, GDP shocks play a significant role in the changes in ED while in causing the responses in GC, GDP shocks are found to be a significant variable.

The same trend as observed from the above findings can be depicted in the following graphical presentation of individual responses of GDP, HL, ED, and GC (Fig. 15.10).

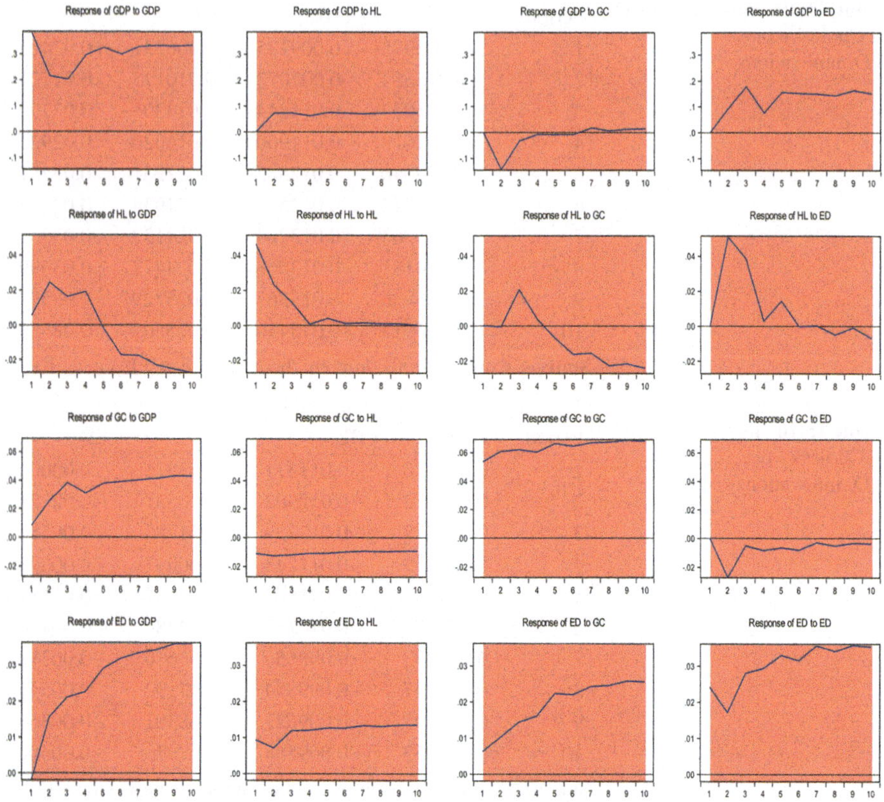

Fig. 15.10 Individual responses of GDP, HL, ED, and GC. (Source: Computations done by the authors using E-views 10)

15.7 Conclusion

The study tried to explore the dynamic relationship between gross domestic product, health, education, and gross capital formation in India from the period 1997 to 2019. This study discovered the existence of long-run association among gross domestic product, health, education, and gross capital formation as evident from ARDL bound test. The findings from VECM confirmed the absence of a causal (Granger) relationship that runs from health, education, and gross capital formation to gross domestic product, implying that health, education, and gross capital formation have no effects on gross domestic product which was not expected. This finding may suggest that investment in health, education, and gross capital formation may be insufficient to produce significant improvement in the country's economic growth. The empirical findings from VECM also revealed a unidirectional causality link that runs from gross domestic product, education, and gross capital formation to health and the study further found a unidirectional causal relationship running from gross domestic product to education and gross capital formation. All these findings suggest that gross domestic product played an important role in determining the health, education, and gross capital formation during the period of study. These results were further supported by the findings of variance decomposition and impulse response function. The study concludes that to achieve sustained economic growth in the long run, the government of India should enhance the budgetary allocation towards health, education, and capital expenditure especially in rural areas because a majority of the people live in rural areas and take appropriate measures to utilize the funds. Policymakers should amend the country's existing health and education policies in such a way that can produce healthy and educated people which will lead to economic development. In addition, the government should encourage private entrepreneurs to contribute to the health and education sector and the CapEx front.

References

Abbas Q (2000) The role of human capital in economic growth: a comparative study of Pakistan and India. Pak Dev Rev 39(4):451–473

Agrawal S, Khan JA (2020) Economic growth and human resource development: an Indian perspective. Int J Creat Res Thoughts 8(9):4286–4294

Apergis N, Padhi P (2013) Health expenses and economic growth: convergence dynamics across the Indian states. Int J Health Care Finance Econ 13(3/4):261–277

Basumallik S (2017) Health and its impact on economic growth in India—an explanation. Int J Creat Res Thoughts 4(4):1248–1257

Bawono S (2021) Human capital, technology, and economic growth: a case study of Indonesia. J Asian Finance Econ Bus 8(5):29–35

Brown RL, Durbin J, Evans JM (1975) Techniques for testing the constancy of regression relationships over time. J R Stat Soc B (Methodol) 37(2):149–192

Engel RF, Granger CWJ (1987) Cointegration and error correction representation: estimation and testing. Econometrica 55:1057–1072

Gangal VLN, Gupta H (2013) Public expenditure and economic growth a case study of India. Glob J Manag Bus Stud 3(2):191–196

Gopalkrishna BV, Rao J (2012) Economic growth and human development: the experience of Indian states. Indian J Ind Relat 47(4):634–644

Haldar SK, Mallik G (2010) Does human capital cause economic growth? A case study of India. Int J Econ Sci Appl Res 3(1):7–25

Idrees AS, Siddiqi (2013) Does public education expenditure cause economic growth? Comparison of developed and developing countries. Se Pak J Commer Soc Sci 7(I):174–183

Indira M, Kumar IBM (2018) An empirical analysis of relationship between higher education and economic growth in India. Int J Res Innov Soc Sci II(VI):90–97

Johansen S, Juselius K (1990) Maximum likelihood estimation and inference on cointegration with applications to the demand for money. Oxf Bull Econ Stat 152:169–210

Karimzadeh M, Karimzadeh B (2013) Impact of trade and human capital on economic growth of India: an empirical analysis. Romanian Econ J 48:201–214

Khan R, Chaudhry IS (2019) Impact of human capital on employment and economic growth in developing countries. Rev Econ Dev Stud 5(3):487–596

Locus RE (1988) On the mechanics of economic development. J Monet Econ 22:3–45

Maitra B, Mukhopadhyay CK (2012) Public spending on education, healthcare and economic growth in selected countries of Asia and the Pacific. Asia-Pacific Dev J 9:19–48

Maksymenko S, Rabbani M (2011) Economic reforms, human capital and economic growth in India and South Korea: a co-integration analysis. J Econ Dev 36(2):39–59
Nyasha S, Odhiambo NM (2019) The impact of public expenditure on economic growth: a review of international literature. Folia Oeconomica Stetinensia 19(2):81–101
Parika A, Singh BP (2020) How does human capital affect economic growth in India? An empirical analysis. Munich Personal RePEc Archive (MPRA), MPRA Paper No. 102428. https://mpra.ub.uni-muenchen.de/10248/
Pesaran MH, Shine Y, SmithPesaran RJ et al (2001) Bounds testing approaches to the analysis of level relationships. J Appl Econ 16(3):289–326
Romer P (1986) Increasing returns and long-run growth. J Polit Econ 94:1002–1037
Romer P (1990) Endegenous technical change. J Polit Econ 98:S71–S102
Sarwar A, Khan MA, Sarwar Z, Khan W (2020) Financial development, human capital and its impact on economic growth of emerging countries. Asian J Econ Banking 5(1):86–100
Seshaiah SV, Reddy TK, Sarma IRS (2018) General government expenditure and economic growth in India: 1980-81 to 2015-15. Theor Econ Lett 8:728–740
Sharma P (2019) Role of human capital in economic growth: a comparative study of India and China. Int J Res Appl Sci Eng Technol 5(11):4042–4048
Sharma P, Sahni P (2015) Human capital and economic growth in India: a co-integration and causality analysis. Ushus J Bus Manag 14(2):1–18
Shukla S (2017) Human capital and economic growth in India. Int J Curr Res 9, Issue II:61628–61631
Solow R (1956) A contribution to the theory of economic growth. Q J Econ 70(1):65–94
Tamang P (2011) The impact of education expenditure on India's economic growth. J Int Acad Res 11(3):14–20
Varkey RS, Joy J, Panda PK (2020) Health infrastructure, health outcome and economic growth: evidence from Indian major states. J Crit Rev 7(11):2002–2010
Viswanath J, Reddy KLN, Pandit V (2009) Human capital contributions to economic growth in India: an aggregate production function analysis. Indian J Industr Relat 44(3):473–486
Widarni EL, Bawono S (2021) Human capital, technology, and economic growth: a case study of Indonesia. J Asian Finance Econ Bus 8(5):0029–0035
Zaman SB, Hossain N, Mehta V, Sharmin SAI (2017) An association of total health expenditure with GDP and life expectancy. J Med Res Innov 1(2):AU7–AU12. https://doi.org/10.5281/zenodo.576546

Dr. Subrata Saha was awarded with the PhD in Economics from the University of North Bengal. Dr. Saha specializes on issues of fiscal policies and effects of Structural changes on fiscal relationships in Southeast Asian Countries and India. The area of research interest is Public Finance and Time Series Econometrics. He is a member of the editorial board of UGC CARE listed journal ENSEMBLE and a life member of the Indian Econometric Society and Indian Economic Association. Dr. Saha is presently working as a Professor of Economics at Raiganj University, West Bengal, India. He has supervised four MPhil and one PhD and presently supervising four PhD scholars at Raiganj University. He has contributed several research papers to National and International Journals and edited research volumes. Besides, he has authored two books in his credit. IRDP, India, has awarded him with prestigious Sarvepalli Radhakrishnan Lifetime Achievement National award in 2018 in recognition of his contribution to his activities towards promoting educational excellence.

Pinki Das secured first class first in Masters (MA) in Economics and was awarded with gold medal from Raiganj University and then successfully completed her MPhil from same university. She is presently pursuing her PhD on the topic entitled 'Contribution of Human capital and Physical capital to Economic Growth in Some Major States of India—An Econometric Study' in Economics Department of Raiganj University in West Bengal, India.

Chapter 16
Exploring the Linkage Between GDP and its Major Determinants with a Special Focus on the New Economic Reforms of 1991

Aamir Jamal, Mudaser Ahad Bhat, and Nufazil Altaf

16.1 Introduction

Almost all the developing nations, including India, share a collective experience of becoming the victim of intensive and extensive exploitation by imperialistic powers for centuries. One can argue that the colonial powers used various strategies for exploiting the third-world nations, and the best among them was the instrument of foreign trade. During the 1950s, many developmental economists (Prebisch 1950; Frank 1956; Emmanuel 1972) argued that the third world nations could not gain from trade as their terms of trade were destined to deteriorate while trading with the industrialized countries. The industrialized countries had a comparative advantage in the production of manufactured goods, and the third-world nations usually exported primary commodities whose income elasticity of demand was less than one (stagnant world demand). As these menaces were associated with trading with colonial powers, it was inevitable that all the developing nations, including India, which recently got independence, would always have viewed foreign trade and foreign investment with fear and suspicion. The fear and doubt against international trade and foreign investment got reflected in terms of the heavy regulation of trade policies (import and export policies) and the foreign investment policies in the country after independence (Athreye and Kapur 2001). Accordingly, after gaining freedom from

A. Jamal
Department of Economics, University of Kashmir, Srinagar, Jammu and Kashmir, India

M. A. Bhat
Department of Data Science, Christ University, Lavasa-Pune, India

N. Altaf (✉)
Department of Humanities, Social Science and Management, NIT Srinagar, Srinagar, Jammu and Kashmir, India
e-mail: nufazilahangar@nitsri.in

M. Mishra et al. (eds.), *Public Policies and Sustainable Development in Post-Reform India*, New Frontiers in Regional Science: Asian Perspectives 71,
https://doi.org/10.1007/978-981-99-3696-0_16

the British, India adopted policies for large-scale industrialization in the country to reduce the dependence on manufactured goods in developed nations (Thakur et al. 2012).

Before 1990 (with some relaxations in the 1980s), trade policy was heavily regulated almost four decades after independence through the restrictive prescriptions of import substitution, import restriction, and export discouragement (Misra and Puri 2011). In the post-reform period, numerous relaxations were provided as far as exports and imports were concerned. Likewise, the inflows of Foreign Direct Investment (FDI) were also heavily regulated in the pre-reform period. This trend changed in the post-reform period when in many sectors, FDI inflows were allowed through an automatic route to boost foreign investors' confidence in the Indian market. Besides, all major determinants of Gross Domestic Product (GDP) such as exports, imports, investment etc. were liberalized in the post-reform period. Since there was a substantial increase in the variables in the post-reform period in absolute terms, it becomes imperative for us to examine the impact of such aggregates on the GDP. Although it is widely accepted that India saw substantial growth rates (in GDP) in the 1980s; however, the growth rate throughout that decade was unstable, culminating in the early 1990s balance of payments crisis (Panagariya 2004). Finally, the impact of the economic reforms on the GDP will be tested by incorporating a dummy variable into the system.

The rest of the paper is structured as follows: Sect. 16.2 presents an empirical literature review, and Sects. 16.3 and 16.4 deal with data sources and research methodology, respectively. In addition, Sect. 16.5 offers data analysis and interpretation based on robust econometric techniques. Lastly, concluding remarks have been presented in Sect. 16.6.

16.2 Literature Review

Naka et al. (1998) used the VECM in their study to deal with the long relationships between a few selected macroeconomic indicators and the Indian stock exchange. Three long-term equilibrium relationships were discovered between the selected macroeconomic variables and the Indian stock market. The domestic market's inflation and output growth were the main factors explaining the Indian stock market's performance.

Onafowora (2003) examined the impact of changes in the RER on the actual trade balances of three ASEAN economies in their bilateral trade with the USA and Japan. A dummy variable was used to capture the shifts in the bilateral trading relations between the nations due to the Asian financial crisis in 1997. The variables were found to have a stable long-run equilibrating relationship. Furthermore, ECT was found to be both negative and significant. Finally, the dummy variable was substantial, which revealed that the Asian financial crisis significantly impacted the nations' real trade balance.

Nunnenkamp and Chakraborty (2008) have tried to assess the validity of the proposition that vast inflows of FDI into the country are believed to promote economic growth. The objectives were achieved by analyzing the industry-specific inflows of foreign direct investment and output. The results revealed that FDI inflows and manufacturing sector output are mutually reinforcing each other. No causal relationship was found in the primary sector between FDI and production.

Manni and Afzal (2012) attempted to assess the impact of economic liberalization on the Bangladeshi economy between 1980 and 2010. Their results revealed that trade liberalization had increased Bangladesh's economic growth, real exports, and imports.

Pala (2013) used cointegration and causality techniques within the VECM framework to explore the linkage stuck between crude oil and the Food Price Index (FPI). The findings from the monthly data revealed the presence of a structural break in the series. The cointegration coefficient was found to be negative at 1990:01 to 2008:08 time periods. Finally, the study indicated that the association between the crude oil (index) and the FPI had changed substantially.

Ming (2014) investigated the impact of foreign direct investment on Taiwan's economic growth using the VECM and annual data from 1978 to 2009. Since VECM estimates are very much responsive to different lags, a proper lag selection was carried out using AIC and BIC lag selection criteria, which indicated that one lag should be used for further estimates. The study suggested that at least one co-integrated vector (relationship) existed among the given variables. Finally, the causality test revealed that GDP and FDI had a causal relationship.

Nyamrunda and Mbogela (2014) used a specified VECM model to examine the impact of lower exchange rates on Tanzanian imports, exports, and output from 1990 to 2011. The lower exchange rate in the Tanzanian economy due to the introduction of structural adjustment policies of the 1980s and early 1990s had not made a significant impact in the long run on both exports and imports of goods and services.

Zikovic et al. (2014) used the VECM approach to unravel the growth, imports, and foreign direct investment knot in a few Central and Eastern European countries (CEE). More precisely, the error correction framework was used to examine the nexus between GDP, NEX (imports coverage ratio), FDI, and GFC. Except for Croatia, the empirical findings revealed that NEX, FDI, and the GFC had a positive long-run influence on GDP growth in all sample economies. In Croatia, the error correction framework revealed that, in contrast to the short-run, the long-run relationship between FDI and GDP was negative and significant.

Choi and Baek (2017) tried to assess the impact of spillover effects on productivity using time series data from 1978 to 2010. The variables used in the study-FDI inflow and exports—were deflated using GDP deflator (2000 = 100). The study's findings revealed that FDI inflow into the country had a significant impact on the total factor productivity via positive spillover effects. The study also pointed towards the implementation of a more open policy as far as FDI inflows into the country are concerned. It is believed that FDI inflows in these sectors would promote economic growth via technological spill overs.

One can argue that from the post-independence era to date, the new economic reforms of 1991 can be considered to be a significant landmark event in Indian economic history. Numerous studies attempted to assess the impact of the new economic reforms on the Indian economy in general, as well as a few sectors in particular. But since the coverage of the reforms was so broad, it was imperative to cover at least the important macroeconomic variables having a significant bearing on the economy's performance. Albeit, earlier studies attempted to compare the performance of the Indian economy in terms of a few key variables during the pre-reform and post-reform periods. However, a comprehensive approach incorporating the various dimensions of the new economic reforms is the need of the hour, for it will provide insights into the positive and negative aspects of the economic reforms in India.

16.3 Data Coverage and Sources

The present study is based on secondary data that has been retrieved from the World Development Indicators (The World Bank 2017). The secondary data obtained has been rechecked from other reputed national and international sources like IMF financial statistics, OECD database, and RBI handbook of statistics for the Indian economy (various publications). The study has chosen four macro-economic variables, GDP, FDI, exports, and imports. It is to be noted that the present study has used annual time series data from 1978 to 2013 for empirical analysis.

16.4 Research Methodology

The vector error correction model and the Wald test statistic were used in the study to scientifically achieve the research objectives. The study has chosen four macroeconomic variables, namely, Gross Domestic Product (LGDP), Imports (LIMP), Exports (LEXP), and Foreign Direct Investment inflow (LFDI). The given variables were first extracted in current billion US dollars ($). Still, they were then deflated using the consumer price index (CPI, 2010 = 100) as a base in order to overcome the problems associated with the data in current figures. The adjusted data were transformed into natural logarithms to overcome non-linearity in relationships and achieve stationarity in variance, (since the data is transformed into natural logarithms, an L is placed as a prefix before every variable). Finally, as an exogenous variable, a dummy variable is incorporated into VECM to capture the effect of new economic reforms on GDP.

The estimation methodology consists of the following steps

- Unit root test
- Lag selection criterion
- Cointegration test
- Vector error correction model (VECM)
- Wald test
- Diagnostic testing

16.5 Data Analysis and Interpretation

16.5.1 Unit Root Test

A time series is said to be stationary when its mean and variance are time-invariant or simply constant over time. In addition, rather than the actual point in time at which covariance is calculated, the value of covariance between two time periods is determined by the distance or gap between the two periods (Gujarati 2012). The real reason for checking the stationarity of a time series is that if it has a unit root (random walk), it can't be used for generalization or forecasting and can only address a specific problem (Diebold and Kilian 2000). In addition to that, if a non-stationary series (random walk) is used in regression analysis, it can lead to spurious or non-sense regression.

There are diverse ways—graphical analysis, correlogram, etc. of scrutinizing whether a time series is stationary or not. However, the present study has used unit root analysis to substantiate the stationarity properties of the specified variables. More precisely, the Augmented Dickey–Fuller test (Dickey and Fuller 1981) is used to carry out this process, and the study uses the ADF test with a constant.

Table 16.1 shows that all variables-LGDP, LIMP, LEXP, and LFDI-have a unit root at a 1% significance level or are non-stationary. Table 16.2 illustrates that at a 1% significance level, the ADF test statistic is greater than the critical value for all variables, asserting that the variables are integrated of the order first.

Table 16.1 ADF test at level

Series	ADF test statistic	Critical values at 1%	Prob*	Decision
LGDP	−2.1633	−3.6463	0.2227	Null hypothesis is accepted
LEXP	−0.0802	−3.6394	0.9437	Null hypothesis is accepted
LIMP	−0.4734	−3.6394	0.8844	Null hypothesis is accepted
LFDI	−0.7448	−3.6793	0.8195	Null hypothesis is accepted

Unit root tests are carried out with a constant (intercept) for all the variables
(Source: Calculation by the authors)
* Indicates significance at 1% level

Table 16.2 ADF test at first difference

Series	ADF test statistic	Critical values at 1%	Prob*	Decision
D(LGDP)	−4.6322	−3.6394	0.0007	Null hypothesis is rejected
D(LEXP)	−3.781	−3.6394	0.0069	Null hypothesis is rejected
D(LIMP)	−4.0730	−3.6394	0.003	Null hypothesis is rejected
D(LFDI)	−5.3805	−3.6793	0.0001	Null hypothesis is rejected

Unit root tests are carried out with a constant (intercept) for all the variables.
(Source: Calculation by the authors)
* Indicates significance at 1% level

Table 16.3 Lag selection criteria

LAG	LOGL	LR	FPE	AIC	SC	HQ
0	−11.51	NA	293e−05	0.912	1.09206	0.9737
1	106.18	200.77	7.45e−08	−5.069	−4.17168*	−4.7633
2	128.81	33.288*	5.26e−08*	−5.4599*	−3.843761	−4.90875*

(Source: Calculation by the authors)
*Specifies the lag order chosen by the criterion

16.5.2 Lag Selection Criteria

It is always prudent to select a proper lag order of all the variables for the ECM and cointegration tests are incredibly responsive to the change in lag orders. They can lead to wrong results due to misspecification of the model. The present study used the AIC (Akaike 1974) for it is one of the best measures for the proper selection of the lag orders (Liew 2004).

From Table 16.3, one can figure out that the SC criterion has selected only one lag. In addition to that majority of criteria, i.e., HQ, FPE, AIC, and LR, have selected two lags. All of these tests are performed at a significance level of 0.05, and as previously stated, the study will use the lowest AIC for further analysis.

16.5.3 Cointegration Test

To begin, we can obtain some co-integrating vectors if the variables are integrated in the same order (Engle and Granger 1987). Due to statistical reasons, the Johansen Juselius test of cointegration (Johansen and Juselius 1990) is preferred over the Engle and Granger method (Bilgili 1998). According to Engle and Granger, there must be a valid error correction model between two and more variables if cointegration is substantiated. Furthermore, Engle and Granger proposed that if cointegration exists between variables over time, there must be either unidirectional or bi-directional feedback between them.

Table 16.4 Johansen Juselius tests for cointegration [Trend assumption: Linear deterministic trend; Series: LGDP, LFDI, LEXP, and LIMP; Unrestricted Co-integration Rank Test (Trace)]

Hypothesized no. of CE(s)	Eigen value	Trace statistic	Critical value at 0.05	Prob**
None*	0.652670	61.03465	47.85	0.001
At most 1	0.433250	26.13781	29.79	0.1246
At most 2	0.187870	7.399192	15.494	0.5317
At most 3	0.015993	0.532052	3.841	0.4657

Trace test statistic confirms the presence of one co-integrating equation(s) at 0.05 level
(Source: Calculation by the authors)
*Indicates rejection of the null hypothesis at the 5% significance level

Table 16.5 Johansen Juselius tests for cointegration [Trend assumption: Linear deterministic trend Series: LGDP, LFDI, LEXP, and LIMP; Unrestricted Co-integration Rank Test (Max-Eigen statistic)]

Hypothesized no. of CE(s)	Eigen value	Max-Eigen statistic	0.05 Critical value	Prob**
None*	0.652670	34.89683	27.58	0.0048
At most 1	0.433250	18.73862	21.13	0.1047
At most 2	0.187870	6.867140	14.26	0.5050
At most 3	0.015993	0.532052	3.841	0.4657

Max-Eigen Statistic confirms the presence of one co-integrating equation(s) at 0.05 level
(Source: Calculation by the authors)
*Indicates rejection of the null hypothesis at the 5% significance level

The null hypothesis that the variables have no co-integrating equation or relationship is spurned by tests (Tables 16.4 and 16.5). The p value for the trace test statistic and the max Eigen test statistic for no co-integrating equation is 0.00. As a result, at the 0.05% level, both tests abandon the very first null hypothesis of no cointegration. The values of trace test statistic $61.034 > 47.856$ and max Eigen test statistic $34.89 > 27.584$, which are both larger than the critical values at the 5% significance levels, also substantiate the results of no cointegration. Nonetheless, as there is a single co-integrating equation/relationship that is greater than 0 and less than the number of variables, we can use the vector error correction model for further analysis.

16.5.4 Vector Error Correction Model (VECM)

Further, if a set of time series is co-integrated of the same order, there exists an equilibrium generating framework known as the Error Correction Mechanism (ECM) that allows the variables to edge closer over time while adjusting the short-run deviations (Engle and Granger 1987). The Error Correction Mechanism (ECM) is suitable when two basic conditions are fulfilled—the time series should be integrated of the same order I(1) and co-integrated as well. Brooks (2008) correctly points out that the Error Correction Framework (ECM) combines long-run equilibrium with short-run dynamics to attain steady-state equilibrium. Since our study has more than one variable in our VAR (Sims 1980) framework, its multivariate counterpart, known as the VECM, would be used.

For the present study, the model is,

$$\begin{aligned} &\mathrm{D(LGDP)} \\ &= \begin{array}{l} C(2) \times \mathrm{D(LGDP(-1))} + C(3) \times \mathrm{D(LGDP(-2))} + C(4) \\ \times \mathrm{D(LFDI(-1))} + C(5) \times \mathrm{D(LFDI(-2))} + C(6) \times \mathrm{D(LEXP(-1))} \\ + C(7) \times \mathrm{D(LEXP(-2))} + C(8) \times \mathrm{D(LIMP(-1))} + C(9) \\ \times \mathrm{D(LIMP(-2))} + C(10) + C(11) \times \mathrm{DUM}. \end{array} \end{aligned} \tag{16.1}$$

The coefficient $C(1)$ is the coefficient of the only co-integrating equation of the model as it was revealed that there exists only one co-integrating equation by the Johansen Juselius maximum likelihood method. Theoretically, the value of C-(1) should be negative and significant. It depicts or measures the rate at which a long-run steady-state is adjusted. The negative and significant coefficient of error correction term is a must because it shows that in the long run, all the variables will move together, and any deviation from this long-run equilibrium path will be automatically corrected. It also reveals the long-run causality (with direction) between the dependent and explanatory variables. Since the coefficient of the only co-integrating equation is negative $C(1) = -0.39$ and is highly significant at a 1% level of significance, the long-run connection between the explanatory variables and the dependent variable can be verified.

To begin with, $C(4)$, which is the lag first of D(LFDI), has a significant impact on GDP at a 5% significance level since the p value for this coefficient is 0.03. Similar to this, the GDP is significantly and positively impacted by the coffiecient of C(7), that is the GDP experiences a notable and favorable influence when the coefficient of exports with a two-period lag is considered. Further, the positive and statistically significant coefficient of the dummy variable suggests that economic reforms have had a positive and beneficial effect on India's economic growth.

The F-statistic can be used to confirm the VECM's overall significance. It examines the joint hypothesis of all independent variables, i.e., whether all explanatory variables can impact the dependent variable jointly.

Table 16.6 reveals that the p value for F-stat is 0.03, indicating that at a 5% level of significance, the null hypothesis that all explanatory variables cannot influence the dependent variable jointly stands rejected. There is a limitation of the F-statistic, as it only tells us whether the model is significant. To put it another way, it tells us whether the predictor variables can influence the dependent variable together. However, it does not reveal how much variation in the dependent variable can be explained by explanatory variables jointly. This problem is tackled with the help of R^2, which clearly states how much variation in (DLGDP) is jointly explained by the explanatory variables (DLEXP, DLFDI, and DLIMP). The value of R^2 is almost

Table 16.6 Vector error correction estimates [Dependent variable D(LGDP); endogenous variables: LGDP, LFDI, LEXP, LIMP]

Coefficient name	Coefficient value	Prob
c(1)*	−0.397895	0.0008
c(2)**	0.654371	0.0469
c(3)	0.465893	0.1773
c(4)**	0.0427703	0.0310
c(5)	0.014534	0.5058
c(6)	0.637907	0.1047
c(7)**	0.580279	0.0358
c(8)	0.118794	0.6859
c(9)	0.259169	0.2922
c(10)*	0.180626	0.0058
c(11)*	0.234833	0.0046

R^2 = 0.5389; Prob (*F*-statistic: 0.031): AIC: −2.130: HQ: −1.96, SC: −1.63
(Source: Calculation by the authors)
Durbin–Watson stat: 2.10. *, ** represent 1 and 5% significance levels

Table 16.7 Wald test statistic: coefficient *C*(2) and *C*(3)

Test statistic	Value	Df	Prob
F test	2.424774	(2,22)	0.11
Chi-square	4.849548	2	0.08

(Source: Calculation by the authors)

0.5389, which is 54% of change/variation in D(LGDP) is jointly explained by D(LIMP), D(LFDI), D(LEXP), and D(LGDP). Besides, the rest of the variation in the Gross Domestic Product can be explained by other variables or factors which are not part of our system.

16.5.5 Wald Test

With the help of the results from vector error correction estimates, we cannot reject or accept the individual null hypothesis linked with three endogenous independent variables. That is, whether they had any significant impact on the dependent variable, it is not possible to show the joint impact of different lags for each regressor on the dependent variable based on VECM results. The Wald test is well-known for demonstrating short-run causality between explanatory and dependent variables; it illustrates the combined significance of the explanatory variables' coefficients on the dependent variable. To find the presence of short-run causality, it uses the Chi-square value of the Wald statistic.

- Table 16.7 shows that, since the Wald test statistic's *p* value is 0.0, we can infer that the current value of D(LGDP) is dependent on previous values of D(LGDP).

Table 16.8 Wald test statistic: coefficient $C(4)$ and $C(5)$

Test statistic	Value	Df	Prob
F test	2.710318	(2,22)	0.08
Chi-square	5.420636	2	0.06

(Source: Calculation by the authors)

Table 16.9 Wald test statistic: coefficient $C(6)$ and $C(7)$

Test statistic	Value	Df	Prob
F test	2.964793	(2,22)	0.07
Chi-square	5.929586	2	0.051

(Source: Calculation by the authors)

Table 16.10 Wald test statistic: coefficient $C(8)$ and $C(9)$

Test statistic	Value	Df	Prob
F test	0.625537	(2,22)	0.544
Chi-square	1.251074	2	0.53

(Source: Calculation by the authors)

- From Table 16.8, one can clearly reject the null hypothesis based on the p value of Chi-square (0.06). Hence, it is reasonable to conclude that the different lags of D (LFDI) have a combined impact on the Gross Domestic Product. Alternatively, there is short-run feedback running from D(LFDI) to D(LGDP).
- In Table 16.9, the Wald test statistic tests the null hypothesis that exports have made no significant impact on the Gross Domestic Product. For every independent variable, a joint significance of two lags has been tested; here, the same procedure will be applied. The results from Table 16.9 indicate that the different coefficients of exports jointly have made a significant impact on the Gross Domestic Product at a 10% level of significance, or in the short run, we can say that exports cause GDP.
- Lastly, Table 16.10 indicates that imports have made no impact on D(LGDP) since the p value of the Chi-square test is 0.53.

16.5.6 Diagnostic Testing

To check the stability of the vector error correction model, it is always desirable to find out whether or not the residuals are normally distributed, whether there is any ARCH effect and whether there is the existence of a serial correlation in the model. Hence, three types of diagnostic tests are carried out, namely, the Normality test, ARCH test, and serial correlation test.

Table 16.11 Jarque–Bera test

Mean	Median	Max	Min	Std.dev	Skewness	Kurtosis	J–B	Prob.
2.36e15	−0.0113	0.149	−0.121	0.060	0.406	3.07	0.917	0.632

(Source: Calculation by the authors)

16.5.6.1 Normality Test

The *p* value of the Jarque–Bera test is 0.632, which is significantly higher than the threshold of 0.05, indicating that the null hypothesis of normally distributed residuals is accepted (Table 16.11).

16.5.6.2 ARCH Test: Heteroscedasticity Testing

The observed value of R^2 is found to be 0.0143; its corresponding probability is 0.907, so we again fail to reject the null hypothesis that there is no ARCH effect in the model, which is also highly desirable.

16.5.6.3 Serial Correlation Test—LM Test

Finally, the Breusch–Godfrey–LM test was used to determine whether the framework specifies any serial correlation; it commences with the null hypothesis that the model includes no serial correlation. The LM test findings reveal that the value of observed R^2 is 1.15, and its corresponding probability is equal to 0.28. So, we again fail to reject the null hypothesis of no serial correlation between the residuals, which is also a good sign for the model.

16.6 Concluding Remarks

The study's primary objective was to scrutinize the short-run and long-run relationship(s) stuck between GDP and its determinants. The Johansen and Juselius test and VECM results confirmed the existence of a long-run equilibrating association between the variables. It was further confirmed by the Wald test statistic that there exists short-run causality from exports, FDI, and GDP (itself) to GDP, and no such casualty was found between imports and GDP. Since our imports chiefly consist of raw materials, machinery and equipment, intermediate inputs, technology, and so on, long-run causality from imports to GDP appears highly realistic in the Indian context. The necessary imports stimulate production and productivity that further enhancing GDP growth in the long run. In the same vein, it is fairly obvious that imports boost exports as well. As a result, in order to put India on a higher GDP growth path, appropriate policies must be formulated, taking into consideration both exports and imports. Moreover, both in the short run and long run, it was found that exports have a positive and significant impact on the GDP. Thus, developing nations like India, instead of pursuing higher growth through the protection of the local industries suffering from the problem of comparative disadvantage, should follow the growth based on boosting exports (export-led growth strategy). Besides, both in the short run and long run, FDI was also found to be significant in explaining the GDP. Hence, the government of India needs to lure more FDI into the country. Finally, the dummy variable that was used as a proxy for economic reforms validated that the reforms had a positive effect on economic growth.

References

Akaike H (1974) A new look at the statistical model identification. IEEE Trans Automat Control 19(6):716–723

Athreye S, Kapur S (2001) Private foreign investment in India: pain or panacea? World Econ 24(3): 399–424

Bilgili F (1998) Stationarity and cointegration tests: comparison of Engle–Granger and Johansen methodology. J Fac Econ Adm Sci 13:131–141

Brooks C (2008) Introductory econometrics for finance. Cambridge University Press, New York

Choi JY, Baek J (2017) Does FDI really matter to economic growth in India? Economies 5(2):1–9

Dickey AD, Fuller AW (1981) Likelihood ratio statistics for auto-regressive time series with a unit root. Econometrica 49(4):1057–1072

Diebold XF, Kilian L (2000) Unit root tests are useful for selecting forecasting models. J Bus Econ Stat 18(3):265–273

Emmanuel A (1972) Unequal exchange: a study of the imperialism of trade. Monthly Review Press, New York

Engle FG, Granger JW (1987) Cointegration and error correction, representation. Estim Econometrica 55(2):251–276

Frank G (1956) Capitalism and underdevelopment in Latin America. Monthly Review Press, New York

Gujarati ND (2012) Basic econometrics. McGraw Hill Education, New Delhi

Johansen S, Juselius K (1990) Maximum likelihood estimation and inference on cointegration with applications to the demand for money. Oxf Bull Econ Stat 52(2):169–210

Liew S (2004) Which lag length selection criteria should we employ? Econ Bull 3(33):1–9

Manni HU, Afzal IN (2012) Effect of trade liberalization on economic growth of developing countries: a case of Bangladeshi economy. J Bus Econ Finance 1(2):37–44

Ming SH (2014) Foreign direct investment, trade, and economic growth in Taiwan. Mod Econ 5(1): 21–23

Misra KS, Puri KV (2011) Indian economy-its development experience. Himalayan Publishing House Pvt Ltd, New Delhi

Naka A, Mukherjee T, Tufte D (1998) Macroeconomic variables and the performance of the Indian stock market. Department of Economics and Finance Working Papers, Paper No, 15. https://scholarworks.uno.edu/econ_wp/15

Nunnenkamp P, Chakraborty C (2008) Economic reforms, FDI, and growth in India: a sector-level analysis. World Dev 36(7):1192–1212

Nyamrunda G, Mbogela L (2014) Impacts of lower exchange rates on exports, imports, and National Output of Tanzania. ACRN J Finance Risk Perspect 3(2):1–9

Onafowora O (2003) Exchange rate and trade balance in East Asia: is there a J-curve. Econ Bull 5(18):1–13

Pala A (2013) Structural breaks, cointegration, and causality by VECM analysis crude oil and food price. Int J Energy Econ Policy 3(3):238–246

Panagariya A (2004) Growth and reforms during the 1980s and 1990s. Econ Polit Wkly 39(25): 2581–2594

Prebisch R (1950) The economic development of Latin America and its principal problem. ECLA, New York

Sims AC (1980) Microeconomics and reality. Econometrica 48(1):1–48

Thakur B, Gupta R, Singh R (2012) Changing face of India's industrial policies: a look. Int J Sci Res Publ 2(12):1–7

The World Bank (2017) World development indicators.. http://databank.worldbank.org/data/reports.aspx?source=world-development-indicators

Zikovic S, Zikovic TI, Grdinic M (2014) A VECM approach to detangling growth, exports, imports, and FDI knot in selected CEE countries. Croat Oper Res Rev 5:161–175

Dr. Aamir Jamal is a faculty member at the Department of Economics, University of Kashmir. Prior to this, he worked as an economics lecturer at Amar Singh College (Cluster University Srinagar). Dr. Aamir Jamal has published several papers in reputed publishing houses (Springer-Nature, Sage, etc.) indexed by SCOPUS, WOS, etc. In addition, he recently earned his Ph.D. from the Central University of Kashmir. He wrote his thesis on the dynamics between the exchange rate volatility and the macroeconomic performance of emerging economies. Among Dr. Aamir Jamal's primary research interests are international trade, political economy, and applied econometrics.

Dr. Mudaser Ahad Bhat earned his M.Phil./Ph.D. in Economics from the Central University of Kashmir. Dr. Mudaser Ahad Bhat is an Assistant Professor at CHRIST University—Lavasa in Pune. Dr. Mudaser Ahad Bhat has served as an economics lecturer in Jammu and Kashmir's higher education department. In addition, Dr. Mudaser Ahad Bhat has passed the National Eligibility Test, the State Eligibility Test, and the Junior Research Fellow Test. He has also published a number of papers in journals that are on the UGC Care list and those indexed by Web of Science like Future Business Journal, Journal of Economic Studies, Organizations and Markets in Emerging Economies, IASSI Quarterly, and others. International economics, macroeconomics, development economics, and econometrics are among Dr. Mudaser Ahad Bhat's research interests.

Dr. Nufazil Altaf is a faculty in the area of Finance and Accounting at the Department of Humanities, Social Sciences, and Management, National Institute of Technology, Srinagar. His research interests include Corporate Finance, Emerging Market Finance, Emerging Industries, Constrained Optimization, Financial Economics, and Applied Econometrics. His research work has been published in international journals of repute. He has also published a book titled Capital Structure Dynamics in Indian MSMEs with Palgrave Macmillan. Besides publishing he is actively presenting his research work in different international and national conferences and seminars. Dr. Altaf has been awarded Highly Commended Paper Award 2020 by Emerald Publishing.

Chapter 17
Evolution of Public Policies for Empowering the Women in Self Help Groups in West Bengal, India

Susmita Chatterjee, Chandan Roy, and Pradip Banerjee

17.1 Introduction

Self Help Groups (SHGs) are the largest informal organizations of people who mutually help each other to improve their living conditions. These groups are piloted by NGOs in order to provide financial services to poor people. The origin of SHG was found in the form of the *Grameen* (Rural) *Bank of Bangladesh*, established by Muhammad Yunus in 1983. SHG movement in India was initiated by Mysore Resettlement And Development Agency (MYRADA) in the mid-1980s to provide financial assistance to economically backward sections of society. The SHG-Bank linkage program began later in 1992 when NABARD issued guidelines for a strategy on the basis of which banks were allowed to lend directly to SHGs in India. Though the SHG scheme was initially targeted as a mechanism of financial intermediation, gradually it became a catalyst of social empowerment along with achieving other developmental goals related to education, health, family planning, etc. (Sinha and Navin 2021). The root of this social empowerment can be traced back to the formation of the Self-Employed Women's Association (SEWA) in 1970. Later, the Government of India made a significant breakthrough in its public policy and introduced Swarnjayanti Gram Swarozgar Yojana (SGSY) in 1999. This particular policy tried to promote women empowerment in rural areas by creating employment and developing the skill of the SHG members. This policy program evolved as a movement in 2011 and named as National Rural Livelihood Mission (NRLM) which

S. Chatterjee
Manindra Chandra College, Kolkata, West Bengal, India

C. Roy (✉)
Raiganj Surendranath Mahavidyalaya, Uttar Dinajpur, West Bengal, India

P. Banerjee
Indian Institute of Management (IIM) Indore, Indore, Madhya Pradesh, India

M. Mishra et al. (eds.), *Public Policies and Sustainable Development in Post-Reform India*, New Frontiers in Regional Science: Asian Perspectives 71,
https://doi.org/10.1007/978-981-99-3696-0_17

gradually became world's largest poverty alleviation policy program. Currently, India has over 6.6 million SHGs with 72 million members. Similarly, West Bengal currently has around 9.17 lakhs SHGs, within which 90% are only women groups involving over 92 lakh women (Mondal 2022). The key contribution to the formation and facilitation of these SHGs in West Bengal has been made by SGSY and SHG-Bank linkage policy.

The impact of microfinance on women empowerment has been widely discussed in the literature, and empirical studies found mixed results (Nilakantan et al. 2013). Comparative backwardness of North Bengal districts has been well discussed in the literature (IAMR 2002) and therefore empowerment enhancing and poverty alleviating role of SHGs are expected to bring a major change in human development in this region. Our basic objective in this chapter would be to determine how much public policy is useful in this region in empowering the rural women. For that, we want to measure the empowerment level of the SHG women residing within backward districts of West Bengal and analyze the role of public policies involved in it. This chapter will try to focus on the SHG activities of the north regional districts of Bengal in light of the evolving public policies for SHG and microcredit. Three north regional districts of West Bengal, namely, Jalpaiguri, Malda, and Murshidabad, have been chosen for this study due to their backwardness and high SHG concentration.

17.2 Impact of SHG on Development: A Review of Past Studies

There is a plethora of research papers, assessments, organizations' impact studies, and implementing agencies' evaluations that offer valuable information on SHGs and their poverty-alleviating and gender-promotional roles over the years. Some of those studies are relevant to this context which is mentioned here.

EDA Rural Systems, along with Andhra Pradesh Mahila Abhivruddhi Society (EDA Rural Systems, APMAS 2006), conducted a study (2006) on four states of India, i.e., Andhra Pradesh, Karnataka, Orissa, and Rajasthan, and found that over 50% of SHG members were below the poverty line, with a majority belonging to SC and ST community. However, only 29% of the household in selected villages of those four states have membership in an SHG, and the most frequently found reason for not joining SHGs was "inflexible rules of banks," and about 10% of memberships were dropped due to migration. Almost 40% of SHGs were found to be weak in terms of bookkeeping of records which ultimately leads to corruption in lending practices. This study indicated high levels of defaults in the payment of loans, and the repayment of loans became a major concern. Although half of the SHGs were operating in profits, the financial value of the members' savings could not be maintained due to high defaults and low-interest rates.

National Bank for Agriculture and Rural Development (NABARD), in its study, namely, "Status of Microfinance in India 2011–2012," indicated the disparities in the geographical spread of the SHG bank linkage program and credit deepening (NABARD 2010). Another report on SHG Federations, entitled "Development Costs and Sustainability," reported that the absence of savings and an appropriate legal framework is a severe constraint on the financial viability of federations of SHGs (Srinivasan and Tankha 2010). All these studies indicate the impediments in the pace of the SHG movement and desired empowerment generation in rural India.

Our focus in this study is to review those sections of literature where the connectivity between SHG and empowerment impact is discussed. Pitt Mark and Khandker (1998) found a positive impact of microfinance on women's autonomy in purchasing decisions, women's access to financial and economic resources, the size of women's social networks, greater freedom of mobility for women and greater likelihood that woman initiates discussion with husband about family planning. A study conducted by NCAER (2008) reflected that the "Bank Linkage Programme" turned out to be a boon for rural women as it increased their access to financial services, reduced household poverty, and boosted their self-confidence, and thereby raised the level of empowerment.

Mehta et al. (2011) conducted a study on the socio-economic status of SHG in Jammu, and he observed the free expression of SHG women regarding their issues. They could raise their monthly saving and availed loans and inspired others to join SHG, which can be reckoned as a sign of empowerment. Swain and Wallentin (2009) also explored the relationship between microfinance and women empowerment in their study. They found the increased volume of saving of SHG women and decreased dependency on money lenders. Women are also found to take decision-making roles in their domestic financial matters. Sahoo (2013) has investigated the same relationship within the SHGs of Orissa state. His study reported that women members had taken loans to start business activities, agricultural work, activities for personal consumption, repair of houses, and payment of medical bills. The easily available credit created a crucial role in the SHG movement.

On the other hand, Kapoor and Kanwar (2018) investigated women empowerment through 446 SHG members in the Kangra district of Himachal Pradesh. They found many advantages for the women joining SHG, viz., exposure to outside work, confidence building, becoming financially secure, getting recognition at the village level, and availing various government schemes. Roy and Biswas (2016) discovered the positive impact of SHG on women empowerment and financial inclusion in West Bengal, as women members have opened bank accounts, availed of loans, started using ATMs, and diversified their sources of income by looking beyond their traditional earning sources. Kaushal and Sharma (2020) analyzed empowerment through Self Help Groups in Himachal Pradesh and found that these groups were not only solving their own problems but also improving their decision-making and habits of taking risks.

However, all the research results are not explicitly representing the positive impact of SHG on women empowerment. Few research outcomes are ambiguous, while few others refute the claim of those who made a positive impact on empowerment. Rahman (1999) found increased spousal conflict (both verbal and physical) among the majority of women borrowers of Grameen Bank. Garikipati (2011), in a study of two drought-prone villages in India, found negative empowerment impacts on women's work time allocation and control of microfinances. Armendariz and Roome (2008) observed that female access to microfinance with male exclusion proved to be counterproductive. Banerjee et al. (2013), in the study of Spandana, found no significant impact of microfinance on measures of women's decision-making over issues of household spending, investment, saving, or education. Nilakantan et al. (2013) showed greater access to microfinance (measured by longer duration of treatment) is associated with zero economic empowerment (measured through enterprise management, credit, and expenditure-related decisions), while an increase in empowerment has been observed in terms of child-related decisions, which according to them was nothing but the rebalancing of power along the traditional gender line.

The polar opposite results of so many research outcomes motivated us to explore whether women SHG members of northern regional districts of West Bengal could achieve adequate empowerment after dealing with microfinance being the beneficiaries of ongoing public policies. We are eager to note whether the level of policies is sufficient to generate adequate empowerment level among them. In the next section, we will briefly analyze the relevant public policies of this sector with its evolution and transformation across the time horizon.

17.3 Public Policies Related to SHGs

Most public policies related to SHGs aim for poverty alleviation and empowerment. However, the SHG movement in India, which emerged under MYRADA in 1985, started much later in West Bengal and the north regional districts of West Bengal, being relatively backward, witnessed all the benefits of forming SHGs more lately.

In West Bengal, the Department of Self-Help Group and Self-Employment was set up in July 2006 under the administrative control of West Bengal Swarojgar Corporation Ltd. (WBSCL). Its primary activities include the provision of interest subsidies for SHG women through West Bengal *Swanirbhar Sahayak Prakalpa* (WBSSP) to reduce the interest burden on loans obtained from banks. Besides, there were provisions for skill enhancement and vocational training in connection with the functional improvement of SHGs. A project, namely, *Muktidhara*, has been launched for the creation and maintenance of sustainable livelihoods of SHG members to eradicate their poverty. A training cum marketing complex, namely, *Karmatirtha* has been established to facilitate training to SHGs in order to develop their skill as well as for the marketing of their products. Thus, WBSCL aims to formulate meaningful policies coordinating all SHG schemes. The SHGs in West Bengal were mainly formed under Swarnjayanti Gram Swarozgar Yojana (SGSY), and NABARD supported bank linkage programs to enhance the economic health and social status of the women using micro-credit and finance services. These institutional measures are expected to raise the decision-making power of the rural women in regional parts of Bengal.

The government of India introduced Integrated Rural Development Program (IRDP) before SGSY in the year 1980, where poor families of rural areas were taken care of through the creation of assets and self-employment. IRDP was transformed into SGSY in 1999, and self-employment through SHGs became the cornerstone of SGSY. But the existing SHGs needed further strengthening and greater financial support. It was at this background that the Union Government approved the restructuring of the SGSY under the new policy, namely, the National Rural Livelihood Mission (NRLM), in 2011. From the present allocation-based strategy, NRLM has been shifted to a demand-driven strategy enabling different states to formulate their own livelihoods and also to focus on targets, outcomes, and time-based delivery.

In 2012–2013, the estimated number of SHGs in West Bengal was nearly 7 lakh, out of which nearly 2 lakh SHGs had been formed under SGSY, approximately 3 lakh had been promoted by the NABARD, around 1.5 lakh SHGs have been formed by the Primary Agricultural Cooperative Societies (PACS), and another 50,000 have been formed by the Small Industries Development Bank of India (SIDBI) (Chakraborty 2013). In 2017–2018, the number of SHGs in West Bengal raised nearly about 8 lakh 47 thousand, while in 2019, it reached 9 lakh 65 thousand (Sarkar and Malik 2019).

In 2014, the Government of India announced an overreaching scheme, namely, "Deendayal Antyodaya Yojana-DAY," to uplift both urban and rural poor through the enhancement of livelihood opportunities through skill development and other means. In 2015, the NRLM program was renamed as "DAY-NRLM." According to the online available data source, the total number of SHGs in West Bengal is currently 9,28,621. Out of 22 districts, we consider eight districts as north regional districts of West Bengal—Alipurduar, Cooch Behar, Darjeeling (GTA), Siliguri (Mahakuma), Dakshin Dinajpur, Uttar Dinajpur, Malda, and Murshidabad. Though Malda and Murshidabad districts are often considered as middle parts of West Bengal since we want to segregate the southern districts (where regional economic backwardness is relatively less), we add these two districts within the northern regional districts of West Bengal in this study. The total number of SHGs in these regions is 2,91,876 (NRLM online data), which is 31% of the state statistics. Table 17.1 shows that Murshidabad district has the largest number of SHGs within North Bengal, followed by Cooch Behar and Malda. Dakshin Dinajpur has the lowest number of SHGs after Darjeeling GTA. The table also reveals that the state average percentage of SHGs having bank accounts is almost the same as that of northern districts.

Table 17.1 SHGs (with bank account status) in northern districts of West Bengal

Sl. no.	District/unit name	Bank account SHG having no bank account	 SHG having bank account	Total SHGs	% of SHGs with bank accounts
1	Alipuruduar	1191	20,556	21,747	94.52
2	Coochbehar	1103	51,332	52,435	97.9
3	Darjeeling GTA	87	8159	8246	98.94
4	Dinajpur Dakshin	564	20,684	21,248	97.35
5	Dinajpur Uttar	3221	31,059	34,280	90.6
6	Malda	1300	50,625	51,925	97.5
7	Murshidabad	1669	91,165	92,834	98.2
8	Siliguri Mahakuma Parishad DMMU	128	9033	9161	98.6
	Northern districts	9263	282,613	291,876	96.8
	West Bengal	**30,429**	**897,588**	**928,017**	**96.72**

Source: Author's calculation from the data available on NLRM (2023) official website (https://nrlm.gov.in)

17.4 Research Methodology

The Women's Empowerment in Agriculture Index (WEAI), launched by International Food Policy Research Institute, Oxford Poverty and Human Development Index, and the United States Agency for International Development, was the first comprehensive and standardized measure to directly measure women's empowerment in the agricultural sector in 2012 (Alkire et al. 2012). Bhattacharya et al. (2013) measured women's empowerment at the individual level using a structural equation model and interpreted empowerment in terms of capability enhancement. Three basic capabilities entitled "health," "knowledge," and "autonomy" have been identified in their study. To estimate the basic capabilities few indicators like food intake, anemia, BMI, educational attainment, functional literacy, application knowledge of family planning, actual decision-making, perceived freedom, and permission regarding mobility have been selected.

Our objective in this chapter is to determine the level of empowerment of SHG women using a simple but comprehensive tool. Roy et al. (2018) developed a simple tool to measure the women empowerment index following WEAI. This is rather a customized index for measuring the empowerment level of SHG women as the chosen indicators were sector-specific. The tool has two broad domains, Input Domain (I_i) and Output Domain (O_i), where three respective sub-domains under Input Domain are (1) Activity Domain (I_1), (2) Knowledge Domain (I_2), and (3) Health Domain (I_3). Again within Activity Sub-Domain, the three indicators are credit access (I_{11}), resource utilization (I_{12}), and repayment decision (I_{13}): within the knowledge domain, three indicators are financial literacy (I_{21}), educational attainment (I_{22}), knowledge about family planning (I_{23}). Within Health Domain,

Table 17.2 Composition of empowerment index for the SHG women

Domain		Weight
Input domain (I_i)	Indicator (I_{ij})	(w_k)
(1) Activity domain (I_1)	Credit access (I_{11})	w_1
	Resource utilization (I_{12})	w_2
	Repayment decision (I_{13})	w_3
(2) Knowledge domain (I_2)	Financial literacy (I_{21})	w_4
	Educational attainment (I_{22})	w_5
	Knowledge about family planning (I_{23})	w_6
(3) Health domain (I_3)	Anemia-free health (Hb >11 mg/dL) (I_{32})	w_7
	Availability of sanitation and safe drinking water (I_{33})	w_8
	(O_{ij})	
Output domain (O_i)	Protest against domestic violence and alcoholism (O_{11})	w_9
(1) Domestic autonomy (O_1)	Household autonomy (O_{12})	w_{10}
	Autonomy in purchase and sales of household resources (O_{13})	w_{11}
	Membership in local political party/NGO (O_{21})	w_{12}
(2) Social interaction (O_2)	Voice against social crimes (O_{22})	w_{13}
	Freedom of mobility without permission (O_{23})	w_{14}

Source: Roy et al. (2018)

the three indicators are healthy body mass index (I_{31}), anemia-free health (I_{32}), availability of sanitation, and safe drinking water (I_{33}).

The two sub-domains under the output domain are (1) Domestic Autonomy and (2) Social Interaction. Within the Domestic Autonomy domain, three indicators are: protest against domestic violence and alcoholism (O_{11}), household autonomy (O_{12}), and autonomy in purchases and sales of household resources (O_{13}); the other three indicators of the Social Interaction Domain are membership in a local political party (O_{21}), the voice against social crime (O_{22}), freedom of mobility without permission (O_{23}).

The composition of the Women's Empowerment Index can be easily understood through Table 17.2. Now Individual Empowerment Index can be calculated utilizing the above indicators.

17.4.1 Individual Empowerment Index (IEI)

$$\textbf{IEI} = \sum\nolimits_{i=1,j=1,k=1}^{3,3,9} \left(w_k I_{ij}\right) + \sum\nolimits_{i=1,j=1,k=10}^{3,3,14} \left(w_k \mathrm{O}_{ij}\right), \tag{17.1}$$

where $\sum_{i=1\text{–}15} w_i = 1$ and $w_1 = w_2 = \ldots\ldots = w_{15}$

$I_{11} = 1$, if the woman gets direct credit access;

$= 0$, otherwise;

$I_{12} = 1$, if she takes the decision about business resource utilization;
$= 0$, otherwise;
$I_{13} = 1$, if she takes repayment decision in the micro-credit business;
$= 0$, otherwise;
$I_{21} = 1$, if she has financial literacy;
$= 0$, otherwise;
$I_{22} = 1$, if she completes her elementary education;
$= 0$, otherwise;
$I_{23} = 1$, if she has knowledge about family planning;
$= 0$, otherwise;
$I_{31} = 1$, if she is anemia free, i.e., her Hb >11.0 mg/dL;
$= 0$, otherwise;
$I_{32} = 1$, if she has sanitation and a safe drinking water facility;
$= 0$, otherwise;
$O_{11} = 1$, if she protests against domestic violence/alcoholism within the household;
$= 0$, otherwise;
$O_{12} = 1$, if she takes the household decision about resources, health, and education;
$= 0$, otherwise;
$O_{13} = 1$, if she takes purchases or sales decisions about domestic resources;
$= 0$, otherwise;
$O_{21} = 1$, if she is a member of local political parties/NGO;
$= 0$, otherwise;
$O_{22} = 1$, if she raises her voice against social crimes (dowry, women abuse, etc.);
$= 0$, otherwise;
$O_{23} = 1$, if she enjoys the freedom to move safely within society without permission;
$= 0$, otherwise;
$\Sigma wk = 1$ and $w_1 = w_2 = \ldots\ldots\ldots = w_k = 1/k$.

Based on the above method, the Individual Empowerment Index **(IEI)** can be assessed separately, whose value will lie between "0" and "1" as it is a weighted average of binary variables. Following WEAI (2012), an empowerment score greater than 0.8 would be labeled as adequate empowerment. In this study, since we are analyzing the empowerment level of a backward region, we consider the benchmark as "0.5" and term it as the "primary level of empowerment." As the value of the index signifying "0" would define "absolute disempowerment" and "1" would define "absolute empowerment," the value 0.5 would define the mid-value of the weighted parameter, which we call "primary level of empowerment."

17.4.2 Women Empowerment Index SHG (WEISHG)

Following Roy et al. (2018), the group index can be constructed using the equation:

$$\textbf{WEISHG} = \text{We} + \text{Wn}(\text{Da}). \tag{17.2}$$

where We = % of women with adequate empowerment, Wn = % of women without adequate empowerment = (1 − We), Da = % of domains in which disempowered women have adequate empowerment.

Note that, 1 ≥ WEISHG ≥0.

17.5 Empirical Rigor

17.5.1 Sample Estimation

The sample size (n) required at the state level (here, North Bengal) has been computed based on the following formula and key parameters:

$$n = t^2 \times p(1-p) \times \text{Deff}/m^2, \tag{17.3}$$

where n = required sample size, t = standard normal value for a one-tailed test at 95% level of confidence, i.e., 1.96, p = current rate (prevalence of motivation level of providers considered to be 0.5), m = margin of error at 5% (standard value of 0.05), Deff = design effect, taken as 1.3.

- The required sample size is 159. Keeping a provision of 5% extra sample for non-response.
- According to the research scope, the findings will be required at the district level as well; hence, a sample size of ~100 at the district level will provide estimates with ~10% margin of error. Considering this, we have covered 50 samples in each study district.

17.5.2 Sampling Methodology

The list of villages with SHG for each study district was taken as the sample frame. In each district, two blocks were selected on the basis of the maximum number of SHGs and the least number of SHGS. In each selected block, five villages were selected through systematic random sampling. In each village, two SHGs were selected randomly; however, priority was given to those SHGs who were engaged in any enterprise activity. A total of five interviews were conducted with the members of SHGs (beneficiaries) who are acting as office bearers.

17.6 Research Findings

Based on the theoretical method, **IEI** for each woman involved with the SHG can be assessed separately, taking equal weights for all indicators. According to Roy et al. (2018), an individual empowerment score above 80% would be considered as adequate empowerment. Here, since we are analyzing the empowerment of a backward region, we consider the score of 50% as a benchmark of the primary level of empowerment. Thus, a woman with a score of 8 and above is supposed to have access to resources and is expected to have a say in family affairs as well as in business decisions. In the focus group, out of 159 SHG women, 125 women have a primary level of empowerment. So, the IEI of 78.6% of women gives an optimistic node. The group empowerment would be 0.86, while disempowered women are observed to have empowerment in 35% of the domains.

17.7 Discussion

We have found the average score in the health domain is approximately "3," whereas the average score in the activity domain is "2," and the average score in the knowledge domain amounted to "1." The differences in scores revealed a particular pattern in women's empowerment. Woman's well-being is a multi-dimensional subject. Care and interventions are needed in childhood, adolescence period, and throughout the reproductive years. Health awareness is essential as health risks are related with childbirth and period of pregnancy and are a foremost reason of concern. However, women need to struggle hard to get access to health care, compared to their male counterparts. Moreover, we see gender-based disparities present in terms of employment, education, and income which hamper the ability of women to protect their health. In this study, we have found that the SHG women are aware of the health care issue and have anemia-free health and proper sanitation and drinking facility.

The study by Wilunda et al. (2021) highlights that women's empowerment may reduce the burden of anemia which is supported by the result of the present study. In the knowledge domain, the study group is not able to get a "moderate" score. Women engaging in women groups like SHGs to improve their livelihoods (property ownership, participation in financial and family decision-making, and contributing to family income), the performance of SHGs in enhancing women's economic empowerment is good enough in this study area. The resource-advantage theory of the firm, developed by Barney (1991) states that the exploitation of resources is needed to achieve the desired sustainable competitive advantage. Thus, the theory claims that a person's achievements be contingent on the resources and capabilities they possess. This is the capability approach. These resources comprise human capital, physical capital, financial capital, and technology as well. People utilize the resources to shape capabilities that generate yields and positive influence on their lives. Women's access to credit and obtain financial training, among others, from the SHG groups, create capital and human resources. The possessions attained create important avenues for women's empowerment. The result of the index with a "moderate" score in the activity domain comprising of credit access and resource utilization shows a positive impact on women's empowerment with financial sustainability, agency, and mobility. For backward rural regions of Bengal where public policies like SGSY, NRLM, and DAY are yet to leave a substantial impact, achievement of a "moderate" score in the empowerment level can be regarded as one step forward towards the goal.

17.8 Conclusion

Empowerment is one of the key objectives behind the formation of Self Help Groups. It was one of the set targets of the Millennium Development Goals, too. Empowerment helps to reduce domestic poverty and infant mortality and enhances nutrition intake and enrollment of children irrespective of their gender. Hence, holistic development is possible when empowerment in the backward rural region takes place in the true sense. Northern districts of West Bengal have been comparatively backward and ignored since the inception of the planning period, as these districts are geographically situated away from the capital of the state. Within this bleak ambiance, the ray of hope which is beaming out from this study is the gaining of empowerment level of around 79% of women within our sample space. The one shortcoming of this study is that the BMI index could not be taken into account. However, still, the research findings give us hope for a better tomorrow. This index is only a summation of the individual empowerment index and not the group index, where the percentage of domains where disempowered women show adequate empowerment could have been added. Nonetheless, 79% of empowerment is not a low level of empowerment. The government, with apposite measures, should take care to build a coherent institutional response that addresses the issue of women's empowerment in a proper way. The involvement and full participation of women in organizations like SHGs are essential. Framing accurate public policies which give distinct attention to the needs of women are imperious for a healthy society. Engagement in SHGs with proper income-earning security is playing a vital role in reducing maternal mortality rates, safe motherhood, and overall healthy life.

Moreover, the COVID-19 situation has created many ups and downs, and therefore this gain of empowerment should not be correlated with the impact of public policies only. We must keep in mind that the COVID-19 pandemic has raised the unemployment level in several sectors, which in turn made many domestic women transform into the breadwinners of their families in West Bengal (Mondal 2022). West Bengal remained one of the top five states both in terms of loan portfolio outstanding and active loan account holders in the microfinance industry (AMFI-WB 2021). North 24 Parganas, Murshidabad, Jalpaiguri, Nadia, South 24 Parganas, Bardhaman, Hooghly, Howrah, and Cooch Behar are the nine top districts in India in terms of loan portfolio outstanding. This helps us to infer that even after the COVID-19 pandemic, the microfinance industry is expanding in West Bengal. During the last 9 months of 2021, 40 lakh women attached to SHGs in rural pockets of West Bengal borrowed Rs. 6000 crores as loans. Rural women of West Bengal tried to ease the financial stress of the family, the burden of children's education, and daily nutrition. Thus, SHG women have not only helped to alleviate social poverty during the COVID pandemic in rural North Bengal but also regained back their empowerment and status within the social matrix of the backward region. This is, undoubtedly, an outcome of state-adopted customized union public policies. Adopting more and more region-specific policies emphasizing regional issues in favor of the poverty-stricken rural women of the backward regions may usher in achieving more significant benefits.

References

Alkire S, Meinzen D, Peterman A et al (2012) The women empowerment in agriculture index. World Dev 52:71–91

AMFI-WB (2021) Annual report 2020–2021. Association of Micro Finance Institution-West Bengal, Kolkata

Armendariz B, Roome N (2008) Gender empowerment in microfinance. Munich Personal RePEc Archive (MPRA) Paper, No. 31040

Banerjee A, Duflo E, Glennerster R, Kinnan C (2013) The miracle of microfinance? Evidence from a randomized evaluation. MIT Press, Cambridge

Barney J (1991) Firm resources and sustained competitive advantage. J Manag 17:99–120. https://doi.org/10.1177/014920639101700108

Bhattacharya J, Banerjee S, Bose M (2013) On assessment of women empowerment at individual level: an analytical exposition. In: Banerjee S, Chakrabarti A (eds) Development and sustainability: India in a global perspective. Springer, New Delhi, pp 385–400

Chakraborty DK (2013) The role of SHGs in poverty alleviation of West Bengal: a study on some selected districts. Bus Stud 23:70–77

EDA Rural Systems, APMAS (2006) Self help groups in India: a study of the lights and shade. CARE, Catholic Relief Services, GIZ-Deutsche Gesellschaft für Internationale Zusammenarbeit GmbH, USAID. https://www.findevgateway.org/paper/2006/01/self-help-groups-india-study-lights-and-shades. Accessed 20 Feb 2022

Garikipati S (2011) Microcredit and women's empowerment: through the lens of time use data from rural India. Dev Change 43(3):719–750. https://twitter.com/DAY_NRLM/status/1342779166719057921?s=20

IAMR (2002) Report of comparative backwardness of North Bengal region. Planning Commission Government of India. https://niti.gov.in/planningcommission.gov.in/docs/reports/sereport/ser/stdy_bkwardnb.pdf. Accessed 31 Jan 2022

Kapoor A, Kanwar P (2018) A brief account of women empowerment through SHGs—a case study of Himachal Pradesh. J Agric Res 41(1):93–96

Kaushal SL, Sharma N (2020) Women empowerment through SHG in HP: an analysis. Productivity 61(2):125–136

Mehta SK, Mishra HG, Singh A (2011) Role of self help groups in socio economic change of vulnerable poor of Jammu region. In: International conference on economics and finance research. IPEDR, pp 76–89

Mondal P (2022) With men jobless, rural women in Bengal turn bread winners. The New Indian Express. https://www.newindianexpress.com/nation/2022/jan/17/with-men-jobless-rural-womenin-bengal-turn-bread-winners-2407699.html. Accessed 17 2022
NABARD (2010) Status of microfinance in India-2009–2010. NABARD, Mumbai
NCAER (2008) Impact and sustainability of SHG bank linkage programme. NCAER, New Delhi
Nilakantan R, Datta SC, Sinha P, Datta SK (2013) The impact of microfinance on women empowerment: evidence from eastern India. Int J Dev Conflict 3(1):27–40
NLRM (2023). https://nrlm.gov.in/outerReportAction.do?methodName=showIndex#gsc.tab=0
Pitt Mark M, Khandker SR (1998) The impact of group-based credit programs on poor households in Bangladesh: does the gender of participants matter? J Polit Econ 106(5):958–996
Rahman A (1999) Women and micro credit in rural Bangladesh: anthropological study of the rhetoric and realities of Grameen Bank lending. Westview Press, Inc., Boulder
Roy NC, Biswas D (2016) Women empowerment through SHG and financial inclusion a case study on Lataguri region in West Bengal. Int J Manag Res Rev 6(6):827–834
Roy C, Chatterjee S, Dutta Gupta S (2018) Women empowerment index: construction of a tool to measure rural women empowerment level in India. ANVESHAK Int J Manag 7(1):199–212. https://doi.org/10.15410/aijm/2018/v7i1/119887
Sahoo A (2013) Self help group and women empowerment: a study of some selected SHGs. Int J Bus Manag Invent 2(9):54–61
Sarkar S, Malik IC (2019) Self help group in West Bengal-PEST analysis. IOSR J Humanit Soc Sci 24(8):42–50
Sinha P, Navin N (2021) Performance of self help groups in India. Econ Polit Wkly 56(5):36–43
Srinivasan G, Tankha A (2010) SHG federations: development costs and sustainability. Access Development Services and Rabobank, New Delhi. https://www.findevgateway.org/sites/default/files/publications/files/mfg-en-paper-shg-federations-development-costs-and-sustainability-2010.pdf
Swain RB, Wallentin FY (2009) Does microfinance empower women? Evidence from self-help groups in India. Int Rev Appl Econ 23(5):541–556
Wilunda C, Wanjohi M, Takahashi R et al (2021) Association of women empowerment with anaemia and haemoglobin concentration in children in sub-Saharan Africa: a multilevel analysis. medRxiv 2021:21264423. https://doi.org/10.1101/2021.10.01.21264423

Dr. Susmita Chatterjee is currently working as an Assistant Professor in the Department of Economics at Maharaja Manindra Chandra College under the University of Calcutta. She also acts as a guest faculty in the Department of Commerce, Calcutta University. She completed her M.Phil. and Ph.D. dissertation from the University of Calcutta and joined IIMC for post-doctoral Research. She supervises Ph.D. students in the Department of Commerce and Department of Economics under the University of Calcutta). Her research interests include applied econometrics, industrial organization, gender studies, and entrepreneurship. She is the author of a large number of articles published in reputed journals of Elsevier, Emerald, Sage, Palgrave, and Springer and three books, and several book chapters in national and international publications. She is also a reviewer of journals (SAGE) and books (OXFORD).

Dr. Chandan Roy is currently the Principal of Raiganj Surendranath Mahavidyalaya, West Bengal. Before joining the post of Principal, he completed almost 22 years of academic trajectory as an Associate Professor and the Head of the Department of Economics at Kaliyaganj College in Uttar Dinajpur, West Bengal. He acquired M.Phil. (Economics) from Jadavpur University and Ph. D. from North Bengal University. His M.Phil. dissertation was on the prospects of Indian leather exports and his Ph.D. thesis was on artisanal silk industry of West Bengal. Dr. Roy actively participated in constructing Uttar Dinajpur District Human Development Report-2010 under the aegis of Planning Commission, Government of India and outlined the draft of Livelihood Chapter and currently engaged in building up Dakshin Dinajpur District Human Development

Report. He worked as a Regional Editor, North Bengal for a reputed Bengali Journal "Artha Bishleshan." Dr. Roy published 35 papers in national and international peer-reviewed journals including a few edited volumes. His published books involve Right to Education: An Accelerator of Social Transformation and Economic Development (2013), International Trade & Inclusive Development (2017), A Study on Bengal Silk Industry: Glorious Past to Deplorable Present (2017), and Saga of Bengal Silk and Handloom Industry (2018). His present work of interest includes women empowerment, education, regional issues of development and sericulture sector.

Dr. Pradip Banerjee is a Professor of Finance and Accounting at the Indian Institute of Management Indore, India. He holds a Ph.D. in finance from Utkal University, India. He has 18 years of teaching experience. His teaching interests are financial accounting, managerial accounting, corporate finance, and business valuation. His research interests include working capital management, auditing, mergers and acquisition, corporate disclosure, and corporate governance. He has published several research articles in national and international journals. He has also published management case studies.

Chapter 18
Gender Inequality in Labour Market and Public Policies: A General Equilibrium Approach

Nilendu Chatterjee, Anindita Nath, and Bappaditya Koley

18.1 Introduction

The world has progressed in many aspects, yet a few areas have remained neglected due to several factors. Participation of the female labour force and gender equality are two such sensitive social aspects that have been creating space for researchers in the field of social studies to intervene. It is not only because inequality does exist in this field but also because such inequality is concerned for a wider proportion of the population worldwide (Neckerman and Florencia 2007; Fajnzylber et al. 2002). Most countries and a large part of the population belonging to the continents of Asia, Africa, and Latin America are still underserved with welfare allotment, and they are cursed with the vicious circle of poverty of various forms (Perry et al. 2006; World Bank 2021; Weiss 2005). Various forms of duality exist in these nations, of which social and financial dualisms are the two main ones. The root causes behind such dualism are social rituals, inequal income distribution, and distortions in the labour market (Dabla-Norris et al. 2015; Bourguignon 2018; Bourguignon and Platteau 2017). Financial dualism, coupled with the vicious cycle of poverty, lead to lower the level of education and nutritional status for a section of the population, and these lead to the discrepancy of working capability as well as working skills for this section (World Health Organization 2002; Sen 1982; Kromydas 2017). Such backwardness puts them behind others, that is, the group that does not suffer from these problems, in the labour market and forces them to earn a lower wage rate (Kundu and Mohanan 2009; Anant et al. 2006; Chaykowski and Powell 1999; Sundari 2020). Another factor that leads to a similar outcome is social ritual—by

N. Chatterjee
Department of Economics, Bankim Sardar College, South 24 Parganas, West Bengal, India

A. Nath · B. Koley (✉)
Department of Geography, Bankim Sardar College, South 24 Parganas, West Bengal, India

M. Mishra et al. (eds.), *Public Policies and Sustainable Development in Post-Reform India*, New Frontiers in Regional Science: Asian Perspectives 71,
https://doi.org/10.1007/978-981-99-3696-0_18

which it is generally believed that women have lower working skills and nutritional level compared to their male counterparts and hence are offered a low wage compared to the male labour force (Jayachandran 2015; Ferrant et al. 2014; Ratho 2020; Sorsa et al. 2015). So, 'Gender Discrimination',[1] which results in 'Wage Discrimination', is a persisting phenomenon in most developing economies.

One cannot deny that public policy or the government has a huge role to play in breaking these vicious circles and wiping away such discrimination. For the last few decades, the developing world has witnessed several policies being taken to eliminate all forms of discrepancies, all of which have contributed to a certain extent (World Bank 2012; Chattopadhyay and Duflo 2004).[2] Most of those policies have been concerned with improving the educational and nutritional status of women in these nations so that these vicious cycles can be overcome (Von Grebmer et al. 2014; Oxford 2019; Knech 2014; World Health Organization 2008, 2021). As a result of this, the attitude and practices in the labour market have witnessed certain changes; however, they are still insufficient to remove discrimination (Kundu and Mohanan 2009; FAO 2015; GEM 2017; ILO 2016). Both the 'sectors with gender discrimination' and the 'sectors with no gender discrimination' exist and function parallelly in the labour market (Jayachandran 2015; Kundu and Mohanan 2009; Esteve-Volart 2009). Clearly, there exist several forms of dualism in the labour market for women (Chakraborty and Chakraborty 2009; Heath and Tan 2020). One can observe an under-representation of the women labour force in a few sectors (Fletcher et al. 2017; Desai et al. 2011; Srivastava and Srivastava 2010); again, there is a surplus of women labour in others (Dasgupta and Verick 2016; Lei et al. 2019; Desai et al. 2011). Sectors that are under the direct observance and guidance of the rules of the government, i.e. technically, the 'organized sectors', such discrimination against women is rare; however, in the 'unorganized sectors' such discrepancies can be observed.[3] Under such scenarios, the role of the Government in the form of public policies becomes even more important to improve the existing conditions and take it to the desired level, especially regarding the women labour force and its participation.

In many cases, especially in developing nations, we see that a significant part of the women is generally engaged in household activities or even in economic activities but for household purposes (Dashora 2013; Reddy et al. 2010; Mencher 1988). Both of these categories do not come under the process of the National Accounting system. However, along the development process, things have been changing gradually. While the women get engaged in economic activities, their

[1] By gender discrimination, we mean non-equal behaviour towards the women due to various reasons.

[2] But not fully.

[3] By 'organised' sector, we mean the sector where government labour rules are followed or that does not do any discrimination against women. By 'unorganised' sector, we mean the sector that does not follow the labour rule, hence it discriminates against women on 5th basis of several factors.

earnings come under the purview of the accounting system.[4] In development economics, we could see the argument that an increase in women labour force signifies a movement towards gender equality or the overall development of the nation (Lewis and Plomien 2009; Kelkar 2005; Inglehart et al. 2003; Kabeer 2021; Das and Pathak 2012; Klasen 2018). But we must not forget that such arguments are not always correct because taking part in economic activities at an early age without proper education actually means backwardness of the economy where women are forced to earn for their family and the economic system is not strong enough to ensure a complete, quality education for women. Poverty forces them to join the labour force before the completion of proper education. Such a process actually reinforces the above-discussed vicious cycle of poverty along with gender discrimination, of various forms, at the workplace. So, if the male labour force is equipped enough for all aspects of human capital, then an increase in the women labour force without proper human capital would actually aggravate the 'gender gap', which is not at all expected from the developmental perspective. Only when both men and women are properly educated and equipped with the necessary human capital would it reduce all forms of disparity and discrimination against women, which would actually mean a real moving forward for society.

Over the last few decades, India has emerged as one of the 'power houses' in the world economy because of its sound and consistent economic growth as well as a high proportion of the working population (Srinivasan 2006; Kshetri and Dholakia 2011; Kennedy 2015; Nandi 2012).[5] Various estimations and predictions suggest that this rising Indian economy will only continue to grow (Lam 2005; Datt and Ravallion 2002). However, along with this growth of the nation, we have seen a fall in the women labour force ratio. Ground-level studies on popular state initiatives like Kanyashree Prakalpa (a conditional cash transfer scheme that emphasizes on continuation of education of women in order to bring a break on the drop-outs as well as promote higher studies among financially poor women and bring them out of poverty) shows that it has led to a fall of above 31% in the combined rates of dropout as well as early marriage in the backward districts of West Bengal (Sen and Dutta 2018). Later, the recognition given by UNESCO as the best Public Service Award in 2017 (UNPSA), further, established the usefulness of this initiative to break the vicious cycle of poverty along with promotion of women education in the backward regions.

This fall has multiple implications. On the one hand, this could be because of an increase in education among women; on the other hand, this could be because of insufficient employment opportunities in the labour market coupled with various forms of social discrimination. We should accept the fact that there are not enough employment opportunities for women in the labour market, coupled with various forms of unequal behaviour towards them, even at the household level (Duflo 2012).

---

[4]Very often, women play the dual role of taking part in household activities as well as in economic activities.

[5]Population in the age group of 25–60.

The census data of India has shown a fall in the women labour force participation ratio.[6] In West Bengal, the Census data confirmed a more than 1.5% fall in women's participation (Census of India 2011). More importantly, Periodic Labour Force Survey (PLFS)[7] data have shown a huge fall in women labour force participation in various districts[8] of West Bengal. PLFS (2020) reports an increase in women labour force participation over the period of 2017–2019. However, during this period, the participation of women labour force aged between 15 and 19 years has fallen. So, there is a mixed interpretation of such reports. It may appear that the overall increase in women labour force participation is good from a societal point of view. Again, it could indicate an early forced drop-out from education. A fall in this ratio could imply a rise in the educational standard of the women for which they are foregoing their present working opportunities and acquiring necessary human capital; again, it could imply a lack of opportunities in the labour market for them and not improvement of education. Whatever the reality may be, all the possibilities are very much associated with public policies. The public or government policy decides the nature of the labour market. It can break the various forms of discrimination and empower women through a proper build-up of human capital and ensure wage inequality for them. We all know that the desired way would be to build up the proper human capital among women through education and other necessary things and then create enough employment opportunities in the labour market along with various policies to ensure no discrimination against women. So, public policies become important and pivotal aspects in not only improving the existing scenarios but also in taking it to the desired level.

In this study, all these aspects will be taken into consideration and discussed with the help of a general equilibrium model. The chapter has the following sequence—in Sect. 18.2, we briefly discuss the existing literature in this field; Sect. 18.3 accommodates the central thought of our study, where we develop and present our model and discuss its various aspects with various possibilities. Finally, Sect. 18.4 makes the concluding comments.

18.2 A Brief Review of Existing Literature

International organizations, namely the United Nations (UN), the World Bank, and the International Labour Organization (ILO), are focusing on gender inequality and the economic importance of female labour. These organizations' significant action resulted in inclusion in the third millennium goal, i.e. 'Promotion of Women's Empowerment and Gender Equality', during the 2005 World Summit, attended by 170 countries (United Nations 2005). The perspective of the World Bank is:

---

[6] See Census of India (1991, 2001) data of 1991 and 2001 for details.

[7] See PLFS, 2019 for details.

[8] Many of these districts are backward.

> Gender equality is a core development objective in its own right. But greater gender equality is also smart economics, enhancing productivity and improving other development outcomes, including prospects for the next generation and for the quality of societal policies and institutions. Economic development is not enough to shrink all gender disparities—corrective policies that focus on persisting gender gaps are essential (World Bank 2012).

Becker (1971) firstly introduced in the concept of discrimination on the grounds of employers' tastes, the basis of the context of traditional or religious, which can operate as social norms in many countries. We consider discrimination as exogenous, while there may certainly be a bunch of factors that can account for discrimination up to some degree. The idea that distortions in the allocation of talent across occupations or sectors have negative growth implications is not new (Murphy et al. 1991; Freshtman et al. 1996), but to our knowledge, this is the first study to use it in order to analyse the consequences of discrimination.

Whenever we are discussing the women labour force, we should focus on a few aspects because the working conditions and scenarios of women are significantly different when we compare them with that of their male counterparts. Amidst several works on women employment, we shall discuss a few of them briefly.

We know that women, in many cases, work in household activities, and therefore their contributions go unreported or even under-reported for being non-monetized in category (Hirway 2002). Therefore, long-run data could be used to get a hold on women's 'invisible work' (Hirway and Jose 2011). In an ambiance of social backwardness in developing nations, variables like religion, caste, and economic dependence play an important part in deciding the nature of women employment (Das 2006; Ghosh 2009). Even marital status is also found important (Panda 1999). Goldin (1994) observed a 'U' shaped relationship between the women labour force and economic growth. However, this study has been criticized by others for not getting enough evidence in favour of his hypothesis. Family income along with family prejudice are also found to be very influential because, with an increase in family income, there is a lower possibility for a woman member to participate the labour market; it may even encourage an existing woman member to leave the labour market (Sarkar et al. 2017; Rodgers 2012). From the economic perspective, there is a lack of enough employment opportunities in the secondary and service sector coupled with disguised employment in the primary sector—these things have contributed to the fall in female labour force participation (Kapsos et al. 2014). Again, economic growth can only generate the demand for women labour in a free economy, but several socioeconomic variables decide the supply of it (Chand and Srivastava 2014).

Jinyoung et al. (2016) have framed a model based on theory and then tested it to the ground-level data from the Asian economies. The paper has involved several aspects of gender inequality and related them to the economic growth of the nation. Their work has focused not only on the importance of gender equality but also on the grounds on which women allocate their daily hours. Their work brings out the fact that if gender inequality can be removed, then it will not only bring a downfall in the population pressure but also increase the national output. They persuade that within a couple of generations, an economy without any gender discrimination can enjoy around a 15% of increase in its growth rate along with over 70% increase in the per capita income.

Gupta and Kothe (2022) have worked with National Sample Survey (NSS) datasets in India and find out the causes as well as the extent of gender discrimination in wage, in rural as well as in urban areas for casual as well as regular workers. Their work has found astonishing results that wage discrimination is more in urban areas than in rural areas, and it is higher in the case of regular employment than in casual work. They have used Theil's index to find out 'within' and 'between' group inequalities using the Oaxaca decomposition method for dividing the wage gaps in different components. Since they have found that the basic wage differential between men and women is above 51%, it cannot reduce the wage inequality by a considerable margin even if the women are adequately educated although women are more benefitted than men for having good educational degrees. This work has expressed the reality that despite having equal talent and working abilities, women receive fewer wages than men based on several grounds, with 'age' as one of the influential factors. The authors seek appropriate public policies that would ensure women participation in the labour market sustainably. Again, they believe that considering the 'household activities' or non-monetized activities by the women in the national income accounting system could actually reduce this level of the wage gap.

In developing nations like India, social norms have an impact on women employment. In such economies, women are engaged in activities with very little growth, which hinders their choices of opportunities (Kapsos et al. 2014). Hence, public policies should be designed in such a way that could break this jinx. One important question arises—how far the social empowerment policies have been successful in empowering women?

A ground-level study in Uttar Pradesh in India suggests that providing non-farm employment opportunities to women and thus enabling them financially have a more significant impact on the development of women as well as reduction of gender inequality that having a female as the head of Gram Panchayat in rural level (Self and Grabowski 2013). Hence, financial autonomy can reduce gender discrimination more than other social policies.

However, in developing nations, we find social schemes with manifold objectives very often. A single scheme with numerous objectives not only dilutes the main objective to be achieved but also increases the private and institutional costs along with the problem of pursuing these objectives (Sekher 2010). Hence, policies with a single, broader objective are more likely to work on the root causes of gender inequality in developing nations (Jayachandran 2015). The author has raised the question of which factors are more responsible for gender inequality—is it the social norms that persist in developing nations? Or is the policy failure make the education, employment, and wage system more masculinities? The author believes that both factors are responsible for gender inequality. Although policy failures can be explained in the case of a few nations, in many poor economies, various backward social norms lead to gender inequality.

In India, these variables vary across states or even across districts due to the existence of diversity between people and regions. Because of immense diversity across regions on the grounds of demography, social prejudice, economic condition, etc., such differences are seen (Sinha 2005). Women of backward communities are eager to grab new employment opportunities because they generally participate in low-wage, low-grade activities. Hence, women of backward communities generally do not want to miss out on new, improved opportunities (Luke and Munshi 2011).

In India, we have seen both an increase in the women labour force and a fall in different periods in different parts of the country. This could be because of the failure of the economy to generate enough employment opportunities; or, it could be social prejudice. Preference for higher studies might also play influential role in this respect. Public policies have always emphasized the need for higher education among women so that they could get absorbed into the labour market with proper human capital and get enough equal opportunities. We have seen that most studies are based on cross-sectional or time-series data over nations or regions. Again, many of the studies are descriptive as well. However, theorizing this issue regarding women labour force of developing economies is still undermined. Through this study, we have made an effort to fill that with the help of a general equilibrium model.

18.3 Model with Duality

18.3.1 Assumptions

Here we begin with the assumption that there are two sectors in the economy—sector U and G. We have used the following notations in our analysis.

U = Unorganized sector with Gender Discrimination.

G = Organised sector with no Gender Discrimination.

M = Total Male labour force in the economy.

F = Total Female labour force in the economy.

X_i = Output level of the i-th sector, where $i = U, G$.

W_F = Wage rate for female labour force.

W_M = Wage rate for male labour force.

P_i = Price of output of the i-th sector, $i = U, G$.

θ = Factor of Efficiency capturing the impact of educational and nutritional efficiency.

θ_1 = Factor of Efficiency for Women.

θ_2 = Factor of Efficiency for Men.

a_{ij} = Per-unit requirement of input—i by sector j. Here, $i = M, F$ and $j = U, G$.

ε = Financial help given by the government to the female (F).

= Equilibrium state.

N = New.

With the above notations, we further proceed to the description as well as working of our model. Both of these sectors use both males (M) as well as females (F) as their labour force but with significant difference in attitude. Sector U

represents 'Unorganised' sector that differentiates between male and female labour force. So, it indulges in and practices gender discrimination and consequential wage discrimination as well. By the words 'Gender Discrimination,' we mean discrimination of attitude and wage that exists in the working environment of sector U. Sector G can be considered as the 'Organised' or Public or Government Sector.[9]

The word 'Organised' implies that it follows every rule of the formal sector; that is, that do not practice any form of Gender discrimination. In the presence of gender discrimination, Sector U produces output X_U by using both M and F, whereas in the absence of any wage as well as gender discrimination, Sector G produces output X_G.

18.3.2 Commodity and Factor Market

Since there is wage discrimination in sector U, we assume that the wage it pays to the female labour force (W_F) is lower than that it offers to the male labour force (W_M), i.e. $W_F < W_M$. Again, in sector G, there is no such discrimination. So, it provides wage W_M to both forms of the labour force.[10] Now, let us assume that the productivity of the women workforce depends upon the level of nutrition and education. The higher the levels of these two variables, the higher the level of productivity. Here we make an effort to catch the impact of these two by θ, which we can name as 'factor of efficiency'.

So, mathematically,

$$a_{\mathrm{FU}}(\theta_1) = W_F. \tag{18.1}$$

Again,

$$a_{\mathrm{MU}}(\theta_2) = W_M. \tag{18.2}$$

Since, as per the assumption, $W_M > W_F$, hence $\theta_2 > \theta_1$, the commodity market equilibrium condition of the 'Unorganised' sector[11] can be written as,

$$a_{\mathrm{FU}}(\theta_1)\ W_F + a_{\mathrm{MU}}(\theta_2)\ W_M = P_U = P^{\#}_U = 1. \tag{18.3}$$

See Eq. (18.3).[12]

[9]Organised sector need not be the public sector or government sector, it could also be the private sector, but it has to come under the category of 'Organised' sector.

[10]Hence, this sector follows equal wage for equal work for both male and female labour force.

[11]Here, we assume that this unorganized sector uses female intensive labour technology since it practices gender discrimination; it needs to pay a lower wage to the female labour force than they need to pay to the male labour force.

[12]#Stands for equilibrium value. Price of unorganised sector (U) is set to equal to 1 or numeraire.

Using Eq. (18.3), the wage equation or factor return for females in sector G, without any gender or wage discrepancy, can be written as,

$$a_{\mathrm{FG}}(\theta_2)W_F = a_{\mathrm{MG}}(\theta_2)W_M = W_M. \tag{18.4}$$

Hence, the goods market equilibrium for sector G can be presented as

$$a_{\mathrm{FG}}(\theta_2)\ W_F + a_{\mathrm{MG}}(\theta_2)\ W_M = P_G = P^{\#}_G. \tag{18.5}$$

Now, if the government decides to provide financial assistance (ε) to the women, it could be illustrated as,

$$a^N_{\mathrm{FG}} = (\theta^{\#}) = W^{\#} = W_M + \epsilon. \tag{18.6}$$

See Eq. (18.6).[13]

Now, we shall focus on the market for factors and its equilibrium scenarios. ε is the fixed but continuous financial help being given to women by the government. Hence, it is a form of subsidy by the government, i.e. $\theta^{\#} \geq \theta_2 > \theta_1$. If this financial assistance continues and it is positive[14] ($\varepsilon > 0$), then women may not choose to work at present; they may decide to go for education and sacrifice work at present for the sake of improving their educational as well as nutritional status and earn a higher wage or equal wage with that of male in future.

So, financial assistance plays a huge role in the decision in the choice of women workforce between work at present and education or capability-development at present and earning big in the future. If $\varepsilon > 0$, the substitution effect dominates over income effect.

The opposite happens in the case of $\varepsilon < 0$, which happens rarely.

Again, if $\varepsilon = 0$, then both the effects weigh out each other which implies women are indifferent between education and work at present.

Now, if the change in ε is positive ($\widehat{\epsilon} > 0$), and it dominates over the changes in W_M ($\widehat{W}_M > 0$), then we can consider this subsided financial scheme as a social reform in the form of a policy implementation because it encourages women to acquire human capital at present and give up working against gender or wage discrimination and look for superlative working opportunities in future where they will earn equal wage with male labour force. From the angle of labour force, this would mean a fall in labour force participation at present. In order to show these with the help of factor market conditions, we make the following assumptions to see the equilibrium scenarios of the labour market from both perspectives, that is, for both male and female labour forces.

Mathematically illustrated as,

[13] Where, N denotes New.

[14] Which generally happens and our assumption as well.

$$a_{\mathrm{FU}}X_U + a_{\mathrm{FG}}X_G = F(\theta_1, \theta_2) \tag{18.7}$$

$$a_{\mathrm{MU}}X_U + a_{\mathrm{MG}}X_G = F(\theta_2). \tag{18.8}$$

Once the government implements its social policy of financial assistance to women, it actually increases the women productivity through an increase in the capital stock, so the productivity of the women labour force raises from θ_1 to $\theta^{\#}$. This change in productivity implies a change in the equilibrium condition for female labour force in the labour market. Hence, the new equilibrium condition for female in the labour market can be written as,

$$a_{\mathrm{FU}}X_U + a_{\mathrm{FG}}X_G = F^N\{(\theta^{\#}, \theta_2)/\theta^{\#} > \theta_2\}. \tag{18.9}$$

If we compare Eq. (18.7) with Eq. (18.9), we get,

$$F(\theta_1, \theta_2) > F^N\{(\theta^{\#}, \theta_2)/\theta^{\#} > \theta_2\}. \tag{18.10}$$

Equation (18.9) implies that because of the fact that $\widehat{\epsilon} > 0$, there will be a fall in the female labour force participation as long as the inequality $\theta^{\#} > \theta_2 > \theta_1$ holds. This also predicts a possible contraction of the unorganized sector that uses female labour-force-intensive technology and practices wage discrepancy. Since there is a prediction of possible contraction of sector U, the above intuition implies that the male labour force that is engaged in the unorganized sector (U), will look to seek employment opportunities in the organized sector (G) because it is formal and hence secure than sector U. So, the organized sector G will survive, and the unorganized one will contract.

18.4 Concluding Remarks

In this study, we have considered a couple of cases. In the first case, we have considered the existence of wage inequality, but in the second case, there is no discrimination against women. We know that two important variables decide the supply of women labour force in a developing economy—education level and nutritional level. We have derived labour market as well as product market equilibrium conditions. We have seen that the presence of a fixed, continuous financial allowance being given to women actually encourages women to choose higher studies over getting into labour market at an early age. Women with financial help look forward to build-up human capital, which has been very desirable from a developmental point of view. In case of no financial help, women are indifferent between the above-mentioned two choices. Hence, financial assistance as a public policy not only enriches the educational level of women but encourages sacrificing low-wage, low-graded employment opportunities at an early age to build up proper human capital so they can cancel the discrimination. Since the sector that practices wage discrimination does not get enough women labour, it may actually shut down this would ask its remaining male labour force to migrate to other economic sectors in search of employment. Hence, we have considered the crucial angles of the women labour market in our study—once, the presence of gender or wage discrimination and later, the absence of it, along with consideration of financial help as a proxy to the public policy.

References

Anant TCA, Hasan R, Mohapatra P, Nagaraj R, Sasikumar SK (2006) Labor markets in India: issues and perspectives. In: Felipe J, Hasan R (eds) Labor markets in Asia. Palgrave Macmillan, London. https://doi.org/10.1057/9780230627383_5

Becker GS (1971) The Economics of Discrimination, (2nd edition), Chicago University Press, London

Bourguignon F (2018) World changes in inequality: an overview of facts, causes, consequences, and policies. CESifo Econ Stud 64(3):345–370. https://doi.org/10.1093/cesifo/ifx028

Bourguignon F, Platteau J (2017) Does aid availability affect effectiveness in reducing poverty? A review article. World Dev 90:6–16. https://doi.org/10.1016/j.worlddev.2015.06.003

Census of India (1991) Census of India 1991. Government of India, New Delhi

Census of India (2001) Census of India 2001. Government of India, New Delhi

Census of India (2011) Census of India 2011. Government of India, New Delhi

Chakraborty I, Chakraborty A (2009) Female work participation and gender differential in earning in West Bengal. J Quant Econ 8(2):98–114

Chand R, Srivastava SK (2014) Changes in the rural labour market and their implications for agriculture. Econ Polit Wkly 49(10):47–54

Chattopadhyay R, Duflo E (2004) Women as policy makers: evidence from a nationwide randomized experiment in India. Econometrica 72:1409–1443

Chaykowski RP, Powell LM (1999) Women and the labour market: recent trends and policy issues. Can Public Policy 25:S1–S25. https://doi.org/10.2307/3552314

Dabla-Norris ME, Kochhar MK, Suphaphiphat MN, Ricka MF, Tsounta ME (2015) Causes and consequences of income inequality: a global perspective. International Monetary Fund, Washington, DC. https://www.imf.org/external/pubs/ft/sdn/2015/sdn1513.pdf

Das MB (2006) Do traditional axes of exclusion affect labor market outcomes in India? World Bank, Washington, DC. https://documents.worldbank.org/curated/en/195941468034790110/pdf/369630sdp970web.pdf

Das D, Pathak M (2012) Gender equality: a core concept of socio-economic development in India. Asian J Soc Sci Hum 1(4):257–264

Dasgupta S, Verick SS (2016) Transformation of women at work in Asia: an unfinished development agenda. SAGE Publications India, New Delhi

Dashora KB (2013) Problems faced by working women in India. Int J Adv Res Manag Soc Sci 2(8): 82–94

Datt G, Ravallion M (2002) Is India's economic growth leaving the poor behind? J Econ Perspect 16(3):89–108. https://doi.org/10.1257/089533002760278730

Desai M, Majumdar B, Chakraborty T, Ghosh K (2011) The second shift: working women in India. Gender Manag 26(6):432–450. https://doi.org/10.1108/17542411111164920

Duflo E (2012) Women empowerment and economic development. J Econ Lit 50(4):1051–1079. https://doi.org/10.1257/jel.50.4.1051

Esteve-Volart B (2009) Gender discrimination and growth: theory and evidence from India. York University, Mimeo. https://bertaev.info.yorku.ca/files/2016/06/disc_january2009.pdf

Fajnzylber P, Daniel L, Norman L (2002) Inequality and violent crime. J Law Econ 45:1–40

FAO (2015) Gender and land statistics recent developments in FAO's gender and land rights database. FAO, Rome. http://www.fao.org/3/a-i4862e.pdf

Ferrant G, Pesando LM, Nowacka K (2014) Unpaid care work: the missing link in the analysis of gender gaps in labour outcomes. OECD Development Centre, Paris. https://www.oecd.org/dev/development-gender/Unpaid_care_work.pdf

Fletcher E, Pande R, Moore CMT (2017) Women and work in India: descriptive evidence and a review of potential policies. SSRN Electron J 2017:3116310. https://doi.org/10.2139/ssrn.3116310

Freshtman C, Murphy K, Weiss Y (1996) Social status, education, and growth. J Polit Econ 104 (1):108–32

GEM (2017) Global entrepreneurship monitor 2016/2017. Women's entrepreneurship report. Global Entrepreneurship Monitor, London. https://www.gemconsortium.org/report/gem-20162017-womens-entrepreneurship-report

Ghosh J (2009) Never done and poorly paid: women's work in globalising India. Womens Unlimited 37(1):247–251. https://doi.org/10.1086/660184

Goldin C (1994) The U-shaped female labor force function in economic development and economic history (no. w4707). National Bureau of Economic Research, Cambridge. https://www.nber.org/papers/w4707

Gupta P, Kothe S (2022) Gender discrimination and the biased Indian Labour Market: evidence from the National Sample Survey. SSRN Electron J 2022:3978324. https://doi.org/10.2139/ssrn.3978324

Heath R, Tan X (2020) Intrahousehold bargaining, female autonomy, and labor supply: theory and evidence from India. J Eur Econ Assoc 18(4):1928–1968. https://doi.org/10.1093/jeea/jvz026

Hirway I (2002) Employment and unemployment situation in 1990s: how good are NSS data? Econ Polit Wkly 37(21):2027–2036

Hirway I, Jose S (2011) Understanding women's work using time-use statistics: the case of India. Fem Econ 17(4):67–92. https://doi.org/10.1080/13545701.2011.622289

ILO (2016) Women at work: trends 2016. International Labour Organization, Geneva. http://www.ilo.org/wcmsp5/groups/public/dgreports/dcomm/publ/documents/publication/wcms_457317.pdf

Inglehart R, Norris P, Ronald I (2003) Rising tide: gender equality and cultural change around the world. Cambridge University Press, Cambridge

Jayachandran S (2015) The roots of gender inequality in developing countries. Annu Rev Econ 7:63–88. https://doi.org/10.1146/annurev-economics-080614-115404

Jinyoung K, Jong WL, Shin K (2016) A model of gender inequality and economic growth. ADB economics working paper series. Paper no. 475. Asian Development Bank, Mandaluyong. https://www.adb.org/sites/default/files/publication/180687/ewp-475.pdf

Kabeer N (2021) Gender equality, inclusive growth, and labour markets. Routledge, Women's Economic Empowerment, pp 13–48

Kapsos S, Silbermann A, Bourmpoula E (2014) Why is female labour force participation declining so sharply in India? International Labour Organization, Geneva. https://www.ilo.org/wcmsp5/groups/public/dgreports/inst/documents/publication/wcms_250977.pdf

Kelkar G (2005) Development effectiveness through gender mainstreaming: gender equality and poverty reduction in South Asia. Econ Polit Wkly 29(4):4690–4699

Kennedy AB (2015) Powerhouses or pretenders? Debating China's and India's emergence as technological powers. Pac Rev 28(2):281–302. https://doi.org/10.1080/09512748.2014.995126

Klasen S (2018) The impact of gender inequality on economic performance in developing countries. Ann Rev Resour Econ 10:279–298. https://doi.org/10.1146/annurev-resource-100517-023429

Knech A (2014) Understanding and fighting poverty–Amartya Sen's capability approach and related theories. Soc Change Rev 10(2):153–176. https://doi.org/10.2478/scr-2013-0016

Kromydas T (2017) Rethinking higher education and its relationship with social inequalities: past knowledge, present state and future potential. Palgrave Commun 3:1. https://doi.org/10.1057/s41599-017-0001-8

Kshetri N, Dholakia N (2011) Regulative institutions supporting entrepreneurship in emerging economies: a comparison of China and India. J Int Entrep 9(2):110–132. https://doi.org/10.1007/s10843-010-0070-x

Kundu A, Mohanan PC (2009) Employment and inequality outcomes in India. In: Joint seminar on employment and inequality, vol 8. Employment, Labour and Social Affairs Directorate and Development Centre, Paris, pp 1–43. https://www.oecd.org/employment/emp/42546020.pdf

Lam D (2005) An economic perspective. Econ Sustain Dev 99:535–562

Lei L, Desai S, Vanneman R (2019) The impact of transportation infrastructure on women's employment in India. Fem Econ 25(4):94–125. https://doi.org/10.1080/13545701.2019.1655162

Lewis J, Plomien A (2009) Flexicurity' as a policy strategy: the implications for gender equality. Econ Soc 38(3):433–459. https://doi.org/10.1080/03085140903020622

Luke N, Munshi K (2011) Women as agents of change: female income and mobility in India. J Dev Econ 94(1):1–17

Mencher J (1988) Women's work and poverty: women's contribution to household maintenance in South India. In: A home divided: women and income in the third world. Stanford University Press, Redwood City, pp 99–119

Murphy K, Shleifer A, Vishny RW (1991) The allocation of talent: implications for growth. The Quart J Econ 106(2):503–503

Nandi S (2012) Comparative analysis of foreign direct investment trends in emerging economies. Proced Soc Behav Sci 37:230–240. https://doi.org/10.1016/j.sbspro.2012.03.289

Neckerman K, Florencia T (2007) Inequality: causes and consequences. Annu Rev Sociol 33:335–357

Oxford (2019) Oxford poverty and human development initiative and UNDP. In: Global multidimensional poverty index 2019: illuminating inequalities. Oxford University Press, Oxford. https://ophi.org.uk/global-multidimensional-poverty-index-2019-illuminating-inequalities/

Panda PK (1999) Poverty and young women's employment: linkages in Kerala. Centre for Development Studies, Trivandrum

Perry GE, Arias OS, López JH, Maloney WF, Servén L (2006) Poverty reduction and growth: virtuous and vicious circles. World Bank, Washington, DC. https://openknowledge.worldbank.org/handle/10986/6997

PLFS (2020) Periodic labour force survey (July 2018–June 2019), periodic labour force survey report. Ministry of Statistics and Programme Implementation, New Delhi

Ratho A (2020) Promoting female participation in urban India's labour force. Observer Research Foundation (ORF) Issue Brief No, 348, 1–14.. https://www.orfonline.org/wp-content/uploads/2020/03/ORF_IssueBrief_348_FemaleLabour.pdf

Reddy NK, Vranda MN, Ahmed A, Nirmala BP, Siddaramu B (2010) Work-life balance among married women employees. Indian J Psychol Med 32(2):112–118

Rodgers J (2012) Labour force participation in rural Bihar: a 30-year perspective based on village surveys. Institute of Human Development, New Delhi. http://www.ihdindia.org/PDFs/Labour_Force_Participation_in_Rural_Bihar_A_Thirty-Year_Perspective_based_on_Village_Surveys.pdf

Sarkar S, Sahoo S, Klasen S (2017) Employment transitions of women in India: a panel analysis. World Dev 115:291–309. https://docs.iza.org/dp11086.pdf

Sekher TV (2010) Special financial incentives for the girl child in India: a review of select schemes. United Nations Population Fund, Mumbai. http://14.139.60.153/bitstream/123456789/11525/1/special_financial_incentives_schemes_for_girls.pdf

Self S, Grabowski R (2013) Female autonomy in rural North India: impact of economic, social, and political factors. J Econ Dev 38(1):59–81

Sen A (1982) Poverty and famines: an essay on entitlement and deprivation. Oxford University Press, Oxford. https://www.prismaweb.org/nl/wp-content/uploads/2017/06/Poverty-and-famines%E2%94%82Amartya-Sen%E2%94%821981.pdf

Sen A, Dutta A (2018) West Bengal's successful Kanyashree Prakalpa programme needs more push from state and beneficiaries. Econ Polit Wkly 53(17):8. https://www.researchgate.net/publication/334965156_West_Bengals_Successful_Kanyashree_Prakalpa_Programme_Needs_More_Push_From_State_and_Beneficiaries

Sinha MG (2005) An analysis of the social sector development in India. Indian J Pub Admin 51(3). https://doi.org/10.1177/0019556120050316

Sorsa P, Mares J, Didier M, Guimaraes C, Rabate M, Tang G, Tuske A (2015) Determinants of the low female labour force participation in India. OECD Economics department working papers.. https://www.oecd.org/officialdocuments/publicdisplaydocumentpdf/?cote=ECO/WKP(2015)25&docLanguage=En. Accessed 21 Feb 2022

Srinivasan TN (2006) China, India and the world economy. Econ Polit Wkly 41(34):3716–3727

Srivastava N, Srivastava R (2010) Women, work, and employment outcomes in rural India. Econ Polit Wkly 45(28):49–63

Sundari S (2020) Structural changes and quality of women's labour in India. Ind J Labour Econ 63: 689–717. https://doi.org/10.1007/s41027-020-00245-2

United Nations (2005) World summit outcome. United Nations, New York. https://www.un.org/en/development/desa/population/migration/generalassembly/docs/globalcompact/A_RES_60_1.pdf

Von Grebmer K, Saltzman A, Birol E, Wiesman D, Prasai N, Yin S, Sonntag A (2014) 2014 Global hunger index: the challenge of hidden hunger, vol 83. International Food Policy Research Institute, Washington, DC

Weiss J (2005) Poverty targeting in Asia. Edward Elgar Publishing, Cheltenham. https://www.adb.org/sites/default/files/publication/159383/adbi-poverty-targeting-asia.pdf

World Bank (2012) World development report 2012: gender equality and development. World Bank, Washington, DC. https://openknowledge.worldbank.org/handle/10986/4391

World Bank (2021) The gradual rise and rapid decline of the middle class in Latin America and the Caribbean. World Bank, Washington, DC. https://openknowledge.worldbank.org/handle/10986/35834

World Health Organization (2002) Health, economic growth and poverty reduction: the report of working group I of the commission on macroeconomics and health. World Health Organization, Geneva. https://apps.who.int/iris/bitstream/handle/10665/42492/9241590092.pdf

World Health Organization (2008) Closing the gap in a generation: health equity through action on the social determinants of health: commission on social determinants of health final report. World Health Organization, Geneva. https://www.who.int/publications/i/item/WHO-IER-CSDH-08.1

World Health Organization (2021) UNICEF-WHO-The World Bank: joint child malnutrition estimates: levels and trends. World Health Organization, Geneva. https://data.unicef.org/resources/jme-report-2021/

Dr. Nilendu Chatterjee is an Assistant Professor in the Department of Economics, Bankim Sardar College (affiliated to the University of Calcutta), West Bengal, India. He has research interests in Resource Economics, International Economics, Econometrics, and Development Economics. He has research interest in both quantitative and qualitative aspects. As a necessary task of the present age research, he has done quite a few works in the field of interdisciplinary research with authors from the field of Geography. He has published a number of research articles in several international journals of economics including International Journal of Sustainable Economies Management, Economic Affairs, Foreign Trade Review, and Journal of knowledge Economy. He has also published a good number of papers in edited volumes published from publishers of international repute such as Springer, Routledge, and many more.

Dr. Anindita Nath is working as a faculty in the Department of Geography at Bankim Sardar College (affiliated to the University of Calcutta), West Bengal, India. Her research interests include coastal hazards and Management, Geospatial application in various geo-environmental fields, climate change, land degradation and management, landslide hazards and management, flood assessment and riverbank erosion, land-use, environmental issues and management, and sustainable development. She contributed a number of national and international research articles and book chapters published by the publishing houses of international reputations. She serves as the reviewer of some reputed journals published by Springer-Nature.

Dr. Bappaditya Koley is the head, Department of Geography, Bankim Sardar College (affiliated to the University of Calcutta) in West Bengal, India. His research interests include landslide hazard risk and management, natural hazards and disaster management, climate change, spatial application of various geo-environmental hazards, integrated coastal hazard and management, applied geomorphology, natural resources mapping, environmental issues, land-use modeling and management of sustainable development. As a co-director, he has completed a Minor Research Project (MRP) funded by the Indian Council of Social Science Research (Eastern Regional Centre, Kolkata), Govt. of India. He has contributed several national and international research articles and book chapters published by the publishing houses of international reputations. Dr. Koley serves as the reviewer of some reputable journal published by Springer-Nature and Taylor & Francis. He is also associated the Guest Editor of the Special Issue "Designing of AIML (Artificial Intelligence and Machine Learning) and Convolutional Neural Network (CNN) Based Architectures and Its Various Applications in the Field of Engineering", under Designs, an Open Access Journal by MDPI.

Chapter 19
A Closer Look at Public and Private Sector Commercial Banks Through Performance Lenses: An Indian Experience in the Post-Reform Era

Sreemanta Sarkar, Debdas Rakshit, and Madhabendra Sinha

19.1 Introduction

The bridge between savers and investors is an important requirement for furthering the progress of any economic system. Mobilization of savings from the people, who spend less than their income to meet the need of those who desire to drive the engine of growth, is the most crucial function of banks and financial institutions. Banks thus put idle saving of the economy into productive channels (Sufian 2009) and affects the allocation of it without affecting the rate of saving. In this way, banks play a crucial role in the economic development of any country (Schumpeter 1934).

The role of banks in the mobilization and allocation of idle savings in an economy is a proven and well-recognized fact (Goswami et al. 2019). The capital formation process gains momentum through the operation of the banking network. In developing countries like India, where the security market fails to stretch its sway over the majority of the population, the role of the banking sector in meeting the investment need of the firms assumes greater significance. The commercial banking sector of this country has been playing this instrumental role as a growth agent since the dawn of the modern banking system (Seenaiah et al. 2015). But this process started getting

S. Sarkar
Department of Economics, Bidhan Chandra College, Asansol, West Bengal, India

Department of Commerce, The University of Burdwan, Burdwan, West Bengal, India

D. Rakshit
Department of Commerce, The University of Burdwan, Burdwan, West Bengal, India

M. Sinha (✉)
Department of Economics and Politics, Visva-Bharati University, Santiniketan, West Bengal, India

M. Mishra et al. (eds.), *Public Policies and Sustainable Development in Post-Reform India*, New Frontiers in Regional Science: Asian Perspectives 71,
https://doi.org/10.1007/978-981-99-3696-0_19

motion after the banking sector nationalization drive in 1969 and accelerated after the initiation of the economic reforms in 1991 (Singh et al. 2016). Even after three decades since the initiation of economic reforms banking sector specifically, commercial banks remain the principal source in meeting the credit needs of the industrial sector. At the end of March 2019, the total outstanding gross bank credit of the industrial sector was to the tune of Rs. 33,049.4 billion, constituting 34.72% of the total credit in this category (Reserve Bank of India [RBI] 2019).

Over the passage of time, India has developed an extensive financial network with wide-ranging financial institutions, including public sector banks, private sector banks, foreign banks, urban and rural cooperative banks, small finance banks, mutual funds, and other non-banking financial institutions (Sarkar and Rakshit 2021). Each category of institution, under the effective control and supervision of the Reserve Bank of India, has been functioning efficiently over the years. The regulatory and supervisory power of RBI has made our financial system strong and robust to withstand different external shocks created in and around the country in different periods of time. The most important of these shocks is the financial crisis of 2007–2008, which, though dismantled the banking and financial organizations of even the most powerful economic giants of the globe, failed to make any formidable dent in the Indian banking sector. The scheduled commercial banks of India effectively withstood (operating profit maintained, return on assets, and asset quality improved) the great financial debacle of 2007–2008 (RBI 2008). The balance sheets of the Indian banks were healthy and affected little by the turbulence in global financial markets (RBI 2009).

But all is not well for the Indian banking sector over the last decade. Diminishing balance sheets since 2012, growing levels of nonperforming assets, and consequent decline in asset quality are making things worse for public sector banks (Ramesh 2019; Pramahender 2021). The mounting volume of impaired loans has now become an area of concern for the banking sector in general and public sector banks in particular (Bajaj et al. 2021), and this has generated tremendous pressure in respect of efficiency and profitability (Rahaman and Sur 2021) of commercial banks in India. For the last decade since 2010, the gross nonperforming assets and net nonperforming assets of all scheduled commercial banks have been persistently rising, and there has been a deterioration of net profit and other profitability indicators like ROA and ROE (Table 19.1). After almost two and half decades since 1993–1994, the net profit of all scheduled commercial banks in India has become negative (RBI 2018).

As against these hard facts, performance appraisal of different types of banks, specifically public and private sector banks, assumes great significance in shaping appropriate policy formulation for the overall development of the economy. The role of the different types of banks and a comparative assessment of their contribution to building an efficient banking segment demands prominence in analyzing the health and soundness of the financial sector of India. This assumes significance specifically in the post-reform era when both types of banks are in keen competition for expanding their market and profitability as well. Keeping this objective into consideration, we attempt to make a comparison of the public sector banks (PSBs) and

Table 19.1 Health of scheduled commercial banks in India from 2010 to 2018

Year	Net profit	Gross NPA	Net NPA	ROA	ROE	NIM
2010	57,109.25	84,700.82	39,126.62	1.05	14.31	2.54
2011	70,331.27	97,973.15	41,799.16	1.1	14.96	2.91
2012	81,658.28	1,42,903.32	65,204.87	1.08	14.6	2.9
2013	91,164.66	1,94,053.31	98,693.86	1.04	13.84	2.79
2014	80,912.68	2,64,381.14	1,42,656.01	0.81	10.69	2.7
2015	89,077.79	3,23,335.16	1,75,841.06	0.81	10.42	2.64
2016	34,148.17	6,11,947.28	3,49,814.43	0.4	3.58	2.58
2017	43,899.5	7,91,791.05	4,33,120.61	0.36	4.16	2.51
2018	−32,437.68	10,39,679.33	5,20,837.65	−0.15	−2.81	2.5

Source: Authors' compilation from RBI (2019) database (amount in '10 millions)

private sector banks (PVBs) of India in terms of performance measures and the main bank-specific factors which may affect these measures. Collecting bank-level data from the RBI database, we have tried to make a comparative assessment of the performance of the PSBs and PVBs of India over the period 2000–2017.

The rest of the paper is structured as follows. Section 19.2 attempts a review of the existing literature. Section 19.3 presents measures and determinants of performance followed by data and methodology in Sect. 19.4, results and discussions in Sect. 19.5, practical and social implications in Sect. 19.7, and conclusion in Sect. 19.7.

19.2 Literature Review

Commercial banks' performance has been drawing researchers' attention since the time of the great depression (Ongore and Kusa 2013). This has got a further fillip with the implementation of the structural adjustment program, under the aegis of IMF, in many countries of the world since 1980 onwards. For the last 40 years, the world has faced many crises, the most notable of which is the East Asian financial crisis during the latter half of the 1990s and the global financial crisis in the first decade of the twentieth century. These blows had significant bearings on the performance of financial institutions, and a large volume of literature has been written on the factors affecting the profitability of banks in different countries of the globe. Studies have been made mostly on the banking sector of a particular country, or a particular region, or across different countries of the world (Dietrich and Wanzenried 2014).

A careful scrutiny of the literature concerning the factors affecting commercial banks' performance reveals that the variables commonly used for the performance are ROA (Pasiouras and Kosmidou 2007; Flamini et al. 2009; Curak et al. 2012; Srinivasan and Britto 2017), ROA and ROE (Athanasoglou et al. 2008; Anbar and Alper 2011; Saeed 2014; Albulescu 2015; Petria et al. 2015; Sanderson and Le Roux

2016; Caporale et al. 2017; Yahya et al. 2017; Brahmaiah 2018; Almaqtari et al. 2019) or ROA, ROE, and NIM (Dietrich and Wanzenried 2011; Ongore and Kusa 2013; Căpraru and Ihnatov 2014; Titko et al. 2015; Tan 2016; Al-Homaidi et al. 2018; Kassem and Sakr 2018; Sarkar and Rakshit 2021). Besides, Demirgüç-Kunt and Huizinga (1999) considered NIM and before-tax profit by asset ratio, Menicucci and Paolucci (2016) took ROE as the performance or profitability measures of commercial banks. In accordance with these works, we have considered ROA, ROE, and NIM as the performance measures of commercial banks.

With regard to bank-specific performance determinants, various authors have used different factors. In line with this literature, we have used asset size or size (Pasiouras and Kosmidou 2007; Flamini et al. 2009; Curak et al. 2012; Căpraru and Ihnatov 2014; Petria et al. 2015; Titko et al. 2015; Almaqtari et al. 2019; Sarkar and Rakshit 2021), asset quality (Anbar and Alper 2011; Ongore and Kusa 2013; Al-Homaidi et al. 2018; Almaqtari et al. 2019; Sarkar and Rakshit 2021), asset management (Yahya et al. 2017; Al-Homaidi et al. 2018; Almaqtari et al. 2019; Sarkar and Rakshit 2021), operating efficiency (Rashid and Jabeen 2016; Al-Homaidi et al. 2018), quality of loan (Petria et al. 2015; Yao et al. 2018; Brahmaiah 2018), capital adequacy (Ongore and Kusa 2013; Dietrich and Wanzenried 2014; Alemu and Aweke 2017; Ebenezer et al. 2017; Al-Homaidi et al. 2018), and business per employee (Rahaman and Sur 2021) as the internal or bank-specific performance determinants.

There are very few studies regarding the comparative assessment of the performance of the public and private sector banks. Bhattacharyya et al. (1997) conducted a study of 70 Indian commercial banks during the period 1986–1991 and found that public sector banks are the most efficient ones, followed by foreign banks and private sector banks. Singh et al. (2016) tried to evaluate the intellectual capital performance of private and public sector banks in India and found the former to be better at creating total information coefficients. Bajaj et al. (2021) make a comparative evaluation of the public sector and private sector commercial banks in terms of determinants of NPA and rate of recovery. They find that the private sector banks experience an increasing trend in the recovery of NPAs compared to the public sector banks. Rautela et al. (2021) try to identify the factors affecting the outsourcing activities of public and private sector commercial banks in India and find that the latter adopt outsourcing more profusely than the former.

A journey into the existing literature indicates that there are numerous pieces of literature regarding the factors affecting the profitability of commercial banks, but there are almost no studies regarding the comparative evaluation of the performance of public and private sector banks. Moreover, a comparative assessment of these banks' groups in terms of measures and drivers of performance is also absent in the existing works. Taking this research gap into consideration, we have tried to make a comparative assessment of the performance of public sector banks (PSBs) and private sector banks (PVBs) operating in India. We attempt to ascertain whether there is any significant difference in the performance of PSBs and PVBs in terms of the commonly used measures and the determinants of performance.

19.3 Performance Measures and Determinants

The study aims to judge whether there is any difference between the public sector and private sector banks in measures of performance and bank-specific performance drivers. Based on the existing literature, we have used return on assets (ROA), return on equity (ROE), and net interest margin (NIM) as the yardstick for the performance of commercial banks. These three measures as are used in the existing works, reflect the financial performance of the commercial banks and give an impression regarding their financial health. Thus, ROA, ROE, and NIM can be taken as the proxy for the performance of commercial banks. With respect to the factors affecting the performance of commercial banks, both bank-specific or internal factors and macroeconomic or external factors have been considered in the current literature. But for the present study, we have used bank-specific factors alone since macroeconomic factors are not specific to individual banks. The following section gives a brief description of the measures and determinants of performance that are used in this analysis. Table 19.2 reports a snapshot view of measures and determinants of performance and the acronym used in the study.

19.3.1 Measures of Performance

19.3.1.1 Return on Assets (ROA)

ROA is defined as the ratio of net profit to total assets and reflects the efficiency with which the resources of a bank are managed to generate profit (Dietrich and

Table 19.2 Description of the measures of performance and performance determinants

Variable	Measurement	Acronym
Performance measures		
Return on assets	Net profit/total assets	ROA
Return on equity	Net profit/capital + reserves and surplus	ROE
Net interest margin	Net interest income/total assets	NIM
Performance determinants		
Asset size	Natural log of total assets	AST
Asset quality	Advance/assets	ASQ
Asset management	Operating profit/asset	ASM
Operating efficiency	Operating expenses/net interest income	OPE
Quality of loan	Net NPA/net advance	QAV
Capital adequacy	Capital funds/risk-weighted assets	CAR
Employees performance	Natural log of (deposit + advance/no. of employees), i.e., natural log of BPE	EMP

Source: Authors' own presentation

Wanzenried 2011). Existing studies on bank performance treats ROA as one of the main performance measures (Pasiouras and Kosmidou 2007; Athanasoglou et al. 2008; Flamini et al. 2009; Dietrich and Wanzenried 2011; Robin et al. 2018; Sarkar and Rakshit 2021).

19.3.1.2 Return on Equity (ROE)

Return on equity is defined as the ratio of net profit to total equity, and it signifies shareholders' return from equity holding (Athanasoglou et al. 2008). The present analysis considers ROE as the ratio of net profit to the sum of capital, reserves, and surplus. Athanasoglou et al. (2008), Căpraru and Ihnatov (2014), Petria et al. (2015), Ebenezer et al. (2017), Gupta and Mahakud (2020) and Sarkar and Rakshit (2021) consider ROE as one of the performance measures of commercial banks.

19.3.1.3 Net Interest Margin (NIM)

Net interest margin is defined as the ratio of net interest to total assets, and it focuses on the profit earned on interest activities (Dietrich and Wanzenried 2014). NIM has been used to serve as the measure of a bank's performance in many studies (Demirgüç-Kunt and Huizinga 1999; Ongore and Kusa 2013; Titko et al. 2015; Tan 2016; Kassem and Sakr 2018; Robin et al. 2018; Le and Ngo 2020).

19.3.2 Performance Determinants

19.3.2.1 Asset Size (AST)

Natural logarithm of the total assets of a bank has been used as a proxy to measure the size of a bank in various studies (Flamini et al. 2009; Curak et al. 2012; Petria et al. 2015; Tan 2016; Almaqtari et al. 2019; Sarkar and Rakshit 2021). Therefore, in continuation with the existing literature, The Natural logarithm of total assets has been used as one of the bank-specific performance determinants in this study.

19.3.2.2 Asset Quality (ASQ)

The proportion of assets that are utilized as advance may be regarded as the measure of asset quality (Almaqtari et al. 2019). The higher the ratio, the higher might be the profitability, provided the banks do not take an undesirable level of risk (Anbar and Alper 2011). Total advance to assets ratio (ASQ) has been used in this study as the measure of asset quality as in prior studies (Ongore and Kusa 2013; Al-Homaidi et al. 2018; Almaqtari et al. 2019; Sarkar and Rakshit 2021).

19.3.2.3 Asset Management (ASM)

The ratio of operating profit to total assets may be used as a proxy for asset management (Al-Homaidi et al. 2018) and may indicate the ability of the banks to manage their resources in generating profit. Asset management has been considered one of the performance drivers of commercial banks in this analysis following (Al-Homaidi et al. 2018; Almaqtari et al. 2019; Sarkar and Rakshit 2021).

19.3.2.4 Operating Efficiency (OPE)

Operating efficiency in the banking sector may be defined as the ratio of operating profit to net interest income (Rashid and Jabeen 2016). The lower the ratio is for a bank, the higher should be its operating efficiency (Almaqtari et al. 2019).

19.3.2.5 Quality of Loan (QAV)

Noncompliance with obligations by the debtor raises the probability of loss to the banks (Petria et al. 2015) and affects its performance adversely. An increase in the burden of unpaid loans has a significant negative impact on the profitability of banks, and for this reason, financial institutions always strive to minimize the burden of stressed assets (Pramahender 2021; Rahaman and Sur 2021). Consequently, net nonperforming assets (Net NPA) to net advances may be taken as an indicator of the loan quality of commercial banks.

19.3.2.6 Capital Adequacy (CAR)

Capital adequacy can be expressed as a ratio of a bank's capital to its risk-weighted assets and can be used to reflect the capital strength of a financial institution to withstand different kinds of risk (Ongore and Kusa 2013). Capital adequacy either in the form of equity to assets (Pasiouras and Kosmidou 2007; Dietrich and Wanzenried 2014; Anbar and Alper 2011; Petria et al. 2015; Ebenezer et al. 2017; Yahya et al. 2017; Almaqtari et al. 2019), capital to total assets (Ongore and Kusa 2013; Alemu and Aweke 2017), or capital to risk-weighted assets (Albulescu 2015; Alshatti 2016; Srinivasan and Britto 2017; Le and Ngo 2020) is commonly used as a performance driver of commercial banks. In line with the existing works, we have used capital to risk-weighted assets as a performance determinant of Indian banks.

19.3.2.7 Employees Performance (EMP)

Business per employee, usually expressed as the ratio of the sum of advance and deposit to the number of employees, may be used to assess the performance of the employees of the commercial banks. It indicates the efficiency with which a bank utilizes its employees (Rahaman and Sur 2021). All banks desire to fetch the highest business per worker, and so business per employee may be taken as a performance determinant of commercial banks. We have used the natural logarithm of business per employee as a proxy for employee performance (EMP).

19.4 Data and Methodology

19.4.1 Data Source

Our objective is to make a comparative assessment of the public and private sector banks in India in terms of performance measures and bank-specific performance determinants. To conduct this analysis, we have taken all public sector banks and private sector banks which were in operation over the entire 18 years period starting from 2000. We have restricted the period of study to 2017 because, since April 2017 onwards, several changes have taken place in the Indian banking sector, especially with respect to public sector banks (Sarkar and Rakshit 2021). Associate banks of State Bank of India (SBI) have been merged into SBI, and there has been the merger of different public sector banks. Changes in the size and market share of the banks resulting from this merger might have a significant influence on the performance of the merged banks. A comparative assessment of the performance of PSBs and PVBs without these merged banks, which are dominant players in the banking industry, is meaningless, and at the same time, extending the time period with the inclusion of these banks may yield inconsistent results. For these reasons, the study period has been taken up to 2017.

All bank-specific data are taken from the Reserve Bank of India database and have been compiled accordingly. We have 450 bank year observations for public sector banks, 288 for private sector banks, and thus 738 bank year observations altogether.

19.4.2 Methodology

To examine whether public sector banks (PSBs) and private sector banks (PSVs) differ significantly with regard to measures of performance (ROA, ROE, NIM) and internal or bank-specific determinants of performance (Asset size, operating efficiency, asset management, asset quality, quality of advance, capital adequacy, employees' performance) we use unequal variances *t*-test or Welch' *t*-test (Satterthwaite 1946).

The test statistic *t* can be shown by the following formula:

$$t = \frac{\overline{b_1} - \overline{b_2}}{\sqrt{\frac{S_1^2}{N_1} + \frac{S_2^2}{N_2}}}, \quad (19.1)$$

where b_i, s_i, and N_i are sample means, sample standard deviations, and no. of observations, respectively, $i = 1, 2$.

Since we have reasonably large unequal sample sizes and unequal sample variances (Tables 19.3 and 19.4), this test appears to be more relevant than Student's *t*-test. The test has several advantages, as found in the literature. Ruxton (2006) suggests that the unequal variance *t*-test is almost parallel to and sometimes better than Student's *t*-test with regard to control of both Type-I and Type-II errors when the underlying distributions are normal. Moreover, this method does not require the test for homogeneity of variance as a prerequisite to deciding about its application. Rather than performing a variance equality test in deciding to use Student's *t*-test or unequal variance *t*-test controls Type I error less effectively than conducting the unequal variance *t*-test in all situations (Moser and Stevens 1992).

19.4.3 Hypotheses

To examine the difference between PSBs and PVBs in terms of performance measures and performance determinants, we frame the following hypotheses:

19.4.3.1 Hypotheses for Performance Measures

$H_{01}{}^{m}$: ROA of PSBs and PVBs does not differ significantly.
$H_{11}{}^{m}$: ROA of PSBs and PVBs differs significantly.
$H_{02}{}^{m}$: ROE of PSBs and PVBs does not differ significantly.
$H_{12}{}^{m}$: ROE of PSBs and PVBs differs significantly.
$H_{03}{}^{m}$: NIM of PSBs and PVBs does not differ significantly.
$H_{13}{}^{m}$: NIM of PSBs and PVBs differs significantly.

19.4.3.2 Hypotheses for Performance Determinants

$H_{01}{}^{d}$: AST of PSBs and PVBs does not differ significantly.
$H_{11}{}^{d}$: AST of PSBs and PVBs differs significantly.
$H_{02}{}^{d}$: ASQ of PSBs and PVBs does not differ significantly.
$H_{12}{}^{d}$: ASQ of PSBs and PVBs differ significantly.

Table 19.3 Two-sample *t*-test for difference of mean for performance measures of PSB and PVB (with unequal variance; unequal Welch)

PM	Bank group	Nob	Mean	SD	95% Conf. interval		*t*-stat	Prob
ROA	PSB	450	00.7319	00.7747	00.6601	00.8037	−04.7589***	00.00
	PVB	288	01.0042	00.7474	00.9175	01.0909		
	Combined	738	00.8382	00.7751	00.7821	00.8942		
	Difference		−00.2722	–	−00.3846	−00.1599		
ROE	PSB	450	13.2502	11.4108	12.1930	14.3073	−00.3558	00.72
	PVB	288	13.5592	11.5757	12.2167	14.9018		
	Combined	738	13.3708	11.4686	12.5420	14.1996		
	Difference		−00.3090	–	−02.0150	01.3969		
NIM	PSB	450	02.7219	00.5735	02.6687	02.7750	−03.1232***	00.00
	PVB	288	02.8734	00.6836	02.7941	02.9527		
	Combined	738	02.7810	00.6227	02.7360	02.8260		
	Difference		−00.1515		−00.2468	−00.0562		

Source: Authors' calculation based on RBI (2019) data

PSB public sector banks, *PVB* private sector banks, *PM* performance measures, *Nob* no of observations, *SD* standard deviation

*, ** and *** denote significant at 10%, 5%, and 1% level

Table 19.4 Two-sample t-test for difference of mean for performance determinants of PSB and PVB (with unequal variance; unequal Welch)

PD	Bank Group	Nob	Mean	SD	95% Conf. Interval		t-stat	Prob
AST	PSB	450	11.3686	01.0822	11.2683	11.4689	14.4540***	00.00
	PVB	288	09.8584	01.5473	09.6790	10.0379		
	Combined	738	10.7793	01.4796	10.6723	10.8862		
	Difference		01.5101	–	01.3048	01.7154		
ASQ	PSB	450	54.9242	09.8871	54.0083	55.8402	−00.1718	00.86
	PVB	288	55.0409	08.3863	54.0683	56.0136		
	Combined	738	54.9698	09.3245	54.2959	55.6436		
	Difference		−00.1166	–	−01.4504	01.2170		
ASM	PSB	450	01.9176	00.6266	01.8595	01.9756	−04.8560***	00.00
	PVB	288	02.2071	00.8788	02.1052	02.3090		
	Combined	738	02.0306	00.7483	01.9765	02.0846		
	Difference		−00.2895	–	−00.4066	−00.1723		
OPE	PSB	450	73.6905	16.8432	72.1301	75.2510	−03.6586***	00.00
	PVB	288	80.3260	27.6724	77.1165	83.5355		
	Combined	738	76.2800	21.9437	74.6942	77.8658		
	Difference		−06.6354	–	−10.2003	−03.0706		
QAV	PSB	450	03.3802	03.2373	03.0802	03.6801	03.3822***	00.00
	PVB	288	02.6200	02.8004	02.2951	02.9448		
	Combined	738	03.0835	03.0946	02.8599	03.3071		
	Difference		00.7602	–	00.3188	01.2015		
CAR	PSB	450	12.1269	01.7869	11.9613	12.2924	−06.0643***	00.00
	PVB	288	13.9320	04.8450	13.3701	14.4940		
	Combined	738	12.8313	03.4443	12.5824	13.0802		
	Difference		−01.8051	–	−02.3906	−01.2196		

(continued)

Table 19.4 (continued)

PD	Bank Group	Nob	Mean	SD	95% Conf. Interval		*t*-stat	Prob
EMP	PSB	450	01.6892	00.8754	01.6081	01.7703	−00.8976	00.36
	PVB	288	01.7395	00.6445	01.6648	01.8143		
	Combined	738	01.7088	00.7932	01.6515	01.7662		
	Difference		−00.0503	–	−00.1604	00.0597		

Source: Authors' calculation based on RBI (2019) data
PSB public sector banks, *PVB* private sector banks, *PM* performance measures, *Nob* no of observations, *SD* standard deviation
*, ** and *** denote significant at 10%, 5%, and 1% level

$H_{03}{}^{d}$: ASM of PSBs and PVBs does not differ significantly.
$H_{13}{}^{d}$: ASM of PSBs and PVBs differs significantly.
$H_{04}{}^{d}$: OPE of PSBs and PVBs does not differ significantly.
$H_{14}{}^{d}$: OPE of PSBs and PVBs differs significantly.
$H_{05}{}^{d}$: QAV of PSBs and PVBs does not differ significantly.
$H_{15}{}^{d}$: QAV of PSBs and PVBs differs significantly.
$H_{06}{}^{d}$: CAR of PSBs and PVBs does not differ significantly.
$H_{16}{}^{d}$: CAR of PSBs and PVBs differs significantly.
$H_{07}{}^{d}$: EMP of PSBs and PVBs does not differ significantly.
$H_{17}{}^{d}$: EMP of PSBs and PVBs differs significantly.

Null hypotheses in Sects. 19.4.3.1 and 19.4.3.2 imply that the average value of the performance measures and determinants are the same for both public and private sector banks, while alternative hypotheses imply that the average values of measures and determinants are not the same for both bank groups. To test these hypotheses, we choose a confidence level of 95% (significance level of 5%), i.e., we are willing to accept a 5% probability of making a Type I error.

19.5 Results and Discussions

Tables 19.3 and 19.4 present the result of a two-sample *t*-test with unequal variances or Welch's *t*-test. Table 19.3 depicts that the average ROA of PSBs and PVBs is 0.73 and 1, respectively, with a difference of −0.27, and this difference is significant at the 1% level. This rejects the null hypothesis $H_{01}{}^{m}$. Thus, PVBs earn higher net profit per unit of assets compared to PSBs during the period under consideration. Moreover, PVBs average ROA meets the international standard of greater than 1% (Singh et al. 2016), but PSBs fail to achieve this as the result suggests. It is also evident from the table that there is not much difference between the mean ROE of both types of banks, and this difference is not significant at all. This leads to the conclusion that the ratio of net profit to the sum total of capital, reserves, and surplus does not significantly differ between PSBs and PVBs. In the case of NIM, PVBs are on top compared to PSBs, and this difference is highly significant, as is clear from Table 19.3. That $H_{03}{}^{m}$ is rejected reveals the fact that net interest incomes per unit of assets significantly differ between these two types of banks, and the higher average NIM value of PVBs in comparison to PSBs signifies that the former earns higher net interest income per unit of assets compared to the latter. Thus, it can be concluded that with respect to ROA and NIM, public-sector banks lag behind private-sector banks, but in the case of ROE these two types of banks do not significantly differ.

The reasons for this difference in performance are obvious if we glance at Table 19.4. It is apparent from the table that PSBs have higher average assets compared to PVBs during the study period, and this difference is highly significant. This leads to the rejection of $H_{01}{}^{d}$. The advance-to-asset ratio (ASQ) for PVBs (55.04) is slightly higher than PSBs (54.92), but this difference (−0.11) is not at all significant. PVBs are seen to earn higher (2.20) average operating profit per unit of the asset (ASM) than PSBs (1.91), and there is a significant difference in the asset management done by these two types of banks. Rejection of $H_{03}{}^{d}$ implies that PVBs manage their assets in a better way to fetch greater operating profits than the PSBs. Private sector banks, as is seen from the table, incur much-operating expenses per unit of net interest earned (OPE), and this difference is significant, the result shows. This rejects $H_{04}{}^{d}$ implying a higher operating efficiency of PSBs compared to their private counterparts.

One fundamental issue that can be ascribed to the difference in the performance of PSBs and PVBs is the volume of stressed assets (RBI 2018). It is seen from the table that the average net NPA and net advance ratio (QAV) of PVBs (2.62) are far less than the PSBs (3.38), and this difference is highly significant. This rejects the null hypothesis $H_{05}{}^{d}$. It pictures the fact that the loan quality of PSBs is inferior in a significant manner compared to PVBs. The result finds support in Ramesh (2019) and Rahaman and Sur (2021). The capitals to risk-weighted assets of PVBs are also seen to be better compared to PSBs (Kaur and Sukhija 2018), and this difference is significant as a result indicates. The average capital adequacy ratio of PVBs is 13.93, whereas it is 12.12 for PSBs. One crucial point is that during the period under consideration, both public sector banks and private sector banks maintained a CAR that is higher than 8% as stipulated in BASEL III norms. Besides, PSBs and PVBs maintained an average capital adequacy ratio as demanded by RBI for public sector banks (12%) in connection with BASEL III norms. However, the private sector banks maintained an average CAR of 13.93, which is much higher than expected by RBI (9%) from them. This fact presents a healthy state of affairs with regard to capital adequacy for scheduled commercial banks in India during the period under consideration.

Business per employee (EMP), defined as the ratio of the total number of employees to the combined sum of the deposit plus advance, is higher for PVBs compared to PSBs. Though the difference in the average value of EMP between the two types of banks is not significant, the higher mean value of EMP for PVBs signifies that the private bank employees may be more aggressive in fetching business than the employees of PSBs. There might be a variety of reasons for this difference. The difference in the average age of employees, cost per employee, work environment, the attitude of the management, etc., might cause a variation in EMP between PSBs and PVBs.

19.6 Practical and Social Implications

Estimation results suggest that Indian private sector banks (PVBs) have shown better performance than the public sector banks (PSBs) during the study period. In the measures of performance (ROA, NIM), private sector banks outperform public-sector banks. As regards bank-specific determinants, the results indicate that PVBs functioned better with regard to asset management (ASM), quality of advance (QAV), and capital adequacy ratio (CAR) in comparison to PSBs during the study period. However, with respect to asset size, PSBs are in a better position compared to PVBs. Though the mean difference with respect to asset quality (ASQ) and employees performance (EMP) is not significant between PSBs and PVBs, the latter achieved a higher average value in these two parameters compared to the former. From this, it might be ascertained that the relatively better performance of private sector banks can be attributed to their capacity to earn higher operating profit per unit of assets, maintain nonperforming assets at a level lower than public sector banks, maintain a higher capital with respect to risk-weighted assets, earning higher business per employee and managing assets in a little better way in comparison to other bank groups.

The results arrived here entail immense practical and social implications specifically for those who believe that the private sector signifies the mark of efficiency. If we consider the results only, then there may be sufficient reason for the supporters of privatization to have ecstasy. But when the banking sector is considered as a whole, the results do not picture the whole truth. In India, public sector banks since the time of nationalization are not solely guided by the idea of profit maximization like private sector banks (Bajaj et al. 2021) but also discharge a host of responsibilities to meet the requirements of a welfare state. Public sector banks have shouldered important responsibilities for the growth and development of this country. Extension of banking network to the remotest, in most cases unprofitable regions (Sarkar and Rakshit 2021), providing advances to the priority sector, and implementation of different welfare schemes announced by the government at different times, are some of the areas where public sector banks have done havoc. Bajaj et al. (2021) find that priority sector loans (PSL) for public sector banks exert a significant impact on the generation of NPA, and the coefficient between NPA and PSL is much higher for PSBs compared to private sector banks. Thus, public sector banks in India should not be judged in terms of profit only, but their performance should be evaluated on a wider social canvas, keeping into consideration a varied range of unprofitable activities they perform for the development of the nation. Private banks may outperform public sector banks in different measures of performance, but this in no way can be a compelling reason for taking the decision of bank privatization. Public sector banks are not only playing a pivotal role in meeting social responsibilities but also represent the trust and confidence of millions of common Indian citizens. Thus, irrespective of the results obtained, there is no reason to embark on rampant privatization specifically for the banking sector of this country.

19.7 Conclusions

The results obtained in this analysis have profound implications for the Indian banking system. The observations convey an important signal to the central bank and also to the planners and policymakers. In a country like India, where the market has weak predictive power regarding banking stress (RBI 2018), these results might be immensely useful in devising appropriate policy measures for the banking sector.

The result, as obtained in this analysis, demands PSBs for efficient management of assets, reduction in the volume of stressed assets, enhancement of quality of assets and advance, diminution of cost, and augmentation of business per employee. Though there is a significant difference in performance between PSBs and PVBs the role of the former should not be squeezed for the greater interest of the economy. Instead, effective steps should be taken to strengthen public sector banks. The steps taken by the government through insolvency and bankruptcy code (IBCs), recapitalization, etc., may prove to be effective for the public sector banks. At the same time, it should be mentioned that there should be healthy competition between different types of banks, and public sector banks should strive to set a leading role not only in respect of performance but also in discharging other social responsibilities in commensuration to the objectives of a welfare state.

References

Albulescu CT (2015) Banks' profitability and financial soundness indicators: a macro-level investigation in emerging countries. Proced Econ Financ 23:203–209

Alemu M, Aweke M (2017) Financial performance analysis of private commercial banks of Ethiopia: CAMEL ratings. Int J Sci Res Publ 7(10):367–395

Al-Homaidi EA, Tabash MI, Farhan NH, Almaqtari FA (2018) Bank-specific and macro-economic determinants of profitability of Indian commercial banks: a panel data approach. Cogent Econ Financ 6(1):1548072

Almaqtari FA, Al-Homaidi EA, Tabash MI, Farhan NH (2019) The determinants of profitability of Indian commercial banks: a panel data approach. Int J Financ Econ 24(1):168–185

Alshatti AS (2016) Determinants of banks' profitability—the case of Jordan. Invest Manag Financ Innov 13(1):84–91

Anbar A, Alper D (2011) Bank specific and macroeconomic determinants of commercial bank profitability: empirical evidence from Turkey. Bus Econ Res J 2(2):139–152

Athanasoglou PP, Brissimis SN, Delis MD (2008) Bank-specific, industry-specific and macroeconomic determinants of bank profitability. J Int Financ Mark Inst Money 18(2):121–136

Bajaj RV, Sanati G, Lodha C (2021) Impact assessment study of NPAs and rate of recovery: are private sector banks in India better off? Glob Bus Rev 2021:0972150920980305

Bhattacharyya A, Lovell CK, Sahay P (1997) The impact of liberalization on the productive efficiency of Indian commercial banks. Eur J Oper Res 98(2):332–345

Brahmaiah B (2018) Factors influencing profitability of banks in India. Theor Econ Lett 8(14):3046

Caporale GM, Lodh S, Nandy M (2017) The performance of banks in the MENA region during the global financial crisis. Res Int Bus Finance 42:583–590

Căpraru B, Ihnatov I (2014) Banks' profitability in selected central and eastern European countries. Proced Econ Finance 16:587–591

Curak M, Poposki K, Pepur S (2012) Profitability determinants of the Macedonian banking sector in changing environment. Proced Soc Behav Sci 44:406–416

Demirgüç-Kunt A, Huizinga H (1999) Determinants of commercial bank interest margins and profitability: some international evidence. World Bank Econ Rev 13(2):379–408

Dietrich A, Wanzenried G (2011) Determinants of bank profitability before and during the crisis: evidence from Switzerland. J Int Financ Mark Inst Money 21(3):307–327

Dietrich A, Wanzenried G (2014) The determinants of commercial banking profitability in low-, middle-, and high-income countries. Q Rev Econ Finance 54(3):337–354

Ebenezer OO, Omar WAWB, Kamil S (2017) Bank specific and macroeconomic determinants of commercial bank profitability: empirical evidence from Nigeria. Int J Financ Bank Stud 6(1):25
Flamini V, McDonald CA, Schumacher LB (2009) The determinants of commercial bank profitability in Sub-Saharan Africa. International Monetary Fund, Washington, DC
Goswami R, Hussain F, Kumar M (2019) Banking efficiency determinants in India: a two-stage analysis. Margin J Appl Econ Res 13(4):361–380
Gupta N, Mahakud J (2020) Ownership, bank size, capitalization and bank performance: evidence from India. Cogent Econ Financ 8(1):1808282
Kassem NM, Sakr A (2018) The impact of bank-specific characteristics on the profitability of commercial banks in Egypt. J Finance Bank Manag 6(2):76–90
Kaur R, Sukhija S (2018) A Comparative Study on the Performance of Selected Public Sector and Private Sector Banks In India. International Journal of Management Studies 82–92
Le TD, Ngo T (2020) The determinants of bank profitability: a cross-country analysis. Cent Bank Rev 20(2):65–73
Menicucci E, Paolucci G (2016) Factors affecting bank profitability in Europe: an empirical investigation. Afr J Bus Manag 10(17):410–420
Moser BK, Stevens GR (1992) Homogeneity of variance in the two-sample means test. Am Stat 46(1):19–21
Ongore VO, Kusa GB (2013) Determinants of financial performance of commercial banks in Kenya. Int J Econ Financ Issues 3(1):237–252
Pasiouras F, Kosmidou K (2007) Factors influencing the profitability of domestic and foreign commercial banks in the European Union. Res Int Bus Finance 21(2):222–237
Petria N, Capraru B, Ihnatov I (2015) Determinants of banks' profitability: evidence from EU 27 banking systems. Proced Econ Finance 20:518–524
Pramahender (2021) Critical perspectives to nonperforming assets of Indian banks, shrinking balance sheet, challenges and way ahead. FIIB Bus Rev 11(2):130–136
Rahaman SM, Sur D (2021) Identifying key drivers of nonperforming assets in Indian public sector banks: a panel data analysis. IIM Kozhikode Soc Manag Rev 2021:22779752211000146
Ramesh K (2019) Bad loans of public sector banks in India: a panel data study. Emerg Econ Stud 5(1):22–30
Rashid A, Jabeen S (2016) Analyzing performance determinants: conventional versus Islamic banks in Pakistan. Borsa Istanbul Rev 16(2):92–107
Rautela P, Sarkar MP, Goel R (2021) Factors affecting the outsourcing activities in public and private sector banks in India. FIIB Bus Rev 2021:23197145211053163
RBI (2008) Report on trend and progress of banking in India 2007–2008
RBI (2009) Report on trend and progress of banking in India 2008–2009
RBI (2018) Report on trend and progress of banking in India 2017–2018
RBI (2019) Report on trend and progress of banking in India 2018–2019
Robin I, Salim R, Bloch H (2018) Financial performance of commercial banks in the post-reform-era: further evidence from Bangladesh. Econ Anal Policy 58:43–54
Ruxton GD (2006) The unequal variance *t*-test is an underused alternative to Student's *t*-test and the Mann–Whitney *U* test. Behav Ecol 17(4):688–690
Saeed MS (2014) Bank-related, industry-related and macroeconomic factors affecting bank profitability: a case of the United Kingdom. Res J Finance Account 5(2):42–50
Sanderson A, Le Roux P (2016) Determinants of banking sector profitability in Zimbabwe. Int J Econ Financ Issues 6(3):845–854
Sarkar S, Rakshit D (2021) Factors influencing the performance of commercial banks: a dynamic panel study on India. FIIB Bus Rev 12(1):85–99
Satterthwaite FE (1946) An approximate distribution of estimates of variance components. Biom Bull 2(6):110–114
Schumpeter JA (1934) The theory of economic development, translated by Redvers Opie. Harvard Econ Stud 46(1600):0404

Seenaiah K, Rath BN, Samantaraya A (2015) Determinants of bank profitability in the post-reform period: evidence from India. Glob Bus Rev 16(5_suppl):82S–92S

Singh S, Sidhu J, Joshi M, Kansal M (2016) Measuring intellectual capital performance of Indian banks: a public and private sector comparison. Manag Finance 42(7):635–655

Srinivasan P, Britto J (2017) Analysis of financial performance of selected commercial banks in India. Theor Econ Lett 7(7):2134–2151

Sufian F (2009) Factors influencing bank profitability in a developing economy: empirical evidence from Malaysia. Glob Bus Rev 10(2):225–241

Tan Y (2016) The impacts of risk and competition on bank profitability in China. J Int Financ Mark Inst Money 40:85–110

Titko J, Skvarciany V, Jurevičienė D (2015) Drivers of bank profitability: case of Latvia and Lithuania. Intellect Econ 9(2):120–129

Yahya AT, Akhtar A, Tabash MI (2017) The impact of political instability, macroeconomic and bank-specific factors on the profitability of Islamic banks: empirical evidence. Invest Manag Financ Innov 14(4):30–39

Yao H, Haris M, Tariq G (2018) Profitability determinants of financial institutions: evidence from banks in Pakistan. Int J Financ Stud 6(2):53

Sreemanta Sarkar is an Associate Professor of Economics, Bidhan Chandra College, affiliated to the Kazi Nazrul University, Asansol, West Bengal, India. Sreemanta Sarkar also serves as the Coordinator of the Undergraduate Studies in Economics of the Kazi Nazrul University. Associate Professor, Sarkar serves as an editorial board member of The Indian Economic Journal. Mr. Sarkar is also a verified reviewer of several Sage Journals. Mr. Sarkar completed his graduation and post-graduation from the Visva-Bharati, a central university, and stood first in both B.A. (Honors) examination and M.A. examination. Mr. Sarkar has completed a UGC minor research project in economics and has several publications in national and international journals. Mr. Sarkar has been teaching Economics at the undergraduate level since the year 2000. His areas of interest include banking and finance, gender issues, economics of education, and environmental economics.

Prof. (Dr.) Debdas Rakshit is currently serving as a Professor of the Department of Commerce, the University of Burdwan, West Bengal, India. Having over 19 years of teaching experience at the post-graduate level and 5 years of industry experience, Dr. Rakshit is also a fellow of the Institute of Cost accountants of India. He stood first class second in M.Com. examination and also obtained his ICWA degree from the Institute of Cost accountants of India in 1994. He has 110 research papers, published in national and international journals, and 5 books to his credit. Prof. Rakshit has supervised 13 doctoral scholars and 5 M.Phil. students till date. Prof. Rakshit's areas of interest include Corporate Restructuring, Financial Statement Analysis, Corporate Performance Management, Banking and Finance, etc.

Dr. Madhabendra Sinha is an Assistant Professor at the Department of Economics and Politics, Visva-Bharati (A Central University), Santiniketan, India; and prior to that he served as an Assistant Professor at the Department of Business Administration, Raiganj University, India. He has been a Senior Research Fellow and PhD in Economics at the National Institute of Technology Durgapur, India. He obtained M.Sc. and M.Phil. in Economics from the University of Calcutta, India, and qualified UGC-NET in Economics. His research interests include open economy economics, development economics, and applied econometrics. He has credits of a couple of research publications in several reputed journals including Journal of Policy Modeling (Elsevier), Social Indicators Research (Springer), Economic Papers (Wiley), Global Business Review (Sage), Applied Intelligence (Springer), Margin: JAER (Sage), Journal of Asian and African Studies (Sage), IJEED (Inderscience), etc. He contributed a number of book chapters published by Springer, Routledge, Emerald, IGI Global, etc. He has participated in several workshops and presented research papers in various conferences and seminars organized by ADBI, IGC, IITs, IIMs, ISI, DSE, IIFT, BIBM and UNCDF, RIS-EXIM Bank, etc. in India, Japan, France, and other countries. He acted as reviewer of different journals published by Taylor & Francis, Wiley, Emerald and Sage. He organized a number of workshops and seminars on research methodology and other issues and gave invited lectures in different universities.

Chapter 20
Elite Capture or Good Governance? Social Security Entitlements in the Coal Mining Region of Jharkhand in India

Arun Kumar Yadav and Vidya Yadav

20.1 Introduction

Despite ongoing worldwide attempts for sustainable economic growth, poverty remains a persistent developmental challenge. In its millennium declaration, the United Nation made "eradicating poverty and hunger" as a top priority. However, due to the incomplete poverty target, it has re-included as a top priority in the UN Sustainable Development Agenda in order to ensure adequate monitoring of "poverty-eradication global government efforts" (United Nations 2016). As a consequence, governments around the world are constantly restructuring their economies in order to control it (United Nations 2003). Simultaneously, government introduces new social assistance programs or strengthening their existing social safety nets to develop the individual resilience capacity of marginalized social sections under good governance approach (The World Bank Group 2015). The *social safety net* is a necessary government-sponsored targeted intervention program that protect an individual or household from two types of negative poverty outcomes (Ghosh 2002; Rogers and Coates 2002), namely, chronic poverty and transient poverty. Chronic poverty results from a permanent inability to work caused by life-cycle events, whereas transient poverty results from a decline in the ability to earn from a marginal status caused by adverse economic circumstances (Subbarao et al. 1997; Devereux 2002).

Article 22 of the Universal Declaration of Human Rights (UDHR) encourages the formation of a social safety net (United Nations 1949). Empirical research reveals

A. K. Yadav
Monitoring and Evaluation (M&E) Office, Patna, Bihar, India

V. Yadav (✉)
Department of Geography, College of Commerce, Arts and Science, Patliputra University, Patna, Bihar, India

M. Mishra et al. (eds.), *Public Policies and Sustainable Development in Post-Reform India*, New Frontiers in Regional Science: Asian Perspectives 71,
https://doi.org/10.1007/978-981-99-3696-0_20

that in the absence of a social safety net, the poor are forced to adjust their production and consumption behavior, focusing on risk avoidance rather than increasing their earnings. As a result, ensuring social security benefits to needy individuals with proper identification is important for their well-being (Subbarao et al. 1997). Moreover, it is necessary to distinguish between the poor and the non-poor to avoid disparities in benefit distribution. However, unequal access to the social safety net among entitled individuals, as well as benefit leakage to fake beneficiaries, appear as the main obstacles for the government in eradicating poverty. Access to safety benefits may vary depending on personal variables such as age, gender, education status, health status, employment status, income level, political and religious affiliation, personal history and personality, family networks, household landholding, and so on (Dasgupta and Beard 2007).

Previous study shows that dominant groups deliberately manipulate administrative decisions to exploite weakness of less powerful groups in order to gain benefits/entitlements; this phenomenon is known as *elite capture* (Dutta 2009; Wong 2010). Elites are usually influential local people who use their intricate networks to persuade the community and national administration to make decisions in their favor (Bardhan and Mookherjee 2000). The influence of elites on the distribution of social benefits is usually a continuous process that can be observed from both a temporal and a spatial perspective (Higley and Burton 2006; Wong 2010). This phenomenon extends beyond the boundaries of the community and typically distributes the benefits to their followers (Hossain 2008). The elite capture of the social safety net is a common phenomenon in developing countries such as India (Duflo et al. 2005; Panda 2015). However, the phenomena of elite capture vary depending on regional socioeconomic and administrative contexts (Rasul and Sharma 2014). Drèze and Khera (2005) found in their study that leakages in the public distribution system (PDS) are generally low in better-off states such as Tamil Nadu and Himachal Pradesh but relatively high in disadvantageous states such as Jharkhand, Uttar Pradesh, and so on.

It has been empirically proven that resourceful regions are more disadvantageous in every aspect, this phenomenon known as the "Resource curse syndrome" (Dutt 2007; Maconachie and Binns 2007). Dhanbad (Jharkhand) is India's most resourceful region due to its significant contribution in coal exploration, it regarded as the "Coal Capital of India." Coal mining is going on in this area since decades and over the time it brings significant changes in its socioeconomic and administrative settings. Yet, this area is recognized as one of the countries' 250 most backward districts out of a total of 640 (GoI 2007). Centre for Science and Environment (CSE 2009) stated in its study that the backwardness of the district is caused by its high level of economic dependence on minerals, which has slowed the economic performance of the region. As a result, the majority of the poor people are concentrated around mines. The failure of poverty reduction programs in this area is due to a lack of proper measures to identify the impoverished people and inequity in the reach of services to them (Bhandari and Chakraborty 2015).

In general, all welfarist schemes directly contribute to the well-being of the 526 million (55%) poor of India (IANS 2015). But explicitly, four direct benefits transfer (DBT) schemes that are always in the spotlight due to coverage gaps or leakage and their associated effects on household well-being are as Ration card,[1] Pradhan Mantri Jan-Dhan Yojana (PMJDY),[2] Mahatma Gandhi National Rural Employment Guarantee Act (MGNREGA),[3] and Rashtriya Swasthya Bima Yojana (RSBY 2008).[4]

Despite the fact that all of the aforementioned social safety schemes are implemented throughout the country, it is especially important in mine-affected areas due to its associated vulnerability. Schemes targeting the proximate population with intention to assist them in escaping from a vicious cycle of poverty (CSE 2009). Hence, the study hypothesizes that households in mine-affected areas make intensive use of all types of social security programs. However, there has been a dearth of specific studies that shows a comparative picture as well as a comprehensive assessment of coverage and leakages of schemes in India. As a result, it becomes necessary to comprehend its comparative utilization scenario between both residential settings (i.e., Mines affected villages and Non-mines affected villages), as well as

[1]Food security scheme: This scheme is currently being implemented with the help of Below Poverty Line (BPL) cards, Antyodaya Anna Yojana (AAY) cards, and Above Poverty Line (APL) cards. The government issued this card based on the household's financial situation. The household's economic cut-off point is defined by the poverty line, which is updated on a regular basis by the government. This system functions as a single-window system for providing subsidies on prescribed food and fuel goods to poor and poorest households at different subsidized rates (PDS 1997). However, it is estimated that approximately 30% of benefits are diverted to non-eligible households (Drèze and Khera 2005).

[2]Economic security scheme: Pradhan Mantri Jan-Dhan Yojana (PMJDY) initiatives are a financial inclusion program with an integrated approach to providing saving instruments and infrastructural support for DBT to marginalized sections of society. The strategy envisions universal banking access, with at least one primary banking account for each household, financial literacy, access to credit, insurance, and pension facilities. In addition, the beneficiaries would receive a RuPay Debit card with built-in life (Rs. 30,000) and accident (Rs. 1 lakh) insurance, as well as a Rs. 5000 overdraft facility (Guha 2015; PMJDY 2016). The government intends to utilize this tool to track the leakage of welfare funds. However, a recent study has found that it is widely used for cleaning up black money following demonetization (Dutta and Das 2017).

[3]Income generation security scheme: The Mahatma Gandhi National Rural Employment Guarantee Act (MGNREGA) is a law enacted plan that provides unskilled willing laborers with an entitlement to 100 days of guaranteed employment every year. This system, which was implemented in 2005, is regarded as the most innovative scheme for developing countries. Because MGNREGA is fundamentally a demand-driven program, employment is provided to needy workers upon request within 15 days. One distinguishing feature of MGNREGA is that it provides a fair opportunity for the rural population to earn income without regard to caste or gender (MoLJ 2005). But it was estimated that around 50% of benefits leak to the unentitled households (Financial Express 2017).

[4]Income generation security scheme: The Mahatma Gandhi National Rural Employment Guarantee Act (MGNREGA) is a law enacted plan that provides unskilled willing laborers with an entitlement to 100 days of guaranteed employment every year. This system, which was implemented in 2005, is regarded as the most innovative scheme for developing countries. Because MGNREGA is fundamentally a demand-driven program, employment is provided to needy workers upon request within 15 days. One distinguishing feature of MGNREGA is that it provides a fair opportunity for the rural population to earn income without regard to caste or gender (MoLJ 2005). But it was estimated that around 50% of benefits leak to the unentitled households (Financial Express 2017).

who is more unfavorable in terms of utilizing social security systems. Who is more likely to benefit from these programs? Is education helpful in obtaining entitlements in the mining region? In light of the above circumstances, current study is carried out with twofold objectives: first, to examine the level and pattern of social security schemes, and second, to investigate the determinants of social security entitlements across households.

20.2 Methods

20.2.1 Study Setting and its Location

Data for the study were collected from Baghmara block of Dhanbad district, Jharkhand, India, during September 2014–February 2015. It is the only block in the Dhanbad district where 33 out of 71 panchayats having a coal-bearing capability and primarily mines operated by Bharat Coking Coal Limited (BCCL). This geographical variation and homogeneity in the mining operation within the block enables a scope of cross-sectional comparative study in the area. Furthermore, according to the Census of India (2011), this block's demographic and socioeconomic features suggest that 33.4% of the total population of 334,309 live in urban areas. The Hindus make up the vast majority of its people (87.5%), followed by Muslims (10.6%). The caste composition of this block reveals that the SC/ST community accounts for 26% of the population. The working-age population accounts for about 39.5% of the population, with the remainder made up of dependents aged 0–15 and 60 and older (see Fig. 20.1).

20.2.2 Sample Group

Initially, the study selected four mines affected villages; this selection was conducted using multilevel sampling technique. Firstly, the study made a list of mines affected 34 villages based on provided information by BCCL till the year 2014. Secondly, in order to assess the current status of villages, the study compared this village list with village-level data opted from the Census of India (2011). The matching exercise between both the village list was done keeping in mind that mining operations can result in the extinction of villages or the change of villages to cities with administrative status. After matching exercise only 20 out of the 34 villages were found to still be in existence. The list of existing 20 villages was then categorized according to mining technique as open-cast mines affected (5), underground mines affected (12), and discontinued mines affected villages (3). Later, this study limited to the villages affected by open-cast mining and underground mining only. Using the probability proportional to size (PPS) sampling technique, study choose two villages from each category (for a total of four mining-affected villages).

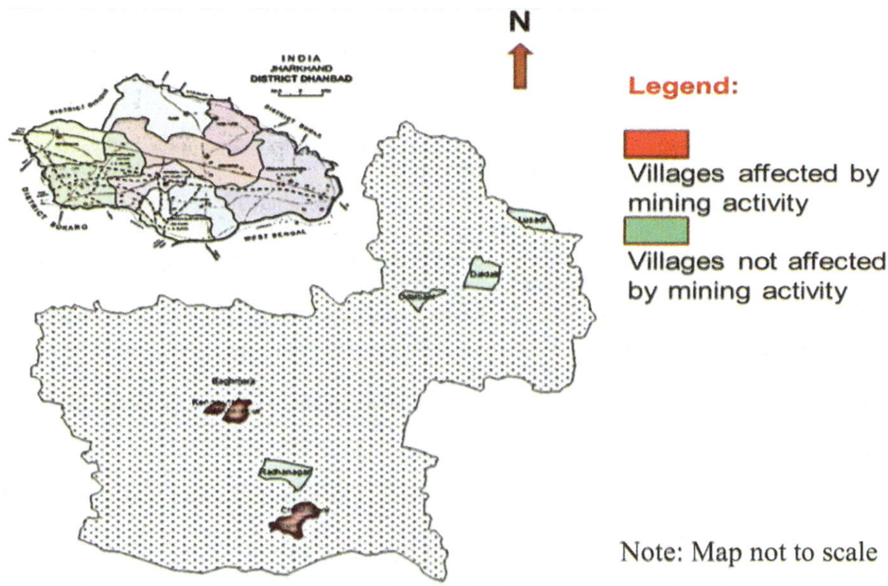

Fig. 20.1 Selected study villages in Baghmara block, Dhanbad, India 2015 (Source: Prepared by the authors)

After the selection of mines affected village study choose four non-mines affected villages based on two criteria: firstly, the villages must be located at least 5 km (aerial distance) away from coal mines. Secondly, the villages should have a similar percentage of the scheduled caste (SC) population cross ponding to mines affected villages.

Following the selection of eight villages, the sampling frame was created through mapping and listing exercises of all households. A pre-determined quota of 52 households sampled was questioned from each village using systematic random sampling from the sampling frame of a village. As a result, the study acquired complete data of 416 households (see Table 20.1).

20.2.3 Data Collection

Study adopted concurrent approach of data collection for quantitative and qualitative information related with social security schemes (SSS) (namely, PMJDY, BPL, MGNREGA, and RSBY) from both the residential settings. The survey instrument was designed to be suitable for the local environment. As a result, it was translated from English to Hindi. The survey instrument was pre-tested with 30 household samples to ensure its applicability. After making all necessary changes based on inputs received during pilot survey related with data forms for accuracy, consistency,

Table 20.1 Hierarchical flowchart for sample selection

Selection	Study area	Criteria/rationale
State	Jharkhand	State affected profoundly by coal mining activities in the country
District	Dhanbad	Known as the coal capital of India due to the highest production of coal
Block	Baghmara	Nearly one-half panchayats of the block have the coal-bearing capacity
Village	4 mining-affected villages	Two affected villages each from the underground and open-cast mining categories
	4 non-mining affected villages	Selected corresponding to mining-affected villages based on the criteria of distance from coal mines and proportion of SC population
Household	52 HH/village	Systematic random sampling based on a sampling frame
Total sample size 416		

Source: Prepared by the authors

and its completeness, researcher conducted the main survey. After the completion of fieldwork important data checks are performed to ensure data quality and, where necessary, the researcher performed extra field visits to clarify data entries. The data was also recorded into the CSPro 6.1 (The Census and Survey Processing System) database, which was developed and supported by the United States Census Bureau and ICF Macro. The quantitative data were analyzed using STATA 14.1 software package.

20.2.4 Ethical Aspects

The study was approved by the International Institute for Population Sciences (IIPS) Students Research Ethics Committee (SREC) in Mumbai, India. The methodological, technical, and ethical soundness of the study were all evaluated by the ethics committee. In addition, prior to conducting the interviews, the study sought informed consent from all participants and assured them of confidentiality.

20.2.5 Outcome

Respondents were questioned about their access and utilization of several social security programs, such as does the household utilize any type of ration card? If so, what kind of ration cards does your family have? For the purpose of analysis, the ration cards associated with BPL and AAY were computed jointly. Is there anyone in the family who has an MGNREGA employment card? Is there anyone in the family that has an RSBY card? Is it possible for any member of a household to open a bank account under PMJDY? Each of the four outcomes in our studies was operationalized as dichotomous (yes/no) variables. Furthermore, using the above information on social security scheme utilization, interaction variables have developed for all-card, to see the amount of utilization of all schemes per household.

20.2.6 Independent Variables

Household heads specified whether they were "male" or "female." Their ages were divided into three groups: 21–34, 35–54, and 55 and older. Caste was also labelled as Scheduled Caste (SC)/Scheduled Tribe (ST), Other Backward Caste (OBC), and General caste. The employment status divided into two categories: regular salaried jobs and irregular salaried jobs. The education level year of schooling of the household head dichotomized as "illiterate" or "literate." Secondly, the presence of a matriculated member in the household dichotomized as "Yes" or "No." The household size divided into three categories: 0–3 members, 4–5 members, and 6 or more members. Farmland sizes are classified as no land, less than 2 acres, and more than 2 acres. Monthly Per Capita Expenditure (MPCE) is divided into three categories: low, medium, and high. The village type is distinguished as mines affected villages and Non-mines affected villages. Other variables that included in the study as a dichotomous form are easy access to local political leaders, membership in a socio-political organization and food security.

20.2.7 Methods

Data analysis plan initiated using bivariate analyses that performed to assess the level of utilization of various social security schemes (SSSs) in households from mines affected and non-mines affected villages. Furthermore, the utilization pattern of SSSs were assessed based on selected household heads and household characteristics. Following that, the concentration index (CI) value of SSSs was computed against monthly per capita expenditure (MPCE) in order to quantify and compare the level of concentration of SSS between both residential settings. The CI value is limited between -1 and 1, and if there is no inequality, the index value will be zero. If the index value is negative, it will be above the line of equality, indicating a disproportionate concentration of the poor in the social security system. In contrast, if a positive result is obtained, the curve will be located below the line of equality (Erreygers 2009).

Furthermore, multiple logistic regression methods were carried out to determine the relationship between different social security schemes and explanatory variables such as household demographic, social and economic characteristics. The logit relationship describes how predictor X was a constant effect on the likelihood of one outcome occurring. It was interpreted in terms of the odds ratio. Moreover, on the basis of different logit regression study tried to estimate predicted the probability of the utilization of different schemes by different caste groups and MPCE rank.

20.3 Results

The bar graph (Figure 20.2) reveals the level of utilization of different SSSs between mine-affected and non-mines affected villages. PMJDY, BPL, and MGNREGA schemes were used more frequently by households in non-mines affected villages by 5%, 4%, and 2%, respectively compare to its counterpart. In contrast, a household from a mine-affected village used the RSBY scheme 2% higher than its counterpart. However, there were no significant differences in the use of all types of cards in both the residential settings. At the 5% level of significance, the chi-square results shows that there is no significant association between village type and social security schemes. The findings contradict the study hypothesis that households in mine-affected villages use all types of social security schemes more intensively compared to households from non-mine-affected villages.

Further, research on banking services extend the findings that prior to initiation of the PMJDY program, level of bank account holding were only 46% in non-mines-affected villages and 53% in mines-affected villages. But, after induction of this scheme, bank account holding level increased by 64% in non-mine-affected villages and 61% in mines-affected villages. Likewise, now actual bank account holding levels are increasing in both residential settings as non-mines affected and mines affected villages by 83% and 86%, respectively.

The utilization pattern of different SSSs by socio-demographic status of household head shows in Table 20.2. The household of SC/ST cast group were utilizing all type of SSSs cards higher (5.4%) compare to other caste groups followed by general caste. Male household heads used slightly higher percent of all the schemes card than

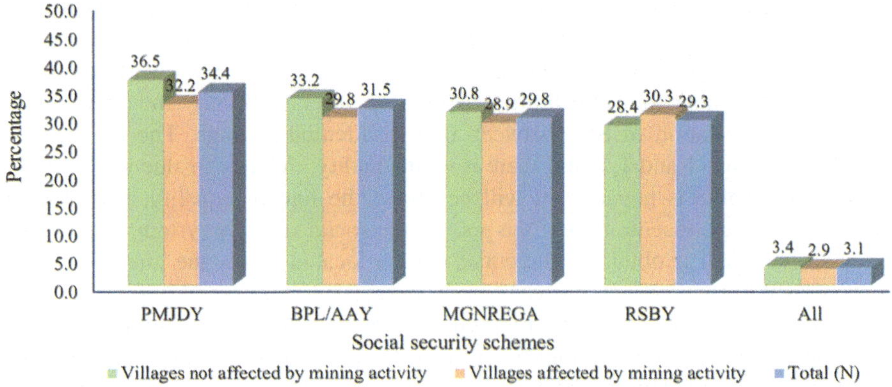

Fig. 20.2 Level of social security scheme in Dhanbad, India 2015 (Source: Prepared by the authors)

Table 20.2 Percentage utilization of different social security schemes by household head characteristics in Dhanbad, India 2015

Schemes	PMJDY	BPL	MGNREGA	RSBY	All
Social group					
SC/ST	41.9	39.1	38.0	28.8	5.4
OBC	30.4	28.5	27.2	34.2	0.6
Forward caste (general)	24.3	18.9	14.9	20.3	2.7
Gender					
Male	33.2	31.6	29.5	29.8	3.2
Female	44.2	30.2	32.6	25.6	2.3
Age of head of household					
21–34 age	38.7	22.7	32.0	18.7	4.0
35–54 age	37.0	35.1	33.2	36.0	3.3
55+ age	27.7	30.8	23.1	24.6	2.3
Educational status					
Illiterate	38.1	44.9	42.4	37.3	5.1
Literate	32.9	26.2	24.8	26.8	2.4
Easily access to local political leader	36.3	67.4	38.5	31.1	7.4
Membership of any socio-political organization	34.1	52.5	34.6	28.5	5.6
Total (*N*)	**34.4 (143)**	**31.5 (131)**	**29.8 (124)**	**29.3 (122)**	**3.1 (13)**

Source: Primary data collected during fieldwork by the author

the female headed households. The younger household head age group 21–34 years, followed by the 35–54 years age group's used schemes comparatively higher as 4% and 3% respectively. The illiterate household head used more all type of schemes than the literate counterpart. Household heads who had easy access to local political leaders used all of the schemes (7%) more than the others. Similarly, those household heads who were members of any social-political organization utilize all type of schemes (6%) more than the others.

Table 20.3 shows the utilization pattern of different SSSs by household characteristics. Household having 4–5 members used comparatively more all type of SSSs, followed by 6+ member households and 1–3-member households by 5%, 1.5%, and 1%, respectively. Only 2% of households with at least one matriculated member used all schemes. Food insecure households, landless households, and low MPCE class households used all type of schemes higher than their counterparts.

Table 20.4 the negative CI value indicates about disproportionate concentration of most of the social security schemes among the low income households. The CI values of different schemes did not showing a consistent pro-poor distribution across households of mine-affected villages. However, BPL and MGNERGA scheme utilization CI values show significantly (p value 0.01) concentration towards low income household of mines affected villages.

Further, in order to identify the prominent determinants of schemes utilization multiple logistic regressions were conducted using selected background

Table 20.3 Percentage utilization of different social security schemes by household characteristics, Dhanbad, India 2015

Schemes	PMJDY	BPL	MGNREGA	RSBY	All
Household size					
1–3 members	34.3	30.0	17.1	20.0	1.4
4–5 members	34.9	30.1	33.5	30.6	4.8
More than 6 members	33.6	34.3	30.7	32.1	1.5
Matriculated member household	32.5	25.7	29.1	27.9	1.9
Food shortage	40.3	44.5	38.7	31.9	4.7
Farmland status					
No land	38.1	30.7	31.8	29.6	4.6
Less than 2 acres	35.3	34.1	32.4	30.1	2.3
More than 2 acres	22.4	26.9	17.9	26.9	1.5
Regular salary job	26.6	13.8	19.2	33.0	2.1
MPCE					
Low	34.5	44.6	36.7	30.9	5.0
Middle	43.2	33.8	30.2	28.1	2.9
High	25.4	15.9	22.5	29.0	1.5
Total (*N*)	**34.4 (143)**	**31.5 (131)**	**29.8 (124)**	**29.3 (122)**	**3.1 (13)**

Source: Data collected during fieldwork by the author

Table 20.4 Concentration values of different social security schemes by MPCE

Types		PMJDY	BPL	MGNREGA	RSBY	All
Villages not affected by mining activity	CI	−0.05	−0.08	−0.11*	−0.02	−0.21
	SE	0.05	0.06	0.06	0.06	0.22
Villages affected by mining activity	CI	−0.07	−0.38***	−0.16***	−0.01	−0.44*
	SE	0.06	0.06	0.06	0.06	0.23
Total	CI	−0.06	−0.22**	−0.14*	−0.01	−0.30
	SE	0.04	0.06	0.07	0.06	0.16

Source: Authors' calculation
Level of significance ***p value <0.01, **p value <0.05, *p value <0.10

characteristics (Table 20.5). Logistic regression of PMJDY finding shows that households from the middle MPCE class had 1.7 times (95%, CI 0.99–2.86) more likely to use the PMJDY scheme than their counterpart. The OBC and general caste had much less likely to use this scheme, with 36% and 45%, respectively.

Logit regression of BPL ration card shows that household heads aged 35–54 years and 55+ years had 2.2 times (95%; CI 0.91–5.40) and 2.4 times (95%; CI 0.88–6.96) more likelihood of using a BPL ration card, respectively. Those household heads had easy access to their political leader significantly 21 times (95%, CI 8.72–55.09) more likelihood of using the ration card. Furthermore, those household heads who were members of any organization had 2.9 times (95% CI 1.31–6.79) more likely to use the ration card. Those households experiencing food insecurity

Table 20.5 The adjusted odds ratio for the utilization of different social security schemes by selected background characteristics in Dhanbad, India 2015 ($N = 416$)

Schemes	BPL	MGNREGA	RSBY	PMJDY	All
Age of head of household					
21–34 years®					
35–54 years	2.22*	0.95	2.78***	1.14	0.77
55 and more years	2.48*	0.63	1.63	0.75	0.78
Social group					
SCs/STs®					
OBCs	0.60	0.64*	1.41	0.64*	0.11*
Forward caste (others)	0.43*	0.36***	0.65	0.55*	0.67
Education of head of household					
Illiterate®					
Literate	1.15	0.45***	0.53**	1.08	0.77
Easy access to local political leaders					
No®					
Yes	21.72***	1.44	1.14	1.17	7.38*
Membership of the socio-political organization					
No®					
Yes	2.98***	1.41	0.73	0.96	2.29
Any household member having matriculation					
No®					
Yes	0.83	1.74*	0.66	1.20	0.79
Household size					
0–3 members®					
4–5 members	0.89	2.15**	1.89*	0.92	4.08
6 and more members	1.05	1.91	1.99*	1.00	0.94
Food shortage					
No®					
Yes	5.17***	2.22***	1.40	1.35	1.76
Regular salaried job					
No®					
Yes	0.18***	0.58*	1.49	0.80	1.09
MPCE					
Low®					
Medium	0.55	1.02	1.18	1.68*	0.30
High	0.20***	0.95	1.49	0.77	0.16
Villages status					
Villages not affected by mining activity®					
Villages affected by mining activity	0.56*	1.14	1.09	0.99	0.40
Log likelihood	**−144.95**	**−225.30**	**−235.83**	**−254.54**	**−41.79**

Source: Data collected during fieldwork by the author

Level of significance ***p value <0.01, **p value <0.05, *p value <0.10

All regressions adjusted for variables sex and farmland holding

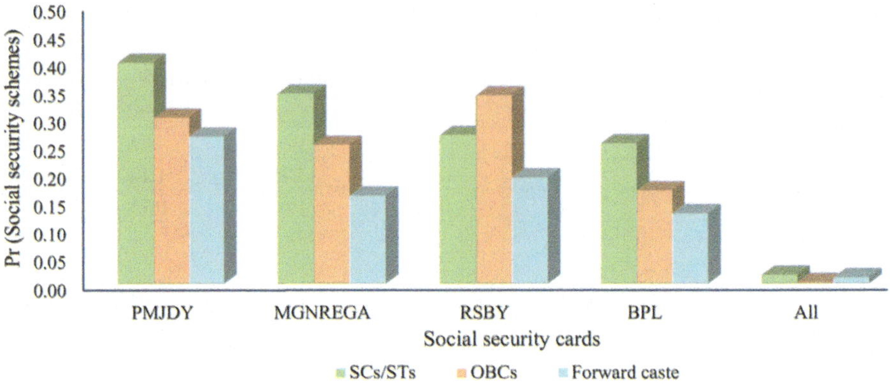

Fig. 20.3 Adjusted predictions of caste with 95% CIs (Source: Prepared by the authors)

had five times (95% CI 2.44–10.96) more likely to use the ration card. The forward caste, regular salaried job, and high MPCE group households were all substantially associated with BPL card usage. Mines affected villages was found to be considerably 44% (95% CI 0.29–1.11) less associated with utilization of ration card.

Logit regression of MGNREGA results reveals that households with any matriculated member had 1.7 times (95% CI 0.98–3.10) increases a likelihood for its card utilization. The 4–5 family household size had 2.1 times (95% CI 1.01–4.55) more likelihood to use it. Those households experiencing food insecurity had 2.2 times (95% CI 1.30–3.77) higher likelihood to use the MGNREGA card. The use of MGNREGA cards was negatively associated with OBCs, general castes, and regular salaried households.

According to the RSBY logit regression, household heads between the ages of 35 and 54 had 2.8 times (95% CI 1.38–5.62) higher likelihood to utilize this card. Households with 4–5 and more than 6 members had 1.8 times (95% CI 0.92–3.89) and 1.9 times (95% CI 0.92–4.28) more likely to use the RSBY card, respectively. Literate household heads were shown to be less likely to use the RSBY system. According to the all-cards regression, those household heads who had easy access to local political leaders had 7.3 times (95% CI 0.98–55.51) more likely to utilize all schemes.

Based on the logistic regression of different schemes predicted probability for households utilization of social security scheme (on the Y-axis) by caste estimated that shown in Figure 20.3. The estimated value by each of the five regressions (such as PMJDY, BPL, MGNREGA, RSBY, and overall) plotted against social group indicators (on the *X*-axis). Except for RSBY scheme, the predicted probability for each of the three caste groups reveals no variance in the hierarchical likelihood of the scheme utilization. It was discovered that likelihood of utilizing PMJDY, MGNREGA, and BPL were higher for SCs/STs, followed by OBCs and general caste. Whereas, OBCs has a higher probability of using RSBY, followed by SCs/STs and general caste. However, the likelihood of using all schemes were highest for SCs/STs households, followed by general caste households.

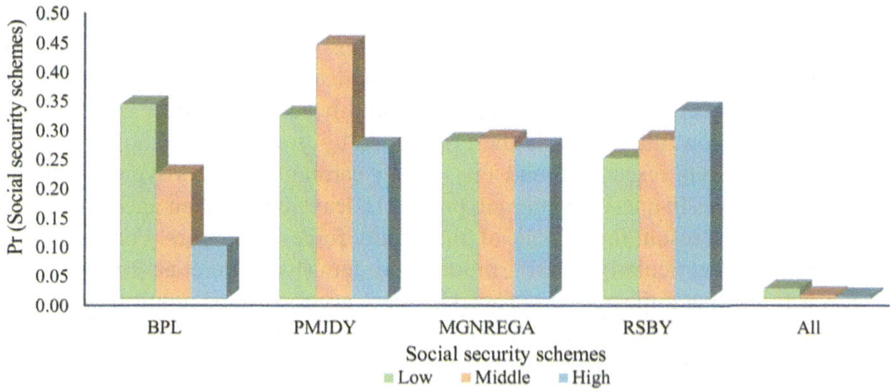

Fig. 20.4 Adjusted predictions of MPCE with 95% CIs (Source: Prepared by the authors)

Figure 20.4 depicts the predicted probability of household ownership of various social security schemes (on the *Y*-axis) based on monthly per capita consumer expenditure (on the *X*-axis). The predicted probabilities demonstrate inconsistency in the likelihood of schemes utilization by different MPCE groups. The estimated probability for BPL schemes shows that the lower MPCE class were more likely to be utilized, followed by the middle and upper MPCE classes. In the case of PMJDY and MGNREGA, the chances of utilization were highest for the middle MPCE class, followed by lower and higher MPCE classes. The likelihood of using RSBY was greatest for the higher level MPCE class, followed by the intermediate and lower MPCE class. However, lower income households had a higher likelihood of using all types of schemes.

20.4 Discussion

In order to examine the extent to which households are covered by various social safety net schemes in the mining region of Dhanbad, Jharkhand, India. The finding shows that despite mining operation in study villages, residing population are socioeconomically vulnerable. Large number of needy households particularly the impoverished, remained outside the scope of the government safety net due to its leakage. The utilization level of different social security schemes was high in the non-mines affected villages except for RSBY scheme. The adjusted odds ratio indicates that probability of BPL card use was significantly low in mine-affected villages compared to its counterpart. However, the use of all schemes is substantially concentrated towards the poor of mine-affected villages although it covers very low in percentage among dwelling population who are genuinely eligible for these schemes.

Furthermore, it was found that more than 35-year household heads primarily utilize BPL and RSBY schemes. This finding is consistent with a previous study on RSBY utilization, which found that individuals under the age of 35, use the RSBY scheme less frequently than older-aged household heads (Mozumdar et al. 2018). The reason for low utilization of these schemes by younger household heads is migration. Previous research found that young earning members typically go to cities from villages in quest of better job prospects, leave behind their aged parents in the villages. As a result, their financial uncertainty forces them to rely on the social safety schemes, particularly on BPL rationing system (Kulkarni et al. 2015).

It was found that if the household head has easy access to local political leaders or if he is a member of any socio-political organization then their favor increases the likelihood to get easy access of social security schemes particularly for BPL ration card. This finding is consistent with prior research, which revealed that membership in any socio-political organization increases the likelihood of obtaining and utilizing social security programs (Karpagam et al. 2016). Alatas et al. (2013) have found that those leaders who hold a formal political position have a greater likelihood of receiving benefits for their followers than informal leaders. The effect of leaders in power is more visible when program benefits are being allocated to households rather than when beneficiaries are being identified. Further findings show that utilization of MNERGA and RSBY cards is directly proportional to household size. Empirical study prove that large household size plays an influencing factor for both enrollment and retention in social security programs due to a higher degree of need and awareness level (Raza et al. 2016). The food insecure households are more likely to use BPL ration card and MGNREGA scheme, but they suffer more due to insufficient and erroneous distribution of entitlement (Srikantha Murthy and Indumati 2011; Upadhyay and Palanivel 2011). Besides, qualitative findings ascertained that "Most of the time, we don't know about the distribution of products other than rice. Those things were typically obtained by a close relative of a fair pricing shop owner and village president" (68 years male respondent).

The adjusted odds ratio indicates that OBCs and forward caste household has a lower likelihood of using the social security scheme than SCs/STs. Furthermore, the predicted odds of entire social security scheme indicates that SCs/STs had a substantially more probability of utilizing social security schemes than OBCs and forward caste groups, with the exception of RSBY program. These findings are similar to earlier studies; nonetheless, the primary reason for the limited utilization of the RSBY scheme by STs/SCs is poor awareness, program design, and enrollment scheduling (Rathi et al. 2012; Thakur 2015). The adjusted odds ratio of MPCE indicates that the middle-income group is more likely to use social security schemes, notably in the case of PMJDY. The predicted probability of social security schemes reveals that BPL ration card utilization has an inverse relationship with household MPCE although schemes such as PMJDY, RSBY, and MGNREGA card usage is directly proportional with MPCE groups, particularly the medium MPCE group. As a result, these programs, particularly PMJDY and MGNREGA, did not provide significant assistance to the most vulnerable members of society, which is consistent with other study (Sekaran et al. 2014; Breitkreuz et al. 2017; Singh and Naik 2018).

20.5 Conclusion

In the global discourse of elite capture on social security schemes and identification of ways to tap leakage for the well-being of the poor. It was found that in countries like India, where democratic decentralization of governance expands, there is political and bureaucratic pressure on the allocation of public services (Bertrand et al. 2007). However, government is trying to tap its leakages by considerable reform in the management of social security schemes, particularly in empowered action group states (EAGs). But current evidence also indicates that reforms in the social security scheme allocation in EAG states, particularly in Jharkhand, is fading and being engulfed in corruption once again (Drèze and Khera 2005). As a result, the current study opens the door to a fresh debate on the elite capture on social security scheme in Dhanbad, Jharkhand.

First and foremost, the study discovered a coverage gap in the social security schemes among eligible households in the study villages. Only a few households utilize all types of schemes, it become possible only due to lot of personal efforts. Furthermore, study discover that individuals with easy access to the local political leader are more likely to capture schemes, whereas those who are merely members of the socioeconomic organization are deprived to take benefit from all types of security schemes. The BPL ration card scheme utilization showed as severe influence of elites, the local political leaders and members of socio-political organization playing prominent roles in it. Since, it is a crucial program for food-insecure households and its requirement is multiple times more to them than food secure households. The MGNERGA is another important scheme for food-insecure households; regardless of other confounding factors, it is more popular among large households. However, qualitative findings ascertained that this scheme is not being implemented in accordance with its requirements in mine-affected areas due to negative mining repercussions. Furthermore, the RSBY scheme's utilization malfunctioned, and its likelihood of utilization is high for the middle MPCE class and OBCs. Furthermore, a qualitative analysis suggests that it is a pro-poor plan, but its leakage and delay in the renewable process have denied entitled needy people from better treatment and reduced its relevance to universal health care (UHC). The PMJDY plan was primarily used and profited by middle MPCE class households. Whereas, lower MPCE class households are expected to benefited more from it, but they are unable to do so since, they are unable to deposit their savings.

In nutshell, finding suggests that these programs are pro-poor in nature, but utilization is inconsistent. Leakages in these social security schemes are cited as one of the causes of the rising food insecurity, which may undermine the state's motive and nature of targeted welfare. As a result, the study strongly recommends expanding the equitable coverage of all social security schemes in order to achieve the target beneficiary. Particularly for PMJDY because the government is constantly changing the method of transferring subsidies and beneifits to beneficiaries in their bank accounts, which is still far from 100% enrolment and utilization. Second, the MGNERGA program was modified to meet the needs of mines affected areas. Third, widespread public participation is essential to raise awareness and understanding among the target population so that, with the support of a social security net, they can improve their living standards.

References

Alatas V et al (2013) Does elite capture matter? Local elites and targeted welfare programs in Indonesia. SSRN Electron J 2013:2326703. https://doi.org/10.2139/ssrn.2326703

Bardhan P, Mookherjee D (2000) Capture and governance at local and national levels. Am Econ Rev 90(1996):135–139

Bertrand M et al (2007) Obtaining a driver's license in India: an experimental approach to studying corruption. Q J Econ 122(4):1639–1676. https://doi.org/10.1162/qjec.2007.122.4.1639

Bhandari L, Chakraborty M (2015) Spatial poverty across India. Livemint, New Delhi. http://www.livemint.com/Home-Page/BH4Yupc3zGc2gs067s6eKN/Spatial-poverty-across-India.html

Breitkreuz R et al (2017) The Mahatma Gandhi National Rural Employment Guarantee Scheme: a policy solution to rural poverty in India? Dev Policy Rev 35(3):397–417. https://doi.org/10.1111/dpr.12220

CSE (2009) Rich lands, poor people. Centre for Science and Environment, New Delhi. http://cseindia.org/mining/pdf/miningpub.pdf

Dasgupta A, Beard VA (2007) Community driven development, collective action and elite capture in Indonesia. Dev Change 38(2):229–249. https://doi.org/10.1111/j.1467-7660.2007.00410.x

Devereux S (2002) Can social safety nets reduce chronic poverty? Dev Policy Rev 20(5):657–675. https://doi.org/10.1111/1467-7679.00194

Drèze J, Khera R (2005) Understanding leakages in the public distribution system. Econ Polit Wkly 50(7):39–42. https://doi.org/10.1177/0144739400020002003

Duflo E, Fischer G, Chattopadhyay R (2005) Efficiency and rent seeking in local government: evidence from randomized policy experiments in India. https://www.imf.org/external/np/res/seminars/2005/weak/edpa.pdf. Accessed 29 June 2017

Dutt KL (2007) Illegal coal mining in Eastern India: rethinking legitimacy and limits of justice. Ecol Wkly 42:57–66

Dutta D (2009) Elite capture and corruption: concepts and definitions. Academia, New York

Dutta T, Das A (2017) Analyzing data of Pradhan Mantri Jan Dhan Yojana. Indian Institute of Technology Bombay, Mumbai

Erreygers G (2009) Correcting the concentration index. J Health Econ 28(2):504–515. https://doi.org/10.1016/j.jhealeco.2008.02.003

Financial Express (2017) MGNREGA leaks as high as 50%, makes strong case for Aadhaar. The Financial Express, New Delhi. https://www.financialexpress.com/opinion/mgnrega-leaks-as-high-as-50-makes-strong-case-for-aadhaar/623357/

Ghosh J (2002) Social policy in Indian development. In: Mkandawire T, United N. R. I. for S. D. (UNRISD) Switzerland (eds) Social policy in a development context. Palgrave Macmillan, London, pp 284–307. https://doi.org/10.1057/9780230523975

GoI (2007) Backward regions Grant Fund, Ministry of Panchayati Raj. Government of India, New Delhi. http://www.panchayat.gov.in/documents/10198/0/BRGFFINALGUIDELINES.pdf

Guha S (2015) The role of Pradhan Mantri Jan Dhan Yojana in financial inclusion: an evaluative study. Glob J Res Anal 4(7):361–362

Higley J, Burton MG (2006) Elite foundations of liberal democracy. Rowman & Littlefield Publishers, Lanham. https://books.google.co.in/books/about/Elite_Foundations_of_Liberal_Democracy.html?id=bmydodBY5FoC&redir_esc=y

Hossain DLA (2008) A tale of three villages: power, difference and locality in rural Bangladesh. J South Asian Dev 3(1):33–51. https://doi.org/10.1177/097317410700300102

IANS (2015) India has one of largest social safety net programmes, Business Standard. IANS, Washington, DC. http://www.business-standard.com/article/news-ians/india-has-one-of-largest-social-safety-net-programmes-115070700985_1.html

Karpagam S, Vasan A, Seethappa V (2016) Falling through the gaps: women accessing care under health insurance schemes in Karnataka. Indian J Gend Stud 23(1):69–86. https://doi.org/10.1177/0971521515612864

Kulkarni S, Raju S, Bammidi S (2015) Social security for the elderly in India. Building knowledge base on ageing in India: increased awareness, access and quality of elderly services. United Nations, New York. http://search.ebscohost.com/login.aspx?direct=true&db=gnh&AN=61035&site=ehost-live

Maconachie R, Binns T (2007) Beyond the resource curse? Diamond mining, development and post-conflict reconstruction in Sierra Leone. Resour Policy 32(3):104–115. https://doi.org/10.1016/j.resourpol.2007.05.001

MoLJ (2005) The National Rural Employment Guarantee Act, 2005. Ministry of Law and Justice, New Delhi. http://nrega.nic.in/amendments_2005_2016.pdf

Mozumdar A et al (2018) Understanding the use of India's National Health Insurance Scheme for family planning and reproductive health services in Uttar Pradesh. Int J Health Plan Manag 33: 823–835. https://doi.org/10.1002/hpm.2531

Panda S (2015) Political connections and elite capture in a poverty alleviation programme in India. J Dev Stud 51(1):50–65. https://doi.org/10.1080/00220388.2014.947281

PDS (1997) Targeted public distribution system. Department of Food and Public Distribution, New Delhi. http://dfpd.nic.in/public-distribution.htm

PMJDY (2016) Pradhan Mantri Jan-Dhan Yojana. Ministry of Finance, New Delhi. https://www.pmjdy.gov.in/about

Rasul G, Sharma E (2014) Understanding the poor economic performance of Bihar and Uttar Pradesh, India: a macro-perspective. Reg Stud Reg Sci 1(1):221–239. https://doi.org/10.1080/21681376.2014.943804

Rathi P, Mukherji A, Sen G (2012) Rashtriya Swasthya Bima Yojana: evaluating utilisation, roll-out and perceptions in Amaravati district, Maharashtra. Econ Polit Wkly 48(39):57–64. https://doi.org/10.2307/41720192

Raza W, van de Poel E, Panda P (2016) Analyses of enrolment, dropout and effectiveness of RSBY in northern rural India. University Library of Munich, Munich. https://mpra.ub.uni-muenchen.de/70081/1/

Rogers BL, Coates J (2002) Food-based safety nets and related programs. World Bank Institute, Washington, DC, p 58. http://nutrition.tufts.edu/sites/default/files/fpan/wp12-safety_nets.pdf

RSBY (2008) Rashtriya Swasthya Bima Yojana, Government website. http://www.rsby.gov.in/about_rsby.aspx. Accessed 13 July 2017

Sekaran V et al (2014) Determinants of enrolment and experiences of Rashtriya Swasthya Bima Yojana (RSBY) beneficiaries in Udupi district, India. Int J Med Public Health 4(1):82. https://doi.org/10.4103/2230-8598.127164

Singh C, Naik G (2018) Financial inclusion after PMJDY: a case study of Gubbi Taluk, Tumkur. SSRN 2018:3151257. https://doi.org/10.2139/ssrn.3151257

Srikantha Murthy PS, Indumati S (2011) Economic analysis of MGNREGA in the drought-prone states of Karnataka, Rajasthan and irrigation-dominated state of Andhra Pradesh. Agric Econ Res Rev 24:531–536. http://planningcommission.nic.in/

Subbarao K et al (1997) Safety net programs and poverty reduction: lessons from cross-country experience. World Bank Group, Washington, DC

Thakur H (2015) Study of awareness, enrollment, and utilization of Rashtriya Swasthya Bima Yojana (National Health Insurance Scheme) in Maharashtra, India. Front Public Health 3:282. https://doi.org/10.3389/fpubh.2015.00282

The World Bank Group (2015) The state of social safety nets. The World Bank Group, Washington, DC. https://doi.org/10.1596/978-1-4648-0543-1

United Nations (1949) United Nations Universal Declaration of Human Rights 1948. Office of the High Commissioner for Human Rights, Geneva, p 11. http://www.un.org/en/universal-declaration-human-rights/

United Nations (2003) World economic and social survey 2003: trends and policies in the world economy. United Nations, New York. https://books.google.co.in/books?id=HP7eBMn6aGUC&pg=PT257&lpg=PT257&dq=restructuring+economy+of+world+against+poverty&source=bl&ots=9gs4e6rNsl&sig=Eji8Uje8ahIdWUsRJkqmghmrZ28&hl=en&sa=X&ved=0ahUKEwiLpcqntfbUAhVDvo8KHS-7AIUQ6AEIODAE#v=onepage&q=restructuri

United Nations (2016) The sustainable development goals report. United Nations, New York. http://www.un.org.lb/Library/Assets/The-Sustainable-Development-Goals-Report-2016-Global.pdf

Upadhyay RP, Palanivel C (2011) Challenges in achieving food security in India. Iran J Public Health 40(4):31–36

Wong S (2010) Elite capture or capture elites? Lessons from the ‘counter-elite’ and ‘co-opt-elite’ approaches in Bangladesh and Ghana. United Nations University World Institute for Development, Helsinki

Arun Kumar Yadav is currently working as a State Programme Coordinator, Monitoring and Evaluation (M&E) Office at Patna, Bihar in Evidence Action. Before this, he was working as an Assistant professor at the Central University of Karnataka, Kalaburagi. He also worked in the Institute of Economic Growth (IEG) New Delhi, as a Research Analyst. He obtained his doctoral degree in Population Studies from the International Institute for Population Sciences, Mumbai. His research area is mainly inclined toward livelihood, migration, urbanization, and public health issues. He jointly published many research papers.

Vidya Yadav is working as an Assistant Professor with P.G. Department of Geography in the College of Commerce, Arts and Science, Patna (Patliputra University), Bihar. She obtained her Doctoral degree in Population Studies from the International Institute for Population Sciences (IIPS), Mumbai. She holds an M.A. degree in Applied Geography from Ravenshaw University, Cuttack, and a Master of Population Studies from IIPS. Her research interest primarily focuses on urban issues, which include urban planning, migration, the living conditions of slum dwellers, and environmental concerns. Apart from that, she has been publishing and presenting many of her research works on various national and international platforms.

Chapter 21
Prioritizing the Bottom of the Pyramid Customers in Online Banking Service: Understanding the Realities with ESQUAL Test in Selected Districts in West Bengal, India

Ahana Sen, Santanu Mallick, and Ranjan Banerjee

21.1 Introduction

Asian countries are increasingly availing of online banking services, and customers in Asian countries are shifting to online banking for their financial transactions for the sake of convenience. All over Asia, usage of branches has gone down by 27%, and dependence on online banking has gone up by 35% in the previous 5 years. In Asia, 25% of the related purchasing decisions are taken by consumers through online devices (Sengupta et al. 2014). The developing nations are presently well aware of the urgency to take part in the journey of online banking (Iqbal and Qureshi 2012). In the context of the paradigm shift from branch to online banking. Online banking has become popular in India as well. Online banking has gained center stage in different states of India. Technological advancement is a continuous process that allows the customers of the banks to tap the advantage of technology as per convenience without time and space constraints (Lin 2013). Digital banking assists customers in avoiding long queues and saves their time, effort, and cost (Gerrard et al. 2006). Online banking enables individuals as well as corporate entities to access their bank accounts anytime and anywhere, to make payments of their utility bills, to manage their money, and to avail of other important services without bearing the trouble of

A. Sen (✉)
Department of Management, Raiganj University, Raiganj, West Bengal, India

S. Mallick
Department of Commerce (Hindi Shift), Banwarilal Bhalotia College, Asansol, West Bengal, India

R. Banerjee
Himalaya Drug Company, Kolkata, West Bengal, India

M. Mishra et al. (eds.), *Public Policies and Sustainable Development in Post-Reform India*, New Frontiers in Regional Science: Asian Perspectives 71,
https://doi.org/10.1007/978-981-99-3696-0_21

physically visiting the branches of the banks (Hamid et al. 2007; Simpson 2002). Digital banking strengthens the relationship between customers and banks (Karjaluoto et al. 2010) and enables banks to cut down the cost of employees and cost of physical branches while at the same time it ensures immediacy and ubiquity (Jayawardhena and Foley 2000; Xue et al. 2011).

Presently, technological upgrades have been influencing the behavior of consumers significantly (Chaouali et al. 2017; Mpinganjira 2015). The increasing capableness of the wireless web provides customers with all-time access to products and services from their computers, laptops, and smartphones. Such advancements are predominantly observed in the banking sector, where online services have captured the main focus (Chaouali et al. 2017; Paul et al. 2016). Both the banking sector and individual customers enjoy the advantages of the emergence of digital banking (for an overview, see Paul and Trehan 2011). The banking sector can tap the advantages of reduced transaction costs, better service quality, and enhanced customer loyalty (Xue et al. 2011). Again, individual customers can also enjoy the advantage of checking account balances, making payments of bills, making application of loans, transferring funds, trading securities, and completing other transactions through web-enabled devices (Tchouassi 2012; Pikkarainen et al. 2004). The Digital India Programme is aimed at empowering society by focusing on digital resources and collaborative platforms, making online banking easy for all. A key component of this program is high-speed internet as a core utility to enable online delivery of various services. It is planned to set up infrastructure for digital identity and financial inclusion and guarantee easy accessibility of common services centers. It is also planned to confirm that cyberspace is made safe and secure, which is very much needed for the success of online banking. Online banking appears to be especially advantageous for the bottom of the pyramid (BoP) customers. Previously, BoP customers have had very little access to financial services, and most of such customers did not avail of banking services. So, the BoP customers very often had to depend on cash and high-interest loans over personal credit and savings (Caskey 2002; Klawitter and Fletschner 2011). It was expected that digital banking might reduce the geographic and cultural barriers which have particularly limited BoP customers' access to offline banking services (Klawitter and Fletschner 2011; Tchouassi 2012). But, BoP consumers' adoption of online banking has lagged behind expectations (Laforet and Li 2005; Tchouassi 2012).

ESQUAL, i.e., Electronic Service Quality (E-S-QUALITY), is constituted on the basis of four pillars or dimensions—efficiency, fulfillment, reliability, and privacy. Efficiency refers to the ease and speed of accessing and using the site. Fulfillment may be explained as the accuracy of services promised. Reliability is the ability to perform service dependably and accurately. Privacy means the assurance that the confidentiality of, as well as access to certain data regarding an entity, is secured. The present study contributes to the evaluation E-S-QUAL's applicability in different settings and to the verification of its factor structure.

Sustainability in different domains is required for the development. The traditional understanding of sustainable development is bounded by some specific issues. This research focuses on the role of online banking in sustainable development by taking into account the huge potential of this sector. The research indicates and evaluates the factors of banking systems.

21.2 Literature Survey

In respect of the adoption of digital banking decisions, the literature mainly speaks of two approaches: (1) Characteristics of the technology and (2) Functional and technological factors (Yousafzai 2012).

The technology acceptance model (TAM) primarily dominates the first approach. It mainly consists of two elements, namely, (1) Perceived ease of use (PEOU) and (2) Perceived usefulness (Giovanis et al. 2012; Kalaiarasi and Srividya 2012; Al-Fahim 2012; Yoon and Steege 2013; Wu et al. 2014; Sharma and Govindaluri 2014; Bashir and Madhavaiah 2015; Rawashdeh 2015). In the literature, these two basic elements have sometimes been indirectly mentioned as compatibility and convenience factors (Oruç and Tatar 2017) or website characteristic factors (Jalil et al. 2014). They have also been referred to as perceived benefit and convenience factors (Kesharwani and Radhakrishna 2013).

The second approach mainly focuses on personal aspects of digital banking adoption. It includes awareness factors (Sharma and Govindaluri 2014), self-efficacy factors (Kesharwani and Radhakrishna 2013), personal openness (Yoon and Steege 2013) factors, and so on. Apart from the personal aspect, social pressure has also received the attention of the researchers (Bashir and Madhavaiah 2015; Sharma and Govindaluri 2014; Kesharwani and Radhakrishna 2013; Wu et al. 2014). Concern for environmental aspects like green factors is also figured in the works of researchers (Yoon and Steege 2013). Perceived risk factors also have been highlighted by some researchers (Fadare et al. 2016; Giovanis et al. 2012; Yoon and Steege 2013; Jalil et al. 2014, Awni Rawashdeh 2015; Kesharwani and Radhakrishna 2013).

Most of the research studies on the adoption of digital banking show that the TAM model has effectively explained around 27% of the variance of actual usage of internet banking among Indian internet users. The predictability rate could be increased by accommodating subjective factors like the image of banks, bank initiative, trust, perceived risk, government support, etc. (Marakarkandy et al. 2017).

Accessibility and reliability strongly influence Indian customers in respect of the adoption of internet banking. The perceived risk factor, however, has a weak influence as compared to other subjective factors (Sikdar and Makkad 2015).

Internet banking adoption rate is more for people who command more economic, cultural, and social resources (Bourdieu 1984; Leonhardt and Chu 2017). This means that economically well-off, intellectually equipped, and with high social backgrounds are more likely to adopt digital banking at a rapid pace (Chu and Zhang 2011; Pitta et al. 2008; Laforet and Li 2005; Tchouassi 2012). As human behavior is largely dependent on the environment in which one operates, so it is in the case of digital banking. People tend to adopt internet banking habits more swiftly and effectively if they have a favorable environment (Ouellette and Wood 1998; Verplanken and Aarts 1999; Wood and Neal 2009). From a financial point of view, it is less risky for consumers to enter into digital transactions which are placed at the higher ladder of financial wealth (Urbany et al. 1996).

In addition, demographic factors also influence the use of internet banking (Hedden and Yoon 2006; Johnson 1990; Lambert-Pandraud et al. 2005). People of the relatively younger group are happier with internet banking. In relation to their senior counterparts as they learn the procedure quickly and easily (Salthouse 1996; Shivapour et al. 2012; Yoon et al. 2009).

In technologically less developed countries, online banking adoption practices take place at a slower pace. This has been evidenced in a study from Pakistan by Akhlaq and Ahmed (2015).

In India, the government launched the UPI system in 2016, a banking system that permits the public to easily transfer money to and from bank accounts. The UPI system surged the digital revolution in India and started the so-called Mobile Banking. The government has also asked the clients to link their bank accounts with their Aadhaar number. With digital banking, a person can easily open a bank account in India, and that too, without even visiting the bank branch. Security in the digital transaction is of paramount importance to the users of digital banking transactions. Banks use many techniques to ensure the security of transactions. However, the customers lack full awareness of these security measures. Therefore, the banks must play a proactive role in educating the customers in order to install confidence in them (Laforet and Li 2005).

The above review of the literature reveals that no major study has yet been conducted so far in West Bengal for testing the ESQUAL of Online Banking Services on bottom-of-the-pyramid customers.

21.3 Objective of the Study

The bottom pyramid segment is becoming crucial for different service sectors as well as for the banking sector. Against this backdrop, the study focuses on identifying factors with reference to ESQUAL scale for this particular selection group. We have adapted an existing ESQUAL scale item.

21.4 Methods

The present study is both empirical and exploratory in nature. This study is based on primary data only. The primary data is sourced by administering a structured questionnaire. While framing the questionnaire, the previous research works in the related areas have been taken into consideration. The collected data is analyzed using factor analysis. For assessing the reliability of the survey instrument, Cronbach

Alpha Coefficients are calculated. The Cronbach Alpha is the most widely used index for determining internal consistency (Kerlinger 1986). Our study area consists of Bankura, Jalpaiguri, Murshidabad, 24 Parganas (N) 24 Parganas (S) Howrah, Hooghly, and Birbhum districts of West Bengal. The study period ranged from 2019 to 2021.

The analysis of the data entails the use of various tools like KMO and Bartlett's test of Sphericity, Factor Analysis, and Reliability test; for the analysis and fulfillment of the objectives of the study. The findings of the study are represented below, with an explanation of each test and its corresponding value.

21.5 Findings

In statistics, Cronbach's α (alpha) is a coefficient of internal consistency. So, for assessing the reliability of the collected data for empirical testing, in the beginning, Cronbach's α (alpha) is calculated for the data with the help of the SPSS (version 15).

Factor Analysis is done as it is the most commonly available tool for data reduction and summarization that may assist anybody in finding out a few major uncorrelated variables. The study relies on some standard statistical and visual tools commonly used in Factor Analysis without avoiding value judgments. One method that has been put forth is to exclude factors with Eigen values less than one as the factors retained in such a way account for more variance than the average for the variables.

Internal consistency of data relating to scale items is very high (Cronbach's Alpha being 0.938), as shown in Table 21.1.

Sample adequacy is verified through KMO and Bartlett's test, and the value is 0.970. Bartlett's test of sphericity is applied to test the null hypothesis that the variables are uncorrelated in the population. In the present study, the chi-square value was 10,380.549 with 91° of freedom. So, it is considered to be statistically significant as $p < 0.01$. A large value of the test statistic in Table 21.2 above leads to the rejection of the null hypothesis, and it may be concluded that the application of

Table 21.1 Reliability statistics

Cronbach's alpha	No. of items
0.983	14

Source: Computed by the authors using the *SPSS* (*v 15*)

Table 21.2 KMO and Bartlett's test

Kaiser–Meyer–Olkin measure of sampling adequacy		0.970
Bartlett's test of sphericity	Approx. chi-square	10,380.549
	d.f.	91
	Sig.	0.000

Source: Computed by the authors using the *SPSS* (*v 15*)

Factor Analysis is suitable. Moreover, a high value of the KMO measure of sampling adequacy implies the suitableness of Factor Analysis.

Interpretation of Output of Factor Analysis: The output of Factor Analysis is obtained by applying the Principal Component Analysis. Table 21.3 shows the output of the Factor Analysis with respect to the questions asked to the respondents. The Total Variance is explained in Table 21.3, and the Rotated Component Matrix is also shown in Table 21.4. In order to identify the number of underlying dimensions, there are a number of different approaches. In the present study, Principal Component Analysis (PCA) method is applied.

A total of 14 elements from factor analysis resulted in five factors viz.: Fulfilment, System Availability and Responsiveness, Privacy, Empathy, and Efficiency. "The Total Variance Explained" table shows the variance explained by the five factors solution. From Table 21.3, it can be observed that the five factors grouping explained approximately 92.070% of the variance. From Table 21.4, it is observed that all the factor loadings were more than 0.5 (only three items were below 0.5 value), which shows moderate to high correlation among them.

Loading of question 3 on components 1 and 2 are similar in nature with the very minute difference in value. So, we have taken question 3 under the umbrella of factor two, i.e., fulfilment in our covariance structure. In the case of factor four, i.e., privacy, it may be the case that the respondents failed to understand the questions and the factor loading amounted to 0.3. We have skipped one question from the third factor because of the lack of commonality in this selected group. There may be some ambiguity among the respondents in the case of factor five, i.e., empathy, and the factor loading amounted to 0.4. So, we have not dropped the item. We are adapting the predetermined questionnaire in a local and cultural context. So, some questions may not be well understood by respondents of this selected study group. Table 21.5 exhibits Cronbach's alpha value for individual factors.

21.6 Conclusion

The outcome of the study is affirmative, and ESQUAL dimensions are well established for this particular study group. The bottom-of-the-pyramid consumers are targeted, and factors of the scale are well explored. The wave of online banking has made banks in India leverage technology by bringing an entire bank into the smartphone. The acceptability of online banking by BoP customers may not be temporary in the near future. We may see more people using this mode of banking because of its opportuneness and efficient process.

The first limitation of the study is the survey area; a few districts of West Bengal have been selected for this study. Pan India validation of the result can be done through a detailed survey in the future. Secondly, the study group is concentrated on the bottom of the pyramid customers, so generalization can be tested in further studies. The research can be extended by relating ESQUAL dimension with customer satisfaction.

Table 21.3 Total variance explained

Component	Initial Eigen values			Extraction sums of squared loadings			Rotation sums of squared loadings		
	Total	% of Variance	Cumulative %	Total	% of Variance	Cumulative %	Total	% of Variance	Cumulative %
1	11.462	81.870	81.870	11.462	81.870	81.870	3.280	23.430	23.430
2	0.505	3.609	85.479	0.505	3.609	85.479	2.762	19.726	43.156
3	0.405	2.893	88.371	0.405	2.893	88.371	2.732	19.513	62.669
4	0.276	1.970	90.342	0.276	1.970	90.342	2.345	16.750	79.420
5	0.242	1.729	92.070	0.242	1.729	92.070	1.771	12.650	92.070
6	0.199	1.424	93.495						
7	0.176	1.258	94.752						
8	0.142	1.013	95.765						
9	0.123	0.876	96.641						
10	0.114	0.817	97.457						
11	0.099	0.710	98.168						
12	0.094	0.668	98.836						
13	0.086	0.617	99.453						
14	0.077	0.547	100.000						

Extraction Method: Principal Component Analysis
Source: Authors' calculation based on survey data

Table 21.4 Rotated component matrix (a)

Questions	Component				
	1	2	3	4	5
Deliver services as promised	0.305	**0.745**	0.308	0.340	0.273
Make no mistakes in my service	0.344	**0.658**	0.329	0.429	0.280
Make accurate promises about my service deliveries	0.609	**0.604**	0.317	0.213	0.169
Taking care of problem promptly	**0.646**	0.316	0.347	0.343	0.358
Being always available to help customers	**0.643**	0.392	0.302	0.333	0.371
Being flexible to accommodate customer preferences	**0.614**	0.314	0.321	0.341	0.457
Inspiring confidence in customers during interactions	0.731	0.268	0.390	**0.299**	0.222
Making customers feel safe in the transactions	0.367	0.348	0.375	**0.705**	0.246
Protecting customer's personal information	0.375	0.501	0.311	**0.645**	0.196
Having personalized interfaces	0.409	0.407	0.450	0.488	**0.337**
Having human assistance available	0.365	0.275	0.361	0.226	**0.756**
Having online help-line services when needed	0.306	0.423	0.569	0.439	**0.344**
Having visually appealing interfaces	0.360	0.344	**0.712**	0.304	0.309
Having interfaces which are easy to use	0.397	0.274	**0.750**	0.281	0.259

Extraction Method: Principal Component Analysis
Rotation Method: Varimax with Kaiser Normalization
a = Rotation converged in eight iterations
The factors with high loading is marked in bold
Source: Authors' calculation

Table 21.5 Cronbach's alpha value for individual factor

Name of the factor	No. of items	Cronbach's alpha
Fulfilment	0.938	3
System availability and responsiveness	0.956	3
Privacy	0.929	3
Empathy	0.928	3
Efficiency	0.946	2

Source: Computed by the authors using the *SPSS* (*v 15*)

References

Akhlaq A, Ahmed E (2015) Digital commerce in emerging economies: factors associated with online shopping intentions in Pakistan. Int J Emerg Mark 10(4):634–647

Al-Fahim N (2012) Factors affecting the adoption of internet banking amongst IIUM' students: a structural equation modelling approach (SEM). J Internet Bank Commerce 17(3):1–15

Bashir I, Madhavaiah C (2015) Consumer attitude and behavioural intention towards internet banking adoption in India. J Indian Bus Res 7(1):67–102

Bourdieu P (1984) Distinction: a social critique of the judgement of taste. Harvard University Press, Cambridge

Caskey J (2002) Bringing unbanked households into the banking system. The Brookings Institution, Washington, DC

Chaouali W, Souiden N, Ladhari R (2017) Explaining adoption of mobile banking with the theory of trying, general self-confidence, and cynicism. J Retail Consum Serv 35:57–67

Chu RW, Zhang XD (2011) Interpretation of the consumption market of Chinese migrant workers: the wealth of bottom of the pyramid. Econ Theory Bus Manag 7:34–46

Fadare OA, Ibrahim MB, Edogbanya A (2016) A survey on perceived risk and intention of adopting internet banking. J Internet Bank Commerce 21(1):1–21

Gerrard P, Cunningham BJ, Devlin FJ (2006) Why consumers are not using internet banking: a qualitative study. J Serv Mark 20(3):160–168

Giovanis AN, Binioris S, Polychronopoulos G (2012) An extension of TAM model with IDT and security/privacy risk in the adoption of internet banking services in Greece. EuroMed J Bus 7(1):24–53

Hamid MRA, Amin H, Lada S, Ahmad N (2007) A comparative analysis of internet banking in Malaysia and Thailand. J Internet Bus 4(1):1–19

Hedden T, Yoon C (2006) Individual differences in executive processing predict susceptibility to interference in verbal working memory. Neuropsychology 20(5):511–528

Iqbal S, Qureshi IA (2012) M-learning adoption: a perspective from a developing country. Int Rev Res Open Distrib Learn 13(3):147–164

Jalil MA, Talukder M, Rahman MK (2014) Factors affecting customer's perceptions towards online banking transactions in Malaysia. J Bus Manag 20(1):25–44

Jayawardhena C, Foley P (2000) Changes in the banking sector-the case of internet banking in the UK. Internet Res 10(1):19–31. https://doi.org/10.1108/10662240010312048

Johnson M (1990) Age differences in decision making: a process methodology for examining strategic information processing. J Gerontol Psychol Sci 45(2):75–78

Kalaiarasi H, Srividya V (2012) A study on factors influencing young user's online banking channel usage in India. J Commerce Account Res 1(3):17–22

Karjaluoto H, Riquelme HE, Rios RE (2010) The moderating effect of gender in the adoption of mobile banking. Int J Bank Mark 28(5):328–341. https://doi.org/10.1108/02652321011064872

Kerlinger F (1986) Foundations of behavioral research, 3rd edn. Holt, Rinehart and Winston, New York

Kesharwani A, Radhakrishna GS (2013) Drivers and inhibitors of internet banking adoption in India. J Internet Bank Commerce 18:1–18

Klawitter M, Fletschner D (2011) Who is banked in low-income families? The effects of gender and bargaining power. Soc Sci Res 40(1):50–62

Laforet S, Li X (2005) Consumers' attitudes towards online and mobile banking in China. Int J Bank Mark 23(5):362–380. https://doi.org/10.1108/02652320510629250

Lambert-Pandraud R, Laurent G, Lapersonne E (2005) Repeat purchasing of new automobiles by older consumers: empirical evidence and interpretations. J Mark 69(2):97–113. http://www.jstor.org/stable/30162047

Leonhardt JM, Chu R (2017) Online banking adoption at the bottom of the pyramid: a survey of Chinese migrant workers. Int J Emerg Mark 12:742–752

Lin H-F (2013) Determining the relative importance of mobile banking quality factors. Comput Stand Interfaces 35(2):195–204. https://doi.org/10.1016/j.csi.2012.07.003

Marakarkandy B, Yajnik N, Dasgupta C (2017) Enabling internet banking adoption: an empirical examination with an augmented technology acceptance model (TAM). J Enterp Inf Manag 30(2):263–294. https://doi.org/10.1108/JEIM-10-2015-0094

Mpinganjira M (2015) Use of e-government services: the role of trust. Int J Emerg Mark 10(4):622–633. https://doi.org/10.1108/ijoem-12-2013-0151

Oruç OE, Tatar Ç (2017) An investigation of factors that affect internet banking usage based on structural equation modeling. Comput Hum Behav 66:232–235

Ouellette J, Wood W (1998) Habit and intention in everyday life: the multiple processes by which past behavior predicts future behavior. Psychol Bull 124(1):54–74

Paul J, Trehan R (2011) Enhancing customer base and productivity through e-delivery channels—study of banks in India. Int J Electron Market Retail 4(2/3):151–164

Paul J, Mittal A, Srivastav G (2016) Impact of service quality on customer satisfaction in private and public sector banks. Int J Bank Mark 34(5):606–622

Pikkarainen T, Pikkarainen K, Karjaluoto H, Pahnila S (2004) Consumer acceptance of online banking: an extension of the technology acceptance model. Internet Res 14(3):224–235
Pitta DA, Guesalaga R, Marshall P (2008) The quest for the fortune at the bottom of the pyramid: potential and challenges. J Consum Mark 25(7):393–401
Rawashdeh A (2015) Factors affecting adoption of internet banking in Jordan: chartered accountant's perspective. Int J Bank Mark 33(4):510–529
Salthouse T (1996) The processing-speed theory of adult age differences in cognition. Psychol Rev 103(3):403–428
Sengupta J et al (2014) Asia financial institutions "digital banking in Asia" winning approaches in a new generation of financial services. McKinsey & Company, Sydney
Sharma SK, Govindaluri SM (2014) Internet banking adoption in India: structural equation modeling approach. J Indian Bus Res 6:155–169
Shivapour S, Nguyen C, Cole C, Denburg N (2012) Effects of age, sex, and neuropsychological performance on financial decision making. Front Neurosci 6(82):1–9
Sikdar P, Makkad M (2015) Online banking adoption A factor validation and satisfaction causation study in the context of Indian banking customers. Int J Bank Mark 33(6):760–785
Simpson J (2002) The impact of the Internet in banking: observations and evidence from developed and emerging markets. Telematics Inform 19:315–330
Tchouassi G (2012) Can mobile phones really work to extend banking services to the unbanked? Empirical lessons from selected sub-Saharan Africa countries. Int J Dev Soc 1(2):70–81
Urbany J, Dickson P, Kalapurakal R (1996) Price search in the retail grocery market. J Mark 60(2):91–104
Verplanken B, Aarts H (1999) Habit, attitude, and planned behavior: is habit an empty construct or an interesting case of goal-directed automaticity? Eur Rev Soc Psychol 10:101–134
Wood W, Neal D (2009) The habitual consumer. J Consum Psychol 19:579–592
Wu M, Jayawardhena C, Hamilton R (2014) A comprehensive examination of internet banking user behaviour: evidence from customers yet to adopt, currently using and stopped using. J Mark Manag 30(9–10):1006–1038
Xue M, Hitt LM, Chen PY (2011) Determinants and outcomes of internet banking adoption. Manag Sci 57(2):291–307. https://doi.org/10.1287/mnsc.1100.1187
Yoon HS, Steege LM (2013) Development of a quantitative model of the impact of customers' personality and perceptions on internet banking use. Comput Hum Behav 29:1133–1141
Yoon C, Cole CA, Lee MP (2009) Consumer decision making and aging: current knowledge and future directions. J Consum Psychol 19(1):2–16
Yousafzai S (2012) A literature review of theoretical models of internet banking adoption at the individual level. J Financ Serv Mark 17:215–226. https://doi.org/10.1057/fsm.2012.19

Dr. Ahana Sen is presently working as an Assistant Professor in the department of Management in Raiganj University, Raiganj. Her area of specialization is Accounting and Finance and research interest lies in the field of Banking and Finance. She is having 5 years of teaching experience. She has presented many research papers in different seminar, conferences at national and international level. She has authored six chapters in different books published from different parts of India.

Dr. Santanu Mallick is an Assistant Professor in the Department of Commerce, Banwarilal Bhalotia College, Asansol, Paschim Burdwan, West Bengal, India. He also held the position of Additional Treasury Officer in Bongaon Treasury under the Department of Finance, Government of West Bengal. He stood second in M.Com examination in 2015 of the University of Calcutta. His research interest lies in Financial Market, Behavioral Finance, Developmental Economics, Women empowerment, etc. He has presented many research papers in different national and international conferences, seminars, and webinars. He has also acted as an editor for an Edited Volume Brain Bloomers.

Mr. Ranjan Banerjee is currently working as Regional Sales Manager, Himalaya Drug Company. He has Graduated from the University of Calcutta with Economics honors and completed Master's program in Economics from the same. He took interest in management and have done Master's in Business Administration from the University of Calcutta. He has published one research article in journal of repute.

Chapter 22
Conjoining People Factor and Human Empowerment for Sustainable Progression: A Public Sector Study

Partha Naskar

22.1 Introduction

In the history of humankind, the role of organizations is deeply rooted in the people factor at the workplace. At the epicenter of all distinctions in the organizational domain lies the people factor, the most crucial component for organizational escalation. Over the years, there has been a gradual transformation towards shaping organizations following the pathway of sustainable agenda goals. At this juncture, the dimensions of public sector houses have been realigned, keeping in mind that the sustainability perspective will foster government deliverables to people at large. The present humanitarian crisis amidst the pandemic environment has led public organizations to be aware, alert, anticipate, agile, adapt, and act accordingly through strategic foresight to combat the uncertainties of the future. It is quite pertinent that the core essentials of government organizations vest on revitalizing the human element in the form of human knowledge, skills, abilities, and individual attitudes with nurturing and fostering of HR functions. To channelize the human element with human empowerment is the call of the hour of the present-day public houses in order to survive and sustain with fruitful recognition, growth, and augmentation in the long run. Public sector organizations today need to reorient themselves towards being more innovative and creative and recreating themselves along the lines of empowered people-based systems that foster pathways for a better tomorrow. The hard time comes with hard lessons through which new vistas, new realities, and new millennium HR practices need to be adapted and collaborated within human empowerment in the public arena, wherein the proponents of the sustainability-survival-sustenance need to be assimilated. The catastrophic effect of the pandemic has changed not only people's lives but also the functioning of workspaces in the public

---

P. Naskar (✉)
Netaji Subhas Administrative Training Institute, Kolkata, West Bengal, India

M. Mishra et al. (eds.), *Public Policies and Sustainable Development in Post-Reform India*, New Frontiers in Regional Science: Asian Perspectives 71,
https://doi.org/10.1007/978-981-99-3696-0_22

field. The changing scenario has posed a fundamental issue that evolution is part of human life as change is important to sustain. The most appropriate HR strategies of the government authorities can be reframed, viz., reveal, recommit, reengage, reconsider, and restart with a futuristic look of human values connoted as "Empowerment." The core idea of inspiring democracy is to empower people. Based on this premise, empowering conditions of the government bodies stand on "people power through popular rights." At the outset of the global pandemic, it is therefore highly desirable, essential, pertinent, and necessary to conduct a study on collaborating HR issues with the potential of human empowerment that led to a pathway towards the development of sustainable goals in the public arena.

22.2 Literature Review

22.2.1 Upholding Humanistic Proponents of Corporate Governance: Issues and Perspectives

The building bricks of a country's development foundation are deeply embedded within the layers of humanistic development in the organizational horizon. The emerging waves of robust change-over in the infrastructural platform has targeted both the public and private arena wherein the notion of corporate governance has been the bell tone of millennium business houses (Bratton and McCahery 1999). An organizational framework offers best when collective efforts, requisite care, upgraded skill, unparallel diligence, and best interests collectively act as a driving force for organizational excellence. A recent panacea of holistic, sustainable development finds its way through corporate governance with a wide spectrum of betterment for the public interest, community, and society at large. The growing tree of corporate governance has spread its branches, ensuring fair treatment, fair business practices, and fair-friendly infrastructural services for building an image of continual progression, transparency, and sustenance in the organizational terrain. Organizations thrive on the workforce (Gugler 2001). The epicenter of an organization's functionality stands on the doctrines of direction, control, and coordination in handling disputes, disagreements, and discontentment arising in the work settings. It has been unanimously agreed that digitalized platforms empower individuals, business houses, and other entities to interact, share, and create resources substituting traditional and age-old hierarchical features and formal authority (Beetham 1999). The multi-faceted attributes of digitalized governance platforms assimilate towards contributing to a common goal and thereby invoking the globally accessible resolution solution of governance. On the threshold of the twenty-first century millennium, the relevance and recognition of the implementation of corporate governance norms characterized by self-regulation proponents need to be examined, oriented, and developed for organizational restoration in the true sense of the term. Further, the underlying strata of "internal governance" vest on the positive correlation between corporate performance and any measure of governance quality (Mintzberg 1996). The standards and practices of corporate governance should not be restricted to geographical boundaries, but the promising tool of corporate governance featuring concepts, structures, and frameworks need to be appropriate, consistent, and beneficial with international benchmarks for galvanizing human empowerment.

22.2.2 *Managing Employee Grievance Aggression and Discontentment: An Optimistic Approach*

The image of an organization is reflected through the vibrant waves of goodwill and trustworthiness-the key enabler for organizational escalation. The essence of the human factor at work is intricately linked with the action, deeds, activities, conduct, and behavioral psychology of the workforce for the attainment of fruitful results in the organizational pathway (Bemmels and Foley 1996). Amidst changing working patterns in organizational work settings, it is the array of attitudes and behavioral phenomena of the workers that matter most in the workplace environment. The pessimistic behavioral pattern in the way of negative behaviors, expressing unethical communicative language, and aggressive activities need to be eliminated to uphold better human relationships at work platforms (Walker and Hamilton 2011). The rules governing the legal provisions need to be compiled at the organizational level for the employees working at work terrain. The worker's role needs to be designed in a comprehensive, structured format with specificity and clarity for ascertaining the attitudinal magnitudes of the workforce (Flanagan et al. 1974). At the organizational platform, the roots of grievances give birth to discontentment, which needs to be addressed with due priority, credibility, and diligence in the course of taking appropriate action in the decision-making mechanism. In the event of handling the mounting grievances, the agenda for the search for remedies work as ways and means of settlement. Twenty-first-century business houses should design proper legal frameworks adhering to the prominent parameters of the code of conduct to restrict uncivil mannerisms in the work arena (Hunter and Kleiner 2004). The epicenter of employee violence and outrage with accumulative waves of unfulfilled demands that arise at the job site result in building hindrances for institutional upliftment with mounting organizational upheavals. Recent studies reveal that the escalating trends of anger, dissatisfaction, and irritation creating an adverse impact on the minds and motivational spirit of the employees and are rising at every corner of the organizational hierarchy (Budd and Colvin 2008). The vital issues concerning workplace violence are often not taken into consideration and deliberately disregarded in the present changing business hemisphere. The inevitable acts of misconception, commotion, ignorance, conflict, and complaints are viable indicators of building the breeding ground of unprecedented activities at the workplace. The optimistic flavor of ethical ideals, loyalty, and commitment need to be nurtured wherein eliminating the adverse forces of disregard, aggravation, and revenge in the occupational zone (Garima 2017). It is quite imperative that tracing the seeds of workplace aggression will invariably minimize the probability of the occurrence of unprecedented behavior and undesirable situations.

22.2.3 *Redefining the Essentials of Discipline Management: Core of Human Empowerment*

The ways and means of value education in the present-day changing environment have undergone radical wanes of transformation through exploration, e-learning, and ethical life management lessons. Organizations today are driven by the guiding principles of ethical knowledge mechanisms gearing human values, morals, and outlook among the workforce for sustainable organizational escalation (Keith and Nerostrom 1995). The avenues of discipline management in the present digitalized business era need to be reoriented, recreated, and rebuilt, which acts as a Bridgeway in creating bondage of harmony, belongingness, and inner-disciplinary instinct within the human resource of an organization. The pathway towards organizational upliftment stands on the foundation of righteousness, consciousness, and togetherness, paving the roadmap for holistic organizational empowerment. In the post-pandemic period, organizations are struggling for sustenance, and amidst fluctuating environment due to identification in the arenas of confusion, embarrassment, puzzlement, and perplexity is the call of the hour (Michael 1999). It can be rightly acclaimed that the relevance of ethical intervention with human empowerment is quite realistic and need to be incorporated for organizational excellence in the coming days. The levels of ethical behavior of an individual can be assessed through the Three-Tier Ethical Scale; the pre-conventional phase focuses on self-development, the conventional phase focuses on moral development, and the post-conventional phase focuses on independent visions of ethical standards. It can be rightly claimed that the vibes of human resource potential have evolved as the lifeblood to regain the decaying ethical values (Hofstede 1997). Such a scenario in the organizational hemisphere may be revived through interactive video, ethical games, moral dilemma discussions, and imparting training at various levels of ethical misapprehension, including towards achieving the desired goal of human empowerment.

22.2.4 *Reorienting Employee Participation for Human Empowerment*

The foundation of the present-day trade-house is erected on the pillars of the business platform, visioning the prime venture of accentuating employee participation in new-fangled dimensions. The projection, scope, and benefits involving the new corporate domain promulgate the pros and cons of the new business ring-tone, which in turn encourages employee involvement in entrepreneurial avenues. The foundation of corporate business houses is focused on the project's incentive package supplemented by the perceptions contributing to personal motivation for work. An entrepreneurial project is designed and formulated with the vision of occupational choice, employee involvement, and interactive phenomenon—all oriented towards fulfillment of elevated business responsibilities (Seibert et al. 2004). To begin with, a new venture needs innovative, independent entrepreneurial attributes to cope with uncertain events on the way to accomplish business endeavors. The working frame of organizational activities can be outlined with the array of functions, viz. planning internal corporate projects, strategic renovation, and designing industrial infrastructural set-up—all aiming to foster the attainment of organizational goals in the business hemisphere. The dual phenomenon governing the corporate climate with the propensity towards recognition of work with a reward system needs to be brought forward for the fulfillment of broader dimensions of corporate entrepreneurship activity (Busck et al. 2010). Collaboration between foundations of incentive system mechanism and prescriptive reward system interplay a motivational role along with real-world decision-making process. The inducement elements ranging from the bonus, risk, and effort all culminated as a stimulating force behind the employee decision-making process to participate in the new mission with innovative vision in the digitalized era. The foundation stone erected for the entrepreneurial venture can be projected from the point of view of the correlation factor existing between the "willingness of participation" and the "project profit sharing factor." The inclination towards involvement aggravates the higher probability of profitability, signifying a positive relationship displaying elevated levels of employee motivation (Welzel and Inglehart 2008).

22.2.5 Integrating Industrial Relations and Human Resources: Pathway Towards Empowerment

The pillars of organizational foundation, the image of institutional goodwill, and the strength of the soil of trust—all bounded by the spirit of togetherness and harmonious relation is coined as industrial relation in emergent business vibes. The treasure behind any foundation lies within its resource fulfilled by the firm hands of human beings residing as manpower in wide-ranging business houses. The notion of industrial relations in the form of unionism, legislation, etc. is increasingly being supplemented by workplace innovations, problem-solving techniques, and encouragement of integration with cooperation in modern organizations. At the threshold of the twenty-first century, the tyranny of employment relationships with conflicting human resource perspectives is the major observation of disagreement between professional relations and individual resources. The dual forces attributing to the

Table 22.1 Visualizing industrial relations at workplace

Industrial relations
Conflicting tools • Union organizing efforts by the associations • Strikes entering at the workfloor • Grievances seeded among the workers
Impact of management schools • Darwin theory–survival of the fittest in the labor market • Scientific management–industrial engineering principles • Human relations—concentrating workers psychological and social requirement
Protective shields • Civil Rights Act (1964) • Employee Retirement Income Security Act (1970) • Occupational Safety and Health Act • Family and Medical Leave Act (1993)
Grievance procedures • Segmentation of unionization • Detection of unfair treatment • Rectification of injustice • Third party arbitration
Web rules • Legitimizing worker claims • Reducing power imbalance • Equitable employer–employee dealings

(Source: Compiled by the author)

accomplishment of organizational goals can be shaped in the form of institutional bondage quoted as Industrial Relations (IR) and work devices designed as Human Resources (HR). The core elements of Industrial Relations and Human Resources in the content and the context of workplace conflict arising in organizational affairs can be identified as Industrial Relations comprising specific variables as depicted in Table 22.1.

The in-equilibrium existing at the junctures of job and job prospects is the root of every dispute at the workaround for the organizational field. The disparity between the individual and the management is created through the walls of power imbalance, hierarchical position, and the age-old philosophy of the master–servant paradox prevailing at the corners of organizational work soil. With the changing waves of time, man being transformed into human assets, personnel departments taking the shape of HR hubs, the goal being redesigned in harmonious correlation (Doellgast 2008). Blending the waves of industrial relations with the vibes of innovation, regardless of collision and conflicts throughout an organization, is the potent driver of human empowerment in the true sense of the term. The proponents of Human Resources at the workplace comprising quite a distinct set of variables are demonstrated in Table 22.2.

Table 22.2 Visualizing human resources at workplace

Human resource
Management approach • Recovery from poor to improved management • Application of the methods of schools of management • Develop work systems with diminishing workplace conflicts
Priority in workers' necessity • Creation of work group for employee assistance • Concern towards non-economic needs • Implementing feedback and appraisal at the organizational hierarchy
Quality of work life • Higher worker satisfaction • Lower employee absenteeism • Unity of interest
Employee contentment quotient • Positive correlation with product and service quality • Negative correlation with voluntary turnover, leave utility, absenteeism • Employee involvement and participation programs (EIP)
Employment relationship • Collaborative involvement of employer–employee • Work practices reflecting mutual power-sharing • Building an effective organizational culture

(Source: Compiled by the author)

22.3 Need of the Study

In the present-day scenario, the content and context of human empowerment are quite pertinent for building sustainable millennium organizations. Moreover, the essentiality of human empowerment intervention in the public arena will foster the effectiveness of the deliverables among the public. It is imperative that wider implementation of human empowerment in the public houses would promote a progressive work environment contributing towards the sustenance and sustainability of the public sector organizations at large.

22.4 Commerce and Industries Department

The state of West Bengal has its growth factor vested in the hands of the Commerce and Industries department. The Commerce and Industries department is primarily oriented towards the promotion and regulation of large and medium-scale industries in the state. With the proponents of new industrial policy and digitalized India, the waves of progressive expansion have strengthened the hands of the Commerce and Industries department of the Government of West Bengal. The department has its key function towards assigning the task of formulating and implementing industrial policies, rules, and regulations along with designing business strategies for the economic development of the state. The apex department of development is vested with responsibility for formulating industrial infrastructure environmental policies conducive to industrial growth, expansion, employability, and sustainability.

22.5 Objectives of the Study

The focal aim of the study is to explore the perspective of human empowerment and its applicability in the public sector with respect to the Commerce and Industries Department of the Government of West Bengal. The primary objective of the paper vests on:

- To investigate the prominent arenas.
- To explain the subdomains/items based on the review of the literature.
- To formulate a comprehensive scale.
- To project the level of human empowerment in the public department.
- To project the level of human empowerment among employee groups in the public department.

22.6 Research Methodology

The present study has been conducted on the platform of a secondary-level literature survey. A comprehensive scale has been crafted taking into account the essential considerations ranging from collective bargaining, the propensity of participation and empowerment, and the relevance of industrial relations. All these considerations are established as independent variables and the factors of human empowerment as dependent variables. The formulation of scale is a modest attempt of the paper and is based on the identification of prominent items with literature review inputs as the major source. The comprehensive, structured scale would be considered as the research tool for the present study.

The formulated scale has been circulated to the respondents in an electronic format comprising HR professionals, academicians, government officials, corporate managers in different organizations, and public bodies in Kolkata. The drafted questionnaire has been formulated based on the opinions about the appropriation of the domain and items in accordance with the Edwards Classical Rules, 1957, for refinement of scale with clear and discrete language construction.

The applicability of the items in the designed scale has been assessed and evaluated through two major statistical techniques, namely item analysis and rating mechanism. The responses were framed with a critical analysis of the domains and items, and the respondents were asked to respond based on their perception and judgmental analysis. With the compilation of responses of the respondents collected through the survey, a final framework for the creation of the Five Pont Scale was conducted. The final questionnaires include the demographic information of the respondents and the particulars of the responses of the respondents based on a rating scale of 1–5. The nomenclature "1" means "Not at all Observed," and "5" means "Extremely Observed." The Test of Reliability has been applied in respect of five identified domains with constructs, and the results reflect that the proposed scale is reliable.

A total sample size of total 216 employees in the categories of A, B, C, and D in the Commerce and Industries Department is considered as the research sample. The responses were collected through telephone, email, and online modes of communication. There have been 54 respondents on average in each of the employee categories. The sampling technique is purposive, stratified, and convenient sampling.

22.7 Findings of the Study

22.7.1 Finding I: Identifying Broad Domains

From the literature elucidated in the paper with the understanding of the related outcome of the research extracts a clear effort has been made to identify the prominent domains considered in the study (Table 22.3).

22.7.2 Findings II: Comprehending the Items

Each of the above domains has been individualistically considered to arrive at a handful of items. The items have been generated from a detailed literature study which has been a significant part of this chapter (Table 22.4).

Table 22.3 Identifying the broad domains

S. no.	Description of the domains
Domain A	Understanding the notion of employee grievance
Domain B	Advocating the proponents of discipline management
Domain C	Upholding the issues of collective bargaining
Domain D	Establishing the foundation of participation and empowerment
Domain E	Building the propensity of industrial relations

(Source: Author's finding)

Table 22.4 Item-wise analysis of each domain

Domain	Item no.	Description of the items
Domain A	A.1	Minimizing employee unrest
	A.2	Reduces confusion and uncertainty among employees
	A.3	Securing the settlement of disputes and grievances by a mutually agreed procedure
	A.4	Eliminating all forms of coercion, intimidation, and violation of rules and regulations of industrial relations
Domain B	B.1	Keeping a check on the superior's attitude and behavior towards their subordinate
	B.2	Enhancing the morale of the employees
	B.3	Strengthening the superior-subordinate relations
	B.4	Fostering employee efficiency
Domain C	C.1	Protecting the interests of workers through collective action
	C.2	Helping to create an understanding between management and employees
	C.3	Acting as a collective force to restrict the exploitation of weaker employees
	C.4	Initiating participative management and good working condition in the department
Domain D	D.1	Improving the quality of working life of the employees with larger involvement in work
	D.2	Securing mutual cooperation of employers and employees in the greater interest of the government
	D.3	Acting as a medium of joint decision-making involved in resolving work-related issues
	D.4	Enhancing the level of commitment of involvement employees at work
Domain E	E.1	Creating a positive employment relationship between work force and management
	E.2	Providing an opportunity for workers participation in management and decision-making
	E.3	Improving workers strength through mutual negotiations and consultation with management
	E.4	Ensuring a feeling of belongingness and togetherness among all the members of the department

(Source: Author's finding)

22.7.3 *Findings III: Designing a Comprehensive Scale*

The author of this chapter has made an attempt to design a scale in the nomenclature of Potential Empowerment Interventions in the Government Department, i.e., "PEI-GD" scale. Each of the above domains has been independently considered to arrive at a handful of items for the scale. The items have been generated from a detailed literature study which has been a significant part of this chapter.

22.7.4 Findings IV: Item-Wise Application

The study reveals that in the arena of minimizing employee unrest and eliminating coercion marks a bold impact in the context of empowerment intervention. On the contrary, areas relating to superior-subordinate relationship, employee efficiency, protecting workers' interest, and joint decision-making less priority has been initiated (Table 22.5).

22.7.5 Findings V: Employee Category-Wise Application

It has been observed that the Group A category of employees has the highest level of empowerment application in the department, whereas the Group C category of employees has the minimum level of empowerment application (Table 22.6).

22.8 Implications of the Study

Against the backdrop of spiraling risks global pandemic, lives, livelihoods, economy, environment, and business committees are confronting serious threats posing for building resilience in the new transformation in the business hemisphere. Consequently, upon the outbreak of the pandemic, organizations are drastically altering strategies and adopting new ways to survive in the long run. The need for preparedness, adaptation, and mobilization of human empowerment and its effective use is one of the prioritized components focusing humanitarian attributes at the organizational platform in turn creates a pathway towards developing sustainable global habitat. The present study has a strong implication in the context of understanding the extent of the real-life application of typical empowerment intervention in the public department of the Government of West Bengal. The implication of the study is that it throws considerable light on the application of empowerment intervention in public work settings. In the last few decades, the founding element of the human empowerment process has been revolutionized with new emancipative values propagating avenues of civil entitlements, perspectives of democratic rights, and dynamics of divergent consequences. The new paradigm of empowering people is embedded within the nucleolus of the untied knot of empowering societal conditions and empowering regime characteristics. The author has made a modest attempt to visualize the core areas where improvement is required in the application of empowerment intervention, and the government may revisit its drive towards initiating empowerment intervention practices in the workplace. It can be rightly connoted that as the world recovers from the catastrophic effect of the pandemic, the relevance of human empowerment through the triple bottom line, i.e., people-planet-profit needs reinforcement.

Table 22.5 Extent of item-wise application of empowerment intervention of each domain

Domain	Item no.	Description of the items	Extent of empowerment intervention
Domain A	A.1	Minimizing employee unrest	Very much observed
	A.2	Reduces confusion and uncertainty among employees	Somewhat observed
	A.3	Securing the settlement of disputes and grievances by a mutually agreed procedure	Less observed
	A.4	Eliminating all forms of coercion, intimidation, and violation of industrial relations	Very much observed
Domain B	B.1	Keeping a check on the superior's attitude and behavior towards their subordinate	Less observed
	B.2	Enhancing the morale of the employees	Somewhat observed
	B.3	Strengthening the superior subordinate relations	Less observed
	B.4	Fostering employee efficiency	Less observed
Domain C	C.1	Protecting the interests of workers through collective action	Less observed
	C.2	Helping to create an understanding between management and employees	Somewhat observed
	C.3	Acting as a collective force to restrict the exploitation of weaker employees	Somewhat observed
	C.4	Initiating participative management and good working condition in the department	Somewhat observed
Domain D	D.1	Improving the quality of working life of the employees with involvement in work	Somewhat observed
	D.2	Securing mutual cooperation of employers and employees for public interest	Less observed
	D.3	Acting as a medium of joint decision-making for resolving work-related issues	Not at all observed
	D.4	Enhancing the level of commitment of involvement employees at work	Less observed
Domain E	E.1	Creating a positive employment relationship between work force and management	Somewhat observed
	E.2	Providing opportunity for workers participation in management and decision-making	Less observed
	E.3	Improving workers strength through mutual negotiation with management	Not at all observed
	E.4	Ensuring a feeling of belongingness and togetherness among employees	Somewhat observed

(Source: Author's finding)

Table 22.6 Employee category having the extent of empowerment intervention with respective domains

Domain	Employee category	Extent of empowerment
Domain A: Understanding the notion of employee grievance	Group A	Somewhat observed
Domain B: Advocating the proponents of discipline management	Group A	Very much observed
	Group B	Somewhat observed
Domain C: Upholding the issues of collective bargaining	Group D	Less observed
	Group C	Less observed
Domain D: Establishing the foundation of participation and empowerment	Group C	Somewhat observed
Domain E: Building the propensity of industrial relations	Group D	Less observed

(Source: Author's finding)

References

Beetham D (1999) Democracy and human rights. Polity Press, Cambridge

Bemmels B, Foley J (1996) Grievance procedure research: a review and theoretical recommendations. J Manag 22(3):359–384

Bratton WW, McCahery JA (1999) Comparative corporate governance and the theory of the firm: the case against global cross reference. Columbia J Transnatl Law 38:213–297

Budd JW, Colvin JS (2008) Improved metrics for workplace dispute resolution procedures: efficiency, equity and voice. Ind Relat J Econ Soc 47(3):460–479

Busck O, Knudsen H, Lind J (2010) The transformation of employee participation: consequences for the work environment. Econ Ind Democr 31(3):285–305

Doellgast V (2008) Collective bargaining and high involvement management in comparative perspective. Ind Relat 47(2):284–319

Flanagan RJ et al (1974) Worker discontent and workplace behavior. Ind Relat 13(2):101–123

Garima B (2017) Grievance handling: motivational tool for employees. Int J Sci Res Publ 7(3): 130–134

Gugler K (ed) (2001) Corporate governance and economic performance. Oxford University Press, Oxford

Hofstede GH (1997) Cultures and organizations. McGraw-Hill, New York

Hunter S, Kleiner BH (2004) Effective grievance handling procedures. Manag Res News 27(2): 85–94

Keith D, Nerostrom JW (1995) Human behaviour at work, 9th edn. McGraw Hill Book Company, New York

Michael JW (1999) Painting the corporate cathedral: the protection of entitlements in corporate law. Oxf J Legal Stud 19:33–35

Mintzberg H (1996) Managing government governing management. Harvard Business Review Classic, Boston

Seibert SE, Silver SR, Randolph WA (2004) Taking empowerment to the next level: a multiple-level model of empowerment, performance and satisfaction. Acad Manag J 47(3):332–349

Walker B, Hamilton R (2011) Employee–employer grievances. Int J Manag Rev 13(1):40–58

Welzel C, Inglehart R (2008) Democratization as human empowerment. J Democr 19(1):126–140

Dr. Partha Naskar is presently holding the post of Joint Director (Accounts) Netaji Subhas Administrative Training Institute, Kolkata under Personnel and Administrative Reforms Department, Government of West Bengal. Obtained B. Com from St. Xavier's College, Kolkata, BBA, MBA in Finance and M.Phil. in Business Administration from Annamalai University. Conferred with Ph.D. in Management from West Bengal State University, Kolkata. Awarded with Doctor of Letters, H.C. (D.Litt) in Human Resource Management from British National University of Queen Mary—the UK and the USA. Dr. Naskar has overall 27+ years' working experience in Finance, Health and Family Welfare, Self Help and Self Employment, Technical Education and Training, Panchayat and Rural Development Departments of GoWB including 6 years knowhow in private sector. He has dealt with HR Policies, Manning Strategies, HRD Initiatives, Managing Manpower Surpluses and Shortages, Recruitment, Transfers, Promotions, Pay Fixations, Seniority Issues, Pension Matters, Staff Welfare Measures and Training and Development. Awarded with 16+ Research and Academic Excellence awards in the domain of human resource management with Indo Asian—Best Researcher Award 2021 InRes Lifetime Achievement Award 2021, Best Innovative Researcher of the 2022, Outstanding Academic Leader of the year 2022 to name few. Published Book titled *Human Resource Interventions in the Government Departments* by LAP Lambert Academic Publishing, KS OmniScriptum Publishing, Latvia, Republic of Moldova Europe. Published 100+ academic research papers in the area of Strategic HRM, Organizational Behavior and Development, Tourism Management, Indian Culture and Religion, HR practices in public sector in National and International Journals, Book Chapter. Presented 62+ conference research papers in the arena of HRM including 12+ international conferences.

The manufacturer's authorised representative in the EU is Springer Nature Customer Service Centre GmbH, Europaplatz 3, 69115 Heidelberg, Germany. If you have any concerns regarding our products, please contact ProductSafety@springernature.com

Printed and bound by CPI Group (UK) Ltd, Croydon, CR0 4YY
30/09/2026
02225319-0018